Introduction to the Hong Kong Basic Law

Introduction to the Hong Kong Basic Law

Danny Gittings

Hong Kong University Press

> For updates to this book, and other interesting material relating to the Hong Kong Basic Law, visit http://www.hkbasiclaw.com

Hong Kong University Press
The University of Hong Kong
Pokfulam Road
Hong Kong
www.hkupress.org

© Hong Kong University Press 2013

ISBN 978-988-8139-48-4 *(Hardback)*
ISBN 978-988-8139-49-1 *(Paperback)*

All rights reserved. No portion of this publication may be reproduced or transmitted in any form or by any means, electronic or mechanical, including photocopy, recording, or any information storage or retrieval system, without permission in writing from the publisher.

British Library Cataloguing-in-Publication Data
A catalogue record for this book is available from the British Library.

10 9 8 7 6 5 4 3 2 1

Printed and bound by Condor Production Ltd., Hong Kong, China

Contents

Preface		vii
Main Abbreviations		ix
Table of Cases		xi
Table of Hong Kong Basic Law Provisions and Related Documents		xvii
Table of Other Legislation and International Agreements, Conventions and Treaties		xxiii
Chapter 1	Introduction	1
Chapter 2	Birth of the Hong Kong Basic Law	9
2.1	The 1997 Deadline	10
2.2	Sino-British Joint Declaration	13
2.3	Drafting the Hong Kong Basic Law	18
2.4	Battles and Changes	21
2.5	Sino-British Disputes	29
2.6	Through Train	33
Chapter 3	What Is the Hong Kong Basic Law?	37
3.1	International Dimension	37
3.2	Domestic Dimension	40
3.3	Constitutional Dimension	46
3.4	Relationship With Chinese Constitution	50
Chapter 4	How High a Degree of Autonomy?	55
4.1	Executive Power	58
4.2	Legislative Power	72
4.3	Judicial Power	80
4.4	Dispute Resolution	85
Chapter 5	System of Government	93
5.1	Chief Executive	95
5.2	Separation of Powers	103
5.3	Small-Circle Selection Process	107

5.4	Hong Kong SAR Government	114
5.5	Elected Legislature	124
5.6	Functional Constituencies	131
5.7	How Powerful a Legislature?	142
Chapter 6	**Role of the Courts**	**153**
6.1	Judicial Independence	155
6.2	Judicial Review	168
6.3	Composition of the Court of Final Appeal	188
6.4	Constitutional Role of the Court of Final Appeal	195
6.5	Limits on Courts	210
Chapter 7	**Interpretation and Amendment**	**219**
7.1	Hong Kong Courts	223
7.2	Standing Committee	230
7.3	Avoiding Interpretations	240
7.4	Judicial Referral	250
7.5	Amendment	258
Chapter 8	**Protection of Human Rights**	**263**
8.1	ICCPR and Bill of Rights	270
8.2	Restrictions on Rights	285
Chapter 9	**What Will Happen After 2047?**	**303**
9.1	Future of Property Rights	304
9.2	What Does 50 Years Mean?	307
9.3	How Much Change?	309
9.4	Parallels With 1997	312
Appendix 1	Full Text of the Hong Kong Basic Law	315
Appendix 2	Full Text of Related Decisions and Interpretations	351
Bibliography		377
Index		389

Preface

The aim of this text is to provide a straightforward introduction to the Hong Kong Basic Law that can be easily understood by those with no prior knowledge of the subject. As a former journalist I have sought to place much emphasis on readability, with the use of acronyms kept to a minimum and much of the additional detail conveyed through comprehensive footnotes in order to provide for a less cluttered text.

As an introductory text, this book does not seek to cover every last detail about the Hong Kong Basic Law. However, based on more than ten years' experience of teaching this subject, I believe it covers all the major areas necessary for a broad understanding of the nature of this important document and the major ways in which it impacts on life in Hong Kong today. For those wishing to use this book as an introduction to more detailed research, extensive reference is made to the many more advanced texts on particular areas.

Although written for an audience wider than students, the structure of the book closely follows the syllabus for many popular courses in both Hong Kong Basic Law and Hong Kong Constitutional Law and should prove particularly useful for those studying these subjects. Among others, these include students studying Hong Kong Constitutional Law for both the PCLL Conversion Examination and the CPE (Graduate Diploma in English and Hong Kong Law), as well as students studying Hong Kong Basic Law on the Diploma in Legal Studies and the Associate of Arts in Legal Studies.

History is, of course, constantly evolving. Important developments can be expected in coming years, especially as Hong Kong moves towards the promised introduction of universal suffrage for the election of first the Chief Executive and then all members of the Legislative Council. I have sought to provide some pointers as to how such events may unfold, based on the current thinking on these issues. But if there is one thing that the experience of the past 15 years has taught us, it is that events in Hong Kong sometimes take a turn which no one could have predicted.

A word on the numerous references to specific provisions in the Hong Kong Basic Law: In order to make it easier for readers to understand exactly which part of these often lengthy provisions is being described, I have followed the common practice of referring to specific paragraph numbers. So, for example, Article 158(3) denotes the third paragraph of Article 158. Where, as is occasionally the case, the Hong Kong Basic Law uses sub-section numbers, these follow the relevant paragraph number. So, for example, Article 24(2)(3) — which was the subject of one of the most important controversies over the Hong Kong Basic Law—refers to the third sub-section of the second paragraph of Article 24.

My thanks go firstly collectively to the many thousands of students to whom I have taught this subject over the past decade. By repeatedly asking me for a simple introductory book on the most important aspects of the Hong Kong Basic Law, you provided the inspiration for me to write this text, and pointed me in the direction of much of its content. I am indebted to Professor Richard Cullen, whose help and encouragement did so much to help me start my academic career, and to Professor Simon N.M. Young, who has generously agreed to supervise me in continuing it. My thanks also go to my colleagues at the College of Humanities and Law of the University of Hong Kong's School of Professional and Continuing Education, especially college head Mrs. Y.L. Cheng, who has been so supportive in so many ways; to Christopher Munn of Hong Kong University Press, for his advice and encouragement in bringing this project to fruition; and to Jessica Wang of Hong Kong University Press for all her patience and assistance during the production process.

Finally, my most heartfelt thanks go to my parents, without whom I would never have come to Hong Kong. For my late mother, Aelfthryth, who tragically passed away shortly before publication, this book is dedicated to her memory. My heartfelt thanks go also to my wife Candy, for her incredible support and encouragement. For my children, Rebecca and Mark, who will be far more directly affected than me by what happens to Hong Kong after 2047, I can only hope that one of the more optimistic scenarios outlined in the final chapter ultimately turns out to be correct.

I have attempted to state the law as it appeared to me as of 31 March 2013. Any mistakes or omissions are, of course, my own.

Danny Gittings
March 2013

Main Abbreviations

The main abbreviations used in the book are:

Cap.	Chapter
HKLJ	*Hong Kong Law Journal*
ICCPR	International Covenant on Civil and Political Rights
ICESCR	International Covenant on Economic, Social and Cultural Rights
NPC	National People's Congress
PLA	People's Liberation Army
PRC	People's Republic of China
SAR	Special Administrative Region

For abbreviations used for court cases, see "Table of Cases" on page xi.

Table of Cases

Abbreviations

AC	Appeal Cases	HCB	High Court Bankruptcy Proceedings
CA	Court of Appeal		
CACC	Court of Appeal Criminal Appeal	HKC	Hong Kong Cases
CACV	Court of Appeal Civil Appeal	HKCFAR	The Authorised Hong Kong Court of Final Appeal Reports
CFA	Court of Final Appeal		
CFI	Court of First Instance	HKCLR	The Hong Kong Criminal Law Reports
DC	District Court	HKEC	Hong Kong Electronic Cases
DCCC	District Court Criminal Case	HKLR	Hong Kong Law Reports
ECHR	European Court of Human Rights	HKLRD	The Authorised Hong Kong Law Reports & Digest
EHRR	European Human Rights Reports		
FACV	Final Appeal (Civil)	HKLY	Hong Kong Law Yearbook
FAMV	Final Appeal Miscellaneous Proceedings (Civil)	HKPLR	Hong Kong Public Law Reports
		HL	House of Lords
FC	Full Court	KB	King's Bench
HC	High Court	PC	Privy Council
HCAL	High Court Constitutional and Administrative Law Proceedings	QB	Queen's Bench
		US	United States Reports

Note: In this and all subsequent tables "n" is used as an abbreviation for "footnote". For example, "10n2" refers to footnote 2 on page 10.

List of Cases

Associated Provincial Picture Houses Ltd v Wednesbury Corp [1948] 1 KB 223 (CA, England)	185n241
Attorney General of Hong Kong v Lee Kwong Kut (1993) 3 HKPLR 72 (PC)	276n80
Azan Aziz Marwah v Director of Immigration [2009] 3 HKC 185 (CFI)	183n226
Burmah Oil v Lord Advocate [1965] AC 75 (HL)	233
C (A Bankrupt), Re [2006] 4 HKC 582 (CA)	115n122

xii Table of Cases

Cathay Pacific Airways Flight Attendants Union v Director-General of Civil Aviation [2007] 2 HKLRD 668 (CA)	185n235
Catholic Diocese of Hong Kong v Secretary for Justice [2012] 1 HKC 301 (CFA)	312
Chan Kam Nga v Director of Immigration (1999) 2 HKCFAR 82 (CFA)	158, 178, 196, 226n44, 232, 234–235, 237, 260n257, 265n13
Chan Kin Sum v Secretary for Justice [2009] 2 HKLRD 166 (CFI)	186, 301
Chan Mei Yee v Director of Immigration (unrep., HCAL 77 and 99/1999, [2000] HKEC 788) (CFI)	274n68
Chan Shu Ying v Chief Executive of the HKSAR [2001] 1 HKLRD 405 (CFI)	128n201
Chan To Foon v Director of Immigration [2001] 3 HKLRD 109 (CFI)	274n67
Chan Wai Yip Albert v Secretary for Justice (unrep., HCAL 36/2005, 19 May 2005) (CFI)	85n204, 244n156
Chan Yu Nam v Secretary for Justice [2010] 1 HKC 493 (CFI)	136n239, 142n267
Chan Yu Nam v Secretary for Justice [2012] 3 HKC 38 (CA)	135–136, 141–142, 227–228
Chan Yu Nam v Secretary for Justice (unrep., FAMV 39 and 40/2011, [2012] HKEC 94) (CFA Appeal Committee)	135n236, 227n50
Cheng Kar Shun v Li Fung Ying [2011] 2 HKLRD 555 (CFI)	147, 229
Cheng v Tse Wai Chun (2000) 3 HKCFAR 339 (CFA)	193n299, 193n303, 199–200, 204
Cheung Hung Ngai v HKSAR [1998] 1 HKLRD 330 (CFA Appeal Committee)	216n469
Chong Fung Yuen v Director of Immigration [2000] 3 HKLRD 661 (CA)	248
Chow Shui v The Queen [1979] HKLR 275 (HC)	263n5
Chu Woan Chyi v Director of Immigration [2009] 6 HKC 77 (CA)	61n38, 207n412
Chu Yee Wah v Director of Environmental Protection [2011] 3 HKC 227 (CFI)	187n258
Chu Yee Wah v Director of Environmental Protection [2011] 5 HKLRD 469 (CA)	187n258
Civil Air Transport Incorporated v Central Air Transport Corporation (1951) 35 HKLR 215 (PC)	214n460
Council of Civil Service Unions v Minister for the Civil Service [1985] AC 374 (HL)	168n109
Democratic Republic of Congo v FG Hemisphere (2011) 14 HKCFAR 95 (CFA)	7, 24n52, 64–65, 84–85, 163n84, 193n298, 194–195, 207–209, 216–217, 247n172, 250, 254n218, 255–257
Democratic Republic of Congo v FG Hemisphere (No 2) (2011) 14 HKCFAR 395 (CFA)	257n236
Director of Immigration v Chong Fung Yuen (2001) 4 HKCFAR 211 (CFA)	6–7, 38n9, 160, 178n185, 193n298, 200–203, 226–230, 239n122, 242, 248–250, 253n214, 254, 261, 265, 281n107, 284
Fateh Mohammad v Commissioner of Registration (2001) 4 HKCFAR 278 (CFA)	265n21

FG Hemisphere v Democratic Republic of Congo [2010] 2 HKLRD 1148 (CA)	209n428
Fok Chun Wa v Hospital Authority [2011] 1 HKLRD A1, [2010] HKEC 713 (CA)	267
Fok Chun Wa v Hospital Authority [2012] 2 HKC 413 (CFA)	267n29
Gurung Kesh Bahadur v Director of Immigration [2001] 3 HKLRD 32 (CA)	39, 48, 228
Gurung Kesh Bahadur v Director of Immigration (2002) 5 HKCFAR 480 (CFA)	39n17, 48n94, 228n55, 285n124–125, 299, 300n220
Harvest Good Development v Secretary for Justice [2007] 4 HKC 1 (CFI)	266n28
Heydon's Case (1584) 3 Coke's Reports 7a (HC, England)	223n25
HKSAR v Barry Peter Miller (unrep., CACC 127/2000, [2002] HKEC 297) (CA)	213n451
HKSAR v Cheung Hung Ngai [1997] HKLY 210 (CA)	216n469
HKSAR v Hung Chan Wa (2006) 9 HKCFAR 614 (CFA)	175, 176n163, 177n172
HKSAR v Lam Kwong Wai (2006) 9 HKCFAR 574 (CFA)	176n164, 287n137, 294n177
HKSAR v Leung Kwok Hung [2004] 3 HKLRD 729 (CA)	287n138
HKSAR v Ma Wai Kwan David [1997] HKLRD 761 (CA)	37, 39–40, 154n13, 173, 179, 214n456, 225
HKSAR v Musa Solomon Dominic (unrep., DCCC 264/1999, 9 November 1999) (DC)	216n468
HKSAR v Ng Kung Siu [1999] 1 HKLRD 783 (CA)	296n196, 297
HKSAR v Ng Kung Siu (1999) 2 HKCFAR 442 (CFA)	8, 77, 159, 193n298, 198–199, 205n390, 239, 254, 294n177, 295–299, 301–302
HKSAR v Yeung May Wan [2004] 3 HKLRD 797 (CA)	207
Ho Choi Wan v Hong Kong Housing Authority (2005) 8 HKCFAR 628 (CFA)	185n237
Ho Po Sang (No 2) v Director of Public Works [1959] HKLR 632 (FC)	172n131
Hong Kong Polytechnic University v Next Magazine Ltd [1997] HKLRD 102 (HC)	275n74
Hua Tian Long (No 2) [2010] 3 HKLRD 611 (CFI)	213, 214n456
John Cheung v United States of America (2000) 213 Federal Reporter Third Series 82 (2nd Circuit, Court of Appeals, US)	63n52
Kelly Brian Edwards v R (unrep., Tax Court of Canada 20001183, 27 June 2002)	63n53
Koo Sze Yiu v Chief Executive of the HKSAR (2006) 9 HKCFAR 441 (CFA)	105n63, 177n171, 177n175, 185
Koon Wing Yee v Insider Dealing Tribunal (2008) 11 HKCFAR 170 (CFA)	176–177
L v C [1994] 2 HKLR 92 (HC)	276n81
Lau Cheong v HKSAR (2002) 5 HKCFAR 415 (CFA)	205
Lau Kong Yung v Director of Immigration (1999) 2 HKCFAR 300 (CFA)	6, 50n110, 87n220, 87n226, 159, 193n298, 194, 197–199, 201, 232n73, 236n96, 237–240, 246, 248n181, 254n217, 281n110, 285n123, 299

xiv   Table of Cases

Lau Kwok Fai v Secretary for Justice (unrep., HCAL 177 and 180/2002, [2003] HKEC 711) (CFI)	94n3
Lee Miu Ling v Attorney General (No 2) (1995) 5 HKPLR 181 (HC)	141
Lee Miu Ling v Attorney General (No 2) (1995) 5 HKPLR 585 (CA)	141n266
Leung Kwok Hung v Chief Executive of the HKSAR (unrep., CACV 73 and 87/2006, [2006] HKEC 816) (CA)	42n48, 105
Leung Kwok Hung v Chief Executive of the HKSAR (unrep., HCAL 107/2005, [2006] HKEC 239) (CFI)	105n61, 105n63, 177
Leung Kwok Hung v HKSAR (2005) 8 HKCFAR 229 (CFA)	176, 185n242, 199n347, 204–205, 206n404, 207, 282n114, 289, 290n154, 292n164, 294n177, 294n180, 295n185, 295n189, 300n221
Leung Kwok Hung v President of the Legislative Council [2007] 1 HKLRD 387 (CFI)	145n284, 174n149
Lo Siu Lan v Hong Kong Housing Authority (2005) 8 HKCFAR 363 (CFA)	99n32, 187n254, 187n256
Marbury v Madison (1803) 5 US 137 (US Supreme Court)	170, 173
Matter of an Application for Leave to Issue a Summons of Prohibition to be Directed to the Magistrate From Further Proceedings in Kowloon Magistracy Cases, In the (1948) 32 HKLR 136 (FC)	168n112
Medical Council of Hong Kong v Chow Siu Shek David (2000) 3 HKCFAR 144 (CFA)	223n24
Mok Chi Hung v Director of Immigration [2001] 2 HKLRD 125 (CFI)	274n68
Ng Ka Ling v Director of Immigration (1999) 2 HKCFAR 4 (CFA)	5–7, 32, 38n9, 39, 48–49, 50n110, 87, 127n197, 158–159, 173–174, 176n167, 178–180, 183, 186n247, 193n298, 195–201, 213–214, 219, 223–226, 231–235, 237–239, 246n163, 247, 251–254, 259–260, 265, 284–285, 296, 298, 311, 313n59
Ng Ka Ling v Director of Immigration (No 2) (1999) 2 HKCFAR 141 (CFA)	49n100, 87n225, 159–160, 181–183
Ng Siu Tung v Director of Immigration (2002) 5 HKCFAR 1 (CFA)	159n47, 186, 203, 206n404, 246–247
Official Receiver & Trustee in Bankruptcy of Chan Wing Hing v Chan Wing Hing (2006) 9 HKCFAR 545 (CFA)	176n161, 300n220
Pacific Century Insurance Co Ltd v Insurance Claims Complaints Bureau [1999] 3 HKLRD 720 (CFI)	168n107
Panday v Gordon [2006] 1 AC 427 (PC)	193n303
PCCW-HKT Telephone Ltd v The Telecommunications Authority (unrep., HCAL 6/2007, [2007] HKEC 993) (CFI)	185n236
Pepper v Hart [1993] AC 593 (HL)	228–229

Pickin v British Railway Board [1974] AC 765 (HL)	171n127
Po Fun Chan v Winnie Cheung (2007) 10 HKCFAR 676 (CFA)	187n257
Public Prosecutor v Zhang Ziqiang (Criminal Case No. 468/1998) (Guangzhou Intermediate People's Court, PRC)	44n59
Qi Yuling v Chen Xiaoqi (Judicial Interpretation No. 25/2001) (Supreme People's Court, PRC)	170n123
R v English Schools Foundation [2004] 3 HKC 343 (CFI)	184n234
R v Hull University Visitor ex parte Page [1993] AC 682 (HL)	168n108
R v Lum Wai Ming [1992] 2 HKCLR 221 (HC)	277n83, 291n161
R v Secretary of State for the Home Department, ex parte Daly [2001] 2 AC 532 (HL)	185n241
R v Secretary of State for the Home Department ex parte Simms [2000] 2 AC 115 (HL)	171n128
R v Sin Yau Ming [1992] 1 HKCLR 127 (CA)	276–277, 281n108, 287, 291
Secretary for Justice v Chan Wah (2000) 3 HKCFAR 459 (CFA)	177, 205, 268n34, 269n40
Secretary for Justice v Commission of Inquiry Re Hong Kong Institute of Education [2009] 4 HKLRD 11 (CFI)	123n173
Secretary for Justice v Lau Kwok Fai (2005) 8 HKCFAR 304 (CFA)	311–312
Secretary for Justice v Oriental Press Group Ltd [1998] 2 HKLRD 123 (CFI)	293
Shum Kwok Sher v HKSAR (2002) 5 HKCFAR 381 (CFA)	289, 290n157–158
Status of the French Mail Streamers, The Daily Press, 12 January 1880 (FC)	273n62
Stock Exchange of Hong Kong v New World Development (2006) 9 HKCFAR 234 (CFA)	81
Sum Tat Man, Re [1991] 2 HKLR 601 (HC)	169n119
Sunday Times v United Kingdom (No 1) (1979–80) 2 EHRR 245 (ECHR)	289n149, 290n155–156
Swire Properties Ltd v Secretary for Justice (2003) 6 HKCFAR 236 (CFA)	280n104
Tam Hing Yee v Wu Tai Wai [1992] 1 HKLR 185 (CA)	275n76
Tam Nga Yin v Director of Immigration (2001) 4 HKCFAR 251 (CFA)	226, 248
Tang Ping Hoi v Attorney General [1987] HKLR 324 (HC)	18, 39, 273n62
Texas v Johnson (1989) 491 US 397 (US Supreme Court)	298n206
Thoburn v Sunderland City Council [2003] QB 151 (Divisional Court, England)	171n128
Ting Lei Miao v Chen Li Hung [1999] 1 HKLRD 123 (CA)	50n110
Town Planning Board v Society for the Protection of the Harbour Ltd (2004) 7 HKCFAR 1 (CFA)	187n253, 187n256
Ubamaka Edward Wilson v Secretary for Security [2013] 2 HKC 75 (CFA)	272n56, 286n132
United States v Eichman (1990) 496 US 310 (US Supreme Court)	298n206
Valente v The Queen [1985] 2 Supreme Court Reports 673 (Supreme Court of Canada)	155, 166
Vallejos Evangeline Banao v Commissioner of Registration (unrep., FACV 19 and 20/2012, [2013] HKEC 429) (CFA)	202n366, 209n429, 243n143, 250n193, 254n18, 265n21

Wilson v Minister for Aboriginal and Torres Strait Islander Affairs (1996) 189 Commonwealth Law Reports 1 (High Court of Australia)	158n40
Wong Yeung Ng v Secretary for Justice [1999] 2 HKLRD 293 (CA)	293n172
Yau Kwong Man v Secretary for Justice [2002] 3 HKC 457 (CFI)	94n4, 101, 157, 280n105
Yeung May Wan v HKSAR (2005) 8 HKCFAR 137 (CFA)	203–205, 207
Yin Xiang Jiang v Director of Immigration [1994] 2 HKLR 101 (CA)	273n63
Zhang Sabine Soi Fan v The Official Receiver (unrep., HCB 472/1989, 31 March 1999) (CFI)	216n468

Table of Hong Kong Basic Law Provisions and Related Documents

Hong Kong Basic Law Provisions

Chapter I	21, 264
Chapter II	21, 40
Chapter III	21, 48, 174n152, 196, 237, 264, 266–267, 270, 272n59, 288n141, 295n187
Chapter IV	21, 47–48, 94, 154
Chapter IV, Section 2	114n119
Chapter IV, Section 4	154n7
Chapter V	21
Chapter VI	21
Chapter VII	21
Chapter VIII	21
Chapter IX	21n38
Preamble	21, 51, 228, 259n250, 308, 313
Preamble, paragraph 2	38n5, 38n8
Preamble, paragraph 3	38n5
Article 1	38, 55
Article 2	3, 38, 55, 80n173, 80n175, 81, 155n20, 188n264
Article 3	38
Article 4	38, 264n10
Article 5	38, 52, 303, 307–309, 313
Article 6	266–267
Article 7	305n17–18
Article 8	47
Article 9	81
Article 11(1)	51
Article 11(2)	47, 72, 77
Article 13(1)	40n22, 61, 217n476, 255–256
Article 13(2)	62n44
Article 13(3)	61, 64
Article 14(1)	40n21
Article 14(2)	80
Article 15	40n23, 67, 71, 116
Article 16	41n31, 59n30
Article 17(1)	72
Article 17(2)	72, 73n123, 82n186
Article 17(3)	26n58, 41n25, 41n29, 47n84, 73–74, 88, 174n150
Article 18(2)	45, 75–76
Article 18(3)	40n24, 41n28, 75–78, 88
Article 18(4)	38n6, 41n27, 79–80
Article 19	80n175, 210, 215n464, 255
Article 19(1)	80n173, 81, 153, 155n20, 174, 188n264
Article 19(2)	44n58, 82, 153–154, 173, 179, 210–211
Article 19(3)	64n60, 81n178, 82, 214–217, 255–256
Article 20	66
Article 21	90
Article 22(1)	41n30
Article 22(2)	41n38
Article 22(3)	33, 41n39
Article 22(4)	41n26, 178n180, 196n327, 224n31, 225n33, 233–236, 248, 253n209, 260, 285n123

Table of Hong Kong Basic Law Provisions and Related Documents

Article 23	1, 26–28, 35, 69n93, 72–73, 75, 106, 123, 143, 295n187, 299n214	Article 40	205n398, 268–269, 310–311
		Article 41	267
		Article 42	288n141
Article 24	264	Article 43(1)	95
Article 24(2)	184	Article 43(2)	67, 89, 95
Article 24(2)(1)	38n10, 200–201, 227, 242, 248–249, 254, 265n14, 265n18	Article 44	95, 115n125, 266n24
		Article 45(1)	67, 95, 108
Article 24(2)(2)	265n19	Article 45(2)	28n65, 112–113
Article 24(2)(3)	38n10, 178n180, 196n327, 200–201, 226n44–45, 232n77, 233–237, 238n108, 239n122–123, 247–248, 253n212, 254n221, 260, 265n13, 265n20	Article 46	96, 243–245
		Article 48(1)	96
		Article 48(3)	100
		Article 48(4)	98, 105n59, 157n30
		Article 48(5)	71, 98, 115n128, 116
		Article 48(6)	98
Article 24(2)(4)	265n22, 266n23	Article 48(7)	97
Article 24(2)(5)	266n23	Article 48(8)	67, 95
Article 24(2)(6)	266n26	Article 48(10)	104, 143
Article 24(3)	264n12	Article 48(11)	147n293
Article 24(4)	266n27	Article 48(12)	101
Article 26	125n185, 136, 227–228, 265	Article 49	74n132, 100–101
		Article 50(1)	100–101, 106
Article 27	48, 208n419, 266, 288n140, 293	Article 50(2)	100
		Article 51	103n50
Article 28	266, 286	Article 52	70n100, 243n147
Article 29	266	Article 52(1)	107
Article 30	105n61, 267, 293n171	Article 52(2)	101
Article 31	39, 48, 228, 267, 285n124	Article 52(3)	100, 103, 106n72
Article 32	267	Article 53(1)	115
Article 32(2)	52n119	Article 53(2)	236, 245, 246n162
Article 33	267	Article 54	97
Article 34	267	Article 55(1)	96
Article 35	267	Article 56(2)	97
Article 35(2)	93, 169	Article 56(3)	97
Article 36	267	Article 59	114
Article 37	52n116, 267	Article 60(1)	114
Article 39	270, 274, 280–281	Article 60(2)	115n128
Article 39(1)	35n113, 63n48, 80n169, 141, 271–272, 274, 278, 280–282, 284, 288, 292	Article 61	33n102, 115, 122n162
		Article 62	114
Article 39(2)	288, 290n158, 292–293, 300	Article 62(1)	98, 117, 157n30

Article 63	114–115	Article 101(1)	154n9
Article 64	125n181, 146	Article 103	312
Article 66	124	Article 105(1)	266, 267n31
Article 67	154n9, 266n25	Article 106	60
Article 68(1)	32, 124, 127–128, 133	Article 108(2)	41n34
Article 72(2)	100	Article 110(2)	41n33, 60
Article 73	124, 142	Article 111(1)	60, 310
Article 73(1)	42, 72, 143, 157n31	Article 116	62
Article 73(2)	103, 142	Article 116(1)	60
Article 73(3)	103, 142	Article 121	306
Article 73(4)	98	Article 122	268n37
Article 73(6)	98n21, 148	Article 123	41n32, 306–307
Article 73(9)	102	Article 124(2)	41n35
Article 73(10)	119, 146–147	Article 126	60n31, 62n45
Article 74	75n133, 98–100, 104, 143–145	Article 129(2)	60n31
		Article 130	41n36
Article 75(2)	145	Article 132(1)	62n43
Article 77	211	Article 133	62
Article 80	80, 153, 157, 174	Article 134(1)	62n44
Article 81(1)	153–154	Article 136(1)	312n57
Article 81(2)	155n18	Article 140	267
Article 82	81–82, 83n191, 188n264, 189, 192	Article 141	52n119
		Article 151	60, 62
Article 83	153	Article 152(1)	62n41
Article 84	81	Article 152(2)	62n41
Article 85	80n173, 81, 155, 211	Article 153(1)	63n47
Article 87(1)	154	Article 153(2)	63
Article 87(2)	267, 284, 293n175	Article 154(1)	230n66
Article 88	82, 98, 161–162	Article 154(2)	60
Article 89	164	Article 155	62
Article 89(2)	164n89	Article 156	62n42
Article 90(1)	154n10, 190n277	Article 157(1)	62n45
Article 90(2)	82, 98n26, 129n204, 161, 164	Article 158	31n84, 158, 173n143, 219, 221–223, 231, 237, 261
Article 92	81, 154, 160		
Article 93(1)	154, 166	Article 158(1)	83–84, 87, 158n42, 175, 182n214, 222, 281n109
Article 96	62–63		
Article 97	128n201	Article 158(2)	81n178, 83, 222–223, 230–231, 237, 250
Article 99(1)	154n11		

Article 158(3)	81n178, 83–84, 85n205, 208n415, 217, 222–223, 225, 231, 234, 236, 240n124, 247n169, 250–257	Annex I(3)	136n239, 228n53
		Annex I(4)	109n90, 110n92
		Annex I(7)	112, 129, 241
Article 158(4)	88	Annex I, amendment	109n89
Article 159	45, 258–262, 281	Annex II	69
Article 159(1)	258, 260	Annex II(I)	126, 128
Article 159(2)	258	Annex II(I)(2)	136n239, 228n53
Article 159(3)	88, 259n248	Annex II(II)	100n36, 134, 145, 148–149, 151
Article 159(4)	46, 259–262, 309, 311n46	Annex II(III)	128–129, 138, 142, 175n158, 241, 314n68
Article 160	21n38		
Article 160(1)	34, 39n15, 41n25, 47, 73n124, 174n150, 278	Annex II, amendment	138n252
		Annex III	43n56, 76, 78n157, 90n249, 210n434, 211n440
Annex I	32, 69, 246n162		
Annex I(1)	109		
Annex I(2)	109		

Initial Drafts of the Hong Kong Basic Law

Basic Law of the Hong Kong SAR of the PRC (Draft) (February 1989)	25–26
Draft Basic Law of the Hong Kong SAR of the PRC (for solicitation of opinions) (April 1988)	23n46
Article 15	59n28
Article 16(3)	74n128
Article 18(3)	215n463
Article 22	26n59
Annex I	23–24
Annex II	24, 125–126

Related Documents Issued by the Chinese Central Authorities

Decision of the NPC Approving the Proposal by the Drafting Committee for the Basic Law of the Hong Kong SAR on the Establishment of the Committee for the Basic Law of the Hong Kong SAR Under the Standing Committee of the NPC (4 April 1990)	88n227–228
Decision of the NPC on the Basic Law of the Hong Kong SAR of the PRC (4 April 1990)	53n126
Decision of the NPC on the Method for the Formation of the First Government and the First Legislative Council of the Hong Kong SAR (4 April 1990)	108n81, 126n190, 128n202
Paragraph 2	31n87
Paragraph 3	32n91
Paragraph 4	32n91
Paragraph 6	28n67, 31n86
Decision of the Preparatory Committee on the Establishment of a Provisional Legislature of the Hong Kong SAR (24 March 1996)	32n92

Table of Hong Kong Basic Law Provisions and Related Documents   xxi

Decision of the Standing Committee of the NPC (31 October 1989)	27n61
Decision of the Standing Committee of the NPC on Issues Relating to the Methods for Selecting the Chief Executive of the Hong Kong SAR and for Forming the Legislative Council of the Hong Kong SAR in the Year 2012 and on Issues Relating to Universal Suffrage (29 December 2007)	68n86, 112n108, 112n112, 130n211, 131n214–215, 134n228
Decision of the Standing Committee of the NPC on Issues Relating to the Methods for Selecting the Chief Executive of the Hong Kong SAR in the Year 2007 and for Forming the Legislative Council of the Hong Kong SAR in the Year 2008 (26 April 2004)	130n211, 134n228
Decision of the Standing Committee of the NPC on the English Text of the Basic Law of the Hong Kong SAR of the PRC (28 June 1990)	308n29
Decision of the Standing Committee of the NPC on the Proposal Advanced by Zheng Yaotang and Other Thirty-two Deputies to the NPC (31 August 1994)	31n85, 127n196
Decision of the Standing Committee of the NPC on Treatment of the Laws Previously in Force in Hong Kong in Accordance With Article 160 of the Basic Law of the Hong Kong SAR of the PRC (23 February 1997)	47n86, 146n292
Annex I	34n109, 278n92
Annex II	34n107, 34n109, 278n92, 279n95
Explanations of Some Questions by the Standing Committee of the NPC Concerning the Implementation of the Nationality Law of the PRC in the Hong Kong SAR (15 May 1996)	66n72
Interpretation by the Standing Committee of the NPC of Article 7 of Annex I and Article III of Annex II to the Basic Law of the Hong Kong SAR of the PRC (6 April 2004)	69–70, 91, 112n111, 129–130, 142, 151, 175n158, 241, 314n68
Interpretation by the Standing Committee of the NPC of Articles 22(4) and 24(2)(3) of the Basic Law of the Hong Kong SAR of the PRC (26 June 1999)	158n44, 160n60, 178n183, 201n364, 203n374, 226n44, 235–237, 239n122, 245, 248, 250n193, 254n216, 260, 285n123
Interpretation of Paragraph 1, Article 13 and Article 19 of the Basic Law of the Hong Kong SAR of the PRC by the Standing Committee of the NPC (26 August 2011)	247n172, 257n235
Interpretation of Paragraph 2, Article 53 of the Basic Law of the Hong Kong SAR of the PRC by the Standing Committee of the NPC (27 April 2005)	236n94, 243–246, 261n261
Official Reply of the State Council Concerning the Area of the "Hong Kong Port Area at the Shenzhen Bay Port" Over Which the Hong Kong Special Administrative Region is Authorized to Exercise Jurisdiction and the Land Use Period (30 December 2006)	313n61
Opinions of the Preparatory Committee for the Hong Kong SAR of the NPC on the Implementation of Article 24(2) of the Basic Law of the Hong Kong SAR (10 August 1996)	230n62, 242n138, 248n177, 250n193
Paragraph 1	248n178
Order of the State Council of the People's Republic of China No. 221 (1 July 1997)	79n163

Table of Other Legislation and International Agreements, Conventions and Treaties

Hong Kong Legislation

Adaptation of Laws (Interpretative Provisions) Ordinance (No. 26 of 1998)	
Section 24	32n98
Bankruptcy Ordinance (Cap. 6)	
Section 30A(10)(b)(i)	176n161
Chief Executive Election (Amendment) (Term of Office of the Chief Executive) Ordinance (No. 4 of 2005)	244n152
Chief Executive Election Ordinance (Cap. 569)	
Section 3(1)	244n150
Section 3(1A)	244n152
Schedule	109n87
Chinese Extradition Ordinance (Cap. 235)	34n111
Coroners Ordinance (Cap. 504)	153n5
Corrupt and Illegal Practices Ordinance (Cap. 288)	34n112
Crimes (Amendment) Ordinance (No. 24 of 1993)	286n127
Crimes Ordinance (Cap. 200)	26n60
Criminal Procedure Ordinance (Cap. 221)	
Section 67C	101n41, 157n36
Crown Proceedings Ordinance (Cap. 300)	
Section 8	212n447
Dangerous Drugs (Amendment) (No. 2) Ordinance (No. 52 of 1992)	277n83
Dangerous Drugs Ordinance (Cap. 134)	276n79, 277n83
Disability Discrimination Ordinance (Cap. 487)	144n280
District Councils Ordinance (Cap. 547)	97n18
District Court Ordinance (Cap. 336)	153n5
Education (Amendment) Ordinance (No. 27 of 2004)	312n56
Employment Ordinance (Cap. 57)	263n1
Family Status Discrimination Ordinance (Cap. 527)	144n280
Film Censorship (Amendment) Ordinance (No. 63 of 1993)	302n233
Government Rent (Assessment and Collection) Ordinance (Cap. 515)	
Section 2	268n33
Heung Yee Kuk Ordinance (Cap. 1097)	
Section 9	268n35

Table of Other Legislation and International Agreements

High Court Ordinance (Cap. 4)	153n5
Section 11A(3)(b)	165n93
Section 12(2)(a)	168n111
Hong Kong Bill of Rights Ordinance (Cap. 383)	7, 29, 34, 35n113, 63, 172, 264, 274–285, 291–294
Section 2(3)	274, 279
Section 3	276, 279
Section 4	279
Section 5(2)(b)	287n134
Section 5(2)(c)	287n134
Section 7	275n73
Section 9	274n70
Section 10	274n70, 282n115
Section 11	274n70
Section 12	274n70, 282n116
Section 13	141n266, 274n70, 283n117
Article 1	282
Article 2	282
Article 2(2)	286n130
Article 2(5)	286n130
Article 3	282, 286n132
Article 4	282
Article 5	282
Article 6	282
Article 7	282
Article 8	275n76, 282, 285n124
Article 9	282
Article 10	283
Article 11	283, 284
Article 11(1)	276n79, 287n136, 293n175
Article 12	283
Article 13	283
Article 14	283
Article 15	283, 286n133
Article 16	275n72, 283
Article 17	275n72, 283
Article 18	283
Article 19	283
Article 20	283
Article 21	283
Article 22	284
Article 23	284
Hong Kong Court of Final Appeal Ordinance (Cap. 484)	34, 153n5, 190–192, 215
Section 1(2)	190n274
Section 4(2)	215n466
Section 6(2)	167
Section 10	191n280
Section 12(1)	191n278

Section 12(3)	191n283
Section 12(4)	191n282
Section 14(1)	190n276
Section 14(2)(a)	164n87, 165n93, 190n276, 207n413
Section 14(4)	191n281
Section 14(5)	190n276
Section 14(11)	190n276
Section 16(1)	190n275
Section 16(1)(c)	191n279, 191n284
Section 16(4)	192n288
Section 18(1)	195n317
Section 22(1)(a)	195n316
Section 22(1)(b)	195n315
Section 23(1)	195n317
Section 23(2)	195n316
Section 32(1)	195n317
Section 32(2)	195n315
Hong Kong Letters Patent 1917–1995	101, 171–172, 263n2
Article VII	276
Article VII(1)	102n44
Article VII(5)	172, 264n7, 277, 280
Article XIV(1)	161n67
Article XVIA(6)(a)	165n91
Hong Kong Reunification Ordinance (No. 110 of 1997)	
Section 3	31n90
Section 8(1)	154n12
Section 10	155n15
Schedule 1	31n89
Hong Kong Royal Instructions 1917–1993	101n43, 171n129
Clause XXIV(2)	144n279
Clause XXVI	263n2
Immigration (Amendment) (No. 3) Ordinance (No. 124 of 1997)	233n78
Section 1(2)	285n123
Immigration Ordinance (Cap. 115)	178
Section 2(4)	265n21
Section 2A(1)	265n17
Schedule 1, paragraph 1(2)(b)	232n77
Schedule 1, paragraph 2(a)	200n357
Schedule 1, paragraph 2(c)	232n77
Schedule 1, paragraph 3(1)	265n22
Interception of Communications and Surveillance Ordinance (Cap. 589)	105n64, 177n177
Interception of Communications Ordinance (Cap. 532)	105n62
Interpretation and General Clauses Ordinance (Cap. 1)	
Section 3	32n99
Section 66	32n98

xxvi   Table of Other Legislation and International Agreements

Judicial Officers Recommendation Commission Ordinance (Cap. 92)
    Section 3(1) — 161n64
    Section 3(1A) — 161n64
    Section 3(3A) — 162n75
Judicial Service Commission (Amendment) Ordinance (No. 121 of 1997) — 161n63
Legislative Council (Amendment) Ordinance (No. 12 of 2012) — 75n138, 145n287
Legislative Council Ordinance (Cap. 542)
    Section 37(1)(e) — 266n25
    Sections 37(2)(f) — 266n25
    Section 37(3) — 266n25
    Section 39(2A) — 75n141
Legislative Council (Powers and Privileges) Ordinance (Cap. 382) — 146
    Section 4 — 211n437
    Section 9 — 146
    Section 12 — 146
    Section 17 — 146
Magistrates Ordinance (Cap. 227) — 153n5
National Flag and National Emblem Ordinance (No. 116 of 1997) — 77
    Section 7 — 77n154, 198n342, 296n194
New Territories Order in Council 1898
    Clause 1 — 10n2
Offences Against the Person Ordinance (Cap. 212) — 204n385
Police Force Ordinance (Cap. 232) — 204n385
Prevention and Control of Disease Ordinance (Cap. 599)
    Section 7(2)(f) — 286n131
Prevention of Bribery Ordinance (Cap. 201)
    Section 4(1) — 153n2
Provision of Municipal Services (Reorganization) Ordinance (Cap. 552) — 128n199
Public Order (Amendment) Ordinance (No. 67 of 1980) — 263n5
Public Order (Amendment) Ordinance (No. 77 of 1995) — 277n86
Public Order (Amendment) Ordinance (No. 119 of 1997) — 279n94, 282n114
Public Order Ordinance (Cap. 245) — 35, 176, 199n347, 204–205, 207n411, 263, 277–278, 289
    Section 13 — 204n388
    Section 14(1) — 204n389
    Section 15(2) — 204n389
Regional Flag and Regional Emblem Ordinance (No. 117 of 1997)
    Section 7 — 296n194
Rules of Procedure of the Legislative Council of the Hong Kong SAR — 145
    Rule 57(6) — 145n284
Rules of the High Court (Cap. 4, Subsidiary Legislation A)
    Order 53, Rule 3(7) — 185n238
Securities (Insider Dealing) Ordinance (Cap. 395) — 176–177

Table of Other Legislation and International Agreements   xxvii

Sex Discrimination Ordinance (Cap. 480)	144n280, 271n50
Societies (Amendment) Ordinance (No. 75 of 1992)	277n86
Societies (Amendment) Ordinance (No. 118 of 1997)	279n94
Societies Ordinance (Cap. 151)	35, 277–278
Summary Offences Ordinance (Cap. 228)	204n385
Village Representative Election Ordinance (Cap. 576)	206n400
Voting by Imprisoned Persons Ordinance (No. 7 of 2009)	301n227

People's Republic of China Legislation

Administrative Litigation Law of the PRC	169
Basic Law of the Macao Special Administrative Region of the PRC	42, 134n224, 258n241, 258n244
Article 84	83n191
Article 144	46n71
Constitution of the PRC 1982	3, 50–54, 258, 287–288
Preamble	180n200
Chapter II	288n141
Chapter III, Section 6	56n9
Article 1	52
Article 2	180n197
Article 10	53n130, 304n6, 306n20
Article 13	304n6, 306n21
Article 25	52n117
Article 31	50n110, 51–54
Article 35	48, 288n140
Article 36	52n120
Article 46	170n123
Article 49	52n118
Article 51	288n142
Article 54	288n143
Article 57	20, 41n40, 180n197
Article 58	249n184
Article 62(2)	53n127, 86n218
Article 62(3)	20, 42n41, 78n159, 258n240
Article 62(7)	86n216, 180n195
Article 62(13)	42n41, 51n113
Article 63(4)	180n195
Article 64	53n124, 258n240, 258n246
Article 67	86n219
Article 67(1)	53n127, 86n218
Article 67(2)	42n47, 78n159
Article 67(3)	42n47, 258n240, 258n244
Article 67(4)	25, 83, 221–222, 239n117
Article 67(7)	43n53, 170n125
Article 67(8)	43n53, 170n125
Article 67(11)	86n216, 180n195

xxviii Table of Other Legislation and International Agreements

Article 72	258n240
Article 85	40n20
Article 89(1)	42n49, 79n162
Article 90	43n50
Article 93	40n20
Article 94	180n198
Article 95	86n215
Article 100	43n52, 72n117
Article 101	86n216
Article 107	43n51
Article 115	76n146
Article 119	57n10
Article 127	82n189
Article 128	86n214, 180n195
Contract Law of the PRC	42n44
Criminal Law of the PRC	42, 210n431
Article 6	44n57
Article 7	44n57, 44n61, 45n65
Article 299	77n153
Criminal Procedure Law of the PRC	
Article 24	44n59
General Principles of the Civil Law of the PRC	42, 220n8, 306n22
Law of the PRC on Assemblies, Processions and Demonstrations	
Article 4	288n144
Law of the PRC on Judicial Immunity from Compulsory Measures Concerning the Property of Foreign Central Banks	76n144
Law of the PRC on the Garrisoning of the Hong Kong SAR	77n148, 211–213
Article 3	40n20
Article 6	80
Article 20	212n441, 212n444
Article 21	212n442
Article 23	212n448–450
Article 25	212n443
Law of the PRC on the National Flag	296n195, 297n199
Legislation Law of the PRC	42
Article 8	42n46
Article 12	258n245
Article 13	258n245
Article 43	236n97
Article 78	42n45
Article 79	42n45, 43n53
Article 83	45n67–68
Article 85	45n68
Article 89(2)	73n123
Marriage Law of the PRC	76n146
Measure Concerning the Execution of Deputies' Duties by the Deputies of the Hong Kong SAR to the NPC	68n87

Measures for the Election of Deputies of the Hong Kong SAR of the PRC to the 12th NPC	78n161, 90n249
Article 5	90n250
Military Service Law of the PRC	
Article 12	78n157
Nationality Law of the PRC	42, 66, 183n226
Organic Law of the People's Courts of the PRC	42n43
Article 35	86n216
Patent Law of the PRC	42n44
Property Rights Law of the PRC	306n22
Regulations of the PRC Concerning Diplomatic Privileges and Immunities	
Article 22(1)(3)	210n434

Foreign Legislation

Australia
Commonwealth of Australia Constitution Act 1900	48n91

Canada
Charter of Rights and Freedoms 1982	
Section 1	291n160
Section 2	48n91
Constitution Act 1867	
Section 91	65n69

Denmark
Greenland Home Rule Act 1978	
Section 18	88n234

Finland
Act on the Autonomy of Aland 1991	
Section 18	72n115
Section 19	74n130
Section 27	72n116

Germany
German Basic Law 1949	
Section 5(i)	48n91

United Kingdom
Constitutional Reform Act 2005	
Section 31	163n82
Schedule 12	163n81
Crown Proceedings Act 1947	212n447
European Communities Act 1972	
Section 2(1)	171n128
Section 2(4)	171n128

Human Rights Act 1998
    Section 3(1) — 171n128
Official Secrets Act 1911 — 26n60
United Kingdom Forces (Jurisdiction of Colonial Courts) Order 1965 — 211n438
War Damage Act 1965 — 233n81

United States
Constitution of the United States of America 1787 — 1, 48, 170
    Article I, Section 8 — 72n118
    Article III — 170n122
    1st Amendment 1791 — 48n91
Judiciary Act 1789 — 170n122
United States–Hong Kong Policy Act 1992 — 63

International Agreements, Conventions and Treaties

Convention for the Extension of Hong Kong Territory 1898 — 10
Convention of Peking 1860 — 10
International Covenant on Civil and Political Rights 1966 — 7–8, 63, 172, 234n85, 270–302
    Article 2(1) — 141n265, 270n48, 282
    Article 3 — 141n265, 282
    Article 4(1) — 287n134
    Article 4(2) — 287n134
    Article 6 — 282
    Article 6(2) — 286n130
    Article 6(5) — 286n130
    Article 7 — 282, 286n132
    Article 8 — 282
    Article 9 — 282
    Article 10 — 282
    Article 11 — 282
    Article 12 — 271n49, 282
    Article 12(3) — 294n179
    Article 13 — 271n49, 282
    Article 14 — 283
    Article 14(1) — 294n184
    Article 14(2) — 293n175
    Article 15(1) — 283, 285
    Article 16 — 283
    Article 17 — 283
    Article 18 — 283, 286n133
    Article 18(3) — 294n184
    Article 19 — 275n72, 283
    Article 19(3) — 198n344, 294n179, 294n181
    Article 21 — 275n72, 283, 290n154, 294n179–180, 294n182

Table of Other Legislation and International Agreements   xxxi

Article 22	283
Article 22(2)	294n179–180, 294n182
Article 23	283
Article 24	283
Article 25	283, 299, 301n224
Article 25(b)	140–141
Article 26	141n265, 284
Article 27	284
Article 28	273n64
Article 40	273n64
International Covenant on Economic, Social and Cultural Rights 1966	270–274
Article 2(1)	274n67
Article 7(a)(i)	271n50
Article 16	273n64–65
Joint Declaration of the Government of the PRC and the Government of the Republic of Portugal on the Question of Macao 1987	134n224
Joint Declaration of the Government of the United Kingdom of Great Britain and Northern Ireland and the Government of the PRC on the Question of Hong Kong 1984	2, 9, 13–18, 21–25, 32, 37–40, 46, 57, 125–127, 172n135, 189–190, 220, 224, 228, 261–262, 264, 271–274, 278, 304–305, 308–309, 311
Paragraph 1	16
Paragraph 2	16
Paragraph 3	16–18
Paragraph 3(1)	38
Paragraph 3(2)	16, 38, 55n1
Paragraph 3(3)	16, 38
Paragraph 3(4)	16, 38
Paragraph 3(5)	16–17, 38
Paragraph 3(6)	17
Paragraph 3(7)	16–17
Paragraph 3(8)	16–17
Paragraph 3(9)	17
Paragraph 3(10)	16–17
Paragraph 3(11)	16, 38n6, 80n168
Paragraph 3(12)	18, 38n4, 303n2, 309n36
Paragraph 5	16
Paragraph 8	18
Annex I	17–18, 259n252
Annex I(I)	125n181, 133n222, 145n289, 228n54, 307
Annex I(II)	17
Annex I(III)	17–18, 155n17, 189n266
Annex I(IX)	62n43
Annex I(XIII)	169n120, 271n53
Annex I(XIV	18, 38n10
Annex II(3)	16

Annex II(6)	16
Annex III	304–305
Annex III(2)	16, 305n11
Annex III(3)	16, 305n11
Annex III(4)	305n11
Optional Protocol to the International Covenant on Civil and Political Rights 1966	273n64
Treaty of Nanking 1842	10, 171n129
Treaty on the Functioning of the European Union 2007	
Article 267	251n199
Vienna Convention on the Law of Treaties 1969	
Article 52	11n3

Chapter 1
Introduction

From deciding who has the right to live in Hong Kong to determining how the government is allowed to spend taxpayers' money, virtually every aspect of life in Hong Kong is affected in innumerable ways by the Basic Law of the Hong Kong Special Administrative Region of the People's Republic of China (or "Hong Kong Basic Law", as it will be called in this book). As the highest law with practical effect in Hong Kong, it sets the framework for Hong Kong's system of government, how its courts operate, and the rights and freedoms enjoyed by its residents, to name just a few examples.

That makes an introductory knowledge of the Hong Kong Basic Law vital for anyone who wishes to understand not only Hong Kong's legal system, but also Hong Kong's way of life and system of government—as well as how these can be expected to evolve in years to come. The good news is that the Hong Kong Basic Law is a relatively youthful document, by comparison with many other constitutional documents around the world. Students of the US Constitution, for instance, must wade through more than 200 years of court cases to understand its provisions. By contrast, in Hong Kong's case, it is still less than 20 years since the Hong Kong Basic Law came into force on 1 July 1997.

That does not mean ignoring everything which happened before that date. As is explained in Chapter 2 on the "Birth of the Hong Kong Basic Law", many of the biggest controversies in modern-day Hong Kong involve issues first fought while the Hong Kong Basic Law was being written between 1985 and 1990. From the arguments over what form democratization should take to the battles over who has the power to interpret the Hong Kong Basic Law, the debates during the drafting process often had a profound effect on where Hong Kong finds itself today.

Take, for instance, the persistent suspicions about any attempt to enact the national security legislation required under Article 23 of the Hong Kong Basic Law. In 2003, such suspicions brought more than half a million protesters onto the streets in a watershed moment which, as we will see in this book, prompted Beijing to tighten its policy towards Hong Kong. The origins of such suspicions can be traced back to the history of the drafting of the Hong Kong Basic Law, which saw much tougher language inserted into Article 23 in the final draft of the Hong Kong Basic Law, primarily to punish Hong Kong people for supporting the Tiananmen protests that were crushed on 4 June 1989.

Official histories tend to portray the emergence of the Hong Kong Basic Law in its final form as the carefully calibrated result of a long and thoughtful process. But the picture presented in this book is of a series of historical accidents which—partly through luck—resulted in a largely fortuitous outcome, although less fortuitous than what might have been achieved had the Hong Kong Basic Law been finalized only a year earlier, before the events of June Fourth.

Those accidents began with the British colonizers agreeing, for reasons of diplomacy, to hold most parts of the territory on a 99-year lease with an expiry date of 30 June 1997—so setting a deadline by which the issue of Hong Kong's future would have to be resolved. They continued with China's emergence from decades of international isolation under the pragmatic leadership of Deng Xiaoping who sought to copy Hong Kong's economic success, just as the future of that success was starting to come into question because of increasing concerns about what would happen after 1997. That a solution presented itself in the shape of the "one country, two systems" formula which China devised for Taiwan was a stroke of luck. Perhaps fortuitously for Hong Kong, Taiwan rejected this formula—so prompting the change of strategy in Beijing that resulted in this formula being applied to Hong Kong instead.

As we will see in Chapter 2, the result of that series of historical accidents was first the Sino-British Joint Declaration, the 1984 international treaty in which Beijing and London agreed on how one country, two systems would be applied in Hong Kong, and then the Hong Kong Basic Law in which those promises were written into a law enacted by China's National People's Congress. Although it endured an often rocky path, with disagreements between Britain and China persisting up until the night of 30 June 1997, that agreement has proved strong enough to survive. More than a quarter of a century later, what is striking is how much the provisions of that 1984 treaty still provide a generally accurate picture of Hong Kong today. It is an agreement that has, to a large extent, stood the test of time and for all its undoubted flaws probably represents a better deal for Hong Kong than might well have been secured at almost any other time in Hong Kong's history.

Some of the more confusing aspects of the Hong Kong Basic Law are its multiple dimensions. In Chapter 3 on "What Is the Hong Kong Basic Law?", this book seeks to disentangle them. As already noted, its origins lie in the 1984 agreement between Britain and China, so providing an international dimension to the Hong Kong Basic Law which means that the Joint Declaration is still sometimes referred to in court cases to help understand the correct meaning of ambiguous provisions in the Hong Kong Basic Law. But the actual legal status of the Hong Kong Basic Law is that of a statute enacted by the National People's Congress, the highest body of constitutional power in China. That gives rise to its domestic dimension, as well as the name "basic law"—which, in fact, more properly describes a whole class of laws enacted by the National People's Congress rather than this one single enactment.

By far the most important dimension from Hong Kong's perspective is the constitutional one, with the Hong Kong Basic Law serving as the highest law with practical effect in Hong Kong, and the benchmark against which the legality of all other laws in Hong Kong are judged. Note, however, the qualification imposed by those three words: with practical effect. As we will see in Chapter 3, the Hong Kong Basic Law is not the highest law of all—a title which, instead, goes to the national constitution, the Constitution of the People's Republic of China 1982. But since most of the provisions in that constitution concern the socialist system on the mainland which are of little practical effect in Hong Kong, that raises difficult—and, to some extent, unanswered—questions about how much of the national constitution actually applies in Hong Kong, and the nature of its relationship with the Hong Kong Basic Law.

At the heart of the Hong Kong Basic Law is the concept of a high degree of autonomy. However, nowhere is this concept precisely defined. Instead, Article 2 of the Hong Kong Basic Law refers only in general terms to Hong Kong enjoying "executive, legislative and independent judicial power, including that of final adjudication". That refers to three of the fundamental powers that international experts on autonomy have identified as central to most autonomous arrangements elsewhere in the world—the right of any area to administer its own affairs, make its own laws and judge its own cases.

As we will see in Chapter 4 on "How High a Degree of Autonomy?", in all three respects the Hong Kong Basic Law confers, at least on paper, extraordinarily wide-ranging powers upon Hong Kong. From exclusive jurisdiction to administer its financial affairs and participate in some international organizations to the power to make laws on almost every subject and the existence of a Court of Final Appeal, Hong Kong enjoys powers which are rarely exercised at a local level under even the most generous autonomy arrangements elsewhere in the world. But we will also see that, in all three respects, much depends on how much self-restraint China chooses to exercise. From its control over the Chief Executive to the power to impose national laws and supplant decisions of the Hong Kong courts with its own interpretations of the Hong Kong Basic Law, the provisions of the Hong Kong Basic Law give Beijing ample means to exercise much greater control over Hong Kong should it wish to do so.

The degree of self-restraint which China has exercised in using these powers has varied. As is explained in Chapter 4, China's self-restraint was at its greatest in the years immediately after 1 July 1997, when the eyes of the world were on Hong Kong. However, it subsequently took a turn towards a more interventionist approach after the huge public protest against national security legislation on 1 July 2003. When Beijing does choose to exercise its powers in a way which reduces the extent of Hong Kong's autonomy—as with a 2004 interpretation from the National People's Congress Standing Committee seizing control of decisions on any changes to the system for electing the Legislative Council—there is no legal mechanism for Hong Kong to challenge this. As we will see, that is one of the biggest shortcomings of the autonomy granted to Hong Kong under the Hong Kong Basic Law since, unlike many autonomous arrangements elsewhere in the world, there is no independent mechanism for resolving any disputes about who exercises any particular power.

One of the most important functions of the Hong Kong Basic Law is to set out the system of government in Hong Kong. Nearly 40% of its 160 provisions are devoted to this, more than any other subject. But as is explained in Chapter 5 on the "System of Government", despite this large number of provisions, there are some important points missing from its description of Hong Kong's system of government. The Hong Kong Basic Law goes into great detail about the powers of the Chief Executive who, as the head of the Hong Kong SAR Government, is responsible for leading Hong Kong. The powers of Hong Kong's legislature, known as the Legislative Council, are described in similar detail. What is missing is a full description of the precise relationship between the Chief Executive's powers and those of the Legislative Council, an omission which has arguably done much to contribute to the repeated conflicts—and persistently poor relations—between the executive and legislature throughout much of the history of the Hong Kong SAR.

China prefers to describe the system of government set out in the Hong Kong Basic Law as one of "executive-led government". That description, inherited from the colonial era, focuses on the powers of the Chief Executive and so has the advantage, from Beijing's perspective, of emphasizing the powers of the one part of Hong Kong's political structure which lies directly under the Central Government's control. As we will see in Chapter 5, the Hong Kong Basic Law does grant the Chief Executive sweeping powers, such as the power to make appointments without any need for approval by the legislature. Those powers are so sweeping, at least on paper, that one comparative study even found that the Hong Kong Basic Law grants the Chief Executive theoretically greater powers than popularly elected presidents in 33 other countries, including the US.

Despite its frequent use by both Chinese and Hong Kong SAR Government officials, the term "executive-led government" does not appear anywhere in the text of the Hong Kong Basic Law. Many scholars, pointing to the other important powers placed in the hands of the Legislative Council and the courts, argue that it is more accurate instead to describe the system of government under the Hong Kong Basic Law as one of "separation of powers"—so placing more emphasis on the division of powers between the executive, legislature and judiciary.

In addition, the small-circle election process which has always been used to choose the Chief Executive so far deprives Hong Kong's leader of the legitimacy that a democratic mandate confers on popularly elected leaders in many other countries. As is explained in Chapter 5, this makes it very difficult in practice for Hong Kong's Chief Executive to exercise many of the sweeping powers granted to the Chief Executive under the Hong Kong Basic Law.

Many members of the Legislative Council are also elected through small-circle elections in functional constituencies, some of which have only a few hundred voters. However, since half of all seats in the legislature are elected through universal suffrage, the overall franchise in Legislative Council polls is currently far higher than in elections for the Chief Executive. That has given the Legislative Council a greater democratic legitimacy which has helped the legislature push the exercise of its powers much further than Beijing appears to have originally envisaged during the drafting of the Hong Kong Basic Law, prompting angry complaints from some mainland scholars.

That may also have been one motive behind Beijing's decision to allow the Chief Executive to be elected by universal suffrage from 2017 onwards, with elections for all seats in the Legislative Council expected to follow the same path at a later date. But, as we will see in Chapter 5, it is far from clear how far the nomination procedures prescribed in the Hong Kong Basic Law will restrict the range of candidates allowed to stand in any future Chief Executive contest, and whether functional constituencies will be abolished when universal suffrage is eventually introduced for elections to all seats in the Legislative Council.

In contrast to its detailed descriptions of the powers of both the Chief Executive and the Legislative Council, the Hong Kong Basic Law says relatively little about the role of the courts. As is explained in Chapter 6 on the "Role of the Courts", this reflects an emphasis on continuity rather than detail since the judicial system that existed in Hong Kong prior to 1 July 1997 was widely viewed as one of the ingredients of Hong Kong's success. As a result, the Hong Kong Basic Law preserves that judicial system largely unchanged, with the exception of the creation of the Court of Final Appeal to succeed the Judicial Committee of the Privy Council in London, which had served as Hong Kong's highest court under colonial rule.

The Hong Kong Basic Law goes to some lengths to seek to protect the independence of the judiciary, particularly when it comes to judicial appointments. These are placed in the hands of an independent commission, so severely limiting the Chief Executive's influence over the process. Once appointed, judges enjoy near absolute job security until they reach retirement age, although their salaries are not similarly protected, a point of some concern to the judiciary, which has unsuccessfully sought to persuade the Hong Kong SAR Government to change this.

As we will see in Chapter 6, the absence of any detailed description of the powers of the courts in the Hong Kong Basic Law has left the courts free to define some of these powers for themselves. That is particularly true in the field of judicial review, an important and growing area of law, where the courts exercise the power to determine the legality of actions of the government and other public bodies. In its landmark January 1999 decision in *Ng Ka Ling v Director of Immigration*,[1] the first case decided by the Court of Final Appeal on the Hong Kong Basic Law and one of the most important cases in Hong Kong's legal history, the court asserted that this power includes the power to invalidate any other Hong Kong laws which it decides are in breach of the Hong Kong Basic Law. Although this power is not explicitly granted to the courts under the Hong Kong Basic Law, and at least one mainland drafter claims it was never China's intention to do so, the court's assertion of the right to exercise this power has never been seriously challenged in Hong Kong since then—and has become an important part of the rule of law in Hong Kong.

In the *Ng Ka Ling* case, the Court of Final Appeal also sought to extend this power even further, controversially claiming the Hong Kong courts have a power to invalidate any actions of the National People's Congress and its Standing Committee which they decide are in breach of the Hong Kong Basic Law. That provoked a furious response

---

1. (1999) 2 HKCFAR 4.

from Beijing, which calls into question whether the courts would ever dare to exercise this power in practice. It also put the Court of Final Appeal on the defensive, especially after a June 1999 interpretation of the Hong Kong Basic Law by the Standing Committee reversed much of the substance of what the court had decided in the *Ng Ka Ling* case.

The result, as is explained in Chapter 6, was a couple of questionable decisions in subsequent politically charged cases, where the Court of Final Appeal appeared to be at least partly motivated by a desire to avoid another confrontation with Beijing so soon. But this period of apparent retreat only lasted from 1999 to 2001, ending when the court demonstrated once more in the important case of *Director of Immigration v Chong Fung Yuen*[2] that it was still willing to take unpopular decisions that risked angering Beijing where this was the inevitable consequence of the clear wording of the Hong Kong Basic Law. After that case, most observers agree the Court of Final Appeal recovered its confidence and, throughout most of the period when it was headed by Andrew Li (the first Chief Justice of the Hong Kong SAR from 1997 to 2010), the court played a strong role in protecting the fundamental freedoms guaranteed under the Hong Kong Basic Law.

Nonetheless, the shadow of the National People's Congress Standing Committee's power to interpret any part of the Hong Kong Basic Law at any time continues to hang over the Hong Kong courts. As is explained in Chapter 7 on "Interpretation and Amendment", there is strong evidence to suggest that it was never the intention of the drafters of the Hong Kong Basic Law to confer such an unrestricted power of interpretation on the Standing Committee, especially the power to determine the meaning of the large parts of the Hong Kong Basic Law which concern matters that fall within Hong Kong's autonomy. Nonetheless, that is the position which has emerged in practice after the Standing Committee's June 1999 interpretation was swiftly accepted by the Court of Final Appeal in an unfortunate decision in the case of *Lau Kong Yung v Director of Immigration*.[3] Decided at a time when the court was still in its period of judicial retreat, that case saw the Court of Final Appeal adopt an even wider view of the Standing Committee's powers than the Standing Committee had, at that time, unequivocally asserted for itself.

Although the accepted position now is that there are no legal limits on the Standing Committee's power to interpret the Hong Kong Basic Law, the Standing Committee has been very cautious about exercising this power so far. The Standing Committee issued only a handful of interpretations during the early years of the Hong Kong SAR and only one of these, in 2004, was at the Standing Committee's own initiative. That 2004 interpretation, on changes to Hong Kong's electoral system, illustrated the importance of Standing Committee interpretations by taking a power which Hong Kong would have been allowed to exercise on its own under the original wording of the Hong Kong Basic Law, and interpreting it in a way which instead gave the Standing Committee the final decision on the matter.

---

2. (2001) 4 HKCFAR 211.
3. (1999) 2 HKCFAR 300.

However, as we will see in Chapter 7, on other issues the Standing Committee has so far declined to intervene, even when it strongly disagreed with decisions of the Hong Kong courts, such as after the *Chong Fung Yuen* case. The Hong Kong SAR Government also seems to have adopted a cautious approach to requesting interpretations from the Standing Committee, generally trying to exhaust all other legal avenues first. The Court of Final Appeal showed similar caution during the early years of the Hong Kong SAR, despite a provision in the Hong Kong Basic Law requiring it to seek an interpretation from the Standing Committee of those provisions in the Hong Kong Basic Law covering matters outside Hong Kong's autonomy, when these are necessary to decide a particular case. In early decisions such as *Ng Ka Ling* and *Chong Fung Yuen*, the Court of Final Appeal always found reasons for concluding that these were not cases which needed to be referred to the Standing Committee.

Only in 2011, did the court finally overcome its reluctance to refer an issue of interpretation to the Standing Committee by a narrow 3 to 2 majority in the case of *Democratic Republic of Congo v FG Hemisphere*.[4] Even then, the Court of Final Appeal was careful to keep as much control as possible over the process, presenting its own views to the Standing Committee on how these provisions should be interpreted in a lengthy judgment which the Standing Committee swiftly endorsed.

One of the most important tasks of the Court of Final Appeal, and indeed the Hong Kong courts as a whole, is to uphold the wide range of fundamental freedoms guaranteed under the Hong Kong Basic Law. As is explained in Chapter 8 on "Protection of Human Rights", these freedoms go beyond the long list of rights specifically mentioned in the Hong Kong Basic Law to include many more in several international human rights treaties such as the International Covenant on Civil and Political Rights, most parts of which continue in force under the Hong Kong Basic Law.

Comprehensive protection of fundamental freedoms in Hong Kong did not start with the Hong Kong Basic Law. In 1991, the enactment of the Hong Kong Bill of Rights Ordinance (Cap. 383) marked Hong Kong's first human rights revolution as it wrote most of the rights listed in the International Covenant on Civil and Political Rights into Hong Kong law, allowing government actions that breached those fundamental freedoms to be challenged in the courts for the first time.

But, as we will see in Chapter 8, the Hong Kong Basic Law marked Hong Kong's second human rights revolution, setting off a further wave of legal challenges, especially over its generous—but often controversial—provisions on who has the right to reside permanently in Hong Kong (which is known as the "right of abode").

That does not mean that the rights listed in the Hong Kong Basic Law can never be restricted. In any society, it is sometimes necessary to restrict even such fundamental rights as freedom of speech and the right to protest if only to protect, for example, the rights and freedoms of others. The Hong Kong Basic Law explicitly recognizes this but

---

4. (2011) 14 HKCFAR 95.

then, again drawing heavily on provisions of the International Covenant on Civil and Political Rights, lays down a succession of stringent tests which must be satisfied before any restriction can be imposed, so ensuring that any restrictions on rights are kept to a minimum.

Since 1 July 1997, the Hong Kong courts have generally adopted a rigorous approach in applying these tests in defence of the fundamental freedoms protected under the Hong Kong Basic Law. But, as is explained in Chapter 8, there have been isolated exceptions such as the Court of Final Appeal's December 1999 decision in the politically sensitive case of *HKSAR v Ng Kung Siu*,[5] which involved a law protecting China's national flag and was decided at a time when the court was still in its period of judicial retreat.

The Hong Kong Basic Law is often referred to as spanning a period of 50 years from 1997, with the implication that everything it says about Hong Kong's separate system and current way of life will suddenly come to an end on 30 June 2047. But, as is explained in the conclusion to this book, Chapter 9 on "What Will Happen After 2047?", the Hong Kong Basic Law does not explicitly mention this date, except in the context of a now outdated provision about renewing some land leases before 30 June 1997.

Nor, despite occasional suggestions by some scholars to the contrary, is there anything in the Hong Kong Basic Law to suggest that its provisions will automatically expire come 30 June 2047. What does become possible after that date are fundamental changes to the Hong Kong Basic Law which are, at least in theory, forbidden before that date.

To some, that is an opportunity for Hong Kong to rid itself of any provisions which have become outdated by that date. Already there have been suggestions that the advent of 30 June 2047 could be used to help solve the problems posed by a provision in the Hong Kong Basic Law protecting the special rights enjoyed by indigenous inhabitants of the New Territories.

But, as we will see in Chapter 9, the issue of how much change to push for in the run-up to 30 June 2047 presents a delicate balancing act. While some changes may be considered desirable, once you start fiddling with the current structure of the Hong Kong Basic Law it raises the risk of providing an opportunity for anyone on the mainland resentful of Hong Kong's privileges to press for other changes (such as curtailing rights and freedoms) which would certainly not be considered desirable in Hong Kong. It is this delicate balancing act which may well prove to be one of the most important issues Hong Kong will have to grapple with in the coming decades.

---

5. (1999) 2 HKCFAR 442.

Chapter 2
Birth of the Hong Kong Basic Law

History is sometimes described as a series of accidents of timing, some fortuitous, others not. In Hong Kong's case, few would dispute that, while the path was often a rocky one, those accidents of history ultimately had a fortuitous outcome. That fortuitous outcome is a remarkable arrangement, known as "one country, two systems", under which Hong Kong is allowed to differ far more radically from the rest of the country of which it is a part—and, in some crucial respects, function almost like an independent nation—than almost anywhere else in the world that is not a country in its own right. It is an arrangement enshrined in an equally remarkable document, the Basic Law of the Hong Kong Special Administrative Region of the People's Republic of China—or Hong Kong Basic Law, as it will be called in this book.

The Hong Kong Basic Law was the product of a brief window of opportunity as China began to emerge from decades of isolation during the early 1980s. Although promulgated by China in 1990, its contents were effectively decided six years earlier in 1984, when Britain and China concluded the Joint Declaration on the Question of Hong Kong. In return for reluctantly promising to return all of Hong Kong to China on 1 July 1997, that 1984 agreement saw Britain persuade an equally reluctant China to make extremely detailed promises about the nature of the "one country, two systems" arrangement that Hong Kong would be permitted to enjoy for at least 50 years beyond that date, together with a commitment to write these promises into a document that would be known as the Hong Kong Basic Law.

It would have been inconceivable for China to have made those promises at any time up until a few years earlier. From shortly after the Communists took power in 1949 through to the end of the Cultural Revolution in 1976, China had been plagued by decades of Maoist-inspired political campaigns aimed at eradicating any trace in the rest of the country of the capitalist system practised in Hong Kong. While Communist rulers tacitly tolerated Hong Kong's continued existence as a separate entity under British rule, any Chinese leader who might have been foolish enough, during those periods of leftist turmoil, to formally advocate enshrining the continued existence of a capitalist system in Hong Kong would have been signing their own arrest warrant.

Only with Deng Xiaoping's rise to power in the late 1970s, and the advent of more pragmatic policies emphasizing economic development, in which Hong Kong was expected to play a major role, did a brief window of opportunity to strike a deal securing the city's future emerge. Just how brief that window of opportunity would be is only evident with the benefit of hindsight. For instance, from today's perspective, it seems almost inconceivable that Chinese leaders would have agreed to such an extraordinary arrangement for Hong Kong had the same negotiations taken place now, when China has already emerged as an economic power in its own right and Hong Kong no longer plays such a critical role as a conduit for foreign investment.

2.1 The 1997 Deadline

That Hong Kong's future should have fallen to be determined by a deadline of 1 July 1997 was the product of another accident of history almost a century earlier. Britain had begun its conquest of Hong Kong by bombarding Qing dynasty China into signing treaties ceding parts of the colony in perpetuity: first Hong Kong Island under the Treaty of Nanking in 1842 concluding Britain's first Opium War with China in 1842, and then the southern tip of Kowloon under the Convention of Peking in 1860 concluding a second Opium War.

By the time it came to the last major extension of Hong Kong's boundaries in 1898, to add the New Territories including all of Kowloon north of the present Boundary Street in Mongkok, the Qing authorities refused to cede any further territory to Britain in perpetuity, for fear of setting a precedent which would be seized upon by other foreign powers. Instead, they offered a 99-year lease, which Britain readily accepted and was written into the Convention for the Extension of Hong Kong Territory as starting from 1 July 1898 — with little attention apparently being paid to the fact that this started the clock ticking on a 30 June 1997 deadline for British rule over most of Hong Kong.

Even then, the significance of that deadline might have been reduced if Britain had drawn a distinction between those parts of Hong Kong ceded in perpetuity under the two earlier treaties, and the land leased under this third treaty. But, with questionable legality[1] and little thought for the future, Britain almost immediately cast aside this distinction. An Order in Council, made by the British government in the name of the Queen on 20 October 1898, declared the New Territories and those parts of Kowloon leased with it integrated into the rest of Hong Kong and to be treated until 30 June 1997 "for all intents and purposes as if they had originally formed part of the said colony".[2] Before long, Boundary Street, the notional border between the ceded and leased parts of Hong Kong had become simply another street in the urban sprawl of Kowloon.

---

1. Wesley-Smith draws an interesting analogy between Britain's rights over the leased territory and a tenant's rights over property owned by another landlord. See Peter Wesley-Smith, *Constitutional and Administrative Law in Hong Kong* (Longman Asia, 2nd edition, 1994) at 27. [Note: Unless otherwise stated, all references following cited source(s) in footnotes are to page number(s) in those source(s).]
2. Clause 1 of The New Territories Order in Council, reprinted in Peter Wesley-Smith, *Unequal Treaty 1898–1997: China, Great Britain and Hong Kong's New Territories* (Oxford University Press, Revised edition, 1998) at 321–322.

That action removed any doubt that when 30 June 1997 arrived, the issue of Hong Kong would have to be dealt with as a whole. But it was not an issue that successive Chinese governments were in any rush to address. From at least the 1920s onwards, those in power in Beijing, first the Kuomintang and then the Communists, refused to recognize the three treaties as granting Britain any legal authority to rule Hong Kong. They argued that these were "unequal treaties", which had been forced upon China against its will and so were invalid, a position which finds some support in modern international law.[3]

Whatever their formal position, those in power in Beijing were careful not to disrupt the status quo. When the People's Liberation Army conquered Guangdong for the Communists in October 1949, they stopped 25 miles north of the border with Hong Kong. Even at the height of the Cultural Revolution in 1967, Chinese Premier Zhou Enlai reportedly intervened to halt plans drawn up by a local army commander to invade Hong Kong.[4]

Whether it was as a conduit for smuggling goods into China in the 1950s, in breach of the international embargo imposed during the Korean War, or as a means of attracting foreign investment after China began to open up its economy in the late 1970s, Hong Kong under British rule served a useful purpose for many decades as China's window on the outside world. That was reflected in China's repeatedly stated official position that, while Britain had no legal right to be in Hong Kong, the status quo should be maintained until some undefined time in the future when "conditions are ripe" for a change.[5]

Deng Xiaoping's rise to power in the late 1970s brought with it a new enthusiasm for forging more cordial ties with the Western world. However, that did not initially arouse any interest in Beijing in addressing the issue of Hong Kong's future. Taiwan was seen as a more immediate priority, especially after the US cut official ties with the island in 1979 in order to open full diplomatic relations with Beijing. Hoping to make the isolated island more receptive towards overtures for reunification, China quickly came up with an early version of a policy—which would later become known as "one country, two systems"—designed to woo Taiwan down this path. First mentioned in general terms in 1979 by the National People's Congress Standing Committee, by 1981 it had taken on the shape of a nine-point plan.

Many of these nine points, such as allowing Taiwan a high degree of autonomy and the right to retain its socio-economic system as well as existing way of life, would eventually be applied to Hong Kong. But that was not the intention at this stage. As far as China

---

3. Article 52 of the Vienna Convention on the Law of Treaties 1969, 1155 United Nations Treaty Series 331, states that: "A treaty is void if its conclusion has been procured by the threat or use of force in violation of the principles of international law embodied in the Charter of the United Nations." However, the Vienna Convention is not retrospective and so does not apply to pre-1969 treaties. See further Yash Ghai, *Hong Kong's New Constitutional Order: The Resumption of Chinese Sovereignty and the Basic Law* (Hong Kong University Press, 2nd edition, 1999) at 11–12.
4. "PLA invasion aired twice", *South China Morning Post*, 23 June 2007.
5. See, for instance, the editorial on this point which appeared in the *People's Daily*, the official newspaper of China's ruling Communist Party, on 8 March 1963.

was concerned, Hong Kong should be satisfied with a few general reassurances. That was most vividly demonstrated in March 1979, during the first official visit to Beijing by a Hong Kong Governor, Sir Murray MacLehose. Deng brushed aside MacLehose's attempt to raise the most pressing problem concerning the 1997 deadline with a vague statement that investors in Hong Kong should "put their hearts at ease".

Such vague reassurances could not solve the problem of the expiry of government land leases in the New Territories and, in practice, throughout the rest of Hong Kong. Fittingly for a city which had built so much of its prosperity upon soaring property prices, it was the issue of land rights which provided the immediate impetus for resolving Hong Kong's future. Apart from one site in Central,[6] all land in Hong Kong was ultimately owned by the British Crown, and sold to its users by the Hong Kong Government, not in perpetuity but on long leases of 75 years, or sometimes even 999 years. That system was a great way of filling the government's coffers, and does much to explain why Hong Kong's taxation rates are among the lowest in the developed world. But it suffered from the drawback that it was generally assumed that leases granted under British rule could only last for as long as Britain had the legal authority to rule Hong Kong.[7] As a result, all land leases in the fast-expanding New Territories were set to expire before 30 June 1997.

Britain cited the land lease issue as its ostensible reason for pushing so hard during the late 1970s and early 1980s to resolve the issue of Hong Kong's future,[8] despite China's lack of interest in discussing the issue and its evident willingness to allow British rule to continue unchallenged for the immediate future. British officials involved in the discussions at the time claim business confidence in Hong Kong was being undermined by the inability to issue leases lasting beyond 30 June 1997, so shortening the timeframe in which any new investment in the New Territories would have to be recouped.[9] Others are more sceptical, noting that there was little public sign of such a lack of confidence, with the Hang Seng Index soaring to new heights in 1978 and 1979, while property prices actually rose faster in the New Territories than Kowloon.[10]

In practice, while the uncertainty over land leases played a part, it seems more likely that the main reason why London pushed the issue so hard at this point was a desire to take advantage of what was described as "a window of opportunity"[11] to settle Hong Kong's future, before developments in China slammed the window shut again. It is

---

6. St. John's Cathedral on Garden Road.
7. See, however, Wesley-Smith, *Constitutional and Administrative Law in Hong Kong* (see note 1) at 59–61 for a brief discussion of the various options that were canvassed as providing a possible legal basis for extending land leases beyond this period.
8. Her Majesty's Government, *White Paper on a Draft Agreement Between the Government of Great Britain and Northern Ireland and the Government of the People's Republic of China on the Future of Hong Kong* (26 Sept 1984) at 2.
9. See, for instance, Robin McLaren, *Britain's Record in Hong Kong* (Royal Institute of International Affairs, 1997) at 12.
10. Robert Cottrell, *The End of Hong Kong: The Secret Diplomacy of Imperial Retreat* (John Murray, 1993) at 41–44.
11. McLaren, *Britain's Record in Hong Kong* (see note 9) at 13.

not that Britain was clairvoyant enough to see how China's economy would grow to a point where Hong Kong's role as a gateway for foreign investment (and, with it, perhaps some of the rationale for allowing "one country, two systems" in Hong Kong) would become relatively less important. Rather, in the words of Sir Percy Cradock, one of the major architects of British policy towards Hong Kong, it was simply a matter of moving quickly to take advantage of the fact that, after decades of instability, China finally had a pragmatic leader in the form of Deng Xiaoping: "We could not be sure how long this situation would last. We would be wise to exploit it while we could."[12]

It was not easy to persuade China to make the issue of Hong Kong's future a priority. A British proposal to solve the land lease problem by extending individual leases in the New Territories beyond 30 June 1997 was rejected by Deng Xiaoping during his 1979 meeting with Governor MacLehose, possibly without even understanding what was actually being proposed.[13] Rebuffed on this specific proposal, Britain continued to press the issue of Hong Kong's future, provoking some annoyance from China. "They are forcing the issue. But we will not be forced," Liao Chengzhi, then China's top official on Hong Kong affairs, was quoted as complaining during this period.[14]

The persistent British pressure paid off. According to Ching (2010), in December 1981 a meeting of the Politburo of China's ruling Communist Party took the historic decision that was to make possible the Sino-British Joint Declaration and the Hong Kong Basic Law.[15] With Taiwan showing no interest in responding to overtures for reunification, and Britain continually pushing the issue of Hong Kong, China decided to deal with Hong Kong first, rather than Taiwan. The "one country, two systems" formula that had been devised for Taiwan was adapted to apply instead to Hong Kong first, and hopefully set such a good example that Taiwan would become more enthusiastic about embracing the same arrangement at a later date.

2.2 Sino-British Joint Declaration

This change of policy finally made possible negotiations between China and Britain over Hong Kong's future. But it did not make them easy. For all its enthusiasm to begin such negotiations, Britain never expected the outcome would be its departure from Hong Kong. From London's perspective, the 19th-century treaties granting Hong Kong to Britain were just as valid as any other international treaties. While the lease on the

---

12. Percy Cradock, *Experiences of China* (John Murray, 1999) at 165.
13. Deng appears to have believed, possibly due to a mistake by his translator, that Governor MacLehose was proposing extending Britain's lease over the New Territories as a whole, as opposed to simply the granting of individual leases within the New Territories. See Cottrell, *The End of Hong Kong* (see note 10) at 55.
14. During a breakfast meeting with top Hong Kong financier Fung King Hey. Quoted in Cottrell, *The End of Hong Kong* (see note 10) at 63.
15. See Frank Ching, "Looking Back: How London and Beijing Decided the Fate of Hong Kong" (April 2010) 18 *Hong Kong Journal*.

New Territories only lasted until 30 June 1997, in theory the 1842 and 1860 treaties allowed Britain to remain in Hong Kong Island and southern Kowloon in perpetuity. The most that London initially envisaged was to exchange sovereignty for administration: by making a formal concession of Chinese sovereignty, that included Hong Kong Island and southern Kowloon, in return for an agreement on a continuing British role in running all of Hong Kong beyond 30 June 1997.

According to Ching (2010), some elements within the Chinese government were initially prepared to consider allowing some kind of continued British role in Hong Kong.[16] But more senior Chinese leaders ultimately decided against this. While Beijing tacitly tolerated the colonial presence in Hong Kong, senior leaders ultimately decided that entering into an agreement that formally recognized and extended Britain's presence would be as bad as signing the original treaties. Hence Deng Xiaoping's famous retort to then British Prime Minister Margaret Thatcher in September 1982, that: "[I]t would mean that the present Chinese government was just like the government of the late Qing dynasty."[17]

That remark came during a stormy meeting in the Great Hall of the People on the edge of Tiananmen Square, after Thatcher explicitly rejected "one country, two systems", or any other formula unless it allowed for a continuing British role in Hong Kong after 1 July 1997.[18] Thatcher then, coincidentally, slipped down the steps of the Great Hall of the People on exiting the meeting—an event widely interpreted as a bad omen in Hong Kong, and which ushered in a period of increasing nervousness over the two countries' fundamental disagreements over Hong Kong's future.

China stuck to its guns, in July 1983 unilaterally announcing a 12-point plan that adapted the "one country, two systems" formula for implementation in Hong Kong.[19] Gone were some of the concessions included in the original version of the formula with Taiwan in mind, notably the promise that the island could retain its own armed forces. In this area, China intended something very different for Hong Kong, with Deng Xiaoping subsequently making it clear that troops from the People's Liberation Army would be stationed in Hong Kong after 30 June 1997.[20] But in other areas, the first indications began

---

16. Ibid. These reportedly included the Department of Treaty and Law, West European Department, Foreign Trade Ministry and Xinhua News Agency.
17. "Our Basic Position on the Question of Hong Kong" (24 Sept 1982) in *Deng Xiaoping on the Question of Hong Kong* (Foreign Languages Press, 1993) at 2.
18. Cradock, *Experiences of China* (see note 12) at 178–180.
19. In a gesture of contempt for Britain, this 12-point plan was first unveiled to a group of visiting Hong Kong secondary school students, and British officials only learnt of its existence through press reports. See Cottrell, *The End of Hong Kong* (see note 10) at 112–113.
20. During a meeting with Sir S.Y. Chung and two other members of Hong Kong's Executive Council in June 1984, Deng dismissed as "sheer nonsense" reported suggestions by former Chinese foreign minister Huang Hua and former defence minister Geng Biao that there would be no need for such forces. See Ming K. Chan, "Different Roads to Home: The Retrocession of Hong Kong and Macau to Chinese Sovereignty" (2003) 12(36) *Journal of Contemporary China* 493, 509.

to emerge of the policies that subsequently would be enshrined in the Joint Declaration and the Hong Kong Basic Law. These included promises that Hong Kong could retain its existing legal system and have its own Court of Final Appeal.

Shaken by the September 1983 Hong Kong dollar crisis, in which the local currency was only saved from collapse by being pegged to the US greenback, Britain quickly gave way. In October, it agreed to negotiate on the basis of China's 12 general principles, conceding a month later that it no longer sought any kind of "authority" in Hong Kong after 30 June 1997.[21]

After that, the talks over Hong Kong's future began to make progress with British negotiators finding, to their amazement, that China appeared to have given no thought to the detailed implementation of "one country, two systems", beyond these 12 general principles. "We had been pushing at the door of a locked room, containing, as we thought, treasures of Chinese planning. Now the door was open and room was found to be virtually empty," recalled Sir Percy Cradock, then Britain's chief negotiator.[22] "This offered us an invaluable opportunity to fill the void with our essentials for post-1997 Hong Kong."

As a result, the detailed arrangements for "one country, two systems" were filled in largely on the basis of briefing papers supplied by British negotiators to their Chinese counterparts. These included, for instance, a British proposal in a paper on Hong Kong's legal system that the future Court of Final Appeal should be able to bolster its expertise by inviting judges from other common law jurisdictions to help hear its cases.[23] Swiftly adopted, this would prove of great significance to the development of Hong Kong's highest court after 1 July 1997.[24] Another concession was to prove of particular significance, both before and after the handover. In the final days of the negotiations, Britain persuaded China to agree to a provision stating that the Legislative Council would be "constituted by elections" after 1 July 1997.[25]

By September 1984, the deal over Hong Kong's future had been done and was published for the world to see. It was to be a further three months before the agreement was formally signed on 19 December 1984, during another visit to Beijing by Thatcher.[26] Even after that, the Joint Declaration did not finally come into force until three days after it was formally ratified on 27 May 1985.

---

21. Cradock, *Experiences of China* (see note 12) at 190–192.
22. Ibid. at 192–193.
23. Cottrell, *The End of Hong Kong* (see note 10) at 134–135.
24. See further "6.3: Composition of the Court of Final Appeal" in Chapter 6 for more on the subsequent controversy over the implementation of this provision in the Joint Declaration and the role played by these judges on the Court of Final Appeal.
25. Cottrell, *The End of Hong Kong* (see note 10) at 171. However, the Joint Declaration did not specify what form these "elections" would take, and this omission subsequently became a cause of controversy during the drafting of the Hong Kong Basic Law.
26. The delay was necessary in order to allow the Joint Declaration to be first approved by the British Parliament and China's NPC Standing Committee. The latter is a permanent body which handles many of the tasks of the NPC between its annual meetings.

The difference in opinion between China and Britain over the legality of the 19th-century treaties under which Britain had originally acquired Hong Kong was papered over in a series of parallel statements at the start of the Joint Declaration on the Question of Hong Kong. While China declared that "it has decided to resume the exercise of sovereignty over Hong Kong with effect from 1 July 1997" (paragraph 1), Britain separately acknowledged that it would "restore Hong Kong to the People's Republic of China" from that date (paragraph 2).

With that agreed, China then officially acknowledged for the first time that Britain would "be responsible for the administration of Hong Kong" until 30 June 1997 (paragraph 4). However, Britain was forced reluctantly to concede the creation of a Sino-British Joint Liaison Group (paragraph 5), consisting of senior diplomats from both countries, to conduct consultations on the implementation of the Joint Declaration and other subjects and to discuss matters relating to a smooth handover in 1997 (Annex II(3)). To allay British fears that this group would develop into a shadow government, it was explicitly described as "an organ for liaison and not an organ of power" that would "play no part in the administration of Hong Kong" (Annex II(6)). China also allowed Britain to issue and extend land leases until 30 June 2047 in return for an annual payment to the Hong Kong Government of "rent" equivalent to 3% of their rateable value (Annex III(2)–III(3)), so resolving the problem that was the ostensible impetus behind the decision to enter into negotiations in the first place.

The real meat of the Joint Declaration was in paragraph 3 of the main text, where China presented the final version of its 12-point plan, now described as "the basic policies of the People's Republic of China regarding Hong Kong". These provided for the future Hong Kong Special Administrative Region (or Hong Kong SAR), as Hong Kong would become known, to enjoy executive, legislative and independent judicial power, including the power of final adjudication (paragraph 3(3)). Crucially, these included exclusive responsibility for internal law and order (paragraph 3(11)), as well as the right to run its own finances independently without paying any taxes to the national authorities (paragraph 3(8)), maintain a separate currency (paragraph 3(7)), issue its own passports and even deal directly with foreign countries on a wide range of issues (paragraph 3(10)). Existing rights and freedoms would be preserved (paragraph 3(5)) and, in contrast to the situation in other parts of China, the Hong Kong SAR would be governed exclusively by "local inhabitants" (paragraph 3(4)). Only defence and foreign affairs (paragraph 3(2)), as well as the appointment of the future Chief Executive and his top officials (paragraph 3(4)), were expressly stated to be China's responsibility.

Judged by today's standards, these "basic policies" might seem like a relatively unremarkable statement of the realities of life in 21st-century Hong Kong. But judged from the perspective of the time when the Joint Declaration was concluded, they were revolutionary. The "basic policies" directly addressed many of the principal concerns of Hong Kong people about their future, especially fears that rights and freedoms would be restricted, Hong Kong's wealth plundered and the PLA put in charge of enforcing law and order. They also provided, at least on paper, for the future Hong Kong SAR to enjoy a degree of autonomy arguably higher than almost any other place in the world that is not a country in its own right.[27]

The basic policies placed a particularly heavy emphasis on preserving Hong Kong's existing economic system as part of this system of autonomy. Four of the 12 points are exclusively concerned with economic and financial issues (see paragraphs 3(6), (7), (8) and (9)) while two more touch on the issue (see parts of paragraphs 3(5) and (10)). That reflects the economic rationale partly underlying China's decision to allow Hong Kong to enjoy a modified version of the formula originally designed with Taiwan in mind, because of the huge economic benefits then flowing to China—especially in terms of foreign investment—through Hong Kong's existing economic system. This would, however, later lead to fears that, by focussing so heavily on economic issues, the underlying basis for Hong Kong's autonomy is fundamentally different from, and arguably weaker than, other places in the world that are also allowed to differ from the country of which they are part.[28] That is especially true if the original economic rationale for granting such autonomy starts to disappear, as may now be happening with Hong Kong's diminishing economic importance to China.

Impressive though they are, the 12 "basic policies" in paragraph 3 are far from the full extent of the promises on autonomy in the 1984 agreement. Less than 1,200 words long, the main text of the Joint Declaration is unusually short for an international treaty of such importance. That reflects Deng Xiaoping's reported aversion to including too much "detail" in any agreement with Britain,[29] a relic of Beijing's initial insistence that Hong Kong should be satisfied with a few general assurances. To assuage Chinese sensitivities, the detailed arrangements for "one country two systems", largely drawn from British briefing papers presented during the negotiations, were instead written into Annex I of the Joint Declaration. Running to more than 4,500 words, under the title "Elaboration by the Government of the People's Republic of China of its Basic Policies Regarding Hong Kong", Annex I is several times longer than the main text which it elaborates upon. It was here that Britain managed to get the detailed promises it sought on the arrangements for post-1 July 1997 Hong Kong—and which would subsequently form the core of the Hong Kong Basic Law—by the simple expedient of avoiding the word "details" and burying them near the back of the Joint Declaration.

Even a quick perusal provides a remarkably detailed—and generally accurate—picture of how "one country, two systems" would be put into practice after 1 July 1997. See, for instance, the detailed description of the sources of law that would be allowed to apply in the Hong Kong SAR in Annex I(II). This specifically mentions "the common law, rules of equity, ordinances, subordinate legislation and customary law". Hong Kong's post-1997 judicial system is set out in similar detail in Annex I(III), including the

---

27. This is discussed further in "Chapter 4: How High a Degree of Autonomy?".
28. See further page 57.
29. British negotiators reported an angry reaction from their Chinese counterparts every time they mentioned the word "detail" during the negotiations (personal communication with senior British negotiator, 1994).

important concession allowing judges from other common law jurisdictions to sit on the future Court of Final Appeal. Also of particular interest are the generous rules on who is entitled to right of abode in the Hong Kong SAR contained in Annex I(XIV), which became the cause of much controversy after 1 July 1997. Crucially, the entire contents of Annex I were explicitly given the same status as the main text of the Joint Declaration (paragraph 8 of the main text).

That was to be of great importance when it came to drafting the Hong Kong Basic Law, the existence of which was mentioned for the first time in paragraph 3(12) of the Joint Declaration. For all its importance, the Joint Declaration only has the status of an agreement between two countries and is not, in itself, a law directly enforceable in the courts. The Joint Declaration does not even use the word "treaty" in its title, largely due to Chinese sensitivities on the subject, although the general consensus is that this does not affect its status as an international treaty, which is binding on the two countries that signed it and registered with the United Nations.[30] But even as an international treaty, in accordance with the long-established position concerning the status of an international treaty at common law, the provisions contained in the Joint Declaration are not directly enforceable in the courts in Hong Kong without an accompanying law. This was reaffirmed shortly after the signing of the Joint Declaration in the case of *Tang Ping Hoi v Attorney General*,[31] when a landowner in the New Territories unsuccessfully sought to force the government to renew his land lease on the terms listed in the Joint Declaration.[32]

Hence the need for the Hong Kong Basic Law, to incorporate the provisions of the Joint Declaration into a law enforceable in the courts of Hong Kong. Crucially, under paragraph 3(12), both China's 12 "basic policies" in paragraph 3 of the Joint Declaration and the lengthy elaboration of them in Annex I must be incorporated in full into the Hong Kong Basic Law, where they would "remain unchanged for 50 years". Since these totalled more than 5,000 words in all, that meant a significant portion of its contents had been already decided even before any work started on drafting the Hong Kong Basic Law.

2.3 Drafting the Hong Kong Basic Law

If negotiating the Joint Declaration was a difficult process, the subsequent task of drafting the Hong Kong Basic Law proved even more explosive. From prolonged disputes over the method for electing the Chief Executive and Legislative Council to the fierce disputes

---

30. Joint Declaration of the Government of the United Kingdom of Great Britain and Northern Ireland and the Government of the People's Republic of China on the Question of Hong Kong 1984, 1399 United Nations Treaty Series 61. See further Roda Mushkat, *One Country Two International Legal Personalities: The Case of Hong Kong* (Hong Kong University Press, 1997) at 141–142.
31. [1987] HKLR 324, 326–328.
32. The case involved a land lease which expired before the formal ratification of the Joint Declaration on 27 May 1985, and so the Hong Kong Government insisted it was entitled to renew on terms less favourable than those stated in the Joint Declaration.

over who would have the power to interpret the Hong Kong Basic Law, most of the major controversies that would re-emerge after 1 July 1997 were fought out for the first time during the drafting process. The battles that began almost as soon as the ink was dry on the Joint Declaration in May 1985 raged on until the promulgation of the final version of the Hong Kong Basic Law on 1 April 1990 and, in some cases, have continued in slightly different forms ever since.

The fact that much of the content of the Hong Kong Basic Law had already been determined in the Joint Declaration did not always make the drafting process easier. Instead, it sometimes only added to the difficulties. For instance, the fact that the Hong Kong courts had been given the power of final adjudication under the Joint Declaration was reportedly cited by at least one mainland drafter[33] as an excuse for restricting the power of the Hong Kong courts to interpret all parts of the Hong Kong Basic Law, in case the courts made a "mistake" which it would then be impossible to correct. Equally, China's reluctant concession during the final days of negotiating the Joint Declaration that the Legislative Council would be "constituted by elections" after 1 July 1997[34] sparked a long and still ongoing battle over what the term "elections" actually means. Started during the drafting process in the late 1980s, this battle continued to rage through the final years of British rule and beyond the 1 July 1997 handover—as great ingenuity was put into devising electoral models involving restricted numbers of voters in order to avoid the early introduction of what most people might have thought the term "elections" actually means: a system of universal suffrage in which almost everyone of voting age who meets basic residency requirements in Hong Kong has the right to cast a vote of broadly equal value.[35]

For all these controversies, the result was a remarkable document which, as will be discussed at length throughout this book, allows Hong Kong to differ far more radically from the rest of the country of which it is a part than almost anywhere else in the world that is not a country in its own right. It is also a document which, generally speaking, improved during the early part of the drafting process, from 1985 to 1988, as China made significant concessions in an attempt to allay concerns in Hong Kong.

However, that changed during the later part of the drafting process, largely due to another accident of timing of history—the huge student-led protests in Beijing's Tiananmen Square and other major Chinese cities in April and May 1989. Demanding political reform and an end to corruption on the mainland, these protests were enthusiastically supported in Hong Kong. As a result, after the bloody suppression of these protests by the People's Liberation Army on 4 June 1989, Beijing was in a less accommodating mood towards the people of Hong Kong who it perceived as having supported an attempt to overthrow the Chinese government. The final stage of the drafting process

---

33. In a conversation with Martin Lee, one of the Hong Kong drafters of the Hong Kong Basic Law. See Martin Lee, "A Tale of Two Articles" in Peter Wesley-Smith and Albert Chen (eds.), *The Basic Law and Hong Kong's Future* (Butterworths, 1988) at 315–317.
34. See further note 25 earlier in this chapter and the accompanying text.
35. See further "5.5: Elected Legislature" in Chapter 5.

was therefore marked by a much tougher stance by China, and the reversal of some of the concessions made during the earlier part of the drafting process. As a result, a drafting process that had begun with such high expectations ended in resignations, recriminations and accusations of the "betrayal" of the people of Hong Kong.

The principal role in the drafting process fell to the Drafting Committee for the Basic Law of the Hong Kong Special Administrative Region (or Basic Law Drafting Committee). This was established by China's National People's Congress, a body which is sometimes described as the country's parliament, and is the highest organ of state power in China under the 1982 Constitution of the People's Republic of China (Article 57). In a legal system with a confusing variety of types of legislation made by different parts of the Chinese state, laws made by the National People's Congress rank above all other types of legislation in China, with the exception of the constitution itself, which is also made by the National People's Congress. Every other law passed by the National People's Congress is known as a "basic law" (see Article 62(3) of the 1982 Constitution), a term which distinguishes them from other—less important—types of legislation in China. This means that, strictly speaking, it is inaccurate to refer to the Hong Kong Basic Law as simply the "basic law", an abbreviation commonly used in Hong Kong. In reality, the Hong Kong Basic Law is simply one of many basic laws enacted by the National People's Congress.[36]

Reflecting the importance China attaches to "one country, two systems" in Hong Kong, the drafting of the Hong Kong Basic Law was handled differently from other laws then being enacted by the National People's Congress. While most Chinese laws in the 1980s were being written by Chinese government ministries, the Hong Kong Basic Law had its own drafting committee from the start, a step then reserved for the most important of basic laws.[37] Its membership was unprecedentedly diverse, with 23 of the 59 committee members coming from Hong Kong. Since the committee reached its decisions by a two-thirds majority, in theory that gave the Hong Kong members a narrow power of veto over anything proposed by the remaining 36 members from the mainland.

In practice, that never happened since the Hong Kong membership was dominated by business leaders, such as Li Ka Shing and Sir Y.K. Pao, and political figures considered sympathetic to Beijing. Yet, even here, there were signs of China's initial willingness to include representatives of a wider spectrum of Hong Kong opinion, most notably the appointment to the drafting committee of Martin Lee and Szeto Wah, who would subsequently emerge as leaders of Hong Kong's pro-democracy movement. A Consultative Committee for the Basic Law of the Hong Kong Special Administrative Region (or Basic

---

36. This raises the issue of whether the Hong Kong Basic Law has any higher status than the other basic laws enacted by the National People's Congress. See further "3.2: Domestic Dimension" in Chapter 3.
37. Although rare in the 1980s, such special drafting committees have since become more common. See Perry Keller "The National People's Congress and the Making of National Law" in Jan Michiel Otto, Maurice V. Polak, Jianfu Chen and Yuewen Li (eds.), *Law-Making in the People's Republic of China* (Kluwer Law International, 2000) at 85–86.

Law Consultative Committee) was also established by the drafting committee at its first full meeting in June 1985, with the ostensible aim of taping into a wider range of Hong Kong opinion. Consisting of 180 members, all from Hong Kong, it played no formal role in drafting the Hong Kong Basic Law but instead collated opinions from the Hong Kong public on its proposed contents.

At its first full meeting, the drafting committee agreed what would prove to be a deadline set in stone, for completing the task of writing the Hong Kong Basic Law by early 1990. Most of the work was then turned over to five sub-groups, established by the drafting committee at its second full meeting in April 1986, to focus on specific areas of the Hong Kong Basic Law. Each sub-group consisted of members of the drafting committee, and was jointly chaired by one representative each from Hong Kong and the mainland. Between them, the five sub-groups met a total of 73 times in all during the drafting process, while the full drafting committee met only nine times, often to approve decisions taken by the sub-groups.

With the basic structure of the Hong Kong Basic Law also decided by the drafting committee at its April 1986 meeting, the sub-groups had the task of drafting the different chapters divided up between them. There was a sub-group on Fundamental Rights and Duties of the Residents which produced Chapter III with the same title, a sub-group on Political Structure which produced Chapter IV with the same title,[38] a sub-group on the Economy which produced Chapter V with the same title, and a sub-group which eventually took responsibility for Education, Science, Culture, Sports, Religion, Labour and Social Services and produced Chapter VI with the same title. There was also a sub-group on the Relationship between the Central Authorities and the Hong Kong SAR. This last group produced not only Chapter II with a similar title, but also the Preamble to the Hong Kong Basic Law, Chapter I on General Principles, Chapter VII on External Affairs and what ultimately became Chapter VIII in the final draft, on Interpretation and Amendment of the Basic Law.

2.4 Battles and Changes

The most bitter and public battles were fought out in the political sub-group over how the future Chief Executive (who would lead Hong Kong after 1 July 1997) should be chosen, as well as the meaning of the word "elections" when it comes to selecting members of future Legislative Councils. After decades of denying democracy to Hong Kong, Britain had finally woken up to the need to make some meaningful step in this direction before it departed. Even while the Joint Declaration negotiations were still ongoing, a Green Paper from the Hong Kong Government in July 1984 on *The Further Development*

---

38. The sub-group on political structure was also given the task of drafting a separate chapter on Supplementary Provisions (Chapter IX in the final draft), which became the shortest chapter in the Hong Kong Basic Law, consisting of only one article in the final draft (Article 160 on the continuation of laws previously in force in Hong Kong, and any obligations under them).

of Representative Government in Hong Kong had emphasized the need to move more quickly towards the introduction of democracy in Hong Kong, possibly even culminating in some form of election of the colonial Governor.[39] In November 1984, shortly before the Joint Declaration was signed, a follow-up White Paper finalized plans for the first elections of any kind to the Legislative Council.

These elections in September 1985 saw the introduction of functional constituencies, in which voting is confined to members of a particular profession or sector of Hong Kong society, and an electoral college limited to several hundred voters.[40] These two systems of indirect elections, in which voting is usually limited to a small section of the population, would subsequently be incorporated into the Hong Kong Basic Law and play an important role in Hong Kong's political system that continues even today.[41] Nonetheless, they resulted in the first election of critical voices to a body which had, until then, consisted entirely of government officials and other members appointed by the Governor. In particular, Martin Lee and Szeto Wah were elected to the new functional constituencies for the legal profession and education sector respectively. Importantly, the Hong Kong Government held out the possibility of taking another major step forward at the next polls in 1988, when some members of the Legislative Council might be chosen through direct elections, in which virtually everyone of voting age who met basic residential requirements would be entitled to vote.[42]

That was a step too far for China. Just two months after those first elections, in November 1985, Beijing's top representative in Hong Kong[43] publicly accused Britain of "deviating" from the Joint Declaration through its plan to introduce political reforms. From China's perspective, everything should be put on hold during the drafting of the Hong Kong Basic Law. Only when the drafting process, which—at that stage—had barely even begun, was completed could Britain introduce electoral reforms, and even then only if they complied with the provisions in the Hong Kong Basic Law.

---

39. This last idea was, however, couched in very tentative terms and only suggested the election of the Governor by members of the Executive and Legislative Council rather than the Hong Kong population as a whole.
40. For the 1985 elections, and subsequent elections in 1988, this electoral college consisted of members of local organizations in Hong Kong—the District Boards (since renamed District Councils) and Urban and Regional Councils (since abolished)—many of whom had, themselves, been elected at a local level.
41. For more on the continuing role today of these two systems of indirect elections, see further "5.3: Small-Circle Selection Process" and "5.5: Elected Legislature" in Chapter 5.
42. The November 1984 White Paper moved forward to 1987 a review of Hong Kong's election system (which originally had been scheduled for 1989) so that any changes could take place in time for the 1988 elections, and suggested these might include the introduction of direct elections.
43. Xu Jiatun, then head of the Hong Kong branch of Xinhua News Agency, the body that functioned as China's chief representative office in Hong Kong, during the final decades of the colonial era.

China apparently then repeated these demands during the next meeting of the Sino-British Joint Liaison Group.[44] This was an early sign that the diplomatic body—officially described in the Joint Declaration as only an "organ for liaison"—would, in practice, assume a far greater role as a vehicle for China restraining Britain's actions in the run-up to 1 July 1997. Britain swiftly backed down. A second Green Paper from the Hong Kong Government in May 1987 on *The 1987 Review of Developments in Representative Government* played down the idea of direct elections in 1988, confusingly burying it as the fifth sub-option among four different choices for the Hong Kong public to consider concerning the future of the Legislative Council. When even that failed to stop a large majority of respondents from supporting the idea, Britain shamefully manipulated the figures. Excluding petitions submitted by pro-democracy groups while counting pre-printed forms printed by pro-Beijing groups, a follow-up White Paper in February 1988 managed to conclude that a majority opposed the introduction of direct elections in 1988.[45] Direct elections were then postponed until 1991, so fulfilling China's demand to wait until after the planned enactment of the Hong Kong Basic Law in 1990 before introducing any reforms.

That only increased the pressure in the political sub-group of the Basic Law Drafting Committee, where bitter battles were being fought out over the shape of the electoral system to be adopted after 1 July 1997 (and also before that date, since Britain had agreed to try to conform with whatever was written into the Hong Kong Basic Law). On one side were the small handful of pro-democracy members, notably Martin Lee and Szeto Wah, pushing for a system of universal suffrage under which virtually everyone of voting age in Hong Kong would be allowed to participate in electing the future Chief Executive and a majority of members of the post-1 July 1997 Legislative Council. Ranged against them was almost everyone else on the drafting committee, including all the mainland members and most of their Hong Kong counterparts. While differing on the precise details, they favoured adopting some variant of the electoral college and functional constituency systems first used for the Legislative Council elections in 1985. This would restrict to a much smaller number of voters those allowed to participate in electing the future Chief Executive and the majority of members of the post-1 July 1997 Legislative Council.

The differences were so intense that it was impossible to settle them in the first draft of the Hong Kong Basic Law, published in April 1988.[46] Instead, Annex I of the first draft listed five alternative models for the selection of the Chief Executive, while Annex

---

44. Mark Roberti, *The Fall of Hong Kong* (John Wiley, 1996) at 159.
45. In fact, of the 368,431 people who registered their views on the issue during this public consultation exercise, an overwhelming 265,078 (including signatories to petitions) supported direct elections in 1988, compared with the 94,565 who were opposed. See further Cottrell, *The End of Hong Kong* (see note 10) at 184–185.
46. The full text of the first draft, which was titled "The Draft Basic Law of the Hong Kong Special Administrative Region of the People's Republic of China (for solicitation of opinions)" is reproduced in Peter Wesley-Smith and Albert Chen (eds.), *The Basic Law and Hong Kong's Future* (Butterworths, 1988) at 329–369.

II offered a further four alternatives for the election of post-1 July 1997 Legislative Council. Nonetheless, amid these competing models, it was already possible to glimpse the first shape of things to come. Apart from the pro-democracy camp's proposal for universal suffrage, the other models in Annex I all favoured some form of electoral college for selecting the Chief Executive, with two alternatives specifically mentioning a 600-member body[47]—an earlier variant on the Election Committee which, initially with 800 members,[48] would ultimately begin choosing the Chief Executive after 1 July 1997. When it came to electing the future Legislative Council, the argument was all about the numbers, as would continue to be the case through 1997 and beyond. While the pro-democracy camp's model pushed for at least 50% of the members of the Legislative Council to be elected through universal suffrage after 1 July 1997, the other alternatives limited this to 25%–30%, with the balance made up of functional constituencies and an electoral college.

It was a similar story in the sub-group on the Relationship between the Central Authorities and the Hong Kong SAR, where bitter battles were fought over the jurisdiction of the Hong Kong courts and the power to interpret the Hong Kong Basic Law—once again foreshadowing the controversies which would erupt after 1 July 1997. Suspicious of the Hong Kong courts, mainland drafters sought to "drill a small hole" in the power of final adjudication granted to the Hong Kong courts under the Joint Declaration, by proposing that the National People's Congress Standing Committee be allowed to directly overturn Hong Kong judgments in a small number of cases.[49] There was also the beginning of what was to prove a long-running battle over the "acts of state" exemption, which places certain types of cases outside the jurisdiction of the Hong Kong courts.[50] This issue proved so controversial that the provision on acts of state was the only part of the Hong Kong Basic Law that initially failed to secure the necessary two-thirds majority during a later meeting of the drafting committee.[51] After 1 July 1997, concerns over this issue faded into the background for more than a decade, until they were revived by a case in which a sharply divided Court of Final Appeal seemed to suggest that Beijing should define the extent of acts of state under the Hong Kong Basic Law.[52]

---

47. The other alternatives suggested choosing the Chief Executive through an even smaller advisory group of 50–100 members which would eventually be replaced by an electoral college of not more than 500 members (Alternative 4), and using an electoral college-like body known as a "Nominating Committee" to choose three candidates who would then be put to a ballot of all voters in Hong Kong (Alternative 5).
48. The size of the Election Committee remained at 800 members, until it was increased to 1,200 members in 2010.
49. See the account by Martin Lee, a member of the sub-group, in Lee, "A Tale of Two Cities" (see note 33) at 317–319.
50. See further note 457 in Chapter 6 for a definition of acts of state.
51. This was the eighth full meeting of the drafting committee in January 1989. The provision restricting the jurisdiction of the Hong Kong courts to hear cases involving "acts of state" was subsequently adopted at the ninth meeting of the drafting committee in February 1990 instead.
52. *Democratic Republic of Congo v FG Hemisphere* (2011) 14 HKCFAR 95. For more on the controversy over this aspect of the case, see further pages 216–217.

Another controversy which began in this sub-group also provided an early foretaste of the tensions that may be inevitable in seeking to reconcile Hong Kong and China's fundamentally different legal systems under the "one country, two systems" formula. While in Hong Kong, like other common law systems, it is the courts which interpret legislation, under the Chinese legal system authoritative interpretation of legislation is primarily a matter for the body which originally enacted the relevant legislation. In the case of laws passed by the National People's Congress, which would naturally include the Hong Kong Basic Law, this is handled by the National People's Congress Standing Committee (see Article 67(4) of the 1982 Constitution).

The tensions caused by these two fundamentally different approaches to interpreting laws were ignored in the Joint Declaration, quite possibly because they were something the British negotiators were unaware of. But in drafting the Hong Kong Basic Law there was no escape. Attempts by Martin Lee to insert a provision giving the Hong Kong courts the primary power to interpret the Hong Kong Basic Law foundered in the face of mainland drafters' suspicion that the Hong Kong courts' power of final adjudication (which they had unsuccessfully sought to narrow) meant it would be impossible to correct any "mistake" made by the courts in interpreting the Hong Kong Basic Law.[53] Instead, the majority of drafters agreed on an ambiguous provision dividing the power of interpretation between the National People's Congress Standing Committee and the Hong Kong courts, the precise meaning of which would become the cause of much controversy after 1 July 1997 and is still being debated today.[54]

In China, like most countries, new laws typically go through several drafts before a final version is enacted, and the Hong Kong Basic Law was no exception. The first draft of the Hong Kong Basic Law was specifically described as being "for solicitation of opinions" when it was published in April 1988, after being approved by the drafting committee at its seventh full meeting. About 73,000 responses followed, during a five-month public consultation exercise in Hong Kong organized by the consultative committee. More than 90% of these were from supporters of pro-democracy groups, many harshly critical of some of the provisions in the first draft.

In some respects, that consultation exercise was a high point of the drafting process with critical opinions being freely expressed and, in many cases, accommodated. At that stage Beijing was still in an accommodative mood. Perhaps anxious to stem the brain drain of Hong Kong professionals immigrating to countries such as Canada and Australia, the drafting committee made significant changes in the second draft of the Hong Kong Basic Law.[55]

---

53. Lee, "A Tale of Two Cities" (see note 33) at 317–319.
54. See further pages 221–223.
55. The Basic Law of the Hong Kong Special Administrative Region of the People's Republic of China (Draft) (Feb 1989).

More than 100 changes were made, 80 of them substantial.[56] On the issue of democratic development, these confirmed what had been left unclear by all the different alternatives listed in the first draft of the Hong Kong Basic Law. The second draft saw the emergence of an Election Committee charged with choosing the Chief Executive, in an almost identical form to that which was eventually implemented after 1 July 1997. In the Legislative Council, it proposed initially limiting elections by universal suffrage to about 25% of the seats.[57]

But, on most other issues, the changes were widely seen as concessions that sought to allay concerns about the potential for China to meddle in Hong Kong's internal affairs after 1 July 1997. The "acts of state" exemption was narrowed so that executive acts of the Central People's Government would no longer be expressly beyond the jurisdiction of the Hong Kong courts. Also narrowed was another provision allowing the National People's Congress Standing Committee to veto new laws enacted in Hong Kong. This was changed so that it no longer applies to the vast majority of Hong Kong laws, which concern matters within Hong Kong's autonomy.[58]

Of even greater long-term significance were the changes to Article 23,[59] the controversial Hong Kong Basic Law provision requiring Hong Kong to have laws protecting China's national security interests. More than virtually any other provision, Article 23 was widely seen as a threat to Hong Kong's separate system. That was particularly true of the requirement in the first draft of the Hong Kong Basic Law for a law prohibiting subversion, the offence of challenging the Central People's Government that has been frequently used on the mainland to jail those who peacefully call for political change. In an effort to allay these concerns, the requirement for a law against subversion was deleted from the second draft of the Hong Kong Basic Law. Instead the wording of Article 23 was rephrased in more specific language to refer to offences which, in most cases, were already covered by existing laws in Hong Kong.[60] In addition, the crucial qualification

---

56. The full text of the most significant changes is reproduced in Ming K. Chan and David J. Clark, *The Hong Kong Basic Law: Blueprint for 'Stability and Prosperity' Under Chinese Sovereignty* (Hong Kong University Press, 1991) at 145–161.
57. The exact figure was 15 out of the 55 seats then proposed for the Legislative Council. See paragraph 6 of the draft Decision of the NPC of the PRC on the Method for the Formation of the First Government and the First Legislative Council of the Hong Kong SAR (Feb 1989). In the second and final drafts of the Hong Kong Basic Law, the rules for the selection of the first Chief Executive and first Legislative Council of the Hong Kong SAR to take office on 1 July 1997 were dealt with in this separate NPC decision attached to the Hong Kong Basic Law, rather than in the main text of the Hong Kong Basic Law.
58. This became Article 17(3) in the second and final drafts of the Hong Kong Basic Law. See further note 128 in Chapter 4 and the accompanying text.
59. This had been Article 22 in the first draft of the Hong Kong Basic Law but, due to renumbering, became Article 23 in the second and final drafts.
60. The rephrased version of Article 23 required laws against treason and sedition, both of which are already covered by the Crimes Ordinance (Cap. 200), as well as secession, which probably falls within the wide-ranging definition of treason under this ordinance. It also required laws against theft of state secrets, which was then covered by the Official Secrets Act 1911, an English law extended to Hong Kong.

was added in the second draft that any new laws would have to be enacted by Hong Kong "on its own", instead of being imposed by the mainland.

Had that wording survived unchanged into the final draft of the Hong Kong Basic Law, much of the later controversy over Article 23 might have been at least partly defused—possibly even including the protest of more than 500,000 Hong Kong people on 1 July 2003 rejecting proposed legislation seeking to implement this provision in the Hong Kong Basic Law. But almost as soon as the National People's Congress Standing Committee published the second draft of the Hong Kong Basic Law in February 1989, events in Beijing took a turn that would lead to a tightening of the language in this and other provisions in the final version of the Hong Kong Basic Law.

As students took to the streets across China in April 1989, in protests sparked by the death of populist reformist leader Hu Yaobang, the debate over the drafting of the Hong Kong Basic Law faded to the sidelines. The consultative committee suspended its work, and two Hong Kong drafters resigned from the drafting committee following the Chinese government's decision to respond to the protests by declaring martial law in parts of Beijing on 20 May 1989. Two more drafters, Martin Lee and Szeto Wah, suspended their participation in the drafting process after the bloody crackdown against the protesters near Tiananmen Square on 4 June 1989.

But the Chinese government refused to extend the drafting process, insisting that the early 1990 deadline for completing the Hong Kong Basic Law remained sacrosanct. When Lee and Szeto, who played prominent roles in organizing the huge Hong Kong protests against the June Fourth crackdown, sought to resume their duties a few months later, they were expelled by the National People's Congress Standing Committee because of their "hostile position toward the Chinese government".[61] The depleted ranks of remaining Hong Kong drafters were then confronted with much less accommodating mainland officials who saw the student-led protests, and, particularly, the massive public support for them in Hong Kong, as a reason for reversing some of the concessions they had previously made over the Hong Kong Basic Law.

The requirement for a law prohibiting subversion against the Central People's Government, which had been taken out of the second draft of the Hong Kong Basic Law in response to objections from Hong Kong, was put back into the final draft. The language of Article 23 was further tightened with the addition of two further offences banning any activities in Hong Kong by, or links with, foreign political organizations— whom Beijing blamed for encouraging the student unrest. Those changes firmly associated Article 23 with the bloody events of 4 June 1989 in the minds of many Hong Kong people. In a vivid demonstration of how events during the drafting of the Hong Kong Basic Law would continue to shape developments in Hong Kong for many decades to come, that linkage came back to haunt the Hong Kong SAR Government 14 years later when intense public opposition forced it to abandon proposed legislation that sought to implement the provisions of Article 23.[62] Robert Allcock, one of the Hong Kong SAR Government law officers most closely involved in this abortive attempt, notes that this

---

61. Decision of the Standing Committee of the NPC (31 Oct 1989).
62. See further note 94 in Chapter 4 and the accompanying text.

linkage with the events of 4 June 1989 was at least partly responsible for the "deep suspicion in Hong Kong that laws to implement Article 23 would be draconian and would be aimed at suppressing dissent".[63]

Other changes included the introduction of a split voting system in the Legislative Council, giving an effective veto power to those returned through mostly small-circle functional constituency elections. This change would prove to have huge practical implications after 1 July 1997, making it extremely difficult to secure the passage of any measures not proposed by the Hong Kong SAR Government.[64] Only on the issue of political development was China prepared to make some concessions. Although the selection of the Chief Executive was left in the hands of the small-circle Election Committee mentioned in the second draft of the Hong Kong Basic Law, of more long-term significance was the addition of a commitment to an "ultimate aim" of selecting the Chief Executive through universal suffrage[65] in the final draft of the Hong Kong Basic Law. On the Legislative Council, after secret last-minute negotiations with Britain,[66] China agreed to a slight increase in the proportion of seats which could be elected by universal suffrage in 1997. This was increased to 33% in an NPC decision attached to the final draft of the Hong Kong Basic Law,[67] compared with the approximately 25% figure mentioned in the NPC decision attached to the second draft.[68]

That fell far short of the demands for a much faster pace of political development being widely voiced by almost all sections of the political spectrum in Hong Kong, where attitudes towards democratization had undergone a sea change in the wake of the events of 4 June 1989.[69] As a result, the drafting process ended in recriminations. Even normally compliant Hong Kong drafters were infuriated by the way in which they had been overruled by their mainland counterparts.[70] In Hong Kong, politicians from

---

63. See "Challenges to Hong Kong's Legal System in view of Hong Kong's Return to Chinese Sovereignty", Conference at the City University of Hong Kong, 9 November 2004.
64. For more on the split voting system, see note 226 in Chapter 5 and the accompanying text.
65. Article 45(2). This goal is, however, qualified by a requirement that candidates for the Chief Executive must first be screened by a "broadly representative nominating committee in accordance with democratic procedures". For more on the possible implications of this provision, see note 113 in Chapter 5 and the accompanying text.
66. Although China's official position was that the drafting of the Hong Kong Basic Law was strictly China's internal affair, in practice there were regular discussions with Britain on key issues during much of the drafting process. See Cradock, *Experiences of China* (see note 12) at 218.
67. Paragraph 6 of the Decision of the NPC on the Method for the Formation of the First Government and the First Legislative Council of the Hong Kong SAR (4 April 1990).
68. See note 57.
69. This was most evident in the general agreement on what became known as the Omelco consensus, a blueprint for much more rapid progress to full democracy which would have seen all members of Hong Kong's legislature popularly elected by 2003. See Roberti, *The Fall of Hong Kong* (see note 44) at 268–275.
70. Ibid. at 284–285. For instance, Raymond Wu, a Beijing loyalist who was one of the joint chairs of the crucial political sub-group, was so angry that he refused to attend the usual press briefing after its last meeting.

across the political spectrum united in expressing their "disappointment", in an emotive Legislative Council debate after the shape of the final draft became clear in February 1990.[71]

Nonetheless, the Hong Kong Basic Law was duly adopted as a national law by the National People's Congress on 4 April 1990 — although it would not, of course, come into effect for another seven years. In another Legislative Council debate hours after its adoption, councillors immediately called for changes to the final draft.[72] But, in reality, it was too late. The law that would govern the implementation of one country, two systems was now set in stone — and the task in the final seven years of British rule would turn to preparing for its implementation.

2.5 Sino-British Disputes

Although the Hong Kong Basic Law was now set in stone, that did not end the controversy over its provisions. Britain had been forced into a fundamental change of policy by the bloody events of 4 June 1989, and the resulting loss of public confidence in China's intentions. One about-turn was the enactment in June 1991 of the Hong Kong Bill of Rights Ordinance (Cap. 383), Hong Kong's first law seeking to protect a wide range of fundamental civil liberties.[73] Mainland drafters of the Hong Kong Basic Law protested furiously at the about-turn on this issue, insisting Britain had previously assured China there was no need for such a law.[74]

China's anger was even more intense over British attempts to exploit ambiguities in the provisions in the Hong Kong Basic Law on the election of the Legislative Council. In 1992, Governor Wilson, who had presided over British acquiescence with China's insistence on a slow pace of democratic development, was removed from office by the British government. His replacement, Chris Patten, a prominent British politician and close friend of the then British Prime Minister John Major, immediately took British policy in a more aggressive direction when it came to expanding democracy in Hong Kong.

Patten did not seek to go against the explicit restriction in the NPC Decision attached to the Hong Kong Basic Law, which limited the number of seats which could be elected by universal suffrage to 33% in 1997.[75] Instead Patten took advantage of the lack of any definition of the functional constituencies which would choose most of the remaining seats. These had always previously been seen as small-circle elections, designed to balance the impact of the popularly elected constituencies by allowing an easy route

---

71. See Legislative Council, *Official Record of Proceedings, Hong Kong Hansard* (28 Feb 1990) at 54–64 and (1 March 1990) at 1–60.
72. See Legislative Council, *Official Record of Proceedings, Hong Kong Hansard* (4 April 1990) at 42–89.
73. For more on the enactment of the Hong Kong Bill of Rights Ordinance, see "8.1: ICCPR and Bill of Rights" in Chapter 8.
74. See, for instance, Shao Tianren, "Legal vacuum fears", *Window*, 10 Nov 1995.
75. See note 67.

for the election of representatives of the business community and other special interest groups. But there was nothing in the Hong Kong Basic Law explicitly defining functional constituencies in these terms. So Patten exploited what he called this "elbow room"[76] to propose that the nine additional functional constituencies which would have to be introduced for the Legislative Council elections in 1995, the last to be held under British rule, should be radically different from any of the existing functional constituencies. Instead of the traditional system of having each constituency elected by a small group of a few thousand voters, Patten proposed dividing up the nine new seats among the whole of Hong Kong's working population, so creating a total electorate of more than 2.7 million.[77] Patten also proposed more modest expansions in the number of those eligible to vote in many of the other existing functional constituencies.[78]

It was a similar story with a further 10 seats, which the NPC decision attached to the Hong Kong Basic Law[79] required to be returned by members of an "election committee" in 1997. It had been previously assumed that this committee would be formed in the same way as the small circle body with the same name charged with choosing Chief Executives after 1997.[80] But nothing had ever been finalized and, once again, neither the Hong Kong Basic Law nor the NPC decision appended to it contained any explicit provisions on this point. So Patten similarly took advantage of this ambiguity to propose a very differently constituted committee for choosing these 10 seats. This consisted solely of members of the local bodies now known as District Councils,[81] virtually all of whom would themselves be elected.[82]

In some respects Patten's proposals were ahead of their time, particularly in exploiting the lack of any formal definition of functional constituencies to redefine such seats as having a much larger franchise than previously had been the case. Eighteen years later, as popular pressure for more democracy once again came up against the road-block of the large role carved out for functional constituencies in the Hong Kong Basic Law, China would agree to embrace even larger functional constituencies than Patten had proposed.[83] But, back in the 1990s, such a concept was still anathema to Beijing. Since China's main purpose in insisting that most seats be returned through functional constituencies and an

---

76. Jonathan Dimbleby, *The Last Governor: Chris Patten and the Handover of Hong Kong* (Little, Brown, 1997) at 109.
77. See Governor Christopher Patten, "Our Next Five Years: The Agenda for Hong Kong", Policy Address, 7 October 1992, at 38.
78. This is usually described as the replacement of corporate voting by individual voting. For an explanation of the change, see further notes 231 and 235 in Chapter 5.
79. See note 67.
80. Britain and China had reached a preliminary understanding on this point in a previous exchange of diplomatic messages known as the "seven letters".
81. They were then known as District Boards.
82. Under these reforms, government appointments to these bodies were abolished. However, these were reintroduced after 1 July 1997. See further note 17 in Chapter 5 and the accompanying text.
83. See further note 252 in Chapter 5 and the accompanying text.

election committee had been to limit the impact of popular democracy in the Legislative Council for a prolonged period after 1997, it angrily rejected Patten's proposals.

In an early example of the significance of its ultimate power to determine the meaning of the Hong Kong Basic Law,[84] the National People's Congress Standing Committee simply declared the election arrangements proposed by Patten to be in breach of that document, without bothering to state which specific provisions in the Hong Kong Basic Law they supposedly breached.[85] That did not stop the elections from going ahead in 1995, under a greatly expanded franchise. But it meant that the legislators returned in those polls could not serve a four-year term, continuing in office beyond 1 July 1997. This had been the original intention, with an NPC Decision appended to the Hong Kong Basic Law containing specific provision for a so-called "through train" for legislators,[86] so as to minimize disruption at the time of the handover.

Instead, a temporary body, the Provisional Legislative Council of the Hong Kong SAR (or Provisional Legislature), was created by a Preparatory Committee established by the National People's Congress Standing Committee in 1996 to prepare for the establishment of the Hong Kong SAR.[87] The Provisional Legislature was designed to fill the gap left by the abolition of the Legislative Council returned by the last elections under British rule, until a new Legislative Council could be elected after 1 July 1997. The Provisional Legislature began meeting in Shenzhen even before that date,[88] and enacted several new laws.[89] Fearful of legal challenges to the validity of any decisions it made outside Hong Kong, these were immediately reaffirmed when the Provisional Legislature met for the first time in Hong Kong in the early morning of 1 July 1997.[90]

That did not stop legal challenges to the Provisional Legislature, an unelected body whose members were chosen by a 400-member Selection Committee. Under the NPC decision appended to the Hong Kong Basic Law, this committee had been originally only intended to nominate the first Chief Executive of the Hong Kong SAR for appointment

---

84. This power, which is most often exercised by issuing formal interpretations of the Hong Kong Basic Law under Article 158, is discussed in detail in "Chapter 7: Interpretation and Amendment".
85. See Decision of the Standing Committee of the NPC on the Proposal Advanced by Zheng Yaotang and Other Thirty-two Deputies to the NPC (31 Aug 1994). Note this is classed as a Decision under the Hong Kong Basic Law, rather than a formal interpretation of its provisions.
86. However, it was explicitly stated in paragraph 6 of the NPC Decision (see note 67) that this through train could only apply "[i]f the composition of the last Hong Kong Legislative Council before the establishment of the Hong Kong Special Administrative Region is in conformity with the relevant provisions of this decision and the Basic Law of the Hong Kong Special Administrative Region", among other conditions.
87. See paragraph 2 of the NPC Decision (see note 67).
88. Its first meeting was held in Huaxia Arts Centre in Shenzhen on 22 February 1997.
89. These included laws on judicial appointments, public holidays, the workings of the Legislative Council and the display of the National Flag in Hong Kong, among other matters. For a full list, see Schedule 1 of the Hong Kong Reunification Ordinance (No. 110 of 1997).
90. Section 3 of the Hong Kong Reunification Ordinance (No. 110 of 1997).

by the Central People's Government.[91] In December 1996, the Selection Committee performed that task by choosing Tung Chee Hwa as the first Chief Executive from a field of four candidates. However, after the breakdown of Sino-British cooperation on electoral matters, the Preparatory Committee expanded the role of the Selection Committee to include also choosing the members of the Provisional Legislature.[92] Critics charged this violated Article 68(1) of the Hong Kong Basic Law, which—reflecting China's last-minute concession to Britain during the Joint Declaration negotiations[93]—requires the post-1 July 1997 Legislative Council to be "constituted by election".[94] But in *Ng Ka Ling v Director of Immigration*,[95] the Court of Final Appeal settled any doubts about the legality of the Provisional Legislature. It ruled that the requirement to be constituted by election did not apply to a temporary body, whose existence had never been envisaged at the time the Hong Kong Basic Law was drafted.[96]

Although ultimately judged legal, the Provisional Legislature left behind an unfortunate legacy for the rule of law in Hong Kong. In April 1998, in its final meeting before being dissolved to make way for an elected successor, the interim body—which was almost entirely lacking in representation from the pro-democracy camp[97]—controversially enacted a bill exempting from many Hong Kong laws much of the Chinese state,[98] including its representative offices in Hong Kong.[99] Chan (2001) argues that this measure

---

91. See paragraphs 3 and 4 of the NPC Decision (see note 67). This only stipulated the method for choosing the first Chief Executive, who would take office on 1 July 1997. The method for choosing subsequent Chief Executives was instead stipulated in Annex I of the Hong Kong Basic Law.
92. Decision of the Preparatory Committee on the Establishment of a Provisional Legislature of the Hong Kong SAR (24 March 1996).
93. See note 25 earlier in this chapter and the accompanying text.
94. For an excellent account of the debate over the legal basis for the establishment of the Provisional Legislature, see Albert H.Y. Chen, "The Provisional Legislative Council of the SAR" (1997) 27 *HKLJ* 1–11.
95. (1999) 2 HKCFAR 4.
96. Ibid. at 43–45.
97. The Democratic Party, then Hong Kong's largest pro-democracy political party, refused to allow its members to stand for selection to the Provisional Legislature and expelled one member, Dominic Chan, who defied this edict. See Todd Crowell and Law Siu Lan, "Into the margins", *Asiaweek*, 21 March 1997.
98. Section 24 of the Adaptation of Laws (Interpretative Provisions) Ordinance (No. 26 of 1998) amended Section 66 of the Interpretation and General Clauses Ordinance (Cap. 1) to exempt the Chinese "state" from all Hong Kong laws which do not expressly, or by necessary implication, apply to the Chinese state. The Hong Kong SAR Government justified this on the grounds that the British "Crown" had enjoyed a similar exemption under Hong Kong law prior to 1 July 1997.
99. Under Section 3 of the Interpretation and General Clauses Ordinance (Cap. 1), the Chinese "state" is defined as including "subordinate organs" which may "exercise functions for which the Central People's Government has responsibility under the Basic Law". This would appear to include the Hong Kong branch of the Xinhua News Agency, which at that time served as Beijing's main representative in Hong Kong and its successor since 2000, the Liaison Office of the Central People's Government in the Hong Kong SAR.

was "clearly inconsistent with Article 22(3) of the Basic Law", which expressly states that such representative offices must abide by Hong Kong laws.[100] This last-minute measure continues periodically to cause further controversy in Hong Kong[101] long after the Provisional Legislature has faded into the history books.

2.6 Through Train

Just as the final phase of the drafting of the Hong Kong Basic Law was dominated by anger and recriminations, so too were the final years of transition. Although the row over elections poisoned relations between Britain and China during the final years of colonial rule, what was remarkable was how much continuity survived.

While the legislators elected in 1995 were prematurely evicted from office on 1 July 1997, the other two branches of Hong Kong's political structure survived largely intact. Contrary to earlier threats, all the top officials in the Hong Kong Government who met the Chinese nationality requirements stipulated in the Hong Kong Basic Law[102] kept their jobs.[103] Despite China's bitter differences with Patten, the new Chief Executive was chosen from the ranks of his former advisers. Tung had served as a member of Patten's Executive Council, the Governor's highest body of advisers, from 1992 until he resigned in 1996, after a famous handshake with then Chinese President Jiang Zemin made clear he was China's preferred choice to become the first Chief Executive.

Another of Patten's former advisers on the Executive Council, Andrew Li, was appointed as the first Chief Justice of the new Court of Final Appeal.[104] Nor were political

---

100. See Johannes Chan, "Prospect for the Due Process Under Chinese Sovereignty" in Steve Tsang (ed.), *Judicial Independence and the Rule of Law in Hong Kong* (Hong Kong University Press, 2001) at 134. However, the Hong Kong SAR Government argued that the legislation was not in breach of Article 22(3) of the Hong Kong Basic Law, because this provision did not require Chinese government offices to be subject to *all* Hong Kong laws.
101. For instance, in 2008 further controversy erupted over the Hong Kong SAR Government's decision that only four further laws (covering relatively innocuous matters such as plants and patents) should be extended to cover the Chinese state. See Albert Wong, "3 Beijing offices above the law, say lawmakers", *South China Morning Post*, 15 March 2008.
102. Under Article 61 of the Hong Kong Basic Law, certain top government posts known as principal official positions, mostly secretaries of government policy bureaux and heads of the disciplined services, must be filled by Chinese citizens who have ordinarily resided in Hong Kong for a continuous period of at least 15 years and have no right of abode overseas.
103. This included Donald Tsang who, at that stage, was widely seen as distrusted by Beijing and vulnerable to losing his job. See Danny Gittings, "Tsang's dramatic change of fortune", *South China Morning Post*, 30 Sept 1998. Ironically, he subsequently went on to succeed Tung Chee Hwa and serve as Hong Kong's Chief Executive from 2005 to 2012.
104. For an excellent account of how the appointment was made despite complications caused by the political differences between China and Britain, see Jill Cottrell and Yash Ghai, "Between Two Systems of Law: The Judiciary in Hong Kong" in P.H. Russell and D.M. O'Brien (eds.), *Judicial Independence in the Age of Democracy: Critical Perspectives From Around the World* (University Press of Virginia, 2001) at 215–216.

disagreements ultimately allowed to stand in the way of China and Britain reaching agreement in 1995 on arrangements for the establishment of the new court. After a bitter debate in the Legislative Council, where critics complained of restrictions on the composition and jurisdiction of the court,[105] these were enacted into law in the Hong Kong Court of Final Appeal Ordinance (Cap. 484), providing for the establishment of the new court from 1 July 1997.

Earlier threats that the Hong Kong Bill of Rights Ordinance (Cap. 383) would be abolished in its entirety also failed to materialize. Using its power under Article 160(1) of the Hong Kong Basic Law,[106] in February 1997 the National People's Congress Standing Committee declared that three sections of the ordinance contravened the Hong Kong Basic Law and so were unable to remain in force beyond 1 July 1997.[107] However, since these three sections only confirmed principles that the courts would apply even without being told to do so by the ordinance, the deletion had little practical impact.[108]

That list of laws was much shorter than originally had been expected. Only 14 laws were abolished in their entirety, while selected provisions in a further 10 laws (such as those three disputed sections in the Bill of Rights) were also declared to be in breach of the Hong Kong Basic Law.[109] Allcock (2004) describes most of these laws as "colonial relics that would not be missed".[110] But while some did fall into this category,[111] others were more akin to sometimes petty score-settling by Beijing, as it sought to erase every last trace from the Hong Kong statute book of the 1995 Legislative Council elections[112] conducted with a larger franchise, which it had so strongly opposed. As a result, Ghai

---

105. These were the restrictions on the number of judges from other common law jurisdictions allowed to sit on the Court of Final Appeal, and on its jurisdiction to hear cases involving acts of state. For more on the debate over these two issues, see "6.3: Composition of the Court of Final Appeal" and "6.5: Limits on Courts" in Chapter 6.
106. This provision grants the Standing Committee the power "[u]pon the establishment of the Hong Kong Special Administrative Region" to decide which pre-existing laws are "in contravention" of the Hong Kong Basic Law and so will not continue as part of the laws of the SAR. It is, however, ambiguous about how far the Standing Committee can continue to exercise this power after 1 July 1997. See further note 84 in Chapter 3.
107. See Annex 2 of Decision of the Standing Committee of the NPC on Treatment of the Laws Previously in Force in Hong Kong in Accordance With Article 160 of the Basic Law of the Hong Kong SAR of the PRC (23 Feb 1997).
108. See further note 98 in Chapter 8 and the accompanying text.
109. Annexes 1 and 2 of Decision of the Standing Committee of the NPC on Treatment of the Laws Previously in Force in Hong Kong (see note 107).
110. Robert Allcock, "Challenges to Hong Kong's Legal System" (see note 63).
111. See, for example, the abolition of the Chinese Extradition Ordinance (Cap. 235), which had not been used for several decades and long since fallen into disuse.
112. Seven of the 24 laws targeted by the Standing Committee in its February 1997 decision related to the 1995 Legislative Council elections. These even included subsidiary legislation made under the Corrupt and Illegal Practices Ordinance (Cap. 288) to guard against any form of electoral corruption.

(1997) notes "that it could be argued that some of the repeals are themselves against the Basic Law".[113]

In two cases, the Standing Committee's actions gave rise to concerns about the future of civil liberties in Hong Kong. Among the 14 laws which had selected provisions declared in breach of the Hong Kong Basic Law were amendments made during the final years of British rule to the Public Order Ordinance (Cap. 245) and Societies Ordinance (Cap. 151), easing restrictions on freedom of assembly and association respectively.[114] The Provisional Legislature then enacted more restrictive versions of these laws.[115]

Although these changes to the Public Order Ordinance (Cap. 245) would lead to persistent tensions between protesters and police during the early years of the Hong Kong SAR, it should not obscure the fact that the overwhelming majority of Hong Kong's pre-existing laws remained unchanged after 1 July 1997. Ultimately, even fierce disagreements between China and Britain did not prevent the Hong Kong Basic Law from being implemented in a way which allowed Hong Kong's legal and judicial system to survive the transfer of sovereignty largely intact. So too did the executive branch of the political structure, with the direct effects of the disagreements being largely confined to replacing the members of the Legislative Council.

During the prolonged period that was the birth of the Hong Kong Basic Law, accidents of timing played a large part. Had it not been for the brief window of opportunity that Britain seized to negotiate Hong Kong's future during the early years after China's emergence from the Cultural Revolution, an agreement on such a generous form of autonomy for Hong Kong might never have proved possible. Another accident of timing that saw the brutal 4 June 1989 crackdown coincide with the final phase of drafting the Hong Kong Basic Law briefly threatened to derail the implementation of one country, two systems. It also added new complications, such as the reworded and tougher version of Article 23 of the Hong Kong Basic Law, which would have important practical implications after 1 July 1997. So too did the bitter disagreements between China and Britain during the final years of colonial rule which were, to some extent, a consequence of the distrust caused in Hong Kong by the June Fourth crackdown.

Throughout all this, the agreement on one country, two systems that was first reached in the Sino-British Joint Declaration, and then enacted into the Hong Kong Basic Law, proved strong enough to survive—although sometimes a little battered around the edges. When questioned about its resilience, Chinese officials noted[116] that one country, two

---

113. See Yash Ghai, "Continuity of Laws and Legal Rights and Obligations in the SAR" (1997) 27 *HKLJ* 136, 145. This argument would appear to be particularly strong in relation to the deletions from the Hong Kong Bill of Rights Ordinance (Cap. 383), an ordinance which the Hong Kong courts have held enjoys constitutional protection under Article 39(1) of the Hong Kong Basic Law. See further note 104 in Chapter 8 and the accompanying text.
114. See further note 86 in Chapter 8.
115. See further note 94 in Chapter 8.
116. Personal conversations with author (1997).

systems was a policy that had been devised by the highest levels of the nation's leadership to be strong enough to apply for at least 50 years, and quite possibly longer.[117] That meant it had to be strong enough to survive any short-term buffeting. Indeed, as it turned out, all the arguments and controversies during this early process of writing the one country two systems into the Hong Kong Basic Law, were only a foretaste of the further difficulties that would test this concept after the Hong Kong Basic Law finally came into force on 1 July 1997.

---

117. For more on the possibility of "one country, two systems" continuing in force beyond the first 50 years, see "Chapter 9: What Will Happen After 2047?".

Chapter 3
What Is the Hong Kong Basic Law?

The Hong Kong Basic Law may be a "unique document", as the Court of Appeal observed in *HKSAR v Ma Wai Kwan David*,[1] the first case to consider its nature after the 1 July 1997 handover. But, for all its importance, the Hong Kong Basic Law is a remarkably difficult document to define. Many describe it as Hong Kong's constitution but, as we will see shortly, that description is not free from dispute. Even calling it simply "the basic law" can be problematic, since it risks confusion with the numerous other Chinese laws that are also called basic laws.

Much of the difficulty in describing the Hong Kong Basic Law stems from its different facets. The product of an international agreement between Britain and China on Hong Kong's future, the Hong Kong Basic Law is also a domestic law that applies throughout all of China and regulates Hong Kong's relations with the rest of the country. In addition, as far as Hong Kong is concerned, it performs the roles often associated with a constitution—setting out Hong Kong's political structure and the rights and duties of its residents. As Chief Judge Chan observed in the *Ma Wai Kwan* case, the Hong Kong Basic Law "has at least three dimensions: international, domestic and constitutional".[2]

To understand the nature of the Hong Kong Basic Law, therefore, it is necessary to examine each of these dimensions in turn, and then consider the difficult relationship that exists between the Hong Kong Basic Law and the document from which it must ultimately draw its legal authority, the 1982 Constitution of the People's Republic of China (or PRC Constitution 1982).

3.1 International Dimension

The international dimension to the Hong Kong Basic Law stems from its birth in the 1984 Joint Declaration on the Question of Hong Kong. This international treaty[3] between Britain and China explicitly provided that its most important contents would be replicated in a "Basic Law of the Hong Kong Special Administrative Region of the People's

---

1. [1997] HKLRD 761, 773.
2. Ibid.
3. The Joint Declaration is generally recognized to have the status of an international treaty, although it does not use the word "treaty" in its title. See further note 30 in Chapter 2 and the accompanying text.

Republic of China".[4] As a result, the Hong Kong Basic Law begins by stating that its purpose is "to ensure the implementation of the basic policies of the People's Republic of China regarding Hong Kong" set out in the Joint Declaration.[5]

That means the Joint Declaration provides the Hong Kong Basic Law with much of its content. Although there are a few areas where critics say the provisions of the Hong Kong Basic Law diverge from those in the Joint Declaration,[6] these are very much the exception. In most areas, one look at the two documents is enough to see how similar they are. Again and again, the wording used in the Joint Declaration is repeated in similar—sometimes even identical—terms in the Hong Kong Basic Law. Chen (2011) describes this as the "Duplication Phenomenon".[7] For instance, many parts of the text of the Preamble and Articles 1–5 of the Hong Kong Basic Law have been copied (with only minor rewording) from the "basic policies" numbers 1–5 listed in paragraph 3 of the Joint Declaration.[8] When controversies have arisen in recent years over the text of a particular provision in the Hong Kong Basic Law, they often can be traced back to wording that has been copied across from the Joint Declaration. For example, the arguments over the residency rights under the Hong Kong Basic Law of firstly children born in China to a Hong Kong parent and secondly Chinese children born in Hong Kong to non-local parents, which gave rise to two of the most important court cases in Hong Kong's constitutional development,[9] both revolved around provisions in the Hong Kong Basic Law which replicated wording originally used in the Joint Declaration.[10]

For that reason, the Joint Declaration, and particularly the basic policies stated in it, remained of some practical importance for many years after 1 July 1997. As an

---

4. Paragraph 3(12) of the Joint Declaration.
5. Paragraphs 2 and 3 of the Preamble.
6. The most often cited is Article 18(4) of the Hong Kong Basic Law which would allow China to assume responsibility for law and order in Hong Kong in the event of a state of war or emergency, even though paragraph 3(11) of the Joint Declaration unequivocally places responsibility for law and order in the hands of the Hong Kong SAR Government (see further note 165 in Chapter 4 and the accompanying text). For further examples, see Yash Ghai, *Hong Kong's New Constitutional Order: The Resumption of Chinese Sovereignty and the Basic Law* (Hong Kong University Press, 2nd edition, 1999) at 67–69 and Roda Mushkat, *One Country, Two International Legal Personalities: The Case of Hong Kong* (Hong Kong University Press, 1997) at 147–148.
7. Albert H.Y. Chen, "The 'Foreign Domestic Helpers Case': The relevance of the NPCSC Interpretation of 1999 and the Preparatory Committee Opinion of 1996" (2011) 41 *HKLJ* 621, 629.
8. For instance, almost the entire wording of paragraph 3(1) of the Joint Declaration is repeated in paragraph 2 of the Preamble of the HK Basic Law. For more on the "basic policies", see "2.2: Sino-British Joint Declaration" in Chapter 2.
9. *Ng Ka Ling v Director of Immigration* (1999) 2 HKCFAR 4 and *Director of Immigration v Chong Fung Yuen* (2001) 4 HKCFAR 211. See further "6.4: Constitutional Role of the Court of Final Appeal" in Chapter 6 for more on the constitutional significance of these two cases.
10. These were Articles 24(2)(3) and 24(2)(1) respectively, which both repeated wording originally used in Annex I(XIV) of the Joint Declaration.

international treaty rather than a law, its provisions cannot be directly enforced in the courts as was demonstrated by the case of *Tang Ping Hoi v Attorney General*.[11] But because of the Joint Declaration's historical connection with the Hong Kong Basic Law, it has been sometimes used by the courts to help interpret disputed provisions in that document. The guiding principles in this respect were laid down by the Court of Final Appeal in *Ng Ka Ling v Director of Immigration*,[12] when it stated that the Joint Declaration could be used as an aid in interpreting both the "context" and "purpose" of provisions in the Hong Kong Basic Law.[13]

One early example of the use of the Joint Declaration to help interpret disputed provisions in the Hong Kong Basic Law came in the *Ma Wai Kwan*[14] case. In that case, the Court of Appeal held that the common law system automatically continued after 1 July 1997, partly on the basis of the unequivocal reference in the Joint Declaration to how "laws currently in force in Hong Kong *will* remain basically unchanged" (emphasis added).[15] Another early example came in *Gurung Kesh Bahadur v Director of Immigration*,[16] where the Court of Appeal relied partly on the fact that the right to travel was listed as one of the basic policies in the Joint Declaration, in interpreting an equivalent reference to the right to travel in Article 31 of the Hong Kong Basic Law as requiring the Immigration Department to readmit Hong Kong residents on their return from travels outside the territory.[17]

As the passage of time makes the 1984 agreement seem increasingly remote, it would not be surprising to see the Hong Kong courts gradually place less emphasis on the Joint Declaration in cases involving interpretation of the Hong Kong Basic Law. That would also reduce one potential flashpoint with Beijing, which has never been entirely

---

11. [1987] HKLR 324. For more on this case, see further note 32 in Chapter 2 and the accompanying text.
12. (1999) 2 HKCFAR 4.
13. Ibid. at 28.
14. [1997] HKLRD 761.
15. Lawyers for defendants charged with the common law offence of conspiracy to pervert the course of public justice had sought to argue that this offence no longer existed after the 1 July 1997 handover, because the wording of the Hong Kong Basic Law was more ambiguous on this point. The English text of Article 160(1) of the Hong Kong Basic Law says that "the laws previously in force *shall* be adopted" (emphasis added). The lawyers argued this meant that, instead of being automatically adopted, a positive act of adoption was required, something which they claimed had not occurred (see *Ma Wai Kwan* at 772). However, as Chief Judge Chan pointed out (at 775), not only is the Joint Declaration unequivocal on this point, but even the Chinese text of the Hong Kong Basic Law, where "the Chinese characters '採用 *cai yong*' (meaning 'adopt') in Article 160(1) are clearly used in the mandatory and declaratory sense", makes clear there is no need for any such act of adoption.
16. [2001] 3 HKLRD 32.
17. Ibid. at 42–43. As a result, the Court of Appeal held that it was unlawful to refuse to readmit a Nepalese resident of Hong Kong after a seven-day absence. The decision was upheld in the Court of Final Appeal in (2002) 5 HKCFAR 480, although without further reference to the Joint Declaration.

comfortable with the international dimension to the Hong Kong Basic Law. Since 1 July 1997, attempts by Britain to invoke the terms of the Joint Declaration in relation to developments in Hong Kong have repeatedly brought denunciations by Chinese government spokesmen, who have described any such international dimension as "interference" in China's "internal affairs".[18] From China's perspective, the purpose of the Joint Declaration was to regulate the process of returning Hong Kong to Chinese sovereignty. With that task completed on 1 July 1997, any international dimension came to an end and it is the domestic dimension of the Hong Kong Basic Law that is now paramount, as a national law that applies both in Hong Kong and throughout the rest of China.

3.2 Domestic Dimension

It is this status as a national law that allows the Hong Kong Basic Law to set down rules governing the relationship between Hong Kong and the rest of the country, which are binding not just on Hong Kong but also the highest bodies of the Chinese state. As Chief Judge Chan put it in *Ma Wai Kwan*, the domestic dimension to the Hong Kong Basic Law "deals with the relationship between the sovereign and an autonomous region which practises a different system".[19]

The importance of this dimension to the Hong Kong Basic Law is reflected in the entire chapter devoted to this subject; Chapter II on the "Relationship Between the Central Authorities and the Hong Kong Special Administrative Region". Supplemented by further provisions elsewhere in the Hong Kong Basic Law, these set out the powers that can be exercised over Hong Kong by Central Authorities in China such as the National People's Congress, its Standing Committee and the Chinese national government, which is officially known as the Central People's Government, or the State Council.[20]

This includes, for instance, control over Hong Kong's defence[21] and foreign affairs,[22] the power to appoint the Chief Executive and the principal officials of the SAR,[23] impose limited types of national Chinese laws[24] and reject certain Hong Kong laws

---

18. See, for example, "China Accuses Britain Over Hong Kong Poll", *BBC*, 7 May 1998.
19. *Ma Wai Kwan* at 773.
20. Under Article 85 of the PRC Constitution 1982, the Central People's Government, or State Council, is "the executive body of the highest organ of state power" and "the highest organ of state administration". Other Central Authorities in China that have a remit in relation to Hong Kong include the Central Military Commission. Under Article 93 of the PRC Constitution 1982, this body directs the armed forces of China. This includes the People's Liberation Army garrison in Hong Kong, a point specifically stated in Article 3 of the Law of the PRC on the Garrisoning of the Hong Kong SAR, one of the small number of Chinese national laws which apply in Hong Kong. See further "4.2: Legislative Power" in Chapter 4 for more on the application of Chinese national laws in Hong Kong.
21. Article 14(1).
22. Article 13(1).
23. Article 15.
24. Article 18(3).

as incompatible with the Hong Kong Basic Law,[25] determine the number of mainland Chinese allowed to settle in Hong Kong[26] and declare a state of war or emergency in extreme circumstances.[27]

These provisions also restrict the power of Chinese authorities, at the local as well as national level, to interfere in Hong Kong affairs. For instance, they place strict limits on what types of national Chinese laws can be applied,[28] as well as the circumstances when Hong Kong laws can be invalidated as incompatible with the Hong Kong Basic Law.[29] There is also a strict prohibition on any branch of the Chinese government, whether at a national or local level, interfering "in the affairs which the Hong Kong Special Administrative Region administers on its own".[30] This bars Chinese authorities from interfering in almost all types of local affairs[31] including, for instance, the extension of land leases,[32] Hong Kong's economic[33] and taxation policies,[34] its handling of shipping[35] and routine civil aviation issues,[36] in addition to numerous other matters.[37] This prohibition even extends to any department of the Central Government, or any local government, setting up offices in Hong Kong without the express permission of the Hong Kong SAR Government, in addition to the Central People's Government[38] — and requires those which are permitted to open such offices to abide by Hong Kong laws.[39]

The Hong Kong Basic Law can impose such restrictions on the powers of even China's highest authorities because of its status as a national Chinese law passed by the National People's Congress, the highest source of constitutional power in China,[40] under its authority: "To enact and amend basic laws concerning criminal offences, civil affairs,

---

25. Articles 17(3) and 160(1).
26. Article 22(4).
27. Article 18(4).
28. Article 18(3).
29. Article 17(3).
30. Article 22(1).
31. Article 16 gives the Hong Kong SAR the power to, "on its own, conduct the administrative affairs of the Region in accordance with the relevant provisions of this Law".
32. Article 123.
33. Article 110(2).
34. Article 108(2).
35. Article 124(2).
36. Article 130.
37. These are among 15 provisions in the Hong Kong Basic Law which explicitly state that specific issues will be handled by the Hong Kong SAR "on its own". In addition, this is strongly implied, although not explicitly stated, in numerous other provisions in the Hong Kong Basic Law.
38. Article 22(2).
39. Article 22(3). However, in 1998, the Hong Kong legislature controversially enacted a law exempting many Chinese government offices in Hong Kong from a large number of Hong Kong laws, which critics charged was in breach of this provision in the Hong Kong Basic Law. See further note 98 in Chapter 2 and the accompanying text.
40. PRC Constitution 1982, Article 57.

the state organs and other matters."[41] That does not make the Hong Kong Basic Law unique, as is sometimes supposed in Hong Kong. The term "basic law" is a generic one which refers to the whole category of laws passed by the full National People's Congress, rather than this one law in particular. Dowdle (2007) notes that: "China has more than sixty 'basic laws' in force at present, of which the Basic Law of the Hong Kong SAR is simply one."[42] These include the Basic Law of the Macao SAR of the PRC, which sets out a similar framework for one country two systems in the former Portuguese enclave, and other laws covering the most important parts of the Chinese legal system such as the Criminal Law, General Principles of the Civil Law, Nationality Law, the Legislation Law on how laws are made, the law on how China's courts operate,[43] and some important economic legislation.[44]

While it is a mistake to think of the Hong Kong Basic Law as unique, the fact that it was enacted by the National People's Congress does give it a high status within the Chinese legal system. Like all basic laws, it ranks second only to the Chinese Constitution and above all the various legislation enacted by other bodies in China.[45] In contrast to the situation in Hong Kong, where Article 73(1) of the Hong Kong Basic Law vests all power to make primary legislation in the hands of the Legislative Council, the law-making system in China is much more splintered. While the full National People's Congress is supposed to make all the laws on the most important issues,[46] its Standing Committee also has sweeping law-making powers.[47] In the absence of any system of separation of powers, such as that which prevents the executive from making primary legislation in Hong Kong,[48] numerous branches of the Chinese government also have the power to make various different types of legislation. These include the State Council,[49] individual

---

41. PRC Constitution 1982, Article 62(3). In the case of the Hong Kong Basic Law, this is supplemented by Article 62(13) giving the NPC the power: "To decide on the establishment of special administrative regions and the systems to be instituted there."
42. Michael Dowdle, "Constitutionalism in the Shadow of the Common Law" in Hualing Fu, Lison Harris and Simon N.M. Young (eds.), *Interpreting Hong Kong's Basic Law: The Struggle for Coherence* (Palgrave, 2007) at 71.
43. PRC Organic Law of the People's Courts, passed in 1979.
44. For example, the PRC Patent Law 1984, and the PRC Contract Law 1999.
45. Articles 78 and 79 of the PRC Legislation Law, passed in 2000. See further note 53.
46. In particular, under Article 8 of the PRC Legislation Law, only the NPC and its Standing Committee are supposed to handle measures involving the criminal and judicial systems, or the restriction of individual freedoms. However, in practice, there have been several instances of other state bodies in China enacting measures to restrict individual freedoms.
47. PRC Constitution 1982, Articles 67(2) and (3). This even gives the Standing Committee the power to supplement and amend basic laws, in between annual meetings of the full NPC.
48. In *Leung Kwok Hung v Chief Executive of the HKSAR* (unrep., CACV 73 and 87/2006, [2006] HKEC 816), the Court of Appeal held that law making in Hong Kong was a task for the Legislative Council, not the Chief Executive. For more on this case, see notes 58–64 in Chapter 5 and the accompanying text.
49. PRC Constitution 1982, Article 89(1).

departments and ministries,[50] and local governments.[51] Local people's congresses, the local equivalents of the National People's Congress, also have the power to make regulations which have legal effect.[52]

This proliferation of law-making bodies creates a confusing situation in China, with different bodies passing pieces of legislation that are sometimes in conflict. However, the fact that the Hong Kong Basic Law was enacted by the National People's Congress ensures that it, like all other basic laws, should prevail in the event of any conflict with a piece of legislation passed by another body in China.[53]

More difficult is the issue of what happens if the Hong Kong Basic Law conflicts with another basic law passed by the National People's Congress since, in that case, both laws would *prima facie* appear to have the same status. That issue arose in one of the first big controversies concerning "one country, two systems" after the 1 July 1997 handover when Hong Kong resident Cheung Tze Keung, popularly known as "Big Spender", together with several gang members, some of them also from Hong Kong, were tried and convicted in a Guangzhou court under PRC Criminal Law for crimes that included kidnapping two Hong Kong tycoons in Hong Kong.[54]

That raised what some called the "chilling precedent"[55] of Hong Kong people being tried for crimes committed in Hong Kong by Chinese courts under PRC Criminal Law, a law which does not have any direct legal effect in Hong Kong.[56] It also suggested an apparent conflict between provisions in two basic laws, firstly those in PRC Criminal Law giving mainland courts jurisdiction over many cases involving crimes committed in

---

50. PRC Constitution 1982, Article 90.
51. PRC Constitution 1982, Article 107.
52. PRC Constitution 1982, Article 100.
53. See Article 79 of the PRC Legislation Law. This provides that national law (which includes both basic laws enacted by the NPC and other laws enacted by its Standing Committee) has higher legal authority than all other forms of legislation in China, with the exception of the Constitution. Under Articles 67(7) and (8) of the PRC Constitution 1982, the Standing Committee has the power to invalidate any other legislation that it judges to be inconsistent with national laws.
54. For a summary of this case, and the controversy surrounding it, see Choy Dick Wan and Fu Hualing, "Cross-Border Relations in Criminal Matters" in Mark S. Gaylord, Danny Gittings and Harold Traver (eds.), *Introduction to Crime, Law and Justice in Hong Kong* (Hong Kong University Press, 2009) at 233–234.
55. See, for instance, Chris Yeung and Billy Wong Wai-yuk, "Chilling 'Big Spender' precedent", *South China Morning Post*, 28 Oct 1998.
56. The PRC Criminal Law is not listed in Annex III of the HK Basic Law, which contains a list of the only Chinese national laws that have direct legal effect in Hong Kong. See further "4.2: Legislative Power" in Chapter 4 for more on the rules regarding the application of Chinese national laws in Hong Kong.

Hong Kong,[57] and secondly those in the Hong Kong Basic Law giving Hong Kong courts jurisdiction over those same cases.[58]

In the "Big Spender" case, the Guangzhou court explained its decision to assert jurisdiction over the case on the grounds that Cheung and his gang had also committed parts of those same crimes on the mainland.[59] But concerns about the apparent conflict between the two basic laws, and whether this could lead to Hong Kong people being put on trial in mainland courts for crimes committed in Hong Kong, were compounded by another case a year later. In that second case mainland resident Li Yuhui, popularly known as the "Telford Gardens poisoner", was tried and convicted in a Shantou court under PRC Criminal Law for crimes committed entirely in Hong Kong.[60] This was another case which, under the Hong Kong Basic Law, clearly could have been tried by the Hong Kong courts instead.[61]

Tsang (2001) argues that the decision to try these two cases on the mainland undermined the special nature of the Hong Kong Basic Law which "is clearly meant to resolve anomalies or discrepancies in law between the PRC and the SAR" in Hong Kong's favour.[62] However, it is equally possible to rationalize these, and subsequent similar cases where crimes committed in Hong Kong were also tried in mainland courts,[63] as cases

---

57. Notably Article 6, which appears to give mainland courts jurisdiction over any cases where either the preparations for, or the consequences of, the crimes take place on the mainland, and Article 7, which gives mainland courts wide extra-territorial jurisdiction over crimes committed by Chinese citizens "outside the territory of the People's Republic of China".
58. Article 19(2) gives the Hong Kong courts jurisdiction over all cases in Hong Kong, with the limited exception of those types of cases (e.g., those involving accredited foreign diplomats) which they were also precluded from hearing prior to 1 July 1997. See further "6.5: Limits on Courts" in Chapter 6.
59. See *Public Prosecutor v Zhang Ziqiang* (Criminal Case No. 468/1998 of the Guangzhou Intermediate People's Court) where the court cited, among other factors, the fact that "the plotting, planning and other preparatory work to implement the offences occurred in the Mainland". As a result, the court concluded it had jurisdiction over all criminal acts by the accused (including those committed in Hong Kong) under Article 24 of PRC Criminal Procedure Law.
60. H.L. Fu, "The Battle of Criminal Jurisdictions" (1998) 28 *HKLJ* 273, 276.
61. Unlike the "Big Spender" case, the court in this case did not explain the legal grounds for its decision to assume jurisdiction over the case. The Hong Kong SAR Government [in Secretary for Justice Elsie Leung, "Viewing the Jurisdictional Issue from a Proper Perspective" (Jan 1999) *Hong Kong Lawyer* 56–57] sought to rationalize the case as an example of the wide extra-territorial jurisdiction granted to mainland courts under Article 7 of PRC Criminal Law (see note 57). However, this rationale raises further issues, since it means treating Hong Kong as "outside the territory of the People's Republic of China" for the purposes of this provision.
62. Steve Tsang, "Commitment to the Rule of Law and Judicial Independence" in Tsang (ed.), *Judicial Independence and the Rule of Law in Hong Kong* (Hong Kong University Press, 2001) at 9.
63. One of the most famous examples was the trial and conviction in a Shenzhen court in 2007 of those responsible for a high-profile murder committed at the Luk Yu teahouse in Hong Kong. However, this case attracted far less controversy than either the "Big Spender" or the "Telford Gardens poisoner" cases, a point discussed further in Danny Gittings, "Changing Expectations: How the Rule of Law Fared in the First Decade of the Hong Kong SAR" (July 2007) 7 *Hong Kong Journal*.

which all involved crimes either partly committed on the mainland or where the suspect was a mainland resident.

In cases involving crimes committed by Hong Kong residents entirely in Hong Kong, there is general consensus that the provisions in the Hong Kong Basic Law should prevail in ensuring that such cases are always tried in Hong Kong,[64] even though it is possible to interpret the PRC Criminal Law in a way that would appear also to give mainland courts jurisdiction over many such cases.[65] Leung (2006)[66] seeks to rationalize this by drawing on the general principle under the Chinese legal system that "special provisions" covering a specific situation will usually prevail in the event of a conflict with "general provisions" covering the situation in the country as a whole.[67] Applying that principle, the Hong Kong Basic Law, as a "special" law governing the specific situation in Hong Kong, would normally prevail over PRC Criminal Law, as well as most other Chinese national laws, since they are "general" laws governing the situation in the country as a whole.

Leung's analysis has its limitations.[68] Nonetheless, in principle, it provides an attractive rationale for asserting the superiority of the Hong Kong Basic Law over other Chinese national laws, including other basic laws, using a principle well established within the Chinese legal system. It also provides one possible rationale for explaining why most Chinese national laws do not apply in Hong Kong, a point explicitly stated in Article 18(2) of the Hong Kong Basic Law,[69] since these can be also categorized as "general" laws over which the more "specific" Hong Kong Basic Law should arguably prevail.

The special status of the Hong Kong Basic Law within the Chinese legal system is further reflected in the provisions in Article 159 which make it more difficult to amend the Hong Kong Basic Law than any other basic law in China,[70] with the sole exception of

---

64. See, for example, Fu, "The Battle of Criminal Jurisdictions" (see note 60) at 276, and Leung, "Viewing the Jurisdictional Issue From a Proper Perspective" (see note 61) at 57.
65. This depends on whether the extra-territorial jurisdiction over Chinese citizens granted to the mainland courts under Article 7 of PRC Criminal Law (see note 57) includes Chinese citizens resident in Hong Kong. However, Fu (see note 60) argues that, in this context, Chinese citizens should be interpreted as only referring to mainland residents.
66. Priscilla Leung Mei-fun, *The Hong Kong Basic Law: Hybrid of Common Law and Chinese Law* (LexisNexis, 2006) at 305.
67. PRC Legislation Law, Article 83.
68. In particular, it would not solve the problem of how to resolve the conflict between the Hong Kong Basic Law and any more recently enacted mainland law, since Article 83 of the PRC Legislation Law also stipulates that new provisions will generally prevail over older provisions. In such circumstances, applying this rationale might invite intervention by the NPC Standing Committee, which (under Article 85 of the PRC Legislation Law) is given the power to resolve any conflicts between a general provision in a newer law and a special provision in an older law.
69. See further "4.2: Legislative Power" in Chapter 4 for more on the restrictions on the application of Chinese national laws in Hong Kong.
70. See further "7.5: Amendment" in Chapter 7 for more on the restrictions on amendments stipulated in Article 159.

the Macao Basic Law.[71] Article 159(4) also purports to make it impossible to amend the Hong Kong Basic Law at all in any way which would breach the basic policies set out by China in the Joint Declaration,[72] the document that gives the Hong Kong Basic Law its international dimension. However Ling (2000)[73] has expressed doubts about whether this particular restriction is legally enforceable.[74]

3.3 Constitutional Dimension

The Hong Kong Basic Law's domestic dimension as a national law has occasionally raised doubts about whether it has any constitutional dimension at all, a conclusion which threatens to undermine the extent to which it protects Hong Kong's high degree of autonomy.[75]

Zhang (1988)[76] has been perhaps the most ardent in denying the existence of any constitutional dimension to the Hong Kong Basic Law, instead describing it as simply one of many basic laws enacted by the National People's Congress. "The draft Basic Law can be nothing but a statutory law," argued Zhang, writing while the Hong Kong Basic Law was still in the early stages of being drafted. "There are those who call the Basic Law Hong Kong's 'little constitution', but as has been seen, this appellation is quite inappropriate."[77]

Some common law scholars have expressed similar views. Dowdle (2007) argues that, "simply calling the Hong Kong Basic Law a 'Basic Law' did not endow it with some uniquely 'constitutional' essence".[78] But Dowdle agrees that its contents, as opposed to its title, do give the Hong Kong Basic Law such a "constitutional essence".[79] From the Hong Kong perspective, it is difficult to see how anyone could deny that to be the case, since the Hong Kong Basic Law performs the roles normally associated with a written constitution.

---

71. Article 144 of the Macao Basic Law imposes similar restrictions on its amendment to those contained in the Hong Kong Basic Law.
72. Under Article 159(4), no amendment to the Hong Kong Basic Law "shall contravene the established basic policies of the People's Republic of China regarding Hong Kong".
73. Bing Ling, "The Proper Law for the Conflict Between the Basic Law and Other Legislative Acts" in Johannes M.M. Chan, H.L. Fu and Yash Ghai (eds.), *Hong Kong's Constitutional Debate: Conflict Over Interpretation* (Hong Kong University Press, 2000) at 163.
74. See further page 262.
75. See further pages 66–67.
76. Zhang Youyu, "The Reasons for and Basic Principles in Formulating the Hong Kong Special Administrative Region Basic Law, and its Essential Contents and Mode of Expression" (1988) 2 *Journal of Chinese Law* 5–19.
77. Ibid. at 7–8.
78. Dowdle, "Constitutionalism in the Shadow of the Common Law" (see note 42) at 71.
79. Ibid.

Although written constitutions vary from country to country, both in form and content, de Smith and Braizer (1994)[80] suggest that they generally have at least two characteristics in common. Firstly, they constitute a higher source of law that is superior to other, ordinary, laws.[81] Secondly, they set out the organization and functions of the different branches of the governmental structure.[82] In addition, constitutions often include a section setting out guarantees of fundamental human rights.[83]

From all these perspectives, the Hong Kong Basic Law fits the definition of a constitution. Its provisions make clear that it constitutes a higher source of law, which prevails over other inconsistent laws in Hong Kong. Article 8 stipulates that sources of law previously in force in Hong Kong prior to 1 July 1997 can only remain in force if they do not "contravene" the Hong Kong Basic Law, while Article 160(1) gives the National People's Congress Standing Committee the power—at least at the time of the 1 July 1997 establishment of the Hong Kong SAR[84]—to invalidate any laws found to be "in contravention" of the Hong Kong Basic Law. In addition, Article 11(2) requires all new laws enacted by the legislature of the Hong Kong SAR to comply with the Hong Kong Basic Law.[85] As a result, both the National People's Congress Standing Committee in 1997,[86] and the Hong Kong courts subsequently,[87] have declared provisions in various Hong Kong laws to be invalid, after finding them to be in contravention of the Hong Kong Basic Law.

Equally, the contents of the Hong Kong Basic Law bear all the hallmarks of a constitution. Chapter IV, the longest chapter in the Hong Kong Basic Law, is devoted to setting out the organization and functions of the different branches of Hong Kong's governmental structure. Consisting of 62 articles, its importance is evident from the fact that Chapter

---

80. Stanley de Smith and Rodney Brazier, *Constitutional and Administrative Law* (Penguin, 8th edition, 1998).
81. Ibid. at 4–5.
82. Ibid.
83. Ibid. at 7.
84. Article 160(1) is ambiguous about who should invalidate any laws found to be inconsistent with the Hong Kong Basic Law *after* 1 July 1997, stating only that: "If any laws are later discovered to be in contravention of this Law, they shall be amended or cease to have force in accordance with the procedure as prescribed by this Law." In practice, this power has been usually exercised by the Hong Kong courts since 1 July 1997, although Article 17(3) also gives the Standing Committee a limited power to invalidate certain categories of laws which it deems inconsistent with the Hong Kong Basic Law. For more on Article 17(3), see further "4.2: Legislative Power" in Chapter 4.
85. This does not, however, directly cover the small number of PRC national laws which are not enacted by the legislature but instead applied in Hong Kong through promulgation by the Chief Executive. See further note 151 in Chapter 4 and the accompanying text.
86. See Decision of the Standing Committee of the NPC on Treatment of the Laws Previously in Force in Hong Kong in Accordance With Article 160 of the Basic Law of the Hong Kong SAR of the PRC (23 Feb 1997), which is described in more detail in "2.6: Through Train" in Chapter 2.
87. See further "6.2: Judicial Review" in Chapter 6 for more on the court's exercise of this power.

IV comprises nearly 40% of the 160 articles in the Hong Kong Basic Law. Its six sections go into considerable detail on the organization and functions of the Chief Executive; Executive Authorities (which refers to what is generally described, in everyday language, as the Hong Kong SAR Government); Legislature; Judiciary; District Organizations responsible for advising on, and running, services at a local level; and Public Servants (which refers to both civil servants and employees of other publicly owned bodies).[88]

In addition, Chapter III of the Hong Kong Basic Law includes generous guarantees of fundamental human rights that are similar, or perhaps even more extensive, than those in many other constitutions.[89] For instance, Article 27 of the Hong Kong Basic Law guarantees freedom of speech, press, assembly, association, procession and demonstration in wording almost identical to that which protects the same rights in theory, although not necessarily in practice,[90] under Article 35 of the PRC Constitution 1982. Most foreign constitutions also contain similar provisions. For instance, freedom of speech and of the press is commonly protected in constitutional documents around the world.[91]

In some respects, the list of rights contained by the Hong Kong Basic Law goes even further than many other constitutions. In *Gurung Kesh Bahadur v Director of Immigration*,[92] the Court of Appeal described the provisions in Article 31 of the Hong Kong Basic Law on the right to travel as "probably wider than those contained in any other constitutional document".[93] That right is not, for instance, explicitly mentioned in the US Constitution, although it nonetheless has been firmly established as a constitutional right by the US Supreme Court.[94]

So it is hardly surprising that the Hong Kong Basic Law is commonly referred to in Hong Kong as the SAR's mini-constitution. In *Ng Ka Ling v Director of Immigration*,[95] the Court of Final Appeal described the Hong Kong Basic Law as both a national law and "the constitution of the Region", noting that: "Like other constitutions, it distributes and

---

88. For more on the provisions on governmental structure, see further "Chapter 5: System of Government".
89. For more on the provisions on rights and duties, see further "Chapter 8: Protection of Human Rights".
90. This is largely because the rights listed in the Chinese constitution are not, in contrast to those listed in the Hong Kong Basic Law, generally enforceable in the courts. See further note 123 in Chapter 6 and note 140 in Chapter 8.
91. See, for example, the 1st Amendment to the US Constitution 1791, Section 5(i) of the German Basic Law 1949 and Section 2 of the Canadian Charter of Rights and Freedoms 1982. A rare exception is the Commonwealth of Australia Constitution Act 1900, which focuses much more on governmental structure and does not explicitly mention either of these freedoms.
92. [2001] 3 HKLRD 32.
93. Ibid. at 43.
94. For a brief summary of the main US Supreme Court cases on this point and their relevance to Hong Kong, see *Gurung Kesh Bahadur v Director of Immigration* (2002) 5 HKCFAR 480, 496–497.
95. (1999) 2 HKCFAR 4.

delimits powers, as well as providing for fundamental rights and freedoms."[96] While that conclusion can be hardly faulted as far as the contents of the Hong Kong Basic Law are concerned, placing too much emphasis on this constitutional dimension can give rise to problems, especially when the use of a shortened title such as "the Basic Law" appears to overlook the fact that it is simply one of many such laws enacted by the National People's Congress.[97]

The potential for such problems is well demonstrated by the reaction to one aspect of the decision in *Ng Ka Ling*, where the Court of Final Appeal used this constitutional dimension to assert a jurisdiction to invalidate any other laws enacted by the National People's Congress if they were found to be inconsistent with the Hong Kong Basic Law: "As with other constitutions, laws which are inconsistent with the Basic Law are of no effect and are invalid."[98] That provoked a brief constitutional crisis, as mainland legal scholars and government officials denounced the Court of Final Appeal's assertion of such a jurisdiction in strident terms.[99] The crisis was only resolved when the court issued an unprecedented supplementary judgment, which essentially rephrased its assertion of such a jurisdiction in more conciliatory terms.[100]

Despite that uproar over the Court of Final Appeal's attempts to use the constitutional dimension to the Hong Kong Basic Law to assert a jurisdiction over actions of the National People's Congress, mainland officials and scholars seem to have softened on the more general issue of whether there is any constitutional dimension to the Hong Kong Basic Law at all.

Li (2000) describes it as a "constitutional legal document" and suggests it is "not groundless" to call the Hong Kong Basic Law a "mini-constitution".[101] This directly contradicts Zhang's assertion to the contrary 12 years earlier.[102] In a survey of the literature of leading mainland law scholars on the subject, Lee and Chen (2007)[103] find broad support for their conclusion that the Hong Kong Basic Law can best be characterized as a "Special Law of the Constitution".[104] What that means is that, while the Hong Kong Basic Law is not a constitution in itself, it plays an important constitutional role in supplementing the provisions of the national constitution when it comes to their application in Hong Kong.

---

96. Ibid. at 26.
97. See further note 42 earlier in this chapter and the accompanying text.
98. *Ng Ka Ling* at 26.
99. See further notes 202–205 in Chapter 6 and the accompanying text.
100. *Ng Ka Ling v Director of Immigration (No 2)* (1999) 2 HKCFAR 141.
101. Li Zaishun, "The Comprehensive Grasping of the 'One Country, Two Systems' Concept Is the Key to the Correct Implementation of the Hong Kong Basic Law", Constitutional Law Conference on Implementation of the Basic Law: A Comparative Perspective, 29 April 2000.
102. See further note 77 earlier in this chapter and the accompanying text.
103. Lee Simon Hoey and Chen Junhao, "The Basic Law Is a Special Law of the Chinese Constitution" in *Seminar on Review and Prospect of the Basic Law: Collection of Articles 2007* (One Country Two Systems Research Institute, 2010) at 487–527.
104. Ibid. at 507–510.

That, in turn, raises the difficult issue of the precise nature of the relationship between the Hong Kong Basic Law and the often conflicting provisions of the PRC Constitution 1982.

3.4 Relationship With Chinese Constitution

The first law listed at the start of Volume 1 of the Laws of Hong Kong is not the Hong Kong Basic Law. Instead, it is the Constitution of the People's Republic of China 1982, the fundamental document that sets out the structure of the Chinese state, the rights and duties of its citizens, and the principles under which the country is governed.

That does not mean the Chinese Constitution is part of the laws of Hong Kong, or that all its provisions apply in Hong Kong. If that were the case, "one country two systems" might well cease to exist, since much of the PRC Constitution 1982 is about the socialist system that is not practised in Hong Kong, and some parts of the constitution are clearly incompatible with Hong Kong's way of life. When controversy first arose[105] about the Hong Kong SAR Government's decision to add the PRC Constitution 1982 to the start of a new edition of the Laws of Hong Kong after the 1 July 1997 handover,[106] the Hong Kong SAR Government insisted the constitution was being included simply "for reference purposes"[107] in order to "enable users to have a complete picture" of Hong Kong's constitutional framework,[108] and that this did not necessarily mean it was actually part of the laws of Hong Kong. The government refused to say whether or not it believed the constitution has legal force in Hong Kong.[109] The issue remains unresolved, with much academic argument about how far the provisions of the PRC Constitution 1982 directly apply in Hong Kong.[110]

---

105. See Margaret Ng, "PRC Constitution Made Part of Laws of Hong Kong?" (Oct 1998) *Hong Kong Lawyer* 21–22, and the question asked by Martin Lee in Legislative Council, *Official Record of Proceedings, Hong Kong Hansard* (10 Feb 1999).
106. Fourteenth issue of the Authorized Loose-leaf Edition of the Laws of Hong Kong, published on 15 June 1998.
107. See Secretary for Constitutional Affairs Michael Suen in Legislative Council, *Official Record of Proceedings, Hong Kong Hansard* (10 Feb 1999).
108. Tony Yen, "The PRC Constitution and Hong Kong Law" (Dec 1998) *Hong Kong Lawyer* 16.
109. Ibid.
110. Ghai argues that the Hong Kong Basic Law "is intended to be self-contained" and that the provisions of the PRC Constitution 1982 do not directly apply in Hong Kong, with the exception of Article 31. See Yash Ghai, "Litigating the Basic Law: Jurisdiction, Interpretation and Procedure" in Chan, Fu and Ghai (eds.), *Hong Kong's Constitutional Debate* (see note 73) at 45. However, his argument is contradicted by several court cases in which the Hong Kong courts have cited various provisions in the PRC Constitution. These include *Ng Ka Ling* (1999) 2 HKCFAR 4, 12, *Lau Kong Yung v Director of Immigration* (1999) 2 HKCFAR 300, 321 and *Ting Lei Miao v Chen Li Hung* [1999] 1 HKLRD 123 (CA). In the later case, Justice Rogers stated (at 140) that "clearly parts of the Constitution are applicable in Hong Kong", although he also suggested that the application of other parts of the constitution "may be altered by the Basic Law". Although part of a dissenting judgment, there is nothing to suggest that the other two judges disagreed on this point.

Whatever the Hong Kong SAR Government's reasons for placing the PRC Constitution 1982 ahead of the Hong Kong Basic Law in the Laws of Hong Kong, it accurately reflects the fact that the Hong Kong Basic Law, like all laws in China, is ultimately enacted under the authority of the PRC Constitution 1982—and highlights some of the difficulties involved in having to rely in this way on a document from such a very different legal system.

Both in its Preamble and again in Article 11(1), the Hong Kong Basic Law makes clear that it is enacted in accordance with the PRC Constitution 1982, citing, in particular, Article 31 of the constitution. This is the vaguely worded provision that was added as part of the passage of a new constitution in 1982,[111] with the intention of enshrining in legal form the policy of "one country, two systems".

The problem is that, whatever its intention, Article 31 makes no mention of one country, two systems. It simply allows the Chinese state to create Special Administrative Regions, a new type of local administrative unit of which Hong Kong became the first on 1 July 1997,[112] and permits the National People's Congress to enact laws prescribing the systems to be followed in such regions.[113] But Article 31 gives no guidance on what systems are allowed under such laws, beyond the vague statement that this will be decided "in the light of the specific conditions". In particular, it does not specifically allow such systems to contravene other parts of the constitution.

The solution adopted by the drafters of the Hong Kong Basic Law was to state in Article 11(1) of that document that, in accordance with Article 31 of the PRC Constitution 1982, the "systems and policies" to be followed in Hong Kong, including the "social and economic systems, the system for safeguarding the fundamental rights and freedoms of its residents, the executive, legislative and judicial systems and the relevant policies" would be based on the Hong Kong Basic Law. This implies that there is no need to follow for Hong Kong to follow the provisions in the PRC Constitution 1982 on these matters. However, the vague wording of Article 31 has long given rise to concern about whether it provides a sufficient legal basis for the enactment of a Hong Kong Basic Law which, in providing for a separate system for Hong Kong, contradicts some of the most fundamental principles in the PRC Constitution 1982.[114]

---

111. The 1982 constitution replaced the 1978 constitution, which had become outdated following the end of the Cultural Revolution and the start of economic reforms in China.
112. Macao became China's second Special Administrative Region on 20 December 1999.
113. This is supplemented by Article 62(13) of the PRC Constitution 1982, which lists one of the NPC's powers as being: "To decide on the establishment of special administrative regions and the systems to be instituted there."
114. See, for instance, Siu K. Lee, "Much Ado About Something" (July 1999) *Hong Kong Lawyer* 26, 27. For a detailed comparison of the provisions in the PRC Constitution 1982 with those in the Hong Kong Basic Law, see Lee and Chen, "The Basic Law Is a Special Law of the Chinese Constitution" (see note 103) at 491–505.

For instance, Article 5 of the Hong Kong Basic Law specifically states that: "The socialist system and policies shall not be practised in the Hong Kong Special Administrative Region, and the previous capitalist system and way of life shall remain unchanged for 50 years."[115] That runs directly counter to Article 1 of the PRC Constitution 1982, which describes the socialist system as the "basic system of the People's Republic of China"—with no mention of any exceptions—and even prohibits "[s]abotage of the socialist system by any organization or individual". Some rights guaranteed under the Hong Kong Basic Law would also appear to run counter to the PRC Constitution 1982. For instance, while the Hong Kong Basic Law guarantees the right of Hong Kong residents "to raise a family freely",[116] the constitution makes provision for China's one-child policy by allowing the state to restrict population growth[117] and imposes a duty on married couples to use birth control.[118] Similarly, while religious freedom is guaranteed in unqualified terms under the Hong Kong Basic Law,[119] it is limited to "normal religious activities" under the PRC Constitution 1982 and subject to several restrictions.[120]

That puts the Hong Kong Basic Law in the uncomfortable position of contradicting many parts of the higher law from which it draws its authority without, given the vague wording of Article 31, any clear legal basis for doing so. As the eminent English legal scholar Sir William Wade stated in a much-quoted opinion to the Law Society of Hong Kong in 1988: "It is thus clear, at least in the eyes of an English lawyer, that the Chinese Constitution and the Basic Law will inevitably be in conflict."[121] Fu (2000) argues that, "the constitutionality of the Basic Law may be doubtful".[122] That would, at least in theory, open the door to provisions in the Hong Kong Basic Law being declared invalid, by reason of their inconsistency with a higher law, in this case the PRC Constitution 1982.

Not surprisingly, this possibility caused much concern during the drafting of the Hong Kong Basic Law and led to several proposals being put forward to try to resolve the

---

115. For more on the meaning of Article 5, see further "9.2: What Does 50 Years Mean?" in Chapter 9.
116. Article 37.
117. Article 25 states that: "The state promotes family planning so that population growth may fit the plans for economic and social development."
118. Article 49 includes a provision stipulating that: "Both husband and wife have the duty to practise family planning."
119. Articles 32(2) and 141.
120. Article 36 states that: "The state protects normal religious activities. No one may make use of religion to engage in activities that disrupt public order, impair the health of citizens or interfere with the educational system of the state."
121. "Opinion on the Draft Hong Kong Basic Law" reprinted in Hungdah Chiu (ed.), *The Draft Basic Law of Hong Kong: Analysis and Documents* (School of Law, University of Maryland, 1988) at 81–91.
122. See for instance Fu Hualing, "Supremacy of a Different Kind: The Constitution, the NPC and the Hong Kong SAR" in Chan, Fu and Ghai (eds.), *Hong Kong's Constitutional Debate* (see note 73) at 98–99.

conflicts between the wording of the Hong Kong Basic Law and the PRC Constitution 1982. One solution would have been to amend the constitution, an idea put forward by Wade,[123] who suggested that the entire Hong Kong Basic Law be treated as an amendment to the constitution,[124] and by the Basic Law Consultative Committee. Other suggestions, also put forward by the Basic Law Consultative Committee, included setting up a committee to try to resolve conflicts between the two documents, and either interpreting the constitution to make clear which parts do not apply in Hong Kong or writing a similar provision into the Hong Kong Basic Law.[125]

None of these suggestions were ultimately accepted. However, China did take one smaller step to address the concerns that had been expressed about the constitutional validity of the Hong Kong Basic Law. This was the adoption of a formal decision of the National People's Congress, on the same day as the promulgation of the Hong Kong Basic Law, which stated that the Hong Kong Basic Law was in accordance with PRC Chinese Constitution 1982 because it was enacted based on the provisions of Article 31 and "in the light of the specific conditions of Hong Kong".[126] Although this made no attempt to address, let alone resolve, the actual conflicts between the Hong Kong Basic Law and the constitution, as a formal decision of China's highest legislative body which is also responsible for supervising the constitution,[127] it did lay to rest any doubts about the constitutionality of the Hong Kong Basic Law.

From the perspective of mainland law scholars, this was never a problem in any case. After all, the wording of the Chinese Constitution does not carry the same legal weight as similar documents in non-Communist countries.[128] Its provisions are not generally enforceable in the courts,[129] and have even been ignored by Chinese leaders when it suited their purposes to do so.[130] If a legal rationale is needed to explain away the

---

123. "Opinion on the Draft Hong Kong Basic Law" (see note 121) at 83.
124. In fact, the Hong Kong Basic Law was passed with the support of more than two-thirds of the members of the NPC, after being submitted by its Standing Committee, so fulfilling the two requirements for an amendment of the PRC Constitution 1982 stipulated in Article 64 of the constitution. However, it was never described as a constitutional amendment by either the NPC or its Standing Committee, and the idea that it can be treated as one has been described as far-fetched. See Lee, "Much Ado About Something" (see note 114) at 28.
125. Consultative Committee for the Basic Law of the Hong Kong SAR, *Final Report on the Relationship Between the Basic Law and the Constitution* (Feb 1987) at 10–12.
126. Decision of the NPC on the Basic Law of the Hong Kong SAR of the PRC (4 April 1990).
127. PRC Constitution 1982, Article 62(2). Under Article 67(1), a similar power is also vested in the NPC Standing Committee.
128. See Albert Chen, *An Introduction to the Legal System of the People's Republic of China* (LexisNexis, 4th edition, 2011) at 49–52.
129. Ibid. at 47–48. See further note 123 in Chapter 6.
130. One of the best known examples is the decision to allow Chinese peasants to lease land during the early stages of economic reforms in the early 1980s even though, at that stage, this was still explicitly forbidden by Article 10 of the PRC Constitution 1982. Only in 1988 was Article 10 finally amended to legitimize a practice that had been already taking place, contrary to the constitution, for several years. See further note 20 in Chapter 9.

conflicts between a Hong Kong Basic Law based upon Article 31 of the constitution and the other provisions elsewhere in the constitution, it can be found in the principle under the Chinese legal system that "special provisions" prevail over conflicting "general provisions".[131] As a result, Li (2000) argues that "Article 31 of the Constitution is a special provision, and the effect of special provisions surpasses that of general provisions."[132]

So, however extensive the conflicts between the wording of the Hong Kong Basic Law and the PRC Constitution 1982, in practice there was never much prospect of this having any effect on the legal status of the Hong Kong Basic Law.

---

131. See further note 66 earlier in this chapter and the accompanying text, on the application of a similar principle in arguing that the "special" nature of the Hong Kong Basic Law allows it to prevail over other more "general" basic laws.
132. Li, "The Comprehensive Grasping of the 'One Country, Two Systems' Concept" (see note 101). Xiao Weiyun [in *One Country, Two Systems: An Account of the Drafting of the Hong Kong Basic Law* (Peking University Press, English edition, 2001) at 83] cites several other examples elsewhere in the PRC Constitution 1982 where "specific provisions" are believed to prevail over conflicting "general provisions".

Chapter 4
How High a Degree of Autonomy?

The granting of a high degree of autonomy to the Hong Kong SAR is one of the first—and most fundamental—principles in the Hong Kong Basic Law. It comes in Article 2, second only to the statement in Article 1 of the most basic principle of all; that Hong Kong is "an inalienable part of the People's Republic of China".

Article 2 states that: "The National People's Congress authorizes the Hong Kong Special Administrative Region to exercise a high degree of autonomy and enjoy executive, legislative and independent judicial power, including that of final adjudication, in accordance with the provisions of this Law." But it offers no detailed definition of exactly what a high degree of autonomy means. Nor does the Joint Declaration, where the term originated.[1]

The lack of any definition in either document is not surprising, given that others have struggled to describe what autonomy means. Heintze (1998) notes it is "not a well-defined legal concept",[2] Hannum and Lillich (1980) observe that autonomy lacks "a generally accepted definition in international law".[3] Nonetheless, it is possible to lay down some broad parameters for the concept. Crawford (2006) explains that: "Autonomous areas are regions of a State, usually possessing some ethnic or cultural distinctiveness, which have been granted separate powers of internal administration, to whatever degree, without being detached from the State of which they are part."[4] In other words, autonomy is where part of a country is given special powers to run some of its local affairs while remaining part of that country.

As that explanation notes, the reason for granting such special powers—which essentially amount to privileges that the people in the rest of the country are not able to enjoy—is because of some distinctive feature of the part of the country that is allowed to exercise such autonomy. Most commonly it is because many of the people who live

---

1. In paragraph 3(2), as one of the basic policies of the PRC regarding Hong Kong. For more on these basic policies, see further "2.2: Sino-British Joint Declaration" in Chapter 2.
2. Hans-Joachim Heintze, "On the Legal Understanding of Autonomy" in Markku Suksi (ed.), *Autonomy: Applications and Implications* (Kluwer Law International, 1998) at 7.
3. Hurst Hannum and Richard B. Lillich, "The Concept of Autonomy in International Law" (1980) 74 *American Journal of International Law* 858. But see Ruth Lapidoth, *Autonomy: Flexible Solutions to Ethnic Conflicts* (United States Institute of Peace, 1997) at 29–33 for a summary of the different definitions that have been put forward.
4. See James Crawford, *The Creation of States in International Law* (Clarendon Press, 2nd edition, 2006) at 323.

in that part of the country are ethnically different from those in the rest of the country.[5] Well-known examples include the autonomy granted to the island of Greenland, which is predominantly inhabited by Inuit (or Eskimo) people—and more than 50 times larger than the rest of Denmark, the country of which it is part. Other examples include the Kurdish region of Iraq, which is predominantly inhabited by a different ethnic group from the rest of the country, and the Palestinian people living in the Gaza Strip and the Israeli-controlled West Bank.

Even where inter-marriage and population movements call into question whether there is still a distinct ethnic group in such regions, it is usually possible to point to continuing cultural differences between the autonomous region and the rest of the country of which it is part. Often these include the use of a different language by part of the population in that region. Well-known examples of this include the regions of Scotland, Wales and Northern Ireland which all enjoy autonomy within the UK.[6] One less well-known example, which merits close study, is the Aland Islands in northern Europe. These tiny islands, inhabited by a predominantly Swedish-speaking population, are part of Finland, but have enjoyed a high degree of autonomy within that country since 1920.[7] This makes them one of the longer-lasting examples of autonomy elsewhere in the world. Ghai (2001) notes that the autonomy arrangements in the Aland Islands are "generally considered to be a success", and provide a useful comparison in evaluating how high a degree of autonomy Hong Kong enjoys under the Hong Kong Basic Law.[8]

But it is important to note that Hong Kong differs in one crucial respect from virtually all of the other autonomous areas elsewhere in the world, as well as from other autonomous areas in China, such as Tibet and Xinjiang. Known as National Autonomous Areas,[9] these areas elsewhere in China are allowed to enjoy a far more limited degree

---

5. See Lapidoth, *Autonomy: Flexible Solutions to Ethnic Conflicts* (see note 3) at 33: "A territorial political autonomy is an arrangement aimed at granting to a group that differs from the majority of the population in the state, but that constitutes the majority in a specific region, a means by which it can express its distinct identity."
6. However Scotland is scheduled to hold a referendum in 2014 on whether it should become independent from the U.K. See "Scotland's independence referendum", *The Economist*, 18 Oct 2012.
7. This was in response to pressure from the islands' population for integration with Sweden. For a detailed description of the autonomy arrangements for the Aland Islands, see Lauri Hannikainen and Fran Horn (eds.), *Autonomy and Demilitarisation in International Law: The Aland Islands in a Changing Europe* (Kluwer Law International, 1997).
8. Yash Ghai, "Resolution of Disputes between the Central and Regional Governments: Models in Autonomous Regions" (2002) 5 *Journal of Chinese and Comparative Law* 1, 2–5.
9. National Autonomous Areas have existed in China since 1947. They are currently provided for under Section 6 of Chapter III of the PRC Constitution 1982, and there are now 159 National Autonomous Areas covering more than 64% of the total area of the territory of China. See She Wenzheng and Bu Xiaolin, "Legislation in National Autonomous Areas of the People's Republic of China" in Jan Michel Otto, Maurice V. Polak, Jianfu Chen and Yuwen Li (eds.), *Law-Making in the People's Republic of China* (Kluwer Law International, 2000) at 131–132.

of autonomy under the PRC Constitution 1982.[10] Indeed, in the case of Tibet, China has rejected repeated calls from the Dalai Lama,[11] the exiled spiritual leader of the Tibetan people, for Tibet to be offered the same degree of autonomy enjoyed by Hong Kong.[12]

Unlike the Eskimos of Greenland, or the Muslims in Xinjiang, to take just two examples, the majority of Hong Kong's population cannot be said to belong to a different ethnic group from the rest of the country of which they are a part. While most people in Hong Kong speak Cantonese, this is part of the Chinese language family as opposed to the much more distinct languages often spoken by the population of other autonomous areas. Heintze (1998) notes: "Hong Kong demonstrates that the subject of autonomy does not have to be determined according to ethnic criteria only."[13]

The reasons behind Hong Kong's autonomy can still be placed within the broad category of "conflict resolution" (i.e., resolving disputes over the status of a particular part of a country) that many scholars see as another common factor underlying many autonomous arrangements the world over.[14] However, the reasons for Hong Kong's autonomy are far more heavily tilted towards economic factors than most other examples of autonomy elsewhere in the world. This is a legacy of Hong Kong's development as a British colony with a free-market economy that China judged to be of great value as a window on the outside world at the time it agreed to grant Hong Kong a high degree of autonomy in the 1984 Joint Declaration.[15] Ghai (1999) argues such economic factors provide a much weaker "moral basis" for Hong Kong's autonomy than the ethnic or cultural factors more commonly used to justify autonomous arrangements elsewhere in the world.[16] He suggests it is one which is likely to come under increasing threat in coming years, "especially as the economic paradigms of the two parts of China converge increasingly".[17]

---

10. See Articles 112–122. For example, under Article 119, National Autonomous Areas have the right to "independently administer educational, scientific, cultural, public health and physical culture affairs in their respective areas".
11. See, for instance, "Dalai Lama yields ground on Tibet self-rule: We will accept China's authority; if it preserves our culture, he says", *South China Morning Post*, 14 March 2005.
12. See, for instance, Information Office of the State Council, *Regional Ethnic Autonomy in Tibet* (23 May 2004) at part V.
13. Heintze, "On the Legal Understanding of Autonomy" (see note 2) at 16. Hannum, however, argues that the differences between the Hong Kong and mainland systems "may be sufficiently great that one can speak of separate 'cultures' as well". See Hurst Hannum, *Autonomy, Sovereignty and Self-Determination* (University of Pennsylvania Press, revised edition, 1996) at 124.
14. See, for example, Hannum (1996) at 123–127, and Markku Suksi, *Sub-State Governance Through Territorial Autonomy: A Comparative Study in Constitutional Law of Powers, Procedures and Institutions* (Springer, 2011) at 141–142 and 214–234.
15. This is reflected in the heavy emphasis in the Joint Declaration on preserving Hong Kong's existing economic systems. See further "2.2: Sino-British Joint Declaration" in Chapter 2.
16. Yash Ghai, *Hong Kong's New Constitutional Order: The Resumption of Chinese Sovereignty and the Basic Law* (Hong Kong University Press, 2nd edition, 1999) at 184.
17. Ibid.

Although the reasons for granting autonomy are often fairly similar in most autonomous areas around the world, the precise content of that autonomy differs in almost every instance. In a study of 22 different autonomous areas, Hannum and Lillich (1980) identified some common characteristics.[18] These characteristics can be broadly summarized[19] as indicating that the following powers are commonly exercised in most autonomous areas:[20]

(1) A locally chosen Chief Executive, with responsibility for administering local laws (although certain specific powers may be reserved for the national government to exercise);
(2) A locally elected legislature with the power to make laws on local matters;
(3) An independent local judiciary with jurisdiction over local matters;
(4) An independent body (such as a court or joint commission) with responsibility for dispute resolution between local and central authorities (such as over who exercises a particular power).

These characteristics provide a widely quoted benchmark for assessing the extent of Hong Kong's autonomy,[21] and the remainder of this chapter will consider how far the provisions in the Hong Kong Basic Law comply with them.

4.1 Executive Power

Executive power, or the power to administer some aspects of local affairs, is a core element of the powers exercised in virtually every autonomous area the world over. Lapidoth (1997) notes that this normally includes the power to run that area's own economic, social and cultural affairs.[22] Based on a survey of 34 autonomous areas around the world,[23] Herzer (2002) offers more detail, noting such autonomous areas typically

---

18. See Hannum and Lillich, "The Concept of Autonomy in International Law" (see note 3) at 886–887.
19. For a more complete description of these characteristics (from which this abbreviated and rephrased summary is drawn), see also Hannum, *Autonomy, Sovereignty and Self-Determination* (see note 13) at 467–468.
20. Ibid. at 468. Although Hannum refers to these as the characteristics of a "fully autonomous" territory, they include some powers which may be exercised by the national government and he notes, "autonomous governments should not expect to be immune from the influence of central governments". As such, this should not be equated with the "absolute", or full, autonomy which mainland legal scholars denounce as effectively equivalent to independence.
21. The Hannum and Lillich criteria are cited in several major textbooks on the Hong Kong Basic Law. See, for example, Ghai, *Hong Kong's New Constitutional Order* (see note 16) at 16 and C.L. Lim and Roda Mushkat, "External Affairs" in Johannes Chan and Lim (eds.), *Law of the Hong Kong Constitution* (Sweet & Maxwell, 2011) at 42.
22. Lapidoth, *Autonomy: Flexible Solutions to Ethnic Conflicts* (see note 3) at 33.
23. This unpublished study was conducted by the International Committee of Lawyers for Tibet.

exercise executive power over education, health care, language policy, taxation, control over natural resources, environmental policy, transportation and law and order.[24]

That does not mean autonomous areas have the power to run all aspects of their own affairs. Hannum and Lillich (1980) point out that autonomy "is not inconsistent with the denial of any local authority over specific areas of special concern to the principal/sovereign government", so long as this does not take the form of "general discretionary powers" to intervene in any area.[25]

Defence and foreign affairs are the two areas which most commonly remain under central government control.[26] However, Hannum and Lillich (1980) note that in many autonomous areas the central government will also retain control over customs, immigration, border security, ports, airports, water and energy resources, as well as monetary, banking and general economic policy.[27]

Judged solely on that basis, Hong Kong enjoys an extraordinarily high degree of executive power. Apart from defence and foreign affairs—and, in the latter case, even this is not entirely outside Hong Kong's control—under the Hong Kong Basic Law, all these powers, which are commonly exercised at a national level in many autonomous areas elsewhere in the world, fall within Hong Kong's control.

The breadth of Hong Kong's executive powers was demonstrated by a provision in the first draft of the Hong Kong Basic Law giving the SAR the power to manage "on its own" affairs in no less than 29 different areas.[28] Following complaints that even such a long list was not comprehensive enough,[29] this unwieldy provision disappeared from later drafts of the Hong Kong Basic Law.[30] But the powers remain, scattered across numerous different provisions in the Hong Kong Basic Law.

---

24. Eva Herzer, *Options for Tibet's Future Political Status: Self-Governance Through an Autonomous Arrangement* (Tibetan Parliamentary & Policy Research Centre, 2002) at 8–22.
25. Hannum and Lillich, "The Concept of Autonomy in International Law" (see note 3) at 887.
26. Lapidoth, *Autonomy: Flexible Solutions to Ethnic Conflicts* (see note 3) at 33.
27. Hannum and Lillich, "The Concept of Autonomy in International Law" (see note 3) at 887.
28. Article 15 of the first draft of the Hong Kong Basic Law stated that: "The Hong Kong Special Administrative Region is vested with executive power. In accordance with the relevant provisions of this Law it shall, on its own, manage public finance, monetary matters, economy, industry and commerce, trade, taxation, postal service, civil aviation, maritime matters, traffic and transport, fishery, agriculture, personnel administration, civil affairs, labour, education, medical and health services, social welfare, culture and recreation, municipal facilities, urban planning, housing, real estate, public order, entry and exit controls, meteorology, communications, science and technology, sports and other administrative affairs."
29. See, for instance, Consultative Committee for the Basic Law of the Hong Kong SAR, *Consultation Report, Volume 1: Report on the Consultation of the Draft Basic Law for Solicitation of Opinions* (Oct 1988) at 44.
30. Article 15 in the first draft of the Hong Kong Basic Law was replaced in the second and final drafts by a simple statement in Article 16 (the different number is due to renumbering between the different drafts of the Hong Kong Basic Law) that: "The Hong Kong Special Administrative Region shall be vested with legislative power. It shall, on its own, conduct the administrative affairs of the Region in accordance with the relevant provisions of this Law."

Chapter V of the Hong Kong Basic Law on the Economy and Chapter VI on Education, Science, Culture, Sports, Religion, Labour and Social Services are overwhelmingly devoted to long lists of provisions on the wide range of executive powers which Hong Kong is allowed to exercise "on its own".[31] The provisions in Chapter VII on External Affairs even give Hong Kong jurisdiction over several issues—notably passports, border controls and some aspects of relations with foreign countries—which are normally handled at a national level almost everywhere else in the world.

Ghai (2005) describes these as "an extraordinary range of substantive powers", some of which can be seen as "indicia of semi-sovereignty".[32] Among the most unique provisions in this respect, Chen (2003) identifies the following powers:[33]

- Hong Kong's exclusive jurisdiction over its finances and the ban on the Central Government levying any form of taxation in Hong Kong (Article 106);
- The continuing existence of the Hong Kong dollar as a separate currency (Article 111(1));
- Hong Kong's existence as a separate customs territory (Article 116(1));
- Hong Kong's power to enter into economic and cultural relations with other countries and participate in some international organizations (Article 151);
- Hong Kong's power to regulate the entry and exit of foreign nationals (Article 154(2)).

While these are all very special powers, a few caveats are necessary. Hong Kong is not the only autonomous area to have a separate currency of its own. Other examples include Scotland and the Faroe Islands. However, as Herzer (2002) notes, in most other cases, the separate currencies that exist in some other autonomous areas "may be used interchangeably, at the same value with the currency of the state, which controls monetary policy".[34] By contrast, Hong Kong controls its own monetary policy (under Article 110(2) of the Hong Kong Basic Law) and the Hong Kong dollar has never been linked to the national currency, China's Renminbi. There is, however, nothing in the Hong Kong Basic Law

---

31. There are, however, a few provisions which also list certain specific powers that are reserved for the Central Authorities. See, for example, the provisions in Articles 126 and 129(2) requiring "special permission of the Central People's Government" before foreign warships or state aircraft can enter Hong Kong.
32. Yash Ghai, "The Imperatives of Autonomy: Contradictions of the Basic Law" in Johannes Chan and Lison Harris (eds.), *Hong Kong's Constitutional Debates* (Hong Kong Law Journal Limited, 2005) at 30.
33. Albert H. Chen, "The Concept of 'One Country Two Systems' and Its Application to Hong Kong" in C. Stephen Hsu (ed.), *Understanding China's Legal System: Essays in Honor of Jerome A. Cohen* (New York University Press, 2003) at 364–365. Chen also cites, as another example, the fact that most Chinese national laws do not apply in Hong Kong. This issue is discussed further in "4.2: Legislative Power", later in this chapter.
34. Herzer, *Options for Tibet's Future Political Status* (see note 24) at 18. Another exception is some of the British Overseas Territories in the West Indies, such as Bermuda and Cayman Islands, which enjoy considerable autonomy from the UK. Partly because of their close economic ties with the US, many of these territories link their currencies to the US dollar instead of the British pound.

that would preclude such a link from being introduced, were it considered desirable at some point in future.[35]

A further caveat is necessary when it comes to Hong Kong's power to regulate the admission of foreign nationals. Although among the powers expressly granted to the Hong Kong SAR Government, in practice it seems clear this power is exercised with a high degree of deference to the wishes of the Central People's Government. That is evident from the repeated refusals to admit those whose presence in Hong Kong might be considered offensive by Beijing, from overseas democracy activists[36] to supporters of Tibetan independence[37] and members of the Falun Gong.[38] It should, however, be noted that this policy of exclusions predates the Hong Kong Basic Law. Even while Hong Kong was still under British rule, it often refused to admit Chinese dissidents based overseas as well as leading figures from Taiwan's Kuomintang.

Some believe that Hong Kong's power to enter into economic and cultural relations with other countries and participate in some international organizations is the "most distinctive feature" of Hong Kong's autonomy under the Hong Kong Basic Law.[39] According to Xu and Wilson (2000): "[T]he HKSAR can be seen to enjoy probably the most extensive external autonomy that has ever existed in an autonomous region in the world, historical or current."[40] Although Article 13(1) of the Hong Kong Basic Law states unequivocally that China "shall be responsible" for foreign affairs relating to Hong Kong, Article 13(3) then carves out what in practice amounts to a large exception to this general principle, by authorizing Hong Kong "to conduct relevant external affairs on its own".

---

35. The option of linking the Hong Kong dollar to China's Renminbi has been put forward by Joseph Yam, former Chief Executive of the Hong Kong Monetary Authority, among others. See Joseph Yam, *The Future of the Monetary System in Hong Kong* (Institute of Global Economics and Finance, Chinese University of Hong Kong, Working Paper No. 9, June 2012) at para. 22.
36. For example, 11 Chinese dissidents were denied visas to attend a conference in Hong Kong in May 1999. See Angela Li, "Legal doubts cited in visa row", *South China Morning Post*, 25 April 1999.
37. For example, three Tibetan activists were denied entry to Hong Kong ahead of the Olympic torch relay in April 2008. See Bonnie Chen, "Three barred", *The Standard*, 30 April 2008.
38. For example, 80 Falun Gong activists were denied entry "for security reasons" in Feb 2003 when they sought to attend a Falun Gong conference in Hong Kong. Some of these activists later unsuccessfully challenged their exclusion by way of judicial review. See *Chu Woan Chyi v Director of Immigration* [2009] 6 HKC 77.
39. Hannum, *Autonomy, Sovereignty and Self-Determination* (see note 13) at 140.
40. See Xiaobing Xu and George D. Wilson, "The Hong Kong Special Administrative Region as a Model of Regional External Autonomy" (2000) 32 *Case Western Reserve Journal of International Law* 1, 6. This conclusion is based on a comparative study by Hurst Hannum [in "The Foreign Affairs Powers of Autonomous Regions" (1988) 57 *Nordic Journal of International Law* 273–277] which identified only three other autonomous areas—two former Soviet republics and the Free Territory of Trieste—which, in theory, exercised wider foreign affairs powers than Hong Kong. However, Xu and Wilson argue (at 6) that, in practice, none of these three were able to do so.

These are generously defined under Article 151 of the Hong Kong Basic Law to include "economic, trade, financial and monetary, shipping, communications, tourism, cultural and sports fields". In all these areas, Hong Kong is allowed—if it wishes—to act almost like a separate country, negotiating agreements on its own with other countries and regions, joining international organizations as a separate member,[41] and even establishing its own economic and trade missions overseas, in all these cases without any need to seek China's approval.[42] Reflecting the importance of Hong Kong's international trading role, specific provision is made in Article 116 of the Hong Kong Basic Law for separate participation in international organizations such as the World Trade Organization and trade agreements, with Hong Kong's own export quotas and preferential tariffs distinct from those of the rest of China. Further provisions in the Hong Kong Basic Law allow Hong Kong to negotiate directly with foreign countries on legal issues such as extradition agreements (Article 96), air services to other countries (Article 133)[43] and visa abolition agreements (Article 155), although in these three areas Hong Kong requires prior authorization from the Central People's Government.[44]

What this means in practice is that a distinction is drawn between foreign affairs, which in the Hong Kong context are narrowly defined as matters of state and international diplomacy (such as which foreign governments are allowed to establish official offices in Hong Kong or send warships on port calls),[45] and most other matters involving

---

41. Under Article 152(2), Hong Kong "may, using the name 'Hong Kong, China', participate in international organizations and conferences *not limited to states*" (emphasis added). Where an international organization only allows countries to be members, Article 152(1) instead allows Hong Kong to be represented by sending members to join the Chinese delegation to those organizations.
42. Under Article 156, Hong Kong is only required to report the establishment of economic and trade offices in foreign countries "to the Central People's Government for the record".
43. However, if these involve air services with stops in other parts of China then, under Article 132(1), the agreement must be instead concluded by the Central People's Government. This reflects similar provisions in Annex I(IX) of the Joint Declaration, and appears to be the result of a compromise in response to initial demands by Chinese aviation authorities for control over all air rights in and out of Hong Kong. See further Robert Cottrell, *The End of Hong Kong: The Secret Diplomacy of Imperial Retreat* (John Murray, 1993) at 170.
44. In the case of air services that do not involve stops in other parts of China, this authorization is already given under Article 134(1). In other cases, authorization needs to be sought through the office of Ministry of Foreign Affairs in Hong Kong, whose role in handling foreign affairs is specifically provided for in Article 13(2).
45. Under Articles 157(1) and 126 respectively, these are matters for the Central People's Government to decide. Neither provision contains any requirement to consult the Hong Kong SAR Government, and there have been a few examples of such decisions which aroused some opposition in Hong Kong. For example, the 1999 decision to allow North Korea to establish a consulate was apparently made despite objections from some in the Hong Kong Police on security grounds. See Anne Swardson, "North Korea to open a consulate in Hong Kong", *Washington Post*, 15 May 1999.

dealings with other countries—which are instead categorized as external affairs and fall within the scope of Hong Kong's autonomy.[46]

The impressive international dimension to Hong Kong's autonomy is further enhanced by Article 153(2), which allows international agreements to continue to be implemented in Hong Kong even if they do not apply in the rest of China.[47] This plays a crucial role in facilitating the protection of civil liberties under the Hong Kong Basic Law, since it allows most parts of several important international human rights agreements to remain in force, a situation specifically provided for under Article 39(1) of the Hong Kong Basic Law.[48] Probably the most significant of these is the International Covenant on Civil and Political Rights, which plays a hugely important role in Hong Kong with most of its provisions incorporated into local legislation through the Hong Kong Bill of Rights Ordinance (Cap. 383).[49]

The breadth of the external affairs powers accorded to Hong Kong by these various provisions in the Hong Kong Basic Law has been recognized in some foreign laws and court judgments. In the US, the United States–Hong Kong Policy Act 1992[50] allows Hong Kong to be treated as separate from the rest of China unless and until the US President determines "Hong Kong is not sufficiently autonomous to justify" continuing such separate treatment.[51] US courts have recognized Hong Kong's capacity to enter into its own extradition agreements under Article 96 of the Hong Kong Basic Law[52] and, in a Canadian case, a tax court held that a treaty with China was not applicable to a Hong Kong company.[53]

Lim and Mushkat (2011) describe the effects of these powers as conferring a separate "international legal personality" on Hong Kong.[54] But the limits to that separate legal

---

46. For more on the distinction between foreign and external affairs and the difficulties in drawing a clear dividing line, see Ghai, *Hong Kong's New Constitutional Order* (see note 16) at 461.
47. However, under Article 153(1), it is for the Central People's Government to decide whether any further international agreements should be extended to Hong Kong, "in accordance with the circumstances and needs of the Region, and after seeking the views of the government of the Region".
48. Article 39(1) states that: "The provisions of the International Covenant on Civil and Political Rights, International Covenant on Economic, Social and Cultural Rights, and international labour conventions as applied to Hong Kong shall remain in force and shall be implemented through the laws of the Hong Kong Special Administrative Region."
49. See further "8.1: ICCPR and Bill of Rights" in Chapter 8 for more on the role of the International Covenant on Civil and Political Rights and the Hong Kong Bill of Rights Ordinance (Cap. 383).
50. 22 United States Code 5701.
51. Ibid. at Section 5722(a).
52. *John Cheung v United States of America* (2000) 213 Federal Reporter Third Series 82. For a useful summary of Hong Kong's status in other US cases, see P.Y. Lo, *The Hong Kong Basic Law* (LexisNexis, 2011) at 753.
53. *Kelly Brian Edwards v R* (unrep., Tax Court of Canada 20001183, 27 June 2002). For a brief summary of this case, see Lim and Mushkat, "External Affairs" (see note 21) at 80.
54. Ibid. at 78.

personality were vividly demonstrated by the Manila hostage tragedy, which saw eight Hong Kong people killed by a hijacker during a bungled rescue operation by Philippines' police in 2010. After failing to take an urgent phone call from then Hong Kong Chief Executive Donald Tsang during the crisis, the Philippine President justified this on the grounds that all such contacts should be conducted via Beijing,[55] a point echoed by some supporters of the Chinese government.[56] Although Beijing reportedly ultimately decided that the fast-moving situation should be treated as a special exception to this normal practice,[57] the incident demonstrated that, even when the lives of local people are at stake, Hong Kong's separate identity on the international stage does not necessarily extend as far as making representations on their behalf.[58]

The extent of Hong Kong's separate international identity is arguably also undermined by the Court of Final Appeal decision in *Democratic Republic of Congo v FG Hemisphere*.[59] This saw a majority on the court conclude that, "[a]s a matter of legal and constitutional principle" it is not possible for Hong Kong to adopt a different position from the Central People's Government on the issue of how far foreign states are immune from the jurisdiction of the courts.[60] Rejecting a vigorous dissent by Justice Bokhary, who unsuccessfully argued that "state immunity" was a matter of external affairs which fell within Hong Kong's powers under Article 13(3) of the Hong Kong Basic Law,[61] the majority seemed somewhat dismissive of the extent of Hong Kong's autonomy under this provision.[62]

---

55. See Raissa Robles, Irene Jay Liu and Phyllis Tsang, "Aquino takes aim at Tsang's letter", *South China Morning Post*, 10 Sept 2010.
56. See, in particular, the comments of Phoenix Television host Anthony Yuen that any such phone call should only have been made by the Chinese President [cited in "Manila hostage crisis", *South China Morning Post*, 28 Sept 2010].
57. See Simon Shen, "Hong Kong's External Space: Defining a Grey Area" (April 2011) 21 *Hong Kong Journal*. Shen sought to justify Tsang's conduct by arguing the external affairs provisions in the Hong Kong Basic Law confer "sub-sovereignty" status on Hong Kong. But this assertion appears at odds with the unitary nature of the Chinese state, and was widely questioned by other commentators. See further Lo, *The Hong Kong Basic Law* (see note 52) at 750.
58. However, Lim and Mushkat [in "External Affairs" (see note 21) at 79] counter that Hong Kong's status as an international legal person exists as a matter of law and so "is not diluted" by this or any other events that have caused commentators to cast doubt on the continued existence of such an identity for Hong Kong.
59. (2011) 14 HKCFAR 95.
60. Ibid. at 182. The majority instead held that the issue involved "facts of state", which lie outside the jurisdiction of the courts under Article 19(3) of the Hong Kong Basic Law. See further "6.5: Limits on Courts" in Chapter 6.
61. Ibid. at 147. For more on this case, and Bokhary's dissenting judgment, see the concluding paragraphs in Chapter 6 and "7.4: Judicial Referral" in Chapter 7.
62. Ibid. at 195, stating: "In so far as the HKSAR has conduct of its external affairs, it does so under powers delegated to the HKSAR by the CPG."

That raises the question of what other issues may be, in future, similarly categorized as foreign affairs rather than external affairs, and so placed outside the scope of Hong Kong's executive powers with possibly damaging consequences for Hong Kong's autonomy.[63] Ghai (1999) notes that the distinction between the two categories "is hard to maintain in practice" and could easily be adjusted if Chinese Central Authorities wish to use this as a means "to rein in" Hong Kong.[64]

It also highlights what is often described as the greatest weakness undermining the extensive powers granted to Hong Kong in the executive and other arenas. Many of these powers, such as Hong Kong's just-discussed power to handle wide categories of external affairs on its own, may be much broader than those which exist almost anywhere else in the world. But Chen (2003) notes, "that the constitutional and legal guarantee for autonomy are less secure" in Hong Kong than many other places.[65] That observation relates primarily to the situation in federal nations—such as the US, Canada and Australia[66]—where the constitutional arrangements governing what powers can be exercised at a local level are very different from countries such as China.

Under a federal system, the division of powers between the national and local levels is part of a power sharing arrangement written into the national constitution.[67] In most cases, the individual states or provinces within a federal country are able to exercise all powers except those explicitly reserved for the national (or federal) government. That means any omissions often work to the advantage of the local authorities, with the individual states or provinces within a federal nation also able to exercise any "residual powers" not allocated under the constitution,[68] although there are exceptions to this general principle.[69]

By contrast, the idea that Hong Kong should enjoy all powers except those expressly reserved for the Chinese authorities—which would include any residual powers not specifically stated in the Hong Kong Basic Law—was firmly rejected during the drafting of

---

63. See, for example, Eric Cheung's argument [in "Undermining our Judicial Independence and Autonomy" (2011) 41 *HKLJ* 411, 416–419] that the majority decision in the Congo case risks "damaging Hong Kong's status as an international trade dispute centre".
64. See Ghai, *Hong Kong's New Constitutional Order* (see note 16) at 461.
65. Chen, "The Concept of 'One Country Two Systems' and Its Application to Hong Kong" (see note 33) at 365.
66. Chen makes an explicit comparison with these three countries in "Constitutional Adjudication in Post-1997 Hong Kong" (2006) 15 *Pacific Rim Law & Policy Journal* 627, 631, concluding that, in this respect, "Hong Kong under OCTS [One Country, Two Systems] does not compare as favorably with states or provinces of the United States, Canada or Australia."
67. Chen, "The Concept of 'One Country Two Systems' and Its Application to Hong Kong" (see note 33) at 365. For a more detailed discussion of the differences between federal countries and other forms of autonomy, see Suksi, *Sub-State Governance Through Territorial Autonomy* (see note 14) at 85–108.
68. See the examples cited in Hannum and Lillich, "The Concept of Autonomy in International Law" (see note 3) at 867–868.
69. One of the most notable exceptions is Canada, where Section 91 of the Constitution Act 1867 gives the federal government a residual power to make any laws necessary for "Peace, Order and good Government of Canada".

the Hong Kong Basic Law on the grounds that "China does not have a federal system but has a unitary system".[70] Under such a unitary system of government, also practised in many other countries such as the UK, all power is ultimately vested in the national government which decides how much autonomy it is willing to delegate (or devolve) to the local level.[71] That means Hong Kong only enjoys those powers specifically stated in the Hong Kong Basic Law, with Article 20 making clear that any additional powers need to be expressly granted by the Chinese Central Authorities.[72]

In practice, Hong Kong enjoys far more extensive powers under the Hong Kong Basic Law than the member states or provinces of federal nations almost anywhere else in the world. As we have seen, in the executive arena Hong Kong exercises many special powers, such as the existence of a separate currency and customs territory as well as the power to deal directly with foreign countries under the broad umbrella of "external relations". These are all powers which cannot be, for example, exercised by individual states or provinces in the US, Canada or Australia.[73] Xiao (2001) argues this means Hong Kong's autonomy "has broken through the common constitutional theory", which normally holds that individual states or provinces in a federal system exercise greater powers than autonomous areas in unitary countries such as China.[74] Zhu (1998) suggests Hong Kong's high degree of autonomy may have fundamentally changed the nature of the Chinese state,[75] while Cohen (1997) believes it marks "the start of the PRC's experimentation with federalism".[76]

Such sweeping conclusions obscure the reality that Hong Kong's autonomy rests on far more shaky legal foundations than the power-sharing arrangements enshrined in

---

70. Wu Jianfan, "Several Issues Concerning the Relationship Between the Central Government of the People's Republic of China and the Hong Kong Special Administrative Region" (1988) 2 *Journal of Chinese Law* 65, 73.
71. Chen notes [in "Constitutional Adjudication in Post-1997 Hong Kong" (see note 66) at 631] that mainland legal scholars prefer to describe this as "delegation of power", in order to clearly differentiate it from the "division of power" between national and local levels that exists in federal nations.
72. Under Article 20, such additional powers may be granted to Hong Kong by the NPC, its Standing Committee or the Central People's Government. One example of this was the granting of the power to determine applications for naturalization as Chinese citizens in Hong Kong to the Immigration Department of the Hong Kong SAR Government under the Explanations of Some Questions by the Standing Committee of the NPC Concerning the Implementation of the Nationality Law of the PRC in the Hong Kong SAR (15 May 1996).
73. Chen, "Constitutional Adjudication in Post-1997 Hong Kong" (see note 66) at 631.
74. Xiao Weiyun, *One Country, Two Systems: An Account of the Drafting of the Hong Kong Basic Law* (Peking University Press, English edition, 2001) at 100.
75. See Zhu Guobin, "Redefining the Central-Local Relationship under the Basic Law—With Special Reference to the Law on Regional National Autonomy" in Priscilla M.F. Leung and Zhu (eds.), *The Basic Law of the HKSAR: From Theory to Practice* (Butterworths, 1998) at 130–135.
76. Jerome Cohen, "Foreword" in Roda Mushkat, *One Country, Two International Legal Personalities: The Case of Hong Kong* (Hong Kong University Press, 1997) at vii.

national constitutions in most federal nations. Unlike the situation in those countries, the Hong Kong Basic Law is not a constitution but instead simply one of many national laws enacted by the National People's Congress,[77] although, as we saw in the previous chapter, some mainland officials and scholars now accept it has a quasi-constitutional status.[78] Li (1999) notes that: "Hong Kong's high degree of autonomy does not change the fact that the SAR enjoys its powers under China's unitary system, powers that can be withdrawn by the centre at any time, unless strict constitutional restraints are in place."[79]

In the absence of the constitutional arrangements that commonly protect the powers exercised at a local level in federal nations, the continued existence of Hong Kong's high degree of autonomy depends far more on two rather uncertain factors. These are, firstly, the extent to which Hong Kong's leaders are prepared to defend that autonomy against encroachment, and secondly, the degree of self-restraint exercised by Beijing.

But the ability of Hong Kong's Chief Executive to defend Hong Kong's autonomy against encroachment is strongly undermined by several provisions in the Hong Kong Basic Law which place the Chief Executive ultimately under Beijing's control. These provisions state that the Chief Executive is accountable to the Central People's Government (Article 43(2))[80] and required to implement its directives (Article 48(8)). Most crucially of all, although chosen through a selection process in Hong Kong, the actual appointment of the Chief Executive is made by the Central People's Government (Articles 15 and 45(1)).

Tamanaha (1989) suggests Hong Kong will never exercise "true autonomy" so long as the Central People's Government continues to exercise such an appointment power.[81] That may overstate the point, since it is not unknown for national governments to exercise similar appointment powers over the leaders of autonomous areas elsewhere in the world.[82] In their conclusions on the common characteristics of an autonomous area, Hannum and Lilllich (1980) note that a locally chosen Chief Executive may be "subject to approval or confirmation" by the national government.[83]

---

77. See further "3.2: Domestic Dimension" in Chapter 3.
78. See note 101 in Chapter 3 and the accompanying text.
79. Li Yahong, "The Central-HKSAR Legislative Relationship: A Constitutional Assessment" in Raymond Wacks (ed.), *The New Legal Order in Hong Kong* (Hong Kong University Press, 1999) at 166.
80. Article 43(2) also requires the Chief Executive to be accountable to the Hong Kong SAR. For more on the conflicting loyalties that may arise as a result, see further "5.1: Chief Executive" in Chapter 5.
81. Brian Z. Tamanaha, "Post-1997 Hong Kong: A Comparative Study of the Meaning of 'High Degree of Autonomy'" (1989) 20 *California Western International Law Journal* 41, 49. Tamanaha suggests that the Central People's Government should only refuse to appoint a Chief Executive on the grounds of mental or physical incapacity or lack of moral integrity, and not for political reasons.
82. See, for example, the case of the autonomous community of Catalonia in Spain, cited by Herzer in *Options for Tibet's Future Political Status* (see note 24) at 49.
83. Hannum and Lillich, "The Concept of Autonomy in International Law" (see note 3) at 887.

The crucial difference is that in those other autonomous areas, any leverage exercised by the national government through its power of appointment is often balanced by a popular election process.[84] With this democratic mandate, the local leader is in a much stronger position to resist any pressure from the national authorities. By contrast, during the first 20 years of the Hong Kong SAR, the Chief Executive—chosen by a committee of several hundred people[85] rather than Hong Kong's population as a whole—lacked an equivalent mandate. That might possibly change after 2017, since Beijing has indicated that it is willing, in principle, to allow the Chief Executive to be elected by voters in Hong Kong through universal suffrage from that date onwards.[86] If a genuine contest is permitted then a popularly elected Chief Executive will have a democratic mandate and, conceivably, more leverage to resist any excessive interference from Beijing.

In terms of the second of the two factors protecting Hong Kong's autonomy in the absence of any formal constitutional safeguards, there was much evidence of self-restraint on Beijing's part during the first six years of the Hong Kong SAR.

During the first few years after 1 July 1997, Chinese leaders ordered Hong Kong deputies to the National People's Congress to keep quiet on local issues, for fear of undermining Hong Kong's high degree of autonomy.[87] Chen (2003) notes that "it is generally accepted" that one of the biggest policy decisions during these early years, the Hong Kong SAR Government's massive intervention in the stock market in support of the Hong Kong dollar in 1998, was "made without any pressure or interference from Beijing".[88]

However, even during these early years, there were occasional signs of interference. The gag order on NPC deputies was soon lifted.[89] After the 1999 banning of the Falun Gong spiritual group on the mainland, Hong Kong came under intense pressure from

---

84. For more on the link between democracy and autonomy, see Chen, "The Concept of 'One Country Two Systems' and Its Application to Hong Kong" (see note 33) at 367.
85. The actual size of the committee varied from 400 members for the first Chief Executive to 1,200 members in 2012. See further "5.3: Small-Circle Selection Process" in Chapter 5.
86. In a December 2007 Decision of the NPC Standing Committee. See further note 108 in Chapter 5 and the accompanying text.
87. See the "Measure Concerning the Execution of Deputies' Duties by the Deputies of the Hong Kong SAR to the NPC" (Nov 1998), cited by Fu Hualing and D.W. Choy, "Of Iron or Rubber? People's Deputies of Hong Kong to the National People's Congress" in Fu, Lison Harris and Simon N.M. Young (eds.), *Interpreting Hong Kong's Basic Law: The Struggle for Coherence* (Palgrave Macmillan, 2007) at 207 and 215–217.
88. Chen, "The Concept of 'One Country Two Systems' and Its Application to Hong Kong" (see note 33) at 359. Then Democratic Party leader Martin Lee, who initially accused the Hong Kong SAR Government of acting at the behest of Beijing, swiftly withdrew this allegation. See Frank Ching, "How Beijing Plays Its Hand: As Seen From Hong Kong" (July 2009) 15 *Hong Kong Journal*.
89. Fu and Choy, "Of Iron or Rubber?" (see note 87) at 217–220.

Beijing to follow suit.[90] A provision that would have allowed the banning of such organizations[91] was then included in national security legislation put forward by the Hong Kong SAR Government in 2003,[92] ostensibly to implement the requirements of Article 23 of the Hong Kong Basic Law.[93] But that legislation proved so unpopular that it was never enacted as, amid general public dissatisfaction with the governance of then Chief Executive Tung Chee Hwa, half a million people took to the streets in protest on 1 July 2003.[94]

That huge public protest marked a watershed moment for the Hong Kong SAR, after which Beijing began to lessen its self-restraint noticeably. According to Cheng (2009), who worked on Hong Kong affairs at the National People's Congress Standing Committee during this period, the events of 2003 "brought an end to the center's former laissez faire policy" and ushered in a new policy where "direct involvement replaced non-intervention".[95] Cheng (2009) notes that "[t]his new policy was first evidenced"[96] when the Standing Committee took the initiative in April 2004 to interpret Annexes I and II of the Hong Kong Basic Law in a way which gave Beijing ultimate control over any changes to Hong Kong's electoral system.[97] This was a power which mainland officials had previously stated fell within the scope of Hong Kong's autonomy, at least in

---

90. Johannes Chan [in "Civil Liberties, Rule of Law and Human Rights: The Hong Kong Special Administrative Region in Its First Four Years" in Lau Siu-kai (ed.), *The First Tung Chee-hwa Administration: The First Five Years of the HKSAR* (The Chinese University Press, 2002) at 105] describes the pressure put on Hong Kong to ban the Falun Gong as "a litmus test to the high degree of autonomy of Hong Kong and the determination of the HKSAR government and the Central Government to uphold two different systems".
91. While not specifically mentioning the Falun Gong, the provision would have given Hong Kong's Secretary for Security a specific power to ban any local organization "affiliated with a mainland organization" which had been banned by the Central Authorities on the grounds of national security. For more on this provision, which proved to be one of the most controversial parts of the legislation, see Lison Harris, Lily Ma and C.B. Fung, "A Connecting Door: The Proscription of Local Organizations" in Fu Hualing, Carole J. Petersen and Simon N.M. Young (eds.), *National Security and Fundamental Freedoms: Hong Kong's Article 23 Under Scrutiny* (Hong Kong University Press, 2005) at 303–330.
92. This was the National Security (Legislative Provisions) Bill, which was tabled in the Legislative Council in February 2003 and ultimately withdrawn in September of that year.
93. Article 23, which was one of the most controversial provisions during the drafting of the Hong Kong Basic Law, requires Hong Kong to enact "on its own" legislation in respect of several national security offences. For the controversy over this provision during the drafting process, see further "2.4: Battles and Changes" in Chapter 2.
94. For a description of these events, See Carole J. Petersen, "Hong Kong's Spring of Discontent: The Rise and Fall of the National Security Bill in 2003" in Fu, Petersen and Young, *National Security and Fundamental Freedoms* (see note 91) at 20–53.
95. Jie Cheng, "The Story of a New Policy" (July 2009) 15 *Hong Kong Journal*.
96. Ibid.
97. See further note 208 in Chapter 5 and the accompanying text.

respect of elections to the Legislative Council.[98] As a result, Chen (2011) describes this as "Beijing's most significant intervention on Hong Kong affairs since the establishment of the HKSAR".[99]

However, not all of Beijing's interventions were unwelcome in Hong Kong. In early 2005, Beijing was widely perceived to have engineered the resignation of the unpopular Tung as Chief Executive, paving the way for his deputy Donald Tsang to replace him.[100] Tsang was, at that stage, much more popular with the Hong Kong public.

A key player in this more interventionist approach is the Liaison Office of the Central People's Government in the Hong Kong SAR.[101] In a 2008 article in a Communist Party publication, Cao Erbao, the Liaison Office's head of research, described the staff working there, together with other Chinese officials involved in Hong Kong affairs, as a "second governing team" that functioned alongside the Hong Kong SAR Government and exercised "important governing powers".[102]

That appeared to be code for direct intervention by the Liaison Office on an increasing range of issues. This included criticizing a local pollster for conducting a survey on Hong Kong peoples' identity[103] and advocating a ban on opinion polls during election campaigns.[104] In one of the most high-profile examples of this increasingly interventionist behaviour, in early 2012 the Liaison Office actively lobbied for Leung Chun Ying to be elected as Chief Executive,[105] with Cao reportedly pressuring officials in the Hong Kong SAR Government to slow a conflict of interest investigation that threatened to cast Leung in a bad light.[106] Leung was widely perceived to have acknowledged the

---

98. See further note 206 in Chapter 5.
99. Albert Chen, "The Development of Representative Government in Hong Kong" in Chan and Lim (eds.), *Law of the Hong Kong Constitution* (see note 21) at 234.
100. Tung resigned on 10 March 2005, three months after his administration was publicly criticized by Chinese leaders for its poor performance. The official reason for his departure was ill health, one of the three permitted reasons for a Chief Executive to resign under Article 52 of the Hong Kong Basic Law. See further Yash Ghai and Jill Cottrell, "The Politics of Succession in Hong Kong" (2005) 35 *HKLJ* 1–6.
101. This office had its origins in the Hong Kong branch of the Xinhua News Agency, which functioned as China's representative office while Hong Kong was under British rule. After 1 July 1997, it was reduced in size and officially given a more limited remit, such as liaising with other mainland representatives in Hong Kong. In Jan 2000, it was renamed and given its current title. See further Christine Loh, *Underground Front: The Chinese Communist Party in Hong Kong* (Hong Kong University Press, 2010) at 72–73 and 202–204.
102. Cao Erbao, "Governing Forces Under the Condition of 'One Country, Two Systems'" (29 Jan 2008) 422 *Study Times*.
103. Ng Kang-chung, "Beijing envoy criticises HKU poll", *South China Morning Post*, 30 Dec 2011.
104. Colleen Lee, "Liaison Office man airs pre-election polling curbs", *South China Morning Post*, 22 March 2012.
105. See Phila Siu and Kelly Ip, "Leung enjoys western lift", *The Standard*, 5 March 2012, reporting that 150 of Leung's 305 nominations for the post of Chief Executive were secured with the support of the Liaison Office.
106. Stuart Lau, "Anger at 'Beijing media meddling'", *South China Morning Post*, 23 March 2012.

importance of this support when he made a high-profile visit to the Liaison Office a day after his victory.[107]

Much depends on how Beijing chooses to exercise its powers under the Hong Kong Basic Law. For instance, although those who will fill the top positions in the Hong Kong SAR Government (known as "Principal Officials")[108] are nominated by the Chief Executive under Article 48(5), the final power to decide whether they are appointed to those posts rests with the Central People's Government under Article 15. In keeping with its initial hands-off approach, there are no known examples of Beijing exercising this veto power during the early years of the Hong Kong SAR. Instead, all the available evidence seems to suggest that the Central People's Government initially endorsed whatever names were put forward by the Chief Executive, even when the nominee was someone who might arouse some suspicions in Beijing.[109]

After the shift to a more interventionist approach, Beijing began to show signs of discarding such self-restraint. From 2007 onwards, there were reports of the Central People's Government rejecting some of the Chief Executive's nominations for Principal Official positions, apparently on the grounds that the nominees were too close to the pro-democracy camp in Hong Kong.[110] However it appeared that Beijing was still prepared to defer to the Chief Executive's wishes in some cases. For example, in 2012 Leung Chun Ying reportedly managed to persuade Beijing to accept one nomination over which it initially had misgivings.[111]

---

107. Phila Siu, "Leung walks into flak over high-profile western visit", *The Standard*, 27 March 2012.
108. For more on the role played by Principal Officials, especially since the introduction of an accountability system in 2002, see further "5.4: Hong Kong SAR Government" in Chapter 5.
109. This included endorsing the nomination, in 1997, of Donald Tsang as Financial Secretary although, at that stage, he was viewed with distrust in Beijing (see further note 103 in Chapter 2). Ironically, Tsang subsequently went on to succeed Tung Chee Hwa and serve as Hong Kong's Chief Executive from 2005 to 2012. In 2005, the Central People's Government also endorsed the nomination of Wong Yan Lung as Secretary for Justice, only a few months after Wong participated in a protest against the NPC Standing Committee's interpretation of the Hong Kong Basic Law. See Carrie Chan, "Wong in Basic Law vow", *The Standard*, 21 Oct 2005.
110. These were the reported rejection of the nominations of Christine Loh as Secretary for Environment in 2007, and Ada Wong as Secretary for Culture in 2012. Loh was later appointed by the Chief Executive as Under Secretary for the Environment in 2012, a more junior post which does not require formal approval by the Central People's Government. See Frank Ching, "Team of choice", *South China Morning Post*, 6 June 2012, and Tony Cheung, "Loh a curious choice for government role but could make an impact in office", *South China Morning Post*, 13 August 2012.
111. Frank Ching, "Team of choice", *South China Morning Post*, 6 June 2012. This was the appointment as Chief Secretary for Administration of Carrie Lam, who was then much more popular with the Hong Kong public, instead of the incumbent Stephen Lam, who was reportedly initially preferred by Beijing. See further note 151 in Chapter 5 and the accompanying text.

4.2 Legislative Power

Legislative power, or a region's power to decide by itself on laws different from those that apply in the rest of the country of which it is a part, is sometimes described as lying at the "core of local autonomy".[112] Hannum and Lillich (1980) note that a "locally elected body with some independent legislative power" is one of the most common characteristics of autonomous areas the world over.[113]

That does not mean the power to enact all laws that apply in those areas. Hannum and Lillich (1980) note that an autonomous area's powers to enact its own laws is generally limited to laws on certain local issues, such as health, education, social services, taxation, trade, environmental protection and local government.[114] For instance, the legislature in the Aland Islands, an area internationally recognized as having a very high degree of autonomy and sometimes compared with Hong Kong, enjoys 27 specified legislative powers.[115] In the Aland Islands, a further 42 legislative powers are reserved for the Finnish national parliament, including laws on marriage, foreign trade, shipping, aviation and most criminal laws.[116]

By contrast, there are no areas which are expressly off-limits as far as Hong Kong's legislative powers are concerned (Article 17(1)). The only explicit restrictions under the Hong Kong Basic Law are that "[n]o law enacted by the legislature" may contravene the Hong Kong Basic Law (Article 11(2)) and that all laws must comply with "legal procedures" (Article 73(1)). These procedures include reporting all new laws to the National People's Congress Standing Committee "for the record" (Article 17(2)).[117] However, in most cases, this is simply a formality, which Article 17(2) specifically states "shall not affect the entry into force of such laws".

What that means in practice is that Hong Kong arguably enjoys far wider law-making powers than perhaps any other autonomous area in the world, enacting laws on issues which usually cannot be legislated at a local level even in federal nations.[118] Perhaps the best example of this is Article 23 of the Hong Kong Basic Law, requiring Hong Kong to enact "on its own" laws covering several national security offences.

---

112. Frederick Harhoff, "Institutions of Autonomy" (1986) 55 *Nordic Journal of International Law* 31.
113. See Hannum and Lillich, "The Concept of Autonomy in International Law" (see note 3) at 886.
114. Ibid. at 887.
115. Act on the Autonomy of Aland (16 August 1991/1144) at Section 18.
116. Ibid. at Section 27.
117. This mirrors a similar provision in Article 100 of the PRC Constitution 1982 requiring local legislation enacted elsewhere in China to be similarly reported to the Standing Committee "for the record".
118. See, for example, Article I, Section 8 of the US Constitution which gives the US Congress jurisdiction over laws covering such matters as the postal service, bankruptcy, copyright, foreign trade and interstate commerce.

Article 23 is not popular in Hong Kong. An attempt to enact legislation implementing this provision in the Hong Kong Basic Law provoked a huge public protest in 2003 that marked a watershed moment in the development of the Hong Kong SAR.[119] To the extent that Article 23 requires the enactment of laws essentially protecting China's interests, this provision is understandably seen as a restriction on Hong Kong's autonomy. But, viewed from another perspective, Article 23 can also be seen as evidence of the extraordinary breadth of Hong Kong's law-making powers under the Hong Kong Basic Law, allowing Hong Kong to enact legislation "on its own" on even this most sensitive of issues, which would normally be handled through national legislation in most other places in the world.[120] Suksi (2011) notes that Article 23 demonstrates how Hong Kong's law-making powers extend even to "this core area of provisions connected to the sovereignty of the State".[121]

China's only direct power over the wide range of legislation enacted in Hong Kong comes in Article 17(3) of the Hong Kong Basic Law. This grants the National People's Congress Standing Committee a limited power to return — and, in effect, veto — certain types of Hong Kong laws if it considers that they are "not in conformity with the provisions of this Law regarding affairs within the responsibility of the Central Authorities or regarding the relationship between the Central Authorities and the Region". Before doing so, it is first required to consult the Committee for the Basic Law of the Hong Kong SAR.[122]

The lack of any explicit time limit for the exercise of this power is a cause for some concern since, on a literal interpretation, Article 17(3) would appear to allow the Standing Committee to intervene at any time to invalidate any law which falls within this category, no matter how long it has been on the statute book. But the emphasis of Article 17 is on the handling of newly enacted laws,[123] and arguably the Standing Committee's power should be interpreted in this light.[124] Suksi (2011) suggests that "a more reasonable

---

119. This was the National Security (Legislative Provisions) Bill. See further note 95 earlier in this chapter and the accompanying text, for more on the effect of these events on Beijing's policy towards Hong Kong.
120. This point is made strongly by Secretary for Justice Elsie Leung in "Understanding 'One Country, Two Systems' Through Hong Kong's Constitutional Development", Basic Law Seminar Presentation, 29 May 2004, at para. 41.
121. Suksi, *Sub-State Governance Through Territorial Autonomy* (see note 14) at 284.
122. See "4.4: Dispute Resolution" later in this chapter for more on the role of the Committee for the Basic Law.
123. As shown by the provision in Article 17(2) on the reporting of newly enacted laws to the Standing Committee for the record. Elsewhere in China, local legislation must be reported to the Standing Committee within 30 days of enactment (see Article 89(2) of the PRC Legislation Law), although this time limit does not apply to Hong Kong.
124. There is, however, uncertainty about whether or not another ambiguously worded provision in the Hong Kong Basic Law, Article 160(1), gives the Standing Committee a broader power to invalidate any law which it holds to be in contravention of the Hong Kong Basic Law. See further note 84 in Chapter 3.

understanding" of Article 17(3) is that it only allows the Standing Committee to invalidate new laws within three months of their enactment.[125]

In any case, the overall effect of Article 17(3) is to limit the effect of the Standing Committee's veto power. Although any law returned "shall immediately be invalidated", the Standing Committee is specifically prohibited from amending it—a restriction designed to protect Hong Kong's wide law-making powers and prevent Beijing from using such amendments as a back-door method of writing laws for Hong Kong.[126] Ghai (2005) notes this restriction "emphasizes the autonomy of Hong Kong".[127] In addition, unlike a similar provision in the first draft of the Hong Kong Basic Law,[128] Article 17(3) does not allow the Standing Committee to return new laws on purely local issues, which do not relate to Hong Kong's relationship with the Central Authorities. This probably excludes the majority of Hong Kong laws from the ambit of this veto power—although it would, of course, ultimately be for the Standing Committee to decide whether or not any particular law falls into the category of those which it is allowed to return.

If narrowly interpreted, the Standing Committee's power under Article 17(3) is not necessarily very different from the practice in many autonomous areas elsewhere in the world. Hannum and Lillich (1980) note it is not uncommon for national authorities to retain the power to veto any actions by a local legislature that "exceed its competence or are otherwise inconsistent with basic constitutional precepts".[129] For instance, laws passed by the Aland Islands can be vetoed by the President of Finland if they exceed the legislative powers of the islands, or relate to security issues.[130]

In practice, the Standing Committee never once invoked this power during the first 15 years of the Hong Kong SAR, although there were suggestions it might become more willing to do so in future.[131] But, in most cases, there is unlikely to be any need for the Standing Committee to invoke this power. In the unlikely event that Beijing objects to any bill passed by the Legislative Council in Hong Kong, it can instead be vetoed by the Chief Executive—who is ultimately accountable to the Central People's Government—refusing to sign it into law.[132] Even this is unlikely to prove necessary, since virtually

---

125. Suksi, *Sub-State Governance Through Territorial Autonomy* (see note 14) at 288.
126. See Wang Shuwen, *Introduction to the Basic Law of the Hong Kong Special Administrative Region* (Law Press, 2nd English edition, 2009) at 228.
127. Ghai, "The Imperatives of Autonomy" (see note 32) at 30.
128. Article 16(3) of "The Draft Basic Law of the Hong Kong SAR of the PRC (for solicitation of opinions)", reproduced in Peter Wesley-Smith and Albert Chen (eds.), *The Basic Law and Hong Kong's Future* (Butterworths, 1988) at 332–333.
129. Hannum and Lillich, "The Concept of Autonomy in International Law" (see note 3) at 887.
130. Act on the Autonomy of Aland (16 August 1991/1144) at Section 19.
131. In November 2012, a senior Chinese official suggested the Standing Committee should more actively exercise its "supervisory right" over Hong Kong legislation. See Zhang Xiaoming, "Enrich the implementation of One Country, Two Systems", *Wen Wei Po*, 22 Nov 2012. Summarized in English in Joshua But, "Fury in Hong Kong at Beijing official's claim of 'foreign interference'", *South China Morning Post*, 23 Nov 2012.
132. Under Article 49 of the Hong Kong Basic Law. For more on this power, and the sequence of events which may follow if the Chief Executive chooses to exercise it, see further pages 100–101.

all bills need the Chief Executive's approval before they can be even introduced into the Legislative Council.[133]

Those important powers granted to the Chief Executive over both the beginning and the end of the legislative process point to what, in practice, amounts to probably the most significant restriction on Hong Kong's legislative powers. Although granted broad powers to legislate on a far wider range of issues than other autonomous areas, Petersen (2005) notes that the power to determine the contents of such legislation rests with "the executive branch, which is primarily accountable to the Chinese government".[134]

It appears that the Central Government does sometimes use its control over the Chief Executive to pressure the executive to enact legislation on areas where Beijing is precluded from acting directly. But this strategy has a mixed record of success. Despite intense pressure from Chinese leaders, the Hong Kong SAR Government never introduced specific anti-Falun Gong legislation following the group's banning in the rest of China in 1999.[135] National security legislation introduced at Beijing's behest in 2003 to implement Article 23 of the Hong Kong Basic Law (which did include a provision that could have been used to target the Falun Gong)[136] proved so unpopular that it was never enacted.[137]

Perhaps the first clear-cut example of Beijing successfully pressuring Hong Kong into enacting politically controversial legislation came in 2012, with the enactment of a law targeting legislators who deliberately resign to trigger by-elections.[138] This followed the 2010 use of this tactic by five pro-democracy legislators to hold what they called a de-facto "referendum" on the future of functional constituencies in the Legislative Council, a move that infuriated Beijing.[139] But even this legislation was much milder than what had been originally proposed,[140] with legislators who resign under such circumstances simply being banned from seeking re-election for a period of six months.[141]

The extraordinarily broad nature of Hong Kong's law-making powers is matched by equally broad restrictions on what Chinese national laws apply in Hong Kong. Under Article 18(3) of the Hong Kong Basic Law, in normal circumstances these are limited to laws "relating to defence and foreign affairs, as well as other matters outside the limits of the autonomy of the Region". Even then, under Article 18(2), such laws normally only

---

133. Under Article 74 of the Hong Kong Basic Law. See further page 144.
134. Carole J. Petersen, "Introduction" in Fu, Petersen and Young (eds.), *National Security and Fundamental Freedoms* (see note 91) at 16.
135. See Benedict Rogers, "We'll do nothing on Falun Gong", *The Standard*, 22 June 2001.
136. See further note 91 earlier in this chapter.
137. For more on these events, see note 94 earlier in this chapter and the accompanying text.
138. Legislative Council (Amendment) Ordinance (No. 12 of 2012).
139. For more on this referendum, see note 251 in Chapter 5 and the accompanying text.
140. Under the Legislative Council (Amendment) Bill 2011, which would have abolished by-elections for such vacancies leading, in many cases, to the seat being given to a political opponent of the legislator who chose to resign. Following public protests, this bill was withdrawn by the Hong Kong SAR Government in Feb 2012.
141. See Section 39(2A) of the Legislative Council Ordinance (Cap. 542).

apply to Hong Kong if they are listed in the Hong Kong Basic Law itself, a provision which adds weight to arguments discussed in the previous chapter for concluding that the Hong Kong Basic Law should be accorded a superior status to other basic laws enacted by the National People's Congress.[142]

The method chosen for implementing this is to list such laws in Annex III of the Hong Kong Basic Law, which is subject to different amendment rules from the main text. Under Article 18(3) of the Hong Kong Basic Law, it is the National People's Congress Standing Committee which decides what laws should be added to, or removed from, the list of laws in Annex III. Before doing so, it is required to consult both the Committee for the Basic Law of the Hong Kong SAR[143] as well as the Hong Kong SAR Government. Even then, a national law added to Annex III will not come into force in Hong Kong until it is implemented through either proclamation by the Chief Executive as a law of the Hong Kong SAR, or enactment of a local version by the Legislative Council.[144]

The result, according to Chen (2003), who cites this as one of the most unique features of Hong Kong's high degree of autonomy, is that more than 99% of national laws do not apply in Hong Kong.[145] That situation is rarely seen in autonomous areas elsewhere in the world, where national laws are usually applied almost in their entirety. A particularly striking contrast can be drawn with the ethnic minority-populated National Autonomous Areas elsewhere in China, that are also allowed to exercise a limited degree of autonomy. While those areas have the power to limit the application of parts of some national laws, usually because they are at odds with local customs,[146] these exceptions are relatively few in number. As a result, it would be reasonable to conclude that around 99% of Chinese national laws do apply in such National Autonomous Areas—the reverse of the situation in Hong Kong, where 99% do not.

At the time of writing, only 12 national laws were listed as applying to Hong Kong in Annex III of the Hong Kong SAR—and only 11 of these have actually been implemented through Hong Kong legislation.[147] These include laws on Chinese nationality, territorial

---

142. See further "3.2: Domestic Dimension" in Chapter 3.
143. See "4.4: Dispute Resolution" later in this chapter for more on the role of the Committee for the Basic Law.
144. A good example is the Law of the PRC on Judicial Immunity from Compulsory Measures Concerning the Property of Foreign Central Banks. This law was added to Annex III of the Hong Kong Basic Law on 27 Oct 2005. However, at the time of writing, seven years later, it had not been implemented through proclamation or legislation and so was still not in force in Hong Kong.
145. Chen, "The Concept of 'One Country Two Systems' and Its Application to Hong Kong" (see note 33) at 364.
146. Under Article 115 of the PRC Constitution 1982. This power is used, for example, to vary how provisions in China's Marriage Law apply to ethnic minorities in some autonomous areas. See She and Bu, "Legislation in National Autonomous Areas" (see note 9) at 137–138.
147. See note 144 above on the one law which so far has not been implemented through Hong Kong legislation.

boundaries, the national flag, anthem, capital, calendar and day, diplomatic and consular privileges and immunities as well as on the garrisoning of the Hong Kong SAR.[148] Most were implemented in Hong Kong through promulgation by the Chief Executive,[149] a process which makes life much easier for the Hong Kong SAR Government, since it means the relevant national law can be implemented unaltered in Hong Kong without any need to consult the Legislative Council.[150] Implementation through proclamation, however, raises troubling questions about whether such laws are necessarily required to comply with the Hong Kong Basic Law, since Article 11(2) only prohibits "law enacted by the legislature" from contravening the Hong Kong Basic Law.[151]

However, two laws on the national flag and emblem were instead adapted for implementation in Hong Kong through the National Flag and National Emblem Ordinance (No. 116 of 1997) enacted by the Legislative Council.[152] This was primarily to add criminal penalties for desecrating the flag and emblem stipulated in other Chinese legislation which does not apply in Hong Kong.[153] Those penalties[154] then gave rise to the first high-profile court case involving the application of Chinese national law in Hong Kong, when two pro-democracy protesters unsuccessfully sought to argue they contravened the rights protected under the Hong Kong Basic Law in the case of *HKSAR v Ng Kung Siu*.[155]

The fact that so few Chinese national laws have so far been applied in Hong Kong also reflects a degree of continuing self-restraint on Beijing's part, self-restraint that appeared to remain in place even after the Central Authorities began to adopt a more interventionist approach on other issues. The vaguely worded third category of national laws that can be legitimately applied to Hong Kong under Article 18(3) of the Hong Kong Basic Law,

---

148. See note 167 later in this chapter, and notes 441–444 in Chapter 6 and the accompanying text, for more on specific provisions in the Law of the PRC on the Garrisoning of the Hong Kong SAR.
149. Three proclamations listing nine of these laws were issued by the Chief Executive in 1997–98. See LN 379 of 1997, LN 386 of 1997 and LN 393 of 1998.
150. However, Suksi [in *Sub-State Governance Through Territorial Autonomy* (see note 14) at 286] argues that implementation through proclamation is less desirable because it "means that the national law is not embedded in the systematic and material environment in which it is supposed to be functioning in the HKSAR".
151. See further Benny Tai, "Chapter One of Hong Kong's New Constitution: Constitutional Positioning and Repositioning" in Ming K. Chan and Alvin Y. So (eds.), *Crisis and Transformation in China's Hong Kong* (Hong Kong University Press and M.E. Sharpe, 2002) at 217–218.
152. See *HKSAR v Ng Kung Siu* (1999) 2 HKCFAR 442, 449 where the Court of Final Appeal observed that: "Legislation as opposed to promulgation was appropriate since the national law had to be adapted for application in the HKSAR."
153. Ibid. at 448–449, noting that in China these are now stipulated in Article 299 of the PRC Criminal Law.
154. Section 7 of the National Flag and National Emblem Ordinance (No. 116 of 1997) stipulates a maximum punishment of up to three years imprisonment.
155. (1999) 2 HKCFAR 442. For more on this case, see further notes 194–202 in Chapter 8 and the accompanying text.

which refers to laws on "other matters outside the limits of the autonomy of the Region", would appear to give Beijing ample room to apply far more national laws than has been the case so far—especially as it would ultimately be up to the Standing Committee to decide whether any particular law falls into this category.[156] One of the most cited laws in this respect is China's Military Service Law which, among other provisions, requires young men in China to enlist for possible service in the People's Liberation Army.[157] Although it seems unlikely this law would ever be applied in Hong Kong in a form that requires conscription, in 2012 the Commander of the PLA's Hong Kong Garrison revealed that Chinese authorities were "studying the issue" of whether the Military Service Law could apply in some modified form to cover those Hong Kong people who wished to volunteer for service in the PLA.[158]

Another apparent loophole in the provisions of Article 18(3) is that the restrictions on what "national laws" may apply to Hong Kong do not seem to prevent the application of other categories of Chinese legislation to Hong Kong. Under the Chinese legal system, the term "national law" only refers to basic laws enacted by the National People's Congress and laws enacted by its Standing Committee.[159] While these are among the most important categories of legislation in China, they are not the only ones. Many other actions of these two bodies use different titles instead. For example, the term "decision" is used to describe some legislation, while other official documents with titles such as "measures" also have legal effect.[160] Since they are not called "national laws", they can be applied to Hong Kong without going through the procedures listed in Article 18(3) of the Hong Kong Basic Law, as has happened on a number of occasions.[161]

---

156. For an example of a much wider definition of this third category of national laws, see the argument advanced in 1991 by Wu Jianfan, an influential mainland drafter of the Hong Kong Basic Law, that this third category could be used by the NPC to apply to Hong Kong a national law establishing a Court of Final Appeal [cited by Johannes M.M. Chan, "The Legal System" in Joseph Y.S. Cheng and Paul C.K. Kwong, *The Other Hong Kong Report 1992* (The Chinese University Press, 1992) at 84–85]. This followed widespread opposition in Hong Kong to the establishment of a Court of Final Appeal on the terms which had been agreed with China. See further notes 269–270 in Chapter 6 and the accompanying text.
157. Under the PRC Military Service Law 1984, Article 12 all Chinese men aged 18–22 can be required to enlist for service in the People's Liberation Army although, in practice, this provision is rarely invoked. For an expression of concern that this could be applied to Hong Kong through Annex III of the Hong Kong Basic Law see, Consultative Committee for the Basic Law, *Consultation Report Volume 1* (see note 29) at 44.
158. Minnie Chan, "Army studying legal issues for locals", *South China Morning Post*, 14 June 2012.
159. Under Articles 62(3) and 67(2) of the PRC Constitution 1982.
160. For a more complete description of the various titles used for actions of the NPC and its Standing Committee, see Albert Chen, *An Introduction to the Legal System of the People's Republic of China* (LexisNexis, 4th edition, 2011) at 143–144.
161. For example, the measures enacted by the NPC laying down the procedure for the election of deputies from Hong Kong. See further note 249 later in this chapter.

That same loophole can be used to extend China's law-making power over Hong Kong to the Central People's Government (or State Council) which, under the PRC Constitution 1982, has the power to make various forms of legislation such as "administrative regulations" and issue other official documents such as "orders" that also have legal effect.[162] Again, since these are not called "national laws", these can be applied to Hong Kong outside the provisions of the Hong Kong Basic Law, although so far the State Council has only done this on relatively uncontentious issues such as Hong Kong's territorial boundaries.[163] Chau (1998) notes that "the Basic Law, as a whole, is silent on the role of lawmaking power of the State Council for the HKSAR".[164]

By far the biggest loophole in the restrictions that normally apply to the application of Chinese national laws in Hong Kong is expressly provided for in Article 18(4) of the Hong Kong Basic Law. This empowers the Standing Committee to declare either a state of war or, far more problematically, a state of emergency "by region of turmoil" within Hong Kong "which endangers national unity or security and is beyond the control of the government of the Region". Once that happens, all the normal restrictions on what national laws may be applied in Hong Kong disappear and the Central People's Government is given complete freedom to apply whatever it considers to be "relevant national laws". Neither the Standing Committee nor the Central People's Government is required to consult Hong Kong before taking such steps, nor is there any limit on how long such laws can remain in force.

Although evidently designed to deal with an extreme situation in which law and order in Hong Kong has already broken down, Article 18(4) gives no guidance on what constitutes the sort of "turmoil" necessary for such powers to be invoked. Weng (2001) argues this gives the Central People's Government "a blank cheque" to apply whatever national laws it wishes, at which point Hong Kong's "autonomy will no doubt be suspended".[165]

If it were ever invoked, it seems likely that Article 18(4) would be used to impose repressive measures such as martial law on Hong Kong. Xiao (2001) notes that the implementation of this provision "may mean constraints on the basic rights and freedoms of citizens".[166] Recognizing that law and order in Hong Kong would have broken down

---

162. See Article 89(1) of the PRC Constitution 1982. For more on the wide law-making powers of the State Council, see Chen, *An Introduction to the Legal System of the People's Republic of China* (see note 160) at 135–137.
163. See, for example, Order of the State Council of the People's Republic of China No. 221 (1 July 1997) setting out the territorial boundaries of the Hong Kong SAR. This, however, reduced the total size of Hong Kong by more than 200 square kilometres from that which applied under British rule. See Gren Manuel, "New borders shrink SAR by twice size of HK Island: Area in Deep and Mirs bays lost to mainland", *South China Morning Post*, 9 August 1997.
164. Chau Pak Kwan, *A Threat to One Country, Two Systems: National Law Making for Hong Kong* (School of Oriental and African Studies, M.A. thesis, April 1988).
165. Byron S.J. Weng, "Judicial Independence Under the Basic Law" in Steve Tsang (ed.), *Judicial Independence and the Rule of Law in Hong Kong* (Hong Kong University Press, 2001) at 57.
166. See Xiao, *One Country, Two Systems* (see note 74) at 166.

(or perhaps unsure if the Hong Kong Police would be prepared to enforce such repressive laws), Article 6 of the Law of the PRC on the Garrisoning of the Hong Kong SAR makes explicit provision for such laws to be enforced by the PLA's Hong Kong Garrison.[167] This constitutes a major exception to the normal principle, under Article 14(2) of the Hong Kong Basic Law, that Hong Kong has sole responsibility for its own law and order, and that the PLA Garrison should not become involved in local Hong Kong affairs.[168]

However, even during a state of war or emergency, there is nothing to suggest that the Hong Kong Basic Law itself would not remain in force, including its provisions protecting human rights.[169] These incorporate strict limits on how far fundamental freedoms can be restricted, even in times of emergency (including, for example, an absolute ban on torture and arbitrary executions).[170] It must, however, be open to question how easy it would be for Hong Kong courts to enforce such restrictions in practice at a time of martial law.[171]

4.3 Judicial Power

Judicial power is another common characteristic of autonomous arrangements the world over. According to Hannum and Lillich (1980): "A free and independent judiciary forms part of the governmental structure of all the politically autonomous entities surveyed."[172] That is true in Hong Kong too, with several provisions in the Hong Kong Basic Law referring to the granting of "judicial power" to the SAR.[173]

The meaning of judicial power is not defined in any of those provisions. Chan (2011) calls it "an extremely difficult concept".[174] However, the Chinese text of Article 80, which states that this power is exercised by the courts of the Hong Kong SAR, uses a term which also can be translated as the "power to adjudicate".[175] That means the power

---

167. Article 6 states that following a declaration of a state of war or emergency, "the Hong Kong Garrison shall perform its duties in accordance with the provisions of the national laws that the Central People's Government decides to apply in the Region".
168. The principle that Hong Kong is responsible for its own law and order is stipulated, without any exceptions, in paragraph 3(11) of the Joint Declaration. As a result, it is sometimes argued that the provisions of Article 18(4) of the Hong Kong Basic Law breach the Joint Declaration. See further note 6 in Chapter 3.
169. See "Chapter 8: Protection of Human Rights" for more on these provisions and, especially, Article 39(1) providing for the continued application of most parts of several international human rights treaties, including the International Covenant on Civil and Political Rights.
170. See further note 134 in Chapter 8, and the accompanying text.
171. Weng [in "Judicial Independence Under the Basic Law" (see note 165) at 57] suggests that after the declaration of a state of emergency: "The independence of the judiciary might well become irrelevant."
172. Hannum and Lillich, "The Concept of Autonomy in International Law" (see note 3) at 869.
173. See Articles 2, 19(1), 80 and 85.
174. Johannes Chan, "The Judiciary" in Chan and Lim (eds.), *Law of the Hong Kong Constitution* (see note 21) at 299.
175. This is "審判權". By contrast, Articles 2 and 19 use the term "司法權".

to receive, hear and determine court cases.[176] Tai (1998) concludes that "adjudicate" best describes the judicial power granted to the Hong Kong SAR,[177] since this term also appears in several other provisions in the Hong Kong Basic Law.[178]

Under Article 85, the courts "exercise judicial power independently, free from any interference". That gives the courts the vital protection of judicial independence, a feature so vital to how the courts operate in Hong Kong that it will be examined in detail in a later chapter.[179] But in terms of assessing the extent of Hong Kong's high degree of autonomy under the Hong Kong Basic Law, the emphasis is on the degree of separation that the Hong Kong courts enjoy from mainland institutions—a separation which is, with one crucial exception, total.

In both Articles 2 and 19(1), the Hong Kong Basic Law refers to Hong Kong exercising "*independent* judicial power" (emphasis added). However, the word "independent" is not used to describe either the executive or legislative power granted to Hong Kong, prompting Ghai (1999) to conclude that the intention behind the Hong Kong Basic Law may have been to make the courts "more autonomous" than other institutions of government in Hong Kong.[180]

That is evidenced from the fact that while, as we saw earlier, the Hong Kong Basic Law gives the Central People's Government extensive powers of control over Hong Kong's Chief Executive,[181] and allows the national legislature to return and invalidate laws enacted by the Hong Kong Legislative Council under certain circumstances,[182] it gives China's national judicial system no role at all in the administration of justice in Hong Kong. Again and again, the Hong Kong Basic Law emphasizes the separate nature of the Hong Kong judicial system through provisions such as those allowing the Hong Kong courts to use English (Article 9), recruit judges from other common law jurisdictions (Article 92), even to sit on Hong Kong's highest court (Article 82), and refer to previous court cases from elsewhere in the common law world (Article 84). In *Stock Exchange of Hong Kong v New World Development*, the Court of Final Appeal described the effect of these and other similar provisions in the Hong Kong Basic Law as being "to establish the constitutional architecture" of a judicial system with "separation from that of the mainland".[183]

---

176. See Benny Tai, "The Jurisdiction of the Courts of the Hong Kong Special Administrative Region" in Alice Lee (ed.) *Law Lectures for Practitioners 1998* (Hong Kong Law Journal Ltd., 1998) at 69–73 for a detailed description of the different aspects of the power to adjudicate in the Hong Kong context.
177. Ibid. at 68.
178. See Articles 2, 19(1), 19(3), 84, 158(2)–(3), all of which use either the term "adjudicate" or "adjudication".
179. See further "6.1: Judicial Independence" in Chapter 6.
180. Ghai, *Hong Kong's New Constitutional Order* (see note 16) at 146.
181. See "4.1: Executive Power" earlier in this chapter.
182. See "4.2: Legislative Power" earlier in this chapter.
183. (2006) 9 HKCFAR 234, 254.

Hannum and Lillich (1980) note that in autonomous areas elsewhere in the world, "members of the highest local court often are appointed by or with the consent of the sovereign government".[184] However, in Hong Kong that is not the case, with Article 88 of the Hong Kong Basic Law clearly stipulating that all judicial appointments will be made locally.[185] Only when it comes to appointments to the Court of Final Appeal, and of the Chief Judge of the High Court, does the National People's Congress Standing Committee need to be notified. Even this is described as a formality, with Article 90(2) of the Hong Kong Basic Law stipulating such notification is only "for the record", which would appear to mean that the Standing Committee does not have any power to veto such appointments.[186] Nonetheless, despite these provisions in the Hong Kong Basic Law, there were disturbing reports that the Central People's Government was asked, and approved, the appointment of Geoffrey Ma as Chief Justice in 2010.[187]

By far the most significant aspect of Hong Kong's judicial autonomy is its power of final adjudication, or the power to finally decide court cases. Under Article 19(2) of the Hong Kong Basic Law, the Hong Kong courts have the power to hear almost all cases in Hong Kong, with the minor exception of those types of cases—such as those involving foreign diplomats—they were unable to hear under British rule and, under Article 19(3), decisions on facts relating to acts of state such as defence and foreign affairs.[188] Under Article 82 of the Hong Kong Basic Law, the Court of Final Appeal, as Hong Kong's highest court, has the power to reach the final decision on all cases heard by the Hong Kong courts. Unlike the situation elsewhere in China, cases from Hong Kong cannot be appealed to higher courts in the Chinese national judicial system headed by the Supreme People's Court in Beijing.[189]

That gives the Hong Kong courts a power which they did not enjoy under British rule, when the court of final appeal was the Judicial Committee of the Privy Council in London, one of Britain's highest courts.[190] It is also a power that few other autonomous areas elsewhere in the world exercise. One survey of autonomous arrangements around the world found only three examples of judiciaries with complete jurisdiction over all

---

184. Hannum and Lillich, "The Concept of Autonomy in International Law" (see note 3) at 869.
185. Although appointed by the Chief Executive, the choice of new judges is essentially a matter for a largely independent commission body known as the Judicial Officers Recommendation Commission. See further note 63 in Chapter 6 and the accompanying text.
186. The term "for the record" is also used elsewhere in the Hong Kong Basic Law to describe other procedures which do not require Standing Committee approval. See, for instance, Article 17(2) [which is described earlier in this chapter in "4.2: Legislative Power"] on the formal reporting of new Hong Kong laws to the Standing Committee.
187. Yvonne Tsui, Joyce Man and Fanny W.Y. Fung, "Geoffrey Ma named as next Chief Justice", *South China Morning Post*, 9 April 2010.
188. See further "6.5: Limits on Courts" in Chapter 6.
189. Under Article 127 of the PRC Constitution 1982, the Supreme People's Court is the highest court in China and has the task of supervising the lower courts. In practice, it hears extremely few cases and most appeals are disposed of by lower-level courts.
190. See further note 16 in Chapter 6.

civil and criminal matters.[191] and these all involved small independent nations which are only considered examples of autonomy, because some of their other powers are exercised by larger, nearby nations.[192] Even under federal systems of government, individual states do not have the power finally to decide all cases and the court of final appeal is usually a national one.[193] For example, in the US, this is the Supreme Court in Washington, DC. As a result, the power of final adjudication granted to the Court of Final Appeal under the Hong Kong Basic Law is often cited by mainland legal scholars in support of their argument that Hong Kong enjoys an even higher degree of autonomy than states in a federal nation.[194]

But the crucial qualification to this glowing picture is that, while Hong Kong courts may be totally free from the control of the mainland courts, the same is not necessarily true when it comes to the power of the national legislature. Under Article 158(1), the final power to interpret the Hong Kong Basic Law belongs to the National People's Congress Standing Committee rather than the Court of Final Appeal. This is part of the Standing Committee's general power, under Article 67(4) of the PRC Constitution 1982, to interpret all laws passed by the National People's Congress and its Standing Committee in line with the general principle that—under the different system of interpretation that exists in China—the final power to issue authoritative interpretations of legislation belongs to the body which enacted that legislation, or a representative of that body.[195]

That does not mean the Hong Kong courts lack the power to interpret the Hong Kong Basic Law. Under Article 158(2), they have a parallel power to interpret on their own those provisions which fall within Hong Kong's autonomy.[196] But when it comes to those provisions which lie outside Hong Kong's autonomy, it is a different matter. Under Article 158(3), before reaching a final judgment, the Court of Final Appeal is required to refer to the Standing Committee for interpretation any provisions necessary to decide

---

191. The Federated States of Micronesia, Andorra and Liechenstein. There are also other autonomous regions with a more limited power of final adjudication. For example, Scotland has its own court of final appeal for almost all criminal (but not civil) cases. See Herzer, *Options for Tibet's Future Political Status* (see note 24) at 17. Note that this survey does not include the Macao SAR which also exercises the power of final adjudication under Article 84 of the Macao Basic Law (a provision which largely replicates the wording of Article 82 of the Hong Kong Basic Law).
192. These are known as "associated states". For example the Federated States of Micronesia is associated with the US under an agreement known as the Compact of Free Association. As a result, the US is responsible for Micronesia's defence and provides social services to its citizens.
193. Hannum and Lillich, "The Concept of Autonomy in International Law" (see note 3) at 871.
194. See Xiao, *One Country, Two Systems* (see note 74) at 98–100 and Wang, *Introduction to the Basic Law of the Hong Kong Special Administrative Region* (see note 126) at 88.
195. See further note 9 in Chapter 7 and the accompanying text.
196. See "7.1: Hong Kong Courts" in Chapter 7 for more on interpretation of the Hong Kong Basic Law by the courts.

the case which concern either affairs that are the responsibility of the Central People's Government, or the relationship between the Central Authorities and Hong Kong.[197]

After more than a decade of managing to avoid such references, a sharply divided court finally invoked this provision for the first time to refer four issues of interpretation of the Hong Kong Basic Law to the Standing Committee in *Democratic Republic of Congo v FG Hemisphere*.[198] The dissenting judgments in that case demonstrated how wary some of Hong Kong's most senior judges remain of allowing the Standing Committee to become involved in Hong Kong court cases, with Justice Bokhary strongly implying that such a referral could be seen as a threat to judicial independence.[199] Lo (2011) describes the *Congo* case as a "watershed event". He argues that the referral to the Standing Committee resulted in a loss of "separate identity" rather than judicial independence, as the "[c]ourts of the HKSAR are no longer to be regarded as outside the PRC system but as PRC courts".[200]

Important though these events were, such a reference procedure is not out of line with the practice in autonomous areas elsewhere in the world. Hannum and Lillich (1980) note that it is common in many autonomous areas for a body responsible to the central authorities to have the final say over issues in court cases involving the relationship between the central authorities and the autonomous area[201]—which is one of the categories for judicial referral listed in Article 158(3) of the Hong Kong Basic Law.

But the Standing Committee's power to affect the outcome of court cases in Hong Kong extends beyond judicial referrals into other areas less commonly subject to control at a national level in autonomous areas elsewhere in the world. Although it might not have been the original intention of the drafters of the Hong Kong Basic Law,[202] it is now generally accepted that Article 158(1) also gives the Standing Committee a free-standing power to interpret any provision in the Hong Kong Basic Law—including those on issues within Hong Kong's autonomy—without waiting for a referral from the Court of Final Appeal.

Such interpretations remain rare.[203] Nonetheless, the effect of applying Article 158(1) so broadly is that no court case involving the Hong Kong Basic Law can be absolutely assured of being immune from the effect of a Standing Committee interpretation. If an interpretation is issued before or during a court case, the court will have no choice but to

---

197. See "7.4: Judicial Referral" in Chapter 7 for more on judicial referral under Article 158(3) of the Hong Kong Basic Law.
198. (2011) 14 HKCFAR 95. See "7.4: Judicial Referral" in Chapter 7 for more on this aspect of the case.
199. Ibid. at 111.
200. P.Y. Lo, "The Gateway Opens Wide" (2011) 41 *HKLJ* 385, 391.
201. Hannum and Lillich, "The Concept of Autonomy in International Law" (see note 3) at 872.
202. See further note 67 in Chapter 7 and the accompanying text.
203. At the time of writing there had been only three free-standing interpretations, in 1999, 2004 and 2005 respectively. For more on these interpretations, see further "Chapter 7: Interpretation and Amendment".

apply that interpretation in deciding the case.[204] If an interpretation is issued after a court case then, although the parties involved in that case will not be affected,[205] the value of that case as a precedent to be followed in subsequent cases will be undermined as, where the decision in that case conflicts with the interpretation, all subsequent cases will instead have to follow the Standing Committee's interpretation.

Even if the Standing Committee does not issue an interpretation, the knowledge that it has the power to do so hangs like a shadow over the Hong Kong courts. In extreme circumstances it could even constrain the Court of Final Appeal from ruling in a way with which the Standing Committee disagrees, in order to avoid the danger of another free-standing interpretation. Tai (2012) suggests that this may be one reason for the court's decision to refer four issues of interpretation of the Hong Kong Basic Law to the Standing Committee in the *Congo* case, for fear that—if it refused to do so—the Standing Committee might instead take the initiative to interpret those provisions, in a way which would be far damaging to the court's authority.[206] As a result, Tai (2012) concludes that the "the courts of the HKSAR can only exercise their autonomous powers under the shadow of an all-powerful sovereign" and the "reality is that the judicial autonomy of the HKSAR relies upon the self-restraint of the Chinese authorities".[207]

4.4 Dispute Resolution

Some disputes are inevitable in any relationship. If left unresolved, they can lead to serious conflict, even divorce. That is true too of the relationship between an autonomous region and the national government of the country of which it is a part. Suksi (2011) notes that autonomy is often granted to such regions as a way of resolving conflicts, sometimes even wars, with the rest of the country.[208] But it would be foolish to believe that autonomy acts as a magic wand which will automatically resolve all aspects of such conflicts.

In some cases, the granting of autonomy can also lead to fresh conflicts, as the national and local governments argue over who has the right to exercise a particular power. Ghai (2002) notes that autonomy systems "are normally complex and complicated".[209] In Ghai

---

204. As happened following the Standing Committee's 2005 interpretation, which brought to an end the case of *Chan Wai Yip Albert v Secretary for Justice* (unrep., HCAL 36/2005, 19 May 2005). See further note 156 in Chapter 7.
205. Article 158(3) states that, "judgments previously rendered shall not be affected".
206. Benny Y.T. Tai, "The Judiciary" in Lam Wai-man, Lui, Percy Luen-tim and Wilson Wong (eds.), *Contemporary Hong Kong Government and Politics* (Hong Kong University Press, 2nd edition, 2012) at 81.
207. Ibid. at 81–82.
208. See Suksi, *Sub-State Governance Through Territorial Autonomy* (see note 14) at 141. For more on the use of autonomy to resolve armed conflicts, see Kjell-Ake Nordquist, "Autonomy as a Conflict-Solving Mechanism—An Overview" in Suksi (ed.), *Autonomy: Applications and Implications* (see note 2) at 59.
209. Ghai, "Resolution of Disputes between the Central and Regional Governments" (see note 8) at 4.

(2005), he concludes that disputes about jurisdiction "are endemic to systems of divided authority".[210] That makes some kind of independent mechanism for resolving national-local disputes an essential element of most autonomous arrangements. Hannum and Lillich (1980) identified this as one of the most common characteristics of autonomous areas around the world, with the final power to resolve such disputes normally being exercised by "a nonlocal court or a joint commission of some kind".[211]

That reference to a nonlocal court often refers to a national constitutional court, which in many countries has the power to resolve any disputes over the extent of a particular area's autonomy.[212] Ghai (2005) notes that, although part of the national power structure, "in most countries operating on the principle of separation of powers, national courts are accepted as independent".[213]

The problem in China is that there is no such system of separation of powers, and the Supreme People's Court is neither independent nor a constitutional court. Instead, like all courts in China, it is constitutionally subordinate to the National People's Congress[214] which, together with its Standing Committee and their local equivalents across China,[215] appoint and remove all judges.[216] Nor does the Supreme People's Court have any constitutional jurisdiction,[217] a task which instead falls to the National People's Congress and its Standing Committee.[218]

What this means in practice is that, in China, any dispute about the extent of an autonomous region's powers will be resolved by either the National People's Congress or, more likely, its Standing Committee.[219] In the Hong Kong context, that is made clear

---

210. Ghai, "The Imperatives of Autonomy" (see note 32) at 39.
211. Hannum and Lillich, "The Concept of Autonomy in International Law" (see note 3) at 887.
212. For example, in Spain and Italy, constitutional courts are responsible for resolving disputes over the powers of the autonomous areas of the Basque Country, Catalonia and South Tyrol respectively. See Hannum, *Autonomy, Sovereignty and Self-Determination* (see note 13) at 272 and 436–437.
213. Ghai, "The Imperatives of Autonomy" (see note 32) at 39.
214. PRC Constitution 1982, Article 128.
215. This is a vast system of local people's congresses (with an estimated total of more than 3 million members) which exist at almost every local administrative level throughout China. See PRC Constitution 1982, Article 95.
216. Generally the court president will be appointed and removed by the corresponding people's congress at that level of government (see PRC Constitution 1982, Articles 62(7) and 101), while its standing committee appoints and removes the other judges on the court (see PRC Constitution 1982, Article 67(11) and PRC Organic Law of the People's Courts, Article 35). For the best-known example of a judge being threatened with removal by a standing committee angered at one of her decisions, see further note 61 in Chapter 6.
217. Chen, *An Introduction to the Legal System of the People's Republic of China* (see note 160) at 61–62. See further note 123 in Chapter 6.
218. PRC Constitution 1982, Articles 62(2) and 67(1).
219. The Standing Committee meets six times a year, whereas the full NPC meets only once. Under Article 67 of the PRC Constitution 1982, the Standing Committee carries out many of the tasks of the full NPC between its annual sessions.

by Article 158(1) of the Hong Kong Basic Law, which has now been accepted by the Hong Kong courts as giving the Standing Committee an unqualified power to determine the meaning of any part of the Hong Kong Basic Law, including those provisions which lie within Hong Kong's autonomy.[220]

Since the Standing Committee is a political rather than judicial body, which ultimately falls under the control of the Communist Party,[221] it hardly meets the description of an independent mechanism for resolving disputes that Hannum and Lillich identified as a common characteristic of other autonomous areas the world over. Chen (2005) notes that, "the sad reality is that the NPC Standing Committee is not able to command respect as an impartial arbiter of constitutional disputes".[222]

In *Ng Ka Ling v Director of Immigration*,[223] the Court of Final Appeal made a brave attempt to fill this vacuum caused by the lack of a constitutional court in China, asserting a constitutional jurisdiction to police the limits of Hong Kong's autonomy which, it claimed, even extended to invalidating any actions of the National People's Congress or its Standing Committee that breach the Hong Kong Basic Law.[224] This caused a brief constitutional crisis, which was only resolved when the court issued a supplementary judgment couched in more conciliatory language.[225] Although the Court of Final Appeal did not officially retreat from its earlier assertion of such a broad constitutional jurisdiction, it must be open to doubt whether it would ever now exercise such a power in practice — especially in light of the court's subsequent acceptance of the Standing Committee's unqualified power to interpret any part of the Hong Kong Basic Law.[226]

The lack of a constitutional court in China has led to a search by many Hong Kong legal scholars for another independent institution which could instead play this vital role of helping resolve any disputes with Beijing over the extent of Hong Kong's power under the Hong Kong Basic Law. Many initially pinned their hopes on the Committee for the Basic Law of the Hong Kong SAR, a body which superficially bears some resemblance to the joint commissions — usually consisting of a mixture of local and national members — which sometimes help resolve similar disputes in a number of other autonomous regions elsewhere in the world.

---

220. In *Lau Kong Yung v Director of Immigration* (1999) 2 HKCFAR 300. For more on this case, including criticism of the court's decision on this point, see further notes 104–125 in Chapter 7 and the accompanying text.
221. See further notes 12–13 in Chapter 7 and the accompanying text.
222. Chen, "The Concept of 'One Country Two Systems' and Its Application to Hong Kong" (see note 33) at 366.
223. (1999) 2 HKCFAR 4.
224. Ibid. at 26–27.
225. *Ng Ka Ling v Director of Immigration (No 2)* (1999) 2 HKCFAR 141. For more on this supplementary judgment, and the reaction to it, see further notes 207–220 in Chapter 6 and the accompanying text.
226. In *Lau Kong Yung* at 323.

Created at the request of the drafters of the Hong Kong Basic Law by a separate decision of the National People's Congress,[227] the Committee for the Basic Law is a working committee under the Standing Committee. It consists of 12 members, half each from Hong Kong and the mainland, appointed by the Standing Committee on the joint nomination of the Chief Executive, President of the Legislative Council and Chief Justice of the Court of Final Appeal.[228] Although explicit provision is made for the inclusion of persons from the legal profession in its membership, this is not required of all members—and it appears Beijing prefers to see the committee consist of a mixture of lawyers and lay people.[229]

Under several provisions in the Hong Kong Basic Law, the National People's Congress and its Standing Committee are required to consult the Committee for the Basic Law before China exercises various powers under the Hong Kong Basic Law, including returning a Hong Kong law declared inconsistent with the Hong Kong Basic Law (Article 17(3)), adding to or removing from the list of national laws that apply in the Hong Kong SAR (Article 18(3)),[230] and interpreting (Article 158(4))[231] or amending (Article 159(3))[232] the Hong Kong Basic Law. Chen (1988) notes that, "the significance of these four areas is that they all represent points of possible conflicts of interest and of opinion between the Central Government and the SAR", although the purely advisory nature of the Committee for the Basic Law means that, "the ultimate power to settle the dispute still lies with the central authority".[233]

According to Ghai (2002), the idea for the Committee for the Basic Law appears to have come from a joint commission in Greenland, charged with resolving disputes with Denmark over the extent of the island's autonomy.[234] A closer parallel might be drawn

---

227. Decision of the NPC Approving the Proposal by the Drafting Committee for the Basic Law of the Hong Kong SAR on the Establishment of the Committee for the Basic Law of the Hong Kong SAR Under the Standing Committee of the NPC (4 April 1990).
228. See Proposal by the Drafting Committee for the Basic Law of the Hong Kong SAR on the Establishment of the Committee for the Basic Law of the Hong Kong SAR Under the Standing Committee of the NPC, which was approved by the NPC in its Decision of 4 April 1990.
229. Carrie Chan, "Ex-democrat Lau to join Basic Law overseer group", *The Standard*, 27 Feb 2007.
230. See "4.2: Legislative Power" earlier in this chapter for more on the Standing Committee's power under Articles 17(3) and 18(3).
231. See "7.2: Standing Committee" in Chapter 7 for more on the Standing Committee's power of interpretation under Article 158.
232. See "7.5: Amendment" in Chapter 7 for more on the NPC's power of amendment under Article 159.
233. Albert Chen, "The Relationship between the Central Government and the SAR" in Wesley-Smith and Chen (eds.), *The Basic Law and Hong Kong's Future* (see note 128) at 135.
234. Ghai, "Resolution of Disputes between the Central and Regional Governments" (see note 8) at 11. This commission, created under Section 18 of the Greenland Home Rule Act 1978, consists of two members each from Greenland and Denmark, as well as three Supreme Court judges. For the text of this provision, and more on the role of the Greenland commission, see Chen, "The Relationship between the Central Government and the SAR" (see note 233) at 113–114.

with the Aland Delegation, another joint commission, consisting of an equal number of representatives from the autonomous islands and the national Finnish government.[235] Like the Committee for the Basic Law, the Aland Delegation plays an essentially consultative role, and lacks the power to take the final decision in disputes over the extent of the island's autonomy.[236] Nonetheless, Hannum (1990) notes that the Delegation "appears to have a significant legal and political role in resolving potential conflicts between the central and Aland governments".[237]

Contrary to initial expectations,[238] that is not a role which the Committee for the Basic Law has so far proved able to play. Lim and Chan (2011) note that it "does not seem to be the intention of the NPCSC to turn the Basic Law Committee into a dispute resolution mechanism".[239] The Committee badly damaged its credibility during the first high-profile dispute over the extent of Hong Kong's autonomy in 1999, when some of its members publicly spoke out in favour of the Standing Committee's first interpretation of the Hong Kong Basic Law[240] even before they had met to discuss the issue,[241] so destroying hopes that it would act in a quasi-judicial manner. Since then, Beijing has increasingly treated the Committee for the Basic Law in a way that one of its Hong Kong members describes as causing some observers to suspect that the Committee is "no more than a rubber-stamp".[242] Meetings are called at short notice, with its members essentially expected to endorse a text the Standing Committee has already prepared, with their role confined to suggesting minor changes in wording.[243]

Ghai (2005) notes that Article 43(2) of the Hong Kong Basic Law makes the Chief Executive accountable to both the Central People's Government and the Hong Kong SAR Government. This means that the Chief Executive is also "indirectly cast" into the role of mediating in disputes between Beijing and Hong Kong, although Ghai (2005) concludes that the Chief Executive is "grossly incapacitated from performing this function".[244] As we have already seen, the lack of a democratic mandate currently makes it very difficult

---

235. For a detailed discussion of the powers and role of the Aland Delegation, see Suksi, *Sub-State Governance Through Territorial Autonomy* (see note 14) at 170–171, 306–307 and 311–313.
236. For a comparison of the similarities and differences between the Committee for the Basic Law and the Aland Delegation, see Ghai, "Resolution of Disputes between the Central and Regional Governments" (see note 8) at 11.
237. Hannum, *Autonomy, Sovereignty and Self-Determination* (see note 13) at 374.
238. For example, Ghai [in *Hong Kong's New Constitutional Order* (see note 16) at 197] suggests that the intention behind the establishment of the committee was "to protect regional autonomy through the rule of law".
239. C.L. Lim and Johannes Chan, "Autonomy and Central-Local Relations" in Chan and Lim (eds.), *Law of the Hong Kong Constitution* (see note 21) at 69.
240. See further "7.2: Standing Committee" in Chapter 7 for more on this interpretation and the events leading up to it.
241. No Kwai-yan, "Move 'not business of courts'", *South China Morning Post*, 19 May 1999.
242. Albert H.Y. Chen, "The NPCSC's Interpretation in Spring 2005" (2005) 35 *HKLJ* 255, 263.
243. Lim and Chan, "Autonomy and Central-Local Relations" (see note 239) at 263.
244. Ghai, "The Imperatives of Autonomy" (see note 32) at 39. See also *Hong Kong's New Constitutional Order* (see note 16) at 293.

for the Chief Executive to resist pressure from the Central Government,[245] and—rightly or wrongly—Chief Executives have been popularly perceived to be too quick to side with Beijing in some disputes over Hong Kong's autonomy.

Nonetheless, there have been occasional examples of the Chief Executive performing such a mediating role, such as in persuading Beijing to allow limited visits by pro-democracy lawmakers who had been banned from the mainland for many years.[246] It remains to be seen whether the advent of a popular mandate for the Chief Executive, if a genuine election by universal suffrage is allowed from 2017 onwards,[247] will mean future Chief Executives are less perceived to be beholden to the Central Government and more capable of carrying out such a mediating role.

It is sometimes suggested that the Hong Kong deputies to the National People's Congress could play a mediating role, since they also have a foot in both camps, being chosen from Hong Kong and sitting in the national legislature. Hong Kong has had deputies in the National People's Congress since 1975,[248] and Hong Kong's continued representation is enshrined in Article 21 of the Hong Kong Basic Law. This provides for "Chinese citizens among the residents of the Hong Kong Special Administrative Region" to elect deputies "to participate in the work of the highest organ of state power".

Only a small minority of Hong Kong Chinese are allowed to participate in this electoral process, under measures adopted by the National People's Congress.[249] These essentially limit the franchise to a slightly enlarged version of the small-circle Election Committee that traditionally has been charged with selecting Hong Kong's Chief Executive.[250] The result, according to Fu and Cullen (2006), is that Hong Kong NPC deputies "do not genuinely represent the territory, as the existing electoral rules effectively limit membership to the 'pro-China' faction within Hong Kong".[251]

---

245. See further page 67.
246. See Frank Ching, "Beginning of a new chapter", *South China Morning Post*, 29 Sept 2005, and Cannix Yau, "Tsang wins the first round", *The Standard*, 3 Oct 2005.
247. See further note 108 in Chapter 5 and the accompanying text.
248. For the history of Hong Kong's deputies to the NPC (who, before 1 July 1997, formed part of the Guangdong delegation), see Fu and Choy, "Of Iron or Rubber?" (see note 87) at 203–205.
249. These measures, laying down the procedure for the election of Hong Kong deputies to the NPC are adopted by the NPC every five years. See, for example, Measures for the Election of Deputies of the Hong Kong SAR of the PRC to the 12th NPC (14 March 2012). Although a source of legislation applicable to Hong Kong, they are not classified as a "national law" and listed in Annex III of the Hong Kong Basic Law. See further note 160 earlier in this chapter and the accompanying text.
250. Ibid., Article 5, which provides for the selection of the deputies by an Electoral Council consisting of those members of the Election Committee who are Chinese citizens, Hong Kong delegates to the Chinese People's Political Consultative Conference, Hong Kong's Chief Executive as well as others involved in the selection of previous NPC deputies. The actual size of this Election Council rose from 435 in 1997 to 1,620 in 2012, with the majority being Election Committee members. See further Fu and Choy, "Of Iron or Rubber?" (see note 87) at 204.
251. Fu Hualing and Richard Cullen, "But Hong Kong Should Seek a Better Way" (April 2006) 2 *Hong Kong Journal*.

This inevitably impedes the extent to which the Hong Kong deputies can act as a "bridging institution"[252] between Hong Kong and the mainland. That was especially true during the early years of the Hong Kong SAR. Adopting a largely hands-off approach towards Hong Kong at that stage, Beijing banned the deputies from speaking out on Hong Kong issues.[253] That policy of self-restraint was later abandoned,[254] and subsequently there have been some incidents where the Hong Kong deputies petitioned mainland authorities over issues that aroused concern in Hong Kong.[255] However, Fu and Choy (2007) note that "the ultimate test for deputies is whether they can change the impression they are merely speaking for the Central Authorities, and not for the people of Hong Kong".[256]

The incscapable conclusion from this overview of the track record of all these various institutions—from the Committee for the Basic Law to the Hong Kong Chief Executive and deputies to the National People's Congress—is that there is no one in Hong Kong who can currently play a genuine mediating role in disputes over its autonomy. Instead, if China wants to take away some of Hong Kong's powers, it can do so unilaterally with no more than a nod in the direction of the Committee for the Basic Law. That happened, most notably, in 2004 when a Standing Committee interpretation took control of decisions on changes to Hong Kong's electoral system,[257] a power which Chinese officials previously had stated fell within the scope of Hong Kong's autonomy in respect of elections to the legislature.[258]

As a result, Hong Kong can be said to broadly satisfy three of the common characteristics of an autonomous area identified by Hannum and Lillich (1980):[259] possessing a locally selected executive, legislature and independent judiciary—all with extremely broad jurisdiction over local matters. But the fourth of those common characteristics, an independent body with responsibility for resolving disputes between local and central authorities, is an area where Hong Kong falls sadly short of the situation that exists in many other autonomous areas elsewhere in the world.

---

252. Ibid.
253. See further note 87 earlier in this chapter.
254. Especially after the huge public protest on 1 July 2003 prompted Beijing to adopt a more interventionist approach. See further note 95 earlier in this chapter and the accompanying text.
255. These include the 2010 jailing in China of Zhao Lianhai, who had campaigned in support of the parents of children affected by contaminated milk. After widespread protests from Hong Kong, including NPC deputies, he was released on medical parole. See Priscilla Jiao and Tanna Chong, "Hong Kong pressure 'key' in U-turn on milk activist", *South China Morning Post*, 24 Nov 2010.
256. Fu and Choy, "Of Iron or Rubber?" (see note 87) at 221.
257. See further note 208 in Chapter 5 and the accompanying text.
258. See further note 206 in Chapter 5.
259. See further note 19 earlier in this chapter and the accompanying text.

Chapter 5
System of Government

Hong Kong's political system is commonly described in a number of different, and arguably conflicting, ways. For the Hong Kong SAR Government and, especially, Chinese national authorities in Beijing, it is an "executive-led" system. This means, among other things, that the executive branch of Hong Kong's political structure (i.e., the Chief Executive and the top, or principal, officials and civil servants who report to the Chief Executive) exercise significant powers without the need for approval by either of the other two branches of Hong Kong's political structure: the legislature (or Legislative Council) and the judiciary. These include exclusive control over the formulation and implementation of government policy, and the sole power to appoint most holders of public office. Partly because of this, Hong Kong's Chief Executive has been sometimes described as exercising greater power domestically than the presidents of the US and many other countries in the world.

But this is far from the whole picture as far as Hong Kong's political system is concerned. Other powers of great importance to the executive in running Hong Kong can only be exercised with the approval of the Legislative Council. These include the power to make laws, levy taxes and spend public funds. The judiciary also exercise significant control, being explicitly given the power under Article 35(2) of the Hong Kong Basic Law to hear challenges to actions of the executive authorities (which are normally described as "judicial review").[1]

These constraints (or checks and balances) on the power of the executive have led some scholars to describe Hong Kong's political system as a "separation of powers". This means a system where significant—distinct—powers are exercised by all three branches of the political structure, as opposed to the executive alone. These powers are then used by the executive, legislature and judiciary to check and balance the actions of the other branches of the political structure and, in particular, curb any excesses. Separation of powers is a system widely practised in many countries, in some cases dating back hundreds of years, having been originally put forward as a defence against "tyranny" being exercised by any one branch of the political system with unchecked powers.[2]

---

1. See further "6.2: Judicial Review" in Chapter 6.
2. The origins of the concept of "separation of powers" are sometimes traced back to the ancient Greek philosopher Aristotle (384–322 BC), but more often attributed to the French political thinker Baron de Montesquieu (1689–1755), who described the concept in more precise terms. See Hilaire Barnett, *Constitutional and Administrative Law* (Routledge, 8th edition, 2011) at 80–82.

This description of Hong Kong's political structure has been endorsed by the courts, where separation of powers has been described as "woven into the fabric of the Basic Law".[3] As a result, the principle of separation of powers has been used by the judiciary to invalidate actions of the executive and laws passed by the legislature that go beyond the permitted powers of those two branches of Hong Kong's political structure under the Hong Kong Basic Law.[4] Nonetheless, separation of powers remains a controversial concept as far as Hong Kong is concerned. Such a system is not practised elsewhere in China, and the existence of a system of separation of powers in Hong Kong has been repeatedly denied by Chinese leaders from Deng Xiaoping downwards, apparently fearful it would weaken the Central Authorities' ultimate control over Hong Kong.[5]

The tensions between these two sometimes competing descriptions—executive-led government and separation of powers—of the political structure laid down in Chapter IV of the Hong Kong Basic Law (which, with 62 articles, is by far the longest chapter in the Hong Kong Basic Law) go some way towards explaining the problems with the present political system in Hong Kong. This is widely seen as unsatisfactory. Scott (2000) describes the system as "uncoordinated, poorly developed, fractious and sometimes dysfunctional".[6] Members of the legislature complain of being treated almost with contempt by the executive. But some legislators are increasingly responding in the same way. A radical minority now regularly resort to high-profile stunts, including throwing objects at the Chief Executive and his top officials. Perhaps more worrying for the executive is the rejectionist attitude taking root among a number of legislators. Officials complain that some legislators often seem more interested in political posturing than constructive cooperation.

As we will see shortly, such problems are a by-product of a deeply flawed political system where legislators only have the power to say "no", rather than play a constructive role in government. The system already has been subject to some change since the Hong Kong Basic Law came into force. In 2002, the outdated system (which, like many parts of Hong Kong's political structure, was inherited from colonial rule) of having civil servants fill all the top posts in the executive was finally replaced with a system of political appointees nominated by the Chief Executive. That has brought Hong Kong a little closer to the "ministerial system" of government widely practised elsewhere in the world. But the change so far has proved a disappointment to many and there is a

---

3. *Lau Kwok Fai v Secretary for Justice* (unrep., HCAL 177 and 180/2002, [2003] HKEC 711) at para. 19.
4. One well-known example is the case of *Yau Kwong Man v Secretary for Justice* [2002] 3 HKC 457. See further note 41 later in this chapter and the accompanying text.
5. See, for example, "Speech at a Meeting with the Members of the Committee for Drafting the Basic Law of the Hong Kong Special Administrative Region", 16 April 1987 in *Deng Xiaoping on the Question of Hong Kong* (Foreign Languages Press, 1993) at 55.
6. Ian Scott, "The Disarticulation of Hong Kong's Post-Handover Political System" (2000) 43 *The China Journal* 29.

widespread consensus that further change is desperately needed,[7] as Hong Kong moves towards the possible introduction of universal suffrage for elections for both the Chief Executive and all seats on the Legislative Council in the years ahead.

5.1 Chief Executive

At the top of Hong Kong's political structure is the Chief Executive. Under the Hong Kong Basic Law, the Chief Executive is the head of the Hong Kong SAR and the region's representative at a national and international level (Article 43(1)). Only Chinese citizens, aged 40 or above, who are permanent residents of Hong Kong with no right of abode in any other country are eligible to serve as Chief Executive. In order to allay concerns that a recent migrant from the mainland might be foisted into the post, they are also required to have been ordinarily resident[8] in Hong Kong for at least 20 years (Article 44).

The Chief Executive is the only one of the three branches of Hong Kong's political structure formally appointed to office by Chinese national authorities, specifically the Central People's Government, although only on the basis of the results of a selection process in Hong Kong (Article 45(1)). The Chief Executive is also the only one of the three branches of Hong Kong's political structure made formally accountable to Chinese national authorities, again the Central People's Government, under the Hong Kong Basic Law (Article 43(2)). The Chief Executive is also required to implement the Central Government's directives on "relevant matters" under the Hong Kong Basic Law (Article 48(8)).

Hence the particular importance of the Chief Executive's position in China's eyes, as the only branch of Hong Kong's political structure which lies directly within its control. That also explains Beijing's adamant insistence that Hong Kong must follow an executive-led system of government, since this is the only way its control over the Chief Executive can be extended to embrace Hong Kong's political structure as a whole.[9]

It also puts the Chief Executive in an impossible position, caught between the often conflicting demands of two masters since, in addition to the Central People's Government, the Hong Kong Basic Law also makes the Chief Executive accountable to Hong Kong (Article 43(2)). However, the experience during the early years of the Hong Kong SAR

---

7. See, for example, Ma Ngok [in *Political Development in Hong Kong: State, Political Society, and Civil Society* (Hong Kong University Press, 2007) at 223–225] on the "multiple contradictions" within the present system.
8. The ordinarily resident requirement can usually be satisfied by living in Hong Kong for the specified period. However, this is subject to some exceptions. See further note 21 in Chapter 8 and the accompanying text.
9. As noted by Chen Zuoer, Deputy Director of the Hong Kong and Macao Affairs Office of the State Council, at a seminar in Beijing on 12 March 2004. Cited by Albert H.Y. Chen in "Executive-led Government, Strong and Weak Governments and Consensus Democracy" in Johannes Chan and Lison Harris (eds.), *Hong Kong's Constitutional Debates* (Hong Kong Law Journal Ltd., 2005) at 10.

was that the holders of the post of Chief Executive appeared well aware that it was the Central Authorities rather than anyone in Hong Kong who ultimately determined whether they got—and kept—their jobs. As a result, successive Chief Executives were accused of paying little more than lip service to their duty of accountability to Hong Kong, while recognizing that the real power lies with Beijing and its representatives in Hong Kong. For example, in what many critics saw as an acknowledgement of this reality, Leung Chun Ying made a high-profile visit to the Central People's Government's Liaison Office in Hong Kong one day after being elected Chief Executive in March 2012.[10]

On paper, the Hong Kong Basic Law vests sweeping powers in the hands of Hong Kong's Chief Executive. His position is best understood by comparison with presidents in countries around the world with a presidential system of government, such as the US. As in those countries, the Chief Executive leads the government (Article 48(1)) and is selected independently of the legislature for a fixed term in office (in Hong Kong, five years—Article 46). By contrast, in countries with a parliamentary system, such as the UK, the government is usually led by a prime minister who emerges from the legislature (in the UK, from the House of Commons), and whose term of office is generally linked to that of the legislature. Although not identical to the American system, Shiu (2010) notes that "the internal operation of Hong Kong's political system is quite similar to the American executive-legislative relations".[11]

Even by comparison with other presidential systems, Hong Kong's Chief Executive exercises greater formal powers. Ma (2002) found that, on paper, Hong Kong's Chief Executive exercises greater power domestically than popularly elected presidents in 33 other countries, including the US.[12] Only two South American states (Chile in 1989, and modern day Paraguay) could be found where presidents exercise greater powers.[13]

That assessment was based especially on the Chief Executive's power to appoint and remove the cabinet and top officials without any need for approval by the Legislative Council. In the US, for instance, although the president chooses members of the cabinet, those appointments must be approved by the US Congress. By contrast, under the Hong Kong Basic Law, the Chief Executive alone determines appointments to the Executive Council (Article 55(1)). This is the body of advisers charged with assisting the Chief

---

10. Phila Siu, "Leung walks into flak over high-profile Western visit", *The Standard*, 27 March 2012. For more on the Liaison Office, see further note 101 in Chapter 4 and the accompanying text.
11. Shiu Sin-por, "Executive-Legislative Relations Under the Basic Law" in *Seminar on Review and Prospect of the Basic Law: Collection of Articles 2007* (One Country Two Systems Research Institute, 2010) at 272.
12. Ma Ngok, "Executive-Legislative Relations: Assessing Legislative Influence in an Executive-Dominant System", in Lau Siu-kai (ed.), *The First Tung Chee-hwa Administration: The First Five Years of the Hong Kong Special Administrative Region* (The Chinese University Press, 2002) at 353 and 368, citing work by Matthew S. Shugart and John Carey, *Presidents and Assemblies: Constitutional Design and Electoral Dynamics* (Cambridge University Press, 1992).
13. Ibid. at 353.

Executive in policy making (Article 54); it meets weekly throughout much of the year and, in practice, functions as the Chief Executive's cabinet. The Chief Executive is required to consult the Executive Council before taking most major decisions (Article 56(2)).[14] However, the Chief Executive is free to reject its advice, prompting Ma (2007) to suggest that, at least in theory under the Hong Kong Basic Law, "the CE can practically rule as a dictator and ignore the opinions of all the others in the executive branch".[15] The only formal restriction under the Hong Kong Basic Law is that, if the Chief Executive chooses to reject the Executive Council's advice, the Chief Executive must put on record the reasons for doing so (Article 56(3)).

The Chief Executive also has a wide-ranging power to appoint and remove other holders of public office (Article 48(7)). These range from the chairman and members of major public bodies, such as the Housing Authority and Hospital Authority, to hundreds of smaller advisory committees. For many years, this appointment power also extended to choosing many members of the District Councils,[16] the local bodies most of whose members are chosen through popular elections. In the past, this allowed the Chief Executive partially to reverse the outcome of those elections, by appointing more government supporters.[17] However, as Hong Kong moves towards the expected introduction of universal suffrage, appointments to the District Councils are scheduled to be abolished from 2016 onwards.[18]

The Chief Executive's powers of appointment amount to a major power of patronage that can be used to reward support for government policy, and punish those who are too critical. In 2003, for instance, then Chief Executive Tung Chee Hwa refused to renew the appointment of then Equal Opportunities Commission Chairperson Anna Wu after the anti-discrimination body had, under her leadership, brought several high-profile actions against the government over its discriminatory practices.[19]

Only in the case of a small number of top government posts known as "principal official" positions is approval required for the Chief Executive's choices.[20] Even then,

---

14. Article 56(2) makes an exception for the appointment, removal and disciplining of officials, as well as the adoption of measures in emergencies.
15. Ma, *Political Development in Hong Kong* (see note 7) at 59.
16. This appointment power was abolished in 1994 by the last British Governor Chris Patten, as part of political reforms which caused a bitter dispute with China (see further "2.5: Sino-British Disputes" in Chapter 2), and subsequently reversed after 1 July 1997. Appointed seats have traditionally constituted about 20% of the membership of District Councils.
17. Fanny W.Y. Fung, Albert Wong and Eva Wu, "Appointees strengthen hand of government in districts", *South China Morning Post*, 15 Dec 2007.
18. Amendments to the District Councils Ordinance (Cap. 547) abolishing appointed seats were introduced into the Legislative Council in February 2013.
19. These include successful challenges against government employment practices and the Education Department's allocation of school places (see Ma Ngok, *Political Development in Hong Kong* (see note 7) at 88–89). However, after Donald Tsang succeeded Tung as Chief Executive, Wu was subsequently appointed to the Executive Council in 2009.
20. See further pages 115–116 later in this chapter for more on which posts in the Hong Kong SAR Government constitute principal official positions.

that approval does not come from the legislature, which is not given any formal role in the appointment or removal of government officials under the Hong Kong Basic Law,[21] in contrast to the situation in most countries with a presidential system of government. Instead, it comes from Chinese national authorities. As a symbol of sovereignty, the Hong Kong Basic Law gives the Central People's Government the formal power to appoint and remove these principal officials, although only on the basis of nominations by the Chief Executive (Article 48(5)). In keeping with its initial policy of self-restraint, all the available evidence suggests that the Central People's Government initially endorsed whatever names were put forward by the Chief Executive in the years immediately after 1 July 1997, even in the case of nominees who were not necessarily Beijing's preferred candidates.[22] However, in more recent years, that appears to have changed with at least two reports of the Central Government rejecting names put forward by the Chief Executive for principal official positions.[23]

An exception is also made for the appointment of judges, in the interests of protecting judicial independence. Although formally appointed by the Chief Executive (Article 48(6)), in this case he or she is normally expected to follow the recommendations of an independent commission consisting primarily of judges and lawyers (Article 88),[24] so denying the free hand that the Chief Executive exercises over most other appointments.[25] In the case of a few senior judges,[26] approval is also required from the Legislative Council and their appointment or removal must be reported to the National People's Congress Standing Committee for the record. However, neither body has so far used this to interfere in the choice of judges for such posts.[27]

Policy formulation is, under the Hong Kong Basic Law, meant to be the exclusive preserve of the executive branch of the government (Articles 48(4) and 62(1))—another example of the Chief Executive's extensive powers. The Legislative Council's official remit on policy matters is limited to receiving and debating the Chief Executive's annual address (Article 73(4)), which sets out in broad terms the executive's policy agenda for the coming year. Legislators are even prohibited from introducing any bills relating

---

21. Although, in practice, the Legislative Council has used its power to "debate any issue concerning public interests", under Article 73(6) of the Hong Kong Basic Law, to debate motions of no confidence in government officials which, if passed, may leave them with little practical choice but to resign. See further note 314 later in this chapter and the accompanying text.
22. See further note 109 in Chapter 4.
23. See further note 110 in Chapter 4.
24. This is known as the Judicial Officers Recommendation Commission. See further note 63 in Chapter 6 and the accompanying text.
25. It may, however, be possible for the Chief Executive to reject the recommendations of this commission in certain circumstances. See further notes 71 and 73 in Chapter 6 and the accompanying text.
26. These are judges on the Court of Final Appeal and the Chief Judge of the High Court (Article 90(2)).
27. In addition, there is some dispute about the circumstances in which the Legislative Council is entitled to refuse to approve a judicial appointment. See further note 65 in Chapter 6.

to government policies without the Chief Executive's written consent (Article 74), a sweeping restriction that has largely put a stop to the private members' bills that played such an important role in influencing the policy agenda in the final years of British rule.[28]

In practice, legislators are often not informed of the details of new government policies until the day they are publicly unveiled—and sometimes not even then, as the executive increasingly skips the formality of briefing legislators in favour of simply announcing policies directly to the public through a press conference. In the past, it was not uncommon for political journalists with good contacts in the executive to have more advance notice of new government policies than Legislative, or even Executive, Councillors.[29]

Even after a policy has been announced, the executive authorities led by the Chief Executive will sometimes try to avoid any need to seek approval from the Legislative Council. Some policies are implemented without any new legislation, or using the executive's powers under existing laws. Even when new legislation is required, the executive may prefer to use a lower-level form of law known as subsidiary legislation which is not subject to such extensive scrutiny by the Legislative Council. One extreme example of this came with the introduction of the Principal Officials Accountability System. This was a fundamental change in the structure of the Hong Kong SAR Government, which is discussed in more detail later in this chapter.[30] Critics said such a fundamental change should have required at least primary legislation, and possibly even an amendment to the Hong Kong Basic Law. Instead, it was implemented through subsidiary legislation, with the Hong Kong SAR Government explicitly stating that there is no requirement for policy decisions of the Chief Executive, however important, to be formally implemented through primary legislation.[31]

As a result, even major policies are sometimes implemented by the executive without being fully debated in the Legislative Council. That includes, for example, the Link REIT privatization of car parks and shopping malls owned by the Housing Authority in 2004–05. In that case, deprived of any effective means of voicing their grievances through the legislature, opponents turned to the courts, bringing a controversial action for judicial review. This delayed the privatization for almost a year,[32] and intensified concerns about whether the courts are being used as a substitute for a properly functioning political process.[33]

---

28. See further note 279 later in this chapter.
29. Based on the author's personal experience as a political journalist at the *South China Morning Post* from 1990 to 2001.
30. See further "5.4: Hong Kong SAR Government".
31. Secretary for Justice Elsie Leung, "Speech on Legal Aspects of the Accountability System at LegCo Motion Debate on the Accountability System", Legislative Council, 30 May 2002. See further note 155 later in this chapter.
32. *Lo Siu Lan v Hong Kong Housing Authority* (2005) 8 HKCFAR 363. See further pages 187–188.
33. For more on such concerns, see further notes 259–260 in Chapter 6 and the accompanying text.

The Chief Executive cannot make laws,[34] a significant constraint on the powers of the executive. But the Chief Executive exercises extensive influence over the legislative process. Shiu (2010) notes that the Chief Executive "is able to lead and control legislation" in most areas, and describes this as one of the main differences between the system of government in Hong Kong and that in the US.[35] When new legislation is required, in most cases it can only be introduced by the Hong Kong SAR Government since, as mentioned earlier, the Hong Kong Basic Law imposes sweeping restrictions on private members' bills (Article 74). Once in the Legislative Council, it enjoys priority over any non-government bills (Article 72(2)) and benefits from a simpler voting procedure designed to maximize the prospects for passing any government bills.[36]

If the Legislative Council nonetheless refuses to pass the government's annual budget or any other important bill,[37] the Chief Executive can dissolve the legislature and call fresh elections in the hope these will return a more cooperative Legislative Council (Article 50(1)). But this is a power which has to be exercised with care. For a start, it can only be used once during the Chief Executive's five-year term of office (Article 50(2)). At a more practical level, if the Chief Executive is unpopular with the Hong Kong public, it runs the risk of returning a new Legislative Council with an even greater number of government opponents.[38] If that new legislature still refuses to pass the government's budget or important bill then, in order to break the impasse, the Hong Kong Basic Law requires the Chief Executive to resign (Article 52(3)).

Other important powers conferred on the Chief Executive under the Hong Kong Basic Law include the power to sign bills (Article 48(3)). No bill can become law until it is signed by the Chief Executive. In the unlikely event that the Legislative Council passes a bill which the Chief Executive disapproves,[39] he or she has the power to refuse to sign

---

34. See further notes 58–64 later in this chapter and the accompanying text.
35. Shiu, "Executive Legislative Relations Under the Basic Law" (see note 11) at 273. This refers, especially, to the fact that in the US it is members of the legislature, not the executive, who usually initiate new bills.
36. Under Annex II(II) of the Hong Kong Basic Law, bills introduced by the government only require the support of a simple majority of legislators in order to be passed. However bills not introduced by the government must secure majority support under a more complicated "split voting system", requiring two separate majorities from different groups of legislators. See further note 226 later in this chapter, and the accompanying text.
37. The term "important" is not defined in the Hong Kong Basic Law. However, the Hong Kong SAR Government argues that it is up to the Chief Executive to decide whether any particular bill falls into this category. See *Legislative Council Panel on Constitutional Affairs, Article 50 of the Basic Law* (July 2005) at para. 10.
38. However, Benny Tai [in "The Development of Constitutionalism in Hong Kong" in Raymond Wacks (ed.), *The New Legal Order in Hong Kong* (Hong Kong University Press, 1999) at 91] argues that the threat of a dissolution may be enough to persuade legislators to change their minds and enact the bill in question.
39. This is unlikely to arise in practice because, under Article 74, no bill relating to government policies can be introduced into the Legislative Council without the Chief Executive's consent. Only if a bill was amended during the course of its passage through the Legislative

it into law on the grounds that it "is not compatible with the overall interests" of Hong Kong (Article 49). The Chief Executive can even dissolve the Legislative Council and call fresh elections if it persists in passing the bill again by a two-thirds majority (Article 50(1)). Once again, this could ultimately lead to the Chief Executive being forced to resign, if the new Legislative Council persists in passing the bill yet again by a two-thirds majority (Article 52(2)). However, this situation is even more unlikely to arise in practice, since the Chief Executive can always back down at any stage and agree to sign the bill.

Like many presidents in countries with a presidential system of government, the Chief Executive exercises a limited judicial power—being empowered to pardon or commute the sentences of criminal offenders (Article 48(12)). Any other sentencing matters must be left to the courts, as was made clear in the case of *Yau Kwong Man v Secretary for Justice*,[40] when the Court of First Instance struck down a statutory provision that sought to give the Chief Executive the power to determine minimum sentences for a limited category of prisoners.[41] In that case, the court held that this was not a power given to the Chief Executive under the Hong Kong Basic Law.

Most of these powers granted to the Chief Executive under the Hong Kong Basic Law are directly copied from those previously exercised by British Governors during colonial rule. In fact, British Governors exercised even more sweeping powers prior to 1 July 1997. These have even been compared to the absolute power wielded by Kings and Queens of England in ancient times, before the advent of parliamentary democracy in Britain.[42]

It was during British rule that the term "executive-led government" most accurately described Hong Kong's political system. Under the Hong Kong Letters Patent, the main constitutional document during the colonial era,[43] the Governor was, in effect, the Chief Executive and legislature rolled into one. Although Hong Kong's first Legislative

---

       Council into a form with which the Chief Executive disapproves might the situation arise. Even then, providing it was a government bill, the Chief Executive could simply choose to withdraw it instead of allowing the bill to be passed.
40.   [2002] 3 HKC 457.
41.   Section 67C of the Criminal Procedure Ordinance (Cap. 221), which purported to give the Chief Executive the power to specify a minimum sentence for prisoners detained at "executive discretion". This is a term originally known as "at Her Majesty's Pleasure", which was used for children under 18 convicted of murder before 1993, when the law was changed to provide for mandatory life sentences for all murderers, whatever their age.
42.   Norman Miners, *The Government and Politics of Hong Kong* (Oxford University Press, 5th edition, 1998) at 98.
43.   The Hong Kong Letters Patent 1917–1995, a short document consisting of only 21 articles, was supplemented by a second constitutional document known as the Hong Kong Royal Instructions 1917–1993, which set out in more detail the rules on the functioning of the executive and legislature during the colonial era. For more on the difference between these two documents, see Peter Wesley-Smith, *Constitutional and Administrative Law in Hong Kong* (Longman Asia, 2nd edition, 1994) at 42–46.

Council came into existence as early as 1843, under British rule it was the Governor who made laws and (until the final years of British rule) appointed its members. Initially, the role of the Legislative Council was restricted to offering "advice", until 1917 when the Governor was required to seek the Legislative Council's consent in making laws.[44] Given this constitutional structure, it would have been inconceivable for a Legislative Council to play any direct role in the removal of a Governor throughout Hong Kong's 150 years of British rule.[45]

By contrast, as we have just seen, under the Hong Kong Basic Law, a Legislative Council that defies the will of the Chief Executive can, in certain circumstances, force the Chief Executive to resign, although only after the legislature's actions have been first endorsed by the Hong Kong public through fresh elections. In addition, under Article 73(9) of the Hong Kong Basic Law, the Legislative Council can also initiate an investigation of the Chief Executive for "serious breach of law or dereliction of duty"[46] and, if the evidence substantiates such charges, pass a motion of impeachment.[47] In January 2013, legislators voted on this procedure for the first time, during an unsuccessful attempt by pro-democracy lawmakers to initiate an impeachment investigation against Chief Executive Leung Chun Ying.[48]

The impeachment process under the Hong Kong Basic Law is similar to the impeachment process that can be used by legislatures to remove a president from office in other countries with a presidential system of government, such as the US and South Korea. The most significant difference in Hong Kong is that, because the Chief Executive is appointed by Chinese national authorities, under Article 73(9) of the Hong Kong Basic Law impeachment by the Legislative Council results in a recommendation to the Central People's Government to remove the Chief Executive, as opposed to immediate dismissal. However, this distinction may prove rather less significant in practice since it is difficult to imagine circumstances in which the Central Government would allow a Chief Executive to remain in office after an impeachment process that uncovered evidence of serious law-breaking or dereliction of duty.

---

44. See Article VII(1) which, after being amended in 1917, stated that: "The Governor, by and with the advice and consent of the Legislative Council, may make laws for the peace, order, and good government of the Colony."
45. It could, however, play an indirect role. In December 1991, Britain announced the removal of Sir David Wilson as Governor, who had been widely criticized by Hong Kong's pro-democracy camp, three months after their strong performance in Hong Kong's first direct elections to the Legislative Council. Wilson was replaced as Governor by Chris Patten, who introduced political reforms designed to accelerate the pace of democratization in Hong Kong.
46. Under Article 73(9), the support of 25% of legislators is needed to initiate a motion for such an investigation, which must then be passed by the Legislative Council. The investigation would be carried out by an independent committee, chaired by the Chief Justice of the Court of Final Appeal.
47. Under Article 73(9), a two-thirds majority is required for the passage of a motion of impeachment.
48. See Eddie Luk, "CY survives", *The Standard*, 10 Jan 2013.

5.2 Separation of Powers

Given these significant differences between the present constitutional structure and that of the colonial era, some scholars have questioned how far the term "executive-led government"—for all China's enthusiasm for the term—still accurately describes Hong Kong's current political system. Wesley-Smith (2005) argues that "it is misleading, and not conducive to clarity of thought, to describe the government system as 'executive-led'".[49]

For all the Chief Executive's supposedly "dictatorial" powers, there are some powers crucial to the functioning of government that the Hong Kong Basic Law prevents the Chief Executive from exercising. Under Article 73(2) of the Hong Kong Basic Law, the government's annual budget is subject to approval by the legislature.[50] This is a power which legislators have not hesitated to threaten to use to extract concessions from a reluctant Hong Kong SAR Government. In 2011, for instance, the government was embarrassingly forced to substantially revise its budget, only a week after it was originally announced, by adding provision for a $6,000 per head cash handout to more than six million people in Hong Kong, in order to avert threats that the budget would be rejected by the Legislative Council.[51]

The requirement in the Hong Kong Basic Law for the budget to be approved by the legislature is similar to that in many other countries, and is often seen as a vital part of a system of checks and balances between the different parts of the political structure. In Hong Kong, the Chief Executive can even be forced to resign if the Legislative Council twice refuses to pass the budget, and fresh elections for the legislature fail to resolve the standoff (under Article 52(3) of the Hong Kong Basic Law).

But the constraints imposed on the government by the Legislative Council's powers in the financial field go further than those exercised by legislatures in many other countries, making this perhaps the area where the Legislative Council exercises the most significant control over the Chief Executive's ability to govern. Under the Hong Kong Basic Law, all taxation and public expenditure must be approved by the Legislative Council (Article 73(3)). In itself, this is an unremarkable statement of the fundamental principle of the legislature acting as a check on the actions of the executive in the financial arena. But the way it is exercised in practice gives the Legislative Council greater powers than its counterparts in many other countries.

Continuing a system that began in the colonial era, many government fee increases and other means of raising new revenue need to be individually approved by the Legislative Council.[52] So too does any additional government spending beyond the amount already

---

49. Peter Wesley-Smith, "The Hong Kong Constitutional System" in Chan and Harris (eds.), *Hong Kong's Constitutional Debates* (see note 9) at 6.
50. The Chief Executive is, however, allowed to approve provisional short-term funding for the government if the Legislative Council has been dissolved (Article 51).
51. Cheung Chi-fai, Tanna Chong and Fanny Fung Wai-yee, "Derision and delight over budget U-turn", *South China Morning Post*, 3 March 2011.
52. Through amendments to subsidiary legislation or the revenue bill implementing the annual budget. See Ma, *Political Development in Hong Kong* (see note 7) at 108.

approved in the annual budget. Ma (2007) describes this as "tantamount to giving Legco the power of line-item veto", since it allows the Legislative Council to go line-by-line through many government revenue-raising proposals and spending requests, vetoing those parts they dislike.[53] Such a power of line-item veto is not commonly exercised by legislatures in the Western world, where legislative control is exercised primarily through the annual process of approving the budget. In Britain, for instance, parliament exercises far less detailed control over public finances, primarily through non-binding reports by parliamentary committees which are often ignored by the government.[54]

One result of these significant constraints on the Chief Executive's powers in the financial arena is that proposals to introduce new taxes have had to be abandoned repeatedly, when it became clear there was insufficient support for them in the Legislative Council. One of the most famous examples was the proposal for a new tax on goods and services (or sales tax), which the executive championed for many years as a way of broadening the sources of government revenue. However, the idea proved so unpopular, with even normally pro-government political parties threatening to vote against it in the legislature, that the executive took the rare step of prematurely abandoning a government consultation exercise on the issue in 2006.[55]

In theory, policy making in the financial arena, as in other areas, is supposed to be exclusively the responsibility of the executive branch of the government. Under the Hong Kong Basic Law, no bill relating to public expenditure can be introduced by individual legislators (Article 74), and no motion regarding revenue or expenditure (Article 48(10)) can be introduced without the Chief Executive's consent. But, in practice, the Legislative Council has on occasion been able to use its power of line-item veto with some success to assert a role in policy making on financial issues. Ma (2007) cites an example of legislators forcing the government to abandon its "polluter pays" policy of using sewage charges to pay for waste-water treatment, by refusing to approve the necessary increase in charges.[56] Lui (2012) concludes that the Legislative Council has proved "more effective" in exercising its powers to monitor government revenue raising and spending than in most other areas.[57]

The limitations imposed on the Chief Executive's ability to govern by what the courts have described as a system of "separation of powers" can be also seen in the fact that,

---

53. Ibid. Ma attributes the granting of these greater powers of control over government finances to Hong Kong's legislature to its history as a body that was originally used by the colonial administration to pacify business representatives opposed to higher government spending.
54. See Miners, *The Government and Politics of Hong Kong* (see note 42) at 130–133 for an excellent description of the differences between the limited degree of control exercised by the British parliament over government finances in the UK, and the much greater degree of control exercised by the Legislative Council in Hong Kong.
55. Chester Yung, "Sales tax sunk", *The Standard*, 6 Dec 2006.
56. Ma, *Political Development in Hong Kong* (see note 7) at 112.
57. Percy Luen-tim Lui, "The Legislature", in Lam Wai-man, Lui and Wilson Wong (eds.), *Contemporary Hong Kong Government and Politics* (Hong Kong University Press, 2nd edition, 2012) at 57.

although the Chief Executive exercises considerable influence over some parts of the legislative process, he or she lacks the power to enact primary legislation. This was highlighted in the case of *Leung Kwok Hung v Chief Executive of the HKSAR*[58] when the court held that an executive order issued by the Chief Executive[59] was purely administrative in nature and not capable of constituting legislation,[60] or even a legal procedure.[61] As a result, the Chief Executive was left powerless in trying to fill a legal vacuum that threatened the ability of Hong Kong's law enforcement agencies to conduct vital covert surveillance activities as part of their work.[62] Recognizing that law making was a task for the Legislative Council, the court instead ordered a suspension of its ruling for six months,[63] to allow time for the legislature speedily to enact a new law filling the legal vacuum.[64]

Although the Legislative Council does pass the vast majority of bills put forward by the executive,[65] it does not necessarily do so quickly, or in their original form. Ma (2007)

---

58. Unrep., CACV 73 and 87/2006, [2006] HKEC 816.
59. The Law Enforcement (Covert Surveillance Procedure) Order issued by the Chief Executive on 5 August 2005, using his power to issue executive orders under Article 48(4) of the Hong Kong Basic Law. This order was subsequently revoked by the Chief Executive on 9 August 2006.
60. *Leung Kwok Hung* (see note 58) at para. 38.
61. Aware of the Chief Executive's lack of law-making powers, the government had sought to argue that the executive order was a "legal procedure" rather than a law. This was an attempt to fall within the wording of Article 30 of the Hong Kong Basic Law, which allows law enforcement agencies to conduct surveillance activities "in accordance with legal procedures". However, when the case was heard at first instance, the court dismissed the idea of a distinction between laws and legal procedures for the purposes of Article 30. See *Leung Kwok Hung v Chief Executive of the HKSAR* (unrep., HCAL 107/2005, [2006] HKEC 239) at paras. 150–151.
62. This followed two District Court cases involving the Independent Commission Against Corruption in 2005. These cases called into question the legality of covert surveillance activities conducted by Hong Kong's law enforcement agencies under existing law. Note, however, that this legal vacuum was partly caused by the Chief Executive's refusal to bring into force the Interception of Communications Ordinance (Cap. 532), a private members' bill passed by the Legislative Council in June 1997. That bill would only have allowed such surveillance activities if they were authorized by a High Court Judge, a restriction which the Hong Kong SAR Government strongly opposed.
63. On appeal to the Court of Final Appeal, in *Koo Sze Yiu v Chief Executive of the HKSAR* (2006) 9 HKCFAR 441, 456–459. This replaced an order issued by the Court of First Instance in *Leung Kwok Hung v Chief Executive of the HKSAR* (see note 61), which had used a different means of delaying the effect of the court judgment for six months — by instead temporarily treating the Law Enforcement (Covert Surveillance Procedure) Order as valid for the purpose of authorizing covert surveillance for that period.
64. This was the Interception of Communications and Surveillance Ordinance (Cap. 589), which was enacted by the Legislative Council on 6 August 2006.
65. For instance, in the 2000–04 session, it passed 131 out of 135 government bills. See Ma, *Political Development in Hong Kong* (see note 7) at 119.

found that it took legislators an average of 237.7 days to scrutinize bills in 2000–04.[66] Many are subject to significant changes, or amendment, during the legislative process. Although most of these amendments are put forward by the government, they are often in response to demands from legislators who might otherwise vote against the bill, and can include changes which the government would prefer not to make.

An extreme example of this came during more than 180 hours of scrutiny by the Legislative Council of the National Security (Legislative Provisions) Bill in early 2003. This controversial bill primarily sought to implement the requirement in Article 23 of the Hong Kong Basic Law for Hong Kong to enact comprehensive laws protecting national security. But it aroused so much opposition during the legislative process that the government was forced to table three revised versions of the bill and 51 amendments,[67] some making major changes to its original proposals.[68] However, all these changes failed to appease the bill's critics. Instead, the highly publicized process of legislative scrutiny arguably only intensified public opposition.[69] As a result, after a massive street protest by more than half a million people on 1 July 2003, legislators who had previously promised to support the bill changed their minds. Lacking enough support in the Legislative Council to secure its enactment, the executive was left with no choice but to withdraw the bill just days before it was due to be put to a vote.[70]

This embarrassing withdrawal of one of the executive's most important legislative initiatives highlighted the gap between the generally sweeping powers which the Chief Executive, in theory, enjoys under the Hong Kong Basic Law and the extent to which they can be exercised in reality. In theory, then Chief Executive Tung Chee Hwa could have allowed the National Security (Legislative Provisions) Bill to be put to a vote and then responded to any refusal to pass it by invoking his power under Article 50(1) of the Hong Kong Basic Law to dissolve the Legislative Council[71] and call fresh elections in the hope of securing a more cooperative legislature. However, this was a meaningless power in this context since, given the intense public hostility to Tung at the time, it would have almost certainly resulted in the election of an even more hostile legislature which might have then forced the Chief Executive to resign.[72]

---

66. Ibid. at 123.
67. Ibid. at 124.
68. For instance, the proposal in the bill on the offence of sedition, which can be committed by inciting others to commit national security offences, was changed so that it would only apply to those who act with this intention in mind, so greatly narrowing the scope of the offence.
69. Ma, *Political Development in Hong Kong* (see note 7) at 124.
70. The Chief Executive initially announced on 7 July 2003 that he was deferring a scheduled vote on the bill two days later. The bill was later formally withdrawn on 5 September 2003. For a full account of this bill and the attempt to enact it, see Fu Hualing, Carole J. Petersen and Simon N.M. Young, *National Security and Fundamental Freedoms: Hong Kong's Article 23 Under Scrutiny* (Hong Kong University Press, 2005).
71. This power can be invoked if the legislature refuses to pass the budget or any other "important" bill. See further note 37 earlier in this chapter.
72. By rejecting the bill a second time and so invoking the resignation provision in Article 52(3) of the Hong Kong Basic Law.

Instead, Tung remained in office for a further 20 months. However, his personal unpopularity that had been highlighted by the 1 July 2003 street protest rendered him a largely powerless Chief Executive, unable to govern effectively due to his lack of public support. Tung finally stepped down in March 2005, officially on the grounds of ill health, one of the few reasons a Chief Executive is permitted to resign under the Hong Kong Basic Law (Article 52(1)). However, the resignation came only three months after Tung had been publicly reprimanded by Chinese leaders over his poor performance in office, and was widely seen as having been engineered by Beijing in response to his growing unpopularity.[73]

Donald Tsang, the career civil servant who succeeded Tung as Chief Executive, was initially much more popular with the Hong Kong public.[74] But such popularity soon evaporated, even before the series of personal scandals that plagued his final months in office,[75] raising questions about whether a Chief Executive chosen through the small-circle selection process that has been always used so far can ever expect to enjoy any more than fleeting popularity with the Hong Kong public.

5.3 Small-Circle Selection Process

As things now stand, becoming Chief Executive through the current selection process seems a sure recipe for destroying whatever popularity an incumbent might have originally had with the Hong Kong public. Tung Chee Hwa and Donald Tsang, the first two Chief Executives of the Hong Kong SAR, both came into office with respectable personal popularity ratings.[76] In both cases, by the time they left office their popularity ratings had sunk so low that they could be reasonably described as widely disliked.[77] In the case of Leung Chun Ying, the third Chief Executive, a similar effect was visible very early on. Initially popular during the election contest, because he was seen as the underdog candidate until his main rival became mired in scandal, Leung's popularity began to fall almost as soon as he was chosen as Chief Executive—and he took office in July 2012 with a popularity rating not much higher than that of Tung and Tsang when they left office.[78]

---

73. See further Yash Ghai and Jill Cottrell, "The Politics of Succession in Hong Kong" (2005) 35 *HKLJ* 1–6.
74. Jimmy Cheung and Gary Cheung, "Tsang's approval at record high", *South China Morning Post*, 22 April 2005.
75. Tsang admitted to "mishandling" dealings with business leaders, after taking trips on their yachts and private jets, and accepting a below market rental of a penthouse in Shenzhen. See Cheung Chi-fai and Tony Cheung, "Quit calls as Tsang says sorry again", *South China Morning Post*, 2 June 2012.
76. Tung and Tsang had average popularity ratings of 65% and 67% respectively during their first six months in office. See Public Opinion Programme (University of Hong Kong), *Popularity of Chief Executive* (1996–2012).
77. Ibid. Tung and Tsang had average popularity ratings of 47% and 44% respectively during their last six months in office.
78. Ibid. In June 2012, Leung had a popularity rating of 51%. See also Tanna Chong and Colleen Lee, "Sharp drop in support for C.Y. Leung, poll finds", *South China Morning Post*, 30 May 2012.

This pattern of unpopularity of Chief Executives in Hong Kong illustrates the importance of election by universal suffrage. In theory, the Hong Kong Basic Law grants the Chief Executive powers that far exceed those of popularly elected presidents in 33 other countries, including the US.[79] In reality, the lack of a democratic mandate probably contributes to making Hong Kong's Chief Executive far weaker than elected leaders elsewhere. Of course, being popularly elected is no guarantee of enduring popularity either, and there are elected leaders in many countries who end their term in office with low approval ratings. Nonetheless, in general, being elected by the people you serve gives most leaders added legitimacy, which often makes it easier for them to govern. That is why popular leaders sometimes exercise influence far beyond their formal constitutional powers.

In Hong Kong, Chief Executives have so far been denied the chance to pursue the same path to popularity. Instead of enjoying the legitimacy that comes from being returned through popular election, Chief Executives have been repeatedly tarred by the perception that they have been, in effect, chosen by the Central People's Government. Under Article 45(1) of the Hong Kong Basic Law, the Central People's Government appoints Hong Kong's Chief Executive after a selection process that is conducted "by election or through consultation" in Hong Kong. In every case so far, that selection process has consisted of a committee of several hundred members, many of whom are seen as all too willing to act at Beijing's behest.[80]

In December 1996, a Selection Committee consisting of just 400 members chose Tung for his first five-year term, in accordance with the terms of an NPC decision appended to the Hong Kong Basic Law.[81] Young and Cullen (2010) describe the one-off selection procedure used on that occasion as "a three-stage exercise which one might liken to a glorified job application and interview process".[82] With the eyes of the world upon Hong Kong in the run-up to the 1 July 1997 handover, it was important to give at least the appearance of a competitive process and three candidates were allowed to proceed through to the final stage of the contest,[83] although Tung's eventual selection was never in any real doubt.[84]

---

79. See note 12 earlier in this chapter.
80. For a classic example of this see Emily Tsang, "We still don't know who to vote for", *South China Morning Post*, 16 March 2012, quoting several Election Committee members as saying they were still awaiting instructions from Beijing as to which candidate to vote for in the 2012 Chief Executive contest.
81. Decision of the NPC on the Method for the Formation of the First Government and the First Legislative Council of the Hong Kong SAR (4 April 1990).
82. Simon N.M. Young and Richard Cullen, *Electing Hong Kong's Chief Executive* (Hong Kong University Press, 2010) at 18.
83. Ibid. The other two candidates were former Chief Justice Sir Yang Ti Liang and businessman Peter Woo.
84. Beijing's support for Tung was first signalled by a famous handshake with then Chinese President Jiang Zemin earlier in 1996. He won the 1996 contest with the support of an overwhelming 320 members of the Selection Committee.

Since then, under Annex I of the Hong Kong Basic Law, the task of choosing subsequent Chief Executives has fallen to a body known as the Election Committee, which initially consisted of 800 members.[85] Annex I(1) requires that committee to be "broadly representative". But, in this context, that term means broadly representative of the views of different sectors of Hong Kong society, rather than of the views of the Hong Kong population as a whole.

For that reason, Annex I(2) provides for a committee drawn equally from four different sectors of Hong Kong society. These are the business sector, professionals, representatives of grassroots interests, and politicians.[86] Most members of the committee are chosen through elections among the voters for many of the same functional constituencies that also choose half of the members of the Legislative Council,[87] so ensuring that this small circle—which has traditionally consisted of around 200,000 voters—are given a privileged position in both sets of elections.[88] However, in a small move towards a more representative committee, in 2010 Annex I(1) was amended to expand the size of the Election Committee to 1,200 members[89]—100 of the additional members coming from the elected members of the local bodies known as District Councils.

In all the contests so far, the Election Committee has performed two functions. Firstly, it has acted as a nominating committee, with those wishing to enter the contest required to secure nominations from at least one-eighth of the members of the committee.[90] Secondly, it has carried out the election of one successful candidate from among those who managed to secure sufficient nominations. That second stage is, of course, only necessary if more than one candidate manages to get enough nominations to enter the contest. In each of the first two selection processes after 1997, only one candidate managed to secure sufficient nominations, which meant they were selected as Chief Executive unopposed.

---

85. In practice, the actual number is normally slightly lower, mainly due to overlapping membership between the different groups eligible for seats on the Election Committee. For example, in 2000, only 794 of the 800 seats were filled. See further Young and Cullen, *Electing Hong Kong's Chief Executive* (see note 82) at 116.
86. Annex I(2) of the Hong Kong Basic Law defines representatives of grassroots interests as those from labour, social services, religious and other sectors. It defines politicians as members of the Legislative Council, representatives of district-based organizations, Hong Kong deputies to the NPC, and representatives of Hong Kong members of the National Committee of the Chinese People's Political Consultative Conference.
87. See further "5.6: Functional Constituencies" later in this chapter. The Election Committee is divided into 38 subsectors listed in the Schedule to the Chief Executive Election Ordinance (Cap. 569); 31 of these subsectors are based around functional constituencies. See further Young and Cullen, *Electing Hong Kong's Chief Executive* (see note 82) at 56–58.
88. Ibid. at 59, noting that, in 2004, there was only a 1.5% difference between the size of the functional constituency electorate and that which selected the Election Committee.
89. Amendment to Annex I of the Basic Law of the Hong Kong SAR of the PRC Concerning the Method for the Selection of the Chief Executive of the Hong Kong SAR (28 Aug 2010).
90. See Annex I(4) of the Hong Kong Basic Law which initially specified a requirement to obtain at least 100 nominations from the 800 member committee. In 2010, this was changed to 150, when the size of the committee was expanded to 1,200 members.

One of the clearest examples of how this small-circle selection process can produce a Chief Executive fundamentally at odds with Hong Kong public opinion came in 2002 when Tung was returned unopposed for what was supposed to be a second five-year term. By that stage, Tung was already starting to become unpopular with the Hong Kong public.[91] But after Chinese leaders publicly expressed their desire for Tung to serve a second term, he received nominations from 714 members of the Election Committee, making it impossible for any other candidate to get enough nominations to stand against him.[92] Much the same happened after Tung's resignation, in the June 2005 selection process for his successor. After Chinese officials publicly expressed their preference for Tung's then deputy, Chief Secretary for Administration Donald Tsang, he received 674 nominations and was returned unopposed after a challenger from the democratic camp[93] failed to secure sufficient nominations.

Since then, the trend has been towards more competitive elections. A major breakthrough came in 2007 when, for the first time, the democratic camp managed to secure sufficient nominations to enter a candidate in the Chief Executive contest,[94] after a concerted campaign for support among voters in the small number of functional constituencies where they are traditionally strong.[95] That set a precedent, which was repeated during the 2012 contest, when a candidate from the democratic camp once again managed to secure sufficient nominations to enter the contest.[96] In both cases, there was never any prospect of the pro-democracy candidate securing the support of a majority of Election Committee members. Instead, the pattern that seemed to be emerging was of a pro-democracy candidate, who had sufficient support to enter the contest but not to win, using this as a platform to denounce the legitimacy of the selection process.[97]

The 2012 contest before an Election Committee expanded in size to 1,200 members also saw the emergence of multiple candidates from the pro-establishment camp for the first time since the 1996 contest. Henry Tang, who had succeeded Tsang as Chief Secretary for Administration, was initially reported to enjoy Beijing's backing and secured the most nominations.[98] But Leung Chun Ying, the Convenor of the Executive

---

91. Tung's popularity fell to an average of 48% in the six months immediately after his re-election in 2002. See Public Opinion Programme (University of Hong Kong), *Popularity of Chief Executive* (1996–2012).
92. Under Annex I(4) of the Hong Kong Basic Law, each member is only allowed to nominate one candidate.
93. This was Lee Wing Tat, then chairman of the Democratic Party.
94. This was barrister Alan Leong from the Civic Party.
95. These are Election Committee subsectors representing professions such as law, education and information technology, where members are elected through individual rather than corporate voting. For an explanation of the difference between these two systems of voting, see note 231 later in this chapter and the accompanying text.
96. This was Albert Ho, then leader of the Democratic Party.
97. For example, Ho used his speech immediately after the announcement of the result of the 2012 contest to denounce the entire selection process as "ugly and disgusting". See "CE-elect appeals for unity", *RTHK*, 25 March 2012.
98. See Gary Cheung, "Tang may have edge in race for top job", *South China Morning Post*, 17 Nov 2011.

Council, who has a history of involvement with the Hong Kong Basic Law going back to its drafting process,[99] was also determined to stand and, after some initial difficulties, managed to secure sufficient nominations to do so.[100] When a series of personal scandals badly discredited Tang in the eyes of the Hong Kong public,[101] Beijing switched its support to the initially more popular Leung with officials from the Liaison Office of the Central People's Government in the Hong Kong SAR—which had begun playing an increasingly active role in Hong Kong affairs[102]—aggressively lobbying members of the Election Committee in support of Leung.[103]

Beijing's switch of support from Tang to Leung during the 2012 Chief Executive contest highlighted how important a factor Hong Kong public opinion has become, even in the current small-circle selection process. In the initial years of the Hong Kong SAR, political reliability seemed to count for far more than popularity as evidenced by the Central Government's strong support for the unpopular Tung—who was widely viewed as beholden to Beijing[104]—securing a second term as Chief Executive in 2002.

But after the huge public protest against national security legislation on 1 July 2003, there was a change of policy by Beijing. One aspect of this was that the Central Government began to play a more active role in Hong Kong affairs.[105] Another aspect was a belated recognition that, without public popularity, it was impossible in practice for any Chief Executive to exercise all the powers granted to the holder of that post under the Hong Kong Basic Law. Cheng (2009), who worked on Hong Kong affairs at the National People's Congress Standing Committee during this period, acknowledges that, "without public support of the executive through an election, an executive-led government could be paralyzed by the legislature and the judiciary".[106]

The first sign of this change of policy was the premature replacement in 2005 of the unpopular Tung, whose term of office was supposed to last until 2007, with the then more popular Tsang. This was despite the fact that Tsang, a British-trained civil servant with a Knighthood from the Queen and a background of promoting colonial policies in Hong

---

99. In 1988, Leung, then aged 34, was appointed Secretary General of the Consultative Committee for the Basic Law of the Hong Kong SAR, which served as an advisory body during the drafting process. For more on this committee, see further pages 20–21.
100. Leung initially submitted 293 nominations compared with 379 for Tang. See Lai Ying-kit, "Leung Chun-ying signs up to become CE candidate", *South China Morning Post*, 23 Feb 2012.
101. Tang's reputation was undermined by revelations of a series of extra-marital affairs and a controversy over a large unauthorized basement in his luxury home which he blamed on his wife. As a result, his popularity dropped far below that of Leung. See Eddie Luk and Phila Siu, "Popularity of Tang tumbles after scandal", *The Standard*, 22 Feb 2012.
102. See further note 101 in Chapter 4 and the accompanying text, for more on the Liaison Office.
103. See Phila Siu and Kelly Ip, "Leung enjoys Western lift", *The Standard*, 5 March 2012.
104. Critics often pointed to the bailout by the Bank of China in the 1980s, which saved Tung's family shipping company from bankruptcy, as evidence of why Beijing believed he was politically reliable.
105. See further page 69.
106. Jie Cheng, "The Story of a New Policy" (July 2009) 15 *Hong Kong Journal*.

Kong that China strongly opposed,[107] was precisely the sort of person who would have failed Beijing's political reliability test in the past.

The second sign came with a historic decision from the National People's Congress Standing Committee in December 2007 allowing that the election of the Chief Executive in 2017 "may be implemented by the method of universal suffrage".[108] Although selection of the Chief Executive through universal suffrage—essentially a popular election as opposed to the small-circle process which has always been used so far—is stated as an "ultimate aim" in Article 45(2) of the Hong Kong Basic Law, this was the first time a date had ever been given for achieving this goal, and one perhaps earlier than Beijing had originally intended. Wang (2008), a prominent mainland legal scholar and former drafter of the Hong Kong Basic Law, says the Central Government took this decision out of recognition that "Hong Kong needs democracy to maintain its stability and prosperity".[109]

That, however, has not ended the uncertainty over whether Hong Kong will enjoy a truly democratic election for its Chief Executive from 2017 onwards. Chen (2008) notes that, while Beijing has signalled it has no objection in principle to the use of universal suffrage from that date onwards, whether this will actually happen "depends on the interaction between Beijing, the CE and Legco in Hong Kong".[110] This is based on Annex I(7) of the Hong Kong Basic Law, as supplemented by the Standing Committee's 2004 interpretation of its provisions, which requires that these three parties reach agreement on any changes to the system for electing the Chief Executive.[111]

One of the most contentious issues in this respect is likely to be the future nomination procedures. Article 45(2) of the Hong Kong Basic Law stipulates that selection of the Chief Executive by universal suffrage should follow "nomination by a broadly representative nominating committee in accordance with democratic procedures". In its December 2007 decision, the Standing Committee ruled that this nominating committee for the future election by universal suffrage "may be formed with reference to" the current Election Committee.[112]

---

107. As Director of Administration in the early 1990s, Tsang was responsible for implementing a British nationality scheme that offered full UK passports to 50,000 Hong Kong families, and which was strongly opposed by Beijing. See further Danny Gittings, "Tsang's dramatic change of fortune", *South China Morning Post*, 30 Sept 1998.
108. Decision of the Standing Committee of the NPC on Issues Relating to the Methods for Selecting the Chief Executive of the Hong Kong SAR and for Forming the Legislative Council of the Hong Kong SAR in the Year 2012 and on Issues Relating to Universal Suffrage (29 Dec 2007).
109. Wang Zhenmin, "The Significance of China's Decision on Universal Suffrage" (April 2008) 10 *Hong Kong Journal*.
110. Albert H.Y. Chen, "A New Era in Hong Kong's Constitutional History" (2008) 38 *HKLJ* 1, 6.
111. Under Annex I(7) any changes to Annex I require the support of two-thirds of members of the Legislative Council, the consent of the Chief Executive and the approval of the Standing Committee. The 2004 Standing Committee interpretation (see further note 208 later in this chapter and the accompanying text) also requires the Chief Executive to report to, and secure the support of, the Standing Committee before initiating this process.
112. Penultimate paragraph of the NPC Standing Committee decision.

What this means in practice is that something based on the current Election Committee is likely to retain the crucial function of determining which candidates are allowed to enter the contest for Chief Executive. But that does not necessarily mean it will continue to use the same nomination procedure used in the contests so far, where the only requirement was that an aspiring candidate secure nominations from at least one-eighth of members of the committee. As was demonstrated during the 2012 selection process, under that procedure it is not too difficult for multiple candidates—including a representative of the democratic camp—to enter the contest.

Chen (2007) notes that the wording of Article 45(2) of the Hong Kong Basic Law, which requires that any election by universal suffrage be preceded by nomination "in accordance with democratic procedures", is wide enough to allow for either the continuing use of the previous nomination procedures or the adoption of new nomination procedures instead.[113] In March 2013, Qiao Xiaoyang, a senior member of the National People's Congress Standing Committee, indicated that Beijing may prefer the adoption of new nomination procedures in which candidates for an election by universal suffrage are nominated by the committee "as a whole".[114] One possibility is that this would take the form of a primary (or preliminary) election, in which the committee votes to decide which of the aspiring candidates will be allowed to enter the main election, an idea first put forward during an earlier government exercise on how to implement universal suffrage.[115] Lo (2008) cites sources close to Beijing as suggesting that the Central Government wants a nomination process which will ensure "that any politically desirable or unacceptable candidates would be screened out".[116]

The suspicion is that new nomination procedures may be used to stop any candidate in the pro-democracy camp from entering an election conducted by universal suffrage, for fear they might win—something Beijing has no real cause to fear under the current small-circle process. Chen (2011) expresses doubt whether Beijing is prepared to allow "full democratization" in Hong Kong unless it can be sure that "full democracy can produce a Government and a legislature dominated by 'patriots'".[117]

---

113. Albert H.Y. Chen, "The phrase 'in accordance with democratic procedures' in Article 45 of the Basic Law" in Hong Kong SAR Government, *Green Paper on Constitutional Development* (July 2007) at Appendix 1, GPA 321.
114. See Gary Cheung and Joshua But, "Qiao Xiaoyang says Beijing forced into universal suffrage debate", *South China Morning Post*, 26 March 2013. For previous comments by Qiao on this issue, see P.Y. Lo, *The Hong Kong Basic Law* (LexisNexis, 2011) at 311.
115. See Hong Kong SAR Government, *Green Paper on Constitutional Development* (see note 113) at 25, citing a proposal to this effect put forward by the Basic Law Institute.
116. See Sonny Lo, *The Dynamics of Beijing–Hong Kong Relations: A Model for Taiwan* (Hong Kong University Press, 2008) at 137.
117. Albert Chen, "The Development of Representative Government in Hong Kong" in Johannes Chan and C.L. Lim (eds.), *Law of the Hong Kong Constitution* (Sweet & Maxwell, 2011) at 246.

That is also likely to be the litmus test for most independent observers, who will find it hard to categorize the election as genuine if the Central Government insists on artificially severe nomination procedures in order to prevent a pro-democracy candidate from entering the contest. Young and Cullen (2010) put the point more colourfully, noting the real question is whether universal suffrage for the Chief Executive from 2017 onwards will be "like choosing between a chocolate, chocolate chip and chocolate peanut-butter ice-cream cone, or choosing between a strawberry, vanilla and rocky road ice-cream cone".[118]

5.4 Hong Kong SAR Government

The Hong Kong Basic Law offers little guidance on the role of the Hong Kong SAR Government. In a relatively brief section on the "executive authorities", as the government is also titled under Article 59, its structure and powers are outlined in relatively vague terms.[119] Headed by the Chief Executive (Article 60(1)), the Hong Kong SAR Government is expressly given only a handful of general responsibilities, such as policy formulation and implementation, conducting administrative affairs, and drafting budgets and proposed legislation (Article 62).

This absence of any specific powers for most parts of the Hong Kong SAR Government reflects the intended dominance of the Chief Executive within the executive branch under the design of the Hong Kong Basic Law. As we saw earlier, the Hong Kong Basic Law does impose significant limitations on the Chief Executive's powers. But this is with reference to the other branches of the political structure—the legislature and judiciary—which are assigned some important powers, such as law making, under a system of separation of powers. Within the executive branch, for the most part it is a different picture. As Ma (2007) notes, according to the Hong Kong Basic Law's design, the Chief Executive has the power to "practically rule as a dictator"[120] over others within the government, and ignore the views of most officials.

The main exception is the Secretary for Justice, the title for the top law officer in the Hong Kong SAR Government. As we will see in the next chapter, the importance of safeguarding the rule of law means that the courts are treated very differently from other branches of the governmental structure under the Hong Kong Basic Law.[121] The same is true of those who decide whether a case should be sent to court. Article 63 of the Hong Kong Basic Law expressly grants the Department of Justice, which is headed by the Secretary for Justice, the power to "control criminal prosecutions, free from any

---

118. Young and Cullen, *Electing Hong Kong's Chief Executive* (see note 82) at 96.
119. See further Section 2 in Chapter IV of the Hong Kong Basic Law and, in particular, Article 60, which sets out a general structure for the Hong Kong SAR Government under the leadership of the Chief Executive, and Article 62 which contains a list of six general powers.
120. See further note 15 earlier in this chapter.
121. See further "6.1: Judicial Independence" in Chapter 6.

interference".[122] That means free from interference even by the Chief Executive who, if he or she was ever suspected of a crime, it would ultimately be the Secretary for Justice's decision whether or not to prosecute.[123]

The Hong Kong Basic Law collectively describes the most senior members of the Chief Executive's team as "principal officials". Under Article 61, they must be Chinese citizens who are permanent residents of Hong Kong with no right of abode in any other country. In order to allay concerns about recent migrants being appointed to these posts, Article 61 requires that they have been ordinarily resident[124] in Hong Kong for at least 15 years, slightly shorter than the 20-year requirement for those wishing to hold the post of Chief Executive.[125]

The most senior of these principal officials are the Chief Secretary for Administration,[126] Financial Secretary and Secretary for Justice respectively, who deputize for the Chief Executive in that order of precedence (Article 53(1)). That makes the Chief Secretary the most senior of these officials. The holder of this post is commonly referred to as the deputy to the Chief Executive, and the post of Chief Secretary is sometimes seen as a stepping stone for those wishing to enter the contest for Chief Executive.[127] Although the Hong Kong Basic Law makes explicit provision for the possibility of deputies to these three principal officials,[128] at the time of writing no such positions have been created. Instead, in 2012, opposition from legislators forced Chief Executive Leung Chun Ying to

---

122. In *Re C (A Bankrupt)* [2006] 4 HKC 582, 590–592, the Court of Appeal held that Article 63 entrenched a constitutional principle that such decisions are made free from any form of political or other pressure. See Wong Yan Lung, "The Secretary for Justice as the Protector of the Public Interest—Continuity and Development" (2007) 37 *HKLJ* 319, 334, where the then Secretary for Justice described this as a "quasi-judicial" power.
123. This issue was addressed by Secretary for Justice Rimsky Yuen immediately after his appointment in June 2012, when asked about the possibility a prosecution might be brought against the Chief Executive over illegal structures at his home. See Hong Kong SAR Government "Transcript of remarks at press conference on Principal Official appointments", 28 June 2012.
124. The ordinarily resident requirement can usually be satisfied by living in Hong Kong for the specified period. However, this is subject to some exceptions. See further note 21 in Chapter 8 and the accompanying text.
125. Under Article 44 of the Hong Kong Basic Law.
126. The English text of the Hong Kong Basic Law refers to this post by the slightly different title of "Administrative Secretary". However, reportedly initially at the insistence of Anson Chan, who served in this post from 1997–2001, the Hong Kong SAR Government instead uses the title of Chief Secretary for Administration. This is similar to the title of Chief Secretary that was used to describe the equivalent post in the colonial administration prior to 1 July 1997. See May Sin-min Hon, "Anson's title 'within law'", *South China Morning Post*, 6 July 1997.
127. Donald Tsang served as Chief Secretary before becoming Chief Executive in 2005. Henry Tang, his successor as Chief Secretary, stood unsuccessfully for Chief Executive in 2012.
128. Article 48(5) refers to the appointment of "Secretaries and Deputy Secretaries of Departments" as principal officials. The three Departments are described in Article 60(2) of the Hong Kong Basic Law as the Department of Administration, Department of Finance and Department of Justice.

shelve, at least temporarily, proposals to introduce the posts of Deputy Chief Secretary and Deputy Financial Secretary.[129]

The other principal officials are a mixture of Directors of Bureaux of the Hong Kong SAR Government, with responsibility for government policy in specific subject areas, and the heads of the Hong Kong Police, Customs and Excise, Immigration Department, Independent Commission Against Corruption and Audit Commission. The Hong Kong Basic Law sets no specific figure on the number of such bureau directors. As of March 2013, there were 12 directors responsible for transport and housing; home affairs; labour and welfare; financial services and the treasury; commerce and economic development; constitutional and mainland affairs; the civil service; development; security; education; food and health; and the environment respectively.[130]

Unlike the situation in many other countries, nominees to these senior governmental posts are not subject to any kind of vetting or approval by the legislature. Ma (2002) cites this as one of the principal factors for concluding that, on paper, Hong Kong's Chief Executive enjoys far greater powers than democratically elected presidents in many other countries.[131]

The only constraint imposed by the Hong Kong Basic Law is that the Chief Executive's nominations for principal official posts must be appointed and removed from office by the Central People's Government (Articles 15 and 48(5)). However, the Central Government rarely seems to have questioned individual choices by the Chief Executive during the early years of the Hong Kong SAR although, more recently, there have been some signs this attitude is beginning to change.[132]

In practice, the main constraint on the Chief Executive's selection of the principal officials so far has been a desire to maintain a high degree of continuity with the previous administration. This meant all of the first three Chief Executives of the Hong Kong SAR Government retained the majority of the incumbents in their posts. That trend started on 1 July 1997 when, anxious to send a message of continuity to Hong Kong and the world, the Central People's Government accepted Tung Chee Hwa's nomination for reappointment as principal officials of the Hong Kong SAR of almost all those holding top positions in the colonial administration.[133]

---

129. See Phila Siu and Tony Cheung, "Leung Chun-ying says restructuring scheme is postponed, not dead", *South China Morning Post*, 18 Oct 2012.
130. See Hong Kong SAR Government, "Central Government appoints new HKSAR team", 28 June 2012.
131. See further note 12 earlier in this chapter and the accompanying text.
132. See further notes 109–110 in Chapter 4.
133. See further "2.6: Through Train" in Chapter 2. The only incumbent not reappointed as a principal official of the Hong Kong SAR Government was Attorney General Jeremy Mathews, a British lawyer who served as the colonial administration's chief law officer until 1 July 1997. His post was renamed Secretary for Justice in order to comply with the wording of the Hong Kong Basic Law, and filled by Hong Kong lawyer Elsie Leung after that date.

That meant the Hong Kong SAR Government initially inherited the century-old system long practised under British rule in Hong Kong, where civil servants filled all the top governmental posts. Most were career civil servants who had spent virtually all their working lives in the Hong Kong Government. Even the small number of outsiders recruited to fill more specialist posts, such as government lawyers, were required to become civil servants for the duration of their work in government. It also meant these civil servants performed a much wider range of tasks than their counterparts in other countries: not only the administrative tasks of policy implementation and running government, which are the standard responsibility of civil servants in much of the world; but also, in the absence of an elected government, politically charged tasks such as policy making, or formulation, which are normally left to elected politicians in most democratic countries.[134]

The Hong Kong Basic Law appears to have been written with the continuation of this system of government by civil servants in mind. Drafted before the introduction of popular elections in Hong Kong,[135] it reflected the system of government which existed in Hong Kong at that time, drawing no distinction between those tasks which are normally carried out by civil servants in other countries and those which are usually left to politicians to perform. Policy formulation and implementation, for instance, are bracketed together in the same sentence of a list of the Hong Kong SAR Government's powers (Article 62(1)).

Even before 1 July 1997, this system was becoming outdated with the advent of a more political environment. Hong Kong civil servants, like their counterparts elsewhere in the world, are supposed to be politically neutral. This neutrality can be summarized as meaning that civil servants do not express their own political opinions or engage in partisan political activities, instead loyally implementing government policies regardless of whether they agree with them or not.[136] This neutrality is one reason why civil servants in most countries generally are not asked to undertake political tasks such as policy formulation. In Hong Kong, it was just about possible to reconcile civil servants' unusual policy-making role with their continued political neutrality in the relatively unpoliticized climate that existed before the early 1990s. Until then, the government dominated a largely unelected Legislative Council and could be confident of securing support for its

---

134. See further Richard Cullen, Xiaonan Yang and Christine Loh, "Executive Government" in Chan and Lim (eds.), *Law of the Hong Kong Constitution* (see note 117) at 252, describing this system as "something of a hybrid part presidential part parliamentary and embedded in a colonial tradition".
135. See further "2.3: Drafting the Hong Kong Basic Law" in Chapter 2.
136. For a fuller definition of civil service neutrality, see Kenneth Kernaghan and John W. Langford, *The Responsible Public Servant* (The Institute for Research on Public Policy, 1990) at 56–57, cited in Cheung Chor Yung, "The Quest for Good Governance: Hong Kong's Principal Officials Accountability System" (2003) 1(2) *China, An International Journal* 249, 267.

policies without any need for civil servants to engage in partisan tasks such as political lobbying.[137]

Such neutrality became increasingly difficult to sustain after the advent of the first popular elections for some seats in the legislature in 1991, and the resulting introduction of party politics in Hong Kong.[138] As the Legislative Council became increasingly politicized, senior civil servants were forced to assume a much more political role and actively lobby politicians and political parties. This new reality was publicly acknowledged for the first time in 2001 when one such civil servant, then Secretary for Security Regina Ip, suggested that it was now necessary for top officials in the Hong Kong SAR Government to "have declared their political stance".[139]

This system of government exclusively by civil servants also became increasingly unsustainable for another reason after 1 July 1997. Criticism of the Hong Kong Government had been relatively muted throughout much of colonial rule. Expectations, it seems, were never particularly high of a government dominated by colonial administrators from half a world away who were often perceived, perhaps unfairly, as having a limited understanding of Hong Kong and its culture.[140] After the establishment of the Hong Kong SAR, it quickly became clear that the Hong Kong public expected much more of a government whose senior echelons were now entirely drawn from long-term Hong Kong residents who spoke the local language.

That was reflected in widespread public dissatisfaction at a series of blunders shortly after 1 July 1997, which reflected poorly on the performance of the then civil service-led government. These included the problem-plagued opening of Hong Kong International Airport at Chek Lap Kok in 1998, for which the then Chief Secretary for Administration had to publicly apologize.[141] In 2000, a series of problems involving public housing culminated in the revelation of a "short-piling scandal", which led to the demolition and rebuilding of two defectively constructed blocks.[142]

As we will see later in this chapter, the Legislative Council played a major role in focussing public anger on the public officials involved in both these incidents.[143] Using

---

137. See, however, the argument that even prior to the early 1990s the idea of civil service neutrality in Hong Kong was a "myth" by Ian Scott, "Civil Service Neutrality in Hong Kong" in Haile K. Asmerom and Elisa P. Reis (eds.), *Democratization and Bureaucratic Neutrality* (Macmillan, 1996) at 277.
138. The first major pro-democracy political party, the United Democrats of Hong Kong, was formed in 1991. This was followed in 1992 by the first major pro-Beijing political party, initially called the Democratic Alliance for the Betterment of Hong Kong.
139. Jimmy Cheung, "Regina Ip breaks civil service ranks to declare political stance", *South China Morning Post*, 1 May 2001.
140. In fact, colonial administrators, serving as what are known as administrative officers, were required to pass a Chinese language test. Those who rose to senior positions had often lived and worked in Hong Kong for several decades.
141. Chief Secretary for Administration Anson Chan, "Speech at LegCo's motion debate", Legislative Council, 3 Feb 1999.
142. Lillian Kwok, "Firm to be sued for piling faults", *The Standard*, 4 July 2000.
143. See further notes 298 and 300 later in this chapter and the accompanying text.

its power to summon witnesses under Article 73(10) of the Hong Kong Basic Law,[144] the council launched investigations that documented the mistakes made by individual officials.[145] The Legislative Council also broke new ground by passing in June 2000, for the first time in its history, a motion of no confidence in two public officials implicated in the short-piling scandal. But because this type of motion is not binding, the Legislative Council could not force those implicated to resign and one of the two censured, career civil servant Tony Miller, refused to do so.[146]

This civil servant's refusal to resign even after being publicly censured intensified popular dissatisfaction with the system of government inherited from the colonial era, under which there was no easy way to force top officials in the Hong Kong Government to take responsibility for even serious errors. In other countries, politically appointed government officials often resign—or are fired—for policy mistakes. But this is less often true of civil servants, who generally enjoy a higher degree of job security, and can only be removed after exhaustive disciplinary procedures. Civil servants are, in any case, not supposed to be responsible for policy blunders,[147] which are the responsibility of elected officials. But in Hong Kong's outdated system of government during the early years of the Hong Kong SAR, there were no politically appointed officials who could take responsibility for policy blunders, a situation which had become unsustainable and in need of reform.

The short-piling scandal, and resulting censure of the officials involved, led directly to the first big change in the structure of the Hong Kong Government after 1 July 1997.[148] Although implemented without amending the Hong Kong Basic Law, this was arguably a bigger change to Hong Kong's governmental structure than some of those which occurred at the time of the 1 July 1997 handover and the introduction of the Hong Kong Basic Law.

Since 2002, it is no longer correct to refer to the Hong Kong SAR Government as a government led by civil servants. Instead, most principal officials are hired on short-term contracts for the same duration as the term of office of the Chief Executive who nominates

---

144. For more on the extent of this power, see further notes 295–297 later in this chapter and the accompanying text.
145. See further notes 298 and 300 later in this chapter and the accompanying text.
146. The other public official censured, Housing Authority Chair Rosanna Wong, resigned a few days before the vote in the Legislative Council. Unlike Miller, she was not a civil servant or formally part of the Hong Kong SAR Government since the Housing Authority, although owned by the government, is run as a separate body.
147. Secretary for Constitutional Affairs Michael Suen subsequently warned that the idea of holding civil servants "responsible and expecting them to step down in the case of serious policy failures is incompatible with the underlying philosophy of a permanent civil service". See "Speech in Respect of the Government Motion on the Accountability System for Principal Officials at the Legislative Council Meeting", Legislative Council, 29 May 2002.
148. In his annual policy address, less than four months after the June 2000 motion of censure, the Chief Executive said he accepted "aspirations for the SAR Government to be subjected to a higher degree of accountability", and began the review of the governmental structure that was to result in the introduction of a new system.

them to the Central People's Government for appointment.[149] It has also become common to see some principal officials lose their jobs when a new Chief Executive takes office, although a desire for continuity means that many others are usually offered fresh contracts by the incoming Chief Executive.

Gone is the near iron rice bowl of job security that formerly protected the civil servants who held these top posts, no matter how poor their work. Now the short-term contracts for most principal officials expressly provide that they can be terminated at any time. In theory, and occasionally in practice, that makes it possible to remove top officials from office if they make serious policy mistakes, or become deeply unpopular with the Hong Kong public.

Although still far from decisive, popularity with the Hong Kong public has become one factor in determining who is appointed to these posts. That was expressly acknowledged by Chief Executive Leung Chun Ying immediately after his election victory in March 2012.[150] It was also evident in the July 2012 appointment as Chief Secretary for Administration of Carrie Lam, who was then the most popular official in the Hong Kong SAR Government, replacing the widely disliked incumbent Stephen Lam.[151]

This major change in the job nature of most principal officials in Hong Kong has made their role a little more similar to government ministers in other countries, such as the UK. That is why the system of principal officials in Hong Kong is sometimes referred to as a "ministerial system", although that is not its official title.

The restructuring of the Hong Kong SAR Government in 2002 to introduce this system, which is officially known as the Principal Officials Accountability System (or POAS), is an example of the breadth of the Chief Executive's powers. Arguably such a major change to the governmental structure should have been implemented through amending the Hong Kong Basic Law. Although it does not expressly require top positions in the Hong Kong SAR to be filled by civil servants, as we saw earlier[152] the Hong Kong Basic Law appears to have been drafted with the intention of maintaining the previous system of government led by civil servants. But, given the difficulties of amending the Hong Kong Basic Law,[153] the Hong Kong SAR Government opted for the simpler expedient of arguing that since the Hong Kong Basic Law does not explicitly prohibit the introduction of a new system of political appointees, there was no need for any such amendment.[154] In a further illustration of the breadth of the Chief Executive's

---

149. This system applies to the Chief Secretary for Administration, Financial Secretary, Secretary for Justice, and their deputies if any, as well as Directors of Bureaux. It does not, however, apply to the five principal officials who head the Hong Kong Police, Customs and Excise, Immigration Department, Independent Commission Against Corruption and Audit Commission respectively.
150. Peter So and Tanna Chong, "We're in same boat, C.Y. tells bureaucrats", *South China Morning Post*, 28 March 2012.
151. See Phila Siu, "Low popularity put paid to Lam, says veteran", *The Standard*, 8 May 2012.
152. See further page 117.
153. These difficulties are described further in "7.5: Amendment" in Chapter 7.
154. For an excellent criticism of this argument, see Christine Loh and Richard Cullen, "Politics Without Democracy: A Study of the New Principal Officials Accountability System in Hong Kong" (2003) 4 *San Diego International Law Journal* 127, 133–134.

powers, this fundamental change to the governmental structure was implemented largely without legislation.[155]

The ministerial system has brought more outsiders into the upper echelons of the Hong Kong SAR Government than ever before. For instance, the first round of appointments in 2002 saw three business executives, a university vice-chancellor and a prominent doctor join the Hong Kong SAR Government.[156] Given the previous dominance of top posts by career civil servants, it was not surprising that many civil servants initially continued to be chosen as principal officials under the ministerial system—although, in most cases, they are now required to quit the civil service before they can take up a principal official post.[157] That was especially true from 2005 to 2012, when Donald Tsang, himself a former career civil servant, served as Chief Executive.[158]

Over time, the role of such civil servants is likely to lessen. In 2012, only five of Leung Chun Ying's 15 initial nominations to those principal official posts that form part of the political appointment system were former civil servants.[159] Since 2008, a major expansion of the accountability system has brought a further influx of outsiders into the Hong Kong SAR Government. Beneath the top tier posts originally designated as politically appointed posts, was added a second layer of politically appointed Under Secretaries (or deputy "ministers"), and a third layer of politically appointed Political Assistants.[160] This makes the Hong Kong system at least superficially similar to that in the UK, where there are also three layers of political appointees at the top of the government.[161]

Although the expansion of the accountability system was initially unpopular with the Hong Kong public, due to controversies over the high salaries and foreign passports of

---

155. Ibid. at 139. The government introduced subsidiary legislation to implement some of the resulting changes, but rejected demands for a new ordinance which would have had to be more fully vetted by the Legislative Council.
156. For a table detailing the first round of appointments, see Ma, *Political Development in Hong Kong* (see note 7) at 67.
157. One exception is the Secretary for the Civil Service, who must be from the civil service, to which he or she can return at the end after serving as a principal official. In addition, some of the five principal official posts not included in the accountability system (see note 149) continue to be filled by civil servants.
158. Ten of the politically appointed posts were filled by former career civil servants after Tsang's re-election as Chief Executive in 2007.
159. However, this included the two top posts of Chief Secretary for Administration and Financial Secretary, which were filled by Carrie Lam and John Tsang respectively. See Hong Kong SAR Government, "Central Government appoints new HKSAR team", 28 June 2012.
160. For the background to this expansion of the accountability system, see Hong Kong SAR Government, *Report on Further Development of the Political Appointment System* (Oct 2007).
161. These are Secretary of State, Minister of State and Parliamentary Under Secretary. See Hong Kong SAR Government, *Consultation Paper on Further Development of the Political Appointment System* (July 2006). This notes (at para. 2.05) the similarity with the system in the UK.

many appointees,[162] the effect has been to open up positions in the upper echelons of the Hong Kong SAR Government to a broader spectrum of Hong Kong society than had ever been the case before. Cullen, Yang and Loh (2011) note: "For all its faults, the POAS helped create Hong Kong's first batch of full-time politicians in the Executive branch."[163] The initial round of appointments in 2008 to these two additional political tiers saw journalists, academics, business executives and financiers brought into the Hong Kong SAR Government. When the posts fell vacant upon the change of Chief Executive in 2012, more than 1,100 people submitted job applications, including some members of the pro-democracy camp.[164] In a further sign of the opening up effect of the expanded accountability system, Christine Loh, a former legislator from the democratic camp and Chief Executive of a prominent think tank, was among those subsequently appointed as Under Secretaries.[165]

The crucial question which remains unclear is to what extent this system of political appointments genuinely deserves its official title as an "accountability system". While Hong Kong's ministers, deputies and assistants may superficially resemble their counterparts in Western democracies such as the UK, in those countries political appointees are accountable to an electorate and may be forced to resign under certain circumstances.

In the UK, this long ago evolved into a constitutional convention (a term used to describe rules of government which are not necessarily written down in law)[166] that ministers should resign to take responsibility for the mistakes of their departments, although

---

162. The Hong Kong SAR Government argued that the new appointees are not covered by the provision in Article 61 of the Hong Kong Basic Law which bans principal officials from holding foreign passports. However, as a result of the controversy, several appointees voluntarily chose to give up their foreign passports. See further Cullen, Yang and Loh, "Executive Government" (see note 134) at 263–264.
163. Ibid. at 268.
164. Two members quit the Democratic Party and Civic Party respectively to apply for politically appointed posts. See Alex Lo, "Democrats' 'desertion' a welcome move", *South China Morning Post*, 15 June 2012.
165. Loh served as a legislator in 1992–95 and 1998–2000, and as Chief Executive of the Civic Exchange think tank from its founding in September 2000 until her appointment as Under Secretary for the Environment in September 2012. She was reportedly nominated by the Chief Executive in 2007 for the more senior post of Secretary for Environment, but her appointment was rejected by the Central People's Government. See further note 110 in Chapter 4.
166. Constitutional law scholars disagree on how to define conventions. One view, originally put forward by the 19th-century English jurist A.V. Dicey, takes a broad view of constitutional conventions as referring to all kinds of customs or practices, which may not be necessarily considered binding. A rival view, proposed by another renowned English jurist, Sir Ivor Jennings, defines constitutional conventions more narrowly as limited to those practices which are supported by constitutional principles and generally considered as binding, with political sanctions often being invoked if they are breached. For a summary of these two views and their possible application to Hong Kong, see Lo, *The Dynamics of Beijing–Hong Kong Relations* (see note 116) at 110–113.

this convention is not always honoured in practice.[167] In Hong Kong, such resignations would have been unthinkable prior to the introduction of a ministerial system in 2002, since most top posts were then held by career civil servants.

Since then there have been mixed signals about whether such a convention is emerging in Hong Kong. Barely a year after the introduction of the ministerial system, two political appointees did resign in July 2003. One, Financial Secretary Antony Leung, admitted he was resigning to take responsibility for a serious mistake, his failure to disclose his purchase of a Lexus saloon shortly before he raised the tax on luxury cars in the annual budget.[168] The other, Secretary for Security Regina Ip, insisted her resignation was for purely personal reasons.[169] However, it came after she had become extremely unpopular with the Hong Kong public for her handling of legislation to implement the requirement in Article 23 of the Hong Kong Basic Law for Hong Kong to have comprehensive laws protecting national security. Indeed her resignation was listed in a government paper on the first year of the new system of political appointments.[170]

These were followed by a third resignation in 2004, after then Secretary for Health, Welfare and Food Yeoh Eng Kiong was severely criticized in a Legislative Council inquiry report for his mishandling of the outbreak of Severe Acute Respiratory Syndrome (or SARS) that killed 299 people a year earlier.[171] Unlike the two previous resignations, this one was explicitly described by the then Chief Executive as being a product of the accountability system.[172] In 2007, former senior civil servant Fanny Law resigned after being criticized by a commission for inquiry for interfering with academic freedom,[173] although this resignation fell into a slightly different category as it did not involve the actions of a political appointee.[174]

---

167. Such resignations have become rare in recent years, with ministers sometimes instead blaming their subordinates and refusing to resign. See Barnett, *Constitutional and Administrative Law* (see note 2) at 288–291.
168. See Lo, *The Dynamics of Beijing–Hong Kong Relations* (see note 116) at 126.
169. See Regina Ip, "Statement by Secretary for Security", Press Conference, 16 July 2003.
170. Hong Kong SAR Government, *Twelve-month Report on the Implementation of the Accountability System for Principal Officials* (July 2003) at para. 44.
171. Legislative Council, *Report of the Select Committee to Inquire Into the Handling of the Severe Acute Respiratory Syndrome Outbreak by the Government and the Hospital Authority* (July 2004).
172. See Hong Kong SAR Government, "CE announces resignation of SHWF", 7 July 2004.
173. The commission concluded that Law had attempted to silence critics of the government's educational policies at the Hong Kong Institute of Education, an accusation which Law denied. See Scarlett Chiang, "Law quits ICAC", *The Standard*, 21 June 2007. The Hong Kong SAR Government subsequently brought a judicial review action, which successfully challenged some aspects of the commission's findings. See *Secretary for Justice v Commission of Inquiry Re Hong Kong Institute of Education* [2009] 4 HKLRD 11, 26–27.
174. Although Law was Commissioner of the Independent Commission Against Corruption at the time of her resignation, this is one of the small number of principal official posts which do not form part of the system of political appointments (see note 149). In addition, the alleged misconduct for which she resigned had occurred earlier, while she was serving in another civil service post.

But there were also many other episodes when principal officials refused to resign after making serious mistakes, or becoming unpopular with the Hong Kong public.[175] As a result, a decade after its introduction, there remained deep scepticism in many quarters in Hong Kong about just how much of a change the system of political appointments had really brought.[176]

Such scepticism centres especially around the most crucial difference between the system of political accountability in Hong Kong and similar systems that exist in democratic countries. In those countries, the appointees are accountable to the electorate—or, at least, a leader who is democratically elected. In Hong Kong, by contrast, principal officials are not accountable to the public, but instead only to a Chief Executive currently returned through a small-circle selection process. That prompts Cullen, Yang and Loh (2011) to conclude that the Hong Kong system is not one which "provides political accountability in a democratic sense" and, rather than solving the issue of lack of accountability, has instead "highlighted the issue of accountability as never before".[177]

That, however, like so many other problems is one which may be at least partially resolved if 2017 does bring the election of a Chief Executive through a system of universal suffrage that is accepted as a genuine contest. If that happens, it will then be possible to argue that Hong Kong's unaccountable officials are, at least, accountable to a leader who is popularly elected.

5.5 Elected Legislature

Under Article 66 of the Hong Kong Basic Law, the Legislative Council is Hong Kong's legislature. Under Article 73, it is given several important responsibilities, including the power to enact, amend and repeal laws, approve taxation, public spending and the annual budget, and monitor the work of the executive branch of the government. But the powers of the Legislative Council are also subject to significant restrictions under the Hong Kong Basic Law, as we will see later in this chapter.

Unlike the other branches of Hong Kong's political structure, all members of the Legislative Council are elected. Indeed, this is expressly required under Article 68(1) of the Hong Kong Basic Law. Like much of the content of the Hong Kong Basic Law, the reasons for this provision date back to the Sino-British Joint Declaration, the document

---

175. One early example was the "penny stocks fiasco" in late July 2002, which saw more than HK$10 billion wiped off the value of local stocks because of the mishandling of a consultation paper on possible changes to how some of them should be listed. The two politically appointed officials involved both refused to accept responsibility for the blunder. For a full description of this incident, see Cheung, "The Quest for Good Governance" (see note 136) at 261–263.
176. See, for example, Tanna Chong and Tony Cheung, "The buck stops where?" *South China Morning Post*, 22 June 2012.
177. Cullen, Yang and Loh, "Executive Government" (see note 134) at 259.

that provides the historical origins for the Hong Kong Basic Law.[178] In the last days of the negotiations over this 1984 agreement on Hong Kong's future, Britain secured a crucial concession from China over the composition of the future Hong Kong SAR's legislature. In a final exchange of messages between the two countries' foreign ministers,[179] less than two weeks before the full text of the Joint Declaration was formally accepted by both sides and made public,[180] China agreed to the insertion of a provision in the Joint Declaration pledging that the future legislature of the Hong Kong SAR "shall be constituted by elections".[181]

Agreed at a time when China was anxious to meet a self-imposed deadline for completing its agreement with Britain,[182] it seems unlikely the consequences of this commitment were carefully considered. Shiu (2010) notes that, while the provision for an elected legislature was agreed without much dispute, "the changes brought about by an elected legislature to executive-legislative relations were not fully taken into account".[183] One top Chinese official subsequently said this provision was only included in the Joint Declaration for the sake of good relations with Britain.[184]

In any case, the practical meaning of this commitment was soon diminished when China adopted a broad meaning of the term "elections". It was made clear that this did not necessarily entail the sort of direct elections (or universal suffrage) that are commonly used to elect legislatures in many other countries, where almost everyone of voting age who meets certain basic nationality or residency requirements[185] is entitled to vote. Various alternative forms of "elections" involving much smaller circles of voters were put forward by Chinese officials and their advisers and incorporated into the first draft of the Hong Kong Basic Law, Annex II of which listed four possible alternative methods of

---

178. See further "2.2: Sino-British Joint Declaration" in Chapter 2.
179. Robert Cottrell, *The End of Hong Kong: The Secret Diplomacy of Imperial Retreat* (John Murray, 1993) at 171.
180. At an initialling ceremony between representatives of the two governments in Beijing on 26 September 1984.
181. Annex I(I) of the Joint Declaration. A second provision was also agreed at the same time that the future Hong Kong SAR Government "shall be accountable to the legislature". This accountability was subsequently limited to four specific areas in Article 64 of the Hong Kong Basic Law.
182. Cottrell, *The End of Hong Kong* (see note 179 above) at 160.
183. Shiu, "Executive-Legislative Relations Under the Basic Law" (see note 11) at 273.
184. This was Xu Jiatun, director of the Hong Kong branch of the Xinhua News Agency and China's de-facto top representative in Hong Kong from 1983 to 1990. Cited in Ming K. Chan and David J. Clark, *The Hong Kong Basic Law: Blueprint for "Stability and Prosperity" Under Chinese Sovereignty* (Hong Kong University Press, 1991) at 11.
185. In many countries, only citizens of that country are eligible to vote. In Hong Kong, eligibility to vote is instead defined, under Article 26 of the Hong Kong Basic Law, in terms of being a Hong Kong permanent resident. For more on permanent residency, also known as right of abode, see further note 17 in Chapter 8 and the accompanying text.

"electing" the Legislative Council—none of which involved all seats in the council being elected through universal suffrage.[186]

The issue rapidly became one of the most controversial ones during the drafting of the Hong Kong Basic Law, especially after the Tiananmen crackdown of 4 June 1989 increased popular pressure in Hong Kong for a more rapid pace of democratization. This was summed up by the Omelco consensus, in which members of the Executive and Legislative Councils called for all seats in the legislature to be chosen through universal suffrage by 2003.[187] Beijing rejected this but, following secret negotiations with Britain,[188] did agree to a slightly faster pace of democratization than it had been previously prepared to concede.[189]

The result was that Annex II(I) of the Hong Kong Basic Law and an accompanying decision of the National People's Congress[190] contained explicit provisions outlining a gradual increase in the percentage of members of the Legislative Council chosen through universal suffrage until 2007. This continued the slow process of democraticising the method by which Hong Kong legislators are chosen, through the use of a confusing variety of different selection methods, which had begun shortly after the conclusion of the Sino-British Joint Declaration in 1984.

Prior to the signing of this 1984 agreement with China, Britain had shown relatively little interest in the introduction of democracy in Hong Kong, apart from a few elections for lower-level tiers of government. For many decades the Urban Council, which was responsible for such mundane matters as public health and street cleaning, was the only body with any elected members.[191] After 1982, it was joined by a system of District Boards (since renamed District Councils) which exercised primarily advisory functions at a local level, and also included some elected members.[192]

At the highest level of government, it was a different story. At that time, all members of the Legislative Council were still appointed by the Governor, so assuring the colonial administration that it was unlikely ever to face any serious opposition to enacting its

---

186. "The Draft Basic Law of the Hong Kong SAR of the PRC (for solicitation of opinions)", reproduced in Peter Wesley-Smith and Albert Chen (eds.), *The Basic Law and Hong Kong's Future* (Butterworths, 1988) at 329–369.
187. For more on the Omelco consensus, and its rejection by China, see Mark Roberti, *The Fall of Hong Kong* (John Wiley, 1996) at 268–275.
188. Percy Cradock, *Experiences of China* (John Murray, 1999) at 229–233.
189. See further note 67 in Chapter 2 and the accompanying text.
190. Decision of the NPC on the Method for the Formation of the First Government and the First Legislative Council of the Hong Kong SAR (4 April 1990).
191. The Urban Council evolved in 1936 from the Sanitary Board, a body first created in 1887. Elections were first introduced in 1952, using a highly restrictive franchise to elect two seats. In 1983, this was expanded so that half of the council's seats were elected by most adults living in Hong Kong's urban areas. See further Miners, *The Government and Politics of Hong Kong* (see note 42) at 155–168.
192. Ibid. at 169–177.

legislative proposals.[193] That only began to change after the 1984 signing of the Joint Declaration, with its recognition that Hong Kong's legislature, in future, would be "constituted by elections".

The first step in this direction came within a year, with the introduction of two forms of indirect elections for around 40% of the seats in the Legislative Council in 1985. These were functional constituencies, in which voting is usually confined to members of a particular profession or sector of Hong Kong society, and an electoral college limited to several hundred voters.[194]

The next stage was the introduction of the first direct elections for 30% of the seats in the Legislative Council in 1991. Subsequent elections in 1995 saw the percentage of legislators returned through direct elections increase very slightly to 33%. More significantly, the abolition of appointments by the government meant that, for the first time, all legislators were now chosen through one form of election or another, with the remaining two-thirds being chosen through functional constituencies and an electoral college.[195] China objected to the expansion of the electorate for some of these functional constituencies and the composition of the electoral college, and the National People's Congress Standing Committee declared the arrangements for the 1995 elections to be in breach of the Hong Kong Basic Law.[196] The result was that the Legislative Council returned through these elections was dissolved on 1 July 1997. It was replaced, for the first year after the resumption of sovereignty, by an unelected body known as the Provisional Legislature, prompting an unsuccessful legal challenge which argued this breached the provision in Article 68(1) of the Hong Kong Basic Law requiring the legislature to "be constituted by election".[197]

---

193. This failure to act earlier to introduce elections for the Legislative Council, even as other British colonies around the world were moving in the direction of greater democracy, was traditionally justified on the grounds that such elections might anger Beijing and precipitate conflicts between pro- and anti-communist elements. See further Steve Tsang, *Democracy Shelved: Great Britain, China, and Attempts at Constitutional Reform in Hong Kong, 1945–1952* (Oxford University Press, 1988) for the leading account of some of the abortive attempts to introduce greater representative government during earlier decades.
194. See further "2.4: Battles and Changes" in Chapter 2 for more on the 1985 elections, and Britain's subsequent acceptance of Chinese demands not to introduce further major changes in the 1988 elections.
195. This electoral college chose 10 out of 60 members of the Legislative Council in the 1995 and 1998 elections, and six out of 60 members of the Legislative Council in the 2000 elections. In the 1995 elections, the electoral college consisted of members of the District Boards. In the 1998 and 2000 elections, the electoral college consisted of members of the Election Committee also responsible for choosing the Chief Executive.
196. Decision of the Standing Committee of the NPC on the Proposal Advanced by Zheng Yaotang and Other Thirty-two Deputies to the NPC (31 Aug 1994).
197. See further note 94 in Chapter 2 and the accompanying text for more on these arguments, which were ultimately dismissed by the Court of Final Appeal in *Ng Ka Ling v Director of Immigration* (1999) 2 HKCFAR 4, 43–45.

In a further step back for public participation in elected government, the Urban Council, together with another newer body known as the Regional Council, which exercised similar functions in the New Territories,[198] were abolished altogether at the end of 1999.[199] This brought to an end the democratic involvement at a local level allowed by these two bodies,[200] despite another unsuccessful court challenge which sought to argue the continued existence of these councils was required under the Hong Kong Basic Law.[201]

Democracy of a sort did return to the Legislative Council, with regular elections being held from 1998 onwards, in accordance with the requirement under Article 68(1) of the Hong Kong Basic Law that the legislature "be constituted by election". But, for many years, the functional constituencies used in these elections were much smaller than those which had existed during the final elections under British rule.

Evidently nervous about allowing too fast a pace of introduction of popular elections, Annex II(I) of the Hong Kong Basic Law and an accompanying decision of the National People's Congress[202] set strict limits on the percentage of seats in the Legislative Council which could be chosen through direct elections prior to 2007. This started at 33% for the elections held in 1998, rising to 40% for the next elections in 2000, and ultimately 50% for the elections held in 2004. That left an important role for functional constituencies in filling the gap. Ever since the Hong Kong Basic Law came into force, functional constituencies have always been used to fill 50% of the seats in the Legislative Council in every election so far.[203] Most of these functional constituencies consist of small-circle elections with the number of voters limited to a few thousand—or, sometimes, even only a few hundred.

However, Annex II(III) of the Hong Kong Basic Law is more flexible about the method for electing the Legislative Council after 2007. Indeed, the original wording of the Hong Kong Basic Law seemed to leave the matter entirely in Hong Kong's hands. Annex II(III) provides that "if there is a need" to make changes to the election methods for the legislature from 2007 onwards, that can be done with the support of two-thirds

---

198. See further Miners, *The Government and Politics of Hong Kong* (see note 42) at 165–167.
199. Under the Provision of Municipal Services (Reorganization) Ordinance (Cap. 552). On 1 July 1997, the Urban and Regional Councils had been already temporarily replaced by provisional bodies, because of China's disagreement with the electoral methods used for both bodies. These were also abolished at the end of 1999.
200. For more on the political impact of the abolition of these two bodies, see Ma, *Political Development in Hong Kong* (see note 7) at 147–149.
201. In *Chan Shu Ying v Chief Executive of the HKSAR* [2001] 1 HKLRD 405, 424, citing Article 97 of the Hong Kong Basic Law which allows the establishment of district organizations. The court held that Article 97 did not create a constitutional obligation to establish such organizations, or to give them any administrative powers.
202. Decision of the NPC on the Method for the Formation of the First Government and the First Legislative Council of the Hong Kong SAR (4 April 1990).
203. The remaining seats not filled by direct elections during the 2000 and 2004 Legislative Council polls were instead chosen by members of the Election Committee that also chose the Chief Executive.

of legislators and the consent of the Chief Executive. According to the original wording of Annex II(III), China's direct involvement was supposed to be limited to the formality of reporting any changes to the National People's Congress Standing Committee "for the record".[204] Importantly, there is no mention in Annex II(III) of any requirement to seek the Standing Committee's approval for such changes. That stands in contrast to an otherwise similar provision in Annex I(7) of the Hong Kong Basic Law, which does require the Standing Committee's approval of any changes to how the Chief Executive is elected after 2007.[205]

This small—but significant—difference between the wording of Annexes I and II of the Hong Kong Basic Law is strongly indicative that Beijing was initially open-minded about the possibility that universal suffrage might be introduced for the election of all seats in the Legislative Council immediately after 2007 and, in any event, expected this to happen more quickly than any move towards universal suffrage for the selection of the Chief Executive. That conclusion is reinforced by earlier promises from Chinese officials that the issue of how the Legislative Council should be chosen from 2007 onward was "a question to be decided by Hong Kong itself".[206]

But, as described earlier in this book,[207] the huge public protest against proposed national security legislation on 1 July 2003 prompted Beijing to adopt a more interventionist approach towards Hong Kong affairs, and the loss of Hong Kong's right to decide by itself how its legislature is elected became the first example of this new policy.

In April 2004, at its own initiative, the National People's Congress Standing Committee issued an interpretation of Annexes I(7) and II(III) of the Hong Kong Basic Law.[208] This interpretation added a crucial additional requirement that must be fulfilled before any changes can be made to the election system for either the Chief Executive or the Legislative Council, a requirement not stated in the original text of the Hong Kong Basic Law. In both Annex I(7) and Annex II(III), there are references to "if there is a need" to make changes. The Standing Committee interpreted this to mean that before even starting the process of amending the electoral system that is listed in both annexes, there is now an additional requirement that the Standing Committee must first decide whether or not there is such a need to make any changes at all, based on a report from Hong Kong's Chief Executive.

---

204. The same term also appears elsewhere in the Hong Kong Basic Law. For example, Article 90(2) requires the appointment and removal of some top judges to be reported to the Standing Committee "for the record", and there has never been any suggestion this gives them any power of approval. See further note 186 in Chapter 4 and the accompanying text.
205. See further note 111 earlier in this chapter.
206. Statement from China's Foreign Ministry in 1994, cited by Frank Ching, "Be consistent", *South China Morning Post*, 30 March 2004. However, former Basic Law drafter Shao Tianren argues this statement has been misinterpreted. See "HK election needs approval from central government", *China Daily*, 9 Feb 2004.
207. See further note 95 in Chapter 4 and the accompanying text.
208. The Interpretation by the Standing Committee of the NPC of Article 7 of Annex I and Article III of Annex II to the Basic Law of the Hong Kong SAR of the PRC (6 April 2004).

That 2004 interpretation is an important example of the very different role that interpretation of laws plays under the Chinese legal system, where it can be used to add words into laws which were not originally there, a task more normally accomplished through amendment of the law in the common law world.[209] Discussing the Standing Committee's interpretation of the words "if there is a need" in this way, Crawford (2005) notes that, in the common law world, "an ordinary interpretation of the text would not attribute any special significance to these words, and would certainly not regard them as imposing a separate prior requirement of approval".[210]

Nonetheless, that was the effect of the 2004 interpretation, which gave the Standing Committee a power of veto over any changes to how the Legislative Council is elected, a power it did not possess in the original text of the Hong Kong Basic Law. This power has since emerged as an important means of imposing strict limits on the extent of any changes to Hong Kong's electoral system, since the Standing Committee's involvement at the beginning of the process of making changes allows it to lay down preconditions as to what type of changes can be even considered.

In two subsequent decisions, the Standing Committee used this power to ban the introduction of universal suffrage for the election of all seats in the Legislative Council polls held in 2008 and 2012 respectively.[211] Crucially, those two decisions also set strict limits on the extent of any changes, by requiring that 50% of the seats in both the 2008 and 2012 elections must continue to be returned through functional constituencies. It is this latter requirement that did much to fuel the arguments over changes to Hong Kong's electoral system in recent years. By freezing in place the requirement for 50% of the Legislative Council to be elected through functional constituencies, which has been in place since 2004, this made it very difficult for members of the pro-democracy camp— who strongly oppose the existence of functional constituencies—to support any changes, so prompting several bitter battles on the issue.

It also led to a fundamental change in strategy as to how to implement universal suffrage in Hong Kong. As we saw earlier, it had initially seemed likely that universal suffrage would be introduced first for elections to all seats in the Legislative Council, since the original text of the Hong Kong Basic Law made it easier to implement universal suffrage for these polls than for those for the Chief Executive. But the 2004 interpretation reversed the situation, with the Standing Committee's subsequent insistence that 50% of seats on the Legislative Council must continue to be elected through functional

---

209. See further notes 7–10 in Chapter 7 and the accompanying text, for more on the very different system of interpretation that exists under the Chinese legal system.
210. James Crawford, *Rights in One Country: Hong Kong and China* (Faculty of Law, University of Hong Kong, 2005) at 13.
211. See Decision of the Standing Committee of the NPC on Issues Relating to the Methods for Selecting the Chief Executive of the Hong Kong SAR in the Year 2007 and for Forming the Legislative Council of the Hong Kong SAR in the Year 2008 (26 April 2004) and Decision of the Standing Committee of the NPC on Issues Relating to the Methods for Selecting the Chief Executive of the Hong Kong SAR and for Forming the Legislative Council of the Hong Kong SAR in the Year 2012 and on Issues Relating to Universal Suffrage (29 Dec 2007).

constituencies, creating a major new obstacle to any changes to how the Legislative Council is elected.

Under the principle of "resolving the simple issues before the difficult ones",[212] in December 2007 then Chief Executive Donald Tsang recommended to the Standing Committee that universal suffrage be implemented for elections for the Chief Executive before those for the Legislative Council.[213] That recommendation was accepted by the Standing Committee in its subsequent decision which, as we saw earlier, gave permission for the possible introduction of universal suffrage for the election of the Chief Executive in 2017.[214] The Standing Committee's December 2007 decision also held "that after the Chief Executive is selected by universal suffrage, the election of the Legislative Council of the Hong Kong Special Administrative Region may be implemented by the method of electing all of the members by universal suffrage".[215] What this means is that the Standing Committee appears to have agreed in principle that universal suffrage can be used to elect all members of the Legislative Council in the 2020 polls, since these are expected to be the first such elections which will be held after 2017. However, as we will see in the next section, it remains unclear whether this will lead to the abolition of functional constituencies after that date.

5.6 Functional Constituencies

Although functional constituencies play such a crucial role under the Hong Kong Basic Law, filling half of the seats in every election to the Legislative Council since 1995, nowhere in the Hong Kong Basic Law does it explain what a functional constituency actually is. As we will see shortly, that leaves room for flexibility. Indeed, the concept of what constitutes a functional constituency has evolved considerably in recent years, and may well continue to do so in future.

A 1999 statement from the Hong Kong SAR Government well captures the traditional concept of functional constituencies, as the term has been applied in most elections to the Legislative Council so far. It describes the aim of functional constituencies as being "to ensure that the economic and professional sectors which are substantial and of importance in the community are represented in the legislature".[216]

---

212. See Hong Kong SAR Government, *Public Consultation Report on the Green Paper on Constitutional Development* (Dec 2007) at 44.
213. Chief Executive Donald Tsang, *Report on the Public Consultation on Constitutional Development and on Whether There is a Need to Amend the Methods for Selecting the Chief Executive of the Hong Kong SAR and for Forming the Legislative Council of the Hong Kong SAR in 2012* (Dec 2007) at paras. 15–16.
214. See note 108 earlier in this chapter and the accompanying text, for more on this aspect of the Standing Committee's December 2007 decision.
215. See para. 1 of the Standing Committee's December 2007 decision.
216. Hong Kong SAR Government, *Administration's Responses to Points raised on 7 May by Members of the Bills Committee on the Legislative Council (Amendment) Bill 1999* (21 May 1999).

Seen in that context, the role of functional constituencies in some senses resembles that of the Election Committee which has been used to choose the Chief Executive so far. As we saw earlier, this committee of several hundred members is divided into four equal sectors, two of which are allocated to the business community and members of the major professions.[217] In both cases, the aim of these small-circle electoral methods favoured under the Hong Kong Basic Law seems to be to ensure the representation of groups who are economically important but numerically small when compared to Hong Kong's population as a whole, and so unlikely to be so strongly represented through a system of popular elections.[218]

That means important business groups such as the Hong Kong General Chamber of Commerce and Chinese General Chamber of Commerce are given their own functional constituencies. So too are many major professions such as lawyers, engineers, accountants, medical practitioners, teachers, architects, surveyors and planners, and social workers.

But the list of professions fortunate enough to be allocated a functional constituency of their own defies easy description, having grown up in an apparently ad-hoc manner as new seats were added at successive elections. Young and Law (2006) note that there is "no single coherent theory that explains what sectors and functions" have their own functional constituency at present, and that the present arrangements seems to be "driven more by political forces and constitutional development than by principled and informed decision making".[219] To take just a couple of examples, several major industries—such as storage, communications, sanitary and environmental services—lacked functional constituencies of their own in recent elections.[220] By contrast, the agricultural and fisheries industry, which is far less economically significant in modern-day Hong Kong, has had its own functional constituency since 1998. With only around 160 voters, the agricultural and fisheries seat also has the distinction of having one of the smallest franchises of any functional constituency in Hong Kong.

Not all functional constituencies are allocated to business and professional groups. Labour unions have their own functional constituency, which currently returns three legislators. So too does the Heung Yee Kuk, which represents the indigenous inhabitants of the New Territories, although this only returns one legislator. Another is chosen by members of the District Councils, the predominantly elected bodies that exercise mainly advisory functions at a local level throughout Hong Kong.

---

217. See further note 86 earlier in this chapter and the accompanying text.
218. See, however, the strong criticism of how far the present functional constituency system achieves this goal in Simon N.M. Young and Anthony Law, "Privileged to vote: Inequalities and anomalies of the FC system" in Christine Loh and Civic Exchange (eds.), *Functional Constituencies: A Unique Feature of the Hong Kong Legislative Council* (Hong Kong University Press, 2006) at 59–109.
219. Ibid. at 104.
220. Ibid. at 75.

The origins of the functional constituency system date back more than 150 years, almost to the beginning of British rule in Hong Kong. From the late 1840s onwards, British Governors began allowing a very few sectors of Hong Kong society (notably the expatriate business community) to nominate their own representatives for appointment as members of the Legislative Council.[221] But the representatives of these privileged sectors of Hong Kong society were still, like all other legislators prior to 1985, appointed to the Legislative Council by successive Governors, who could always reject any nominees they disliked.

As we have seen, the Joint Declaration required the legislature of the future Hong Kong SAR to be "constituted by elections".[222] As a result, in 1985, the previous informal system of the Governor appointing representatives of various sectors to the Legislative Council was replaced with a more formal and expanded system under which a much wider range of groups and sectors of society elected their own representatives directly to the Legislative Council. This marked the birth of the modern system of functional constituencies, which remains in place today.

Functional constituencies began as a way of bringing more democracy to the Legislative Council. Their introduction in the 1985 elections to the Legislative Council resulted in the first election of opposition voices to a body which had, until then, consisted entirely of government officials and other members appointed by the Governor. In particular, Martin Lee and Szeto Wah were elected to the new functional constituencies for the legal profession and education sector respectively, and went on to become leading figures in Hong Kong's pro-democracy camp for several decades.[223]

However, after their introduction in 1985, functional constituencies quickly became a way of slowing the pace of democratization in the Legislative Council. Over the next decade, the number of functional constituency seats expanded rapidly from the 12 first created in 1985 to 21 functional constituency seats in 1991. Their numbers were then further expanded to 30 functional constituency seats in 1995, comprising 50% of all seats in the Legislative Council, a percentage which has remained unchanged ever since. These functional constituencies were used to fill most of the gap left by the scrapping of appointed seats on the Legislative Council. These appointed seats had to be abolished because Article 68(1) of the Hong Kong Basic Law required a legislature "constituted by election", so making it impossible for the Hong Kong SAR Chief Executive to continue the practice that existed under British rule, whereby the colonial Governor appointed

---

221. This began with local Justices of the Peace nominating their own candidates for appointment by the Governor to the Legislative Council, and was later extended to allow the Hong Kong General Chamber of Commerce to do likewise. See Leo F. Goodstadt, "Business friendly and politically convenient — the historical role of functional constituencies" in Loh and Civic Exchange (eds.), *Functional Constituencies* (see note 218) at 43.
222. See further note 179 earlier in this chapter and the accompanying text, for more on the inclusion of this provision in Annex I(I) of the Joint Declaration during the final stages of the negotiation of this agreement.
223. See further "2.4: Battles and Changes" in Chapter 2 for more on the 1985 elections.

many members of the Legislative Council.[224] However, since China was not prepared to concede that all the appointed seats should be immediately replaced by members of the Legislative Council returned through popular elections, functional constituencies emerged as the main alternative.[225]

Under the Hong Kong Basic Law, these legislators returned through functional constituencies exercise considerable power, having what amounts to a power of veto over many measures put to a vote in the Legislative Council. Although bills proposed by the government only require the support of a simple majority of all legislators, under Annex II(II) of the Hong Kong Basic Law all motions, bills and amendments proposed by individual members of the Legislative Council can only be passed if they secure the support of two separate majorities — one among the legislators returned through direct elections,[226] and a second among the legislators returned through functional constituencies. This split voting system makes it very difficult for anything proposed by individual legislators to be passed if the government opposes it — since, although there are exceptions, on balance legislators from the functional constituencies tend to be more sympathetic to the government's stance on many issues. For instance, a study by Chaney (2004) found that functional constituency legislators tended to side with the Hong Kong SAR Government in 95% or more of votes on amendments to its bills during the period from 2000 to 2004.[227] The importance of this split voting system as a means of helping the government get its measures through the legislature is highlighted by the fact that the National People's Congress Standing Committee, in two successive decisions, has mandated that this voting system must remain unchanged until at least 2016.[228]

Since the franchise for most functional constituencies remains extremely small, the practical effect of this split voting system is to give functional constituency legislators, many of whom have been returned by only a few thousand voters, the power to veto measures put forward by their counterparts in the geographical constituencies, who often have been returned by more than one thousand times as many voters. Those geographical constituencies — Hong Kong Island, Kowloon East, Kowloon West, New Territories East

---

224. By contrast, the wording of the 1987 Sino-Portuguese Joint Declaration on the Question of Macao made no mention of a wholly elected legislature, and so the Basic Law of the Macao SAR allows its Chief Executive to continue appointing some members of Macao's legislature.
225. The number of appointed seats decreased from 22 in 1985, to 20 in 1988, and finally 18 in 1991. These remaining appointed seats were then abolished altogether in 1995.
226. The wording of Annex II(II) actually requires the support of a majority of legislators returned through both direct elections and the Election Committee. However, the role of the Election Committee in electing some members of the Legislative Council ended after the 2000 elections. See further note 195 earlier in this chapter.
227. See the analysis of voting on committee-stage amendments in Christopher Chaney, *The Hong Kong Executive Authorities' Monopoly on Legislative Power: Analysis of the Legislative Council's Second Term Voting Records* (Centre for Comparative and Public Law, University of Hong Kong, Occasional Paper No. 13, June 2004).
228. These are the Standing Committee's decisions of 26 April 2004 and 29 December 2007. See further note 211 earlier in this chapter.

and New Territories West—all have electorates of at least 400,000 and, in some cases, more than twice that number.[229] By contrast, 22 functional constituencies had fewer than 10,000 registered voters in recent years, and 12 of these had fewer than 1,000.[230]

The small size of these seats is exacerbated by the corporate voting system still used in elections for most functional constituencies. This means that the right to vote in those seats is mostly allocated to corporate bodies (hence the name, corporate voting) and other organizations in the sectors of society represented by those constituencies.[231] In some cases, a few individuals who are members of these organizations may also be allowed to vote in a personal capacity. But these constitute only a fraction of those working in these industries. Young and Law (2006) cite the example of how only a tiny percentage of the more than 14,000 people working in financial services in Hong Kong are eligible to vote in the functional constituency allocated to this industry: "There seems to be no reasonable explanation for saying that 80 persons in the sector should be privileged with the right to vote in the FC while the remaining 99.5% should not."[232]

Not surprisingly, those seats which use predominantly corporate voting tend to be among the smallest of all the functional constituencies. None have more than 5,000 voters and 10 have fewer than 1,000 voters, including four with fewer than 200 voters.[233] In many cases, there is no election at all. In the 2012 elections, for example, 16 candidates were returned unopposed because there was only one candidate for each of these seats.[234]

Corporate voting for functional constituencies was briefly abolished from 1995 to 1997 as part of a package of electoral reforms introduced by Chris Patten, the last British Governor of Hong Kong.[235] However, this was strongly opposed by Beijing and reversed after 1 July 1997, with the result that corporate voting remains the system for electing many functional constituencies today. Attempts to challenge corporate voting in the courts have met with little success. In *Chan Yu Nam v Secretary for Justice*,[236] the

---

229. In 2012, the number of registered electors for the geographical constituencies ranged in size from 437,967 in Kowloon West to 987,330 in New Territories West. See Hong SAR Government, "2012 final registers of electors published today", 18 July 2012.
230. Figures as of 2012. See Hong Kong SAR Government, "Voter Registration Statistics: Functional Constituency", 18 July 2012.
231. However the actual votes are still cast by individuals who are authorized representatives (or agents) of those corporate bodies and other organizations. See further Young and Law, "Privileged to vote" (see note 218) at 93–102, for an explanation of the corporate voting system and some of the problems which it creates.
232. Ibid. at 85.
233. Figures as of 2012. See further Hong Kong SAR Government, "Voter Registration Statistics: Functional Constituency", 18 July 2012.
234. See further Hong Kong SAR Government, "287 validly nominated candidates for Legislative Council elections", 7 August 2012.
235. See, however, Young and Law, who argue [in "Privileged to vote" (see note 218) at 94] that what was actually abolished during this period was agency voting (under which corporate bodies and other organizations appoint agents to vote on their behalf) rather than the system of corporate voting as a whole.
236. [2012] 3 HKC 38. An application for leave to appeal the case was subsequently dismissed by the Court of Final Appeal (unrep., FAMV 39 and 40/2011, [2012] HKEC 94).

Court of Appeal dismissed an argument that corporate voting contravenes Article 26 of the Hong Kong Basic Law on the right to vote, a provision which makes no mention of corporate bodies or other organizations being allowed to exercise this right.[237] Instead the court described corporate voting as having played a "central role" in the development of a system of functional constituencies where the main emphasis was on representing the interests of "economic and other stakeholders" rather than those of individuals.[238] Noting that corporate voting is indirectly mentioned in two annexes,[239] the court held that it was clear the Hong Kong Basic Law intended to provide for the "continuation beyond 1997 of corporate participation" in elections.[240]

Not all functional constituencies have such a tiny electorate. A smaller number have long been elected through a system of individual voting, which means that everyone in the sector of society represented by that constituency is eligible to vote, as opposed to simply representatives of corporate bodies. These functional constituencies tend to be far larger, and more inclined to elect representatives from the pro-democracy camp. For instance, the seat for the education sector, which is the largest functional constituency allocated to a specific profession, has more than 90,000 voters. For many years, this one seat constituted nearly 40% of the total functional constituency electorate.[241]

Periodic attempts have been made to expand even further the numbers allowed to vote in some seats so as to try to transform the functional constituency system required under the Hong Kong Basic Law into something closer to universal suffrage. The first such attempt was the creation of nine huge functional constituencies[242] — with a potential total electorate of 2.7 million — as part of the controversial electoral reforms introduced by Governor Chris Patten for the 1995 elections to the Legislative Council.[243] These

---

237. Article 26 states that: "Permanent residents of the Hong Kong Special Administrative Region shall have the right to vote and the right to stand for election in accordance with law." However in *Chan Yu Nam* (at 66) the Court of Appeal noted that: "Article 26 does not say that 'only' permanent residents may take part in voting in Hong Kong."
238. *Chan Yu Nam* at 64.
239. Annexes I(3) and II(I)(2) both refer to "corporate bodies" in the English text of the Hong Kong Basic Law. The term used in the Chinese text （法定團體） is less clear on this point, but still indicates that some statutory bodies have the right to vote. See *Chan Yu Nam* at 68–69, and the more detailed discussion in the Court of First Instance on this point in *Chan Yu Nam v Secretary for Justice* [2010] 1 HKC 493, 519.
240. *Chan Yu Nam* (CA) at 68. For more on the purposive approach adopted by the court during this case, see further notes 52–54 in Chapter 7 and the accompanying text.
241. It was followed by the health services functional constituency which, with more than 35,000 voters, constituted a further 16% of the total functional constituency electorate during the 2008 Legislative Council polls. See further Electoral Affairs Commission, *Report on the 2008 Legislative Council Election Held on 7 September 2008* (4 Dec 2008) at 105.
242. The creation of nine additional functional constituency seats was necessary in 1995 because the total number of such seats grew from 21 to 30 to fill part of the gap created by the abolition of all remaining appointed seats.
243. See Governor Christopher Patten, "Our Next Five Years: The Agenda for Hong Kong", Policy Address, 7 Oct 1992, at 38–39.

grouped together often diverse industries (for example, one seat was allocated to what appeared to be a catch-all category of community, social and personal services) and gave everyone working in them a vote.[244] The effect was that most of those excluded from voting in previous functional constituency polls acquired the right to vote, although some groups (such as housewives, retirees and students) were still excluded.

Those huge functional constituencies proved short-lived, since China's opposition ensured that the legislature elected through this expanded franchise was dissolved on 1 July 1997 and replaced by a temporary, and unelected, body known as the Provisional Legislature.[245] It enacted legislation either abolishing, or greatly reducing, the size of the nine new functional constituencies created in 1995.[246] The effect was that the total number registered to vote in all the functional constituencies shrank to 138,984 in the first elections under the Hong Kong Basic Law, barely a tenth of the 1.15 million who had registered to vote in the much larger functional constituencies used in the 1995 polls.[247]

Although short-lived, the huge functional constituencies that briefly existed during the final years of British rule illustrated an important point. This was that the lack of any formal definition of functional constituencies in the Hong Kong Basic Law leaves scope for introducing more democracy simply by redefining what constitutes a functional constituency, providing there is the political will to do so. Such political will was absent in 1995, largely due to a lack of trust between Britain and China at that time. But it ultimately proved present in 2010, when agreement was reached on the introduction of even larger functional constituencies than the ones Beijing had so strongly opposed during the final years of British rule. This broke the political deadlock over making changes to how the Legislative Council is elected.

As we have already seen, the two decisions issued by the Standing Committee requiring that 50% of seats in the Legislative Council continue to be chosen through functional constituencies have so far placed a major obstacle in the path of agreeing on any changes.[248] That 50% requirement meant that any increase in the number of seats returned through popular elections must be accompanied by a corresponding increase in the number of functional constituencies. That was something members of the democratic camp repeatedly proved unwilling to accept, as increasing the number of functional constituencies seemed like a move in the opposite direction from their preferred path of

---

244. The other eight new functional constituencies also grouped together a wide variety of occupations. They were: 1) primary production, power and construction; 2) textiles and garments; 3) manufacturing; 4) import and export; 5) wholesale and retail; 6) hotels and catering; 7) transport and communication; and 8) financing, insurance, real estate and business services.
245. See further note 94 in Chapter 2 and the accompanying text, for more on the Provisional Legislature and the controversy over its legality under the Hong Kong Basic Law.
246. Six of the nine were abolished altogether, while three (textiles and garments; import and export; and wholesale and retail) were retained in name, but drastically reduced in size so that each had fewer than 5,000 voters.
247. See "Appendix 5" in Loh and Civic Exchange (eds.), *Functional Constituencies* (see note 218).
248. See further note 211 earlier in this chapter and the accompanying text.

abolishing such constituencies altogether. Since Annex II(III) of the Hong Kong Basic Law stipulates that the support of two-thirds of legislators is required for any changes to how the Legislative Council is elected, change is all but impossible without the support of at least some members of the pro-democracy camp which, in all elections so far, has managed to control at least one-third of the seats in the legislature.

That obstacle stymied one attempt by the Hong Kong SAR Government in 2005 to make changes to how the Legislative Council is elected. At that time, strenuous opposition from the pro-democracy camp—largely over the proposed addition of the five additional functional constituency seats chosen by members of the District Councils in order to balance the introduction of five additional directly elected seats—meant the government failed to secure the support of the necessary two-thirds of legislators.[249] A similar fate almost befell a second attempt by the Hong Kong SAR Government in 2010, when it once again sought to introduce initially similar changes to how the Legislative Council is elected.[250] That prompted a furious response from the pro-democracy camp, with five of its members infuriating Beijing by resigning from their seats in the legislature; these five legislators then portrayed the resulting by-elections as a "referendum" on the future of functional constituencies.[251]

But other members of the pro-democracy camp indicated they were willing to compromise, in return for a major expansion in the size of the electorate for these five new functional constituency seats. Once it became clear this was the only way to break the political deadlock over the issue, Beijing eventually agreed to allow this.[252] The result was that the electorate for the five additional functional constituency seats—which was originally only going to consist of around 400 members of District Councils—was massively expanded to include every voter in Hong Kong who did not already have the right

---

249. For an account of the Hong Kong SAR Government's 2005 proposal, which also sought to enlarge the size of the Election Committee that selects the Chief Executive to 1,600 members, and its failure to secure sufficient support in the Legislative Council, see Albert H.Y. Chen, "The Fate of the Constitutional Reform Proposal of October 2005" (2005) 35 *HKLJ* 537–543.
250. These closely resembled the defeated 2005 proposals, although the increase in the size of the Election Committee (to 1,200 members) was smaller than proposed in 2005, while appointed members of the District Councils were (unlike in 2005) to be excluded from voting for the five new functional constituency seats. For more on the similarities and differences between the two proposals, see Albert H.Y. Chen, "Constitutional Developments in Autumn 2009" (2009) 39 *HKLJ* 751, 760–765.
251. These May 2010 by-elections, popularly known as the "Five District Referendum", saw more than 500,000 voters support the complete abolition of functional constituencies. However they were unpopular with much of the Hong Kong public, resulting in a low voter turnout of only 17.1%. See further Albert H.Y. Chen, "An Unexpected Breakthrough in Hong Kong's Constitutional Development" (2010) 40 *HKLJ* 259, 260.
252. Chen (2010) at 261–264. Annex II was then amended to add five more functional constituency and five more directly elected seats. See Amendment to Annex II to the Basic Law of the Hong Kong SAR of the PRC Concerning the Method for the Formation of the Legislative Council of the Hong Kong SAR and Its Voting Procedures (28 Aug 2010).

to vote in another functional constituency, or around 3.2 million people in all. In the 2012 Legislative Council elections, more than 1.6 million people turned out to vote for these new seats, with the successful candidates all receiving more than 220,000 votes.[253] Often called "super functional constituencies", these seats do retain some of the traditional characteristics of a functional constituency, since the right to nominate candidates and stand for election is limited to members of District Councils.[254] But in terms of who is allowed to vote in these super functional constituencies, they go further than the huge functional constituencies which China so strongly opposed in 1995, since even the few groups (such as housewives, retirees and students) denied the right to vote during that previous attempt to expand the franchise for functional constituencies are now eligible to vote.

That marks a major shift in what China accepts as constituting a functional constituency. But Chen (2010), who initially doubted such huge seats would be compatible with the Standing Committee's requirement for 50% of the Legislative Council to be elected through functional constituencies, notes "there is nothing to prevent the Central Government and the HKSAR Government from adopting a more open, flexible and creative interpretation of functional constituencies".[255]

The result is that Hong Kong now has a system of "one person, two votes", since the right to vote in a functional constituency is no longer confined to certain sectors of the population, but instead enjoyed by all the same people who also have the right to vote in geographical constituencies. Chen (2010) describes this as a system of "*quasi*-universal suffrage",[256] and it is a development likely to have important implications for the debate over what form full universal suffrage will take when it is eventually introduced for the election of all seats in the Legislative Council.

As we saw earlier, the Standing Committee has ruled that universal suffrage can be introduced for elections to all seats in the Legislative Council after the introduction of universal suffrage for the selection of the Chief Executive. This has been interpreted to mean any time from the Legislative Council elections in 2020 onwards. Although the Standing Committee has not yet indicated what form such universal suffrage should take, there have been repeated hints that this may involve a continuing role for functional constituencies.

---

253. See Hong Kong SAR Government, "LegCo Election results: District Council (second)", 10 Sept 2012.
254. The restrictions on who can nominate candidates and stand for election were cited by the Hong Kong SAR Government as evidence that these five seats are still functional constituencies rather than elections through universal suffrage. See Secretary for Justice Wong Yan Lung, "Speech at Press Conference on Constitutional Reform Package", Press Conference, 21 June 2010.
255. See Chen, "An Unexpected Breakthrough in Hong Kong's Constitutional Development" (see note 251) at 264 and 268, explaining his initial doubt was based on the fact that these super functional constituencies were very different from the concept of functional constituencies that Beijing had always previously adopted.
256. Ibid. at 265.

In an important speech in 2010, Qiao Xiaoyang, then Deputy Secretary General of the Standing Committee recognized for the first time that universal suffrage requires a system of not just universal voting rights, but also equal voting rights.[257] This recognition that universal suffrage must include equal voting rights implies an acceptance that functional constituencies cannot continue in their present form once universal suffrage is introduced.[258] That is not necessarily because the present system fails to provide for universal voting rights, something which has been arguably achieved since the introduction of super functional constituencies for the 2012 Legislative Council polls gave every elector a second vote. But the present system still fails to provide for equal voting rights, since the votes of the 1.6 million who voted in the super functional constituencies in the 2012 election have only a fraction of the value of those in other functional constituencies, where the franchise is still limited to a few thousand voters.[259]

That does not necessarily imply functional constituencies might not continue to exist in some modified form although, at a minimum, they would clearly have to be modified to provide for more similarly sized constituencies. In that same 2010 speech, Qiao praised functional constituencies as "conducive to the balanced participation of various strata and sectors".[260] He also seemed to indicate a continuing role for such constituencies in some form under a future system of universal suffrage, asserting that it is internationally recognized that "reasonable restrictions" can be imposed on the right to vote, with different countries allowed to adopt different approaches to implementing universal suffrage in accordance with their respective circumstances.[261]

It is difficult to see how any form of functional constituencies—even if modified to provide for more equally sized constituencies—could be compatible with the International Covenant on Civil and Political Rights, one of the most important international human rights treaties that continues to apply in Hong Kong. Article 25(b) of the ICCPR explicitly provides that the right to "universal and equal suffrage" applies not only to the right to vote but also the right to stand for election.[262] As such, it seems

---

257. Ibid. at 262.
258. This point has been explicitly acknowledged by the Hong Kong SAR Government on several occasions. See, for example, the comments by Chief Secretary for Administration Henry Tang in Legislative Council, *Official Record of Proceedings, Hong Kong Hansard* (14 April 2010) at 6688.
259. This point is made strongly by the Hong Kong Bar Association in its commentary on Qiao's speech. See Hong Kong Bar Association, *Hong Kong: A Step Taken in Development of Political System* (July 2010).
260. See "Qiao Xiaoyang's explanation of the NPC's decision", *South China Morning Post*, 30 Dec 2007.
261. For an English translation of Qiao's comments on this point, see Lo, *The Hong Kong Basic Law* (see note 114) at 308.
262. Article 25(b) refers to the right of citizens (which, in the Hong Kong context, should be interpreted as meaning permanent residents) to enjoy without distinction or unreasonable restrictions, the right: "To vote and to be elected at genuine periodic elections which shall be by universal and equal suffrage and shall be held by secret ballot, guaranteeing the free expression of the will of the elector."

functional constituencies could only comply with this provision in the ICCPR if almost anyone was allowed to stand for election to them, which would defeat the whole purpose of functional constituencies.

Although the continued application of the ICCPR to Hong Kong is specifically provided for in Article 39(1) of the Hong Kong Basic Law, the Hong Kong SAR Government argues this does not mean the requirements in Article 25(b) of the ICCPR apply to Hong Kong. That argument is based on a reservation (or exception) entered by Britain when the ICCPR was first applied to Hong Kong in 1976.[263] Since there were no elections in Hong Kong at that time, Britain noted that Article 25(b) of the ICCPR did not apply to Hong Kong "in so far as it may require the establishment of an elected Executive or Legislative Council in Hong Kong". The Hong Kong SAR Government argues that reservation originally entered by Britain in 1976 continues to apply today, and means there is no requirement under the ICCPR for Hong Kong to hold elections or, if it does, to use universal and equal suffrage.[264]

However, the United Nations Human Rights Committee, which monitors compliance with the ICCPR by countries around the world, strongly disagrees. It argues that, while this reservation meant there was no requirement to introduce such elections, once they are held—as has been the case in Hong Kong since 1985—they must still comply with the requirement to hold any elections under a system of universal and equal suffrage, which it is generally acknowledged that the existing system of functional constituencies fails to do.[265]

While the view of the United Nations Human Rights Committee on this point won some support from the Hong Kong courts in the case of *Lee Miu Ling v Attorney General (No 2)*,[266] more recently the Court of Appeal seems to have assumed that the reservation relating to universal suffrage remains in force in the case of *Chan Yu Nam v Secretary for*

---

263. See further notes 48–49 in Chapter 8 and the accompanying text, for more on the initial application of this international treaty to Hong Kong, and the reservations entered by Britain at that time.
264. For a detailed, and critical, account of the Hong Kong SAR Government's position on this issue, See C.L. Lim, "Right to Vote and Right to Political Participation" in Chan and Lim (eds.), *Law of the Hong Kong Constitution* (see note 117) at 853–859.
265. Ibid. at pages 853–854. The UN Human Rights Committee has made this point repeatedly since 1995. See, for example, UN Human Rights Committee, *Concluding Observations of the Human Rights Committee on the Fourth Periodic Report Relating to Hong Kong of the United Kingdom and Northern Ireland* (9 Nov 1995), reproduced in (1995) 5 HKPLR 641, 644, which found that Hong Kong's electoral system also breached three further provisions prohibiting discrimination in the ICCPR (Articles 2(1), 3 and 26).
266. (1995) 5 HKPLR 181, 197–198. In the High Court, Justice Keith described an equivalent provision in Section 13 of the Hong Kong Bill of Rights Ordinance (Cap. 383) as a "dead letter". Although the case was appealed to the Court of Appeal (in (1995) 5 HKPLR 585) it did not take issue with Justice Keith's reasoning on this point.

Justice.[267] In any event, ever since the National People's Congress Standing Committee's interpretation of Annex II(III) of the Hong Kong Basic Law in 2004,[268] it is clear that the ultimate power to decide on how Hong Kong's legislature is elected lies with the Standing Committee. Judging from the hints dropped so far, it seems the Standing Committee envisages some continued role for functional constituencies.[269]

5.7 How Powerful a Legislature?

Hong Kong has an executive-led system of government in which the Chief Executive and the executive authorities exercise more sweeping powers than the other branches of the political structure. But, as we saw earlier, under the system of separation of powers prescribed in the Hong Kong Basic Law,[270] the legislature exercises important checks and balances over these powers that often impose significant constraints on the executive's freedom of action.

While its powers are severely limited in some areas, the reality since 1 July 1997 is that overall the Legislative Council has probably acted as a more significant constraint on the actions of the Chief Executive and the executive branch than the drafters of the Hong Kong Basic Law originally envisaged. Shiu (2007) argues that "the executive branch has been passive and weak after Hong Kong's return to China", while the Legislative Council has "acted like a sovereign parliament" and exceeded the powers explicitly granted to it under the Hong Kong Basic Law.[271]

The powers explicitly granted to the Legislative Council are set out in Article 73 of the Hong Kong Basic Law, with the most significant being its financial and legislative powers. As we saw earlier,[272] the legislature exercises tight control over the government's budget, taxation and public expenditure (Articles 73(2)–(3)). Many government requests to raise or spend funds require individual approval, giving the Legislative Council tantamount to a power of "line-item veto" that goes further than the power legislatures in

---

267. [2012] 3 HKC 38. The point was not directly at issue in this case, which concerned the legality of the system of corporate voting used in many functional constituencies (see notes 237–240 earlier in this chapter and the accompanying text). Nonetheless the Court of Appeal made repeated references to the reservation (at 50, 52, 60–61 and 68) without any suggestion that it no longer applies. When the case was heard in the Court of First Instance, Justice Cheung stated that it was "unnecessary to express any view" on this point ([2010] 1 HKC 493, 527).
268. See further note 208 earlier in this chapter and the accompanying text.
269. In addition to Qiao's praise of functional constituencies in his 2010 speech (see note 260), see also the comments of Zhang Xiaoming, Deputy Director of the Hong Kong and Macao Affairs Office of the State Council, that functional constituencies should be retained because they represent sectors of society responsible for 90% of Hong Kong's gross domestic product. See Carrie Chan, "Future of functional seats disputed", *The Standard*, 31 Dec 2007.
270. See further "5.2: Separation of Powers" earlier in this chapter.
271. Shiu, "Executive-Legislative Relations Under the Basic Law" (see note 11) at 270–271.
272. See further note 53 earlier in this chapter and the accompanying text.

many other countries exercise over government finances. This power acts as a constraint on the executive's policy-making powers in the financial arena with the government sometimes having to abandon important policy initiatives, such as a sales tax, because there was no prospect of securing support for them in the legislature.[273]

Under the Hong Kong Basic Law, the powers explicitly granted to the Legislative Council in the financial arena are primarily negative powers. That means the legislature has the power to negate (or veto) financial proposals put forward by the executive. But it is not allowed to respond in a more positive manner, by putting forward alternative proposals of its own on financial issues. Instead, all bills on public expenditure must come from the Hong Kong SAR Government (Article 74) and any motions regarding revenues or expenditure require the approval of the Chief Executive (Article 48(10)), so denying the Legislative Council any direct policy-making role on financial matters. As we saw earlier, the legislature can sometimes circumvent this restriction, by using its veto power to force the Hong Kong SAR Government to put forward revised proposals that are more to the legislature's liking, so indirectly inserting itself into the policy-making process in the financial arena.[274]

Such occasional exceptions aside, this power to act mainly in a negative manner (by rejecting government proposals) rather than in a positive manner (by putting forward alternative proposals of its own) acts as a significant constraint on the role of the legislature. Much the same applies to some of the Legislative Council's other most important powers under the Hong Kong Basic Law, so helping to explain some of the difficulties that the executive and the legislature have experienced in working together since 1 July 1997. Li (2001) suggests that confining the Legislative Council's powers to this negative role "unavoidably leads to an irresponsible legislature" since, deprived of the power to initiate (and take responsibility) for policy proposals of their own, legislators tend to focus on making "unrealistic demands of the government of the day".[275]

Another important area where the Legislative Council's powers are confined primarily to the negative is its power under Article 73(1) of the Hong Kong Basic Law to "enact, amend or repeal laws". As we saw earlier, the fact that under the system of separation of powers, only the Legislative Council can make primary legislation (and the Chief Executive is not given any such law-making powers) can sometimes impose serious limitations on the executive's ability to govern.[276] Although the Legislative Council passes the vast majority of bills presented by the executive, there have been some striking exceptions. One of the most famous of these was when then Chief Executive Tung Chee Hwa was forced to withdraw the controversial National Security (Legislative Provisions) Bill in 2003, which sought to implement provisions in Article 23 of the Hong Kong Basic

---

273. See further note 55 earlier in this chapter and the accompanying text.
274. See further note 56 earlier in this chapter and the accompanying text.
275. Li Pang-kwong, "The Executive-Legislature Relationship in Hong Kong: Evolution and Development" in Joseph Cheng (ed.), *Political Development in the HKSAR* (The Chinese University Press, 2001) at 94.
276. See further notes 58–64 earlier in this chapter and the accompanying text.

Law, after it became clear there was not enough support in the Legislative Council to secure its enactment.[277]

The Legislative Council's powers are confined to the negative in this area (i.e., deciding whether to accept or reject bills put forward by the executive) because under the Hong Kong Basic Law it is virtually impossible for individual legislators to introduce their own bills, known as private members' bills, into the legislature on most issues. Under Article 74, they are forbidden from introducing any bills relating not only to public expenditure but also political structure and the operation of the government. Even private members' bills relating to any other aspects of "government policies"—a broad term which can cover almost any issue—require the prior written approval of the Chief Executive, which is rarely given.[278]

In practice these restrictions cover the vast majority of possible bills, and have put a stop to the situation that existed in the mid-1990s, when private members' bills were subject to fewer restrictions[279] and played an important part in shaping the policy agenda. For instance, proposals which originated as private members' bills from former legislator Anna Wu in 1994 were subsequently adopted by the government and resulted in the passage of Hong Kong's first anti-discrimination laws and the creation of the Equal Opportunities Commission.[280] In 1995–97, immediately before the Hong Kong Basic Law came into force, 50 private members' bills were introduced into the Legislative Council, and 22 of these became law.[281] By contrast, in 1998–2000, just two private members' bills managed to overcome the restrictions in Article 74 of the Hong Kong Basic Law and succeed in being tabled for discussion in the Legislative Council.[282]

The Hong Kong SAR Government has even tried to argue that Article 74 of the Hong Kong Basic Law prevents legislators from moving amendments to government bills without the Chief Executive's consent.[283] However, this restriction has not been

---

277. See further notes 67–70 earlier in this chapter and the accompanying text.
278. For a rare example of such permission being given, see Angela Li, "Tung supports first private members' bill", *South China Morning Post*, 8 June 2000.
279. The main restriction prior to 1 July 1997 was a "charging effect" restriction. This meant legislators needed express authorization from the Governor to introduce private members' bills or amendments "the object or effect of which may be to dispose of or charge any part" of public revenue within Hong Kong. See Clause XXIV(2) of the Hong Kong Royal Instructions 1917–1993.
280. The Sex Discrimination Ordinance (Cap. 480) and Disability Discrimination Ordinance (Cap. 487) were enacted in 1995, and the Equal Opportunities Commission was established the following year to implement both these ordinances and the Family Status Discrimination Ordinance (Cap. 527), which was enacted in 1997.
281. Andrew Cheng Kar-foo, "Lawmakers who can't make law", *South China Morning Post*, 4 August 2001.
282. Ibid.
283. On the grounds that otherwise legislators could use such amendments to achieve what they are not allowed to do directly through private members' bills. See Legislative Council Secretariat, *Procedure in Dealing With the Introduction of Members' Bills as Provided in Article 74 of the Basic Law and the Interpretation of Article 48(10) of the Basic Law* (22 July 1998) at para. 8.

accepted by the Legislative Council[284] which, under Article 75(2) of the Hong Kong Basic Law, has the power to write its own rules of procedure governing how such bills are handled, among other matters. But, in practice, the split voting system laid down in Annex II(II) of the Hong Kong Basic Law makes it very difficult for most such amendments to be passed. This system means such amendments must secure the support of a majority of legislators elected through functional constituencies, in addition to a majority of the legislators returned through direct elections.[285] Since the majority of legislators from the functional constituencies are generally more inclined to side with the government, such amendments rarely secure enough votes to pass under the split voting system. For instance, from 2000 to 2004, only two of the 41 amendments proposed by individual legislators were passed, compared with 171 of the 173 amendments proposed by the Hong Kong SAR Government.[286]

However, although amendments proposed by legislators are rarely passed, the power to put forward such amendments can still have an important impact. In 2012, radical pro-democracy legislators began using this power as a filibustering technique, proposing more than 1,300 amendments to a bill which they strongly opposed.[287] Discussion of these amendments paralysed the work of the legislature for several weeks, until the Legislative Council President exercised his powers under the council's Rules of Procedure to bring the discussion to a premature end.[288]

One area where the Legislative Council has succeeded in exercising powers that go beyond those explicitly granted to it under the Hong Kong Basic Law is in holding the executive accountable for its actions and, especially, its mistakes. Under the Sino-British Joint Declaration, the executive is supposed to be accountable to the legislature.[289] But

---

284. Ibid. at para. 21. However, the Legislative Council did voluntarily agree to continue the more limited "charging effect" restriction on amendments that existed prior to 1 July 1997 (see note 279). Under Rule 57(6) of the Rules of Procedure of the Legislative Council, legislators need the written consent of the Chief Executive before they can introduce any amendment "to dispose of or charge any part of the revenue or other public moneys of Hong Kong". In *Leung Kwok Hung v President of the Legislative Council* [2007] 1 HKLRD 387, 405 this restriction was described as "founded on the separation of powers", since it is the role of the executive to make proposals on how public funds should be spent.
285. For more on the power that the split voting system places in the hands of functional constituency legislators who are often elected by a very small number of voters, see further page 134.
286. See the analysis of committee-stage amendments in Chaney, *The Hong Kong Executive Authorities' Monopoly on Legislative Power* (see note 227) at 9–11.
287. This was a bill banning legislators who deliberately resign to trigger by-elections from standing for re-election for six months, which was eventually enacted as the Legislative Council (Amendment) Ordinance (No. 12 of 2012). See further page 75.
288. See further Legislative Council President Jasper Tsang, *President's Ruling on Closing the Joint Debate at the Committee Stage of the Legislative Council (Amendment) Bill 2012* (22 May 2012).
289. Annex I(I). This was agreed during the final weeks of the negotiations over the Joint Declaration, together with another provision in the same article stating that the legislature "shall be constituted by elections". See further notes 179 and 181 earlier in this chapter and the accompanying text.

under Article 64 of the Hong Kong Basic Law, such accountability is confined to four specific areas. These are implementing laws passed by the Legislative Council that have been brought into force, seeking approval for taxation and public expenditure, presenting regular policy addresses to the legislature and answering questions raised by its members.

However, the Legislative Council has managed to use the other powers granted to it under the Hong Kong Basic Law to hold the executive accountable in ways that go far beyond the four specific areas mentioned in Article 64 of the Hong Kong Basic Law. For instance, the legislature's power to summon witnesses "to testify or give evidence" under Article 73(10) of the Hong Kong Basic Law has been used to continue the practice that began in the 1990s of establishing committees (usually known as Select Committees) to invoke the Legislative Council's special powers in investigating matters of public concern.

These special powers, contained in the Legislative Council (Powers and Privileges) Ordinance (Cap. 382), give the legislature the power to summon almost anyone in Hong Kong—including government officials—to give evidence before the council or its committees and demand the production of any required documents (Section 9), on pain of arrest (Section 12) and up to 12 months in jail if they fail to comply (Section 17). These were powers used to great effect by the Legislative Council in the final years of British rule to uncover the truth about events that the colonial administration tried to keep quiet, notably the 1994 sacking of a senior Independent Commission Against Corruption investigator Alex Tsui and the surprise retirement in 1996 of then Director of Immigration Laurence Leung.[290]

Initially, the continued exercise of such powers by the Legislative Council under the Hong Kong Basic Law seemed in doubt. The Legislative Council (Powers and Privileges) Ordinance was included in an early draft of the list of Hong Kong laws not expected to be adopted as laws of the Hong Kong SAR on the grounds that they contravened the Hong Kong Basic Law.[291] However, anxious to maximize continuity in the legal system by retaining as many laws as possible, the ordinance was dropped from the final list of laws that the National People's Congress Standing Committee ruled inconsistent with the Hong Kong Basic Law and so of no legal effect after 1 July 1997.[292]

That means the legislature still has the same sweeping powers to summon witnesses and demand the production of documents under the Legislative Council (Powers and Privileges) Ordinance. In theory, the Hong Kong Basic Law gives the Chief Executive the power to intervene to stop government officials from being forced to testify or give

---

290. See Ma Ngok, *Political Development in Hong Kong* (see note 7) at 114.
291. Connie Law, "Alarm at plan to shackle Legco", *South China Morning Post*, 16 August 1995.
292. See Decision of the Standing Committee of the NPC on Treatment of the Laws Previously in Force in Hong Kong in Accordance With Article 160 of the Basic Law of the Hong Kong SAR of the PRC (23 Feb 1997), which is described in more detail in notes 107–113 in Chapter 2 and the accompanying text.

evidence before the Legislative Council,[293] suggesting that the drafters of the Hong Kong Basic Law may not have intended to allow the legislature to exercise such broad powers to hold the executive accountable in this way. In practice, since 1 July 1997, Chief Executives seem to have found it politically impossible to prevent the legislature from summoning government officials to testify or give evidence on issues that have aroused serious public concern.[294]

The extent of this power to summon witnesses under Article 73(10) of the Hong Kong Basic Law was put to the test in the case of *Cheng Kar Shun v Li Fung Ying*,[295] where a witness who did not want to obey a summons from a Legislative Council committee unsuccessfully challenged its power to do so in the courts.[296] In a ringing endorsement of the Legislative Council's distinct powers under the separation of powers principle, Justice Cheung held that the courts, "do not, as a rule, interfere with the internal workings of the legislature".[297]

In the years since the Hong Kong Basic Law came into force, the Legislative Council has repeatedly used its powers of summoning witnesses and demanding the production of documents to force the executive to be more accountable for its mistakes. The report of the Legislative Council's first Select Committee inquiry after 1 July 1997, into the problem-plagued opening of Hong Kong International Airport at Chek Lap Kok in 1998,[298] forced a public apology from Hong Kong's then Chief Secretary for Administration.[299] The hearings held by its second Select Committee inquiry after 1 July 1997, into a "short piling scandal" and other problems involving public housing,[300] helped focus public

---

293. Article 48(11) allows the Chief Executive: "To decide, in the light of security and vital public interests, whether government officials or other personnel in charge of government affairs should testify or give evidence before the Legislative Council or its committees."
294. In 2004, then Chief Executive Tung Chee Hwa did insist that it would be "constitutionally inappropriate" for him to appear in person before a formal session of the Legislative Council Select Committee investigating the government's handling of the outbreak of Severe Acute Respiratory Syndrome a year earlier. But Tung instead agreed to hold an informal meeting with members of the Select Committee. See Patsy Moy, "Tung to meet SARS panel behind closed doors", *South China Morning Post*, 9 May 2004.
295. [2011] 2 HKLRD 555.
296. Ibid. at 611, rejecting the argument that the power granted under Article 73(10) of the Hong Kong Basic Law could only be exercised by the full Legislative Council, rather than its individual committees.
297. Ibid. at 617. For more on this case, see Chen, "Constitutional Developments in Autumn 2009" (see note 250) at 751–759.
298. Legislative Council, *Report of Select Committee to Inquire Into the Circumstances Leading to the Problems Surrounding the Commencement of the Operation of the New Hong Kong International Airport at Chek Lap Kok Since 6 July 1998 and Related Issues* (Jan 1999).
299. Chief Secretary for Administration Anson Chan, "Speech at LegCo's motion debate", Legislative Council, 3 Feb 1999.
300. Select Committee on Building Problems of Public Housing Units, established by a resolution of the Legislative Council on 7 Feb 2001.

anger on the public officials involved. This led to a motion of no confidence being passed against them, even before the inquiry's work was complete.[301] This, in turn, prompted the Chief Executive to announce a fundamental review of governmental structure[302] that resulted in the introduction of a "ministerial system", which was supposed to foster greater accountability in the upper echelons of the Hong Kong SAR Government.[303]

One of the most direct examples of the Legislative Council using its powers of investigation to impose greater accountability on the executive came when it forced the resignation of one of the Hong Kong SAR Government's principal officials in 2004. This resignation was the immediate result of the publication of the report of its third Select Committee inquiry after 1 July 1997, an investigation into the Hong Kong SAR Government's and Hospital Authority's mishandling of the outbreak of Severe Acute Respiratory Syndrome (or SARS) that killed 299 people in 2003.[304] The severe criticism in that report of then Secretary for Health, Welfare and Food Yeoh Eng Kiong's mishandling of the SARS outbreak made it politically impossible for him to remain in office, and he reluctantly resigned within days of the publication of the report.[305]

The Hong Kong Basic Law does not give the Legislative Council any direct role in the appointment or removal of government officials. Instead, under the system of executive-led government, these are supposed to be a matter solely for the Chief Executive and, in the case of the top posts known as principal official positions, the Central People's Government.[306] So the legislature's success in using its powers of investigation to occasionally play a role in this area is a striking example of how the Legislative Council can exercise an influence that appears to go beyond the powers it is explicitly given under the Hong Kong Basic Law.

The same is true of the legislature's power to "debate any issue concerning public interests" under Article 73(6) of the Hong Kong Basic Law. Such debates on motions about issues of public interest have long formed an important part of the Legislative Council's weekly meetings.[307] Like bills and amendments put forward by Legislative Council, these motions are subject to the split voting system set out in Annex II(II) of the Hong Kong Basic Law. This requires the support of a majority of the generally

---

301. See further note 146 earlier in this chapter and the accompanying text.
302. See further note 148 earlier in this chapter and the accompanying text.
303. See further pages 119–124.
304. Legislative Council, *Report of the Select Committee to inquire into the handling of the Severe Acute Respiratory Syndrome outbreak by the Government and the Hospital Authority* (July 2004).
305. See further note 172 earlier in this chapter and the accompanying text.
306. See further pages 96–97 for more on how the Chief Executive's appointment powers are seen as an important example of the executive-led system of government which China says is enshrined in the Hong Kong Basic Law.
307. Under Rule 13 of the House Rules of the Legislative Council of the Hong Kong SAR, a maximum of two such debates can normally be held during each of the council's regular meetings, although Legco's President may allow more under special circumstances.

pro-government legislators elected through functional constituencies[308] and has led to the defeat of many motions which, although they commanded the support of a majority of legislators as a whole, were unable to overcome this hurdle.[309]

Even when they are passed, these motions on issues of public interest have no binding effect and the government is free to ignore them. Nonetheless, such motions can play a role in shaping the political agenda, and sometimes have an impact on government policy making.[310] For this reason, government officials will usually attend the debates, lobby for support and respond to the issues raised.[311]

Over the years, such debates have covered a wide range of issues of public interest, from housing and social welfare problems to calls for a faster pace of democracy. In recent years, they have also been used on several occasions to express a lack of confidence in senior government officials who are seen to have committed serious mistakes. Such motions of no confidence are fundamentally different from those in countries with a parliamentary system of government, such as the UK. In the UK, the passage of a no confidence motion in the government by the House of Commons will directly lead to the government's resignation and the calling of fresh elections.[312] In Hong Kong, by contrast, such motions of no confidence are only symbolic, just like motions on any other matters of public interest debated by the Legislative Council. As we have seen, the Hong Kong Basic Law does not give the legislature any formal role in the appointment and removal of government officials, making it impossible for such motions of no confidence to have any binding effect.

---

308. For more on the split voting system, see further note 226 earlier in this chapter and the accompanying text.
309. An extreme example came in Oct 2004, when legislators from the democratic and pro-Beijing camps united behind a motion calling for a minimum wage and cap on working hours. Although this secured the support of 27 of the 30 legislators returned through geographical constituencies, it was defeated because of the opposition of 16 of the 30 legislators from the functional constituencies meant it failed to secure the necessary majority in that sector. See Legislative Council, *Official Record of Proceedings, Hong Kong Hansard* (13 Oct 2004) at 226.
310. A prominent example of this came in Dec 1991, when the Legislative Council passed a motion opposing an agreement between Britain and China on the composition of the Court of Final Appeal (see Legislative Council, *Official Record of Proceedings, Hong Kong Hansard* (4 Dec 1991) at 1012). As a result, the Hong Kong Government abandoned plans to establish the Court of Final Appeal before the handover, and the court did not ultimately come into existence until 1 July 1997. See further notes 270–274 in Chapter 6 and the accompanying text.
311. See, however, the exceptional example of two motion debates in 1995 and 1997 on the role of the Chinese Communist Party in which no government officials spoke, and none were present for the 1997 debate. See Chris Yeung, "Officials 'coy' on communists", *South China Morning Post*, 27 April 1995 and "Bid to clarify communists' role defeated", *South China Morning Post*, 6 March 1997.
312. For example, a motion of no confidence passed by the House of Commons on 28 March 1979 led to the resignation of the then Labour government and parliamentary elections which brought a Conservative government led by Margaret Thatcher to power.

Nonetheless, the political reality is that it would be difficult for any government official to stay in office after being publicly censured by the Legislative Council.[313] Then Secretary for Justice Elsie Leung was in no doubt that she would have had to resign had the legislature passed the motion of no confidence moved against her in March 1999.[314] In June 2000, then Housing Authority Chair Rosanna Wong resigned when it became clear that a motion of no confidence in her was about to be passed by the legislature. The other target of that no confidence motion, a career civil servant, refused to resign. But his refusal to resign caused further public anger and led directly to a fundamental review of the governmental structure.[315] This resulted in the introduction of a "ministerial system" under which it is sometimes easier to remove top officials from office.[316]

The Legislative Council's use of its power to debate issues of public interest in order to move motions of no confidence that place intense pressure on government officials to resign is another example of how the legislature has, in practice, succeeded in going beyond the powers explicitly granted to it under the Hong Kong Basic Law. These make no mention of the power to move such no confidence motions. It seems unlikely the drafters of the Hong Kong Basic Law ever envisaged the Legislative Council using its powers in this way. One prominent former drafter, Xiao Weiyun, has strongly argued that such no confidence motions are in breach of the Hong Kong Basic Law because they interfere with the power to appoint and remove government officials,[317] which is meant to be a matter solely for the Chief Executive and the Central People's Government. Shiu (2007) complains that such motions allow "interference with personnel power that does not belong to the legislature".[318]

However, such objections have been rare so far. Instead, even the Hong Kong SAR Government initially defended the right of the legislature to debate such no confidence motions, on the grounds that they have no legal effect.[319] The reality is that the Legislative Council's success in exercising powers beyond those explicitly granted to it under the

---

313. Even when such motions are defeated, they may still weaken beyond repair the position of the official in question. For example, then Financial Secretary Antony Leung resigned in July 2003, two months after the defeat of a motion of no confidence against him in Legco. See further note 168 earlier in this chapter and the accompanying text.
314. Personal conversation with the author. The motion was defeated by 29 votes to 21. See also Cliff Buddle, "No escaping the legal minefield", *South China Morning Post*, 12 July 2002.
315. See further notes 146–148 earlier in this chapter and the accompanying text.
316. See further pages 119–124.
317. Jimmy Cheung, "Courts and Legco 'can't interpret Basic Law'", *South China Morning Post*, 17 Jan 2004. See further, "A tribute to the guardian of Basic Law", *China Daily* (Hong Kong edition), 7 Feb 2005, following Xiao's death, explaining his view that the Legislative Council should be restricted to debating motions on issues within Hong Kong's autonomy, and not discuss other matters.
318. Shiu, "Executive-Legislative Relations Under the Basic Law" (see note 11) at 271.
319. See the comments of then Chief Secretary for Administration Donald Tsang describing Xiao's criticisms as "of reference value only", in Legislative Council, *Minutes of Special Meeting of the Legislative Council Panel on Constitutional Affairs* (28 Jan 2004) at paras. 23 and 26.

Hong Kong Basic Law met with relatively little challenge in the early years of the Hong Kong SAR.

It may, however, explain China's insistence on imposing additional restrictions on any moves towards greater democracy in the election of members of the legislature, which go beyond those explicitly stated in the Hong Kong Basic Law. Whether it is in moving no confidence motions or setting up Select Committees to hold inquiries, the driving forces are primarily those legislators who have been popularly elected. Had it not been for the split voting system in Annex II(II) of the Hong Kong Basic Law, which requires that all such motions must also secure the support of a majority of members elected through functional constituencies, there would have most likely been many more defeats for the Hong Kong SAR Government in the Legislative Council in recent years.[320] That explains China's insistence that functional constituencies must continue to elect half of the Legislative Council for now, and may be retained even under a future system of universal suffrage. It also explains the 2004 interpretation from the National People's Congress Standing Committee giving it the power to control any changes to how the legislature is elected, a power not mentioned in the original wording of Hong Kong Basic Law.[321]

When the Hong Kong Basic Law was originally drafted, with its provisions emphasizing the powers of the Chief Executive under an executive-led system of government, it must have seemed relatively harmless to allow Hong Kong to decide by itself how the relatively less powerful Legislative Council should be elected after 2007. At that stage, the general expectation appears to have been that Hong Kong was likely to have universal suffrage for the election of all seats in the Legislative Council long before Beijing allowed universal suffrage for the selection of the Chief Executive. But the legislature's success in pushing its powers beyond those explicitly permitted under the Hong Kong Basic Law has changed the picture. Now the Standing Committee exercises equally tight control over electoral methods for the Legislative Council as those for the Chief Executive. With the legislature no longer seen as so powerless, now it is the Chief Executive who can be elected by universal suffrage first, in 2017, in a belated recognition that only such popular election can provide him with the legitimacy to rule effectively.[322] The truly democratic elections for all seats in the Legislative Council will be delayed until after the Chief Executive has first been given a chance to secure a popular mandate.

---

320. An analysis by Chaney [in *The Hong Kong Executive Authorities' Monopoly on Legislative Power* (see note 227) at 15–16] found that legislators, who only succeeded in passing two of their own amendments to government bills from 2000 to 2004, would instead have succeeded with 15 amendments if there was no split voting system.
321. See further note 208 earlier in this chapter and the accompanying text.
322. See further note 106 earlier in this chapter and the accompanying text.

Chapter 6
Role of the Courts

The Hong Kong Basic Law says relatively little about the role of the courts. Wesley-Smith (2004) describes it as "almost impenetrably obscure in relation to the courts and judiciary".[1]

The courts are described only in general terms as the "the judiciary of the Region" (Article 80), exercising "independent judicial power, including that of final adjudication" (Article 19(1)). The Hong Kong Basic Law grants to those courts jurisdiction over — or the right to try — "all cases in the Region"[2] (Article 19(2)), subject only to a small number of exceptions.[3]

The structure of the courts is outlined in only very general terms. Brief reference is made to the existence of a Court of Final Appeal, Court of Appeal and Court of First Instance (these last two courts being collectively known as the High Court), district courts, magistrates' courts and other special courts[4] (Article 81(1)). But it is left to local Hong Kong laws, instead of the Hong Kong Basic Law, to fill in the details about the structure, powers and functions of these courts (Article 83).[5]

That reflects the emphasis on continuity rather than detail in the Hong Kong Basic Law. The judicial system that existed in Hong Kong under British rule was often cited as one of the ingredients of Hong Kong's success,[6] so it was always clear that one of the goals of "one country, two systems" would be to try to ensure its survival largely

---

1. Peter Wesley-Smith, "Judges and Judicial Power Under the Hong Kong Basic Law" (2004) 34 *HKLJ* 83–84.
2. The Chinese text of Article 19(2) is ambiguous and might better be translated as "all cases *of* the Region" (emphasis added) since some statutory provisions, such as Section 4(1) of the Prevention of Bribery Ordinance (Cap. 201), allow the Hong Kong courts to exercise jurisdiction over certain crimes committed outside Hong Kong. See further Benny Tai, "The Jurisdiction of the Courts of the Hong Kong Special Administrative Region" in Alice Lee (ed.), *Law Lectures for Practitioners 1998* (Hong Kong Law Journal Ltd., 1998) at 74–75.
3. For more on these restrictions, see further "6.5: Limits on Courts" later in this chapter.
4. Special courts refer to the Coroners' Court, which investigates certain categories of deaths, and tribunals under the purview of the judiciary, such as the Lands and Labour Tribunals.
5. The main laws on the structure, powers and functions of the Hong Kong courts include the Magistrates Ordinance (Cap. 227), Coroners Ordinance (Cap. 504), District Court Ordinance (Cap. 336), High Court Ordinance (Cap. 4) and Hong Kong Court of Final Appeal Ordinance (Cap. 484).
6. For two examples of this, see M.J. Enright, E.E. Scott and D. Dodwell, *The Hong Kong Advantage* (Oxford University Press, 1997) at 108–109, and Wang Shuwen, *Introduction to the Basic Law of the Hong Kong Special Administrative Region* (Law Press, 2nd English edition, 2009) at 492.

unchanged after 1 July 1997. As a result, the section in the Hong Kong Basic Law on the judiciary[7] lays great stress on the need for continuity, going much further in this respect than the equivalent sections on other parts of Hong Kong's political structure.[8]

All the judges and other members of the judiciary who sat in Hong Kong's courts before 1 July 1997 were specifically guaranteed the right to keep their jobs (Article 93(1)). They are also subject to much milder Chinese nationality restrictions on who can hold the top posts than apply to the other branches of the political structure under the Hong Kong Basic Law. While all principal official posts in the Hong Kong SAR Government and 80% of the seats in the Legislative Council must be filled by Chinese nationals with no right of abode overseas,[9] in apparent recognition of the large number of expatriate judges at the time of the 1997 handover only two posts in the judiciary are subject to the same nationality requirement. These are the heads of Hong Kong's two highest courts, the Chief Justice of the Court of Final Appeal and the Chief Judge of the High Court.[10] In contrast to the requirement that most new civil servants must be Hong Kong permanent residents,[11] Article 92 of the Hong Kong Basic Law specifically provides for the continued recruitment of judges from common law jurisdictions elsewhere in the world.

The courts too were left largely unchanged by the Hong Kong Basic Law. With the exception of the Court of Final Appeal, all the other courts listed in Article 81(1) are simply continuations of those that existed in Hong Kong under British rule.[12] They are given jurisdiction over exactly the same types of cases as before (Article 19(2)) — a point that has proved of great significance in exercising certain powers of judicial review[13] — and required to apply the same principles in both civil and criminal cases as they did under British rule (Article 87(1)).

This all adds up to a picture of a judicial system that was subject to far less change under the Hong Kong Basic Law than other branches of Hong Kong's political structure.

---

7. Section 4 of Chapter IV of the Hong Kong Basic Law.
8. The Chief Executive, Executive Authorities and Legislative Councils, which are the subjects of Sections 1–3 of Chapter IV of the Hong Kong Basic Law.
9. Articles 101(1) and 67.
10. Article 90(1). However some Chinese legal scholars have suggested that the nationality requirement should be extended to all judges on the Court of Final Appeal. See Colleen Lee, "Appeal court judges should all be Chinese nationals, scholars say", *South China Morning Post*, 5 Nov 2012.
11. Article 99(1).
12. Although, in some cases, these courts are given different names under the Hong Kong Basic Law. The term Supreme Court, which under British rule was used to describe both the Court of First Instance and the Court of Appeal, could not continue to be used because of the potential for confusion with the Supreme People's Court in Beijing. See Wang, *Introduction to the Basic Law of the Hong Kong Special Administrative Region* (see note 6) at 502. As a result, the former Supreme Court was renamed as the High Court, consisting of a Court of First Instance and a Court of Appeal under Section 8(1) of the Hong Kong Reunification Ordinance 1997 (No. 110 of 1997).
13. See the case of *HKSAR v Ma Wai Kwan David* [1997] HKLRD 761, which is explained further in notes 142–146 later in this chapter and the accompanying text.

On 3 July 1997, the first working day after the handover, the same courts continued sitting,[14] with the same judges to hear the same cases that had begun before the handover.[15] The only exception was in the one area where it was impossible to avoid change. Under British rule, Hong Kong's court of final appeal was the Judicial Committee of the Privy Council in London.[16] Since China was unwilling to see this continue after the end of British rule, it agreed to the creation of a Court of Final Appeal in Hong Kong in the Sino-British Joint Declaration.[17]

This was the one area of Hong Kong's previous judicial system where major changes became necessary under the Hong Kong Basic Law.[18] As a result, perhaps the biggest challenge for Hong Kong's judicial system after 1 July 1997 was the successful establishment of this court.[19]

6.1 Judicial Independence

Although the Hong Kong Basic Law says relatively little about the role of the judiciary, it does expressly provide that the courts exercise "independent" judicial power. This point is considered sufficiently important that it is reiterated in three separate provisions.[20] Hsu (2004) describes it as a "cardinal feature" of the Hong Kong Basic Law.[21] Article 85 of the Hong Kong Basic Law, one of these three provisions, adds that such power is exercised by the courts "free from any interference".

The meaning of independent judicial power, more commonly known as "judicial independence", is not defined in the Hong Kong Basic Law. However, in an important Canadian court case on the subject, *Valente v The Queen*,[22] the Supreme Court of

---

14. Although in some cases under different names. See further note 12 above.
15. Section 10 of the Hong Kong Reunification Ordinance (No. 110 of 1997), which was passed by the Provisional Legislative Council in the early hours of 1 July 1997, specifically guaranteed that "the continuity of legal proceedings, the criminal justice system, the administration of justice and the course of public justice shall not be affected by the resumption of the exercise of sovereignty over Hong Kong by the People's Republic of China".
16. The Judicial Committee of the Privy Council hears appeals from British colonies and some members of the British Commonwealth. Until 2009, such appeals were usually heard by Law Lords from the House of Lords, which was then the highest court in Britain for most domestic appeals. Since the establishment of a Supreme Court of the United Kingdom in 2009, appeals are usually heard by justices from that court.
17. Annex I(III) of the Joint Declaration. See further "2.2: Sino-British Joint Declaration" in Chapter 2.
18. This is explicitly recognized in Article 81(2) of the Hong Kong Basic Law which, in seeking to preserve the "judicial system previously practised in Hong Kong", makes an exception "for those changes consequent upon the establishment of the Court of Final Appeal of the Hong Kong Special Administrative Region".
19. See further "6.4: Constitutional Role of the Court of Final Appeal" for more on the challenges that the court faced in the years immediately after its establishment.
20. Articles 2, 19(1) and 85.
21. Berry F.C. Hsu, "Judicial Independence under the Basic Law" (2004) 34 *HKLJ* 279, 280.
22. *Valente v The Queen* [1985] 2 Supreme Court Reports 673.

Canada offered some guidance. It described judicial independence as "not merely a state of mind or attitude in the actual exercise of judicial functions, but a status or relationship to others, particularly to the executive branch of government, that rests on objective conditions or guarantees".[23] That last point is particularly important in ensuring that the courts can function independently, given the executive branch's extensive involvement in the legal process. In most countries, the executive prosecutes virtually every criminal case and is a party to many of the most important cases in the civil arena. Without such guarantees of judicial independence it is unlikely, for instance, that Hong Kong would have experienced such explosive growth in the number of judicial review cases brought against the government and other public bodies in recent years.[24]

Freedom from interference by the executive is not something the courts in Hong Kong always necessarily enjoyed in the past. Cottrell and Ghai (2001) note that "[j]udicial independence was not a hallmark of colonial rule", citing the frequency with which judges were appointed from within the executive branch of the government under British rule.[25] Barnes (1976) argues that during earlier decades in colonial Hong Kong, those judicial officers who ruled against the executive branch too frequently put their promotion prospects at risk.[26]

Only since 1 July 1997 has judicial independence been constitutionally protected under the Hong Kong Basic Law. Even now, despite the importance it places upon this cardinal principle, the Hong Kong Basic Law only provides for some (but far from all) of the specific protections often considered essential elements of judicial independence in other common law jurisdictions.[27]

Judicial independence is also an important part of the system of separation of powers laid down in the Hong Kong Basic Law.[28] This is a system in which each of the three branches of the political structure—the executive, legislature and judiciary—function largely independently of each other, and act as checks and balances on any abuse of powers by the other branches of the political structure. In the case of the judiciary, such checks and balances are exercised especially through the process of judicial review, under which the courts rule on the validity of the acts, decisions and omissions of the executive and legislature, as well as other public bodies.[29]

---

23. Ibid. at 685. For more on this case, and its relevance to Hong Kong, see Peter Wesley-Smith, "Individual and Institutional Independence of the Judiciary", in Steve Tsang (ed.), *Judicial Independence and the Rule of Law in Hong Kong* (Hong Kong University Press, 2001) at 99–101.
24. See further "6.2: Judicial Review" later in this chapter.
25. Jill Cottrell and Yash Ghai, "Between Two Systems of Law: The Judiciary in Hong Kong" in P.H. Russell and D.M. O'Brien (eds.), *Judicial Independence in the Age of Democracy: Critical Perspectives from Around the World* (University Press of Virginia, 2001) at 208.
26. E.E. Barnes, "The Independence of the Judiciary in Hong Kong" (1976) 6 *HKLJ* 7, 19.
27. See further notes 98–102 later in this chapter and the accompanying text, for an example of an omission from the Hong Kong Basic Law concerning the protection of judicial independence, in relation to the financial security of judges.
28. See further "5.2: Separation of Powers" in Chapter 5.
29. See further "6.2: Judicial Review" later in this chapter.

Under this system of separation of powers, no branch of the political structure is allowed to interfere in the powers granted to the other branches under the Hong Kong Basic Law. That means, for instance, the judiciary has no business making policy, a matter which is reserved for the executive under the Hong Kong Basic Law.[30] The courts must also be careful not to usurp the primary role in law making given to the legislature under the Hong Kong Basic Law.[31] Equally it means that neither the executive nor the legislature is permitted to interfere in the exercise of "judicial power", a power which under Article 80 of the Hong Kong Basic Law is granted to the courts alone.

Although the Hong Kong Basic Law does not expressly define judicial power,[32] it does make clear this includes the power to adjudicate (or decide) court cases.[33] Since part of adjudicating court cases is deciding what remedy or punishment, such as a prison sentence, should be imposed, that too is a power which only can be exercised by the courts.[34] Any attempt by the executive or legislature to interfere in the exercise of these powers is a breach of the Hong Kong Basic Law. That was demonstrated in *Yau Kwong Man v Secretary for Security*,[35] where the Court of First Instance declared a statutory provision[36] giving the Chief Executive the power to specify minimum sentences for a limited category of child prisoners[37] inconsistent with the exclusive granting of judicial power to the courts under Article 80 of the Hong Kong Basic Law.

This separation of powers under the Hong Kong Basic Law is somewhat undermined by the frequency with which judges are appointed to positions by the executive branch of government. This is a relatively common practice in Hong Kong since, given their high reputation in the community, judges are often seen as the most appropriate figures to head government inquiries or other bodies where an impartial figure is needed.[38] But it risks undermining the judiciary's independence from the executive, especially when judges are called upon to take up sensitive appointments relating to the investigation of

---

30. Articles 48(4) and 62(1). See further "5.1: Chief Executive" in Chapter 5.
31. Article 73(1).
32. For more on the difficulties of defining the exact meaning of judicial power, see further note 174 in Chapter 4 and Hsu, "Judicial Independence under the Basic Law" (see note 21) at 285.
33. See the Chinese text of Article 80 of the Hong Kong Basic Law which is described further in note 175 in Chapter 4 and the accompanying text.
34. For a comprehensive description of the different aspects of the power to adjudicate, see Tai "The Jurisdiction of the Courts of the Hong Kong Special Administrative Region" (see note 2) at 69–73.
35. [2002] 3 HKC 457.
36. Section 67C of the Criminal Procedure Ordinance (Cap. 221).
37. These were prisoners detained at "executive discretion". This was a term originally known as "at Her Majesty's Pleasure" and used for children under 18 convicted of murder before 1993, when the law was changed to provide for mandatory life sentences for all murderers, whatever their age.
38. As of 2009, judges held 12 statutory and a further 12 non-statutory appointments outside the judiciary. Most are similar to judicial work (e.g., Chairman of the Insider Dealing Tribunal). However, a few involve unrelated work (e.g., Chairman of the Advisory Committee on Post-service Employment of Civil Servants). See Hong Kong SAR Government, *Statutory and Non-statutory Appointments of Judges to Offices Outside the Judiciary* (13 Jan 2009).

crime and law enforcement,[39] and could be potentially open to challenge as breaching the Hong Kong Basic Law.[40]

However, the main exception to a strict system of separation of powers — and probably the biggest threat to judicial independence in Hong Kong — is the power to interpret the Hong Kong Basic Law itself. Under the common law system, interpretation of legislation is part of judicial power. That means, under any system of separation of powers, interpretation of laws should be normally a matter for the courts alone. Chan (2000) describes this as "the very root of the common law system".[41] But Article 158 of the Hong Kong Basic Law modifies this common law position to the extent that the power to interpret the Hong Kong Basic Law is split between the National People's Congress Standing Committee and the Hong Kong courts, with the former enjoying the ultimate power of interpretation.[42] That reflects the system on the mainland, where there is no separation of powers, and authoritative interpretation of legislation is instead primarily a matter for the body that enacted it.[43]

The threat this can pose to judicial independence in Hong Kong was vividly demonstrated by the events of 1999, when the Standing Committee interpreted[44] two provisions of the Hong Kong Basic Law relating to the right to live in Hong Kong of many children born in mainland China. The Standing Committee's interpretation reversed the Court of Final Appeal's interpretation of these provisions a few months earlier in the cases of *Ng Ka Ling v Director of Immigration*[45] and *Chan Kam Nga v Director of Immigration*.[46] That

---

39. This concern has been raised particularly in relation to the Commissioner on Interception of Communications and Surveillance, a judge who oversees compliance by the police and other law enforcement agencies with the legal requirements for interception of communications and covert surveillance. See Norma Connolly, Ravina Shamdasani and Ambrose Leung, "Spying bill undermines judicial separation", *South China Morning Post*, 4 Aug 2006; and Margaret Ng, "Our judiciary is paying the price for spy law", *South China Morning Post*, 11 Nov 2007.
40. In *Wilson v Minister for Aboriginal and Torres Strait Islander Affairs* (1996) 189 Commonwealth Law Reports 1, 10–20, the High Court of Australia held that the separation of powers under the Australian system means that, under some circumstances, judges may not be appointed by the executive to conduct inquiries. For further discussion of this case, and whether a similar principle might apply in Hong Kong, see Sir Anthony Mason, "The Role of the Common Law in Hong Kong" in Jessica Young and Rebecca Lee (eds.), *The Common Law Lecture Series 2005* (Faculty of Law, University of Hong Kong, 2006) at 21–24.
41. Johannes Chan, "Judicial Independence: Controversies on the Constitutional Jurisdiction of the Court of Final Appeal of the Hong Kong Special Administrative Region" (2000) 33 *International Law* 1015, 1018.
42. Under Article 158(1) of the Hong Kong Basic Law. See further "7.2: Standing Committee" in Chapter 7.
43. See further notes 9–10 in Chapter 7 and the accompanying text.
44. The Interpretation by the Standing Committee of the NPC of Articles 22(4) and 24(2)(3) of the Basic Law of the Hong Kong SAR of the PRC (26 June 1999).
45. (1999) 2 HKCFAR 4.
46. (1999) 2 HKCFAR 82.

meant these two earlier cases could no longer be used as precedents by other children in a similar situation,[47] so depriving possibly hundreds of thousands of children with a Hong Kong parent of the right to move to Hong Kong. It may also have had an impact on the Court of Final Appeal's decisions in some subsequent cases. The court's decisions in *Lau Kong Yung v Director of Immigration*[48] and *HKSAR v Ng Kung Siu*,[49] two important cases decided later in 1999, were widely criticized as unnecessarily conceding crucial issues relating to Hong Kong's high degree of autonomy[50] and civil liberties,[51] in order to avoid any further confrontations with the Standing Committee.

The practical limits on the judicial independence guaranteed in the Hong Kong Basic Law were further highlighted by the intense political pressure placed on the Court of Final Appeal over another part of its *Ng Ka Ling* judgment. This sought to extend the court's power of judicial review to include invalidating any actions of the National People's Congress and its Standing Committee which breach the Hong Kong Basic Law.[52] Such an assertion of judicial power runs counter to the system on the mainland, where the courts are subordinate to these bodies, and provoked severe criticism from Beijing.[53]

Under the principle of judicial independence, judges cannot publicly defend their decisions when they come under attack, since that would involve venturing into the political arena. Rather, it is the "constitutional responsibility" of the executive branch of the government to come to the defence of the courts "whether or not the decision in question is in its favour", as then Chief Justice Andrew Li pointedly noted in a speech the following year.[54] That was a responsibility which the executive branch failed to fulfil in 1999, leaving the attacks on the Court of Final Appeal unanswered, including strong personal criticism of the Chief Justice.[55] Instead of defending the court, the executive branch requested that it issue a supplementary judgment in *Ng Ka Ling v Director of*

---

47. Although the rights of the parties to these earlier two cases were preserved, in *Ng Siu Tung v Director of Immigration* (2002) 5 HKCFAR 1, 26 the Court of Final Appeal held that their "precedential value" is "displaced by a Standing Committee interpretation".
48. (1999) 2 HKCFAR 300.
49. (1999) 2 HKCFAR 442.
50. In *Lau Kong Yung*, the Court of Final Appeal (at 323) described as "unqualified" the Standing Committee's power to interpret the Hong Kong Basic Law, so conceding that this included those parts of the Hong Kong Basic Law within Hong Kong's autonomy. For more on this case, and criticism of the court's reasoning, see further notes 333–340 later in this chapter and notes 104–125 in Chapter 7, together with the accompanying text.
51. In *Ng Kung Siu* the Court of Final Appeal upheld the restrictions on civil liberties in two laws, which make it a criminal offence to desecrate the national and regional flags. For more on this case, and criticism of the court's reasoning, see further notes 190–209 in Chapter 8 and the accompanying text.
52. *Ng Ka Ling* at 26–28. For more on this aspect of the judgment, see further notes 186–194 later in this chapter and the accompanying text.
53. See further notes 202–205 later in this chapter and the accompanying text.
54. See Chief Justice Andrew Li, "Speech at the Opening of the Legal Year", 17 Jan 2000, at para. 4.
55. See Johannes Chan, "Judicial Independence" (see note 41) at 1022–1023.

Immigration (No 2).[56] This rephrased the court's original remarks on the National People's Congress and its Standing Committee in more conciliatory language, in what essentially amounted to a political statement to appease China's anger with the court. Tai (2012) concludes that these events demonstrate that in cases involving a "direct conflict between the Mainland's and HKSAR's interests, the HKSAR Government would not be a trustworthy partner in protecting Hong Kong's judicial autonomy".[57] However, in cases where is no such direct conflict, the Hong Kong SAR Government has shown signs in recent years of being more willing to fulfil its constitutional responsibility to defend the principle of judicial independence from attacks.[58]

Many observers saw the events of 1999 as a serious blow to judicial independence in Hong Kong.[59] It certainly marked a low point for the young court, which was then barely two years old. It would be another two years before the Court of Final Appeal began to recover its confidence and was once again prepared to defy the Standing Committee, in a more cautious manner, in the case of *Director of Immigration v Chong Fung Yuen*.[60]

Yet even during the worst of the attacks on the court, no judge ever had any serious cause to fear losing their jobs—unlike the situation in mainland China, where judges sometimes have been threatened with dismissal for issuing rulings that anger local authorities.[61] This highlights the fact that, although there are some specific shortcomings, overall the provisions on the appointment and removal of judges in the Hong Kong Basic Law are among its stronger provisions in terms of protecting judicial independence.

The Hong Kong Basic Law states that judges and other members of the judiciary[62] "shall be chosen on the basis of their judicial and professional qualities" (Article 92).

---

56. (1999) 2 HKCFAR 141. For more on this supplementary judgment, and the reaction to it, see further notes 207–220 later in this chapter and the accompanying text.
57. Benny Y.T. Tai, "The Judiciary" in Lam Wai-man, Lui, Percy Luen-tim and Wilson Wong (eds.), *Contemporary Hong Kong Government and Politics* (Hong Kong University Press, 2nd edition, 2012) at 77.
58. As, for example, in Chief Secretary for Administration Carrie Lam's defence of judicial independence as a "core value" following strong criticism of the Hong Kong judiciary by former Secretary for Justice Elsie Leung. See further Johnny Tam, "Chief Secretary Carrie Lam defends Hong Kong's judicial independence", *South China Morning Post*, 8 Oct 2012.
59. See, for example, Johannes Chan, "Judicial Independence" (see note 41) at 1022–1023.
60. (2001) 4 HKCFAR 211. In this case, the Court of Final Appeal approved the Court of Appeal's refusal to follow part of the earlier interpretation issued by the Standing Committee in 1999, on the grounds that this involved a different sub-section of the same provision in the Hong Kong Basic Law. See further notes 175–178 in Chapter 7 and the accompanying text.
61. The most famous example was the suspension from office in 2003 of Luoyang Intermediate People's Court Judge Li Huijuan by the Henan Provincial People's Congress Standing Committee in response to her ruling invalidating a regulation passed by the Henan Provincial People's Congress which contradicted a national regulation. Judge Li was ultimately reinstated following protests from Chinese legal scholars. See further Albert Chen, *An Introduction to the Legal System of the People's Republic of China* (LexisNexis, 4th edition, 2011) at 148 and Jim Yardley, "A judge tests China's courts, making history", *New York Times*, 28 Nov 2005.
62. The term "other members of the judiciary" refers to those such as magistrates who also sit in a decision-making capacity in court hearings, but are not known as judges. See further note 88 later in this chapter.

It also largely preserves the system which has existed in Hong Kong since 1976, under which the choice of who should fill most judicial vacancies is essentially a matter for a largely independent body now known as the Judicial Officers Recommendation Commission.[63] The commission is chaired by the Chief Justice, as head of the judiciary, and also includes the Secretary for Justice as well as seven other members appointed by the Chief Executive: two judges, a solicitor and a barrister, and three lay members not "connected in any way with the practice of law".[64] Although the commission recommends who should fill most judicial vacancies, the actual appointments are made by the Chief Executive, continuing the practice that existed before 1 July 1997, when such appointments were made by the colonial Governor.

Under Article 90(2) of the Hong Kong Basic Law, appointments to the Court of Final Appeal and as Chief Judge of the High Court also must be endorsed by the Legislative Council and reported to the National People's Congress Standing Committee for the record. Although neither body has ever sought to interfere in the choice of judges for such posts, this does appear to give legislators the power to reject judicial appointments in some circumstances.[65] In addition, there have been reports of the Central People's Government being consulted over at least one judicial appointment, although there is nothing in the Hong Kong Basic Law that provides for this.[66]

During Hong Kong's colonial era, this commission had a limited role. It was not mentioned in the constitutional document then in force,[67] and there was never any suggestion that Governors were required to follow its advice.[68] That changed after 1 July 1997 when the Hong Kong Basic Law explicitly stated the commission's key role in the choice of judges. Under Article 88, "judges shall be appointed by the Chief Executive on

---

63. This body was originally established as the Judicial Service Commission in 1976. On 1 July 1997, it was renamed as the Judicial Officers Recommendation Commission under the Judicial Service Commission (Amendment) Ordinance (No. 121 of 1997).
64. Section 3(1) of the Judicial Officers Recommendation Commission Ordinance (Cap. 92). Under Section 3(1A), the Chief Executive is required to consult the Law Society and Bar Association before appointing the solicitor and barrister members of the commission.
65. The Hong Kong SAR Government has argued that the Legislative Council can only refuse to endorse an appointment if "the requirements set out in the Basic Law regarding judicial appointments have not been followed". See Hong Kong SAR Government, *Legal and Administrative Matters Relating to the Appointment of Judges of the Court of Final Appeal* (3 June 2000) at para. 14. However, many legislators argue that the Legislative Council can also refuse to approve judicial appointments in other circumstances. See Legislative Council, *Minutes of Special Meeting of the Legislative Council Panel on Administration of Justice and Legal Services* (3 June 2000) at paras. 13–27.
66. This was the appointment of Geoffrey Ma as Chief Justice in 2010. See further note 187 in Chapter 4 and the accompanying text.
67. Under Article XIV(1) of the Hong Kong Letters Patent 1917–1995, the Governor had very wide powers in the appointment of judges.
68. Cottrell and Ghai (in "Between Two Systems of Law" (see note 25) at 210) describe the situation as "remarkably devoid of constitutional safeguards".

the recommendation of an independent commission".[69] That seems to leave open the possibility that the Chief Executive could reject a recommendation from this commission,[70] although this would be only likely to happen in the most exceptional circumstances.[71] What is less clear is whether the wording of Article 88 still leaves room for what colonial Governors were free to do in the past[72] — namely for the Chief Executive to choose his or her own preferred candidate for appointment as a judge, instead of someone chosen by the commission.[73]

The presence of the Secretary for Justice, who, as the government's top law officer, can hardly be said to be independent of the executive, has raised questions about whether the commission's composition entirely complies with the requirement in Article 88 of the Hong Kong Basic Law that judges must be nominated by an "independent commission".[74] In addition, Chan (2011) notes that the three lay members appointed by the Chief Executive have the power to veto any proposed appointments,[75] even if such appointments are supported by all the judges and lawyers sitting on the commission, although there is no evidence this has ever happened.[76]

Despite these shortcomings, overall the arrangements for appointing judges in Hong Kong appear to compare favourably with those in many major Western democracies, especially in terms of minimizing the role of the executive in the appointment process.[77]

---

69. Hsu (in "Judicial Independence under the Basic Law" (see note 21) at 289) suggests a possible difference in the wording of the Chinese text of Article 88, which instead states that judges "*are* appointed by the Chief Executive" (emphasis added).
70. See Legislative Council, *Minutes of the Special Meeting of the Legislative Council Panel on Administration of Justice and Legal Services* (17 June 2000) at paras. 4–10.
71. Ibid. at para. 5, where the Hong Kong SAR Government suggested one possible scenario could be where a judicial appointee becomes involved in a major controversy after the commission has already made its recommendation to the Chief Executive.
72. See further note 67.
73. Cottrell and Ghai (in "Between Two Systems of Law" (see note 25) at 212) note that, for regular judicial appointments, "the advice of the commission is not binding". However they add that, in practice, its recommendations "are treated as binding" by the Chief Executive. See also the suggestion by Senior Counsel Ronny Tong (in Eddie Luk, "Retirement looms for judge", *The Standard*, 28 March 2012) that it is theoretically possible "for the Chief Executive to appoint anyone" as a judge.
74. See, for example, Wesley-Smith, "Individual and Institutional Independence of the Judiciary" (see note 23) at 109. The executive's response is that having a member of the executive on the commission does not infringe judicial independence and is appropriate, given the importance of the role of the Secretary for Justice. See Hong Kong SAR Government, *Paper Prepared by the Director of Administration on "Process of Appointment of Judges"* (22 April 2002).
75. Under Section 3(3A) of the Judicial Officers Recommendation Commission Ordinance (Cap. 92), only two dissenting votes or abstentions are necessary to stop any proposed appointment or promotion.
76. Johannes Chan, "The Judiciary" in Chan and C.L. Lim (eds.), *Law of the Hong Kong Constitution* (Sweet & Maxwell, 2011) at 307.
77. See Eva Liu and Cheung Wai-lam, *The Process of Appointment of Judges in Hong Kong and Some Foreign Countries: Overall Comparison* (Research and Library Services Division, Legislative Council Secretariat, 12 May 2001), especially Table 3.

In a confidential 2010 US diplomatic telegram, which was later leaked on the Internet, senior American diplomats noted that prominent members of the legal community in Hong Kong "took pains to note the apolitical nature of the process, drawing a respectful (if pointed) contrast with judicial nominations in the United States".[78] This refers to the fact that, in the US, federal judges are chosen by the President, often on explicitly political criteria.[79] In the UK, new judges were also traditionally chosen by a member of the executive.[80] Only in 2006 was an independent Judicial Appointments Commission established, a body in some ways similar to the much longer established Judicial Officers Recommendation Commission in Hong Kong.[81] Although this Judicial Appointments Commission now chooses new judges, a member of the British government still retains the power to force the commission to choose another candidate.[82]

Nonetheless, concerns about whether political considerations might be occasionally creeping into the judicial appointments process in Hong Kong arose for the first time in 2012, when Justice Kemal Bokhary, often described as the most liberal judge on the Court of Final Appeal, was forced to step down from his permanent post upon reaching the retirement age of 65, especially after it emerged that he was being replaced by a slightly older judge.[83] Suspicions were enhanced by the timing, with Bokhary being informed of the decision only a few months after he dissented from the court's first reference of an issue of interpretation of the Hong Kong Basic Law to the National People's Congress Standing Committee.[84] It also came around the time Bokhary was publicly criticized in

---

78. US Consulate in Hong Kong, *Upon This Rock: Hong Kong Rule of Law Remains Solid (Part 1)* (26 Feb 2010).
79. From 1789 to 1994, 97 of the 108 judges appointed by US Presidents to the US Supreme Court, and confirmed by the US Senate, had the same political party background as the US President who appointed them. See Eva Liu, *The Process of Appointment of Judges in Some Foreign Countries: The United States* (Research and Library Services Division, Legislative Council Secretariat, 24 April 2001).
80. Appointments were made by the Queen on the advice of the Lord Chancellor or, in the case of judges in the Court of Appeal and above, on the advice of the Prime Minister.
81. The Judicial Appointments Commission consists of 15 members, including at least five from the judiciary, two from the legal profession and five lay members (including a chairman) who have never held judicial office or been a practising lawyer (Schedule 12 of the Constitutional Reform Act 2005).
82. Under Section 31 of the Constitutional Reform Act 2005, if the Lord Chancellor exercises his power to reject a recommendation by the Judicial Appointments Commission, the commission must put forward another nominee instead.
83. This was Justice Robert Tang, then vice-president of the Court of Appeal. Bokhary was, however, appointed as a non-permanent judge of the Court of Final Appeal (see further notes 279–283 later in this chapter and the accompanying text, for more on non-permanent judges). For an example of expressions of concern, see Austin Chiu, "Hong Kong faces loss of liberal voice in the top court", *South China Morning Post*, 28 March 2012.
84. In *Democratic Republic of Congo v FG Hemisphere* (2011) 14 HKCFAR 95. In *Recollections* (Sweet & Maxwell, 2013) at 580, Bokhary says he was informed a few months after this dissent that his term of office in his permanent post would not be extended.

China's state-run media following the leaking of his private remarks to US diplomats.[85] One lawyer described the decision to replace him with an older judge as "inexplicable"[86] while Bokhary, who made clear he would have preferred to stay as a permanent judge on the court, expressed concern about the effect on judicial independence, "if other judges become less independent because they fear something similar may happen to them".[87]

Once appointed, judges in Hong Kong enjoy security of tenure under the Hong Kong Basic Law.[88] This means they generally keep their jobs until they resign or reach retirement age, and can be only removed prior to this in exceptional circumstances. Under Article 89 of the Hong Kong Basic Law, these are limited to "inability to discharge his or her duties, or for misbehaviour". In keeping with the need to minimize the direct role of the executive in such matters, even in these exceptional circumstances only a tribunal appointed by the Chief Justice, and consisting of at least three local judges,[89] can recommend that a judge be dismissed. The judge's removal from office is then formally made by the Chief Executive, in accordance with the tribunal's recommendation. As with appointments, under Article 90(2) of the Hong Kong Basic Law, the removal of any judge on the Court of Final Appeal or the Chief Judge of the High Court also must be endorsed by the Legislative Council and reported to the National People's Congress Standing Committee for the record.

Since the Hong Kong Basic Law came into effect on 1 July 1997, no judge has ever been removed from office prior to reaching retirement age. Even looking back into Hong Kong's colonial history, it is more than 100 years since a judge was last forced out of office.[90] However, Chan (2011) notes that the provisions in Article 89 of the Hong Kong

---

85. See, for example, Lau Nai Keung, "Judge's improper encounters show his lack of judgement", *China Daily Hong Kong edition*, 13 Sept 2011. The most controversial aspect of these remarks involved a revelation that the judges on the Court of Final Appeal had considered resigning following the NPC Standing Committee's first interpretation of the Hong Kong Basic Law. See further note 330 later in this chapter and the accompanying text.
86. Senior Counsel Audrey Eu, cited in Austin Chiu and Adrian Wan, "New judge older than judge he's replacing", *South China Morning Post*, 29 March 2012.
87. Quoted in Eddie Luk, "I wasn't asked to stay on, says liberal judge", *South China Morning Post*, 29 March 2012. In *Recollections* (see note 84) at 586, Bokhary notes that the Chief Justice "can only recommend", implying it may have been the Chief Executive who decided not to allow him to remain as a permanent judge. Under Section 14(2)(a) of the Hong Kong Court of Final Appeal Ordinance (Cap. 484), the Chief Executive makes such decisions "in accordance with the recommendation of the Chief Justice".
88. However, this protection only applies to "judges". The term is not defined in the Hong Kong Basic Law, but Chan (2011) argues [in "The Judiciary" (see note 76) at 308] that, based on the provisions preserving the previous judicial system, it most likely refers to judges in the District Court and above. This means magistrates and adjudicators in those tribunals that form part of the court system do not enjoy any job security under the Hong Kong Basic Law.
89. In the case of similar allegations against the Chief Justice, the tribunal must consist of at least five local judges and will be instead appointed by the Chief Executive (Article 89(2)).
90. The most famous example was the 1847 suspension from office of then Chief Justice John Hulme, after he refused to follow a request from then Governor Sir John Davies in handling a court case. However, this suspension was reversed within six months. In 1912, then Chief Justice Sir Francis Piggott was removed by the British Government when he refused to retire. For a summary of these events, see Chan, "The Judiciary" (see note 76) at 310.

Basic Law protecting judges from being prematurely removed from office are, in some respects, not as strong as those which applied prior to 1 July 1997, when judges from outside Hong Kong could sit on such tribunals and any judge removed from office had a further right of appeal to the Judicial Committee of the Privy Council.[91]

Note, however, that the job security afforded to judges by the Hong Kong Basic Law only applies until they reach retirement age, which is 65 for most judges in Hong Kong, much lower than the retirement age for judges in many other jurisdictions.[92] As was demonstrated by the controversy over Justice Bokhary's enforced retirement in 2012, there is no right to remain in office after reaching 65. However the Judicial Officers Recommendation Commission (or, in some cases, the Chief Justice) do have the discretion to recommend to the Chief Executive that an extension be granted in specific cases.[93]

In addition, no provision in any constitutional document can protect against judges being pressured into resigning before they reach retirement age. Although there is no evidence so far of this having occurred since 1 July 1997, there were occasional instances of this happening before that date.[94] On one occasion, a judge caught reading a book during a trial was not assigned any further court cases, leaving him little choice but to resign.[95] In 1988, then Chief Justice Sir Denys Roberts publicly admitted some judicial resignations "have been pushed rather than because they wanted to go". [96]

While the provisions in the Hong Kong Basic Law protecting against interference by the executive in the appointment and removal of judges in some respects exceed those in

---

91. Ibid. at 309. Article XVIA(6)(a) of the Hong Kong Letters Patent 1917–1995 provided that judges from the UK and other parts of the British Commonwealth could sit on any panel formed to consider whether a judge should be removed from office.
92. In the UK, the retirement age for most judges is 70. In the US, there is no retirement age for federal judges and some continue in office into their eighties.
93. Recommendations are made by the commission, except in the case of the permanent judges on the Court of Final Appeal, where the recommendations are instead made by the Chief Justice. With the approval of the Chief Executive, judges on the Court of Final Appeal can have their term of office extended for up to two periods of three years beyond the age of 65 (under Section 14(2)(a) of the Hong Kong Court of Final Appeal Ordinance (Cap. 484)), while judges on the High Court can have their term of office extended for up to five years (under Section 11A(3)(b) of the High Court Ordinance (Cap. 4)). However, the judiciary says such extensions will only be requested in "exceptional circumstances". See Austin Chiu, "Age crisis prompts fears for judiciary", *South China Morning Post*, 9 April 2012.
94. See the three examples in 1987–1988 cited by Nihal Jayawickrama, "Public Law", in Raymond Wacks (ed.), *The Law in Hong Kong 1969–1989* (Oxford University Press, 1989) at 67–71.
95. Ibid. at 69–70. The judge in question, Justice Patrick O'Dea, resigned at the age of 47, 18 years before his normal retirement age.
96. Ibid. at 70, citing *South China Morning Post*, 9 March 1988. In a further case in 1996, District Judge Brian Caird took early retirement after the then Governor announced the establishment of a tribunal, which could have led to his removal from office. See Emma Batha, "Cover-up claimed as inquiry into Caird's behaviour dropped", *South China Morning Post*, 24 Dec 1996.

many countries, there are other aspects to judicial independence where the Hong Kong Basic Law does not offer so much protection. Some might say there is limited value in guaranteeing judges' continued employment if the executive is free to cut their salaries to a pittance, or interfere with how the judiciary is administered. Perhaps for this reason, in *Valente v The Queen*,[97] the Supreme Court of Canada identified three essential criteria for judicial independence. These are not only (1) security of tenure; but also (2) financial security; and (3) institutional independence relating to administration. When it comes to these latter two criteria for judicial independence, in contrast to its generally strong provisions on security of tenure, the Hong Kong Basic Law affords little or no protection.

This omission is particularly glaring for financial security, since many other major common law jurisdictions have constitutional provisions or laws prohibiting any reduction in judicial remuneration. A 2003 consultancy report commissioned by the Hong Kong Judiciary on the issue, and conducted by Sir Anthony Mason, a non-permanent judge on the Court of Final Appeal, described this as an "essential element of judicial independence".[98] However, the Hong Kong Basic Law contains only a very limited provision—similar to that which also applies to all civil servants—protecting judicial remuneration from being reduced below the level which applied on 1 July 1997 (Article 93(1)). A recommendation in the 2003 consultancy report that this be supplemented by a law providing more general protection against any reduction in judicial remuneration[99] was rejected by the executive branch of the Hong Kong SAR Government,[100] prompting a public expression of disappointment by the judiciary.[101]

Instead, judicial remuneration continues to be determined by the Chief Executive on an annual basis, after considering the recommendations of an advisory body known as the Standing Committee on Judicial Salaries and Conditions of Service. However, the Chief Executive is free to ignore the Standing Committee's advice in deciding judicial remuneration, in contrast to the situation with judicial appointments where it is much more difficult for the Chief Executive to ignore the advice of the body that makes recommendations on appointments. Like all government spending, judicial remuneration is subject to annual approval by the Legislative Council. However, in 2008, the Hong Kong

---

97. *Valente v The Queen* [1985] 2 Supreme Court Reports 673. See further note 23 earlier in this chapter.
98. Sir Anthony Mason, *Consultancy Report: System for the Determination of Judicial Remuneration* (Hong Kong Judiciary, Feb 2003) at 56.
99. Ibid. at 56–58.
100. The executive accepted that most common law jurisdictions do prohibit any reduction in judicial pay. However, it argued that some international judicial instruments do recognise that such a reduction would be permissible as part of a general reduction in public expenditure. See Hong Kong SAR Government, *Legislative Council Brief: System for the Determination of Judicial Remuneration and Interim Arrangement for the 2008–09 Judicial Service Pay Adjustment Exercise* (20 May 2008).
101. See Hong Kong Judiciary, *Statement on the Administration's Decision on the New System for the Determination of Judicial Remuneration* (20 May 2008).

SAR Government agreed to reform this system so that it would no longer be necessary to hold a separate vote on the issue each year.[102]

Institutional independence in relation to administration, the third essential element of judicial independence identified by the Supreme Court of Canada, is somewhat better protected in Hong Kong. The Chief Justice, as head of the judiciary, is ultimately responsible for the administration of the courts under Section 6(2) of the Hong Kong Court of Final Appeal Ordinance (Cap. 484), although he is assisted in day-to-day tasks by a civil servant known as the Judiciary Administrator. The main problem here lies in the judiciary's lack of control over its budget. Like judicial remuneration, this is decided by the executive on an annual basis, and subject to approval by the Legislative Council. Like all public spending, this is at risk of being cut when money is tight. For instance, total spending on the judiciary was reduced by 14% from 2002 to 2007, at a time when the Hong Kong SAR was trying to curb its budget deficits. These cuts led to magistrates' courts being closed and a public warning by then Chief Justice Andrew Li about the resulting increase in waiting times for court hearings.[103]

That all adds up to a mixed picture for judicial independence in Hong Kong. Security of tenure is generally well protected although, even here, some have expressed concern following the decision not to allow Justice Bokhary to stay on past his retirement age in 2012. In terms of provisions on financial security, Hong Kong lags behind many other common law jurisdictions. And hanging over everything is the shadow of the mainland legal system, where there is no judicial independence, at least in the way in which the term is generally understood in Hong Kong. That explains the difficulties which leaders in Beijing sometimes have in accepting the concept of judicial independence in Hong Kong. That is evidenced, for example, by then Chinese Vice President Xi Jinping's suggestion in July 2008 that the judiciary should help "support" the executive and legislature.[104] Tai (2012) suggests that these comments may suggest that "the Chinese authorities are still not satisfied with the performance of the HKSAR judiciary" and concludes that, unless and until there is significant change in the system of government in China, "the judicial autonomy of the HKSAR can only continue to be built on sand".[105] And, as was demonstrated by the events of 1999, for all the guarantees of judicial independence written into the Hong Kong Basic Law, the reality of Hong Kong's constitutional position sometimes imposes limits on how far judicial independence can be exercised in practice in cases involving issues considered particularly sensitive by Beijing.

---

102. Instead, the Hong Kong SAR Government agreed that judicial remuneration should be approved in advance, through what is known as a standing appropriation.
103. Chief Justice Andrew Li, "Speech at the Opening of the Legal Year", 17 Feb 2005.
104. See the statement issued by the Hong Kong Bar Association in response to these remarks, *Press Statement Regarding Judicial Independence* (9 July 2008).
105. Tai, "The Judiciary" (see note 57) at 82.

6.2 Judicial Review

Judicial review is one of the most fundamental principles underpinning the rule of law in most modern legal systems. For more than 100 years, it has been widely recognized that an integral part of any independent judicial system is that the actions of those who govern a society are subject to challenge in the same courts that hear cases involving ordinary members of that society.[106] From this evolved the view that one important role of the courts is to ensure that the executive branch of the government and other public bodies which exercise similar functions[107] do not act beyond the scope of the powers that they have been given by law (this is known as the doctrine of ultra vires[108]). In modern times, the courts initially used three grounds to judge whether an action is ultra vires. These three grounds are whether that action is: (1) illegal, (2) irrational, or (3) followed the wrong procedures.[109] They are now supplemented by further categories which have begun to emerge in recent years.[110]

Although Hong Kong courts have long had the jurisdiction to review administrative acts of the executive authorities and other public bodies,[111] for a long time this power was rarely exercised. Judicial rule was almost non-existent in Hong Kong prior to the 1950s,[112] and remained extremely rare for several decades afterwards.[113] Chan (2008)

---

106. See, for example, the classic definition of the rule of law given by the famous English constitutional law scholar A.V. Dicey in 1885. This emphasized equality before the law in terms of the executive branch of the government being subject to the same courts as its citizens. See A.V. Dicey, *An Introduction to the Study of the Law of the Constitution* (Macmillan, 10th edition, 1959) at 187–196.
107. Judicial review is not confined to actions of the executive branch of the government, and also can be used to challenge the actions of statutory bodies or those which exercise functions similar to those which could be exercised by the government. See, for example, *Pacific Century Insurance Co Ltd v Insurance Claims Complaints Bureau* [1999] 3 HKLRD 720. However, in Hong Kong, the majority of judicial review applications are directed against the government. See Benedict Lai, "Recent Trends and Developments of Judicial Review in Hong Kong", 20th Biennial Lawasia Conference, 5–8 June 2007, at para. 6 and Polly Hui, "Judicial review legal aid bids on the rise", *South China Morning Post*, 3 March 2008.
108. For a classic definition of the ultra vires principle, see *R v Hull University Visitor ex parte Page* [1993] AC 682, 701.
109. This third category is known as procedural impropriety. For the classic statement of these three categories, see Lord Diplock in *Council of Civil Service Unions v Minister for the Civil Service* [1985] AC 374, 410–411. For a more detailed description of these three categories in the Hong Kong context, see Richard Gordon and Johnny Mok, *Judicial Review in Hong Kong* (LexisNexis, 2009) at 69–88.
110. Notably, proportionality and legitimate expectation, two further categories of judicial review. See further notes 242–247 later in this chapter and the accompanying text.
111. Under Section 12(2)(a) of the High Court Ordinance (Cap. 4), the Court of First Instance exercises civil jurisdiction "of a like nature and extent as that" of the High Court of Justice in England. This includes the power of judicial review.
112. For a rare exception, see *In the Matter of an Application for Leave to Issue a Summons of Prohibition to be Directed to the Magistrate From Further Proceedings in Kowloon Magistracy Cases* (1948) 32 HKLR 136.
113. A survey of the Hong Kong Law Reports found only 29 reported judicial review cases in the

attributes the rarity of judicial review during the earlier decades of Hong Kong's colonial history to a combination of cultural, political and legal factors. A population dominated by refugees from mainland China displayed the "traditional Chinese cultural inclination to avoid confrontation in courts as much as possible".[114] He notes that the relatively closed political system, and a legal system then conducted entirely in English, further discouraged most Hong Kong people from attempting to challenge actions of the executive in the courts.[115]

By the time the Hong Kong Basic Law came to be written, this was slowly beginning to change. As the Hong Kong Government embarked on social programmes, such as public housing and greater regulation of society, the amount of legislation greatly increased.[116] So too did the scope of the discretionary powers exercised by public officials, which might be susceptible to challenge in the courts.[117] The number of judicial review cases, although still tiny by today's standards, began to rise. The 1980s saw more judicial review cases than the previous 30 years combined.[118] In 1988, there were 29 applications for judicial review. Two years later, there were 75 applications.[119]

Judicial review as it then existed in Hong Kong, like so many other aspects of Hong Kong's existing way of life, was specifically preserved under the Hong Kong Basic Law. Reflecting a similar provision in the Sino-British Joint Declaration,[120] Article 35(2) guarantees the right of Hong Kong residents "to institute legal proceedings in the courts against the acts of the executive authorities and their personnel". That was not something difficult for China to accept given the situation that was beginning to emerge in mainland China at the time when the Hong Kong Basic Law was being drafted, where the Administrative Litigation Law 1989 made certain types of actions of the executive authorities on the mainland susceptible to judicial review in the Chinese courts.[121]

1950s, 27 in the 1960s, and 28 in the 1970s. See Benny Tai Yiu-ting, "The Development of Constitutionalism in Hong Kong" in Raymond Wacks (ed.), *The New Legal Order in Hong Kong* (Hong Kong University Press, 1999) at 54.

114. Johannes Chan, "Administrative Law, Politics and Governance: The Hong Kong Experience" in Tom Ginsburg and Albert Chen (eds.), *Administrative Law and Governance in Asia* (Routledge, 2008) at 144–145.

115. Ibid.

116. Hong Kong's former Chief Justice has noted the substantial growth in the size of the statute book since the 1970s as one factor explaining the increase in the number of judicial review cases. See Chief Justice Andrew Li, "Speech at the Ceremonial Opening of the Legal Year", 9 Jan 2006.

117. Ibid.

118. Lai, "Recent Trends and Developments of Judicial Review in Hong Kong" (see note 107) at footnote 3.

119. Figures cited by Justice Barnett in *Re Sum Tat Man* [1991] 2 HKLR 601, 613.

120. Annex I(XIII).

121. For an excellent analysis of the significance of the Administrative Litigation Law and its limitations, see Chen Jianfu, *Chinese Law: Towards an Understanding of Chinese Law, Its Nature and Development* (Kluwer Law International, 1999) at 155–162.

What the Hong Kong Basic Law made no mention of was a second and broader type of judicial review that was still virtually unknown in Hong Kong at that stage, and which is never practised elsewhere in China. This is constitutional review, which involves challenging the legality of not simply an action by the government or a public body, but the law used to justify that action. Under the first, and narrower, type of judicial review, the court is only asked to decide whether a particular action of the government or a public body went beyond the powers granted to that body by law. But under the broader concept of constitutional review, it is possible to argue that even if an action was authorized by a particular law, that law (or, at least, some parts of that law) should be held invalid because it contravenes a higher constitutional document, so rendering the action invalid. In some circumstances, this can also offer a viable defence for defendants in criminal cases who cannot, or do not, deny committing the offence with which they are charged. Rather than protest their innocence, such defendants can instead argue that the relevant section of the law under which they are being charged is invalid because it breaches a higher constitutional document, usually by contravening the civil liberties protected by that document.

Constitutional review requires, naturally enough, a higher constitutional document against which the legality of other laws can be judged. Perhaps the most famous example of this is the US Constitution, with the US Supreme Court deciding more than two centuries ago, in the famous case of *Marbury v Madison*,[122] that laws which contravene the constitution can be declared unenforceable by the courts.

However, in some countries it is not the role of the courts to decide whether or not other laws contravene a constitutional document. In particular, in mainland China, provisions in the constitution are not generally enforceable in the courts.[123] The first known case of a judge in mainland China trying to exercise a power similar to constitutional review, in a case involving two conflicting laws, resulted in the suspension from work of the judge in question.[124] Instead, it is the role of the National People's Congress Standing Committee to invalidate many types of legislation if they conflict with the constitution.[125]

---

122. (1803) 5 US 137. The case involved a successful challenge to the Judiciary Act 1789, which the court found unconstitutional because it sought to give the Supreme Court more authority than is permitted under Article III of the US Constitution.
123. This was first decided by the Supreme People's Court in 1955. It was reinforced in 2008 when the court withdrew earlier guidance it had offered to a lower court in the case of *Qi Yuling v Chen Xiaoqi* (Judicial Interpretation No. 25/2001), which had been partly based on Article 46 of the PRC Constitution 1982. See further Chen, *An Introduction to the Legal System of the People's Republic of China* (see note 61) at 61–62.
124. See note 61 earlier in this chapter on the case involving Luoyang Intermediate People's Court Judge Li Huijuan. This case can be considered analogous to constitutional review, although it involved invalidating local legislation which conflicted with national legislation rather than with the PRC Constitution 1982.
125. Under Articles 67(7) and 67(8) of the PRC Constitution 1982, the Standing Committee has the power to annul any local legislation, as well as national legislation made by the State Council or other branches of the Central People's Government, that contravenes the constitution.

In Britain too, constitutional review has long been extremely difficult because Britain, unlike most countries in the world, traditionally lacked a written constitutional document against which the legality of other laws could be judged. In addition, the concept of parliamentary sovereignty, which means there are no legal limits on the power of the British parliament,[126] made it extremely difficult for the English courts to question the validity of laws passed by the British parliament.[127] However, in recent years, English judges have begun to treat a few laws passed by the British parliament as constitutional-like documents, which parliament intends to prevail over other laws unless expressly stated otherwise.[128]

Despite being a British colony, constitutional review has long been theoretically possible in Hong Kong. Unlike Britain, Hong Kong has always had a written constitution against which the validity of other laws could be judged, the Hong Kong Letters Patent.[129] However, the Letters Patent was a "crude and rudimentary constitution"[130] consisting of just 21 articles and—until the final years of British rule—no provisions protecting human rights. That meant there was nothing in the colonial constitution which other laws might

---

126. See the classic definition of parliamentary sovereignty in Dicey, *An Introduction to the Study of the Law of the Constitution* (see note 106) at 39–40.
127. See, for example, *Pickin v British Railway Board* [1974] AC 765, where the House of Lords concluded that parliamentary sovereignty prevented it from questioning the validity of a law which it was alleged that parliament had passed following fraudulent misrepresentations by one of the parties involved.
128. This particularly applies to Sections 2(1) and 2(4) of the European Communities Act 1972, which give primacy to European Union legislation over acts of the British parliament in the event of a conflict between the two, and Section 3(1) of the Human Rights Act 1998, which requires all other acts of parliament to be interpreted in a way consistent with the human rights protected by this act. These were described as "constitutional statutes" by Lord Justice Laws in *Thoburn v Sunderland City Council* [2003] QB 151, 187–189. Because of their special status, the courts will normally apply such "constitutional statutes" in preference to any other act of parliament with which they conflict, unless that other act of parliament expressly states that it is meant to prevail. See Lord Hoffman in *R v Secretary of State for the Home Department ex parte Simms* [2000] 2 AC 115, 131.
129. This was originally published as a Royal Charter dated 5 April 1943, immediately after the British and Chinese governments exchanged formally ratified copies of the Treaty of Nanking ceding Hong Kong Island to Britain. A revised version of the Hong Kong Letters Patent was subsequently published in 1917, and continued to apply until the end of British rule. The Hong Kong Letters Patent 1917–1995 was supplemented by a second constitutional document known as the Hong Kong Royal Instructions 1917–1993. However, some doubt has been expressed about whether the Royal Instructions were legally binding in the same way as the Letters Patent. See Yash Ghai, *Hong Kong's New Constitutional Order: The Resumption of Chinese Sovereignty and the Basic Law* (Hong Kong University Press, 2nd edition, 1999), note 8 at 15.
130. Albert Chen, "The Interpretation of the Basic Law—Common Law and Mainland Chinese perspectives" (2000) 30 *HKLJ* 380, 417. Chan (2008) describes it as "an archaic form of constitution, setting out nothing but the barebones of governance", in "Administrative Law, Politics and Governance" (see note 114) at 149.

contravene, and so no cases of constitutional review by the Hong Kong courts throughout most of colonial rule.[131]

That changed in 1991 when, in response to popular pressure for greater protection of human rights, Article VII of the Hong Kong Letters Patent was amended to add a new provision in Article VII(5) giving constitutional protection to most parts of the International Covenant on Civil and Political Rights, an international human rights treaty which had long applied in Hong Kong.[132] This amendment specifically stated that "[n]o law of Hong Kong shall be made after" this amendment "that restricts the rights and freedoms enjoyed in Hong Kong in a manner which is inconsistent with that Covenant as applied to Hong Kong".[133] This amendment to the Letters Patent was accompanied by the enactment of the Hong Kong Bill of Rights Ordinance (Cap. 383).[134] This wrote most parts of the International Covenant on Civil and Political Rights (which previously only had the status of a treaty in Hong Kong[135]) into Hong Kong law, so making them directly enforceable in the courts for the first time.

Chen (2000) describes these events of 1991 as "the first constitutional revolution in Hong Kong", since it "inaugurated the era in Hong Kong's legal history of judicial review of legislation on the basis of constitutional guarantees of human rights".[136] Largely as a result of this amendment to the Letters Patent and the accompanying enactment of the Hong Kong Bill of Rights Ordinance, the final years of British rule saw a surge in the number of judicial review cases[137]—including the first cases of constitutional review—as litigants challenged the legality of both government actions and laws restricting human rights which were now constitutionally protected. Chan (2008) describes this "enhanced scope to review legislation under the new constitutional set-up" as posing "a major challenge to the judiciary" which forced the judiciary to "re-examine its role and limits".[138] Some judges had difficulty adjusting to the advent of constitutional review. In a much criticized statement, Hong Kong's then Chief Justice Yang Ti Liang publicly expressed

---

131. There were, however, a few cases in which the courts had to interpret provisions in the Hong Kong Letters Patent. See, for example, *Ho Po Sang (No 2) v Director of Public Works* [1959] HKLR 632.
132. The International Covenant on Civil and Political Rights was first applied to Hong Kong by Britain in 1976, subject to some "reservations" (or exceptions) stating that a few provisions in the covenant did not fully apply in Hong Kong. See further notes 48–49 in Chapter 8 and the accompanying text.
133. See further pages 276–277 for more on the 1991 amendment to the Letters Patent.
134. See further pages 274–276 for more on the enactment of this ordinance.
135. At common law, international treaties are not directly enforceable in the courts in Hong Kong without an accompanying law as evidenced, for example, by the refusal of the Hong Kong courts to directly enforce provisions in the 1984 Sino-British Joint Declaration. See further notes 31–32 in Chapter 2 and the accompanying text.
136. Chen, "The Interpretation of the Basic Law" (see note 130) at 418.
137. A survey of the Hong Kong Law Reports found 153 reported judicial review cases from 1990 to June 1997, compared with only 62 in the 1980s. See Tai, "The Development of Constitutionalism in Hong Kong" (see note 113) at 54.
138. Chan, "Administrative Law, Politics and Governance" (see note 114) at 149.

concern that when the courts start invalidating laws they are straying into the area of lawmaking, a task more properly left to the legislature.[139] Another judge went even further, describing the Bill of Rights as a charter for criminals that upset stability and law and order in Hong Kong.[140]

However, the judiciary overcame these challenges, and by 1997 the power of constitutional review had become firmly established—through the human rights litigation during the final years of British rule—as part of the jurisdiction of the Hong Kong courts.[141] That was to prove crucial to the continued exercise of the power of constitutional review by the Hong Kong courts after the Hong Kong Basic Law came into force on 1 July 1997, since Article 19(2) effectively provides that the Hong Kong courts continue to exercise the same jurisdiction under the Hong Kong Basic Law as they did under British rule. In *HKSAR v Ma Wai Kwan David*,[142] the Court of Appeal accepted a submission from the Hong Kong SAR Government that, since the courts had prior to 1 July 1997 exercised the power of constitutional review in relation to Hong Kong laws which conflicted with the Hong Kong Letters Patent, this meant they now had a similar "power to determine the constitutionality of SAR made laws vis-à-vis the Basic Law".[143] Chen (2000) describes this as "the *Marbury v Madison* of the constitutional history of the HKSAR",[144] in a reference to the famous US Supreme Court case on the issue of constitutional review almost two centuries earlier,[145] because "it dealt with the most crucial issue in the new constitutional order of Hong Kong, and the proposition it upheld has never been challenged by any party in subsequent cases".[146]

Evidently aware of the importance of the issue, the Court of Final Appeal chose to reiterate the power of the Hong Kong courts to invalidate legislation inconsistent with the Hong Kong Basic Law in *Ng Ka Ling v Director of Immigration*,[147] the first substantive case involving the Hong Kong Basic Law to be heard by the new court. Rather than

---

139. See Chris Yeung, "Sparks fly as Chief Justice states case", *South China Morning Post*, 18 Nov 1995. For criticism of the Chief Justice's statement see Connie Law, "Sir Ti Liang argument nonsense, says experts", *South China Morning Post*, 18 Nov 1995. For a more general account of judicial hostility towards the Bill of Rights, as reflected in some court decisions, see Johannes Chan, "Hong Kong's Bill of Rights: Its Reception of and Contribution to International and Comparative Jurisprudence" (1998) 47 *International & Comparative Law Quarterly* 306, 311–320.
140. Cited by Chan (1998) at 317.
141. Chen, "The Interpretation of the Basic Law" (see note 130) at 419.
142. [1997] HKLRD 761.
143. Ibid. at 793. Justice Nazareth found this power "to flow from the second paragraph of art. 19". However, he rejected the government's argument that the power of constitutional review could also be found in Article 158, which gives the courts what he described as "a bare power to interpret the Basic Law". For more on the power of the courts to interpret the Hong Kong Basic Law, and how it is exercised, see further "7.1: Hong Kong Courts" in Chapter 7.
144. Chen, "The Interpretation of the Basic Law" (see note 130) at 424–425.
145. See note 122 earlier in this chapter.
146. Chen, "The Interpretation of the Basic Law" (see note 130) at 425.
147. (1999) 2 HKCFAR 4.

simply justifying this as a continuation of the power of constitutional review exercised by the Hong Kong courts prior to 1 July 1997, Chief Justice Li argued that the power of constitutional review was an integral part of the independent judicial power granted to the Hong Kong courts under Articles 19(1) and 80 of the Hong Kong Basic Law:

> In exercising their judicial power conferred by the Basic Law, the courts of the Region have a duty to enforce and interpret that Law. They undoubtedly have the jurisdiction to examine whether legislation enacted by the legislature of the Region or acts of the executive authorities of the Region are consistent with the Basic Law and, if found to be inconsistent, to hold them to be invalid. The exercise of this jurisdiction is a matter of obligation, not of discretion so that if inconsistency is established, the courts are bound to hold that a law or executive act is invalid at least to the extent of the inconsistency. Although this has not been questioned, it is right that we should take this opportunity of stating it unequivocally. In exercising this jurisdiction, the courts perform their constitutional role under the Basic Law of acting as a constitutional check on the executive and legislative branches of government to ensure that they act in accordance with the Basic Law.[148]

This important passage, which has been cited by the Hong Kong courts in many subsequent cases to justify exercising the power of constitutional review,[149] is a plausible interpretation of the power granted to the courts under the Hong Kong Basic Law, and one which has been generally accepted in Hong Kong. However, nowhere in the Hong Kong Basic Law does it explicitly state that the courts have the power to invalidate legislation inconsistent with the Hong Kong Basic Law. Instead, the only provisions in the Hong Kong Basic Law that explicitly refer to the power to invalidate legislation inconsistent with the Hong Kong Basic Law place this power in the hands of the National People's Congress Standing Committee in certain—apparently limited—circumstances.[150] This reflects the situation in mainland China where the power of constitutional review belongs to the National People's Congress Standing Committee, not the courts.[151]

As a result, it is far from clear whether it was really the intention of the drafters of the Hong Kong Basic Law to grant the power of constitutional review to the Hong Kong courts.[152] Some prominent former mainland drafters, most notably Xiao Weiyun, have

---

148. Ibid. at 25.
149. See, for example, *Leung Kwok Hung v President of the Legislative Council of the Hong Kong SAR* [2007] 1 HKLRD 387, 394.
150. See Article 17(3), which gives the Standing Committee a power to invalidate limited categories of Hong Kong laws (see further "4.2: Legislative Power" in Chapter 4), as well as Article 160(1) which gave the Standing Committee the power to invalidate any pre-existing laws found to be "in contravention" of the Hong Kong Basic Law at the time of the establishment of the Hong Kong SAR on 1 July 1997 (see further note 106 in Chapter 2). Article 160(1) is ambiguous about whether it continues to confer the same power on the Standing Committee after that date (see further note 84 in Chapter 3).
151. See further notes 123–125 earlier in this chapter and the accompanying text.
152. The first draft produced by the Basic Law Drafting Committee appeared to preclude any possibility of constitutional review, at least in respect of the rights listed in Chapter III of the Hong Kong Basic Law. See Albert H.Y. Chen, "A Disappointing Draft of Hong Kong's Bill of Rights" (1988) 17 *HKLJ* 133–136.

strongly argued that (as elsewhere in China) this is a power which can only be exercised by the National People's Congress Standing Committee, and that the Hong Kong courts are breaking the Hong Kong Basic Law every time they invalidate legislation inconsistent with the Hong Kong Basic Law.[153] Shiu (2010) questions "the legal basis for the Hong Kong courts to establish by themselves the power of constitutional review".[154]

However, such objectors have been so far confined to a relatively small number of voices, whose views have never yet been publicly endorsed by the Central Government. Within Hong Kong, the exercise of the power of constitutional review by the courts is generally accepted as an integral part of the judicial system.[155] Shiu (2010), one of that relatively small number of objectors, complains that this power "has been confirmed, declared as part of the system in a high-profile and active manner".[156]

That does not mean such a power can never be taken away. As demonstrated by previous interpretations of the Hong Kong Basic Law, the National People's Congress Standing Committee can always use its ultimate power of interpretation under Article 158(1) of the Hong Kong Basic Law[157] to intervene at any time and take away powers which had previously fallen within the scope of Hong Kong's high degree of autonomy.[158] Nonetheless, after more than 15 years of this power being exercised by the Hong Kong courts without any public objections from Beijing, it is possible to be cautiously optimistic that constitutional review may have become difficult to take away.

That does not mean that using constitutional review to invalidate sections of laws is ever likely to become a frequent occurrence. In *HKSAR v Hung Chan Wa*, Justice Bokhary observed that "[s]triking down a law is a course of last resort".[159] Young (2011) notes that "declarations of unconstitutionality" (the term used to describe when the court declares part of a law to be invalid because it is inconsistent with a constitutional document such as the Hong Kong Basic Law) only arose in nine cases before the Court of Final Appeal during its first decade of hearing constitutional cases.[160] Although most of these involved

---

153. See Xiao Weiyun, "A Brief Discussion of the Judgments of the Court of Final Appeal and the NPCSC Interpretation" (2002) 5 *Journal of Chinese and Comparative Law* 93, 94, and Chen, "The Interpretation of the Basic Law" (see note 130) at 424, especially note 221.
154. Shiu Sin-por, "Executive-Legislative Relations Under the Basic Law" in *Seminar on Review and Prospect of the Basic Law: Collection of Articles 2007* (One Country Two Systems Research Institute, 2010) at 271.
155. Johannes Chan, "Basic Law and Constitutional Review" (2007) 37 *HKLJ* 407, 410.
156. Shiu, "Executive-Legislative Relations Under the Basic Law" (see note 154) at 271. In July 2012, Shiu was appointed as head of the Central Policy Unit, the Hong Kong SAR Government's think tank, reporting directly to the Chief Executive.
157. See further "7.2: Standing Committee" in Chapter 7.
158. The clearest example of this is the Standing Committee's 2004 interpretation giving the Standing Committee control of any changes to the system for electing the Legislative Council, a power which fell within the scope of Hong Kong's autonomy under the original wording of Annex II(III) of the Hong Kong Basic Law. See further note 208 in Chapter 5 and the accompanying text.
159. (2006) 9 HKCFAR 614, 634.
160. Simon N.M. Young, "Constitutional Rights in Hong Kong's Court of Final Appeal" (2011) 27 *Chinese (Taiwan) Yearbook of International Law and Affairs* 67, 87. Note, however, that this constituted 20% of all human rights cases heard by the court during this period.

cases brought against the Hong Kong SAR Government, in one instance it was a government agency which successfully sought a declaration of unconstitutionality from the court, as the easiest way of avoiding having to enforce a legal provision that was fraught with practical problems.[161] Young (2011) notes this shows "that even public authorities can often have an interest in ensuring that unconstitutional laws are struck down".[162]

Where possible, instead, the "courts will strive to give laws a constitutional reading"[163] that makes them compatible with the Hong Kong Basic Law, even if this means adopting what is called a remedial interpretation. This involves going beyond the normal rules of interpretation used by the courts and, for example, reading a different meaning into the wording of the law (or sometimes even slightly changing its wording) in order to make it consistent with the Hong Kong Basic Law.[164] However, this has not yet become a common practice in Hong Kong, with the Court of Final Appeal only resorting to remedial interpretation on four occasions during its first decade of hearing constitutional cases.[165]

Even where the courts do decide to issue a declaration of unconstitutionality, they will generally try and keep the parts of the law affected to a minimum. In *Leung Kwok Hung v HKSAR*, the Court of Final Appeal invalidated just two words in the Public Order Ordinance (Cap. 245), leaving the bulk of the law untouched.[166] That technique is known as "severance", since the unconstitutional part of the law is severed from the remainder of the law, which is allowed to remain in force providing it passes the test of being distinct enough to survive independently of the invalidated provisions.[167]

In an extreme example of the court's efforts to keep any declaration of invalidity to a minimum, in *Koon Wing Yee v Insider Dealing Tribunal*[168] the Court of Final Appeal invalidated a more minor provision in the Securities (Insider Dealing) Ordinance (Cap. 395) than the provisions which were actually successfully challenged as unconstitutional

---

161. *Official Receiver & Trustee in Bankruptcy of Chan Wing Hing v Chan Wing Hing* (2006) 9 HKCFAR 545. The case involved a successful application by the Official Receiver for a declaration of unconstitutionality in respect of Section 30A(10)(b)(i) of the Bankruptcy Ordinance (Cap. 6), which extended a person's bankruptcy period every time they left Hong Kong without giving notice, something very difficult to monitor in practice.
162. Young, "Constitutional Rights in Hong Kong's Court of Final Appeal" (see note 160) at 73.
163. *Hung Chan Wa* at 634.
164. See *HKSAR v Lam Kwong Wai* (2006) 9 HKCFAR 574, 606–612 for a statement of the court's power to make remedial interpretations and an example of such an interpretation being applied. For more on the use of remedial interpretation by the Court of Final Appeal, see Kevin Zervos, "Constitutional Remedies under the Basic Law" (2010) 40 *HKLJ* 687, 699–703.
165. Young, "Constitutional Rights in Hong Kong's Court of Final Appeal" (see note 160) at 89.
166. (2005) 8 HKCFAR 229, 265–266. As a result, opinions differ about the human rights significance of this judgment. See further note 393 later in this chapter and the accompanying text.
167. Ibid. See also *Ng Ka Ling v Director of Immigration* (1999) 2 HKCFAR 4, 37.
168. (2008) 11 HKCFAR 170.

in that case.[169] Speaking extra-judicially, Justice Bokhary, one of the judges in this case, described this as the "striking down of a statutory provision which was not objectionable in itself" with the aim of "preserving the bulk and most important parts of the statutory scheme".[170]

The court has also experimented with other ways to limit the effect of any declaration of unconstitutionality. These include temporarily suspending its declaration to allow time for the enactment of a new law,[171] and possibly limiting the effect of such a declaration on previous court cases.[172]

On the relatively few occasions when the courts have exercised their power to strike down parts of laws that they conclude are inconsistent with the Hong Kong Basic Law, the Hong Kong SAR Government has mostly accepted the consequences. Most notably, a declaration of unconstitutionality by the Court of Final Appeal in *Secretary for Justice v Chan Wah*[173] forced the Hong Kong SAR Government fundamentally to change the system for village elections in the New Territories.[174] A ruling by the High Court in *Leung Kwok Hung v Chief Executive of the HKSAR*[175] that an executive order issued by the Chief Executive authorizing telephone tapping and other forms of interception of telecommunications was against the Hong Kong Basic Law[176] forced the government to hastily push through a new law introducing a more tightly controlled system of intercepting communications.[177]

---

169. Ibid. at 207–210. The case involved a successful challenge that it was a breach of the applicants' human rights to apply a lower (civil) standard of proof in cases before the Insider Dealing Tribunal that could lead to the imposition of criminal penalties. Instead of severely disrupting the work of the tribunal by invalidating the parts of the ordinance which had been successfully challenged in this case, the court simply invalidated the criminal penalties, so removing any human rights issue. For criticism that the court may have gone too far in this case, see Zervos, "Constitutional Remedies under the Basic Law" (see note 164) at 703–707.
170. Justice Kemal Bokhary, "Current State of Judicial Review in Hong Kong", Speech to Peking University School of Transnational Law, 15 Sept 2009 at 13.
171. As in *Koo Sze Yiu v Chief Executive of the HKSAR* (2006) 9 HKCFAR 441, 456–459, where the court suspended its declaration for six months. See further note 63 in Chapter 5.
172. This is known as prospective overruling, because the effect of the court decision does not apply to most previously decided court cases. In *HKSAR v Hung Chan Wa* (2006) 9 HKCFAR 614, 630–631, the Court of Final Appeal left open the issue of whether the Hong Kong courts have this power. See further Zervos, "Constitutional Remedies under the Basic Law" (see note 164) at 707–710.
173. (2000) 3 HKCFAR 459.
174. See further note 400 later in this chapter.
175. Unrep., HCAL 107/2005, [2006] HKEC 239. The case was appealed up to the Court of Final Appeal, primarily on the issue of whether the court had the power temporarily to delay enforcement of its ruling, where it was heard as *Koo Sze Yiu* (see note 171).
176. This was the Law Enforcement (Covert Surveillance Procedure) Order issued by the Chief Executive on 5 August 2005. See further note 59 in Chapter 5.
177. This was the Interception of Communications and Surveillance Ordinance (Cap. 589), which was enacted by the Legislative Council on 6 August 2006.

However, the Hong Kong SAR Government has been more cautious about accepting court rulings on residency rights in Hong Kong, especially where large numbers are involved. That was demonstrated by the government's reaction to the Court of Final Appeal rulings in *Ng Ka Ling* and the accompanying case of *Chan Kam Nga v Director of Immigration*,[178] which invalidated sections of the Immigration Ordinance (Cap. 115) restricting the right of many mainland-born children with a Hong Kong parent to reside in Hong Kong[179] because they violated the court's interpretation of two provisions in the Hong Kong Basic Law.[180] On that occasion, the Hong Kong SAR Government refused to implement the court's rulings because of the huge numbers involved and the impact this would have on Hong Kong.[181] Instead, the Chief Executive sought a fresh interpretation of the relevant provisions in the Hong Kong Basic Law from the National People's Congress Standing Committee.[182] This effectively reversed key parts of the court ruling by holding that the restrictions were compatible with the Hong Kong Basic Law,[183] so preventing other children in the same situation from using these cases as a precedent.[184] That showed how, while the Hong Kong SAR Government may usually choose to comply with court rulings in cases involving the Hong Kong Basic Law, the Standing Committee's ultimate power of interpretation gives it an alternative in the rare cases where it feels unable to accept the effects of the court judgment.[185]

---

178. (1999) 2 HKCFAR 82.
179. See *Ng Ka Ling* at 33–43 and *Chan Kam Nga* at 89–92.
180. These were Article 24(2)(3) on the category of children entitled to the right of abode in Hong Kong, and Article 22(4) on the power of mainland authorities to control entry into Hong Kong from the mainland. See further notes 77–78 in Chapter 7.
181. The Hong Kong SAR Government estimated that 690,000 people would immediately become eligible for residence in Hong Kong as a result of the court's rulings in these two cases, followed by a further 980,000 after seven years. See "Assessment of Service Implication in Relation to the Judgement of the Court of Final Appeal on the Right of Abode Issue Tabled at the Legislative Council" (6 May 1999), reproduced in Johannes M.M. Chan, H.L. Fu and Yash Ghai (eds.), *Hong Kong's Constitutional Debate: Conflict Over Interpretation* (Hong Kong University Press, 2000) at 274–283.
182. Through a report by the Chief Executive to the State Council stating that "the HKSAR is no longer capable of resolving the problem on its own". See "Report on Seeking Assistance from the Central People's Government in Solving Problems Encountered in the Implementation of the Basic Law of the Hong Kong SAR" (20 May 1999), reproduced in Chan, Fu and Ghai (eds.), *Hong Kong's Constitutional Debate* (see note 181) at 474–477.
183. See The Interpretation by the Standing Committee of the NPC of Articles 22(4) and 24(2)(3) of the Basic Law of the Hong Kong SAR of the PRC (26 June 1999). For more on this interpretation, see further note 90 in Chapter 7.
184. See further note 168 in Chapter 7 and the accompanying text.
185. In *Director of Immigration v Chong Fung Yuen* (2001) 4 HKCFAR 211, 221 the Court of Final Appeal sought to rationalize this by indirectly drawing a comparison with the well-established position at common law that a government can propose legislation to reverse the effects of a court judgment. See notes 367–370 later in this chapter and the accompanying text.

Ng Ka Ling also saw the Court of Final Appeal seek to extend the boundaries of constitutional review even further, by controversially arguing that the courts have the power to invalidate any actions of the National People's Congress and its Standing Committee that they judge to be in breach of the Hong Kong Basic Law.[186] In doing so, the Court of Final Appeal overruled the Court of Appeal on this point.[187] In *HKSAR v Ma Wai Kwan David*,[188] the Court of Appeal had held that actions of the National People's Congress fell within one of the few restrictions on the jurisdiction of the courts under the Hong Kong Basic Law. This is Article 19(2), which states that, "restrictions on their jurisdiction imposed by the legal system and principles previously in force in Hong Kong shall be maintained".[189]

In *Ma Wai Kwan*, then Chief Judge Chan held that the courts could not challenge an action of the British parliament while Hong Kong was under British rule.[190] So this was a restriction on their "jurisdiction imposed by the legal system and principles previously in force", which continued after 1 July 1997 under Article 19(2) with the only difference being that, instead of applying to the British parliament, it now applied to China's parliament, the National People's Congress.

However, in *Ng Ka Ling*, the Court of Final Appeal rejected this argument on the grounds that the two situations were not the same. While Hong Kong was a British colony before 1 July 1997 and, as a result, naturally had no constitutional right to autonomy or any general power to challenge actions of the British parliament, the new situation was "fundamentally different".[191] After 1 July 1997, Hong Kong is not a Chinese colony, but instead part of China with a "constitution" (as the court called the Hong Kong Basic Law) guaranteeing a high degree of autonomy. This meant that the old restrictions, which only applied in a colonial setting, were no longer relevant.[192] Furthermore, the court asserted that: "As with other constitutions, laws which are inconsistent with the Basic Law are of no effect and are invalid."[193] The Court of Final Appeal said this meant that, in choosing to pass the Hong Kong Basic Law and to give the Hong Kong courts "independent judicial power", the National People's Congress had therefore chosen to give the Hong Kong courts the power to invalidate (at least in relation to their enforcement in Hong Kong) any actions inconsistent with the Hong Kong Basic Law, even including those committed by the National People's Congress itself, or its Standing Committee.[194]

This was a clever attempt to fill what otherwise would be a vacuum. Since it is difficult to imagine the courts in China being prepared to enforce the Hong Kong Basic

---

186. *Ng Ka Ling* at 26–28.
187. Ibid. at 27.
188. [1997] HKLRD 761.
189. For more on the effect of Article 19(2) in restricting the courts from hearing certain specific types of cases, see further "6.5: Limits on Courts" later in this chapter.
190. *Ma Wai Kwan* at 780–781.
191. *Ng Ka Ling* at 27.
192. Ibid.
193. Ibid. at 26.
194. Ibid.

Law, or indeed any other law, against the National People's Congress or its Standing Committee,[195] there would be no way of restraining any breaches of the Hong Kong Basic Law by these two bodies unless the Hong Kong courts performed this role. However, the Court of Final Appeal's judgment overlooked the fact that the Hong Kong Basic Law does not have the status of a constitution within the Chinese legal system. Instead, it is simply one of many Basic Laws passed by the National People's Congress.[196] In any event, the PRC Constitution 1982 provides that all branches of the Chinese state are answerable to the National People's Congress or its local counterparts,[197] including even the military.[198] So it seems inconceivable that the drafters of the Hong Kong Basic Law would ever have intended to allow even the lowest court in Hong Kong (the Court of Final Appeal referred to this power being exercised by all the courts of Hong Kong[199]) to challenge the National People's Congress in a way which no other body of the Chinese state is permitted to do, at least under the constitution.[200]

The *Ng Ka Ling* judgment recognized that this assertion of a right to invalidate actions of the National People's Congress and its Standing Committee was "controversial".[201] So it was not surprising that the *Ng Ka Ling* case drew a swift response from Beijing. In a statement issued by the official Xinhua News Agency only eight days after the judgment, four mainland legal scholars accused the Court of Final Appeal of breaching the Chinese constitution and placing itself above the National People's Congress and its Standing Committee in a way that effectively amounted to a declaration of independence from the rest of China.[202] This was followed by similar criticism from the State Council,[203]

---

195. Under the PRC Constitution 1982, the Supreme People's Court, China's highest court, is responsible to the NPC (Article 128), which appoints and removes its President (Articles 62(7) and 63(4)). The other judges on the court are appointed and removed by the NPC Standing Committee (Article 67(11)).
196. See further "3.2: Domestic Dimension" in Chapter 3. See also on this point, Albert H.Y. Chen, "The Court of Final Appeal's Ruling in the 'Illegal Migrant' Children Case" and Bing Ling, "The Proper Law for the Conflict Between the Basic Law and Other Legislative Acts", in Chan, Fu and Ghai (eds.), *Hong Kong's Constitutional Debate* (see note 181) at 76, 154 and 169.
197. PRC Constitution 1982, Articles 2 and 57 (the latter article was cited in *Ng Ka Ling* at 12).
198. PRC Constitution 1982, Article 94.
199. *Ng Ka Ling* at 26.
200. In reality, of course, the supreme authority in China rests with the Chinese Communist Party, which is officially given a leading role in the Preamble to the PRC Constitution 1982. Some scholars argue this allows bodies such as the Supreme People's Court to ignore the authority of the NPC as long as they follow the wishes of their real boss, the Chinese Communist Party. See Nanping Liu, *Opinions of the Supreme People's Court: Judicial Interpretation in China* (Sweet & Maxwell Asia, 1997) at 59–63.
201. *Ng Ka Ling* at 26.
202. See Xiao Weiyun and others, "Why the Court of Final Appeal Was Wrong: Comments of the Mainland Scholars on the Judgment of the Court of Final Appeal", Xinhua News Agency, 6 Feb 1999, translated in Chan, Fu and Ghai (eds.), *Hong Kong's Constitutional Debate* (see note 181) at 54–55.
203. Mark O'Neill, "Beijing says abode ruling was wrong and should be changed", *South China Morning Post*, 9 Feb 1999.

the highest arm of the Central Government, and the Legislative Affairs Commission of the National People's Congress Standing Committee,[204] a powerful body responsible for drafting and scrutinising laws. There were also proposals to place the issue on the agenda of the National People's Congress, so that it could pass a motion formally condemning the court.[205]

In order to defuse what was widely described as a "constitutional crisis",[206] the Hong Kong SAR Government took the unprecedented step of going back to the Court of Final Appeal and asking it to reopen the case and clarify those sections of its judgment which had caused such controversy. This was an "exceptional course", as the court noted in responding to the government's application in *Ng Ka Ling v Director of Immigration (No 2)*, since normally a court will not comment on its judgment after delivering it, unless the same issues arise again in a later case.[207] It is difficult to point to any comparable instances of courts elsewhere in the common law world agreeing to take such a step, and the only example the government could cite was when Britain's House of Lords had agreed to reopen a case because one of the judges had failed to declare a possible conflict of interest.[208] The Hong Kong Bar Association strongly criticized the government's application for fear it would set a dangerous precedent, and encourage losing parties to go back to the court to seek similar clarifications in other cases.[209]

However, the Court of Final Appeal, like highest courts elsewhere, has an "inherent jurisdiction"[210] to depart from previous practice. This means there is nothing to prevent the court, if it wishes to do so, from deciding to reopen a case in order to "clarify" it. Clearly under considerable pressure following the criticism by mainland legal scholars and officials, the court said it recognized that sections of its original judgment had "given rise to much controversy",[211] and so was prepared to take "the exceptional course under our inherent jurisdiction"[212] of explaining them further.[213]

---

204. May Sin-Mi Hon, "Beijing calls for change to abode ruling", *South China Morning Post*, 14 Feb 1999.
205. Political Desk, "Deputy fights to get ruling placed on NPC meeting agenda", *South China Morning Post*, 13 Feb 1999.
206. See, for instance, No Kwai-yan, "Concern for judicial system after mainland experts say migrants verdict challenges China's National People's Congress", *South China Morning Post*, 8 Feb 1999.
207. (1999) 2 HKCFAR 141.
208. See Hong Kong SAR Government's submission to the Court of Final Appeal, reprinted as "Court Should Have Option to Reopen Cases", *The Standard*, 27 Feb 1999. The case referred to was *re Pinochet* [1999] UKHL 1.
209. "Bar Statement on Government's Application to CFA", reprinted in Chan, Fu and Ghai (eds.), *Hong Kong's Constitutional Debate* (see note 181) at 255.
210. *Ng Ka Ling (No 2)* at 142.
211. Ibid.
212. Ibid.
213. Although often described as a "clarification", the court's supplementary judgment did not actually use this word.

The court then expressly acknowledged the power of the National People's Congress Standing Committee to issue binding interpretations of the Hong Kong Basic Law,[214] and stated that the courts had no authority to question them.[215] Crucially, the two-paragraph supplementary judgment concluded by also recognizing "the authority of the National People's Congress or the Standing Committee to do any act which *is in accordance* with the provisions of the Basic Law and the procedure therein"[216] (emphasis added).

But the form of words used by the court cleverly avoided directly addressing the issue that had caused the controversy in the first place. Faced with controversy over its assertion that Hong Kong's courts have the power to invalidate actions of the National People's Congress and its Standing Committee *not* in accordance[217] with the Hong Kong Basic Law, the Court of Final Appeal responded by saying that it had no authority to invalidate any action of the National People's Congress or its Standing Committee that *is* in accordance with the Hong Kong Basic Law. This did not directly contradict its earlier assertion of a power to invalidate actions *not* in accordance with the Hong Kong Basic Law.

The general reaction to the court's supplementary judgment was that it had successfully made a peace offering to Beijing in order to defuse the constitutional crisis, without formally retreating from its earlier position.[218] It was undoubtedly successful in achieving the first of these two objectives. Within a day of the supplementary judgment, the Legislative Affairs Commission of the National People's Congress Standing Committee issued a statement describing it as "a necessary step",[219] and the top Chinese official in charge of Hong Kong affairs signalled a few days later that Beijing now considered the crisis over.[220]

However, opinions are divided over how much damage the court did to its reputation by making such a peace offering. Chen (2000) sees it as a "legitimate and appropriate way to deal with the problem" arguing it is in many ways similar to the reference procedures that exist in Canada and India, where governments in those countries can refer issues of constitutional and public importance to the court for an opinion.[221] Chan (2000), by contrast, believes the court's independence was "thrown into doubt" because the court

---

214. *Ng Ka Ling (No 2)* at 142. This power derives from Article 158(1) of the Hong Kong Basic Law. See further "7.2: Standing Committee" in Chapter 7.
215. Ibid.
216. Ibid.
217. "Inconsistent" was the term actually used in the original judgment. See *Ng Ka Ling* at 26.
218. See, for instance, Editorial, "Best Way Out", *South China Morning Post*, 27 Feb 1999. However, Chen (2000) draws a distinction between the precise wording used in the original and supplementary judgments. See Chen, "The Court of Final Appeal's Ruling in the 'Illegal Migrant' Children Case" (see note 196) at 95.
219. Chris Yeung, "Beijing hint of end to abode row", *South China Morning Post*, 28 Feb 1999.
220. May Sin-mi Hon, "Qian adds to easing of abode dispute", *South China Morning Post*, 1 March 1999.
221. See Chen "The Court of Final Appeal's Ruling in the 'Illegal Migrant' Children Case" (see note 196) at 93.

showed it "is unable to withstand political pressure and is prepared to take a political course which has flimsy legal ground and which is beyond the role of the Court".[222]

While the clarification did not formally contradict the court's earlier assertion of a power to invalidate actions of the National People's Congress and its Standing Committee that breach the Hong Kong Basic Law, Ghai (2000) expresses doubts as to whether, in reality, the Court of Final Appeal would ever now really dare to exercise that power.[223] When questioned on the issue in a press interview eight years later, Chief Justice Li also downplayed the prospect of such a power ever being exercised.[224] While still insisting the courts have the jurisdiction to invalidate actions of the National People's Congress, the Chief Justice added "this was unlikely to arise ... as such acts would probably be covered by an interpretation by the NPC Standing Committee, which would be binding on the courts".[225] Remarkably, for more than a decade after *Ng Ka Ling (No 2)*, the issue of the power of the courts to invalidate actions of the National People's Congress and its Standing Committee never again arose in any other case before the Court of Final Appeal. Perhaps this indicates a desire on all sides to avoid reviving such a sensitive issue. When the issue did finally arise in passing in a High Court case in 2008,[226] despite the formal legal position preserved in *Ng Ka Ling (No 2)*, Justice Cheung appeared uncertain whether the Hong Kong courts really had the jurisdiction to deal with an alleged breach of the Hong Kong Basic Law by the National People's Congress Standing Committee.[227]

Ng Ka Ling was an exceptional case, in which the huge numbers of children involved coupled with what China perceived as a challenge by the Court of Final Appeal to the authority of the National People's Congress almost guaranteed controversy. But, *Ng Ka Ling* aside, what has been notable about the growth in judicial review in Hong Kong is how it took many years before it began to arouse controversy.

---

222. Johannes M.M. Chan, "What the Court of Final Appeal Has Not Clarified in Its Clarification: Jurisdiction and Amicus Intervention" in Chan, Fu and Ghai (eds.), *Hong Kong's Constitutional Debate* (see note 181) at 180–181.
223. Yash Ghai, "The NPC Interpretation and its Consequences" in Chan, Fu and Ghai (eds.), *Hong Kong's Constitutional Debate* (see note 181) at 213.
224. Cliff Buddle, "Judicial independence 'guaranteed'", *South China Morning Post*, 15 June 2007.
225. Ibid.
226. *Azan Aziz Marwah v Director of Immigration* [2009] 3 HKC 185, 202–203. The case involved an application for judicial review of the Immigration Department's refusal to issue a Hong Kong SAR passport to the son of a naturalized Chinese citizen The issue was briefly raised during the case as to whether an interpretation of PRC Nationality Law issued by the NPC Standing Committee breached the Hong Kong Basic Law by discriminating in favour of those of ethnic Chinese origin.
227. Ibid. No decision was necessary on this point, because the applicant had failed to raise the issue of alleged discrimination prior to the court hearing or provide any evidence in support of it. Nonetheless, citing *Ng Ka Ling (No 2)*, Justice Cheung observed that the issue raised the question of "whether the courts have the necessary jurisdiction to deal with these questions by way of judicial review".

While the number of constitutional review cases has remained small, although the small number belie the fact that these include some of the most important judgments in recent years, for many years the number of judicial review cases as a whole rose rapidly. Most such cases involve challenges to the actions of the executive branch of the government and other public bodies, rather than challenges to the legality of laws.

The annual number of applications for permission to lodge a judicial review reached 149 cases in 2005,[228] almost equivalent to the total reported number of judicial review cases from 1950 to 1989.[229] Much, but not all, of this growth can be attributed to the introduction of the Hong Kong Basic Law. Much longer and more detailed than the colonial constitutional document it replaced, especially in its extensive protection of human rights, the Hong Kong Basic Law provides much more material for bringing legal challenges against the actions of the executive and public bodies. The early years after the Hong Kong Basic Law came into force saw a peak of several thousand judicial review applications annually, the vast majority of which involved claims for right of abode under Article 24(2) of the Hong Kong Basic Law.[230]

Other factors have also played a part in this extraordinary growth in judicial review in Hong Kong. Legal aid has funded many cases; otherwise it would have been extremely difficult for applicants with little money to initiate judicial reviews.[231] The advent of a bilingual legal system has made the courts seem more approachable for the majority of the population.[232] Then Chief Justice Andrew Li (2006) also observed that there has been a broader cultural change in Hong Kong society, which has seen the traditional Chinese reluctance to resort to the courts fade away as, "with better education, citizens have higher expectations of public institutions and are more conscious of their rights and freedoms".[233]

This growth in judicial review has inevitably seen a great increase in the variety of participants and types of such cases. To quote just a few examples, parents have challenged the expulsion of their child from school,[234] airline crew have disputed changes to

---

228. However the annual figure declined for several years afterwards, falling to 110 cases in 2011. See Austin Chiu, "Judicial review cases in sharp fall", *South China Morning Post*, 19 July 2012.
229. A survey of the Hong Kong Law Reports found 146 reported judicial review cases from 1950 to 1989. See Tai, "The Development of Constitutionalism in Hong Kong" (see note 113) at 54.
230. For example, 3,752 of the 3,848 judicial review cases brought in 2001 involved right of abode issues. See Ma Ngok, *Political Development in Hong Kong: State, Political Society, and Civil Society* (Hong Kong University Press, 2007) at 85.
231. However, most applications for legal aid to bring judicial review cases are rejected, suggesting the number of judicial review cases would be even higher if restrictions on eligibility for legal aid were relaxed. See Polly Hui, "Hearing impaired", *South China Morning Post*, 3 March 2008.
232. See Lai, "Recent Trends and Developments of Judicial Review in Hong Kong" (see note 107) at para. 9.
233. Li, "Speech at the Ceremonial Opening of the Legal Year 2006" (see note 116).
234. *R v English Schools Foundation* [2004] 3 HKC 343.

their required rest periods during long flights.[235] Other examples include telecommunication companies challenging the size of the fees they are allowed to charge for connecting calls that originate on a rival network,[236] and public housing tenants challenging the Housing Authority's refusal to conduct regular reviews that might have resulted in a reduction in rents during a period of economic hardship.[237] Judicial review applications have also been made much easier by the relaxed attitude adopted by the courts as to who can bring such cases.[238] In *Koo Sze Yiu v Chief Executive of the HKSAR*, simply being a concerned member of the public was enough to challenge the legality of covert surveillance by law enforcement agencies.[239]

Inevitably, such challenges to government policies bring the courts into the political arena. So too does the expanding scope of judicial review, where Hong Kong has followed (and, in some cases, led) other jurisdictions in the common law world in recognizing new grounds for judicial review which involve much greater scrutiny of the merits of government actions. Gone are the days when judicial review was essentially confined to considering government actions by the three criteria of whether they were: (1) illegal, (2) irrational, or (3) followed the wrong procedures.[240] Now, irrationality, which the courts had interpreted in such an extreme fashion that it hardly ever applied,[241] has been increasingly replaced by proportionality in human rights cases.[242] This sets a

---

235. *Cathay Pacific Airways Flight Attendants Union v Director-General of Civil Aviation* [2007] 2 HKLRD 668.
236. *PCCW-HKT Telephone Ltd v The Telecommunications Authority* (unrep., HCAL 6/2007, [2007] HKEC 993). For an account of this case, see Gordon and Mok, *Judicial Review in Hong Kong* (see note 109) at 221–222.
237. *Ho Choi Wan v Hong Kong Housing Authority* (2005) 8 HKCFAR 628. For more on this case, which had potentially major implications for the approximately 30% of Hong Kong's population who live in public rental housing, see further Chan, "Basic Law and Constitutional Review" (see note 155) at 440–441.
238. Under Order 53, Rule 3(7) of the Rules of the High Court (Cap. 4, Subsidiary Legislation A), an applicant in a judicial review case must have "sufficient interest in the matter to which the application relates". As a result, much depends on how widely this requirement for "sufficient interest" (or standing) is defined by the courts.
239. (2006) 9 HKCFAR 441. For more on this case (which was known as *Leung Kwok Hung v Chief Executive of the HKSAR* in the lower courts), see further notes 58–64 in Chapter 5 and the accompanying text.
240. See note 109 earlier in this chapter for the classic statement of these three categories.
241. See the classic definition of irrationality in *Associated Provincial Picture Houses Ltd v Wednesbury Corp* [1948] 1 KB 223, 230 as only applying to "a conclusion so unreasonable that no reasonable authority could ever have come to it". This extreme definition of irrationality, which became known as "Wednesbury unreasonableness", has been since criticized in the English courts as too restrictive. See the comments of Lord Cooke in *R v Secretary of State for the Home Department, ex parte Daly* [2001] 2 AC 532, 549.
242. See the Court of Final Appeal's statement on the use of the proportionality test in judging the necessity of any restrictions on human rights in *Leung Kwok Hung v HKSAR* (2005) 8 HKCFAR 229, 252–254. For further examples of the use of proportionality in human rights cases in Hong Kong, see Gordon and Mok, *Judicial Review in Hong Kong* (see note 109) at 198–204.

much lower threshold for showing that government actions were disproportionate, or that they went further than was necessary to achieve the objective being pursued. Chan (2007) notes that it "will inevitably involve value choices and value judgment over the relative importance of competing considerations".[243] So, for example, in *Chan Kin Sum v Secretary for Justice*, the court held that, although the government was entitled to prevent some prisoners from voting, an indiscriminate ban on all prisoners voting was disproportionate and so impermissible.[244] Although initially confined to human rights cases, Chan (2008) predicts that the proportionality principle will expand to cover all types of judicial cases.[245]

In another area, the Court of Final Appeal has led the common law world in developing legitimate expectation as a new ground for judicial review, allowing applicants to bring cases based simply on promises made by government officials. So, in *Ng Siu Tung v Director of Immigration*,[246] some of the children who no longer had any legal right to reside in Hong Kong as a result of the National People's Congress Standing Committee's interpretation of the relevant provisions in the Hong Kong Basic Law were nonetheless successful. This was on the grounds that prior assurances by government officials had given them a legitimate expectation of being allowed to remain in Hong Kong.[247]

Initially, the court's increased involvement in political issues did not bring any of the accusations of meddling by "unelected judges" that often have been seen in major Western democracies such as the US and Britain.[248] Chan (2007) suggests that is, at least partly, because unlike those countries neither the executive branch of government nor the legislature in Hong Kong are currently elected entirely by universal suffrage.[249] Far from seeking to minimize the judiciary's involvement in political issues, the lack of alternative channels to challenge government policies in the absence of full democracy in Hong Kong has led to issues that might be resolved through the political process in elected democracies instead being fought out through the courts.[250] Mason (2011),

---

243. Chan, "Basic Law and Constitutional Review" (see note 155) at 426.
244. [2009] 2 HKLRD 166, 221–222.
245. Chan, "Administrative Law, Politics and Governance" (see note 114) at 165.
246. (2002) 5 HKCFAR 1.
247. The applicants were claiming the right of abode in Hong Kong, and had been advised by government officials that there was no need to join the *Ng Ka Ling* litigation because they would be treated in the same way as the parties to that case. However, they were denied the right of abode after the Hong Kong SAR Government sought an interpretation from the NPC Standing Committee that prevented the outcome of the *Ng Ka Ling* litigation from applying to anyone other than the parties in that case (see further "7.2: Standing Committee" in Chapter 7 for more on the *Ng Ka Ling* case and the subsequent interpretation by the Standing Committee). For an excellent analysis of the significance of the *Ng Siu Tung* case, see Christopher Forsyth and Rebecca Williams, "Closing Chapter in the Immigrant Children Saga: Substantive Legitimate Expectations and Administrative Justice in Hong Kong" (2002) 10(1) *Asia Pacific Law Review* 29–47.
248. See Chen, "The Interpretation of the Basic Law" (see note 130) at 419–420.
249. See Chan, "Basic Law and Constitutional Review" (see note 155) at 410.
250. Ibid. at 446.

who has frequently served on the Court of Final Appeal as a non-permanent judge from overseas,[251] notes that "there is a tendency in Hong Kong to look to the courts for relief in circumstances where in Australia we would be looking to the political process for a solution".[252]

Frustrated by the government's unwillingness to listen to their warnings about the consequences of further harbour reclamation, an environmental pressure group resorted to judicial review to focus public attention on the issue and force a change in government policy.[253] Similarly, two public housing tenants opposed to the Link REIT privatization of most of the Housing Authority's shopping centres and car parks successfully used an application for judicial review to delay the proposed listing in 2004–05.[254] Since this privatization did not require the approval of the Legislative Council, and attempts to oppose it through the legislature proved ineffective, opponents of the privatization resorted to challenging it through the courts instead.[255] Although the applicants in both cases were either partially or wholly unsuccessful, they still achieved their apparent goal of rallying public opposition against the government's handling of these issues.[256]

More recently, this growing trend to seek to resolve political issues through the courts has produced the first signs of a backlash. In 2007 the Court of Final Appeal tightened the criteria for bringing an application for judicial review in an apparent attempt to filter out some of the more extreme cases coming before the courts.[257] In 2011, a judicial review case halted construction of the bridge linking Hong Kong with Zhuhai and Macao until it was reversed on appeal.[258] Some politicians accused those involved in this case of putting the interests of the Hong Kong public at risk, since delays in the project that appeared

---

251. For more on the important role on the Court of Final Appeal played by Sir Anthony Mason, a former Chief Justice of Australia, see further notes 295–298 later in this chapter and the accompanying text.
252. Sir Anthony Mason, "A non-permanent fixture on the CFA", Interview in (August 2010) *Hong Kong Lawyer* 20, 22.
253. *Town Planning Board v Society for the Protection of the Harbour Ltd* (2004) 7 HKCFAR 1. For an excellent account of the use of this case to focus public attention on the issue, see Chan, "Basic Law and Constitutional Review" (see note 155) at 439–440.
254. *Lo Siu Lan v Hong Kong Housing Authority* (2005) 8 HKCFAR 363.
255. For more on the inability of legislators to block the proposed privatisation through the political process, see Anthony BL Cheung and Max WL Wong, "Judicial Review and Policy Making in Hong Kong: Changing Interface Between the Legal and the Political" (2006) 28 *Asia Pacific Journal of Public Administration* 117, 124–125.
256. The applicants in *Lo Siu Lan* lost their case but, by delaying the proposed privatization, still succeeded in severely embarrassing the government. The applicants in *Society for the Protection of Harbour* were only partially successful. See further Chan, "Basic Law and Constitutional Review" (see note 155) at 440.
257. In *Po Fun Chan v Winnie Cheung* (2007) 10 HKCFAR 676, 685–686, the Court of Final Appeal replaced the "potential arguability" test with an "arguability" test which it stated "undoubtedly imposes a higher threshold" for bringing a judicial review case.
258. *Chu Yee Wah v Director of Environmental Protection* [2011] 3 HKC 227, reversed on appeal in [2011] 5 HKLRD 469. The case involved the environmental impact assessment conducted by the government for the project.

to be at least partly attributable to the case resulted in a multi-billion dollar increase in construction costs.[259] There were signs these sentiments were shared by others in Hong Kong, with a law scholar reporting that many secondary school teachers who attended his seminars echoed such criticisms of the case and even questioned the need for judicial review.[260]

Looking forward, the possible introduction of universal suffrage from 2017 onwards[261] may have some impact on the number of judicial review cases if it makes the political process a more viable alternative for resolving some of the disputes which currently end up in the courts. A more democratic system of government could also remove one of the strongest arguments for the court's active role in political issues. Cullen (2007) notes that any introduction of universal suffrage poses "a challenge as demanding as it is unusual" for the Court of Final Appeal since "a key political factor driving judicial authority and power is set to weaken dramatically".[262] However, Cheung and Wong (2006) believe that the increasingly political role being forced upon the courts is unlikely to diminish even if Hong Kong becomes more democratic because "interest groups which are losing the 'political' game will not be likely to submit themselves to the outcome of the political process and will still resort to the judicial process in order to exhaust their final opportunity".[263]

That suggests many are likely to continue to take their grievances with the government to the courts. Having staked out its claim to a strong constitutional role for the courts, the Court of Final Appeal is now finding that the flaws in Hong Kong's political system are pushing that role far further than what the court originally may have envisaged.

6.3 Composition of the Court of Final Appeal

The creation of a Court of Final Appeal with the power of final adjudication in both civil and criminal cases is perhaps the most significant feature of the provisions on Hong Kong's judicial system in the Hong Kong Basic Law.[264] It gives Hong Kong a power which is rarely exercised by autonomous areas elsewhere in the world, and which is often

---

259. See, for example, Lau Nai-keung, "Public the big loser in wrangle over bridge", *South China Morning Post*, 29 April 2011.
260. Jolie Ho, "HKU professor points to bias against rule of law among liberal arts teachers", *South China Morning Post*, 12 Feb 2013.
261. See further note 108 in Chapter 5 and the accompanying text, for more on the possible introduction of universal suffrage for the election of the Chief Executive.
262. Richard Cullen, "When political change challenges our courts", *South China Morning Post*, 14 April 2007.
263. Cheung and Wong, "Judicial Review and Policy Making in Hong Kong" (see note 255) at 131.
264. See especially Article 82, which vests the Court of Final Appeal with the power of final adjudication. This power is also mentioned in Articles 2 and 19(1), although without specifically referring to the Court of Final Appeal.

seen as one of the most special features of Hong Kong's high degree of autonomy under the Hong Kong Basic Law.[265]

Given this significance, it was probably inevitable that the creation of the Court of Final Appeal should also cause some of the most significant controversies in the early years of the implementation of the Hong Kong Basic Law. These saw the new court struggle (sometimes uncertainly) to define its role in an environment which, especially due to the National People's Congress Standing Committee's power to interpret the Hong Kong Basic Law, no other final appellate court elsewhere in the common law world has ever had to operate.

The controversy over the Court of Final Appeal began even before its creation, with a prolonged battle over the court's composition. Like so many other provisions in the Hong Kong Basic Law, the origins of the Court of Final Appeal date back to the Sino-British Joint Declaration.[266] Since the power of final adjudication was not exercised in Hong Kong prior to 1 July 1997, judges in Hong Kong had no experience of sitting in a final appellate role. So China accepted a suggestion from Britain to include in the Joint Declaration a provision allowing judges from other common law jurisdictions to be invited to sit on the Court of Final Appeal.[267] The rationale was that Hong Kong judges would benefit from the expertise of having judges with experience of courts of final appeal elsewhere in the common law world sitting alongside them on Hong Kong's new Court of Final Appeal. That was incorporated into Article 82 of the Hong Kong Basic Law, which allows that the court "may as required invite *judges* from other common law jurisdictions to sit on the Court of Final Appeal" (emphasis added).

In keeping with its lack of detailed provisions on the judiciary,[268] neither the Joint Declaration nor the Hong Kong Basic Law elaborate on how many such judges can be invited to sit on the court, or under what circumstances. That was widely interpreted in Hong Kong as meaning there were no limits on the number of such judges who can be invited, especially as both the Joint Declaration and the Hong Kong Basic Law refer to inviting overseas *judges* in the plural. However, Britain, anxious to reach an agreement that would allow the court to be established in the early 1990s and so build up its authority prior to 1 July 1997, soon discovered that China envisaged only a very limited role for overseas judges. As a result, a 1991 agreement between Britain and China on the establishment of the court proposed limiting the number of overseas judges who can be invited to sit on the court to a maximum of one in any case. This restriction was opposed by a majority of members in the Legislative Council,[269] and denounced as being in breach of the Joint Declaration and the Hong Kong Basic Law by the two organizations

---

265. This is a power that few other autonomous areas elsewhere in the world exercise, at least in relation to both civil and criminal cases. See further note 191 in Chapter 4 and the accompanying text.
266. Annex I(III).
267. See further note 23 in Chapter 2 and the accompanying text.
268. See further note 1 earlier in this chapter and the accompanying text.
269. See Legislative Council, *Official Record of Proceedings, Hong Kong Hansard* (4 Dec 1991) at 1012.

representing Hong Kong's legal profession, the Law Society and the Hong Kong Bar Association.[270] Whether it was actually in breach of either the Joint Declaration or the Hong Kong Basic Law depends on how the word *judges* is interpreted since, even under the 1991 agreement, there is nothing to stop more than one overseas judge sitting on the court—just not in the same case.[271]

The practical effect of this fierce opposition to the 1991 agreement was to delay the creation of the Court of Final Appeal for several years, as this initial attempt to establish the court was abandoned and Britain and China instead became embroiled in battles over other issues.[272] Only as 1997 drew closer did such opposition soften. After a further agreement in 1995 between Britain and China, which included the same restriction on the number of overseas judges allowed to sit on the court, the Law Society changed its stance and supported the new agreement. After a fierce debate in the Legislative Council, the government was able to secure the passage of the Hong Kong Court of Final Appeal Ordinance (Cap. 484), the law establishing the new court.[273] By this time, China considered it too late to establish the court before the end of British rule and so the ordinance did not come into force until 1 July 1997.[274]

The ordinance provides for a five-member court, which will normally consist of the Chief Justice, three other permanent judges and one non-permanent judge.[275] The permanent judges are full-time members of the court, who normally serve until they retire at the age of 65 or resign.[276] In accordance with the nationality restrictions in the Hong Kong Basic Law, the Chief Justice must be a Chinese national.[277] The other permanent judges

---

270. For more on opposition to the 1991 agreement, see Johannes M.M. Chan, "The Legal System" in Joseph Y.S. Cheng and Paul C.K. Kwong, *The Other Hong Kong Report 1992* (The Chinese University Press, 1992) at 83–84.
271. See, for instance, the opinion delivered by Sir William Wade, *The Court of Final Appeal of Hong Kong* (24 Oct 1991), where the eminent English Queen's Counsel held (at para. 8) that a restriction allowing no more than one overseas judge to sit on the Court of Final Appeal in any individual case "could be held to come within the Basic Law at the very lowest level of literal construction". However, he also noted (at para. 6) that interpreting the Hong Kong Basic Law "in the spirit of the high degree of autonomy" would point to allowing a larger number of overseas judges.
272. Most notably arguments over the electoral arrangements proposed by the last British Governor, Chris Patten, which began shortly after he took up the post in 1992. See further "2.5: Sino-British Disputes" in Chapter 2.
273. For more on the 1995 agreement, and its acceptance by the Legislative Council, see Leo F. Goodstadt, "Prospects for the Rule of Law: the Political Dimension" in Tsang (ed.), *Judicial Independence and the Rule of Law in Hong Kong* (see note 23) at 191–194.
274. Hong Kong Court of Final Appeal Ordinance (Cap. 484), Section 1(2).
275. Ibid., Section 16(1).
276. Ibid., Sections 14(1), 14(5) and 14(11). Under Section 14(2)(a), the retirement age of 65 can be extended for up to six years under certain circumstances. See further notes 83–87 earlier in this chapter and the accompanying text, for the controversy in 2012 over the failure to give such an extension to Justice Bokhary.
277. Article 90(1). This also applies to the Chief Judge of the High Court.

can be either Chinese or foreigners, providing they have previously worked in Hong Kong as either a judge in the Court of Appeal or Court of First Instance, or as a barrister who has worked in the local legal profession for at least 10 years.[278]

Only the fifth, non-permanent, member of the court can be an overseas judge invited from another common law jurisdiction. Even then, this need not always be the case. This judge is chosen by the Chief Justice,[279] from two lists consisting of a total of up to 30 non-permanent judges.[280] These are not permanent posts and judges serve on these lists for three years at a time, although this can be renewed multiple times.[281] While one list consists of overseas judges living outside Hong Kong with experience of serving in a higher court in another common law jurisdiction,[282] the other list consists primarily of retired Hong Kong judges.[283] The intention behind the existence of these two separate lists appears to have been to further limit the presence of overseas judges on the Court of Final Appeal, since it means there is no requirement for an overseas judge to be invited to sit on the court in every case. But the choice of the fifth judge in every case is entirely at the discretion of the Chief Justice.[284] Chan (2007) describes Andrew Li, the first Chief Justice of the Hong Kong SAR, as having taken a "policy decision" that this discretion should be exercised to invite an overseas rather than a Hong Kong judge to be the fifth, non-permanent, member of the court in virtually every substantive case.[285] As a result, an overseas judge joined the Court of Final Appeal for 97% of the cases it heard from July 1997 to June 2010.[286] Young and Da Roza (2010) describe the role of the other panel of Hong Kong judges as of "diminishing importance".[287] However, this other panel still performs a useful subsidiary role, since it provides a panel from which a substitute can be

---

278. Hong Kong Court of Final Appeal Ordinance (Cap. 484), Section 12(1).
279. Ibid., Section 16(1)(c).
280. Ibid., Section 10.
281. Ibid., Section 14(4).
282. Ibid., Section 12(4) defining such higher courts as, "a court of unlimited jurisdiction in either civil or criminal matters". They are also required never to have been a judge or permanent magistrate in Hong Kong.
283. Ibid., Section 12(3). In addition to retired Hong Kong judges, current Justices of Appeal and barristers who have worked in the local legal profession for at least 10 years are also eligible for inclusion on this list. However, the appointment of current Justices of Appeal to the panel of non-permanent judges for the Court of Final Appeal has been criticized by some in the legal profession as blurring the distinction between the two courts. See Albert Wong, "Lawmakers voice doubts over dual role for judges", *South China Morning Post*, 5 May 2010.
284. Ibid., Section 16(1)(c) gives the Chief Justice complete discretion in choosing if the fifth, non-permanent, judge in any particular case comes from the list of non-permanent Hong Kong judges or the list of judges from other common law jurisdictions.
285. Chan, "Basic Law and Constitutional Review" (see note 155) at 420.
286. Simon N.M. Young and Antonio Da Roza, "Judges and Judging in the Court of Final Appeal: A Statistical Picture" (August 2010) *Hong Kong Lawyer* 23, 24.
287. Ibid. at 29.

quickly brought in to make up the numbers on the court if one of the permanent judges is not available to hear any particular case.[288]

Although Article 82 of the Hong Kong Basic Law allows judges from any common law jurisdiction to sit on the Court of Final Appeal, initially only judges from Australia, England and New Zealand were invited to do so. This was justified on the grounds that these three countries "have close affinity with Hong Kong in terms of their laws, legal tradition and procedure".[289] Contrary to earlier fears, the Court of Final Appeal has had little difficulty attracting a panel of eminent overseas judges. Early examples included former Chief Justices from England[290] and Australia,[291] as well as one of New Zealand's most famous judges.[292]

Although restricted to a maximum of one judge in any case, those overseas judges have exercised far greater influence than their limited numbers would suggest. In 77 cases from 1997 to 2009, the overseas judge either authored or co-authored the majority judgment, which represents the views of most (or, more often, all) judges on the court.[293] Young and Da Roza (2010) suggest that their influence may be even greater than this, since "given their distinction as senior international jurists, [they] have probably influenced much of the decision-making, even when they had no direct role in the majority judgment".[294] This is particularly true of Sir Anthony Mason, a former Chief Justice of Australia, who for many years was a semi-permanent fixture on the Court of Final Appeal, and has written extensively about its work.[295] Although a non-permanent judge, invited to join the court on a case-by-case basis, Mason achieved the extraordinary feat

---

288. This is permitted under Section 16(4) of the Hong Kong Court of Final Ordinance (Cap. 484). See Justice Kemal Bokhary, *Hong Kong's Legal System: The Court of Final Appeal* (New Zealand Centre for Public Law, Occasional Paper No. 13, Nov 2002) at 6. According to Young [in "Constitutional Rights in Hong Kong's Court of Final Appeal" (see note 160) at 80], a non-permanent Hong Kong judge joined the court for 36% of all constitutional cases from 1999 to 2009.
289. See Secretary for Justice Elsie Leung, "Speech Moving a Resolution Under the Hong Kong Court of Final Appeal Ordinance (Cap. 484) in the Provisional Legislative Council", 23 July 1997, at para. 11.
290. Lord Woolf of Barnes was appointed a non-permanent judge of the Court of Final Appeal in July 2003. At that stage he was still Lord Chief Justice of England and Wales, but retired from this post two years later.
291. Sir Anthony Mason, who was appointed a non-permanent judge of the Court of Final Appeal in July 1997, and Sir Gerard Brennan, who was appointed in September 2000.
292. Lord Cooke of Thorndon, who was appointed a non-permanent judge of the Court of Final Appeal in July 1997.
293. Young and Da Roza, "Judges and Judging in the Court of Final Appeal" (see note 286) at 25.
294. Ibid. at 30.
295. See, for example, Sir Anthony Mason, "The Place of Comparative Law in the Developing Jurisprudence on the Rule of Law and Human Rights in Hong Kong" (2007) 37 *HKLJ* 299–317; and "The Rule of Law in the Shadow of the Giant: The Hong Kong Experience" (2011) 33 *Sydney Law Review* 623–644.

of writing more majority judgments in human rights cases than most of the court's permanent judges.[296] Young (2011) describes his influence on the court as "enormous",[297] and it is notable that Mason participated in most of the court's more controversial cases that are discussed in this book.[298]

The presence of an overseas judge on the Court of Final Appeal for virtually every major case has been mostly welcomed in Hong Kong.[299] Justice Bokhary, who sat alongside them during his 15 years on the court, has said that "their names are indelible in our history".[300] Voicing a common sentiment, Chan (2011) comments: "The overseas judges have played an important role in developing the jurisprudence of the Hong Kong courts. Their participation has enriched Hong Kong's local jurisprudence, and enhanced the reputation and independence of the court."[301]

The extent to which the presence of overseas judges has helped enhanced the international reputation of Hong Kong's Court of Final Appeal, is partly demonstrated by the significant number of its judgments which have been followed by courts in other countries.[302] Lo (2010) notes several instances where English judges who delivered judgments in the Court of Final Appeal helped to ensure those decisions received wider international attention by subsequently citing them with approval while hearing other cases back in London.[303]

---

296. Mason authored or co-authored 12 majority judgments in human rights cases from 1999 to 2009, more majority judgments than any other judge except then Chief Justice Li (although Justice Bokhary delivered more judgments in total, when separate concurring and dissenting judgments are taken into account). See Young, "Constitutional Rights in Hong Kong's Court of Final Appeal" (see note 160) at 79–80.
297. Ibid. at 80.
298. These include, for example, *Ng Ka Ling v Director of Immigration* (1999) 2 HKCFAR 4, *Lau Kong Yung v Director of Immigration* (1999) 2 HKCFAR 300, *HKSAR v Ng Kung Siu* (1999) 2 HKCFAR 442, *Director of Immigration v Chong Fung Yuen* (2001) 4 HKCFAR 211 and *Democratic Republic of Congo v FG Hemisphere* (2011) 14 HKCFAR 95.
299. For an early exception, see the criticism by Ma Lik, (in "A Judgment found wanting", *Hong Kong iMail*, 5 Dec 2000) of the Court of Final Appeal's decision in *Cheng v Tse Wai Chun* (2000) 3 HKCFAR 339, a case where the leading judgment was delivered by Lord Nicholls of Birkenhead, an overseas judge from the House of Lords. For more on this case, see further note 350 later in this chapter and the accompanying text.
300. Bokhary, "Hong Kong's Legal System" (see note 288) at 6.
301. Chan (2011), "The Judiciary" (see note 76) at 294.
302. As of 2010, Hong Kong Court of Final Appeal judgments had been cited at least 36 times in UK courts and at least 18 times in Australian courts. See P.Y. Lo, "The impact of CFA jurisprudence beyond Hong Kong" (August 2010) *Hong Kong Lawyer* 36, 36–37.
303. Ibid. Perhaps the best known example is Lord Nicholls of Birkenhead's judgment in the Court of Final Appeal case of *Cheng v Tse* (see notes 299 and 350) which was then referred to with approval in *Panday v Gordon* [2006] 1 AC 427, 436, a Privy Council case presided over by Lord Nicholls.

However the overseas judges appear very conscious that, when serving on the Court of Final Appeal, it is necessary to act "primarily as a Hong Kong judge, serving its community and seeing legal problems through a Hong Kong lens", in the words of Sir Anthony Mason, who has far more experience of serving in this capacity than anyone else.[304] In particular, the overseas judges seem to have trod a careful path when it came to the more politically sensitive cases heard by the court. Young (2011) notes they have never once dissented in any human rights case,[305] although that is not particularly remarkable in a Court of Final Appeal which Ghai (2012) describes as "known for consensus among its members".[306] Nor have the overseas judges allowed their common law background to stand in the way of reaching conclusions that might be considered more in tune with Hong Kong's constitutional realities and less likely to arouse objections from Beijing.

In the Court of Final Appeal's controversial judgment in *Lau Kong Yung v Director of Immigration*,[307] which has been criticized in some quarters as unnecessarily undermining Hong Kong's autonomy,[308] Mason noted that the court's conclusion on the unrestricted nature of the National People's Congress Standing Committee's power to interpret the Hong Kong Basic Law "may seem strange" to those familiar with the common law system.[309] He then proceeded to justify the decision partly on the basis of the nature of the Hong Kong Basic Law as "a national law enacted by the PRC", in a concurring judgment which was strongly praised by the Hong Kong SAR Government.[310]

More recently, it was not the overseas judge but instead two Hong Kong judges who dissented from the Court of Final Appeal's decision to refer an issue of interpretation to the National People's Congress Standing Committee for the first time in the case of *Democratic Republic of Congo v FG Hemisphere*.[311] With the court split over the issue, it was the vote of the overseas judge, who was once again Mason (as in most of the court's controversial cases), which provided a 3 to 2 majority in favour of referral to the Standing Committee.[312] This was despite the fact that, as Chen (2011) argues persuasively, some

---

304. Mason, "A non-permanent fixture on the CFA" (see note 252) at 22. The same point was made by Chief Justice Andrew Li in "The Chief Justice's Address at His Farewell Sitting", 16 July 2010, at 9.
305. Young, "Constitutional Rights in Hong Kong's Court of Final Appeal" (see note 160) at 81.
306. Ghai notes (in "Solid foundation", *South China Morning Post*, 17 April 2012) that only 5%–6% of Court of Final Appeal cases result in a dissenting judgment. For more detail on this point, see Jill Cottrell and Yash Ghai, "Concurring and Dissenting Judgments in the Court of Final Appeal" (August 2010) *Hong Kong Lawyer* 31, 34–35.
307. (1999) 2 HKCFAR 300.
308. For more on this case, and criticism of the court's reasoning, see further notes 333–340 later in this chapter and notes 104–125 in Chapter 7, together with the accompanying text.
309. *Lau Kong Yung* at 345.
310. Ibid. Then Secretary for Security Regina Ip specifically drew journalists' attention to Mason's concurring judgment, and praised it as "excellent", during a government press briefing for English-language journalists attended by the author on 3 December 1999.
311. (2011) 14 HKCFAR 95. The dissenting judges were Justice Bokhary and Justice Mortimer, a non-permanent Hong Kong judge who joined the case because the Chief Justice was unable to do so (see further note 428 later in this chapter).
312. See further "7.4: Judicial Referral" in Chapter 7.

aspects of the majority judgment "had to stretch—or go beyond—the existing English common law".[313]

Mason's decisions in these two cases can be defended as consistent with his description of the role of an overseas judge as being one of "seeing legal problems through a Hong Kong lens".[314] But these two decisions also suggest that, for all their invaluable contributions to building up the international reputation of the Court of Final Appeal, it is difficult to conclude that overseas judges have been at the forefront of efforts within the court to defend Hong Kong's high degree of autonomy.

6.4 Constitutional Role of the Court of Final Appeal

Once the Court of Final Appeal came into existence on 1 July 1997, the controversy shifted to its role and the way the court exercised its powers. These powers are defined in general terms in the Hong Kong Court of Final Appeal Ordinance (Cap. 484). This empowers the court to hear civil appeals on questions of "great general or public importance" and criminal appeals on questions of either "great and general importance" or "substantial and grave injustice".[315] Only in cases involving $1 million or more is there an automatic right of appeal to the Court of Final Appeal.[316] In all other cases, leave to appeal is discretionary, and is decided by either an Appeal Committee consisting of three judges from the court, or the Court of Appeal in civil cases.[317]

These general provisions on what types of appeals the court can hear are only part of the picture as far as the role of the Court of Final Appeal is concerned. As Bokhary (2002) notes: "The Court of Final Appeal is both a court exercising general appellate jurisdiction and a constitutional court."[318] This means that, in addition to its general role in hearing appeals from the lower courts, the constitutional role of the Court of Final Appeal also needs to be considered. It is this later role which has given rise to most of the controversies concerning the Court of Final Appeal since 1 July 1997.

The Court of Final Appeal did not have a chance to assert its constitutional role until the first substantive case on the Hong Kong Basic Law came before the court in *Ng Ka Ling v Director of Immigration*.[319] Recognizing the significance of that moment, Chief

---

313. See Albert H.Y. Chen, "Focus on the Congo Case: Introduction" (2011) 41 *HKLJ* 369, 372–373 referring to the statements in the majority judgment that the Hong Kong courts were required to follow the PRC's policy on the extent of immunity for foreign governments, and should treat this as an act of state outside the jurisdiction of the Hong Kong courts. For more on this aspect of the judgment, see further notes 474–475 later in this chapter and the accompanying text.
314. Mason, "A non-permanent fixture on the CFA" (see note 252) at 22.
315. Hong Kong Court of Final Appeal Ordinance (Cap. 484), Sections 22(1)(b) and 32(2).
316. Ibid., Sections 22(1)(a) and 23(2).
317. Ibid., Sections 18(1), 23(1) and 32(1).
318. Bokhary, "Hong Kong's Legal System" (see note 288) at 5.
319. (1999) 2 HKCFAR 4.

Justice Li began his judgment in that case by describing it as of "momentous importance" for the "development of constitutional jurisprudence in the new order" under the Hong Kong Basic Law.[320] Tai (2002) categorizes three separate aspects to the Court of Final Appeal's constitutional role that were identified by the court in this case, as guardian of: 1) Hong Kong's high degree of autonomy; 2) the rule of law; and 3) human rights.[321] The first of these three aspects of the court's constitutional role formed the basis for an important part of the court's ruling in this case, when it rejected any need to refer an issue of how to interpret the Hong Kong Basic Law to the National People's Congress Standing Committee because this would constitute "a substantial derogation from the Region's autonomy".[322] The court also explicitly referred to the third aspect of its constitutional role in laying down the important principle (which subsequently would be cited in many other human rights cases) that the courts "should give a generous interpretation to the provisions in Chapter III" of the Hong Kong Basic Law on civil liberties "in order to give to Hong Kong residents the full measure of fundamental rights and freedoms so constitutionally guaranteed".[323]

The court's assertion in *Ng Ka Ling* that its constitutional role includes the power to invalidate any Hong Kong laws that are found to be inconsistent with the Hong Kong Basic Law has been mostly accepted in Hong Kong, despite the lack of any explicit provisions to this effect in the Hong Kong Basic Law.[324] The same cannot be said of the court's attempt in this case to extend its constitutional role even further, to also invalidate any actions of the National People's Congress and its Standing Committee which breach the Hong Kong Basic Law.[325] That provoked a furious response from Beijing, which forced the Court of Final Appeal to rephrase this assertion of such an expansive constitutional role in more conciliatory terms in an unprecedented supplementary judgment.[326]

Beijing's furious response to this aspect of the *Ng Ka Ling* judgment ushered in an uncertain period for the court. Such uncertainty increased after the National People's Congress Standing Committee's June 1999 interpretation of two provisions in the Hong Kong Basic Law[327] reversed key parts of the court's ruling in *Ng Ka Ling* and the accompanying case of *Chan Kam Nga v Director of Immigration*.[328] Taking direct aim at the Court of Final Appeal's assertion of a constitutional role in defending Hong Kong's high degree of autonomy, which was one of the main reasons why the court refused to refer an

---

320. Ibid. at 12.
321. Benny Y. T. Tai, "Chapter One of Hong Kong's New Constitution: Constitutional Positioning and Repositioning", in Ming Chan and Alvin Y. So (eds.), *Crisis and Transformation in China's Hong Kong* (Hong Kong University Press and M.E. Sharpe, 2002) at 195.
322. *Ng Ka Ling* at 33. For more on the court's decision on this point, and criticism of it, see further notes 208–214 in Chapter 7 and the accompanying text.
323. *Ng Ka Ling* at 29.
324. See further notes 150–156 earlier in this chapter and the accompanying text.
325. See further notes 186–194 earlier in this chapter and the accompanying text.
326. See further notes 207–220 earlier in this chapter and the accompanying text.
327. Articles 22(4) and 24(2)(3). See further notes 89–90 in Chapter 7 and the accompanying text.
328. (1999) 2 HKCFAR 82.

issue of interpretation of the Hong Kong Basic Law to the Standing Committee during these cases, the June 1999 interpretation accused the Court of Final Appeal of breaching the Hong Kong Basic Law by refusing to make such a referral.[329]

The Standing Committee's June 1999 interpretation marked a low point for the Court of Final Appeal. According to Justice Kemal Bokhary, one of the permanent judges on the court, he and his colleagues seriously considered resigning in response to the Standing Committee interpretation, but ultimately decided not to do so for fear of being "replaced by less independent or competent jurists".[330]

It also placed the Court of Final Appeal in a difficult position. While courts are supposed to decide cases purely on their legal merits, many scholars agree that after Beijing's attacks on the *Ng Ka Ling* judgment, the Court of Final Appeal began to consider more carefully the political consequences of its decisions.[331] For instance, the court could have found strong legal grounds for rejecting the Standing Committee's June 1999 interpretation on the basis that, on a proper reading of the Hong Kong Basic Law, it exceeded the powers granted to the Standing Committee.[332] But such an act of defiance would have almost certainly provoked some kind of hostile response from the Chinese Central Authorities.

So, instead of risking another confrontation, the Court of Final Appeal chose to retreat, adopting what Chan (2007) describes as "an almost defeatist attitude"[333] in *Lau Kong Yung v Director of Immigration*[334] six months later. That case saw the court not only accept the legality of the June 1999 interpretation by the Standing Committee, but go much further in holding that there are no legal limits to the Standing Committee's powers of interpretation under any circumstances.[335] Ling (2007) describes the latter conclusion, which arguably goes much further than was intended by the drafters of the Hong Kong Basic Law, as "misguided and damaging" to Hong Kong's high degree of autonomy.[336] It also went much further than was actually necessary to decide this case,

---

329. As a result, the court was forced to concede that it might need to reconsider its position on when such a reference to the Standing Committee is required. See further notes 217–218 in Chapter 7 and the accompanying text.
330. See US Consulate in Hong Kong, *Rule of Law in Hong Kong* (28 August 2007, released by the Wikileaks website in 2011), reporting private remarks by Bokhary to a US diplomat. Bokhary subsequently confirmed the judges had considered resigning in an interview with *ATV*'s "Newsline" (4 Nov 2012).
331. See, for instance, Tai, "Chapter One of Hong Kong's New Constitution" (see note 321) at 211 and Po Jen Yap, "Constitutional Review Under the Basic Law: The Rise, Retreat and Resurgence of Judicial Power in Hong Kong" (2007) 37 *HKLJ* 449, 474.
332. For more on that argument, which is put forward persuasively by Ling Bing, "Subject Matter Limitation on the NPCSC's Power to Interpret the Basic Law" (2007) 37 *HKLJ* 619, 625–633, see further notes 65–68, 107–108 and 115–116 in Chapter 7, as well as the accompanying text.
333. Chan, "Basic Law and Constitutional Review" (see note 155) at 420.
334. (1999) 2 HKCFAR 300.
335. Ibid. at 323.
336. Ling, "Subject Matter Limitation on the NPCSC's Power to Interpret the Basic Law" (see note 332) at 620.

which only involved the legality of the June 1999 interpretation, prompting Cohen (2000) to complain that the court "unnecessarily prostrated itself before Beijing".[337]

The decision in *Lau Kong Yung* has its defenders. Chen (2006) describes it as the "only approach consistent" with constitutional reality in China.[338] But, for many other observers, it marked a low point for the court. Chan (2007) notes: "There is no trace in this judgment of the same spirit in *Ng Ka Ling* of venturing into a brave new world."[339] Instead, the Court of Final Appeal seemed willing to retreat as far as was necessary to placate Beijing, for fear that another confrontation with Chinese Central Authorities so soon after the controversy over the *Ng Ka Ling* case would have gravely undermined the court's authority and ability to protect the rule of law in Hong Kong. If the price of such a retreat was sacrificing some of its role in protecting Hong Kong's high degree of autonomy, the decision in *Lau Kong Yung* suggests that was a price the Court of Final Appeal was prepared to pay. Forced by Beijing's furious response to its decision in *Ng Ka Ling* to choose between the three aspects of its constitutional role that the court had originally outlined in that case, Tai (2002) suggests that the Court of Final Appeal chose to prioritize its role as guardian of the rule of law in Hong Kong ahead of protecting Hong Kong's high degree of autonomy and human rights.[340]

That impression was reinforced only two weeks after the *Lau Kong Yung* judgment by the Court of Final Appeal's decision in *HKSAR v Ng Kung Siu*.[341] In this case, it was the role of guardian of Hong Kong's human rights which the court appeared willing to sacrifice in order to avoid another confrontation with the Chinese Central Authorities. Overturning the Court of Appeal, in *Ng Kung Siu*, the Court of Final Appeal upheld the legality of a localized version of a Chinese national law[342] that restricted civil liberties by criminalizing any desecration of the Chinese national flag.[343] Once again this case saw the court retreat further than was necessary to avoid another confrontation with Beijing, adopting such a broad definition of one permissible restriction on civil liberties that it could be used to justify not just protecting the national flag but also many other potential restrictions on civil liberties.[344]

---

337. Cohen argues that the Court of Final Appeal could have accepted the legality of the Standing Committee's June 1999 interpretation, without conceding the more general point that there are no limits on the Standing Committee's power to interpret the Hong Kong Basic Law. See Jerome A. Cohen, "Hong Kong's Basic Law: An American Perspective", International Symposium to Commemorate the 10th Anniversary of the Promulgation of the Hong Kong SAR Basic Law, 1 April 2000.
338. Albert H.Y. Chen, "Constitutional Adjudication in Post-1997 Hong Kong" (2006) 15 *Pacific Rim Law & Policy Journal* 627, 645.
339. Chan, "Basic Law and Constitutional Review" (see note 155) at 420.
340. Tai, "Chapter One of Hong Kong's New Constitution" (see note 321) at 205.
341. (1999) 2 HKCFAR 442. For more on this case, and criticism of the court's reasoning, see further notes 190–209 in Chapter 8 and the accompanying text.
342. Section 7 of the National Flag and National Emblem Ordinance (No. 116 of 1997).
343. *Ng Kung Siu* at 455–462.
344. The key issue involved how to define "*ordre public*", an ambiguous term which is listed as a permissible reason for restricting freedom of expression under Article 19(3) of the International Covenant on Civil and Political Rights. See further note 202 in Chapter 8 and the accompanying text.

Clearly troubled by the implications of this, one of the judges on the court, Justice Bokhary, sought to limit the effects of the decision, describing the restriction on damaging the national flag as being only "just within the outer limits of constitutionality".[345] Ghai (2012) describes Bokhary's separate judgment in this case as a "near dissent" in which, "[c]onscious of the need to show solidarity with his colleagues given the political context, he did not dissent from their verdict, but did not agree with their reasoning".[346] Nonetheless, it is telling that even Bokhary, who in later cases would emerge as a champion of looser restrictions on human rights,[347] did not actually dissent from the decision in *Ng Kung Siu*, despite his evidently strong reservations.

Chan (2007) describes Bokhary's failure to dissent in *Ng Kung Siu* as evidence of how the court "needed time" as it searched "for a new balance between aligning itself as a court of final adjudication and respecting the sovereignty of the Central Government".[348] Forced on the defensive by China's hostile response to the *Ng Ka Ling* judgment, the Court of Final Appeal had been compelled to give some ground on its defence of Hong Kong's high degree of autonomy in *Lau Kong Yung*, and on the protection of civil liberties in *Ng Kung Siu*. But it soon became clear that this was a temporary retreat, rather than a permanent abandonment of the court's role in defending these two goals.

The first sign came less than a year later in *Cheng v Tse Wai Chun*.[349] While *Ng Kung Siu* may have narrowed the permissible boundaries for freedom of expression in Hong Kong, *Cheng v Tse* saw the court move in the opposite direction. The case involved a defamation action against Albert Cheng, a popular pro-democracy radio talk-show host, who was alleged to have acted out of malice. By adopting a narrower definition of malice than previously had been used elsewhere in the common law world,[350] the Court of Final Appeal made it easier to defeat such actions for defamation, and so widened the permissible boundaries for freedom of expression in Hong Kong. Chang (2000) describes the decision in *Cheng v Tse* as a "landmark decision",[351] while Tai (2002) notes it provided an opportunity for "the CFA to show to the world that it has not given up its constitutional position as the guardian of human rights in Hong Kong".[352]

Cheng v Tse was a politically less sensitive case than *Ng Kung Siu* that involved primarily common law issues, rather than the Hong Kong Basic Law, and so was of less

---

345. *Ng Kung Siu* at 468.
346. Ghai, "Solid foundation" (see note 306).
347. See, especially, Bokhary's dissenting judgment in *Leung Kwok Hung v HKSAR* (2005) 8 HKCFAR 229, 298–300, questioning the Commissioner of Police's power to impose restrictions on public protests under the Public Order Ordinance (Cap. 245).
348. Chan, "Basic Law and Constitutional Review" (see note 155) at 422.
349. (2000) 3 HKCFAR 339.
350. Ibid. at 360–361. The court held that even a statement made with intent to injure would not necessarily amount to malice (and so defeat the defence of fair comment in defamation cases) if it reflected an honestly held opinion.
351. Denis Chang, "Has Hong Kong Anything Special or Unique to Contribute to the Contemporary World of Jurisprudence?" (2000) 30 *HKLJ* 347.
352. Tai, "Chapter One of Hong Kong's New Constitution" (see note 321) at 209.

interest to Beijing. Nonetheless, the court's expansion of the permissible boundaries of freedom of expression in this case was bold enough to incur the wrath of one prominent pro-Beijing politician in Hong Kong. A Hong Kong deputy to the National People's Congress complained that the judgment protected "irresponsible statements" and was particularly enraged that an overseas judge had delivered the ruling on behalf of the court.[353]

If *Cheng v Tse* marked a first step in the Court of Final Appeal's recovery from the setbacks that followed its decision in *Ng Ka Ling*, its decision in *Director of Immigration v Chong Fung Yuen*[354] a year later marks a more fundamental turning point. Chen (2006) suggests this case "may be said to symbolize the restoration of the self-confidence of the Hong Kong courts after the 'trauma' of 1999".[355]

Once again, the court upheld mainland-related claims for right of abode under the Hong Kong Basic Law. The provisions at issue were ostensibly similar: Article 24(2)(1) of the Hong Kong Basic Law in *Chong Fung Yuen* as opposed to Article 24(2)(3) in *Ng Ka Ling*. But there the similarities between the two cases end. *Ng Ka Ling* clearly involved huge numbers, with the Hong Kong SAR Government estimating the court's decision in this case granted the right of abode to up to 1.67 million Chinese children born on the mainland to at least one Hong Kong parent.[356] By contrast, *Chong Fung Yuen* granted right of abode to, at that stage, the relatively small number of Chinese children born in Hong Kong to parents without the right to live in Hong Kong.[357] At the time of the *Chong Fung Yuen* judgment, the numbers involved were estimated at only 555 a year.[358] That meant initially there was none of the same concern about being swamped by large numbers, which the Hong Kong SAR Government had so successfully used to turn public opinion against the Court of Final Appeal's decision in *Ng Ka Ling*. But courts cannot look into the future and foresee the social impact of their judgments, which saw the number of mainland mothers giving birth in Hong Kong increase rapidly in subsequent years, so giving rise to many of the same concerns a decade later.

In *Chong Fung Yuen*, the Court of Final Appeal also showed signs of having learnt from the furore which followed the *Ng Ka Ling* judgment, especially in being much more careful to couch its references to the National People's Congress Standing Committee in

---

353. Ma Lik, "A judgment found wanting", *Hong Kong iMail*, 5 Dec 2000. The judgment in this case was delivered by an English Law Lord, Lord Nicholls of Birkenhead. For more on the controversy over allowing such overseas judges to sit on the Court of Final Appeal, see further notes 269–273 earlier in this chapter and the accompanying text.
354. (2001) 4 HKCFAR 211.
355. Chen, "Constitutional Adjudication in Post-1997 Hong Kong" (see note 338) at 647.
356. See further note 181 earlier in this chapter.
357. Although Article 24(2)(1) of the Hong Kong Basic Law grants the right of abode to all "Chinese citizens born in Hong Kong", Schedule 1, paragraph 2(a) of the Immigration Ordinance (Cap. 115) at that time qualified this right by limiting it, in most cases, to those persons whose "father or mother was settled or had the right of abode in Hong Kong at the time of the birth of the person or at any later time".
358. *Chong Fung Yuen* at 226.

deferential terms. Having already conceded in *Lau Kong Yung* the Standing Committee's unrestricted power to interpret the Hong Kong Basic Law,[359] the Court of Final Appeal made no attempt to draw back from this general principle. Instead *Chong Fung Yuen* saw the court reiterate that the Standing Committee's power "extends to every provision in the Basic Law".[360] That assertion has been criticized by some as evidence that the Court of Final Appeal had abandoned any effort to reclaim its role as guardian of Hong Kong's high degree of autonomy.[361] But it is also possible to see this assertion in a more positive light, as evidence of the court's efforts to find a new middle path that would balance deference to the Chinese Central Authorities with continuing to defend Hong Kong's high degree of autonomy.

The court's balancing act between these two competing considerations is evident in many parts of the *Chong Fung Yuen* judgment. Having demonstrated its respect for the general principle of the Standing Committee's supremacy, the Court of Final Appeal then proceeded to limit the practical effect of this principle. In *Chong Fung Yuen*, the court once again refused to refer the Hong Kong Basic Law provision at issue to the Standing Committee for an interpretation, on the grounds that this was not the type of provision where such a reference was required.[362] Instead the Court of Final Appeal reiterated that it would continue to interpret the Hong Kong Basic Law according to common law principles.[363] Despite its strong reaffirmation of the binding nature of Standing Committee interpretations, *Chong Fung Yuen* also saw the court refuse to follow part of the wording of the June 1999 interpretation that had been issued by the Standing Committee after *Ng Ka Ling*. This was on the basis that since the earlier interpretation involved Article 24(2)(3) of the Hong Kong Basic Law, it was not binding in a case which instead involved Article 24(2)(1) of the Hong Kong Basic Law.[364]

Unsurprisingly, the Standing Committee was unhappy with this fresh act of defiance by the Court of Final Appeal—albeit defiance couched in more respectful terms than in *Ng Ka Ling*. A statement from the Standing Committee's Legislative Affairs Commission

---

359. (1999) 2 HKCFAR 300, 323.
360. *Chong Fung Yuen* at 222.
361. Ling (2007) describes the court's statement on this point as "misconceived". See Ling, "Subject Matter Limitation on the NPCSC's Power to Interpret the Basic Law" (see note 332) at 624.
362. *Chong Fung Yuen* at 225–229. The Court of Final Appeal rejected a "substantive effect" test put forward by the Hong Kong SAR Government, which would have classified most provisions in the Hong Kong Basic Law as provisions that must be referred to the Standing Committee for an interpretation. See further notes 222–223 in Chapter 7 and the accompanying text.
363. Ibid. at 224.
364. Ibid. at 227–228. This was despite the fact that the Preamble to the June 1999 interpretation did suggest that the Standing Committee believed Article 24(2)(1) of the Hong Kong Basic Law should be interpreted in a way which, contrary to the Court of Final Appeal's conclusion in *Chong Fung Yuen*, would deny the right of abode to those children without a parent who is either settled or has the right of abode in Hong Kong. See further notes 177–178 in Chapter 7 and the accompanying text.

the day after the *Chong Fung Yuen* judgment expressed "concern" at the court's refusal to apply the June 1999 interpretation.[365] But, other than this statement, no action was taken at the time. In particular, the Standing Committee did not immediately respond by issuing a formal interpretation overruling the court. This suggests that, at least in the short term, the Court of Final Appeal had correctly judged how far it could go in reasserting its constitutional role as guardian of Hong Kong's autonomy without provoking any substantive response from the Standing Committee. However it is unclear if this will continue to be true in the long term, since the Hong Kong SAR Government has already sought to reopen the issue of the extent of the binding effect of Standing Committee interpretations. In early 2013, it unsuccessfully requested the Court of Final Appeal to refer the issue back to the Standing Committee for interpretation.[366]

Of particular importance to the court's recovery from the "'trauma' of 1999" was its characterization in *Chong Fung Yuen* of the Standing Committee's power of interpretation as "legislative interpretation" that can "clarify or supplement laws".[367] That means treating the Standing Committee's interpretations of the Hong Kong Basic Law in almost the same way as if they were actual legislation. Since it is widely accepted in the common law world that legislation can reverse the effects of court decisions, treating the Standing Committee interpretations like legislation makes it much easier to accept that these too can reverse the effects of court decisions, without seriously undermining the common law system expressly preserved under the Hong Kong Basic Law. Chan (2007) notes that: "This characterisation of the NPCSC's interpretation as a legislative process provides a theoretical justification for the court to reconcile the primacy of the common law in the HKSAR and respect for the sovereign power."[368]

Chong Fung Yuen was a landmark decision for the evolving constitutional role of the Court of Final Appeal, because it provided both a "theoretical justification"[369] for accepting the reality of the Standing Committee's power of interpretation and a practical approach for limiting the effect of such interpretations as much as possible without incurring any retaliatory measures from Beijing. As a result, Chan (2007) describes the decision in *Chong Fung Yuen* as the "jurisprudential liberation of the constitutional role of the Court of Final Appeal".[370]

With the Court of Final Appeal now adopting what many commentators describe as a more "pragmatic"[371] approach, the legal battles over the Standing Committee's power of interpretation came to an end for many years. Chen (2006) describes the court as

---

365. See "HK Government—Abode Right Case Is Over", Xinhua News Agency, 21 July 2001.
366. See *Vallejos Evangeline Banao v Commissioner of Registration* (unrep., FACV 19 and 20/2012, [2013] HKEC 429) at para. 111, where the court rejected the request because it was "simply unnecessary" to decide the case.
367. *Chong Fung Yuen* at 221.
368. Chan, "Basic Law and Constitutional Review" (see note 155) at 417.
369. Ibid.
370. Ibid. at 422.
371. Ibid. at 445. See also Yap, "Constitutional Review Under the Basic Law" (see note 331) at 450.

adopting a middle path of being "neither too proud nor too humble",[372] as it sought to strike a balance between deference to Chinese Central Authorities and continuing to defend Hong Kong's high degree of autonomy whenever possible. A further sign of that middle path came in the next major interpretation-related case. In *Ng Siu Tung v Director of Immigration*,[373] the Court of Final Appeal ruled that one group of about 1,000 mainland children covered by the Standing Committee's June 1999 interpretation nonetheless should be given the right to live in Hong Kong, because of promises made to them by the Hong Kong SAR Government.[374] However, conscious of the large numbers involved, the majority on the court denied the right to live in Hong Kong to a second group of more than 600,000 children who were covered by similar (although less specific) promises.[375] Describing the distinction between the two groups as "highly technical at best",[376] Yap (2007) portrays this as another politically motivated decision by the Court of Final Appeal, arguing the court realized that upholding the rights of this second group of more than 600,000 "would in effect be denying the central tenor of the NPC Interpretation, a prospect the court could no longer stomach".[377]

Chan (2007) sees *Chong Fung Yuen* as also marking a turning point in the third aspect of the court's constitutional role — that of protecting civil liberties — with the court subsequently having "regained its confidence as a guardian of fundamental rights".[378] However, opinions are divided on this point. Yap (2007) takes a sharply different view, describing the court as "generally conservative" on human rights issues, especially in cases with law and order implications.[379]

Some subsequent cases do give an impression of a Court of Final Appeal which, as in *Cheng v Tse*, appears anxious to reclaim its constitutional role as an aggressive defender of human rights in Hong Kong. In *Yeung May Wan v HKSAR*,[380] for instance, the Court of Final Appeal delivered a ringing endorsement of the importance of protecting freedom of speech and the freedom to demonstrate, noting that: "These freedoms are at the heart of Hong Kong's system and it is well established that the courts should give a generous interpretation to the constitutional guarantees for these freedoms in order to give to Hong Kong residents their full measure."[381]

---

372. Chen, "Constitutional Adjudication in Post-1997 Hong Kong" (see note 338) at 680.
373. (2002) 5 HKCFAR 1.
374. Ibid. at 54–55.
375. Ibid. At issue were representations made by the Hong Kong SAR Government that these children would be treated in the same way as the parties to the *Ng Ka Ling* litigation. This case is also highly significant because it marked a major step in the development of substantive legitimate expectation as an additional ground for judicial review. See further note 247 earlier in this chapter and the accompanying text.
376. Yap, "Constitutional Review Under the Basic Law" (see note 331) at 463. This also appears to be close to the view of Justice Bokhary, who delivered a partially dissenting judgment in this case. See *Ng Siu Tung* at 90–121.
377. Yap, "Constitutional Review Under the Basic Law" (see note 331) at 463.
378. Chan, "Basic Law and Constitutional Review" (see note 155) at 422.
379. Yap, "Constitutional Review Under the Basic Law" (see note 331) at 450.
380. (2005) 8 HKCFAR 137.
381. Ibid. at 148.

The decision in *Yeung May Wan* was of particular political significance because it involved an appeal against convictions for obstruction by protesters from the Falun Gong, which although banned on the mainland remains legal in Hong Kong,[382] and had been demonstrating outside the Central People's Government's Liaison Office when the arrests occurred. Overturning the convictions, the Court of Final Appeal emphasized the importance of upholding "the freedom to express views which may be found to be disagreeable or even offensive to others or which may be critical of persons in authority"[383] — a description almost tailor made for the Falun Gong.

The court's judgment in that case is rightly seen as an important reaffirmation of the rule of law in Hong Kong. Chen (2006) notes that the "political significance of the Yeung case exceeds its constitutional and legal significance" and the Court of Final Appeal's decision "testifies to the equality of all—including the most vocal opponents of the Chinese government—before the law in Hong Kong, as well as the independence of the judiciary and the rigorous legal protection of human rights in SAR".[384] However, as in *Cheng v Tse*, *Yeung May Wan* was not a case primarily about the Hong Kong Basic Law.[385] Yap (2007) suggests this made it much easier for the Court of Final Appeal to take such a strong stance in this case.[386]

A more mixed picture emerges from another case on freedom to demonstrate decided by the Court of Final Appeal two months later. Unlike *Yeung May Wan*, *Leung Kwok Hung v HKSAR*[387] revolved much more directly around the human rights safeguards written into the Hong Kong Basic Law. At issue was the legality of provisions in the Public Order Ordinance (Cap. 245) requiring organizers of public protests of more than 30 people to notify the Commissioner of Police in advance,[388] and giving the Commissioner certain powers to ban or restrict such protests.[389] The Court of Final Appeal did find that one of the criteria listed in the ordinance for banning or restricting protests was too ambiguous to comply with the human rights safeguards written into the

---

382. Despite intense pressure from Beijing, Hong Kong never enacted legislation banning the Falun Gong, although the Hong Kong SAR Government did try to include a provision which could have been used to target this group in the proposed national security legislation which was abandoned after huge public protests in 2003. See further note 91 in Chapter 4 and the accompanying text.
383. *Yeung May Wan* at 148.
384. Chen, "Constitutional Adjudication in Post-1997 Hong Kong" (see note 338) at 667.
385. The case involved charges of obstruction of a public place under the Summary Offences Ordinance (Cap. 228) and, when the protesters resisted being arrested, charges of willfully obstructing and assaulting a police officer under the Offences Against the Person Ordinance (Cap. 212) and the Police Force Ordinance (Cap. 232).
386. Yap, "Constitutional Review Under the Basic Law" (see note 331) at 466–467.
387. (2005) 8 HKCFAR 229.
388. Section 13.
389. Under Sections 14(1) and 15(2), a ban or restriction can only be imposed if the Commissioner of Police considers it "necessary in the interests of national security or public safety, public order or the protection of the rights and freedoms of others".

Hong Kong Basic Law.[390] The case was also of importance for the court's declaration that the concept of proportionality should now be used in human rights cases.[391] This makes it much easier to challenge government actions through judicial review by arguing that they are disproportionate, in other words that they went further than was necessary to achieve the objective pursued.

But on the central issue in *Leung Kwok Hung*, the majority found in favour of the Hong Kong SAR Government, upholding the legality of the police's power to ban or restrict protests under the Public Order Ordinance.[392] Yap (2007) is harshly critical of this aspect of the court's decision in *Leung Kwok Hung*—contrasting it unfavourably with the *Yeung May Wan* judgment two months earlier—and noting that "despite the Court's emphasis on the 'cardinal importance' of the 'precious' right to freedom of assembly and how it lies at the foundation of a democratic society, the rhetoric rang hollow in light of the actual decision reached by the Court".[393] Others less critical of the court still find far more convincing the dissenting judgment of Justice Bokhary in this case, who argued the police's power to ban or restrict protests was incompatible with the human rights safeguards in the Hong Kong Basic Law.[394]

Other examples of the Court of Final Appeal adopting an apparently conservative approach towards human rights include *Lau Cheong v HKSAR*,[395] where the court upheld the mandatory life sentence for murder.[396] But there are also numerous cases in which the court took a much more radical approach in defence of human rights in Hong Kong. In addition to the cases of *Cheng v Tse* and *Yeung May Wan*, the case of *Secretary for Justice v Chan Wah*[397] is of particular note. That case saw the Court of Final Appeal rule against election arrangements in the New Territories which discriminated in favour of indigenous inhabitants[398] by denying other villagers the right to vote.[399] As a result, the

---

390. *Leung Kwok Hung* at 263–264. The offending criteria was a reference to "*ordre public*" as a permissible reason for banning or restricting protests, a concept which the Court of Final Appeal had previously described as "imprecise and elusive" in *HKSAR v Ng Kung Siu* (1999) 2 HKCFAR 442, 459. The words "*ordre public*" were subsequently removed from the ordinance.
391. *Leung Kwok Hung* at 252–254. For more on proportionality, see further notes 242–245 earlier in this chapter and the accompanying text.
392. Ibid. at 267–268.
393. Yap, "Constitutional Review Under the Basic Law" (see note 331) at 466.
394. *Leung Kwok Hung* at 269–303. For example, Albert Chen comments that the majority judgment on this point "lacks legal rigor". See "Constitutional Adjudication in Post-1997 Hong Kong" (see note 338) at 671.
395. (2002) 5 HKCFAR 415.
396. Ibid. at 452–454.
397. (2000) 3 HKCFAR 459.
398. See further note 33 in Chapter 8 and the accompanying text, for an explanation of the meaning of indigenous inhabitants of the New Territories and their special treatment under Article 40 of the Hong Kong Basic Law.
399. *Chan Wah* at 471–474.

Hong Kong SAR Government was forced fundamentally to reform the system for village elections in the New Territories in order to comply with the court's ruling.[400]

The mixed picture presented by these different human rights cases is described by Chen (2006) as showing a Court of Final Appeal which is "moderately liberal — neither radically liberal nor conservative".[401] Young (2011) suggests it reflects what he calls the "mainstream view" within the Court of Final Appeal during the early years of the Hong Kong SAR.[402] This is "a liberal yet pragmatic viewpoint that is close to the center of the political spectrum", and was expounded primarily by Andrew Li, who served as Chief Justice until 2010, and Sir Anthony Mason, the overseas judge who — as we saw earlier — was a semi-permanent fixture on the court throughout much of this period.[403]

That "mainstream view" was not always shared by Justice Kemal Bokhary, the most liberal judge on the Court of Final Appeal during this period, and author of a handful of high-profile dissents in a number of important human rights cases.[404] Speaking extra-judicially, Bokhary has described his dissents as having "always been in favour of the parties invoking rights and freedoms" and justified them on the grounds that "progress sometimes lies in the direction pointed to by a dissent".[405] Young (2011) describes Bokhary's approach as one "which draws a higher baseline of minimum rights protection than the mainstream view and shows particular concern for the interests of right of abode claimants and criminal defendants".[406]

However, the main contrast during the first decade of the Hong Kong SAR was not between different judges on the Court of Final Appeal, but rather with the more conservative approach towards human rights cases often taken by the Court of Appeal. Chan (2007) notes this contrast was "quite noticeable, and many appeals from the Court of Appeal are allowed, not so much that the Court of Appeal has erroneously applied the law, but rather that the Court of Final Appeal has made a different value choice".[407]

---

400. The Village Representative Election Ordinance (Cap. 576) introduced a new system of dual elections to elect two representatives for each village, with one representative being elected by all village residents and the other representative only by indigenous inhabitants and their spouses.
401. Chen, "Constitutional Adjudication in Post-1997 Hong Kong" (see note 338) at 680.
402. Young, "Constitutional Rights in Hong Kong's Court of Final Appeal" (see note 160) at 81.
403. Ibid. For more on Sir Anthony Mason's role on the Court of Final Appeal, see further notes 295–298 earlier in this chapter and the accompanying text.
404. These included dissents in *Ng Siu Tung v Director of Immigration* (2002) 5 HKCFAR 1, 90–121 (see further note 376) and *Leung Kwok Hung v HKSAR* (2005) 8 HKCFAR 229 at 269–303 (see note 394). However, Ghai notes (in "Solid foundation" (see note 306)) that Bokhary, although well-known for such dissents, is "not essentially a dissenter" and was also the main writer of majority judgments during his period on the court.
405. Bokhary, "Current state of Judicial Review in Hong Kong" (see note 170) at 15–16.
406. Young, "Constitutional Rights in Hong Kong's Court of Final Appeal" (see note 160) at 81.
407. Chan, "Basic Law and Constitutional Review" (see note 155) at 426.

One good example of this contrasting approach was the Court of Appeal's decision in the *Yeung May Wan* case.[408] While this contained valuable passages on the importance of protecting fundamental freedoms, a panel of Justices of Appeal led by then Chief Judge of the High Court Geoffrey Ma upheld several of the convictions against the Falun Gong protesters, despite conceding that their original arrests had been unlawful. Equally troubling was the Court of Appeal's 14-month delay in deciding the case — presumably because of concerns about its political sensitivity — which prompted expressions of international concern.[409]

In contrast to the Court of Appeal's caution, the Court of Final Appeal swiftly reached a very different decision in the *Yeung May Wan* case, delivering judgment within a month of the appeal hearing and quashing all remaining convictions against the Falun Gong protesters.[410] Then Chief Justice Li was sharply critical of the Court of Appeal's "unacceptable" procrastination in deciding the case. He even expressed scepticism about Chief Judge Ma's explanation that the long delay in hearing the case in the Court of Appeal had been caused by the need to wait for a decision in the *Leung Kwok Hung* case.[411]

So it was no surprise that when Li retired as Chief Justice in 2010 to be succeeded in this role by Ma, there were expressions of concern that Ma's more conservative approach towards human rights — and perhaps also a less vigorous defence of Hong Kong's high degree of autonomy — would come with him from the Court of Appeal to the Court of Final Appeal.[412] Such concerns were heightened by a series of subsequent retirements from the Court of Final Appeal, especially the controversial decision in 2012 not to allow Justice Kemal Bokhary to remain in his permanent post beyond the retirement age of 65, instead replacing him with a slightly older judge from the Court of Appeal.[413]

Perceptions of a possible change of stance by the Court of Final Appeal were brought to the fore by the court's 2011 decision in *Democratic Republic of Congo v FG Hemisphere*.[414] That case saw a sharply divided court decide to refer issues of

---

408. *HKSAR v Yeung May Wan* [2004] 3 HKLRD 797.
409. See, for example, Her Majesty's Government, *Six-monthly Report on Hong Kong: January–June 2004* (July 2004) at 18. Also Cliff Buddle, "Is justice delayed, justice denied, to Falun Gong 16?", *South China Morning Post*, 25 July 2004.
410. (2005) 8 HKCFAR 137, 176.
411. Ibid. at 178. Although the *Leung Kwok Hung* case also concerned the right to protest, it involved very different legal issues relating to the Public Order Ordinance (Cap. 245). As a result, Chief Justice Li concluded that "the reason given is not objectively a sufficient justification for the delay".
412. See, for example, the comments of Senior Counsel Ronny Tong quoted in Patsy Moy, "New chief justice gives oath on lawyer wife", *The Standard*, 9 April 2010, citing the Court of Appeal's decision to uphold a ban on several Falun Gong protesters entering Hong Kong in *Chu Woan Chyi v Director of Immigration* [2009] 6 HKC 77.
413. Under Section 14(2)(a) of the Hong Kong Court of Final Appeal Ordinance (Cap. 484), it is the Chief Justice who recommends to the Chief Executive whether permanent judges on the Court of Final Appeal should be allowed to stay in office beyond their retirement age. See further notes 83–87 earlier in this chapter and the accompanying text.
414. (2011) 14 HKCFAR 95.

interpretation of the Hong Kong Basic Law to the National People's Congress Standing Committee for the first time,[415] something the court had always avoided doing until then.[416]

In deciding by a narrow 3 to 2 majority that a common law rule allowing foreign governments sometimes to be sued in the Hong Kong courts should give way to the Chinese government's position that this was not permissible, the court placed heavy emphasis on a strongly worded letter from the Ministry of Foreign Affairs warning of the "serious prejudice to the overall interests of China" that would otherwise ensue.[417] Cheung (2011) describes this letter as having "stepped beyond the line" by telling the Court of Final Appeal how the Chinese government expected to see the case decided, and suggests it left "the sword of Damocles hanging over the head" of the court.[418]

The majority's strong reliance on this letter from the Chinese government brought a strong riposte from Bokhary, one of the dissenting judges in the case, who warned that it could gravely undermine human rights protections if the courts decided cases simply on the basis of what would avoid prejudice or embarrassment to the executive.[419] The dissenting judge seemed to suggest that he saw the court's decision in the *Congo* case as a fundamental test of judicial independence, with the unspoken implication that, by deferring to Beijing's wishes, the majority on the court had failed this test:

> It has always been known that the day would come when the Court has to give a decision on judicial independence. That day has come. Judicial independence is not to be found in what the courts merely say. It is to be found in what the courts actually do.[420]

Writing extra-judicially, Sir Anthony Mason, the overseas judge who sat on the court during that case and voted with the majority in the Court of Final Appeal's 3 to 2 decision, has responded to the implication in Bokhary's remarks.[421] While agreeing that the Congo case may have "symbolic significance" because it marked the first time that the Court of Final Appeal had referred an issue of interpretation to the Standing Committee, Mason argues that "it is difficult to see that judicial independence was compromised".[422]

---

415. Under the judicial referral procedure in Article 158(3) of the Hong Kong Basic Law. For more on this procedure, see further "7.4: Judicial Referral" in Chapter 7.
416. Most notably through the use of a predominant provision test, which took a very restrictive approach towards when such referrals would be required. See further notes 210–214 in Chapter 7 and the accompanying text.
417. *FG Hemisphere* at 174–178 and 203–205 on the majority's view that the contents of the letter should be treated as "facts of state" binding on the court. For more on facts of state, see further "6.5: Limits on Courts".
418. Eric T.M. Cheung, "Undermining our Judicial Independence and Autonomy" (2011) 41 *HKLJ* 411, 412–413.
419. *FG Hemisphere* at 150 citing the example given by Lord Pannick, counsel for *FG Hemisphere*, of how the exercise of freedom of speech under Article 27 of the Hong Kong Basic Law may sometimes result in comments that prejudice or embarrass China's interests.
420. Ibid. at 111.
421. Mason, "The Rule of Law in the Shadow of the Giant: The Hong Kong Experience" (see note 295) at 639.
422. Ibid.

Bokhary's concern about possible threats to judicial independence extends beyond the *Congo* case. Speaking after being controversially forced to step down from his permanent post upon reaching the retirement age of 65,[423] he warned in October 2012 that a "storm of unprecedented ferocity" was gathering over the rule of law in Hong Kong.[424] This was in response to strong criticism of Hong Kong judges by former Secretary for Justice Elsie Leung, who accused them of making "mistakes" and having a poor understanding of the relationship between Hong Kong and the mainland.[425]

It is worth noting that the Court of Final Appeal's decision in the *Congo* case aroused only a muted response in Hong Kong,[426] with none of the same controversy that surrounded earlier Standing Committee interpretations of the Hong Kong Basic Law.[427] Since the new Chief Justice did not sit in the *Congo* case, it would be premature to conclude—based on this case alone—that this marks the start of a more deferential approach by the court towards China's interests.[428] That conclusion is strengthened by the court's subsequent refusal to accept the government's request to refer an issue of interpretation to the Standing Committee in *Vallejos Evangeline Banao v Commissioner of Registration*, a case in which the new Chief Justice did sit.[429]

Nonetheless it probably would be unrealistic to expect that the Court of Final Appeal under Ma's leadership will remain unchanged in all respects from the court led by his predecessor. Mason (2011) notes that: "No Chief Justice is a graven image of his predecessor", and that experience elsewhere in the world generally has been that a change of Chief Justice leads to some changes in the court. However he notes that these are often changes of style rather than substance and predicts that, given the collegial nature of Hong Kong's Court of Final Appeal, "a strong sense of continuity will inevitably prevail".[430]

---

423. For more on this controversy, see further notes 83–87 earlier in this chapter and the accompanying text.
424. Austin Chiu, "Retiring Court of Final Appeal judge Kemal Bokhary warns of legal turmoil", *South China Morning Post*, 25 Oct 2012.
425. Ng Kang-chung, "Elsie Leung attacks double standards of Law Society and Bar Association", *South China Morning Post*, 13 Oct 2012.
426. Diana Lee, "Reactions muted to top court's Beijing call", *The Standard*, 9 June 2011.
427. One significant difference was that none of these previous interpretations had been requested by the Court of Final Appeal. For more on these previous interpretations, and the reaction to them, see further "7.2: Standing Committee" and "7.3: Avoiding Interpretations" in Chapter 7.
428. Ma did not sit in this case because his wife had been one of the judges who heard the case when it was heard by the Court of Appeal as *FG Hemisphere v Democratic Republic of Congo* [2010] 2 HKLRD 1148. Benny Tai suggests [in "The Constitutional Game of Article 158(3) of the Basic Law" (2011) 41 *HKLJ* 377, 382] this made it easier for the court to seek an interpretation from the Standing Committee because it meant there was no danger of any resulting criticism "affecting his personal authority".
429. Unrep., FACV 19 and 20/2012, [2013] HKEC 429 at paras. 109–112. The Court of Final Appeal held that a referral was "simply unnecessary" to decide the case, which involved the right of abode of foreign domestic helpers in Hong Kong.
430. Mason, "A non-permanent fixture on the CFA" (see note 252) at 21–22.

6.5 Limits on Courts

Article 19 of the Hong Kong Basic Law places very few limits on the power of the Hong Kong courts to hear cases. Under Article 19(2), they have jurisdiction "over all cases in the [Hong Kong Special Administrative] Region, except that the restrictions on their jurisdiction imposed by the legal system and principles previously in force in Hong Kong shall be maintained".[431] This provision reflects a central theme in China's approach towards drafting the Hong Kong Basic Law—its belief that the powers of the different branches of Hong Kong's political structure, and the restrictions on the exercise of those powers, should to a large extent resemble those that applied to the equivalent institutions in Hong Kong under British rule.

In the case of the courts, this serves an important practical purpose. It has been long recognized in Hong Kong and elsewhere in the world that certain groups of people have to be exempt from the jurisdiction of the courts under certain circumstances in order to carry out their work, and Article 19(2) allows this practice to continue under the Hong Kong Basic Law. Foreign diplomats and representatives of major international organizations, for instance, would not agree to be based in Hong Kong (or elsewhere in the world, for that matter) if they were at risk of being arrested and prosecuted under local laws in the course of their work. So, as was the case under British rule, they continue to enjoy "diplomatic immunity", which means they are exempt from the jurisdiction of the Hong Kong courts in almost all circumstances.

Diplomatic immunity was traditionally an uncontroversial issue in Hong Kong, only occasionally arousing minor anguish over issues such as foreign diplomats refusing to pay their parking tickets.[432] However, that changed following an alleged assault by Grace Mugabe, the wife of the president of Zimbabwe, on a photographer in Hong Kong in 2009.[433] After consulting the Chinese Ministry of Foreign Affairs, the Hong Kong SAR Government refused to prosecute Mugabe on the grounds that she enjoyed diplomatic immunity under one of the small number of Chinese national laws which applies in Hong Kong.[434]

---

431. However, this does not mean the Hong Kong courts have *exclusive* jurisdiction over all cases in Hong Kong. The laws of other jurisdictions outside Hong Kong may also give their courts jurisdiction to try cases involving some crimes committed in Hong Kong. This is particular true under the PRC Criminal Law, which gives mainland courts wide jurisdiction over crimes committed anywhere in the world. See further "3.2: Domestic Dimension" in Chapter 3.
432. Gren Manual, "Parking diplomats rule the waivers", *South China Morning Post*, 15 Feb 1998.
433. For an account of this incident, and the subsequent enquiry by a Legislative Council panel, See C.L. Lim and Roda Mushkat, "External Affairs" in Chan and Lim (eds.), *Law of the Hong Kong Constitution* (see note 76) at 102–104.
434. The Regulations of the PRC Concerning Diplomatic Privileges and Immunities, which are listed in Annex III of the Hong Kong Basic Law. (For more on the application of Chinese national laws in Hong Kong, see further "4.2: Legislative Power" in Chapter 4.) Article 22(1)(3) of these regulations gives the Central People's Government broad discretion to decide which "visiting foreigners" should enjoy immunity from the jurisdiction of the courts.

Similarly, it long has been recognized in both Hong Kong and internationally that if judges are to feel free to carry out their work, they need to be exempt from civil cases being brought over anything said or done in their courts.[435] This restriction on the jurisdiction of the Hong Kong courts is incorporated into the Hong Kong Basic Law, Article 85 of which states: "Members of the judiciary shall be immune from legal action in the performance of their judicial functions."[436] In addition, in order to ensure that they can speak freely in the course of their work, Legislative Councillors have long enjoyed immunity from prosecution for anything they say before the council or its committees,[437] just as members of parliaments in many other countries enjoy similar protection. Again this restriction on the jurisdiction of the Hong Kong courts is incorporated into the Hong Kong Basic Law, although in a slightly more limited form with Article 77 providing that Legislative Councillors "shall be immune from legal action in respect of their statements at meetings of the Council".

Initially, somewhat more controversial was the use of Article 19(2) to exclude from the jurisdiction of the Hong Kong courts actions while on duty of members of the garrison of the People's Liberation Army. Again this is a common practice internationally and, in some respects, similar to the situation that existed in Hong Kong under colonial rule when the Commanding Officer of the British Forces had the right to refuse to allow the Hong Kong courts to hear cases involving crimes committed by members of the British garrison while on duty,[438] although in practice he would usually waive that right in serious cases.[439]

This restriction on the jurisdiction of the Hong Kong courts has continued since 1 July 1997, and is incorporated into the Law of the PRC on the Garrisoning of the Hong Kong SAR, another of the small number of Chinese national laws that applies in Hong Kong.[440] This law provides that criminal offences committed by members of the garrison

---

435. For further details on this and other restrictions on the jurisdiction of the Hong Kong courts, see further Tai "The Jurisdiction of the Courts of the Hong Kong Special Administrative Region" (see note 2) at 81–100.
436. Interestingly, the protection under Article 85 applies not only to judges in the higher courts but also to magistrates and other judicial officers in the lower courts. The term "in performance of their judicial functions" is not defined. However, Ghai and Cottrell argue (in "Between Two Systems of Law" (see note 25) at 214) that this may not matter because judges can be expected to "construe any ambiguity in favor of the wider immunity".
437. Under Section 4 of the Legislative Council (Powers and Privileges) Ordinance (Cap 382).
438. Under Section 3(1)(a) of the United Kingdom Forces (Jurisdiction of Colonial Courts) Order 1965. Under Sections 3(1)(b) and 3(1)(c) of the Order, he also had the right to refuse to allow the Hong Kong courts to hear cases involving offences against someone associated with the armed forces, or involving property owned by either the British government or its armed forces.
439. Secretary for Security Peter Lai in Legislative Council, *Official Record of Proceedings, Hong Kong Hansard* (20 Nov 1996) at 106.
440. Under Annex III of the Hong Kong Basic Law.

while on duty will instead be heard by Chinese military courts,[441] and that members of the garrison arrested by Hong Kong police must be handed over to the garrison as soon as their identity is confirmed.[442] It is also for the garrison, at least initially, to decide whether or not a soldier was on duty at the time the crime was committed.[443] However, if the garrison decides that the soldier was not on duty, then any case involving alleged crimes committed against Hong Kong residents or other people outside the garrison can, as was the case under British rule, be heard in the Hong Kong courts.[444] The first reported case of this occurred in 2006, when an off-duty member of the garrison was convicted of theft in Tsuen Wan Magistrates' Court after being caught stealing a key ring during a visit to Hong Kong Disneyland.[445]

The provisions in the Garrison Law allowing for trials in Chinese military courts had caused concern in the run-up to 1 July 1997, because of fears about how the People's Liberation Army would behave.[446] This was coupled with concern that the provisions in the Garrison Law on civil cases involving members of the garrison imposed greater restrictions on the Hong Kong courts than was the case under colonial rule, when torts committed by members of the British garrison were always subject to the jurisdiction of the Hong Kong courts, even if the solider was on duty at the time when the tort occurred.[447] By contrast, under the Garrison Law, while torts committed by members of the garrison while they are off duty are still heard in the Hong Kong courts,[448] those committed by members of the garrison while on duty instead fall under the jurisdiction of the Supreme People's Court in Beijing.[449] However, the Chinese courts are supposed to use Hong Kong law, rather than Chinese law, to determine the amount of compensation payable.[450]

In practice, these provisions have not proved nearly as controversial as was initially feared, since the tight discipline exercised by the People's Liberation Army over

---

441. Garrison Law, Article 20.
442. Ibid., Article 21.
443. Ibid., Article 25, which makes certificates to this effect issued by the garrison "valid evidence" in court proceedings "unless the contrary is proved".
444. Ibid., Article 20.
445. "Soldier Fined for Shoplifting at Disneyland", *Associated Press*, 19 March 2006.
446. See, for instance, the motion expressing concern at the draft Garrison Law, passed by the Legislative Council on 20 Nov 1996. *Official Record of Proceedings, Hong Kong Hansard* (20 Nov 1996) at 75–113.
447. Secretary for Security in Legislative Council (see note 439) at 107. However, while individual members of the British garrison could be sued in the Hong Kong courts, Section 8 of the Crown Proceedings Ordinance (Cap. 300) prevented any proceedings being brought against the garrison as a whole and these instead had to be pursued in the British courts through the Crown Proceedings Act 1947.
448. Garrison Law, Article 23.
449. Ibid.
450. Ibid.

its Hong Kong garrison meant that there were no reported criminal cases involving any of its soldiers until the Disneyland theft case in 2006. It has been even suggested that, in practice, the situation is now better than it was under colonial rule, when there were numerous court cases involving crimes and at least one murder[451] committed by off-duty members of the British garrison. For instance, then Chief Executive Donald Tsang remarked in October 2005: "Every weekend there were brawls in the bars with the British soldiers. We have had not one single incident involving Chinese soldiers, not even traffic tickets. ... With the British, it was every week."[452]

However, in 2010, controversy erupted over another China-related restriction on the jurisdiction of the Hong Kong courts. Unlike the other restrictions discussed so far, which are directly imposed by provisions in either the Hong Kong Basic Law or other Chinese national laws that apply in Hong Kong, this restriction was decided by the courts as a common law principle.

In the case of *Hua Tian Long (No 2)*, the Court of First Instance held that all bodies established under the Central People's Government are immune from the jurisdiction of the Hong Kong courts, even if they operate as businesses.[453] The practical implications of this decision, which led to the release of a ship seized for breach of contract after the owners showed they were under the direct control of a Chinese government ministry, are potentially huge. Cheung, Gu and Zhang (2010) argue that it puts Hong Kong courts in an inferior position to their mainland counterparts, which do have jurisdiction over government-operated businesses, and "will adversely affect Hong Kong's reputation as an international finance centre".[454]

The court reached this decision on the basis that the ancient common law doctrine of Crown immunity, which exempted much of the British state from the jurisdiction of the Hong Kong courts under colonial rule, now automatically transfers to all branches of the Chinese state.[455] But that is a highly questionable conclusion, which appears to ignore the clear decision of the Court of Final Appeal in *Ng Ka Ling v Director of Immigration* that those restrictions which were only imposed on the courts by virtue of the fact that Hong

---

451. *HKSAR v Barry Peter Miller* (unrep., CACC 127/2000, [2002] HKEC 297). The case involved a murder committed by a member of the British garrison in April 1997 who then returned to Britain and was ultimately extradited back to Hong Kong to stand trial after a lengthy legal battle. See Wendy Shair, "Former soldier extradited", *The Standard*, 23 May 1999.
452. Robert Matas, "Democracy not around the corner, Hong Kong chief says", *The Globe and Mail*, 24 Oct 2005.
453. [2010] 3 HKLRD 611, 634.
454. Eric Cheung, Gu Weixia and Zhang Xianchu, "Crown immunity without the crown" (Nov 2010) *Hong Kong Lawyer* 12, 17.
455. *Hua Tian Long (No 2)* at 613, where the court held that "the establishment of the new constitutional order did not alter this position". Note that the issue of the future of Crown immunity in Hong Kong after 1 July 1997 has long been a contentious one. See further note 98 in Chapter 2 and the accompanying text.

Kong was a British colony cannot automatically continue under the "fundamentally different" system which now exists under the Hong Kong Basic Law.[456]

Returning to the restrictions on the courts directly stated in the Hong Kong Basic Law, Article 19(3) imposes one further restriction by stipulating that Hong Kong courts "shall have no jurisdiction over acts of state such as defence and foreign affairs". The wording of this provision is slightly confusing because it does not mean the courts cannot hear cases involving acts of state. Instead what it means is that where an act of state arises in a court case, the courts cannot decide the facts relating to that act of state (these are known as "facts of state"). Under Article 19(3) of the Hong Kong Basic Law, the court must obtain a certificate from the Chief Executive (who will first consult the Central People's Government) on these facts of state, which will then be binding on the court. In other words, the court can still pass judgment, but has no jurisdiction to decide certain important facts relating to the case.

Acts of state have been long recognized at common law as covering certain areas of primarily defence and foreign affairs that involve matters of government policy, and so properly lie outside the jurisdiction of the courts.[457] Wesley-Smith (1994) explains the reason for this: "The state cannot speak with two voices on such a matter, the judiciary saying one thing, the Executive another—and the judicial ought to defer to the executive branch because of the latter's responsibility for determining such questions."[458] Typical examples of acts of state at common law include declarations of war, the making of treaties, recognition of foreign governments and their diplomatic representatives.[459]

Such issues of defence and foreign affairs have long been outside the jurisdiction of the Hong Kong courts at common law,[460] and to the extent that Article 19(3) simply continues that same restriction it hardly can be seen as any kind of threat to the rule of law in Hong Kong. What has been controversial ever since the drafting of the Hong Kong Basic Law is whether Article 19(3) of the Hong Kong Basic Law goes further than the position at common law in restricting what types of cases the courts can decide by themselves and, if so, how much further. Luo (1993), a former Vice President of the

---

456. (1999) 2 HKCFAR 4, 27. See further page 179 earlier in this chapter on this point. In *Hua Tian Long (No 2)*, the court instead cited (at 632) from the Court of Appeal decision in *HKSAR v Ma Wai Kwan David* [1997] HKLRD 761, apparently ignoring the fact that it had been overruled on this point by the Court of Final Appeal in *Ng Ka Ling*. However, for a defence of the decision in *Hua Tian Long (No 2)*, see Oliver Jones, "In defence of Crown liability" (Jan 2011) *Hong Kong Lawyer* 41–47.
457. For a useful description of different meanings of the term "act of state", see Peter Wesley-Smith, *Constitutional and Administrative Law in Hong Kong* (Longman Asia, 2nd edition, 1994) at 91–104.
458. Ibid. at 99.
459. *Halsbury's Laws of England* (5th edition, reissue), Vol. 8(2), Acts of State at para. 370A.
460. See, for example, *Civil Air Transport Incorporated v Central Air Transport Corporation* (1951) 35 HKLR 215, a case which revolved around an act of state, whether Britain still recognized the Kuomintang government or the new Communist rulers of China at the time of the events giving rise to the litigation in late 1949.

Supreme People's Court, notes that mainland legal scholars are divided over the meaning of acts of state under Chinese law with some favouring a much broader definition than at common law.[461] This broader definition also includes "all kinds of decisions of the central government of a country", so potentially placing far more cases in the category of those which the courts are not allowed to decide by themselves.[462]

That broader definition of acts of state was evident in the first draft of the Hong Kong Basic Law, where the equivalent provision[463] placed not only defence and foreign affairs but also "cases relating to executive acts of the Central People's Government" outside the jurisdiction of the Hong Kong courts. This additional category was removed from later drafts of the Hong Kong Basic Law, following fierce debate over the wording of this provision.[464] But Article 19(3)'s reference to "acts of state *such as* defence and foreign affairs" in the final draft of the Hong Kong Basic Law continued to raise concern that, in addition to defence and foreign affairs, the courts also would be barred from deciding by themselves cases involving other further unspecified categories of acts of state. Indeed, it is difficult to read any other meaning into the use of the words "such as" in the English text, a point made equally clear by the use of the term "etcetera" (等) in the Chinese text of Article 19(3).[465]

This was another cause of the fierce opposition from the pro-democracy camp and many in the legal profession to the enactment of the Hong Kong Court of Final Appeal Ordinance (Cap. 484) in 1995 since, in order to comply with the Hong Kong Basic Law, this ordinance uses the same wording as Article 19(3), stating that: "The court shall have no jurisdiction over acts of state such as defence and foreign affairs."[466] The concern expressed by opponents of the agreement between Britain and China on the establishment of the Court of Final Appeal was that the potentially open-ended nature of the acts of state exception under the Hong Kong Basic Law ripped a hole in the jurisdiction of the courts, and that it could be used to defeat any cases brought against the Hong Kong SAR Government, or even the many companies in Hong Kong that are owned by the Chinese state. This fear was put most starkly by barrister and then leader of the Democratic Party

---

461. Luo Haocai, *The Chinese Judicial Review System* (Peking University Press, 1993) at 308, excerpted and translated in Wang Guiguo, "A Comparative Study on the Act of State Doctrine—With Special Reference to the Hong Kong Court of Final Appeal" in Wang and Wei Zhenying, *Legal Developments in China: Market Economy and Law* (Sweet & Maxwell Asia, 1996) at 273.
462. Ibid.
463. This was Article 18(3), due to the different numbering of articles in the first draft of the Hong Kong Basic Law.
464. Article 19 was the only article in the draft Hong Kong Basic Law not adopted by a two-thirds majority at a meeting of Basic Law drafters in January 1989. See Xiao Weiyun, *One Country, Two Systems: An Account of the Drafting of the Hong Kong Basic Law* (Peking University Press, English edition, 2001) at 168.
465. The relevant provision in the Chinese text reads: "香港特別行政區法院對國防、外交等國家行為無管轄權。"
466. Section 4(2).

Martin Lee: "The 'etcetera' in the Chinese text on acts of state is left deliberately vague, so that if you are, say, owed money by a state-owned company or if you want to sue the People's Bank of China, you could be out of luck."[467]

Such concerns initially proved misplaced after 1 July 1997, as for many years the only cases involving acts of state under the Hong Kong Basic Law were uncontroversial decisions on whether to recognize certain individuals as foreign diplomats,[468] decisions which clearly belong to the executive rather than the judiciary. When one appellant tried, in 1998, to put forward the argument Martin Lee had so feared, namely that a contract with a Chinese state-owned enterprise constitutes an act of state, this was swiftly dismissed by the courts.[469]

One vital safeguard is that at common law it has long been a matter for the courts to determine what constitutes an act of state.[470] The traditional position at common law is that only after the court has decided for itself that any particular case involves an act of state is it required to ask the executive for a certificate regarding the relevant facts of state. Scholars, including those familiar with the Chinese legal system, initially suggested that this would continue to be the situation under the Hong Kong Basic Law, so leaving the definition of acts of state in the hands of the Hong Kong courts and making it much less likely that definition would be radically expanded.[471]

However the Court of Final Appeal decision in *Democratic Republic of Congo v FG Hemisphere*[472] appears to have greatly reduced the extent of this safeguard. In that case, instead of deciding for itself what constitutes an act of state, the court instead asked the National People's Congress Standing Committee to rule on one particular instance of what constitutes an act of state under Article 19(3) of the Hong Kong Basic Law. At issue was the extent of the immunity enjoyed by foreign governments from legal action in the Hong Kong courts. Although somewhat confusingly known as "state immunity", this is an issue which had been resolved by the courts by themselves at common law in the past, rather than by categorizing it as an act of state requiring a certificate from the executive.[473]

---

467. Martin Lee, "Courting disaster", *South China Morning Post*, 14 June 1995.
468. *Zhang Sabine Soi Fan v The Official Receiver* (unrep., HCB 472/1989, 31 March 1999) and *HKSAR v Musa Solomon Dominic* (unrep., DCCC 264/1999, 9 Nov 1999).
469. *Cheung Hung Ngai v HKSAR* [1998] 1 HKLRD 330 (CFA Appeal Committee) and *HKSAR v Cheung Hung Ngai* [1997] HKLY 210 (CA). Since Cheung had not raised the act of state issue at his original trial, both courts dismissed his application for leave to appeal without any substantive consideration of the act of state issue. Nonetheless, the Court of Appeal did express "very grave doubts" as to whether a contract with a Chinese state-owned company constituted an act of state beyond the jurisdiction of the courts.
470. Ghai, *Hong Kong's New Constitutional Order* (see note 129) at 319.
471. See, for example, Wang, "A Comparative Study on the Act of State Doctrine" (see note 461) at 284.
472. (2011) 14 HKCFAR 95.
473. See the powerful dissenting judgment of Bokhary on this point (at 136–137) where, based on a review of the case law on state immunity, he concludes that the issue "does not involve any Basic Law interpretation at all let alone any interpretation to be sought from the Standing Committee".

But, in the *Congo* case, by a narrow 3 to 2 majority the Court of Final Appeal found that the contents of a strongly worded letter from the Chinese Ministry of Foreign Affairs placed before the court during the appeal hearing should be treated as facts of state, even though it had never been requested by the court through the procedure stipulated in Article 19(3).[474] Largely based on the contents of this letter, the majority in the sharply divided court provisionally concluded that the Chinese position of absolute immunity, which means foreign governments can never be sued in the courts, should take priority over the more limited form of immunity which had previously existed at common law in Hong Kong.[475]

Perhaps most worryingly, before reaching a final judgment on this point, the majority on the court then asked the National People's Congress Standing Committee to rule on whether it was correct in provisionally concluding that the issue of state immunity fell within the scope of acts of state under Article 19(3) of the Hong Kong Basic Law.[476] This was the first time the Court of Final Appeal had ever referred an issue to the Standing Committee under the provision on judicial referral in Article 158(3) of the Hong Kong Basic Law, which requires it to seek interpretations from that body in certain limited circumstances.

Chan (2011) notes that making a referral on this point "may further restrict the jurisdiction of Hong Kong courts".[477] Bokhary (2013), who dissented from the decision, says it means "what belongs to" two systems has been instead "assigned by the court" to one country and "it is difficult to see how the loss can ever be recovered".[478] The concern is that the Court of Final Appeal appears to have relinquished the power that the courts had previously enjoyed at common law to define the scope of acts of state, and may instead leave it to the Standing Committee to determine (and perhaps even expand) this definition in future. However, the other message that comes through very clearly from the court's judgment in the *Congo* case is that by far the biggest restriction on the jurisdiction of the courts under the Hong Kong Basic Law is not acts of state or anything else contained in Article 19. Instead, it is what is now generally accepted as the unrestricted power of the Standing Committee to interpret any part of the Hong Kong Basic Law, an issue which we will examine in detail in the next chapter.

---

474. Ibid. at 204. For the text of the letter, see 174–178.
475. Ibid. at 182. This more limited form of immunity, known as restrictive immunity, restricts the immunity enjoyed by foreign governments in the courts so that it does not apply to certain litigation relating to commercial transactions.
476. Ibid. at 232–233. The act of state issue was one of four questions referred by the court to the Standing Committee, the others primarily related to questions involving the interpretation of Article 13(1) on foreign affairs.
477. Chan, "The Judiciary" (see note 76) at 318.
478. Bokhary, *Recollections* (see note 84) at 580.

Chapter 7
Interpretation and Amendment

How the Hong Kong Basic Law is interpreted, or most crucially, who interprets the Hong Kong Basic Law, has been one of the most consistently controversial issues, from its drafting back in the 1980s through to today. The article on interpretation, which ultimately became Article 158 in the final draft of the Hong Kong Basic Law, was the subject of more argument than almost any other during the drafting process.[1] Issues involving interpretation of the Hong Kong Basic Law have been at the heart of some of the major controversies that have erupted in recent years, from the repeated disputes over who has the right to live in Hong Kong to the long-running arguments over how to change Hong Kong's electoral system.

One reason why the issue has proved so controversial is that interpretation affects every aspect of the Hong Kong Basic Law. Few, if any, laws are written in language that is clear enough to cover every possible situation which may arise after their enactment. That is especially true of constitutional instruments such as the Hong Kong Basic Law, which state general principles covering a wide range of issues. "Gaps and ambiguities are bound to arise", as Hong Kong's Court of Final Appeal stated in the seminal case of *Ng Ka Ling v Director of Immigration*.[2] When such ambiguities arise, how they are resolved can determine the meaning of any part of the Hong Kong Basic Law including, for instance, how far the apparently generous provisions on human rights really protect fundamental freedoms in Hong Kong.

Another reason why interpretation has proved so controversial is that it is one of the very few areas where there is some interface between the two different legal systems that exist in Hong Kong and the rest of China, and which most other provisions in the Hong Kong Basic Law seek to keep separate from one another. In contrast to so many other issues covered by the Hong Kong Basic Law, interpretation is not the exclusive responsibility of either Hong Kong or mainland Chinese authorities. Instead, it is a power shared by institutions in Hong Kong and the mainland—although, as we will see, not necessarily equally.

---

1. For a flavour of these arguments, see an account by one of the key participants in Martin Lee, "A Tale of Two Articles", in Peter Wesley-Smith and Albert Chen (eds.), *The Basic Law and Hong Kong's Future* (Butterworths, 1988) at 309–325.
2. (1999) 2 HKCFAR 4, 28.

Given the huge differences that still exist between these two systems, it should be no surprise that this sometimes leads to conflict. As then Secretary for Justice Elsie Leung once noted in a moment of candour: "It is unavoidable that the Mainland organs and legal sectors and the local institutions and legal sectors will sometimes have different interpretations of the provisions of the Basic Law."[3] Given that reality, perhaps the biggest surprise is not that there have been some conflicts over how to interpret the Hong Kong Basic Law since 1997. Instead, it is that such conflicts have so far been confined to a handful of occasions.

Who interprets the Hong Kong Basic Law was one of the few important issues not mentioned in the 1984 Joint Declaration, the Sino-British agreement that went into exhaustive detail about most other aspects of Hong Kong's future after 1997.[4] That omission, which subsequently became a cause of frustration to some lawyers in Hong Kong,[5] is perhaps symptomatic of the lack of understanding in some quarters of the very different way in which laws are interpreted under the Chinese legal system.

For many lawyers in Hong Kong, it initially seemed guarantee enough that the Joint Declaration provided for the continuation of the common law system in Hong Kong after 1 July 1997, and the creation of a Court of Final Appeal with the power to finally decide all cases that fall within its jurisdiction. Under the common law system, it is only the courts which can interpret legislation and, in most circumstances, only when deciding court cases. Ghai (2007) notes that this "might have given at least the Hong Kong public the impression that the final power to interpret the Basic Law would be with the Hong Kong courts" after 1997.[6]

But it soon became clear that this overlooked the very different system that applies in the rest of China, where interpretation of legislation is not necessarily linked to deciding court cases. In China, most courts lack the power to issue authoritative interpretations of legislation.[7] Even the one exception, the Supreme People's Court, issues many of its interpretations outside court cases and in a form unrecognizable to most common law lawyers.[8]

---

3. Secretary for Justice Elsie Leung, "Statement on the Term of the New Chief Executive", Press Conference, 12 March 2005, at para. 15.
4. See further "2.2: Sino-British Joint Declaration" in Chapter 2.
5. See, for instance, Martin Lee's complaint that the issue "should have been settled between the Chinese and British Governments during their negotiations over Hong Kong in 1984" in Lee, "A Tale of Two Articles" (see note 1) at 323.
6. Yash Ghai, "The Political Economy of Interpretation" in Hualing Fu, Lison Harris and Simon N.M. Young (eds.), *Interpreting Hong Kong's Basic Law: The Struggle for Coherence* (Palgrave Macmillan, 2007) at 128.
7. This was explicitly stated by the Supreme People's Court in "A Reply From the Supreme People's Court that Local Courts at Various Levels Shall Not Make Judicial Interpretations" (31 March 1987), cited by Chen Jianfu, *Chinese Law: Context and Transformation* (Martinus Nijhoff, 2008) at 201.
8. Some of these "interpretations" are longer than the original text of the law they purport to interpret. For example, a 200-article "interpretation" of the 156-article long PRC General Principles of the Civil Law, was issued by the Supreme People's Court in April 1988. See Chen Jianfu (2008) at 200.

Under the Chinese legal system, it is the body that enacts a particular piece of legislation, or a representative of that body, which has the power to issue binding interpretations explaining the meaning of that legislation in an authoritative manner,[9] with the emphasis overwhelmingly on reflecting the intention behind the law, sometimes even to the extent of defying the plain meaning of its wording. Mason (2011) summarizes the Chinese system of interpretation as one which holds that "the institution which best understands what the legislative intention was, is the institution which enacted the law".[10]

In the case of laws passed by the National People's Congress, including the Hong Kong Basic Law, the representative body of the National People's Congress responsible for interpreting these laws is its Standing Committee. Article 67(4) of the PRC Constitution 1982 specifically tasks the Standing Committee with responsibility for interpreting all laws passed by the National People's Congress and its Standing Committee.

That led to some bitter battles during the drafting of the Hong Kong Basic Law about how to resolve the conflict between the Hong Kong and mainland legal systems over which body would be responsible for interpreting the Hong Kong Basic Law, including warnings by some mainland drafters that the Hong Kong courts might "get it wrong" if they were given an unrestricted power to interpret the Hong Kong Basic Law.[11] These battles were made more intense by the fact that the two bodies involved, the Hong Kong courts and the National People's Congress Standing Committee, could hardly be more different from one another. On the one hand, the Hong Kong courts, which are responsible for interpretation under the common law system, function independently of the government and are not supposed to take political considerations into account. On the other hand, the Standing Committee, which is responsible for interpretation under the Chinese legal system, is a legislative body that is part of China's political structure and functions in a manner far removed from a court. Although officially elected by the full National People's Congress, in reality its membership list is approved beforehand at a high level within the Chinese Communist Party by its Central Committee.[12] As a result, Ghai (2000) concludes that the Standing Committee is "correctly perceived to be a political body under the control of the Central Government and the Communist Party".[13]

The eventual solution, which was portrayed as a compromise by mainland drafters at the time,[14] was Article 158, the sole article in the Hong Kong Basic Law on the issue of

---

9. See Joseph Y.S. Cheng, "The Constitutional Relationship Between the Central Government and the Future Hong Kong Special Administrative Region Government" (1988) 20 *Case Western Reserve Journal of International Law* 65, 79.
10. Sir Anthony Mason, "The Rule of Law in the Shadow of the Giant: The Hong Kong Experience" (2011) 33 *Sydney Law Review* 623, 629.
11. Lee, "A Tale of Two Articles" (see note 1) at 315–317.
12. John Burns, "China's *Nomenklatura* System" (1987) 36(5) *Problems of Communism* 36, 42.
13. Yash Ghai, "Litigating the Basic Law: Jurisdiction, Interpretation and Procedure", in Johannes M.M. Chan, H.L. Fu and Yash Ghai (eds), *Hong Kong's Constitutional Debate: Conflict Over Interpretation* (Hong Kong University Press, 2000) at 36.
14. See, for instance, Xiao Weiyun, *One Country, Two Systems: An Account of the Drafting of the Hong Kong Basic Law* (Peking University Press, English edition, 2001) at 173.

interpretation. Although long—at 230 words, Article 158 is among the longest provisions in the Hong Kong Basic Law—it is far from explicit on certain crucial matters. Article 158 does make clear that both systems will play some role in interpreting the Hong Kong Basic Law. But, beyond that, this highly complex[15] provision is itself open to competing interpretations over the precise division of responsibilities as to who interprets which parts of the Hong Kong Basic Law, and is best described as an uneasy compromise between the two legal systems.

It starts, in Article 158(1), with an unhelpfully brief statement of the Standing Committee's ultimate power to interpret the Hong Kong Basic Law. That simply reflects the general principle in relation to interpretation under the Chinese legal system stated in Article 67(4) of the PRC Constitution 1982. But there is no elaboration on when that power (which is rarely used by the Standing Committee, even in relation to other laws)[16] will be exercised in practice, or whether it is subject to any kind of restrictions, especially in the context of the overall framework for "one country, two systems" in Hong Kong.

Article 158 then goes on to delegate to the Hong Kong courts a considerable part of the Standing Committee's interpretative powers. Under Article 158(2), the courts are empowered to interpret *on their own* all provisions in the Hong Kong Basic Law that fall within Hong Kong's autonomy, without any need to consult the Standing Committee. Only in the case of the "relatively few"[17] provisions concerning matters outside Hong Kong's autonomy are the courts required, under Article 158(3), to consult the Standing Committee.[18] Even then, that only applies to cases involving a final judgment, so effectively limiting the requirement to consult the Standing Committee to a tiny number of cases heard by the Court of Final Appeal.[19]

What the wording of Article 158 leaves unclear is whether the delegation to the Hong Kong courts of such wide-ranging powers to interpret large parts of the Hong Kong Basic Law on their own means that, as would normally be the case in China,[20] the Standing Committee has chosen to give up its own power to interpret those parts of the Hong Kong Basic Law that lie within Hong Kong's autonomy, and will instead confine itself to

---

15. See Johannes Chan's characterization of Article 158 in "Basic Law and Constitutional Review" (2007) 37 *HKLJ* 407, 415.
16. From 1949 to 2000, there were no more than nine instances of interpretation of laws by the Standing Committee. See Albert Chen, *An Introduction to the Legal System of the People's Republic of China* (LexisNexis, 4th edition, 2011) at 155–156.
17. See Solicitor General Robert Allcock, "Application of Article 158 of the Basic Law", Constitutional Law Conference on Implementation of the Basic Law: A Comparative Perspective, 29 April 2000, at para. 11.
18. The precise definition of those categories of provisions that fall outside Hong Kong autonomy under Article 158(3) is explained on page 231.
19. See further "7.4: Judicial Referral" later in this chapter for a more detailed discussion of the circumstances when the Court of Final Appeal is required to refer an issue to the Standing Committee for interpretation under Article 158(3).
20. See further note 65 later in this chapter and the accompanying text.

interpreting the smaller number of provisions that lie outside Hong Kong's autonomy. Or whether Article 158 still gives the Standing Committee a parallel power to intervene and interpret any part of the Hong Kong Basic Law at any time, including the many provisions (such as those on human rights) on matters that lie within Hong Kong's autonomy, and which would normally be left to the Hong Kong courts to interpret.

It is this crucial ambiguity which lies at the heart of some of the major controversies over interpretation since 1997. Although now resolved as a matter of law, as we will see it still has important—and troubling—implications for the true extent of Hong Kong's autonomy under the Hong Kong Basic Law.

7.1 Hong Kong Courts

For all their significance, Standing Committee interpretations are rare. Instead, on the vast majority of occasions it is the Hong Kong courts which are interpreting the Hong Kong Basic Law in deciding cases, as they are authorized to do under Articles 158(2) and (3) of the Hong Kong Basic Law.

The courts take a purposive approach towards interpreting the Hong Kong Basic Law, supplemented by a generous interpretation of its human rights provisions.[21] The importance of adopting a purposive approach was explained by the Court of Final Appeal in its first major case involving the Hong Kong Basic Law, *Ng Ka Ling v Director of Immigration*. In that case, the court emphasized the constitutional nature of the Hong Kong Basic Law, noting that: "As is usual for constitutional instruments, it uses ample and general language. It is a living instrument intended to meet changing needs and circumstances."[22]

That means the "adoption of a purposive approach is necessary because a constitution states general principles and expresses purposes without condescending to particularity and definition of terms".[23] Or to put it more simply, a purposive approach is necessary to fill in the gaps left by the lack of definition, or detail, in the Hong Kong Basic Law.

While the Court of Final Appeal has been consistent in stating the need to use a purposive approach in interpreting the Hong Kong Basic Law, it has been less consistent in how it applied that purposive approach in practice. In another case involving the interpretation of a Hong Kong statute the following year, the court described the purposive approach as a modern development of the "mischief rule in particular".[24] That refers to one of the oldest rules of statutory interpretation, with cases in the English courts dating back more than 400 years.[25] The mischief rule was the first to recognize that it is sometimes

---

21. *Ng Ka Ling v Director of Immigration* (1999) 2 HKCFAR 4, 28–29.
22. Ibid. at 28.
23. Ibid.
24. *Medical Council of Hong Kong v Chow Siu Shek David* (2000) 3 HKCFAR 144, 153.
25. See, for example, *Heydon's Case* (1584) 3 Coke's Reports 7a, which is generally regarded as the leading statement of the mischief rule.

necessary to consider the purpose why a particular provision in a law has been enacted,[26] although generally only by reference to what is stated in other parts of the same law.[27]

The purposive approach allows the courts to go much further than the mischief rule in trying to ascertain the reasons for the enactment of a particular provision, by also considering material in other documents (which is known as "extrinsic material"). In *Ng Ka Ling*, the Court of Final Appeal explained the application of the purposive approach as follows: "[I]n ascertaining the true meaning of the instrument, the courts must consider the purpose of the instrument and its relevant provisions as well as the language of its text in the light of the context, context being of particular importance in the interpretation of a constitutional instrument."[28]

The court made clear that such purpose could be established not just by looking at the wording of the particular provision in the Hong Kong Basic Law at issue in a case, but also by reference to "other provisions of the Basic Law or relevant extrinsic materials including the Joint Declaration".[29] The same considerations could also be taken into account in considering how to interpret one provision in the Hong Kong Basic Law in the context of the wording of other provisions[30] (this is known as a "contextual approach").

What the court left unclear in *Ng Ka Ling* was what comes first in its purposive approach towards interpreting the Hong Kong Basic Law: the wording of a particular provision, or the purpose behind its enactment? While both factors will often point in the same direction, it is also possible for evidence to emerge of a purpose which conflicts with the plain wording of a particular provision. This raises the question: Which of these two factors—wording or purpose—should ultimately prevail in such circumstances?

In *Ng Ka Ling*, the Court of Final Appeal appeared unsure on this point. Some parts of the judgment laid great emphasis on the importance of following the "ordinary language" of the Hong Kong Basic Law, particularly in deciding one of the most crucial issues in the case, whether children born in mainland China to a Hong Kong Chinese parent require permission from mainland authorities before they can lawfully move to Hong Kong.[31] But Ghai (2000) notes that other parts of the *Ng Ka Ling* judgment disregarded the "plain meaning" of the Hong Kong Basic Law,[32] most notably in refusing to refer

---

26. This was described in terms of the "mischief" at common law which the legislation was designed to remedy, so giving rise to the name "mischief rule".
27. Particularly the statement of purpose in the Preamble to the law.
28. *Ng Ka Ling* at 28.
29. Ibid.
30. Ibid.
31. Ibid. at 33–35. The issue revolved around the wording of Article 22(4), which allows mainland authorities to restrict the entry into Hong Kong of "people from other parts of China". The Court of Final Appeal decided that children born in China to a Hong Kong Chinese parent "are not, as a matter of ordinary language, people from other parts of China", and therefore not subject to this provision. It reinforced this conclusion by reference to what it described as the purpose of the Hong Kong Basic Law in granting a high degree of autonomy to Hong Kong.
32. Yash Ghai, "Litigating the Basic Law" (see note 13) at 35.

a provision on matters outside Hong Kong's autonomy to the Standing Committee for interpretation,[33] as would seem to be required by the wording of Article 158(3) of the Hong Kong Basic Law.[34]

The Court of Final Appeal justified its refusal to refer this provision to the Standing Committee in *Ng Ka Ling* by an extreme application of the purposive approach, in which the purpose behind Article 158(3) appeared to be accorded greater priority than its wording. That purpose was described by the court exclusively in terms of protecting Hong Kong's high degree of autonomy, a purpose which the Court of Final Appeal believed would be undermined if it was required too frequently to refer issues of interpretation to the Standing Committee.[35]

But a high degree of autonomy, important though it is, is not the only purpose of the Hong Kong Basic Law. As Chen (2000) points out, in a powerful attack on this aspect of the *Ng Ka Ling* judgment, a more balanced approach might have given equal weight to another purpose of the Hong Kong Basic Law, which also allows Chinese Central Authorities "to exercise supervisory powers to ensure that the limits of autonomy are not exceeded".[36] In other cases, the courts have interpreted the purpose of the Hong Kong Basic Law in very different terms. In *HKSAR v Ma Wai Kwan David*, for instance, the court described the purpose of the Hong Kong Basic Law in terms of ensuring "continuity" across 1 July 1997 to safeguard "stability and prosperity" in Hong Kong.[37]

That highlights the inherent problem with a wide version of the purposive approach which, at its most extreme, allows judges to decide almost whatever they want. Ghai (2000) notes that: "[C]ourts assume wide discretion when they apply the purposive rules. It is up to them to decide what the purpose of the legislation is" and the courts can even "ignore the plain meaning of the legislation if they think it is not in accordance with what they formulate as the purpose of the law".[38] Such a wide formulation of the purposive approach also makes it more difficult to distinguish the common law system of interpreting legislation from that which prevails in mainland China where, as we will see shortly, an almost overwhelming emphasis is often placed on purpose (or legislative intent), even to the extent of sometimes rewriting the wording of laws to accord with such purpose.[39]

---

33. This was Article 22(4), which is described in note 31 above.
34. See further "7.4: Judicial Referral" later in this chapter for more on Article 158(3) and this aspect of the *Ng Ka Ling* judgment.
35. See *Ng Ka Ling* at 33, where the court held that a referral to the Standing Committee in this case "would be a substantial derogation from the Region's autonomy and cannot be right".
36. Albert H.Y. Chen, "The Court of Final Appeal's Ruling in the 'Illegal Migrant' Children Case" in Chan, Fu and Ghai (eds.), *Hong Kong's Constitutional Debate* (see note 13) at 133–134. For a more detailed discussion of the supervisory powers that the Hong Kong Basic Law allows Chinese Central Authorities to exercise over Hong Kong, see further "Chapter 4: How High a Degree of Autonomy?".
37. [1997] HKLRD 761, 772.
38. Yash Ghai, "Litigating the Basic Law" (see note 13 above) at 30.
39. See further note 135 later in this chapter and the accompanying text.

Clarification came two years later when the Court of Final Appeal, perhaps anxious to emphasize the difference between the Hong Kong and mainland legal systems when it comes to the interpretation of laws, subtly redefined how it applies the purposive approach in the case of *Director of Immigration v Chong Fung Yuen*.[40] Gone was the heavy, almost exclusive, emphasis on purpose that was evident in some parts of the *Ng Ka Ling* judgment. Ghai (2007) notes that, "in contrast to *Ng Ka Ling*" this later decision "places the primary emphasis on the language of the text".[41] As the court explained in an important passage in *Chong Fung Yuen*, the purpose (or legislative intent) behind the law is only relevant in so far as it helps explain that language:

> Their task is not to ascertain the intent of the lawmaker on its own. Their duty is to ascertain what was meant by the language used and to give effect to the legislative intent as expressed in the language. It is the text of the enactment which is the law and it is regarded as important both that the law should be certain and that it should be ascertainable by the citizen.[42]

What that means is that while the purpose behind the Hong Kong Basic Law can still be relevant in helping to understand the language of the law, once the meaning of that language is clearly established, the courts are bound to give effect to it, even if this leads to consequences which the judges would prefer to avoid. So, for instance, in *Tam Nga Yin v Director of Immigration*,[43] another case decided on the same day as *Chong Fung Yuen*, a majority of judges on the Court of Final Appeal reluctantly denied residency rights to children born outside Hong Kong and adopted by Hong Kong parents. This was because the majority on the court found that the only possible meaning of the wording "*born outside Hong Kong of*" (emphasis added) used in the relevant provision in the Hong Kong Basic Law[44] was that it only granted residency rights to children *born of*—rather than adopted by—Hong Kong parents.[45]

---

40. (2001) 4 HKCFAR 211.
41. Yash Ghai, "The Intersection of Chinese Law and the Common Law in the Hong Kong Special Administrative Region: Question of Technique or Politics" (2007) 37 *HKLJ* 363, 386.
42. *Chong Fung Yuen* at 213.
43. (2001) 4 HKCFAR 251.
44. This is Article 24(2)(3), a provision also at issue in a different context in the earlier cases of *Ng Ka Ling v Director of Immigration* (1999) 2 HKCFAR 4 and *Chan Kam Nga v Director of Immigration* (1999) 2 HKCFAR 82, which led to the first interpretation of the Hong Kong Basic Law by the Standing Committee in June 1999 (see further notes 89–90 later in this chapter and the accompanying text). However, in *Tam Nga Yin*, the Court of Final Appeal held (at 256) that this 1999 interpretation was not relevant to the case because it did not address the issue of adopted children (see further note 180 later in this chapter).
45. *Tam Nga Yin* at 263, where the majority made clear that if the language of Article 24(2)(3) had been ambiguous, they would "lean in favour of an interpretation that adopted children are included". Justice Bokhary dissented in this case, arguing (at 264–265) that the wording of Article 24(2)(3) was wide enough to cover adopted children. Despite losing in court, the case had a happy ending for the adopted children involved as an outpouring of public support led to a change in government policy that allowed them to stay in Hong Kong. See Chow Chung-yan, "Tears of joy as Agnes finally gets to call Hong Kong 'home'", *South China Morning Post*, 26 Oct 2001.

Similarly in *Chong Fung Yuen*, the court held that the only possible meaning of the clear and unambiguous language used in Article 24(2)(1) of the Hong Kong Basic Law, which states that "Chinese citizens born in Hong Kong" are entitled to permanent residency, was that this applied to all Chinese children born in Hong Kong, even if their parents had no connection with the city, and were only visiting Hong Kong in order to give birth.[46] The decision in *Chong Fung Yuen* would prove to have major social implications. Although the numbers involved were relatively small at the time of the judgment,[47] the court's decision paved the way for a large influx of mainland mothers seeking to give birth in Hong Kong in subsequent years. Within a few years, the situation had become so serious that pregnant Hong Kong mothers were complaining about a shortage of hospital beds[48] and, by 2012, there were growing calls for the National People's Congress Standing Committee to intervene to reverse the effects of the court's decision.[49]

But in holding that their task was confined to interpreting the language actually used in the Hong Kong Basic Law, what the Court of Final Appeal was essentially saying in *Chong Fung Yuen* was that it is not the task of the courts to deal with the consequences that might arise if the language used in the Hong Kong Basic Law did not accurately reflect the intention of the drafters of that document. That does not mean the intention behind a particular provision in the Hong Kong Basic Law will never be taken into account by the courts. In *Chong Fung Yuen*, the key point was that the court held there was only one possible meaning of the wording in dispute. Where the wording of a particular provision is not entirely clear, considerations of the purpose behind that provision can still assume considerable importance, and even tilt the balance in favour of adopting a less obvious interpretation of the wording in dispute.

So, for example, in *Chan Yu Nam v Secretary for Justice* the Court of Appeal dismissed a challenge to the legality of allowing companies and other organizations to vote in elections for many functional constituencies in the Legislative Council through a system known as corporate voting.[50] Viewed in isolation, the most obvious interpretation of Article 26 of the Hong Kong Basic Law might have tended to support this challenge. The wording of this provision only refers to certain individuals (namely Hong Kong permanent residents) having the right to vote, and does not directly state that this right can be exercised by companies or other organizations.[51] But, in contrast to the decision in

---

46. *Chong Fung Yuen* at 233, where the court held that, "[t]he meaning of the provision is not ambiguous, that is, it is not reasonably capable of sustaining competing interpretations".
47. Ibid. at 226, where the court noted figures for births since 1 July 1997, which suggested the number of children involved would be around 555 per annum.
48. See, for example, Dennis Chong, "Birth pains", *The Standard*, 15 April 2011.
49. Tanna Chong, Simpson Cheung and Johnny Tam, "NPC asked for second look at Law's baby rule", *South China Morning Post*, 12 March 2012.
50. [2012] 3 HKC 38 An application for leave to appeal the case was subsequently dismissed by the Court of Final Appeal (unrep., FAMV 39 and 40/2011, [2012] HKEC 94). For an explanation of the corporate voting system, see further note 231 in Chapter 5 and the accompanying text.
51. However as the court noted in *Chan Yu Nam* (at 66), nor does Article 26 explicitly exclude the possibility of companies or other organizations having the right to vote. See further note 237 in Chapter 5.

Chong Fung Yuen, the Court of Appeal held that the wording of the provision at issue in this case was not entirely clear, and susceptible to different possible meanings.[52] Stressing the importance of looking at "the whole of the Basic Law" rather than any one provision in isolation, the court concluded that Article 26 should be interpreted in the context of other provisions that indirectly refer to corporate voting elsewhere in the Hong Kong Basic Law, as "part of a mosaic" allowing for the continuation of this system of voting.[53]

Where the wording of a particular provision in the Hong Kong Basic Law is ambiguous, extrinsic materials may still sometimes be relevant in interpreting the purpose behind that provision. In *Chan Yu Nam*, the Court of Appeal devoted a substantial part of its judgment to examining a wide range of extrinsic materials on the history of elections to the Legislative Council, including the provisions on this issue in the Joint Declaration.[54] That 1984 agreement with Britain is one of the most important extrinsic materials, since the primary purpose of the Hong Kong Basic Law (as stated in its Preamble) is to implement the policies on "one country, two systems" that the Chinese government originally set out in the Joint Declaration. For instance, in *Gurung Kesh Bahadur v Director of Immigration*, the court adopted a broad interpretation of the meaning of the right to travel in Article 31 of the Hong Kong Basic Law partly on the basis of the repeated references to this right in the Joint Declaration.[55]

A small portion of what was said during the enactment of the Hong Kong Basic Law may also be relevant. Put simply, if the wording of a particular provision in the Hong Kong Basic Law is open to different possible interpretations, authoritative statements during the enactment process may help to establish which of those interpretations most accurately reflects the original purpose behind the drafting of that particular provision. A parallel can be drawn with the situation in other countries where courts are often willing to consider, to a greater or lesser extent, evidence of the original intention of the drafters of a law. In England, the legal system on which the Hong Kong courts still rely most heavily for precedents, ever since the landmark decision of the House of Lords in *Pepper v Hart* the courts have been allowed to look at clear statements made in parliament by the promoter (or presenter) of a piece of legislation during the enactment process for assistance in interpreting provisions in that legislation which are unclear.[56] But statements by

---

52. Ibid. at 66–67.
53. Ibid. at 47 and 68. See, in particular, the references to "corporate bodies" in Annex I(3) and Annex II(I)(2) in the English text of the Hong Kong Basic Law. These are described in more detail in note 239 in Chapter 5.
54. Ibid. at 49–64. See, in particular, the court's citing (at 51–52) of the provision in Annex I(I) of the Joint Declaration requiring the Legislative Council to be "constituted by elections". For more on this important provision, see further note 179 in Chapter 5 and the accompanying text.
55. [2001] 3 HKLRD 32, 43 (CA) Upheld by the CFA in (2002) 5 HKCFAR 480. See further note 17 in Chapter 3 and the accompanying text.
56. [1993] AC 593, 640.

anyone else, or any other discussion that took place during the process of enacting the law, are strictly irrelevant as far as the English courts are concerned.[57]

In Hong Kong, the courts appear to adopt a broadly similar approach as far as the Hong Kong Basic Law is concerned. In *Chong Fung Yuen*, the Court of Final Appeal explicitly included, in the permissible extrinsic materials to which the courts are allowed to refer, a lengthy statement made by Basic Law Drafting Committee Chairman Ji Pengfei in presenting the Hong Kong Basic Law to the National People's Congress shortly before its enactment in 1990.[58] Titled an "Explanation" of the Hong Kong Basic Law and related documents, this speech arguably performs a broadly similar role in relation to the Hong Kong Basic Law as the statements made to the UK Parliament to which the English courts are allowed to refer under the principle laid down by the House of Lords in *Pepper v Hart*.[59]

But the Ji Pengfei speech only represents a tiny fraction of what was stated by members of the Basic Law Drafting Committee during the lengthy process of writing the Hong Kong Basic Law. In common with their English counterparts, the Hong Kong courts have so far proved reluctant to open the floodgates to detailed examination of the mass of material that accumulates during the drafting of any law. That is because to admit such a large quantity of extrinsic material would inevitably detract from the primary focus that the courts have, at least since the *Chong Fung Yuen* case, placed on the actual language used in the Hong Kong Basic Law, and the need that the meaning of any particular provision "should be certain and that it should be ascertainable" from its wording.[60]

As the Court of First Instance noted in *Cheng Kar Shun v Li Fung Ying*, expressing reservations about an unsuccessful argument based around a detailed analysis of the drafting history of the Hong Kong Basic Law: "[I]f the true interpretation of the law can only be ascertained after a lengthy examination and reconstruction of the drafting history as well as the lawmaker's thinking process, it is difficult to see how the law is certain and ascertainable to the citizen."[61]

Such reservations become even stronger when the materials presented to the court were written after the drafting of the Hong Kong Basic Law had been completed. In

---

57. For a useful summary of the conditions laid down by the House of Lords in *Pepper v Hart* and their subsequent application in other English cases, see Simon N.M. Young, "Legislative History, Original Intent and the Interpretation of the Basic Law" in Fu, Harris and Young (eds.), *Interpreting Hong Kong's Basic Law* (see note 6) at 19–23.
58. (2001) 4 HKCFAR 211, 224.
59. Young (see note 57) describes (at 25) this as a "literal" application of the *Pepper v Hart* criteria to the Hong Kong Basic Law. But, noting the important role in drafting the Hong Kong Basic Law that was played by sub-groups of the Basic Law Drafting Committee, he argues in favour of a broader approach that would also allow the courts to refer to documents of these sub-groups.
60. *Chong Fung Yuen* at 223.
61. *Cheng Kar Shun v Li Fung Ying* [2011] 2 HKLRD 555, 603. For more on this case, see further notes 296–297 in Chapter 5 and the accompanying text.

Chong Fung Yuen, the Court of Final Appeal cautioned that there was a particular need to be "prudent" in considering such documents because "under a common law system which includes a separation of powers, the interpretation of laws once enacted is a matter for the courts".[62]

That is not the case under the Chinese legal system, where most courts lack the power to issue authoritative interpretations of laws. Mason (2006), one of the judges in the *Chong Fung Yuen* case, notes that the court's primary focus on the language used in the Hong Kong Basic Law stands "in contrast to other systems which may place more weight on the way in which the instrument came into existence or on post-enactment materials".[63]

7.2 Standing Committee

The issue of interpretation led to bitter arguments during the drafting of the Hong Kong Basic Law.[64] After that, controversy over this issue initially faded away. Amid all the other battles in the run-up to 1997 over issues such as elections to the Legislative Council, concern about the potential impact of the Standing Committee's power of interpretation on Hong Kong's legal system was largely relegated to the sidelines. That was especially so since many assumed that the way in which the final draft of the Hong Kong Basic Law was written restricted the Standing Committee's interpretative powers to a relatively small part of the Hong Kong Basic Law, and severely limited the circumstances under which such a power could be exercised.

As we have already seen, under Article 158(2), the Standing Committee delegated to the Hong Kong courts the important power to interpret on their own all provisions in the Hong Kong Basic Law that fall within Hong Kong's autonomy. Ling (2007) notes that the normal position in China is that when one body delegates a power to another body, then the body which originally possessed that power will no longer exercise that power themselves.[65] Many such examples can be found scattered throughout the Hong Kong Basic Law.[66] This suggests that once the Standing Committee delegated such

---

62. *Chong Fung Yuen* at 223. As a result, the court refused (at 233) to follow an opinion issued in 1996 (see note 138) by the Preparatory Committee, a body established by the NPC Standing Committee to prepare for the establishment of the Hong Kong SAR. This opinion advocated denying residency rights to the category of children at issue in this case.
63. Sir Anthony Mason, "The Role of the Common Law in Hong Kong" in Jessica Young and Rebecca Lee (eds.), *The Common Law Lecture Series 2005* (Faculty of Law, University of Hong Kong, 2006) at 12.
64. See further "2.4: Battles and Changes" in Chapter 2.
65. Ling Bing, "Subject Matter Limitation on the NPCSC's Power to Interpret the Basic Law" 37 *HKLJ* 619, 633–639.
66. For example, the delegation by the Central People's Government to the Hong Kong SAR Government of the authority to issue Hong Kong SAR passports under Article 154(1) means that the Central People's Government has never, so far, exercised the power to issue such passports itself.

wide-ranging interpretative powers to the Hong Kong courts under Article 158(2), it was no longer able to interpret those same provisions, which concern matters that fall within Hong Kong's autonomy and constitute the vast majority of the provisions in the Hong Kong Basic law. This is often described as a *subject-matter limitation* on the Standing Committee's power to interpret the Hong Kong Basic Law, and there is strong evidence to suggest it was the original intention of the drafters of the Hong Kong Basic Law to impose such a limitation on the Standing Committee.[67] For instance, the existence of such a subject-matter limitation which would prevent the Standing Committee from interpreting those provisions in the Hong Kong Basic Law that fall within Hong Kong's autonomy was explicitly mentioned in a 1989 report from the sub-group of the Basic Law Drafting Committee responsible for writing the final version of Article 158.[68]

The existence of such a subject-matter limitation is crucial because it would limit the Standing Committee's role in interpreting the Hong Kong Basic Law to the much smaller number of provisions in the Hong Kong Basic Law that concern issues which are outside Hong Kong's autonomy. These are more precisely defined in Article 158(3) as provisions concerning:

(1) Affairs which are the responsibility of the Central People's Government; or
(2) The relationship between the Central Authorities and Hong Kong.

These two categories are known as "excluded provisions",[69] because they are the only parts of the Hong Kong Basic Law which the Court of Final Appeal is excluded from always interpreting entirely by itself.

Even when it comes to these two categories of excluded provisions, which would only seem to cover relatively few articles in the Hong Kong Basic Law, the Standing Committee's role initially seemed to be limited. Under Article 158(3), the Court of Final Appeal is assigned an important gatekeeper role in deciding when issues which arise during court cases involving excluded provisions must be referred to the Standing Committee for interpretation. In *Ng Ka Ling*, the court emphasized that "it is for the Court of Final Appeal and for it alone to decide"[70] when such a referral is necessary. Since, under the common law system, interpretation of laws only occurs during court cases, this seemed to suggest that, even in these two limited categories of excluded provisions, there is a *procedural limitation* on the Standing Committee's power to interpret the Hong Kong Basic Law. This procedural limitation is that the Standing Committee cannot

---

67. See the detailed analysis of the drafting history of Article 158 in Ling, "Subject Matter Limitation" (see note 65) at 625–633.
68. *Report by the Subgroup on the Relationship Between the Central Authorities and the HKSAR on the Amendment of Articles* (Basic Law Drafting Committee Secretariat, 1989) cited in Ling, "Subject Matter Limitation" (see note 65) at 631. See further Ling's analysis of the significance of the wording used in this report at 631–632.
69. *Ng Ka Ling v Director of Immigration* (1999) 2 HKCFAR 4, 30.
70. Ibid. at 31.

simply decide to interpret the Hong Kong Basic Law on its own initiative. Instead, it has to wait for a referral from the Court of Final Appeal before it can interpret any particular provision in the Hong Kong Basic Law, a referral that the "predominant provision test"[71] formulated by the court in *Ng Ka Ling* suggested would be an extremely rare event.

But that conclusion ignores the reality that under the Chinese legal system, interpretation of laws is not necessarily linked to court cases, and often occurs quite independently of any specific case.[72] Thus, if the Standing Committee simply follows the same system that it applies to interpreting other laws in China, there is no need to wait for a referral by the Court of Final Appeal, or for any court case at all.[73] In any case, the Court of Final Appeal's arguably over-zealous assertion of its gatekeeper role in *Ng Ka Ling* quickly triggered a chain of events which swept away any possibility of legal limits on the extent of the Standing Committee's powers to interpret the Hong Kong Basic Law.

Fearing that the decision in *Ng Ka Ling* and the closely related case of *Chan Kam Nga v Director of Immigration* to Hong Kong parents,[74] which was also decided on the same day, opened the floodgates to an uncontrollable influx of more than one million children born on the mainland to Hong Kong parents,[75] the Hong Kong SAR Government looked for ways to reverse the effects of the court's judgments in these cases.[76] The Court of Final Appeal had invalidated provisions in the Immigration Ordinance (Cap. 115) which restricted the number of such children entitled to permanent residency rights,[77] and made

---

71. Ibid. at 33. For more on this aspect of the *Ng Ka Ling* judgment, and criticism of it, see further notes 208–214 later in this chapter and the accompanying text.
72. For an excellent analysis of interpretations of other laws issued by the Standing Committee, see Yang Xiaonan "Legislative Interpretations by the Standing Committee of the National People's Congress in China" (2008) 38 *HKLJ* 255–285.
73. That conclusion is supported by Yash Ghai (in *Hong Kong's New Constitutional Order: The Resumption of Chinese Sovereignty and The Basic Law* (Hong Kong University Press, 2nd edition, 1999) at 198) where he states that the Standing Committee's "power may be exercised in the absence of litigation" (cited with approval in *Lau Kong Yung v Director of Immigration* (1999) 2 HKCFAR 300, 324).
74. (1999) 2 HKCFAR 82.
75. It was estimated that 692,000 children would immediately acquire the right to live in Hong Kong as a result of these judgments, followed by a further 983,000 children seven years later. See Hong Kong SAR Government, "Estimates of the Number of Mainlanders with Right of Abode" (6 May 1999), reproduced in Chan, Fu and Ghai (eds.), *Hong Kong's Constitutional Debate* (see note 13) at 265.
76. See Hong Kong SAR Government, "Right of Abode: The Solution" (18 May 1999), reproduced in Chan, Fu and Ghai (eds.) at 310–319.
77. In *Chan Kam Nga*, the court invalidated what was known as the "time of birth" restriction, by holding (at 92–93) that the wording in Schedule 1, paragraph 2(c) of the ordinance restricting such rights to those children with a parent who was already a Hong Kong permanent resident "at the time of the birth" of the child was inconsistent with Article 24(2)(3) of the Hong Kong Basic Law. In *Ng Ka Ling* (at 40–43), the court reached a similar conclusion in respect of a provision in Schedule 1, paragraph 1(2)(b) preventing illegitimate children with a Hong Kong father from claiming the right of abode.

it more difficult for even those who were entitled to such residency rights to enter Hong Kong.[78] The court reached this decision on the basis that these provisions contravened its interpretation of Articles 22(4) and 24(2)(3) of the Hong Kong Basic Law. This meant the Hong Kong SAR Government could not solve the problem by simply proposing further legislation in Hong Kong to reintroduce similar restrictions, since that would again run foul of the court's interpretation of Articles 22(4) and 24(2)(3). Instead, the only way to prevent any possibility of a mass influx, which was portrayed by the Hong Kong SAR Government as having unacceptable social and economic consequences for Hong Kong,[79] was to displace the court's interpretation of the relevant provisions in the Hong Kong Basic Law.

Where similar situations have arisen elsewhere in the common law world, with governments struggling to cope with the effects of court judgments which were perceived as leading to intolerable social and economic consequences, the usual response has been to pass new legislation or amend the wording of the law in question so that it no longer allows for such unacceptable consequences. That need not undermine the authority of the court which delivered the original judgment, since the court will still be seen to have correctly interpreted the wording of the law as it stood at the time the case was decided. Changing the law after a court judgment simply recognizes that a sovereign legislature generally has the power to pass new legislation or amend the wording of existing legislation, and the courts will then follow this new legislation or wording in subsequent cases.[80] In Britain, for instance, the government famously reacted to a court defeat that laid it open to large compensation claims in the case of *Burmah Oil v Lord Advocate* by successfully persuading the UK Parliament to enact fresh legislation removing any liability for such claims.[8]

Adopting the same response to the *Ng Ka Ling* judgment would have meant amending the wording of the Hong Kong Basic Law to prevent uncontrolled entry of mainland-born

---

78. In *Ng Ka Ling*, the court invalidated what was known as the "one-way permit" restriction by holding (at 33–37) that provisions requiring most such children to obtain a one-way permit from mainland authorities before they were allowed to reside in Hong Kong (added by the Immigration (Amendment)(No. 3) Ordinance (No. 124 of 1997), which was rushed through the Provisional Legislature on 10 July 1997 to try to prevent a mass influx of these children) could not be justified by reference to Article 22(4) of the Hong Kong Basic Law. The court held that Article 22(4) did not apply to this category of children. See further note 31 earlier in this chapter.
79. See Hong Kong SAR Government, "Assessment of Service Implication in Relation to the Judgment of the Court of Final Appeal on the Right of Abode Issue Tabled at the Legislative Council" (6 May 1999), reproduced in Chan, Fu and Ghai (eds.), *Hong Kong's Constitutional Debate* (see note 13) at 274–283.
80. See further on this point Chan, "Basic Law and Constitutional Review" (see note 15) at 417.
81. [1965] AC 75. Following the House of Lords decision that the British government was required by law to pay compensation for damage inflicted by British forces during World War II, the UK Parliament enacted the War Damage Act 1965 changing the law so that no compensation payments were necessary.

children into Hong Kong. Such a response, which was advocated even by some government critics, would most likely have been relatively uncontroversial given the general consensus at the time that Hong Kong could not cope with the consequences of such a mass influx of children from the mainland.[82]

That option foundered in the face of the restrictions on amending the Hong Kong Basic Law.[83] Those restrictions are intended to protect Hong Kong's autonomy by making it more difficult to undermine the guarantees of Hong Kong's separate system enshrined in the Hong Kong Basic Law. But, in this case, those restrictions arguably helped undermine the very autonomy they were intended to protect. Citing the difficulties involved in amending the Hong Kong Basic Law,[84] the Hong Kong SAR Government opted for the much more controversial option of asking the Standing Committee to cast aside any perceived limitations on its interpretative powers, and declare that the Court of Final Appeal had got it wrong in how it interpreted Articles 22(4) and 24(2)(3) in its decisions in *Ng Ka Ling* and *Chan Kam Nga*.[85]

That this scenario was never envisaged by the drafters of the Hong Kong Basic Law was evident from the circuitous procedure used by the Hong Kong SAR Government. The Hong Kong Basic Law only mentions one direct route for referring an issue of interpretation from Hong Kong to the Standing Committee. That route is when the Court of Final Appeal chooses to exercise its power under Article 158(3) to refer excluded provisions on issues outside Hong Kong's autonomy to the Standing Committee. But the court pointedly refused to do this during the *Ng Ka Ling* case, based on the highly restrictive test that it adopted for when to make such referrals.[86]

So the Hong Kong SAR Government took a more circuitous route to the Standing Committee. This began with Chief Executive first reporting to the State Council

---

82. Two strong critics of the government's handling of the issue, the Democratic Party and the Hong Kong Bar Association, both advocated amending Article 24(2)(3) of the Hong Kong Basic Law to reduce the number of mainland-born children entitled to right of abode in Hong Kong. See, for example, Hong Kong Bar Association, "A Constitutionally Acceptable Solution" (13 May 1999), reproduced in Chan, Fu and Ghai (eds.), *Hong Kong's Constitutional Debate* (see note 13) at 378–382.
83. See further "7.5: Amendment" later in this chapter.
84. See Hong Kong SAR Government, "Right of Abode: The Solution" (18 May 1999), reproduced in Chan, Fu and Ghai (eds.), *Hong Kong's Constitutional Debate* (see note 13) at 312–313.
85. Ibid. at 315–319. However, the Hong Kong SAR Government did not ask the Standing Committee to declare that the Court of Final Appeal had misinterpreted Article 24(2)(3) of the Hong Kong Basic Law in invalidating a restriction preventing illegitimate children of Hong Kong fathers from claiming the right of abode (see further note 77), a restriction which the court had held to be in breach of the rights protected under the International Covenant on Civil and Political Rights. For more on the role of the ICCPR in Hong Kong, see further "8.1: ICCPR and Bill of Rights" in Chapter 8.
86. For more on this aspect of the *Ng Ka Ling* judgment and criticism of it, see further notes 208–214 later in this chapter and the accompanying text.

(or Central People's Government) that the Hong Kong SAR "is no longer capable of resolving the problem on its own".[87] It was then the State Council, rather than the Chief Executive, which approached the Standing Committee seeking a fresh interpretation of Articles 22(4) and 24(2)(3).[88] The Standing Committee duly obliged with an interpretation in June 1999,[89] which declared that the correct interpretation of these two provisions in the Hong Kong Basic Law was, for the most part, the one that the Hong Kong SAR Government had applied prior to the Court of Final Appeal's decisions in *Ng Ka Ling* and *Chan Kam Nga*, in restricting the number of children eligible for permanent residency and making it more difficult for them to enter Hong Kong.[90]

That June 1999 interpretation from the Standing Committee is a good example of the very different approach to interpretation of laws that often applies under the Chinese legal system. Yang (2008) notes that such interpretations often lack legal reasoning in the main body of the interpretation.[91] Mason (2011) describes the Chinese approach to interpretation as "more policy orientated than the common law approach".[92]

As we saw earlier, although the Court of Final Appeal appeared somewhat unsure about how to balance considerations of wording with those of intention in its approach to interpretation in the *Ng Ka Ling* case, some parts of that judgment placed heavy emphasis on following the "ordinary language" of the Hong Kong Basic Law.[93] By contrast, the Standing Committee's June 1999 interpretation made no attempt to analyse the wording of the provisions in the Hong Kong Basic Law that were at issue, although it would later

---

87. See "Report on Seeking Assistance from the Central People's Government in Solving Problems Encountered in the Implementation of the Basic Law of the Hong Kong SAR" (20 May 1999), reproduced in Chan, Fu and Ghai (eds.), *Hong Kong's Constitutional Debate* (see note 13) at 474–477.
88. See further note 157 later in this chapter on whether it may also be possible for the Chief Executive directly to approach the Standing Committee with a request for an interpretation, without going through the State Council.
89. The Interpretation by the Standing Committee of the NPC of Articles 22(4) and 24(2)(3) of the Basic Law of the Hong Kong SAR of the PRC (26 June 1999).
90. Ibid. at paras. 1 and 2, essentially holding that the "time of birth" and "one-way permit" restrictions (see notes 77 and 78 respectively) were in accordance with its interpretation of Articles 22(4) and 24(2)(3) of the Hong Kong Basic Law. However, the Standing Committee did not address the issue of the ban on the illegitimate children of Hong Kong fathers acquiring the right of abode, which had also been invalidated by the Court of Final Appeal in *Ng Ka Ling*, since the Hong Kong SAR Government did not raise this issue in its request for an interpretation (see note 85).
91. Yang, "Legislative Interpretations by the Standing Committee of the National People's Congress in China" (see note 72) at 283–284. However, Yang notes that such legal reasoning is sometimes contained in an accompanying explanation or report.
92. Mason, "The Rule of Law in the Shadow of the Giant" (see note 10) at 630. For an excellent summary of the available literature on the Standing Committee's approach to interpretation of laws, see P.Y. Lo, *The Hong Kong Basic Law* (LexisNexis, 2011) at 813–816.
93. This was particular true in relation to the court's interpretation of Article 22(4) of the Hong Kong Basic Law. See further note 31 earlier in this chapter and the accompanying text.

make at least a perfunctory attempt to do so in one subsequent interpretation.[94] Instead, the Standing Committee's June 1999 interpretation simply declared that the Court of Final Appeal had got the "legislative intent" of Articles 22(4) and 24(2)(3) of the Hong Kong Basic Law wrong, and the correct interpretation of both provisions was one which did not allow all of these mainland-born children uncontrolled entry to Hong Kong.[95]

That solved the Hong Kong SAR Government's immediate problem since it meant that it could once again ask the Legislative Council to enact legislation restricting the entry of these children into Hong Kong, based on the Standing Committee's new interpretation of Articles 22(4) and 24(2)(3).[96] But it came at the price of giving the Standing Committee a far broader role in interpreting the Hong Kong Basic Law than had been previously recognized, with troubling implications for Hong Kong's high degree of autonomy.

The main problem is not the procedure which the Hong Kong SAR Government used to obtain an interpretation from the Standing Committee. Although the original request took a rather circuitous route from Hong Kong, the State Council's eventual action, in proposing a motion of interpretation to the Standing Committee, is expressly permitted under Chinese law.[97] Nor can it really be argued that such an interpretation must wait for a request from Hong Kong's Court of Final Appeal when interpretations are generally issued independently of court cases under the Chinese legal system.[98]

Far more troubling was the subject matter that was actually interpreted by the Standing Committee, and the implications of this for the critical issue of whether there is any subject-matter limitation on the Standing Committee's power to interpret those parts of the Hong Kong Basic Law which concern matters that lie within Hong Kong's autonomy. Of the two provisions interpreted by the Standing Committee, one presented little problem. Article 22(4), on the Central People's Government's undisputed right to control the entry of mainland Chinese into Hong Kong, clearly involved a matter outside Hong Kong's autonomy and so falls within the definition of excluded provisions under Article 158(3) which the Standing Committee are expressly empowered to interpret.

---

94. This was the Standing Committee's 2005 interpretation of Article 53(2) of the Hong Kong Basic Law. See further notes 161–165 later in this chapter and the accompanying text, for more on the extent to which this interpretation made a limited attempt to analyse the wording of various provisions in the Hong Kong Basic Law.
95. The term "legislative intent" appears twice in the 1999 interpretation, in the Preamble and para. 2 respectively.
96. Within three weeks of the Standing Committee's interpretation, the Legislative Council enacted fresh legislation essentially reintroducing the "time of birth" and "one-way permit" restrictions. For an account of this legislation, see *Lau Kong Yung v Director of Immigration* (1999) 2 HKCFAR 300, 327–328, where it was unsuccessfully challenged by lawyers for some of the children affected.
97. Article 43 of the PRC Legislation Law gives various branches of the Chinese state, including the State Council, the power to submit requests for legislative interpretation to the Standing Committee.
98. See further notes 7–8 earlier in this chapter and the accompanying text.

The problem lay with Article 24(2)(3), the other provision interpreted by the Standing Committee. This is the third in a list of six categories of people with the right to live permanently in Hong Kong without restrictions (which is often called right of abode) at the start of Chapter III of the Hong Kong Basic Law.[99] That chapter contains the majority of the human rights guarantees enshrined in the Hong Kong Basic Law.[100] Those guarantees are one of the most important elements of Hong Kong's high degree of autonomy, and were described by the Court of Final Appeal in *Ng Ka Ling* as lying "at the heart of Hong Kong's separate system".[101] In the accompanying case of *Chan Kam Nga*, the Court of Final Appeal described the right of abode as "the fundamental right without which the full array" of other rights cannot be exercised.[102]

Yet, when the Standing Committee drastically reduced the numbers entitled to exercise that fundamental right in its June 1999 interpretation, the immediate response of the Court of Final Appeal was what Chan (2007) aptly describes as "almost defeatist".[103] In *Lau Kong Yung v Director of Immigration*,[104] perhaps one of the court's most unfortunate judgments, the Court of Final Appeal essentially conceded that the Standing Committee could do what it likes when it comes to interpreting the Hong Kong Basic Law, even if this means taking away guarantees that lie at the heart of Hong Kong's separate system. Dismissing arguments that limitations on the Standing Committee's power of interpretation were part of the high degree of autonomy granted to Hong Kong under the Hong Kong Basic Law, Chief Justice Li described the Standing Committee's interpretative powers as "not restricted or qualified in any way" by the power delegated to the Hong Kong courts under Article 158(2) to interpret on their own all parts of the Hong Kong Basic Law that fall within Hong Kong's autonomy.[105]

That conclusion by the court appears at odds with the original intention of the drafters of the Hong Kong Basic Law who, as we saw earlier,[106] did appear to envisage some limits on the Standing Committee's power to interpret the Hong Kong Basic Law.[107] The court's conclusion also appears to go further than the position stated by the Standing Committee itself. Ling (2007) argues that the Standing Committee has never unequivocally asserted

---

99. For more on right of abode and the six categories of persons listed in Article 24(2), see further notes 18–23 in Chapter 8 and the accompanying text.
100. See further pages 266–267 for a list of the human rights protected under Chapter III of the Hong Kong Basic Law.
101. *Ng Ka Ling* at 28–29. It should, however, be noted that the court did not include the different categories of permanent residents in this description.
102. *Chan Kam Nga* at 87.
103. Chan, "Basic Law and Constitutional Review" (see note 15) at 420.
104. (1999) 2 HKCFAR 300.
105. Ibid. at 323.
106. See further notes 67–68 earlier in this chapter and the accompanying text.
107. Although the court did consider the drafting history of the Hong Kong Basic Law in *Lau Kong Yung*, Ling argues persuasively that it is doubtful whether the court was presented "with the full legislative history that led to the adoption of Article 158". See Ling, "Subject Matter Limitation" (see note 65) at 625.

that it has the power to interpret those parts of the Hong Kong Basic Law that it considers as falling within Hong Kong's autonomy.[108] It was, however, welcome news to the Hong Kong SAR Government, which had pointedly stated that the Standing Committee has the power to interpret the Hong Kong Basic Law "before, during or after" any court case.[109]

However flawed the legal reasoning behind the decision in *Lau Kong Yung* on this issue, from this point onwards it became the accepted position in Hong Kong that there are no restrictions on the Standing Committee's power to interpret the Hong Kong Basic Law. In this sense, *Lau Kong Yung* represents the historic submission of the Hong Kong courts to the ultimate authority of the Standing Committee. That this was not an easy conclusion for the court to reach is evident from the comments of Sir Anthony Mason, the overseas judge who sat on the court during this case.[110] While agreeing that there are no limits on the Standing Committee's power to interpret the Hong Kong Basic Law, Mason conceded that granting such unrestricted powers of interpretation to a non-judicial body, which can be exercised outside court cases, "may seem strange" to those familiar with the common law system.[111] However, he argued that "it follows inevitably" from not only Article 158 but also the nature of the Hong Kong Basic Law as "a national law enacted by the PRC".[112]

The decision in *Lau Kong Yung* has its defenders. Chen (2006) describes it as the "only approach consistent" with constitutional reality in China.[113] But there are also numerous critics. Cohen (2000), for instance, who had been harshly critical of the *Ng Ka Ling* judgment, which he complained was unnecessarily "provocative", criticizes the court for veering to the other extreme in *Lau Kong Yung* with a judgment which "unnecessarily prostrated itself before Beijing".[114]

Ling (2007) describes the Court of Final Appeal's concession of unlimited interpretative powers to the Standing Committee as "repugnant to the foundational values and principles upon which the entire system of the Hong Kong Special Administrative Region rests".[115] He also comprehensively attacks the legal reasoning used by the court[116] in a

---

108. Ibid. at 639–644. However this conclusion depends on what view is taken of the reasons for the Standing Committee including Article 24(2)(3) of the Hong Kong Basic Law in its 1999 interpretation. See further notes 122–123 later in this chapter.
109. Ng Kang-chung, "Tung 'can appeal for NPC ruling anytime'", *South China Morning Post*, 13 June 1999.
110. For more on the important role on the Court of Final Appeal played by Sir Anthony Mason, a former Chief Justice of Australia, see further notes 295–298 in Chapter 6 and the accompanying text.
111. *Lau Kong Yung* at 345.
112. Ibid.
113. Albert H.Y. Chen, "Constitutional Adjudication in Post-1997 Hong Kong" (2006) 15 *Pacific Rim Law & Policy Journal* 627, 645.
114. Jerome A. Cohen, "Hong Kong's Basic Law: An American Perspective", International Symposium to Commemorate the 10th Anniversary of the Promulgation of the HKSAR Basic Law, 1 April 2000.
115. Ling, "Subject Matter Limitation" (see note 65) at 645.
116. Ibid. at 624–646. Ling describes (at 624) the Court of Final Appeal's position on this issue as "untenable" and "misconceived".

way which it is hard to see how the Court of Final Appeal could convincingly refute were the issue ever to be argued again before the court in a subsequent case. Writing extra-judicially, Sir Anthony Mason, one of the judges in the *Lau Kong Yung* case, has noted Ling's criticism, but made no attempt to respond to the main thrust of his argument.[117]

Yet the *Lau Kong Yung* judgment needs to be viewed in the context of the time when it was delivered. Coming so soon after the Court of Final Appeal had been severely criticized by mainland scholars and officials for statements which they perceived as challenging Chinese sovereignty in the section of the *Ng Ka Ling* judgment on the constitutional jurisdiction of the courts,[118] the court was clearly anxious to avoid doing anything which might provoke another confrontation with China. That was equally evident in another controversial judgment two weeks after *Lau Kong Yung* in *HKSAR v Ng Kung Siu*,[119] a case involving a challenge to the legality of laws protecting both the Chinese national and Hong Kong flags, another issue of intense interest to Beijing.[120]

What is particularly unfortunate about the *Lau Kong Yung* case is that an excessively cautious court chose to retreat even further than was actually necessary to avoid a further confrontation with Beijing. Cohen (2000) notes that further confrontation could have been avoided just as easily if the court had instead reached the more modest conclusion that this particular interpretation by the Standing Committee was in accordance with the Hong Kong Basic Law.[121] This more modest conclusion would have been relatively uncontentious since the Standing Committee appears, although its statements on the subject are not entirely clear, to have taken the view that the 1999 interpretation only involved excluded provisions in the Hong Kong Basic Law on issues outside Hong Kong's autonomy.[122] These excluded provisions are ones which—although there may be disputes about precisely which provisions fall into this category[123]—it is generally

---

117. See Mason, "The Rule of Law in the Shadow of the Giant" (see note 10) at 629, stating simply that Ling's arguments are inconsistent with decisions of the Court of Final Appeal and the court's interpretation of Article 67(4) of the PRC Constitution 1982. This does not, of course, in any way answer Ling's argument that those court decisions were wrongly decided.
118. For more on China's criticism of this aspect of the *Ng Ka Ling* judgment, see further notes 202–205 in Chapter 6 and the accompanying text.
119. (1999) 2 HKCFAR 442.
120. For more on this case, and criticism of the court's reasoning, see further notes 190–209 in Chapter 8 and the accompanying text.
121. Cohen, "Hong Kong's Basic Law: An American Perspective" (see note 114).
122. See the discussion in *Director of Immigration v Chong Fung Yuen* (2001) 4 HKCFAR 211, 227–229. At issue is whether the Standing Committee regards Article 24(2)(3) of the Hong Kong Basic Law as an excluded provision outside Hong Kong's autonomy. Ling [in "Subject Matter Limitation" (see note 65) at 640–643] argues that it is clear the Standing Committee does, and so it did not believe that its 1999 interpretation involved any Hong Kong Basic Law provisions that fall within Hong Kong's autonomy.
123. In *Ng Ka Ling* at 32, the Court of Final Appeal described Article 24(2)(3) as a provision which falls within Hong Kong's autonomy, a position possibly at odds with the Standing Committee's characterization of this provision in its 1999 interpretation.

accepted that the Court of Final Appeal does not have the power to interpret entirely by itself.[124]

Instead Gewirtz (2001), among others, criticizes the court for "pre-emptively" conceding to the Standing Committee an unrestricted power to interpret even those parts of the Hong Kong Basic Law that lie entirely within Hong Kong's autonomy.[125] That damaging concession rightly aroused concerns in Hong Kong about the effect upon judicial independence and the rule of law if the Standing Committee were to begin widely and frequently exercising this unrestricted power.

7.3 Avoiding Interpretations

Although the events of 1999, culminating in the court's submission in the *Lau Kong Yung* case, swept away any possibility of legal limitations on the Standing Committee's power to interpret the Hong Kong Basic Law, subsequent events proved that this did not have the apocalyptic effect on Hong Kong's legal system that some had initially feared.

Interpretation of the Hong Kong Basic Law has remained primarily a matter for the Hong Kong courts and, for many years, interpretations by the Standing Committees were extremely rare. Wong Yan Lung, the second Secretary for Justice of the Hong Kong SAR, successfully fulfilled a pledge to avoid seeking any such interpretations from the Standing Committee during his seven years as the Hong Kong SAR Government's top law officer.[126] Upon his retirement as the first Chief Justice of the Hong Kong SAR in 2010, Andrew Li noted that "the view is widely held that this power of the Standing Committee should only be exercised in exceptional circumstances".[127] As of March 2013, the Standing Committee had only interpreted the Hong Kong Basic Law on four occasions.

That could still change. In the absence of any legal limits on the Standing Committee's power to interpret the Hong Kong Basic Law, much depends on how much self-restraint Beijing is prepared to exercise in deciding how and when to use this power. As we saw earlier, on some issues Beijing has cast aside its previous policy of self-restraint and begun to adopt a more interventionist approach towards Hong Kong affairs.[128] But when it comes to the Standing Committee exercising its power to interpret the Hong Kong Basic Law, it seems that fear of stirring up an adverse reaction in Hong Kong has so far meant that this policy of self-restraint has survived for much longer.

---

124. The precise definition of these excluded provisions, listed in Article 158(3) of the Hong Kong Basic Law, is explained on page 231.
125. Paul Gewirtz, "Approaches to Constitutional Interpretation: Comparative Constitutionalism and Chinese Characteristics" (2001) 31 *HKLJ* 200, 222–223.
126. For an example of this pledge, see Secretary for Justice Wong Yan Lung, "One Country, Two Systems", Speech to Chatham House, 9 June 2006. Wong served as Secretary for Justice from October 2005 to June 2012.
127. "Chief Justice Andrew Li: Departing With No Regrets" (August 2010) *Hong Kong Lawyer* at 17.
128. See further notes 95–110 in Chapter 4 and the accompanying text.

That was evident from the strong public reaction to the Standing Committee's second interpretation of the Hong Kong Basic Law, issued in 2004.[129] Unlike all other interpretations by the Standing Committee so far, this 2004 interpretation was not issued in response to a request from anyone in Hong Kong. Instead the interpretation was issued at the Standing Committee's own initiative,[130] and is described by Chen (2011) as "Beijing's most significant intervention on Hong Kong affairs since the establishment of the HKSAR".[131]

Faced with strong public pressure in Hong Kong for early moves towards fully democratic elections for both the Chief Executive and all seats in the Legislative Council,[132] the Standing Committee moved to make this more difficult. This 2004 interpretation of Annexes I(7) and II(III) of the Hong Kong Basic Law gave the Standing Committee far greater power over any changes to Hong Kong's electoral systems, particularly in respect of the Legislative Council, than had been mentioned in the original wording of those two annexes.[133] That demonstrated a particularly troubling characteristic of interpretation under the Chinese legal system. In contrast to interpretation under the common law system, which is usually limited to explaining the existing wording of a law,[134] Yang (2008) notes that interpretations by the Standing Committee sometimes add "new content that had not been in the original texts" of the laws that are interpreted.[135]

The 2004 interpretation also demonstrated the political price that interpretations by the Standing Committee can exact, as it was widely credited with swelling attendance at the June Fourth candlelit vigil in Victoria Park that year, as well as a huge anti-government street protest on 1 July.[136] Given the rarity of Standing Committee interpretations

---

129. The Interpretation by the Standing Committee of the NPC of Article 7 of Annex I and Article III of Annex II to the Basic Law of the Hong Kong SAR of the PRC (6 April 2004).
130. This interpretation was initiated by the Standing Committee's Council of Chairpersons, a powerful body which plays an important role in shaping the Standing Committee's agenda.
131. Albert Chen, "The Development of Representative Government in Hong Kong" in Johannes Chan and C.L. Lim (eds.), *Law of the Hong Kong Constitution* (Sweet & Maxwell, 2011) at 234.
132. For the background to this interpretation, which followed the huge public protest against national security legislation on 1 July 2003, see further note 94 in Chapter 4 and the accompanying text.
133. See further page 129 for a description of the content of this interpretation, which gave the Standing Committee the power to decide "if there is a need" to make any changes to Hong Kong's electoral system.
134. A rare exception is remedial interpretation under the common law system, when the courts exceptionally go beyond their normal rules of interpretation, and may even sometimes slightly change the wording of a law, to save it from being invalidated for inconsistency with a constitutional document such as the Hong Kong Basic Law. See further notes 164–165 in Chapter 6 and the accompanying text.
135. Yang, "Legislative Interpretations by the Standing Committee of the National People's Congress in China" (see note 72) at 283–284.
136. Polly Hui, "Basic Law interpretation was our own June 4, says Bishop", *South China Morning Post*, 5 June 2004.

for many years afterwards, it seems reasonable to conclude that, for many years, the wish to avoid any backlash in Hong Kong played a role in restraining the Standing Committee from issuing more frequent interpretations during that period.

Strong evidence to support this comes from the Standing Committee's angry reaction to the Court of Final Appeal's decision in *Director of Immigration v Chong Fung Yuen* that Article 24(2)(1) of the Hong Kong Basic Law should be interpreted as granting the right of abode to all Chinese children born in Hong Kong, even if both their parents are not resident and have no connection with Hong Kong.[137] That ran directly counter to guidelines on this point previously issued by a committee of the National People's Congress,[138] and prompted a statement of "concern" from the Standing Committee's Legislative Affairs Commission in response to the judgment.[139] But that statement was not a legally binding interpretation. Despite the Standing Committee's publicly professed unhappiness with this aspect of the *Chong Fung Yuen* judgment, it made no immediate attempt to issue a formal interpretation declaring the court wrong, in a clear indication of the Standing Committee's self-imposed restraint. Chen (2001) describes the Standing Committee as having at that time "exercised self-restraint in the interests of the autonomy of Hong Kong and the Rule of Law".[140]

Another factor making it difficult for the Standing Committee to issue an immediate interpretation reversing the effect of *Chong Fung Yuen* was the lack of any such request from the Hong Kong SAR Government in the immediate aftermath of the judgment. Having seen the Court of Final Appeal reject its attempt to argue during the case that Article 24(2)(1) fell into the category of those excluded provisions which must be referred to the Standing Committee for interpretation,[141] the Hong Kong SAR Government proved reluctant to undermine the court's authority by approaching the Standing Committee for an interpretation immediately after the case was over.[142]

That self-restraint remained true for many years afterwards, even as the number of mainland mothers seeking to give birth in Hong Kong in order to obtain residency rights for their children continued to grow, causing increasing social problems. However, in early 2013, there were signs of that self-restraint beginning to crumble as the Hong Kong

---

137. (2001) 4 HKCFAR 211, 230–233. For more on the court's interpretation of Article 24(2)(1) of the Hong Kong Basic Law in this case, see further note 46 earlier in this chapter and the accompanying text.
138. Opinions of the Preparatory Committee for the Hong Kong SAR of the NPC on the Implementation of Article 24(2) of the Basic Law of the Hong Kong SAR (10 August 1996).
139. See further note 365 in Chapter 6 and the accompanying text.
140. Albert H.Y. Chen, "Another Case of Conflict Between the CFA and the NPC Standing Committee?" (2001) 31 *HKLJ* 179, 186.
141. *Chong Fung Yuen* at 227–229. See further note 222 later in this chapter and the accompanying text.
142. See Angela Li and Antoine So, "Abode appeal to Beijing ruled out", *South China Morning Post*, 22 July 2001. Then Secretary for Security Regina Ip subsequently told the author that the Hong Kong SAR Government chose not to request an interpretation from the Standing Committee because there was "no community consensus" on the issue at the time of the *Chong Fung Yuen* judgment. Interviewed on "Backchat", *RTHK Radio 3*, 9 March 2012.

SAR Government unsuccessfully tried to persuade the Court of Final Appeal to refer the issue to the Standing Committee during another case.[143]

The Hong Kong SAR Government also showed some caution when it came to the Standing Committee's third interpretation of the Hong Kong Basic Law, issued in 2005.[144] That involved the very specific issue of how long a replacement Chief Executive should serve if his predecessor resigns without completing a full five-year term in office. Article 46 of the Hong Kong Basic Law would appear to be unequivocal on this point, stating without qualification that: "The term of office of the Chief Executive of the Hong Kong Special Administrative Region shall be five years." For those trained in the common law tradition of respect for the wording of statutory legislation, that wording would seem to leave little room for doubt. Not surprisingly, almost every lawyer in Hong Kong who expressed an opinion on this point concluded that the clear meaning of Article 46 of the Hong Kong Basic Law is that every new Chief Executive must be chosen for a full five-year term, even when their predecessor resigns prematurely.[145]

But that is not the system in mainland China, where the successor to a senior government official who leaves office without completing a full term will normally only serve for the remainder of his predecessor's term in office.[146] For example, if a mainland official leaves office after serving only three years out of a five-year term, a replacement would normally be chosen to serve the remaining two years of that term. That was broadly the situation Hong Kong faced in early 2005, when Hong Kong's first Chief Executive, Tung Chee Hwa resigned prematurely after serving slightly less than three years of his second five-year term in office, apparently under pressure from Beijing because of his unpopularity with the Hong Kong public.[147]

Almost as soon as Tung's intention to resign became known, mainland law scholars and officials began arguing that, despite the apparently clear wording of Article 46, the correct interpretation of the Hong Kong Basic Law was that the same system should apply in determining the term of office of his successor as is used to fill posts that are prematurely vacated on the mainland. That meant they wanted the new Chief Executive initially to only serve the approximately two years that remained of Tung's term, instead of immediately beginning a new five-year term in office. Ghai (2007) argues this also

---

143. *Vallejos Evangeline Banao v Commissioner of Registration* (unrep., FACV 19 and 20/2012, [2013] HKEC 429) at paras. 109–112. See further note 429 in Chapter 6.
144. Interpretation of Paragraph 2, Article 53 of the Basic Law of the Hong Kong SAR of the PRC by the Standing Committee of the NPC (27 April 2005).
145. The main exception is Robert Morris, who puts forward a contrary argument in "The 'Replacement' Chief Executive's Two-Year Term: A Pure and Unambiguous Common Law Analysis" (2005) 35 *HKLJ* 17–26.
146. See Leung, "Statement on the Term of the New Chief Executive" (see note 3) at para. 5.
147. After being selected for a second five-year term in 2002, Tung resigned on 10 March 2005 citing ill health, one of the three permitted reasons for a Chief Executive to resign under Article 52 of the Hong Kong Basic Law. However, his resignation followed public criticism by Chinese leaders, and was widely perceived to be at the Central Government's behest. See Yash Ghai and Jill Cottrell, "The Politics of Succession in Hong Kong" (2005) 35 *HKLJ* 1–6.

served a useful political purpose from China's perspective because it kept the new Chief Executive "on a short leash—he had to prove his loyalty before he served a full term".[148]

Embarrassingly for the Hong Kong SAR Government, it had previously subscribed to the common law interpretation of Article 46,[149] and even put forward legislation which had been enacted stating that any new Chief Executive would be chosen for a five-year term.[150] Under pressure from Beijing, the government then changed its position to fall in line with the views expressed by mainland scholars and officials,[151] and proposed fresh legislation to change the position in Hong Kong law.[152] Then Secretary for Justice Elsie Leung justified this change in stance on the grounds that the Hong Kong Basic Law should be interpreted "in the context of the institutional framework and rules of statutory interpretation of the mainland"[153] and expressed regret that China's views on the issue had not been taken into account earlier.[154] That rather alarming statement seemed to suggest that the Hong Kong SAR Government no longer believed common law principles were relevant to understanding the correct meaning of the Hong Kong Basic Law. But the Secretary for Justice was quick to limit its effect, noting that the Hong Kong SAR Government would continue to use common law principles in applying those parts of the Hong Kong Basic Law (especially the provisions on human rights) that cover issues within Hong Kong's autonomy.[155]

The interpretation from the Standing Committee which followed shortly afterwards, when a legal challenge to the government's change of stance threatened to derail the planned election for Tung's successor,[156] was limited in its effect. Once again initiated by the Hong Kong SAR Government through the circuitous route of first reporting a problem to the State Council,[157] this solved the immediate threat of a constitutional crisis

---

148. Ghai, "The Political Economy of Interpretation" (see note 6) at 137. After serving the two years that remained of Tung's term, the new Chief Executive, Donald Tsang, was subsequently chosen to serve a full five-year term from 2007 to 2012.
149. Leung, "Statement on the Term of the New Chief Executive" (see note 3) at para. 2.
150. Section 3(1) of the Chief Executive Election Ordinance (Cap. 569).
151. Leung, "Statement on the Term of the New Chief Executive" (see note 3) at para. 13.
152. Chief Executive Election (Amendment) (Term of Office of the Chief Executive) Ordinance (No. 4 of 2005) added a new Section 3(1A) into the Chief Executive Election Ordinance, providing for a shortened term of office for a Chief Executive whose predecessor had left office prematurely.
153. Leung, "Statement on the Term of the New Chief Executive" (see note 3) at para. 3.
154. Ibid. at para. 16.
155. See, for instance, Secretary for Justice Elsie Leung, "Letter to Hong Kong: The Chief Executive's Term of Office and the Rule of Law", *RTHK Radio 3*, 20 March 2005, at para. 13.
156. *Chan Wai Yip Albert v Secretary for Justice* (unrep., HCAL 36/2005, 19 May 2005), in which a member of the pro-democracy camp sought to argue that the Chief Executive Election (Amendment) (Term of Office of the Chief Executive) Bill (see note 152) was in breach of the clear meaning of Article 46 of the Hong Kong Basic Law.
157. This was the same route adopted by the Hong Kong SAR Government to initiate the first interpretation of the Hong Kong Basic Law in 1999 (see note 87 earlier in this chapter and the accompanying text). However it may also be possible for the Chief Executive to directly approach the Standing Committee with a request for an interpretation of the Hong Kong

that might otherwise have arisen, since a protracted legal battle would probably have made it impossible to choose a new Chief Executive within six months of Tung's resignation, as required under Article 53(2) of the Hong Kong Basic Law. At the request of the Hong Kong SAR Government, this third interpretation of the Hong Kong Basic Law was strictly limited to the immediate crisis at hand.[158] In particular, it made clear that this interpretation did not necessarily apply to how the same problem should be resolved if it arose again in future.[159]

The content of the 2005 interpretation also differed markedly from the Standing Committee's two previous interpretations of the Hong Kong Basic Law. In reaching its conclusion that the new Chief Executive should initially only serve for the approximately two remaining years of Tung's five-year term, the Standing Committee sought for the first time to justify its interpretation with some analysis of the wording of the relevant provisions of the Hong Kong Basic Law. That marked a significant evolution from the Standing Committee's first interpretation of the Hong Kong Basic Law in 1999, which had made no real effort to analyse the wording of the provisions being interpreted and instead justified its conclusions solely on the basis of the "legislative intent" behind the Hong Kong Basic Law.[160]

The thrust of the Standing Committee's analysis in its 2005 interpretation was that Article 46, the clearly worded provision upon which the arguments of the common law lawyers placed so much reliance, could not be considered by itself.[161] Instead, Article 46 had to be considered in the context of other provisions in the Hong Kong Basic Law,

---

Basic Law, as this has already been done by the Macao Chief Executive in November 2011, in relation to considering interpreting two provisions in the Macao Basic Law. See further Hong Kong Bar Association, *The Bar's Position Paper on the "Procedure for Seeking an Interpretation of the Basic Law under Article 158(1) of the Basic Law"* (25 May 2012) at note 5.

158. Acting Chief Executive Donald Tsang, *Report to the State Council Concerning the Submission of a Request to the Standing Committee of the NPC Regarding the Interpretation of Article 53(2) of the Basic Law of the Hong Kong SAR of the PRC* (6 April 2005). This report is notable for its emphasis on how the Hong Kong SAR Government considers the request for a Standing Committee interpretation as very much a last resort, noting that it was only requested after an unsuccessful search for "viable options other than an interpretation". See, however, Albert H.Y. Chen, "The NPCSC's Interpretation in Spring 2005" (2005) 35 *HKLJ* 255, 256–257 for other options the government could have pursued instead.

159. The last sentence of the 2005 interpretation stated that, if the selection method for choosing the Chief Executive was changed after 2007, then the system for filling any similar vacancy would be determined in accordance with the new selection method.

160. For more on the role of legislative intent in the Standing Committee's 1999 interpretation, see further note 95 earlier in this chapter and the accompanying text.

161. This was explicitly stated in an earlier statement which preceded the interpretation. See Legislative Affairs Commission of the Standing Committee of the NPC, *Statement on Term of Office of the Chief Executive Returned at a By-election Upon the Occurrence of a Vacancy* (12 March 2005), summarized in English in "Beijing's case for Tung's successor to serve two-year term", *South China Morning Post*, 24 March 2005.

which are not explicit on how long a Chief Executive should stay in office.[162] Since considering how to interpret one provision in the context of the wording of other provisions (which is known as a "contextual approach") is an important part of the common law approach to interpreting the Hong Kong Basic Law,[163] some see the 2005 interpretation as a small first step towards narrowing the differences between the Hong Kong and Chinese systems of interpretation. Lin and Lo (2007) argue that the "interpretation methodologies are quite similar in the Mainland and the HKSAR", even if they sometimes lead to different results.[164]

That would appear to be overstating the position. Ghai (2007) notes that, while the 2005 interpretation did mark the first time that a Standing Committee interpretation made some attempt to analyse the wording of the relevant provisions in the Hong Kong Basic Law, this analysis was still "perfunctory and one-sided".[165] Chen (2005) comments, "that it is almost impossible that a Hong Kong court would arrive at the same interpretation".[166] Certainly the Standing Committee's analysis of the wording of the relevant provisions in the Hong Kong Basic Law is still a world away from how a common law court would consider all possible interpretations of any wording in dispute before reaching a conclusion. That indicates how much further the Standing Committee still needs to travel before the gap between the systems of interpretation on the mainland and in Hong Kong can really be described as having substantially diminished.

Not only have Standing Committee interpretations been few in number, but for many years the courts found ways to diminish the practical effect of the few interpretations which the Standing Committee issued. That is not to suggest that the courts ever directly challenged the unlimited power of the Standing Committee to interpret any part of the Hong Kong Basic Law, a point conceded in *Lau Kong Yung* and never subsequently retracted.[167] In *Ng Siu Tung v Director of Immigration*, the Court of Final Appeal accepted that the effect of a Standing Committee interpretation was to "destroy the precedential effect" of any part of a court judgment which conflicted with the Standing Committee's binding interpretation of the Hong Kong Basic Law.[168]

Instead, the courts were more subtle in their approach. This subtle approach included turning to common law principles to grant rights no longer available under the Hong Kong Basic Law because of a Standing Committee interpretation. In *Ng Siu Tung*, the

---

162. Specifically Article 53(2), which was the main focus of the interpretation, and Annex I. Both these provisions deal with the selection of the Chief Executive, but do not state any term of office.
163. In *Ng Ka Ling*, the Court of Final Appeal stated that context is "of particular importance in the interpretation of a constitutional instrument". See further note 28 earlier in this chapter and the accompanying text.
164. Lin Feng and P.Y. Lo, "One Term, Two Interpretations: The Justifications and the Future of Basic Law Interpretation" in Fu, Harris and Young (eds.), *Interpreting Hong Kong's Basic Law* (see note 6) at 150–151.
165. Ghai, "The Intersection of Chinese Law and the Common Law" (see note 41) at 399.
166. Chen, "The NPCSC's Interpretation in Spring 2005" (see note 158) at 261.
167. For more on this case, and criticism of the court's reasoning, see further notes 104–125 earlier in this chapter and the accompanying text.
168. (2002) 5 HKCFAR 1, 26.

Court of Final Appeal adopted this approach in respect of around 1,000 children born in mainland China who fell into broadly the same category as the successful applicants in *Ng Ka Ling*. These children had lost their right to immediately claim permanent residency in Hong Kong under Article 24(2)(3) of the Hong Kong Basic Law when the Court of Final Appeal's interpretation of this and another related provision were reversed by the Standing Committee's first interpretation of the Hong Kong Basic Law in June 1999.[169] Although now denied any residency rights under the Hong Kong Basic Law, the Court of Final Appeal nonetheless found that this relatively small group of children had been given a "legitimate expectation" at common law that they would be allowed to remain in Hong Kong based on letters (or "specific representations") that they had previously received from the Hong Kong SAR Government.[170]

In holding such a legitimate expectation constituted a substantive right at common law which could be enforced through judicial review, Hong Kong's Court of Final Appeal broke new ground in *Ng Siu Tung* as the first final appellate court in the common law world to allow such expectations to be enforced through judicial review. Forsyth and Williams (2002) note that the case showed how—following the court's concession of unlimited interpretative powers to the Standing Committee—protection of rights through "a common law doctrine, has certain advantages over protection by means of the Basic Law".[171] This is because, while rights granted under the Hong Kong Basic Law can be easily curtailed by means of a Standing Committee interpretation, this is more difficult in the case of rights granted at common law.[172]

---

169. Since Article 158(3) of the Hong Kong Basic Law states that "judgments previously rendered shall not be affected" by a Standing Committee interpretation, the applicants in *Ng Siu Tung* argued this meant they should not be affected by the Standing Committee's interpretation. However, by a 4 to 1 majority the court held that the phrase "shall not be affected" in Article 158(3) should be more narrowly interpreted as only applying to those children who were parties to any court cases decided before the Standing Committee interpretation. See *Ng Siu Tung* at 24–27.
170. *Ng Siu Tung* at 38–40 and 54–55. Most of these letters, written by the Legal Aid Department in 1998–99, advised applicants that there was "no need" for them to bring their own court cases at that time because similar issues were already being litigated in *Ng Ka Ling* and a related case.
171. See Christopher Forsyth and Rebecca Williams, "Closing Chapter in the Immigrant Children Saga: Substantive Legitimate Expectations and Administrative Justice in Hong Kong" (2002) 10(1) *Asia Pacific Law Review* 29, 45. Note, however, that the court declined to uphold the residency rights of around 600,000 children who had only received more general reassurances (or representations) from the Hong Kong SAR Government (as opposed to specific letters). Yap (2007) suggests this was because upholding the rights of this much larger group of children, even at common law, would have been seen as a direct challenge to the Standing Committee. See further notes 375–376 in Chapter 6 and the accompanying text.
172. Although not necessarily impossible, since the Standing Committee could still issue an interpretation stating that the provisions of the Hong Kong Basic Law have supplanted the common law position on a particular issue. This is broadly what happened in the Standing Committee's 2011 interpretation issued at the request of the Court of Final Appeal in the case of *Democratic Republic of Congo v FG Hemisphere* (2011) 14 HKCFAR 95. See further note 228 later in this chapter and the accompanying text.

The courts also initially sought to limit the binding effect of Standing Committee interpretations. Lo (2007) describes their approach as one of "conceding compliance only in identical circumstances".[173] In *Chong Fung Yuen v Director of Immigration*,[174] the Court of Appeal confined the binding effect of the Standing Committee's 1999 interpretation of Articles 22(4) and 24(2)(3) of the Hong Kong Basic Law to those two specific provisions.[175] That approach, which was then adopted by the Court of Final Appeal in dealing with the case,[176] allowed the courts to refuse to follow a sentence in the Preamble to the Standing Committee's 1999 interpretation. Applying that sentence, which referred back to an opinion previously issued by a committee of the National People's Congress,[177] would have forced the court to reach a different conclusion on the meaning of Article 24(2)(1) of the Hong Kong Basic Law.[178] In *Tam Nga Yin v Director of Immigration*,[179] the Court of Final Appeal arguably went even further. Although *Tam Nga Yin* directly involved Article 24(2)(3), one of the two provisions which had been at the heart of the Standing Committee's 1999 interpretation, the court still held that this earlier interpretation was irrelevant to the main issue in this case, since it involved a different aspect of Article 24(2)(3).[180]

These cases demonstrate that, at least in 2001, when the Court of Final Appeal had only recently conceded the Standing Committee's unlimited power to interpret the Hong Kong Basic Law,[181] the courts were still anxious to limit the binding effect of such Standing Committee interpretations as much as possible. In effect, the courts took the approach in those cases of treating the Standing Committee like a superior court, where only the core of its judgments (the *ratio*, or reasons for the decision in any case) are binding on the lower courts. Anything else stated by the Standing Committee in its

---

173. P.Y. Lo, "Rethinking Judicial Reference: Barricades at the Gateway" in Fu, Harris and Young (eds.), *Interpreting Hong Kong's Basic Law* (see note 6) at 172.
174. [2000] 3 HKLRD 661.
175. Ibid. at 680.
176. In *Director of Immigration v Chong Fung Yuen* (2001) 2 HKCFAR 211, 223. However, this point was never actually argued before the Court of Final Appeal in this case, since it had already been conceded by the Hong Kong SAR Government after losing in the Court of Appeal.
177. This was a 1996 opinion from the Preparatory Committee established to prepare for the change of sovereignty (see further note 138 earlier in this chapter).
178. Ibid. at paragraph 1, which stated that children born in Hong Kong to "people residing temporarily in Hong Kong" should not be entitled to permanent residency. Instead the Court of Final Appeal concluded in *Chong Fung Yuen* (at 230–233) that the "clear meaning" of Article 24(2)(1) was that even children of Chinese visiting Hong Kong to give birth were entitled to the right of abode under this provision. See further pages 227 and 242.
179. (2001) 4 HKCFAR 251.
180. Ibid. at 256, rejecting an argument from the Hong Kong SAR Government that the Standing Committee's 1999 interpretation had "by implication dealt with adopted children", the issue that was the subject of this case. See further note 44 earlier in this chapter.
181. In *Lau Kong Yung v Director of Immigration* (1999) 2 HKCFAR 300, 323. For more on this case, and criticism of the court's reasoning, see further notes 104–125 earlier in this chapter and the accompanying text.

interpretation is no more binding on the Hong Kong courts than comments by any judge in a superior court. At most, it can be regarded as *obiter* (or comments by the way), to borrow another phrase from the common law system, although the courts appeared reluctant to do even this in *Chong Fung Yuen*.[182]

The Court of Final Appeal's decision in *Chong Fung Yuen* angered the Standing Committee, whose Legislative Affairs Commission issued a statement of "concern" in response.[183] It is also problematic in another respect since the Standing Committee is not a court, but rather a part of China's legislature.[184] That point is made elsewhere in the *Chong Fung Yuen* judgment, where the Court of Final Appeal describes the Standing Committee's power of interpretation as "legislative interpretation" that can "clarify or supplement laws".[185] Chan (2007) argues this means the court is characterizing the Standing Committee's interpretations of the Hong Kong Basic Law in almost the same way as if they were actual legislation.[186] That is an important point, since it is widely accepted in the common law world that legislation can reverse the effects of court decisions.[187] So treating the Standing Committee interpretations like legislation makes it easier to accept that these too can reverse the effects of court decisions, without seriously undermining the common law system expressly preserved under the Hong Kong Basic Law.[188]

But, as Yap (2007) notes, the judges cannot have it both ways.[189] If Standing Committee interpretations are treated like the judgments of a superior court, then the courts were arguably entitled to disregard the Standing Committee's comments on Article 24(2)(1) on the grounds that these are no more binding than *obiter* in any court case. But judges are not normally free to disregard any part of statutory legislation in the same way. So if the court chooses to characterize Standing Committee interpretations as legislation, as it appears to have done in *Chong Fung Yuen*, then it should follow every last word of any interpretation by the Standing Committee, including the sentence in the 1999 interpretation that would have required the court to reach a different conclusion on the meaning of Article 24(2)(1).[190]

---

182. See especially the Court of Appeal's rejection (at 685–687) of an argument from the Hong Kong SAR Government that the other parts of the Standing Committee's interpretation "should be treated as obiter dicta of the highest order".
183. See further note 365 in Chapter 6 and the accompanying text.
184. Under Article 58 of the PRC Constitution 1982: "The National People's Congress and its Standing Committee exercise the legislative power of the state."
185. *Chong Fung Yuen* at 221.
186. Chan, "Basic Law and Constitutional Review" (see note 15) at 417.
187. See further note 80 earlier in this chapter and the accompanying text.
188. See further notes 368–370 in Chapter 6 and the accompanying text.
189. Po Jen Yap, "Constitutional Review under the Basic Law: The Rise, Retreat and Resurgence of Judicial Power in Hong Kong" (2007) 37 *HKLJ* 449, 461–462.
190. Chan (2007) responds (in "Basic Law and Constitutional Review" (see note 15) at 418–419) that while a Standing Committee Interpretation "is legislative in nature, it is not the same as legislation". He argues that factual or procedural issues covered by such an interpretation are not intended to be treated as legislation and, as a matter of evidence, it is for the courts to determine which parts of any interpretation fall into this non-binding category.

In any case, at the time of writing it remained unclear whether the court's enthusiasm for limiting the binding effect of Standing Committee interpretations during the early years of the Hong Kong SAR would continue, especially if concerns that changes in the composition of the Court of Final Appeal may lead it to adopt a less vigorous stance in defending Hong Kong's high degree of autonomy do eventually turn out to be true.[191] As we will see in the next section of this chapter, the Court of Final Appeal has already overcome its previous reluctance to seek interpretations from the Standing Committee in the case of *Democratic Republic of Congo v FG Hemisphere*.[192] Following this, in *Vallejos Evangeline Banao v Commissioner of Registration* the government sought to reopen the issue of the extent of the binding effect of Standing Committee interpretations by requesting that the Court of Final Appeal refer the issue of which parts of the 1999 interpretation are binding to the Standing Committee for interpretation.[193] Although the court did not do so on this occasion, on the grounds that it was not necessary to decide the case,[194] it remains to be seen if the court will be willing to do so if the issue arises again in a more directly relevant case.

In addition, while characterizing Standing Committee interpretations as little different from a legislature in any other common law jurisdiction exercising its undisputed power to enact fresh legislation reversing the unacceptable effects of a court judgment is a useful way of trying to make them seem less threatening to the common law system, even Chan (2007) — a strong proponent of this view — concedes such an approach has its limits.[195] Elsewhere in the common law world, fresh legislation would normally only be enacted after a court case was over, and not while it is still ongoing. But Standing Committee interpretations can be issued in the midst of a court case. Indeed, Article 158(3) makes express provision for this. In those circumstances, the task of how to reconcile interference in the judicial process by a legislative body with the continuation of the common law system in Hong Kong becomes much more challenging. It is a task which the Court of Final Appeal largely managed to avoid for the first 14 years after the establishment of the Hong Kong SAR in 1997.

7.4 Judicial Referral

As we saw earlier, although Article 158(2) gives the Hong Kong courts wide-ranging power to interpret *on their own* all provisions in the Hong Kong Basic Law that fall within Hong Kong's autonomy, this is not always true of other provisions on matters outside Hong Kong's autonomy.

---

191. See further note 412 in Chapter 6 and the accompanying text.
192. (2011) 14 HKCFAR 95. See further pages 255–257.
193. *Vallejos Evangeline Banao v Commissioner of Registration* (unrep., FACV 19 and 20/2012, [2013] HKEC 429) at para. 99. This is a case on right of abode for foreign domestic helpers, an issue covered by the 1996 opinion from the Preparatory Committee (see note 138 earlier in this chapter) endorsed by the Standing Committee in its 1999 interpretation.
194. Ibid. at para. 111.
195. Chan, "Basic Law and Constitutional Review" (see note 15) at 416.

Article 158(3) defines such provisions as those concerning:

(1) Affairs which are the responsibility of the Central People's Government; or
(2) The relationship between the Central Authorities and Hong Kong.

These two categories are known as "excluded provisions",[196] because they are the only parts of the Hong Kong Basic Law which the courts are excluded from always interpreting entirely by themselves. Instead, where an interpretation of one of these excluded provisions "will affect the judgments on the cases" (or, in other words, is necessary to decide a case), Article 158(3) requires that the court must "before making their final judgments which are not appealable, seek an interpretation of the relevant provisions from the Standing Committee of the National People's Congress through the Court of Final Appeal of the Region".

From its wording, it appears that the judicial referral procedure in Article 158(3) only applies to the Court of Final Appeal, and Hong Kong's other courts are not required to refer issues of interpretation to the Standing Committee even when these fall within the two categories of "excluded provisions". In *Ng Ka Ling*, the Court of Final Appeal noted that "there is no limitation on the power of the lower courts to interpret all the provisions of the Basic Law".[197] This puts Hong Kong's lower courts in the ironic position of having wider powers to interpret the Hong Kong Basic Law than Hong Kong's highest court.

The judicial referral procedure in Article 158(3) was described by drafters of the Hong Kong Basic Law as modelled on the judicial referral procedure practised in Europe for many decades.[198] Under that procedure, before delivering a final judgment, the courts in member states of the European Union must refer issues of interpretation of European Union law to the European Court of Justice for a preliminary ruling.[199] The rationale in both cases is ostensibly similar. Just as issues of interpretation of those provisions in the Hong Kong Basic Law outside Hong Kong's autonomy are a national matter which need to be referred to a national body before the court delivers a final judgment, issues of interpretation of European Union law are a European matter which need to be referred to a pan-European body before the court delivers a final judgment.[200]

But any similarities end there. Crawford (2005) describes any comparison with the European Court of Justice as "a rather distant analogy".[201] Chan (2007) notes

---

196. *Ng Ka Ling v Director of Immigration* (1999) 2 HKCFAR 4, 30.
197. Ibid.
198. Wang Shuwen, *Introduction to the Basic Law of the Hong Kong Special Administrative Region* (Law Press, 2nd English edition, 2009) at 216.
199. Currently under Article 267 of the Treaty on the Functioning of the European Union 2007 (which originated as Article 177 of the Treaty Establishing the European Economic Community 1957).
200. Wang, *Introduction to the Basic Law of the Hong Kong Special Administrative Region* (see note 198) at 216–217.
201. James Crawford, *Rights in One Country: Hong Kong and China* (Faculty of Law, University of Hong Kong, 2005) at 9.

that "[u]nder the European system, the referral is part of the judicial process" with the issue of interpretation simply being referred to another court, at which the parties to the case will have the right to appear. "In contrast, the NPCSC is a political body which will decide the question of interpretation behind closed doors."[202]

Characterizing Standing Committee interpretations as "legislative interpretations" (i.e., the action of a legislature rather than a court)[203] may make such interpretations seem less threatening to the survival of the common law system in Hong Kong when those interpretations are delivered *after* a court case is finished. But referring issues of interpretation to a legislature *during* a court case under Article 158(3) is a different matter. As Chan (2007) points out, this raises serious concerns about the right to a fair hearing, as it risks depriving the parties to the case "of an opportunity to be heard by the NPCSC on an issue which will be crucial to the outcome of the hearing".[204]

Evidently alive to such concerns, during the early years of the Hong Kong SAR the Court of Final Appeal displayed what Lo (2007) describes as an "institutional reluctance"[205] to refer any issues of interpretation to the Standing Committee under Article 158(3). In *Ng Ka Ling*, the Court of Final Appeal emphasized that it saw the power of the courts to interpret the Hong Kong Basic Law on their own as "an essential part of the high degree of autonomy granted to the Region".[206] So essential that Ghai (2000) describes the court as disregarding the "plain meaning" of the wording of Article 158(3) in *Ng Ka Ling* so as to avoid referring an issue of interpretation to the Standing Committee.[207]

That wording would suggest that Article 158(3) only imposes two conditions which must be satisfied before the court is required to refer an issue of interpretation to the Standing Committee. In *Ng Ka Ling* these were described as the:

(1) Classification condition: Is this Hong Kong Basic Law provision classified as an excluded provision, which falls into one of the two categories of provisions listed in Article 158(3) as outside Hong Kong's autonomy?
(2) Necessity condition: Is it necessary to interpret this Hong Kong Basic Law provision because it will affect the judgment in the case?[208]

In *Ng Ka Ling*, the court was evidently anxious to involve referring to the Standing Committee for interpretation one of the Hong Kong Basic Law provisions necessary to decide this case, which even the court provisionally accepted could be classified as an

---

202. Chan, "Basic Law and Constitutional Review" (see note 15) at 416. See further Lo, "Rethinking Judicial Reference" (see note 173) at 163.
203. Chan, "Basic Law and Constitutional Review" (see note 15) at 417.
204. Ibid. at 416.
205. Lo, "Rethinking Judicial Reference" (see note 173) at 163.
206. *Ng Ka Ling* at 32.
207. Ghai, "Litigating the Basic Law" (see note 13) at 35.
208. *Ng Ka Ling* at 30–32, noting also a further requirement that the question of interpretation is "arguable" and not "plainly and obviously bad".

excluded provision on matters that lie outside Hong Kong's autonomy.[209] So the court added in a further condition not mentioned anywhere in the text of the Hong Kong Basic Law. Adopting a highly purposive interpretation of the Hong Kong Basic Law, that focussed almost exclusively on maximizing Hong Kong's high degree of autonomy by minimizing judicial referrals to the Standing Committee, the court added in what became known as the "predominant provision test". This held that where a case involves multiple provisions in the Hong Kong Basic Law, all that matters for the purposes of Article 158(3) is the classification of the predominant (or main) provision at issue in the case.[210]

According to that test, only if the predominant provision at issue in any case is classified as falling into one of the two categories of excluded provisions outside Hong Kong's autonomy is it necessary to refer the issue to the Standing Committee for interpretation. But the court controversially concluded that there was no need to refer such excluded provisions to the Standing Committee for interpretation if they are not the predominant provision at issue in any particular case.[211] Unsurprisingly, the Court of Final Appeal then concluded that the predominant provision at issue in *Ng Ka Ling* was one which was accepted by both sides in this case as falling within Hong Kong's autonomy.[212] This neatly avoided any need for a referral to the Standing Committee, and the court then proceeded to interpret on its own all the Hong Kong Basic Law provisions at issue in this case, including the one which it had provisionally accepted was an excluded provision on matters that lie outside Hong Kong's autonomy.

Ghai (1999), a strong defender of other aspects of the *Ng Ka Ling* judgment, notes that such an interpretation of an excluded provision by the court is "precisely what it must not do" and "its correctness may be doubted".[213] Chen (2000) is more sharply critical. In a strong attack on almost every aspect of the reasoning used in *Ng Ka Ling* to justify refusing to seek an interpretation from the Standing Committee, he accuses the court of being confused, mistaken and acting in breach of Article 158(3).[214]

---

209. Ibid. at 32. This was Article 22(4), which gives mainland authorities the power to restrict the entry into Hong Kong of "people from other parts of China". How to interpret the wording of this provision, in particular whether it includes children born in mainland China to a Hong Kong Chinese parent, was an important part of the *Ng Ka Ling* case. See further note 31 earlier in this chapter.
210. Ibid. at 33. For more on the court's reasoning in adopting this interpretation of Article 158(3), see further note 35 earlier in this chapter and the accompanying text.
211. Ibid.
212. This is Article 24(2)(3) on the right of abode of children born outside Hong Kong to a Hong Kong Chinese parent. It is, however, unclear whether the Standing Committee views this provision as falling inside Hong Kong's autonomy. See further note 122 earlier in this chapter.
213. Yash Ghai, "Commentary" [1999] 1 HKLRD 360, 363–364.
214. Chen, "The Court of Final Appeal's Ruling in the 'Illegal Migrant' Children Case" (see note 36) at 113–141. Some of Chen's criticism of the court's ruling on this point was subsequently acknowledged as meriting "serious consideration" by the Court of Final Appeal in *Chong Fung Yuen* at 229.

If the Court of Final Appeal's reason for adopting the predominant provision test was to keep the provisions in the Hong Kong Basic Law at issue in *Ng Ka Ling* out of the hands of the Standing Committee, it failed. One consequence of the court refusing to refer interpretation of the disputed provisions to the Standing Committee before delivering its judgment in *Ng Ka Ling* was that the Hong Kong SAR Government then proceeded to refer those same provisions to the Standing Committee for a fresh interpretation after the case was over.[215] This was a highly controversial action which almost certainly did much more damage to Hong Kong's autonomy than any referral by the court would have done.

After the Preamble to that interpretation criticized the court's failure to seek an interpretation from the Standing Committee during the *Ng Ka Ling* case "in compliance with the requirement of Article 158(3)",[216] the Court of Final Appeal subsequently conceded that it might need to reconsider its predominant provision test when "an appropriate case" arises.[217] But the court has been in no hurry to do this, which would most likely entail admitting it had misinterpreted Article 158(3) in *Ng Ka Ling*. Instead the court simply held that the issue was not directly relevant, in four subsequent cases that touched on the issue of Standing Committee interpretations.[218]

The Court of Final Appeal's twisting of the wording of Article 158(3) in *Ng Ka Ling* was only the most extreme example of its institutional reluctance to refer issues of interpretation to the Standing Committee during the early years of the Hong Kong SAR. In *HKSAR v Ng Kung Siu*,[219] a case decided 11 months later, the judges reacted with horror to a suggestion from government lawyers during the case that an issue of the application of national law in Hong Kong should be referred to the Standing Committee for interpretation under Article 158(3). "To refer this question would make us look like a bunch of clowns", Justice Ching was quoted as saying.[220]

In *Chong Fung Yuen*, the Court of Final Appeal rejected in more measured language the Hong Kong SAR Government's argument that Article 24(2)(1), the sole provision in the Hong Kong Basic Law at issue in this case, fell into the category of excluded provisions outside Hong Kong autonomy which must be referred to the Standing Committee for interpretation under Article 158(3). This was despite some—albeit conflicting—evidence that the Standing Committee viewed Article 24(2)(1) as falling into the category of excluded provisions.[221]

---

215. The referral was initiated through a report from the Chief Executive to the State Council. See further note 87 earlier in this chapter and the accompanying text.
216. The Interpretation by the Standing Committee of Articles 22(4) and 24(2)(3) (see note 89).
217. *Lau Kong Yung v Director of Immigration* (1999) 2 HKCFAR 300, 324.
218. Ibid. See also *Chong Fung Yuen* at 230, *Democratic Republic of Congo v FG Hemisphere* (2011) 14 HKCFAR 95, 231–232 and *Vallejos Evangeline Banao* at para. 103.
219. (1999) 2 HKCFAR 442. For more on this case, see further notes 190–209 in Chapter 8 and the accompanying text.
220. Cliff Buddle, "NPC role in flag case floated", *South China Morning Post*, 22 Oct 1999.
221. *Chong Fung Yuen* at 228. At issue was an ambiguity in the wording of the Preamble to the Standing Committee's 1999 interpretation of the Hong Kong Basic Law, which left it unclear whether the Standing Committee viewed Article 24(2)(3) as falling into the category of excluded provisions. See further note 122 earlier in this chapter.

That case saw the rejection of the Hong Kong SAR Government's attempt to widen the categories of excluded provisions, with the court holding that it was the subject matter of a particular provision which determined whether or not that provision should be referred to the Standing Committee for interpretation under Article 158(3) and not the effect of that provision.[222] That is a crucial distinction, because focussing on the effect of a provision is a far broader test which, had it been accepted by the court, could have led to "most if not all the articles in the Basic Law"[223] being categorized as excluded provisions, so requiring very frequent references to the Standing Committee for interpretation under Article 158(3).

It took 14 years before the Court of Final Appeal overcame its institutional reluctance to refer issues of interpretation to the Standing Committee for interpretation under Article 158(3). Even when it finally did so in 2011 for the first time in the case of *Democratic Republic of Congo v FG Hemisphere*,[224] the court was sharply divided on the point, concluding by a narrow 3 to 2 majority that four specific questions involving Articles 13(1) and 19 of the Hong Kong Basic Law should be referred to the Standing Committee for interpretation.[225]

In contrast to the previous cases where the issue of a possible referral to the Standing Committee had arisen, in the *Congo* case there was no real argument about how to classify the two main provisions in the Hong Kong Basic Law that had been raised during this case. Since Article 13(1) concerned issues of foreign affairs while Article 19(3) involved acts of state, it was clear that these were excluded provisions that would need to be referred to the Standing Committee *if* they would affect the judgment in the *Congo* case.

Instead, one of the main arguments in the Court of Final Appeal during the *Congo* case was about the necessity condition laid down in Article 158(3), and whether these two provisions were necessary to decide the case at all. It was this issue which so sharply divided the court, with the minority holding the case could be decided through common law principles which did "not involve any Basic Law interpretation at all", so rendering irrelevant the question of whether to refer any issues of interpretation of the Hong Kong Basic Law to the Standing Committee, because there were no such issues necessary to decide the case.[226] For Justice Bokhary, who penned the most strongly worded dissent, this was a fundamental issue of judicial independence and he alluded to how the majority's decision to refer aspects of the case to the Standing Committee might be viewed:

---

222. Ibid. at 229, rejecting the Hong Kong SAR Government's argument that a "substantive effect test" should be used to decide whether a provision must be referred to the Standing Committee for interpretation under Article 158(3). This test would be based upon what effect a provision has on affairs which are the responsibility of the Central People's Government or the relationship between the Central Authorities and the SAR.
223. Ibid.
224. (2011) 14 HKCFAR 95.
225. Ibid. at 232–233.
226. Ibid. at 138. The case involved the existence of restrictive state immunity, which allows foreign governments to be sued for commercial transactions, a principle which had been established by the courts at common law before 1997.

"Judicial independence is not to be found in what courts merely say. It is to be found in what the courts actually do. In other words, it is to be found in what the courts decide."[227]

It is a mark of how far the Court of Final Appeal's thinking had evolved since *Ng Ka Ling*, when the court seemed anxious to avoid a referral to the Standing Committee at all costs, that Justice Bokhary was now in the minority. This time when offered an easy path in the *Congo* case to avoid referring an issue of interpretation to the Standing Committee, simply by concluding that the issue could be decided at common law, a path which the court would most likely have jumped at a decade earlier, the majority on the court instead concluded that Articles 13(1) and 19(3) of the Hong Kong Basic Law were necessary to decide the case.[228] Since these two articles are clearly excluded provisions on issues outside Hong Kong's autonomy, once the majority on the court had concluded that they were necessary to decide the case, that then inevitably meant the issue of how to interpret them had to be referred to the Standing Committee under Article 158(3).[229]

The biggest surprise came in the procedure adopted by the court for referring these issues to the Standing Committee for interpretation. Since the referral procedure in Article 158(3) was expressly modelled on the preliminary reference procedure used by national courts within the European Union,[230] it might have been thought that the Court of Final Appeal would refer any issues of interpretation to the Standing Committee at a preliminary stage during the court hearing. Instead, the Court of Final Appeal did the opposite in the *Congo* case. Noting that the "language of Article 158(3) plainly permits this court to express its view on the question"[231] before referring the issue to the Standing Committee for interpretation, the Court of Final Appeal proceeded to hear the case in full and deliver a lengthy judgment stating the court's view on how the relevant provisions in the Hong Kong Basic Law should be interpreted.[232] Although the judgment described these conclusions as "tentative and provisional",[233] pending a ruling from the Standing

---

227. Ibid. at 111.
228. Ibid. at 182 and 210–213. The majority essentially concluded that this was an issue of foreign affairs, and so the common law position of restrictive state immunity (see note 226) must give way to China's stance that foreign governments should never be sued through the courts. The majority was heavily influenced by three letters to this effect from China's Ministry of Foreign Affairs, which they held should be treated as "facts of state" that the court cannot decide by itself. For more on facts of state, see further page 214.
229. Ibid. at 232.
230. See note 198 earlier in this chapter and the accompanying text.
231. *Congo* case at 230.
232. National courts within the European Union do sometimes express their own "provisional conclusions" when using the preliminary reference procedure to refer issues of interpretation to the European Court of Justice. See P.Y. Lo, "The Gateway Opens Wide" (2011) 41 *HKLJ* 385, 390. However, these are generally much shorter and limited to a maximum of ten pages. See Andrew Le Sueur, *A Report on Six Seminars About the UK Supreme Court* (Legal Studies Research Paper No. 1/2008, Queen Mary School of Law, Dec 2008) at 51.
233. *Congo* case at 165–166.

Committee on whether the court had correctly interpreted the Hong Kong Basic Law, it gave every other appearance of being a full judgment—even to the extent of laying out the orders which would be implemented in the event of a favourable Standing Committee ruling.[234] When the Standing Committee's interpretation duly endorsed the judgment's provisional conclusions,[235] the court did not even need to reconvene, simply issuing a brief supplementary judgment confirming its earlier conclusions as final.[236]

That procedure goes a long way to allay concerns about the damage that a referral to the Standing Committee for interpretation could inflict on the right to a fair hearing in any case.[237] While the parties to a case may not have a right to put their arguments directly to the Standing Committee, the effect of delaying a referral under Article 158(3) until the *Congo* case was essentially over was that their arguments were fully aired in court before the case was referred to the Standing Committee, and indirectly reflected to the Standing Committee in the court's lengthy provisional judgment. Lo (2011) notes that the Court of Final Appeal made sure that the questions it referred to the Standing Committee were "narrowly and specifically phrased, in order to elicit 'correspondingly written' answers from the NPCSC".[238] In other words, the Court of Final Appeal simply asked the Standing Committee to endorse the conclusions the court had already reached.

That sets a useful precedent for any future cases in which the court has to refer issues to the Standing Committee for interpretation under Article 158(3) of the Hong Kong Basic Law. In the *Congo* case, since the court's provisional ruling essentially followed the stance already taken by China's Ministry of Foreign Affairs during the case,[239] there was never really much doubt about the Standing Committee's likely answer. But if, as may happen at some point, the Court of Final Appeal has to refer another issue of interpretation to the Standing Committee where its provisional conclusions are less palatable to Beijing, the fact that any such reference is accompanied by a lengthy judgment setting out the court's reasoning may cause the Standing Committee to hesitate before publicly rejecting the court's provisional conclusions, even though the Standing Committee has every legal right to do so.

In this way, while the *Congo* case marks an important turning point in the Court of Final Appeal's willingness to refer issues of interpretation to the Standing Committee, it seems possible that the court is still trying—through procedural means—to limit the Standing Committee's scope for interpretation under Article 158(3) of the Hong Kong Basic Law.

---

234. Ibid. at 235.
235. Interpretation of Paragraph 1, Article 13 and Article 19 of the Basic Law of the Hong Kong SAR of the PRC by the Standing Committee of the NPC (26 August 2011).
236. *Democratic Republic of Congo v FG Hemisphere (No 2)* (2011) 14 HKCFAR 395, 400.
237. See further note 204 earlier in this chapter and the accompanying text.
238. Lo, "The Gateway Opens Wide" (see note 232) at 390.
239. In three letters presented during the case. See further note 228.

7.5 Amendment

Nowhere is the special status of the Hong Kong Basic Law more apparent than in the severe restrictions on how it can be amended. Instead of following the procedures for amending laws that are set out in the national constitution,[240] the Hong Kong Basic Law is almost the only law in China which contains its own built-in amendment procedures.[241] As a consequence, while the national constitution is clearly the superior law, in some respects the Hong Kong Basic Law is even more difficult to amend than the constitution.[242]

Under Article 159(1), only the National People's Congress is allowed to amend the main text of the Hong Kong Basic Law.[243] While this may restrict Hong Kong's autonomy, since it prevents Hong Kong from amending its own constitutional document, it also makes the Hong Kong Basic Law much more difficult to amend than other laws passed by the National People's Congress—which can all be amended by its Standing Committee without waiting for the next annual session of the full National People's Congress.[244] The procedure for initiating amendments to the Hong Kong Basic Law is also much more restrictive than for other Chinese laws. While ordinary members of the National People's Congress are allowed to initiate amendments to other laws,[245] and even the constitution,[246] this is not the case with the Hong Kong Basic Law. Instead, under Article 159(2), the right to initiate amendments to the Hong Kong Basic Law is confined to the Standing Committee, State Council and Hong Kong SAR. In the case of Hong Kong, the rules on initiating an amendment are highly restrictive—requiring the support of the Chief Executive, two-thirds of the members of the Legislative Council, and a similar proportion of Hong Kong deputies to the National People's Congress. Chan

---

240. See PRC Constitution 1982, Articles 62(3), 64, 67(3) and 72.
241. The only other exceptions are the Macao Basic Law and the constitution itself. See further H.L. Fu, "The Form and Substance of Legal Interaction Between Hong Kong and Mainland China: Towards Hong Kong's New Legal Sovereignty" in Raymond Wacks (ed.), *The New Legal Order in Hong Kong* (Hong Kong University Press, 1999) at 99.
242. See further "3.4: Relationship with Chinese Constitution" for more on the issue of possible conflicts between the Hong Kong Basic Law and the national constitution.
243. Different rules apply to the three annexes to the Hong Kong Basic Law, which all have their own amendment procedures.
244. Again, with the exception of the Macao Basic Law. Under Article 67(3) of the PRC Constitution 1982, amendments by the Standing Committee are not supposed to "contravene the basic principles" of laws enacted by the NPC. However, in practice, this restriction is sometimes ignored. See Chen Jianfu, *Chinese Law: Towards an Understanding of Chinese Law, Its Nature and Development* (Kluwer Law International, 1999) at 116.
245. See PRC Legislation Law, Article 13. Under Article 12, several other bodies are also allowed to initiate amendments to other laws. These include Special Committees of the NPC, the Central Military Commission and Supreme People's Court.
246. See PRC Constitution 1982, Article 64. It should, however, be noted that amendments to the Constitution will only be passed if they are supported by two-thirds of all delegates to the NPC while amendments to other laws (including the Hong Kong Basic Law) can be enacted by a simple majority.

(2012) notes that: "It is almost impossible to meet this procedural requirement in most cases."[247]

These procedural restrictions on amending the Hong Kong Basic Law[248] are supplemented by a potentially important substantive restriction on such amendments in Article 159(4). This imposes an absolute ban on any amendments which "contravene the established basic policies of the People's Republic of China regarding Hong Kong". That refers to the fundamental principles of one country, two systems in Hong Kong originally stipulated in the Sino-British Joint Declaration in 1984, the international treaty on Hong Kong's return to China,[249] and subsequently written into the Hong Kong Basic Law.[250] These basic policies protect many areas fundamental to Hong Kong's separate system and existing way of life including, to name just a few examples, extensive human rights guarantees, Hong Kong's separate judicial system with its power of final adjudication, and exclusive responsibility for law and order.[251]

If enforceable, this substantive restriction in Article 159(4) is by far the most significant restriction on amendments. That is because it means the large parts of the Hong Kong Basic Law which reflect these basic policies,[252] and cover most of the areas where any changes would most severely erode Hong Kong's autonomy and separate way of life, cannot be amended in any major way for at least 50 years beyond 1 July 1997.[253] That appears to have been the conclusion of the Court of Final Appeal in *Ng Ka Ling v Director of Immigration*, when the court cited Article 159(4) in one of the most controversial sections of its judgment, as one of the grounds for asserting a jurisdiction to invalidate actions of the National People's Congress and its Standing Committee if they contravene the Hong Kong Basic Law.[254]

---

247. Johannes Chan, "Mainland mothers giving birth in Hong Kong" (Sept 2012) *Hong Kong Lawyer* 24, 33.
248. Article 159(3) adds a further procedural restriction, requiring that, before any amendment is placed on the NPC's agenda, it must first be considered by the Committee for the Basic Law of the Hong Kong SAR. See further notes 227–228 in Chapter 4 and the accompanying text, for more on the creation of this committee and its composition.
249. See further "2.2: Sino-British Joint Declaration" in Chapter 2.
250. See the Preamble to the Hong Kong Basic Law, which explicitly states that the purpose of this law is "to ensure the implementation of the basic policies of the People's Republic of China regarding Hong Kong".
251. For more on the basic policies, see further pages 16–17.
252. How much of the Hong Kong Basic Law is affected would depend on whether this includes everything reflecting China's 4,500 word "elaboration" of these basic policies in Annex I of the Joint Declaration. Ghai (1999) observes that, if this is included, it would be impossible to amend "most provisions of the Basic Law". See Ghai, *Hong Kong's New Constitutional Order* (see note 73) at 181.
253. For more on the position after 50 years, see further "Chapter 9: What Will Happen After 2047?".
254. (1999) 2 HKCFAR 4, 26. Although this was not directly stated, the implication of the court citing Article 159(4) was that the court had the jurisdiction to invalidate any amendments to the Hong Kong Basic Law by the NPC which contravene these basic policies. For more on this aspect of the *Ng Ka Ling* judgment, see further notes 186–194 in Chapter 6 and the accompanying text.

Wang (2009), an influential mainland drafter of the Hong Kong Basic Law, describes the purpose behind the restrictions in Article 159 as being "to prevent rush amendment" and "substantial change in the principle and essence" of the Hong Kong Basic Law.[255] But, if that was the purpose behind these restrictions, it is far from clear that they achieve this objective. Instead, by making it so time-consuming and difficult to amend the Hong Kong Basic Law, these restrictions have arguably encouraged the use of less satisfactory alternatives to amendment when problems have arisen with the wording of a particular provision in the Hong Kong Basic Law which needed to be urgently addressed.

That is best demonstrated by what happened after the Court of Final Appeal's decision in *Ng Ka Ling*.[256] Then, there was general agreement that Hong Kong could not cope with the social consequences of the Court of Final Appeal's interpretation of Articles 22(4) and 24(2)(3) of the Hong Kong Basic Law, which potentially opened the doors to a mass influx of more than one million children born on the mainland.[257] Had it not been for the Article 159(1) requirement that all amendments must be adopted by the full National People's Congress, the problem could possibly have been quickly resolved by asking the Standing Committee to amend the Hong Kong Basic Law, a task it is allowed to perform in relation to almost all other laws enacted by the National People's Congress. Amending the Hong Kong Basic Law would also have been comparable with the practice elsewhere in the common law world, where governments sometimes respond to court decisions that pose unacceptable social consequences by seeking to amend the law in question.[258]

But the Hong Kong SAR Government rejected this option, partly because the fact that only the full National People's Congress is allowed to amend the Hong Kong Basic Law means the first opportunity to do this would not come until its next session nearly a year later.[259] Instead, it opted for the different, and far more controversial, path of seeking a new interpretation of Articles 22(4) and 24(2)(3). Because, unlike amendment, interpretation of the Hong Kong Basic Law can be carried out by the Standing Committee, which meets every two months, this meant the effect of the court ruling could be swiftly reversed in 1999—although at some cost to confidence in Hong Kong's legal system.[260]

It was a similar story in early 2005, when the Hong Kong SAR Government was faced with a legal challenge which threatened to derail the impending election of a Chief Executive. Once again arguing it could not afford to wait almost a year for the National People's Congress to amend the Hong Kong Basic Law provision at issue in this case, the

---

255. Wang, *Introduction to the Basic Law of the Hong Kong Special Administrative Region* (see note 198) at page 220.
256. See further notes 77–78 earlier in this chapter for more on this decision.
257. See further note 75 earlier in this chapter on the Hong Kong SAR Government's estimates of the number of children eligible for residency rights as a result of the decision in *Ng Ka Ling* and the related case of *Chan Kam Nga v Director of Immigration* (1999) 2 HKCFAR 82.
258. See the example cited in note 81 earlier in this chapter and the accompanying text.
259. See Hong Kong SAR Government, "Right of Abode: The Solution" (see note 84) at 313. This also raises the issue of whether an amendment would contravene the ban in Article 159(4) on any amendments that contravene the basic policies (see further note 252).
260. See further "7.2: Standing Committee" earlier in this chapter for more on the 1999 interpretation and its aftermath.

government instead opted for the quicker route of seeking another interpretation from the Standing Committee.[261]

Some might argue this hardly matters, since whether the Standing Committee uses amendment or interpretation to change the meaning of legislation are just two different ways of achieving the same goal. That was the argument which the Court of Final Appeal seemed to be leaning towards in *Director of Immigration v Chong Fung Yuen*, when it described the Standing Committee's action as "legislative interpretation".[262]

But Chen (2006) notes amendment should normally be considered preferable to interpretation as it "provides for more transparency and room for public debate on the bill containing the proposed amendment".[263] In addition, in using interpretation to bypass the amendment procedures in Article 159, the government also bypassed all the restrictions on amendments written into that article, since Article 158 on interpretation does not stipulate any express restrictions on how or when the Hong Kong Basic Law can be interpreted by the Standing Committee. In particular, there is no equivalent of the substantive restriction in Article 159(4), which seeks to prevent any amendment to the Hong Kong Basic Law that contravenes the established basic policies of the People's Republic of China regarding Hong Kong which were originally stipulated in the Joint Declaration. This lack of safeguards in relation to how the Hong Kong Basic Law is interpreted suggests that it would, in theory, be possible to achieve through interpretation what is theoretically forbidden through amendment. In other words, that interpretation could be used to redefine (and erode) the fundamental principles that protect "one country, two systems" in Hong Kong.

In practice, it may nonetheless be possible to make such sweeping changes through amendment of the Hong Kong Basic Law since it is far from clear whether the prohibition in Article 159(4) against making major amendments is legally enforceable. Just as the doctrine of parliamentary sovereignty has traditionally meant that there are no legal limits on the power of the UK Parliament to make or unmake any law,[264] so Chen (2000) argues that in China a doctrine of Congressional supremacy means there are no limits on the power of the National People's Congress, "to make or unmake any law whatsoever on any matter whatsoever".[265]

---

261. See further pages 243–246 for more on the Standing Committee's 2005 interpretation.
262. (2001) 4 HKCFAR 211, 221. See further notes 368–370 in Chapter 6 and the accompanying text, for more on the significance of the court's characterization of Standing Committee interpretations in this way.
263. Chen, "Constitutional Adjudication in Post-1997 Hong Kong" (see note 113) at 647.
264. See the classic statement on the absolute sovereignty of the UK Parliament put forward by the famous 19th-century jurist A.V. Dicey in *An Introduction to the Study of the Law of the Constitution* (Macmillan, 10th edition, 1959) at 39–40.
265. Albert H.Y. Chen, "The Court of Final Appeal's Ruling in the 'Illegal Migrant' Children Case: Congressional Supremacy and Judicial Review" in Chan, Fu and Ghai (eds.), *Hong Kong's Constitutional Debate* (see note 13) at 80.

What this means is that while any amendment to the Hong Kong Basic Law that contravened China's basic policies would doubtless be both politically controversial and a breach of China's obligations under the Joint Declaration, it would not necessarily be unlawful. Instead, as a sovereign legislature, the National People's Congress would simply be exercising its lawful power to repeal the contrary provision contained in Article 159(4) of the Hong Kong Basic Law, which purports to prevent such changes. As Ling (2000) notes, the attempt to entrench large parts of the Hong Kong Basic Law against fundamental change for the first 50 years after 1997, is "not legally binding on a future NPC".[266]

As such, the provisions in Article 159 seeking to protect against any fundamental changes to the Hong Kong Basic Law for at least the first 50 years after 1 July 1997 are best viewed more as a declaration of principle by China than as a legally binding restraint on any major changes to how "one country, two systems" is applied in Hong Kong.

---

266. Bing Ling, "The Proper Law for the Conflict Between the Basic Law and Other Legislative Acts of the National People's Congress" in Chan, Fu and Ghai (eds.), *Hong Kong's Constitutional Debate* (see note 13) at 163.

Chapter 8
Protection of Human Rights

For almost 150 years, Hong Kong lacked any broad laws protecting human rights.[1] Unlike constitutions the world over, which usually contain extensive provisions on civil liberties, Hong Kong's main constitutional document during the colonial era contained no reference to human rights throughout most of that period.[2]

Instead, such legal protection of human rights as then existed in Hong Kong came primarily through the development by the courts of common law principles such as the presumption of innocence.[3] But these offered only limited protection since common law principles can always be overridden by statutory legislation. Chan and Lim (2011) note that as recently as the mid-1980s, "Hong Kong had some of the most draconian controls over the activities of lawful societies and public assemblies".[4] For a long time, the Public Order Ordinance (Cap. 245) even made it a crime for three or more people to gather in public and discuss public affairs without permission from the police, so theoretically making it an offence to discuss current events over a family meal in a *dim sum* restaurant.[5]

---

1. There were, however, certain provisions in some ordinances providing for specific protection of individual rights. See, for example, the provisions in the Employment Ordinance (Cap. 57) providing employees with limited protection against dismissal or other discrimination on the grounds of pregnancy or involvement in trade union activities.
2. This was the Hong Kong Letters Patent 1917–1995. Interestingly a second constitutional document during the colonial period, known as the Hong Kong Royal Instructions 1917–1993, did contain one provision relating to human rights. This was Clause XXVI, which made it more difficult to pass laws discriminating against those not of European birth. For more on these two documents, see further note 43 in Chapter 5 and note 129 in Chapter 6.
3. See Johannes Chan and C.L. Lim, "Interpreting Constitutional Rights and Permissible Restrictions" in Chan and Lim (eds.), *Law of the Hong Kong Constitution* (Sweet & Maxwell, 2011) at 467 for a description of some of the main common law principles used by the courts to protect human rights.
4. Ibid.
5. See Johannes Chan, "Civil Liberties, Rule of Law and Human Rights: The Hong Kong Special Administrative Region in Its First Four Years" in Lau Siu-kai (ed.), *The First Tung Chee-hwa Administration: The First Five Years of the HKSAR* (The Chinese University Press, 2002) at 99 citing the extraordinary case of *Chow Shui v The Queen* [1979] HKLR 275 where passengers on two coaches were convicted of illegal assembly. Outrage over this case in the legal profession led to the easing of restrictions on freedom of assembly in the Public Order (Amendment) Ordinance (No. 67 of 1980).

The lack of broad legal protection for civil liberties in Hong Kong only changed after the bloody Tiananmen crackdown in June 1989 intensified public fears to the point where Britain was forced to shift its stance and concede the need for a comprehensive human rights law.[6] That law, the Hong Kong Bill of Rights Ordinance (Cap. 383), and the accompanying amendment protecting its contents in the colonial constitution,[7] marked what Chen (2006) describes as "the first constitutional revolution in Hong Kong".[8] For the first time in Hong Kong's history, a wide range of fundamental rights became enforceable in the courts and the 1990s saw a huge increase in the number of judicial review cases as government actions, and even laws, were successfully challenged in the courts for breaching these rights.[9]

To the surprise of some, the Bill of Rights survived the transfer of sovereignty on 1 July 1997 mostly unscathed and remains an important part of the legal framework protecting human rights in Hong Kong. It has been joined since that date by the Hong Kong Basic Law which, with its own extensive provisions on civil liberties, now constitutes the primary source of legal safeguards of human rights in Hong Kong.

The importance afforded to protecting human rights is evident almost from the start of the Hong Kong Basic Law, where this is one of the first General Principles mentioned in Chapter I of the document.[10] An entire chapter is then devoted to repeating, and in some cases expanding upon, the guarantees of specific rights originally set out in the Sino-British Joint Declaration, the 1984 agreement on the terms of Hong Kong's return to China.[11]

Titled "Fundamental Rights and Duties of the Residents", Chapter III of the Hong Kong Basic Law begins by setting out in Article 24 who is a Hong Kong resident, and eligible to enjoy the wide range of rights listed in this chapter. Those with the most rights are known as permanent residents, and eligible for Hong Kong identity cards stating they have the right of abode in Hong Kong.[12] The importance of this right is evident from the fact that it has been the subject of more litigation than any other provision in

---

6. For a detailed description of Britain's change of stance in 1989 on the need for a Bill of Rights by one of the key participants in this process, see Nihal Jayawickrama, "The Bill of Rights" in Raymond Wacks (ed.), *Human Rights in Hong Kong* (Oxford University Press, 1992) at 63–76.
7. This was Article VII(5) of the Hong Kong Letters Patent 1917–1995, which fundamentally changed the nature of a constitutional document that until then, had been devoid of any reference to human rights, and is described in more detail later in this chapter.
8. Albert H.Y. Chen, "Constitutional Adjudication in Post-1997 Hong Kong" (2006) 15 *Pacific Rim Law & Policy Journal* 627, 653.
9. For more on the growth of judicial review as a result of the Bill of Rights and Article VII(5), see further notes 136–137 in Chapter 6 and the accompanying text.
10. See Article 4, which states: "The Hong Kong Special Administrative Region shall safeguard the rights and freedoms of the residents of the Hong Kong Special Administrative Region and of other persons in the Region in accordance with law."
11. See further "2.2: Sino-British Joint Declaration" in Chapter 2.
12. Article 24(3).

the Hong Kong Basic Law, including such landmark cases as *Ng Ka Ling v Director of Immigration*[13] and *Director of Immigration v Chong Fung Yuen*.[14]

The right of abode has been called a "core right" by the Court of Final Appeal,[15] and described as "the right, in the eyes of its law, to call that place home: coming and going at will; staying as long as you like".[16] What this means in practice is that permanent residents have the right to remain in Hong Kong without being subject to any kind of restrictions and can never be removed from Hong Kong against their will.[17] In addition, under Article 26 of the Hong Kong Basic Law, only permanent residents have the right to vote and stand for election in Hong Kong.

Under Article 24(2), six categories of persons enjoy the right of abode in Hong Kong. The overwhelming majority are Chinese citizens either born in Hong Kong[18] or ordinarily resident for a continuous period of at least seven years,[19] together with their children born anywhere in the world.[20] While most people can satisfy the ordinarily resident requirement by living in Hong Kong for seven years, this is not true of everyone. Prisoners, illegal immigrants, refugees and—most controversially—foreign domestic helpers are among those who are not regarded as ordinarily resident, and so cannot qualify for right of abode regardless of how long they live in Hong Kong in one of these capacities.[21]

Non-Chinese who fulfil the same requirement of seven years ordinary residency can also acquire the right of abode in Hong Kong if they enter Hong Kong with valid travel documents and meet the additional requirement of taking Hong Kong as their place of permanent residence.[22] Unlike Chinese, their children are only automatically entitled to

---

13. (1999) 2 HKCFAR 4. This case involved the children of Hong Kong Chinese born outside Hong Kong, the third of the six categories of permanent residents listed in Article 24(2). For more on the impact of *Ng Ka Ling* and the closely related judgment in *Chan Kam Nga v Director of Immigration* (1999) 2 HKCFAR 82, see further note 75 in Chapter 7 and the accompanying text.
14. (2001) 4 HKCFAR 211. This case involved Chinese children born in Hong Kong, the first of the six categories of permanent residents listed in Article 24(2). For more on the impact of this case, see further note 48 in Chapter 7 and the accompanying text.
15. *Ng Ka Ling* at 34.
16. *Chan Kam Nga* at 87.
17. See Section 2A(1) of the Immigration Ordinance (Cap. 115) for the full definition of right of abode.
18. Article 24(2)(1).
19. Article 24(2)(2).
20. Article 24(2)(3).
21. Section 2(4) of the Immigration Ordinance (Cap. 115). In *Fateh Mohammad v Commissioner of Registration* (2001) 4 HKCFAR 278, 283–284 the Court of Final Appeal agreed that prisoners and other detainees do not satisfy the requirements for ordinary residency. In *Vallejos Evangeline Banao v Commissioner of Registration* (unrep. FACV 19 and 20/2012, [2013] HKEC 429) the Court of Final Appeal held that foreign domestic helpers do not satisfy the requirements for ordinary residency.
22. Article 24(2)(4). The Hong Kong Basic Law gives no guidance on what constitutes taking Hong Kong as a place of permanent residence. However, under paragraph 3(1) of Schedule 1 of the Immigration Ordinance (Cap. 115), applicants for this category of right of abode may be required to show they have a habitual residence in Hong Kong, along with their spouse and young children, as well as a reasonable means of income and proof of having paid taxes.

right of abode until they reach the age of 21.[23] Non-Chinese permanent residents enjoy slightly fewer rights than their Chinese counterparts, as they are not allowed to stand for election as Chief Executive[24] or for most seats in the Legislative Council.[25]

Others lawfully resident in Hong Kong who do not fall into any of these six categories,[26] often because they have not yet fulfilled the seven-year residency requirement, are known as non-permanent residents. They are eligible for a different type of identity card, which does not confer any right of abode.[27] Apart from the right to vote and stand for election, they enjoy all the same rights as permanent residents, with Article 25 expressly stating that "[a]ll Hong Kong residents shall be equal before the law". These rights, which are set out in the remainder of Chapter III as well as elsewhere in the Hong Kong Basic Law, include:

- The right to private property ownership (Article 6), including the acquisition, use, disposal and inheritance of such property as well as compensation for any lawful deprivation[28] of such property (Article 105(1));
- Freedom of speech, press, publication, association, assembly, procession, demonstration, to form and join trade unions and to strike (Article 27);
- Freedom of the person from torture, the right not to be subjected to arbitrary or unlawful arrest, body searches, detention, imprisonment, deprivation of life or other restrictions on freedom of the person (Article 28);
- Freedom from arbitrary or unlawful search of, or intrusion into, homes or other premises (Article 29);

---

23. Article 24(2)(5). However, if such children are living in Hong Kong at the age of 21 they may well be able to instead qualify for right of abode through the criteria in Article 24(2)(4).
24. Article 44 limits candidates for Chief Executive to Chinese citizens over the age of 40, who have no right of abode in any foreign country and have been ordinarily resident in Hong Kong for at least 20 years.
25. Article 67 restricts the number of legislators who are not Chinese citizens or have right of abode in a foreign country to a maximum of 20% of the total membership of the Legislative Council. Under Sections 37(1)(e), 37(2)(f) and 37(3) of the Legislative Council Ordinance (Cap. 542), this restriction is implemented by only allowing non-Chinese to contest 12 specified functional constituency seats in Legislative Council elections.
26. The sixth category, Article 24(2)(6), is a residual provision designed to preserve the rights of others who had the right of abode in Hong Kong before 1 July 1997 and do not fall into any of the first five categories. However, it only applies to those who do not have a right of abode anywhere else in the world which, in practice, means certain members of ethnic minority groups and refugees.
27. Article 24(4).
28. The Chinese text of Article 105(1) uses the term *zhengyong* (徵用). In *Harvest Good Development v Secretary for Justice* [2007] 4 HKC 1, 33–35 the Court of First Instance held that this term has a narrower meaning than deprivation, and only applies to the expropriation of property for public use. For more on this case, including academic criticism of the decision, see Anne Cheung, "Language" in Chan and Lim (eds.), *Law of the Hong Kong Constitution* (see note 3) at 137–139.

- Freedom and privacy of communication, except under limited circumstances involving public security or investigation of criminal offences (Article 30);
- Freedom of movement within Hong Kong and emigration overseas, as well as the right to travel, enter and leave Hong Kong with valid travel documents, unless restrained by law (Article 31);
- Freedom of conscience, religious belief and to preach, conduct and participate in religious activities in public (Article 32);
- Freedom of choice of occupation (Article 33);
- Freedom to engage in academic research, literary and artistic creation and other cultural activities (Article 34), as well as protection of the lawful rights and interests of authors in their literary and artistic creations (Article 140);
- The right to confidential legal advice, choice of lawyers, access to the courts, judicial remedies, legal action against the acts of the executive authorities and their personnel (Article 35), as well as the right to a fair trial and to be presumed innocent until convicted (Article 87(2));
- The right to social welfare, including welfare benefits and retirement security, in accordance with the law (Article 36);
- Freedom of marriage and the right to raise a family freely (Article 37).

In most cases, these rights apply not just to Hong Kong residents but also to visitors and everyone else (such as illegal immigrants) who are physically present in Hong Kong. When it comes to freedom from torture, or the right to a fair trial, to name two examples, whether or not someone is living in Hong Kong should make no difference to the exercise of such fundamental rights. As the Court of Appeal noted in *Fok Chun Wa v Hospital Authority*: "[I]t is not possible to envisage circumstances in which it would be lawful to deprive a non-resident of the freedom from arbitrary detention or imprisonment".[29]

That is not true of all the other rights listed in the Hong Kong Basic Law. Immigration controls are routinely applied to visitors, and the right to freely enter Hong Kong listed in Article 31 of the Hong Kong Basic Law does not apply to non-residents. Equally, the right to social welfare listed in Article 36 of the Hong Kong Basic Law only applies to Hong Kong residents.[30] More generally, Article 41 provides that non-residents can be excluded from enjoying some of the rights listed in Chapter III of the Hong Kong Basic Law.[31] However, Chan and Lim (2011) argue persuasively that any such exclusion must

---

29. [2011] 1 HKLRD A1, [2010] HKEC 713 at para. 70. The appeal was dismissed by the Court of Final Appeal in [2012] 2 HKC 413.
30. Ibid. at para. 68, dismissing a challenge to the constitutionality of the much higher fees which the Hospital Authority charges non-resident mothers giving birth in Hong Kong.
31. However, there is no equivalent provision allowing non-residents to be excluded from enjoying the much smaller number of rights listed in other chapters in the Hong Kong Basic Law, notably the property-related rights in Articles 6 and 105(1) and the right to a fair trial and to be presumed innocent under Article 87(2).

satisfy broadly the same tests which, as we will see later in this chapter, apply to all restrictions on rights under the Hong Kong Basic Law.[32]

Perhaps the most curious human rights provision in the Hong Kong Basic Law is the only one safeguarding the rights of a particular interest group, Article 40 protects "[t]he lawful traditional rights and interests of the indigenous inhabitants of the 'New Territories'". This refers to special privileges enjoyed by descendants through a male line of those villagers living in the New Territories at the time it was occupied by Britain in 1898.[33]

It is difficult to see any legal rationale for this group being singled out for special treatment under the Hong Kong Basic Law, especially since they now constitute only a minority of the population of the New Territories. Many such "indigenous inhabitants" do not even live in the New Territories, or in Hong Kong for that matter, but sometimes return from overseas to claim their privileges.[34] The reasons for including this provision in the Hong Kong Basic Law appear to be political. Article 40 is, in effect, a reward to the Heung Yee Kuk, the powerful statutory body representing the interests of people in the New Territories,[35] for being among the earliest supporters of Hong Kong's return to China.[36]

By far the biggest problem with Article 40 is that it makes no attempt to define the scope of the "traditional rights and interests" which it seeks to protect. Some are relatively uncontentious, with indigenous inhabitants long recognized as enjoying the traditional custom of being buried near their village, as well as certain exemptions from rates and government rent.[37]

---

32. Chan and Lim, "Interpreting Constitutional Rights and Permissible Restrictions" (see note 3) at 472.
33. Under Section 2 of the Government Rent (Assessment and Collection) Ordinance (Cap. 515), an indigenous inhabitant is defined as "a person who was in 1898 a resident of an established village in Hong Kong or who is descended through the male line from that person".
34. Because indigenous inhabitants are defined in terms of who their ancestors are, rather than where they live, there is no need for an indigenous inhabitant ever to have lived in the New Territories at all. In *Secretary for Justice v Chan Wah* (2000) 3 HKCFAR 459, 463, the Court of Final Appeal noted that only a minority of the indigenous inhabitants linked to one of the two villages in the case still lived in that village.
35. The Heung Yee Kuk was incorporated as a statutory body under the Heung Yee Kuk Ordinance (Cap. 1097), Section 9 of which gives the organization the function of representing all "the people of the New Territories". However, in practice, the bulk of its membership consists of indigenous inhabitants, even though they now constitute only a minority of the total population of the New Territories.
36. See Johannes Chan, "Protection of Basic Rights" in Peter Wesley-Smith and Albert Chen (eds.), *The Basic Law and Hong Kong's Future* (Butterworths, 1988) at 217.
37. The exemption from government rent, or any increase in rent in the case of certain property held by an indigenous inhabitant since 30 June 1984, is specifically mentioned in Article 122 of the Hong Kong Basic Law. For a full list of the traditional rights and interests that may fall within the scope of Article 40, see Johannes Chan, "Rights of New Territories Indigenous Inhabitants" in Chan and Lim (eds.), *Law of the Hong Kong Constitution* (see note 3) at 889–891.

Far more controversial is what many consider the most valuable of these traditional rights, known as the Small House Policy. This allows every male indigenous inhabitant aged 18 or above one concessionary grant of land to build a small house in the village where his male ancestors originally lived.[38] In recent years, this has led to rapid development of many villages in the New Territories, with resulting environmental and other social problems.[39]

It is far from clear whether the Small House Policy does fall within a proper legal definition of the traditional rights and interests protected under Article 40, especially in respect of more recent aspects of the policy which only date back a few decades.[40] Chan (2011) argues persuasively that any right under Article 40 only extends to allowing an indigenous inhabitant to build a small house on his own land without any need to pay the normal land premium to the government,[41] and not to the far more common practice of such indigenous inhabitants obtaining a plot of land from the government on concessionary terms.[42]

In recent years, there have been increasing concerns that the Small House Policy has become unsustainable, since some estimates put the number of indigenous inhabitants entitled to such concessionary land grants at up to 240,000.[43] But rather than challenge whether the policy is really protected under Article 40, the Hong Kong SAR Government has instead floated the idea of curtailing it in future on the grounds that the rights granted under the Hong Kong Basic Law are not necessarily guaranteed beyond 30 June 2047.[44]

---

38. Ibid. at 891–895 for a more detailed description of the Small House Policy.
39. For an excellent description of these problems, see Lisa Hopkinson and Mandy Lao Man Lei, *Rethinking the Small House Policy* (Civic Exchange, 2003) at 14–27.
40. The Hong Kong Government has previously expressed uncertainty over whether or not the Small House Policy is covered by Article 40 of the Hong Kong Basic Law, and said this is a matter for the courts to decide. See Hopkinson and Lao, *Rethinking the Small House Policy* (see note 39 above) at 30–32. In *Secretary for Justice v Chan Wah* (2000) 3 HKCFAR 459, 477, the Court of Final Appeal described the Small House Policy as falling within the scope of Article 40. However, since this case involved the unrelated issue of electoral rights in New Territories' villages (see further note 400 in Chapter 6 and the accompanying text, on the impact of this case), Chan (2011) argues that these remarks were *obiter* that is not binding in future cases. See Chan, "Rights of New Territories Indigenous Inhabitants" (see note 37) at 889.
41. Chan (2011) at 894–895. Now known as the Free Building Licence, the origins of this policy can be traced back to before Britain's conquest of the New Territories in 1898, when landowners in this area were allowed to build on their farms without any restrictions.
42. Ibid. at 896–900. Known as a Private Treaty Grant, and allowing each indigenous inhabitant to apply to the government for one plot of land at two-thirds of the normal market value, this policy only came into existence in the 1970s, to replace a system of village auctions which had existed since the 1950s. As a result, Chan (2011) argues it is too recent to qualify as one of the "traditional rights and interests" protected under Article 40.
43. Ambrose Leung, "Village poll electors expected to double", *South China Morning Post*, 12 Feb 2003.
44. See further note 41 in Chapter 9 and the accompanying text.

8.1 ICCPR and Bill of Rights

In addition to the long list of rights which, as we saw in the last section, are directly mentioned in various articles of the Hong Kong Basic Law, Chapter III contains another extremely important provision. In perhaps the most important rights-related provision in the entire document, Article 39 supplements these rights directly mentioned in the Hong Kong Basic Law by adding in most of the contents of several international human rights treaties.

These include what are often considered two of the world's most important international human rights treaties: the International Covenant on Civil and Political Rights (ICCPR) and the International Covenant on Economic, Social and Cultural Rights (ICESCR), both adopted by the United Nations General Assembly in 1966. Together with the more general principles stated in the Universal Declaration of Human Rights, adopted by the United Nations almost 20 years earlier, these three documents are often referred to as an International Bill of Rights—setting out basic standards of civil liberties that should be followed in countries around the world.

The ICCPR protects a wide range of basic freedoms including the rights to life, liberty, equality, privacy, peaceful assembly, freedom of association, movement, to marry, found a family, vote and participate in public affairs. Also protected are freedom from slavery, inhuman or degrading treatment or punishment, arbitrary arrest or detention and imprisonment due to debt, as well as freedom of thought, conscience, religion, opinion and expression. The rights of children and members of religious, ethnic and linguistic minorities are specifically safeguarded.[45]

The ICESCR supplements this with a further long list of rights. These include the right to work for fair wages in safe and healthy working conditions, form and join trade unions, strike, receive social security, education, an adequate standard of living including food, clothing and housing, to be free from hunger and take part in cultural life. It specifically states that all these rights should be equally enjoyed by both men and women.[46] However, the rights listed in the ICESCR are worded in more general terms than those in the ICCPR, raising questions about whether they should be seen as enforceable rights or simply "aspirations" which countries should aim to achieve at some point in the future.[47]

Britain, which played an important role in helping draft the two international covenants, signed and ratified both documents almost as soon as they came into force in 1976. That meant most parts of both the ICCPR and ICESCR immediately applied not only in Britain but also in all its colonies around the world,[48] including Hong Kong. In common

---

45. For the full text, see International Covenant on Civil and Political Rights 1966, 999 United Nations Treaty Series 171.
46. For the full text, see International Covenant on Economic, Social and Cultural Rights 1966, 993 United Nations Treaty Series 3.
47. See further notes 67–68 later in this chapter and the accompanying text.
48. Unlike some other international treaties, it was not possible for Britain entirely to exclude the application of the ICCPR in any of the colonies under its jurisdiction. See Article 2(1), which states that the rights under the ICCPR apply "to all individuals within its territory *and subject to its jurisdiction*" (emphasis added).

with many other countries, Britain did enter "reservations" (or exceptions) preventing a few parts of these two covenants from applying in full. In relation to Hong Kong, these included exceptions in relation to immigration legislation[49] and, in a sign of how different attitudes were towards gender equality in those days, another in relation to equal pay for men and women in the private sector.[50] By far the most significant reservation was a stipulation that there is no requirement for "the establishment of an elected Executive or Legislative Council in Hong Kong". The precise meaning of this reservation is still hotly debated today, and may have important implications for what form universal suffrage takes in future elections for all seats in the Legislative Council.[51]

With the exception of the small number of provisions covered by these reservations, from 1976 onwards both the ICCPR and ICESCR were part of the framework of human rights protection that applied to Hong Kong. This meant that when China promised in the Joint Declaration, the 1984 agreement on the terms of Hong Kong's return to China,[52] that existing rights and freedoms would continue to be protected in Hong Kong after 1 July 1997, one part of such continuity in human rights protection was a promise that the provisions of the ICCPR and ICESCR "as applied to Hong Kong shall remain in force".[53]

That guarantee was then written into Article 39(1) of the Hong Kong Basic Law, with the addition of more than 40 international labour conventions which also applied to Hong Kong during British rule.[54] These treaties—which, unlike the ICCPR and ICESCR, are not specifically mentioned by name in the Hong Kong Basic Law—protect a wide range of workers' rights, including the right to form and join trade unions and engage in collective (or joint) bargaining with employers.[55]

---

49. These limited the right to freedom of movement (contained in Article 12 of the ICCPR) where this was necessary to comply with immigration legislation, and specifically excluded immigrants in Hong Kong from the right to appeal against deportation (under Article 13 of the ICCPR).
50. This reservation stated that Britain reserved "the right to postpone the application" of Article 7(a)(i) of the ICESCR in a number of territories, including Hong Kong, "in so far as it concerns the provision of equal pay to men and women for equal work in the private sector". This was subsequently rendered largely irrelevant in Hong Kong by the enactment of the Sex Discrimination Ordinance (Cap. 480) in 1995. However, the reservation officially remained in force in Hong Kong until China abandoned it upon ratifying the ICESCR in 2001.
51. For more on the argument over the different possible meanings of this reservation, see further notes 264–265 in Chapter 5 and the accompanying text.
52. See further "2.2: Sino-British Joint Declaration" in Chapter 2.
53. Annex I(XIII).
54. For more on these treaties, see Yash Ghai, *Hong Kong's New Constitutional Order: The Resumption of Chinese Sovereignty and the Basic Law* (Hong Kong University Press, 2nd edition, 1999) at 412–414.
55. However, Hong Kong has not had any laws giving workers a right to collective bargaining, since a private members' bill providing for this was repealed in 1997. See further Po Jen Yap, "Freedom of Assembly and Association" in Chan and Lim (eds.), *Law of the Hong Kong Constitution* (see note 3) at 707–708.

The use of the term "as applied to Hong Kong" in both the Joint Declaration and the Hong Kong Basic Law made clear that the principle of continuity in human rights protection only required that these international treaties would continue to apply in Hong Kong to the same extent after 1 July 1997 as they did before that date.[56] This meant that the "reservations" which Britain had used to prevent a small number of provisions from applying to Hong Kong in full during colonial rule, such as the stipulation that there is no requirement for the establishment of an elected Executive or Legislative Council in Hong Kong, would continue to prevent those provisions from applying in full after 1 July 1997.

To the disappointment of some in Hong Kong,[57] China refused to write the text of the ICCPR and ICESCR directly into the Hong Kong Basic Law, arguing this was "unnecessary" and would make the Hong Kong Basic Law "too long and cumbersome".[58] However, in a concession which would prove to have far-reaching implications, the drafters of the Hong Kong Basic Law did agree to add one additional clause to the wording of Article 39(1), which went further than what had been originally promised in the Joint Declaration. This additional clause stated that, as well as remaining in force beyond 1 July 1997, the provisions of the ICCPR, ICESCR and international labour conventions as applied to Hong Kong "shall be implemented through the laws of the Hong Kong Special Administrative Region".[59]

Despite this addition of what would prove to be a crucial clause to the wording of Article 39(1), China made clear that it expected to see a continuation after 1 July 1997 of the longstanding situation under which most parts of the ICCPR and ICESCR were not directly implemented through Hong Kong law.[60] For all their importance, it has long been the position in the common law world that international treaties do not confer rights capable of being enforced in the courts unless and until they are implemented (or incorporated) into local law.[61] In Hong Kong, this fundamental principle has been recognized by the courts for more than 100 years.[62]

---

56. See *Ubamaka Edward Wilson v Secretary for Security* [2013] 2 HKC 75, 96–101 where the Court of Final Appeal rejected the argument that a narrower meaning should be given to the term "as applied to Hong Kong" in a case involving a reservation to the ICCPR relating to immigration legislation (see note 49).
57. See, for example, Albert Chen, "A Disappointing Draft of Hong Kong's Bill of Rights" (1987) 17 *HKLJ* 133–136.
58. Simon F.S. Li, "Some Thoughts on Rights Under the Basic Law" cited in Jayawickrama, "The Bill of Rights" (see note 6) at 66.
59. This wording did not appear in the first two drafts of Chapter III produced by the drafting committee's sub-group on Fundamental Rights and Duties of the Residents. After lobbying from Hong Kong, it was added to the third draft produced by the sub-group in August 1987. See Chan, "Protection of Basic Rights" (see note 36) at 198 and 219.
60. See, for example, Wang Shuwen, *Introduction to the Basic Law of the Hong Kong Special Administrative Region* (Law Press, 2nd English edition, 2009) at 335–336.

This meant that, although most parts of both the ICCPR and ICESCR had applied to Hong Kong as international treaties since 1976 that did not make the rights listed in these two covenants enforceable in the Hong Kong courts. As a result, for the first 15 years that they applied to Hong Kong, the two covenants had only a minimal impact on Hong Kong's legal system.[63] In the absence of any rights enforceable in the courts, the only legal obligation that these covenants initially imposed was a requirement that Britain, as with all parties to the ICCPR and ICESCR, make regular reports on the human rights situation to the appropriate UN monitoring body.[64] Arguing that it was not then a party to either of these covenants, China was initially reluctant to take over these reporting obligations from Britain after 1 July 1997, although it ultimately agreed to do so.[65]

---

61. This is often called the "transformation theory" and can be seen as one aspect of the separation of powers between the executive and legislature. Since it is the executive branch of government which ratifies international treaties, it is necessary for the legislature to transform the contents of such treaties into local law before they can affect individual rights. See Chan and Lim, "Interpreting Constitutional Rights and Permissible Restrictions" (see note 3) at 468. One example of the transformation theory is the Joint Declaration, the contents of which did not become enforceable at law until they were largely replicated in the Hong Kong Basic Law.
62. See the case of *Status of the French Mail Streamers*, The Daily Press, 12 Jan 1880, cited by Roda Mushkat, *One Country Two International Legal Personalities: The Case of Hong Kong* (Hong Kong University Press, 1997) at 171–172. See also the more recent case of *Tang Ping-hoi v Attorney General* [1987] HKLR 324, 326–328 (discussed further in note 32 in Chapter 2 and the accompanying text) rejecting an application to enforce a provision in the Joint Declaration.
63. However, that does not mean they were of no legal significance at all. While the contents of an international treaty cannot be directly enforced at law, the courts will try, where possible, to interpret any laws in a way compatible with an applicable treaty. In addition, where the law is unclear on a particular point, the court may use a treaty to help decide the case. See, for example, *Yin Xiang Jiang v Director of Immigration* [1994] 2 HKLR 101, 106 and Chan and Lim, "Interpreting Constitutional Rights and Permissible Restrictions" (see note 3) at 468–469.
64. This is the UN Human Rights Committee in the case of the ICCPR (see Articles 28 and 40) and UN Committee on Economic, Social and Cultural Rights in the case of the ICESCR (see Article 16). Britain chose not to ratify an Optional Protocol to the International Covenant on Civil and Political Rights 1966, 999 United Nations Treaty Series 302, which would have allowed Hong Kong residents to raise complaints about violations of rights protected under the ICCPR directly with the UN Human Rights Committee.
65. In December 1997, China notified the UN Secretary General that it was willing to submit reports on the implementation of the ICCPR and ICESCR in Hong Kong. China subsequently ratified the ICESCR in 2001. This means the ICESCR now applies not just in Hong Kong but also the rest of China, and the Chinese Government is directly bound by the reporting obligations in Article 16. However, this is not yet true of the ICCPR. Although China took the initial step of signing the ICCPR in 1998, it has not yet taken the essential follow-up action of ratifying the covenant, without which it cannot be brought into force in the rest of China.

Since neither the ICCPR nor the ICESCR had been incorporated into Hong Kong law at the time of both the negotiations that led to the Joint Declaration or throughout most of the drafting of the Hong Kong Basic Law, it seems China believed that the requirement to submit reports to the relevant UN bodies was the only legal obligation which would arise from allowing most parts of these two international covenants to remain in force in Hong Kong beyond 1 July 1997. Shiu (2001) argues: "That was the understanding which the Chinese Government agreed to as part of the Joint Declaration, and is reflected in Article 39 of the Basic Law."[66]

When it comes to the ICESCR, that remains the position in Hong Kong today. Since this covenant has never been incorporated into Hong Kong law, the rights listed in the ICESCR remain largely unenforceable in the Hong Kong courts. The courts have held that the very general wording used in the ICESCR—which includes many rights, such as an adequate standard of living, that are difficult to define precisely—makes its provisions incapable of being enforced at law.[67] In a series of judgments, the courts have instead described the rights listed in the ICESCR as "aspirational" or "promotional" in nature, and stated that they do not create any "absolute obligations",[68] although this is strongly disputed by the relevant UN monitoring body.[69]

However, to China's fury, the position in respect of the ICCPR was fundamentally changed by the enactment of the Hong Kong Bill of Rights Ordinance (Cap. 383) in June 1991. As originally enacted, this law stated twice—both in its long title and in Section 2(3) of the ordinance—that its purpose "is to provide for the incorporation into the law of Hong Kong of provisions of the International Covenant on Civil and Political Rights as applied to Hong Kong". Just as was the case with the Joint Declaration and Article 39(1) of the Hong Kong Basic Law, the use of the term "as applied to Hong Kong" meant an exception was made for the small number of provisions in the ICCPR about which Britain had originally entered reservations to prevent them from applying to Hong Kong in full.[70]

---

66. Shiu Sin-por, "Judicial activism creates court chaos", *South China Morning Post*, 20 Feb 2001. See also Wu Jianfan, "The Bill of Rights: China responds to criticism of PWC's legal proposals", *Window*, 10 Nov 1995.
67. See, in particular, the reference in Article 2(1) to "achieving progressively the full realization of the rights" listed in the ICESCR. In *Chan To Foon v Director of Immigration* [2001] 3 HKLRD 109, 132, the Court of First Instance interpreted this as meaning that rights listed in the ICESCR only need to be implemented as and when any "existing social difficulties" are overcome.
68. Ibid. at 132–134. See also *Chan Mei Yee v Director of Immigration* (unrep., HCAL 77 and 99/1999, [2000] HKEC 788) at para. 46, and *Mok Chi Hung v Director of Immigration* [2001] 2 HKLRD 125, 135.
69. See the UN Committee on Economic, Social and Cultural Rights, *Concluding Observations on the Initial Report of the Hong Kong Special Administrative Region* (11 May 2001) at paras. 16 and 27.
70. These reservations are listed in Sections 9–13 in Part III of the ordinance.

Apart from that small number of reservations, the wording of Part II of the ordinance, which is called "The Hong Kong Bill of Rights", and contains the list of rights incorporated into Hong Kong law, is almost a carbon copy of the rights listed in the ICCPR. In most cases,[71] the main difference between the list of rights in the two documents is the numbering system used for the various rights.[72] That was why the enactment of the Hong Kong Bill of Rights Ordinance marked such a revolution in human rights protection in Hong Kong, since it meant that most of the wide range of rights listed in the ICCPR, which had applied as a largely unenforceable international treaty since 1976, became part of Hong Kong law from 1991 onwards, so making those rights enforceable in the courts for the first time.

The impact of the Hong Kong Bill of Rights Ordinance was slightly lessened by a provision[73] added to the final draft of the law in response to pressure from the business community, stating the ordinance only applies to the government, public authorities[74] and those acting on their behalf.[75] This means that the rights listed in the ICCPR still cannot be directly enforced in the courts in disputes between private citizens.[76] But simply making the rights listed in the ICCPR enforceable in cases involving the government and public authorities was more than enough to have a significant impact on Hong Kong's legal system. Chan (1996) counts nearly 250 court cases involving the Bill of Rights

---

71. There are a very few exceptions, where the Hong Kong Bill of Rights uses slightly different wording from the ICCPR. See Dinusha Panditaratne, "Basic Law, Hong Kong Bill of Rights and the ICCPR" in Chan and Lim (eds.), *Law of the Hong Kong Constitution* (see note 3) at 432–433.
72. For example, Article 19 of the ICCPR on freedom of opinion and expression becomes Article 16 of the Bill of Rights, while Article 21 of the ICCPR on the right of peaceful assembly becomes Article 17 of the Bill of Rights.
73. Section 7.
74. This includes many bodies exercising functions similar to government. In *Hong Kong Polytechnic University v Next Magazine Ltd* [1997] HKLRD 102, 106, Justice Keith gave the example of bodies which are brought into the "public domain" through either being funded by the government in some form, or subject to government monitoring or control, or some other form of public accountability.
75. This restriction did not appear in the original draft of the ordinance. For more on the pressure that led to its introduction see Andrew Byrnes, "And Some Have Bills of Rights Thrust Upon Them: The Experience of Hong Kong's Bill of Rights" in Philip Alston (ed.), *Promoting Human Rights Through Bills of Rights: Comparative Perspectives* (Oxford University Press, 1999) at 341.
76. As shown by the case of *Tam Hing Yee v Wu Tai Wai* [1992] 1 HKLR 185, 189 where the court held that an order banning a debtor from leaving Hong Kong was not inconsistent with the freedom of movement protected under Article 8 of the Hong Kong Bill of Rights since it had been imposed at the request of his creditor, and so amounted to a dispute between private citizens. The Bill of Rights was amended to reverse the effects of this decision and explicitly state that it did cover disputes between private citizens, by a private members' bill passed shortly before 1 July 1997. However, this amendment was almost immediately suspended, and subsequently repealed, by the Provisional Legislature, when it began meeting in Hong Kong after that date.

during the first four years after it came into force.[77] The Bill of Rights was one of the major reasons behind the surge in the number of judicial review cases in the 1990s,[78] as litigants used the new ordinance to challenge a wide variety of rights' infringements.

The extent of this revolution was highlighted in *R v Sin Yau Ming*,[79] the first case involving the ordinance to reach the Court of Appeal, where the Bill of Rights was described as ushering in an "entirely new jurisprudential approach" in which the contents of the ICCPR were now superior to laws enacted by the Hong Kong legislature.[80] That was not primarily because of what was stated in the Bill of Rights itself. Although Section 3 of the ordinance originally provided that all laws enacted before the Bill of Rights are repealed if they are inconsistent with it, that provision simply reflected the long standing common law principle that the courts in Hong Kong and elsewhere have traditionally applied in relation to other laws, in holding that a new law will normally prevail over an earlier inconsistent law.[81]

Instead, the superiority that the Bill of Rights enjoys over other laws comes from what is known as "constitutional entrenchment". This means that the contents of the Bill of Rights are entrenched (or protected) by being referred to in a constitutional document that has a superior status to other laws. Prior to 1 July 1997, this was the Hong Kong Letters Patent, the main constitutional document throughout most of the colonial era. Until the enactment of the Bill of Rights, this document had been devoid of any provisions protecting civil liberties.[82] But that radically changed in 1991 when, to accompany the enactment of the Bill of Rights, Article VII of the Letters Patent was amended to give the contents of this ordinance a superior status to any other inconsistent legislation which might be enacted at a later date — so, in effect, reversing the usual common law principle that a new law will normally prevail over an earlier inconsistent law.

---

77. Johannes Chan, "The Hong Kong Bill of Rights 1991–1995: A Statistical Overview" in George Edwards and Johannes Chan, *Hong Kong's Bill of Rights: Two Years Before 1997* (Faculty of Law, University of Hong Kong, 1996) at 8–19.
78. See the figures cited in note 137 in Chapter 6.
79. [1992] 1 HKCLR 127. The case involved a number of presumptions in the Dangerous Drugs Ordinance (Cap. 134) that the court found inconsistent with the right to a presumption of innocence protected under Article 11(1) of the Hong Kong Bill of Rights. For an account of the most significant aspects of this case, see Richard Swede "One Territory — Three Systems? The Hong Kong Bill of Rights" (1995) 44 *International & Comparative Law Quarterly* 358, 363–367.
80. *Sin Yau Ming* at 141. However, some subsequent cases showed less judicial enthusiasm for the Bill of Rights, in particular the Privy Council appeal in *Attorney General of Hong Kong v Lee Kwong Kut* (1993) 3 HKPLR 72 which saw Lord Woolf warn (at 100) that "issues involving the Hong Kong Bill should be approached with realism and good sense, and kept in proportion". For more on the caution, and even hostility of some judges towards the Bill of Rights, see further note 139 in Chapter 6.
81. This is known at common law as the doctrine of "implied repeal", under which a newer law is normally implied to have repealed any inconsistent provisions in earlier laws even if it does not specifically refer to that earlier law. See *L v C* [1994] 2 HKLR 92, 99 for an example of the use of the doctrine of implied repeal by the Hong Kong courts.
82. See further note 2 earlier in this chapter.

Referring to the ICCPR, this 1991 addition of a new Article VII(5) to the Letters Patent specifically stated that "[n]o law of Hong Kong shall be made after" this amendment "that restricts the rights and freedoms enjoyed in Hong Kong in a manner which is inconsistent with that Covenant as applied to Hong Kong". Within a year, the High Court had confirmed this meant that a 1992 law enacted after the Bill of Rights was invalid because it infringed one of the rights protected by the Bill of Rights, and so infringed this new provision in the Letters Patent invalidating any law inconsistent with the ICCPR as applied to Hong Kong.[83]

The result was that the Bill of Rights had a major impact on Hong Kong's laws. By 1997, 38 laws had been amended to comply with the ordinance.[84] These included major changes to the Public Order Ordinance (Cap. 245) and Societies Ordinance (Cap. 151), two laws which had previously imposed significant restrictions on freedom of assembly and association in Hong Kong.[85] In both cases, requirements to seek police approval before holding a public protest or registering an organization were swept away, and replaced with milder provisions simply requiring that the police be notified in advance.[86]

China strongly objected to these amendments,[87] which only reinforced its suspicion of the Bill of Rights. Mainland drafters of the Hong Kong Basic Law complained bitterly that when China agreed in both the Joint Declaration and the Hong Kong Basic Law to allow most parts of the ICCPR to remain in force beyond 1 July 1997, all they agreed to was the situation which existed throughout most of the period during which these two documents were being written—when the covenant only applied to Hong Kong as a largely unenforceable international treaty rather than a law enforceable in the courts.[88]

---

83. *R v Lum Wai Ming* [1992] 2 HKCLR 221, 228. Ironically, this law, the Dangerous Drugs (Amendment) (No. 2) Ordinance (No. 52 of 1992), had been enacted to replace some of the provisions in the Dangerous Drugs Ordinance (Cap. 134) which were declared inconsistent with the Bill of Rights in *Sin Yau Ming*. See further note 79.
84. Chief Executive's Office, *Civil Liberties and Social Order: Consultation Document* (April 1997) at 5.
85. See further note 5 earlier in this chapter and the accompanying text. For a detailed account of the significant restrictions that the Public Order Ordinance imposed on freedom of assembly before the enactment of the Bill of Rights, see Roda Mushkat, "Peaceful Assembly" in Wacks (ed.), *Human Rights in Hong Kong* (see note 6) at 410–438.
86. See the Public Order (Amendment) Ordinance (No. 77 of 1995) and the Societies (Amendment) Ordinance (No. 75 of 1992). Although prior police approval was no longer required after these amendments to the two ordinances, both laws still allowed the government to respond to such notification by banning a particular protest or organization under certain limited circumstances.
87. See, for instance, the "Statement of the Legal Sub-Group of the Preliminary Working Committee Concerning the Bill of Rights Ordinance" (17 Oct 1995), reproduced in Andrew Byrnes and Johannes Chan (1995) *Bill of Rights Bulletin* 3(4) at Appendix A, which complains that "these major amendments will weaken the administration of Hong Kong and are not conducive to the stability of Hong Kong".
88. See Wu, "The Bill of Rights" (see note 66).

As far as China was concerned, Britain had tricked them by changing the way the ICCPR was implemented in Hong Kong after the process of writing the Hong Kong Basic Law had been almost completed.[89]

Nonetheless, since China had already agreed in Article 39(1) of the Hong Kong Basic Law to allow most parts of the ICCPR to remain in force in Hong Kong beyond 1 July 1997, it was difficult entirely to reject a law which largely replicated the contents of that treaty. To do this might even have been in breach of the clause in Article 39(1) stating that the ICCPR as applied in Hong Kong, "shall be implemented through the laws of the Hong Kong Special Administrative Region"—which is precisely what the Bill of Rights does.[90]

As a result, instead of abolishing the Bill of Rights, China reluctantly concluded that most parts of the ordinance should be allowed to remain in force beyond 1 July 1997.[91] Article 160(1) of the Hong Kong Basic Law unequivocally gives the National People's Congress Standing Committee the power to declare any law that existed in Hong Kong prior to 1 July 1997 inconsistent with the Hong Kong Basic Law, either in whole or in part. The effect of such a declaration is that all of the law, or the relevant parts, depending on the nature of the Standing Committee's declaration in relation to that particular law, cease to have any legal effect after that date.

The Standing Committee did not hesitate to invoke this power to invalidate other laws that China disliked. In early 1997, it declared 24 laws either wholly or partly inconsistent with the Hong Kong Basic Law, and of no legal effect after 1 July 1997.[92] These included all the laws used to implement the 1995 elections to the Legislative Council, which had been the subject of a furious political dispute between Britain and China.[93] Also invalidated were the amendments to the Public Order Ordinance (Cap. 245) and Societies Ordinance (Cap. 151) easing restrictions on freedom of assembly and association which China so disliked. These were replaced by fresh amendments to both laws,

---

89. The first draft of the Hong Kong Bill of Rights Ordinance was published by the Hong Kong Government in March 1990, only a few weeks before the final draft of the Hong Kong Basic Law was enacted by the NPC on 4 April 1990.
90. This clause, which went further than what had been promised in the Joint Declaration, was added during the drafting process. See note 59 earlier in this chapter and the accompanying text.
91. See further Shao Tianren, "Legal vacuum fears", *Window*, 10 Nov 1995, in which this influential mainland drafter of the Hong Kong Basic Law argues that it is necessary to take a "restrained" approach towards the Bill of Rights "taking into account that the relevant ordinance has been in existence for some length of time".
92. Annexes 1 and 2 of Decision of the Standing Committee of the NPC on Treatment of the Laws Previously in Force in Hong Kong in Accordance With Article 160 of the Basic Law of the Hong Kong SAR of the PRC (23 Feb 1997). See further note 112 in Chapter 2 and the accompanying text.
93. For more on the background to this dispute, see further "2.5: Sino-British Disputes" in Chapter 2.

which essentially reintroduced the earlier requirement to seek police approval before holding a public protest or registering an organization.[94]

But when it came to the Hong Kong Bill of Rights Ordinance (Cap. 383), the Standing Committee adopted a more cautious approach. No changes were made to list of rights that had been copied from the ICCPR into Part II of the ordinance. This means that all the rights protected under the Bill of Rights continued as part of the laws of Hong Kong after 1 July 1997, and the list of rights protected under the Bill of Rights remains the same today as it was when the ordinance was first enacted in 1991.

Instead, the Standing Committee confined itself to declaring three specific provisions in Part I of the ordinance inconsistent with the Hong Kong Basic Law, and of no legal effect after that date.[95] These were the three provisions—Sections 2(3), 3 and 4—which China claimed gave the ordinance a superior status over other laws.[96] But such claims were based on a fundamental misunderstanding of how Hong Kong's legal system works. As we have already seen,[97] Section 3 simply repeated the long-established common law position that new laws normally prevail over any earlier inconsistent laws. As a result, deleting this provision from the ordinance makes no difference, because it only describes what the courts would normally do anyway, whether or not this is explicitly stated in the law. Much the same was true of the other two sections deleted from the ordinance by the Standing Committee.[98]

Chan and Lim (2011) describe the deletion of these three sections as "simply a cosmetic face-saving measure which has no effect whatsoever on the operation of the Hong Kong Bill of Rights after 1997".[99] Nor did the other change that occurred in 1997

---

94. These requirements had existed in earlier versions of both laws. See further notes 5 and 85 earlier in this chapter and the accompanying text. While the Societies (Amendment) Ordinance (No. 118 of 1997) explicitly reintroduced the requirement to seek police approval when registering an organization, the Public Order (Amendment) Ordinance (No. 119 of 1997) nominally preserved the pre-1997 situation under which protest organizers were only required to notify police. However, they were now also required to obtain a "Certificate of No Objection" from police, so essentially requiring police approval. Chan (2002) describes this as a "disguised licensing system" in "Civil Liberties, Rule of Law and Human Rights" (see note 5) at 100.
95. See Annex 2 of Decision of the Standing Committee of the NPC on Treatment of the Laws Previously in Force in Hong Kong (see note 92).
96. See Shao, "Legal Vacuum Fears" (see note 91), who argues that, "[t]hese sections have virtually guaranteed the ordinance a superior status".
97. See note 81 earlier in this chapter and the accompanying text.
98. As previously noted (see page 274), Section 2(3) only repeats what is already stated in the long title, which remains part of the ordinance. Section 4, which requires the courts to try and interpret new legislation in a manner consistent with the ICCPR as applied to Hong Kong, also only describes the general principle noted earlier (see note 63) that, wherever possible, the courts will normally try to interpret legislation in a manner consistent with any applicable international treaties. See further Peter Wesley-Smith, "Maintenance of the Bill of Rights" (1997) 27 *HKLJ* 15–16.
99. Chan and Lim, "Interpreting Constitutional Rights and Permissible Restrictions" (see note 3) at 470.

have any effect on the status of the Bill of Rights. This was the ending of the constitutional protection that the ordinance had, until then, enjoyed under Article VII(5) of the Hong Kong Letters Patent, which—together with all other parts of the colonial constitution—ceased to have any legal effect in Hong Kong after that date.

Had this constitutional protection from the Letters Patent not been replaced by anything else, this could have seriously diminished the effectiveness of the Bill of Rights. Those same common law principles which allow the Bill of Rights to prevail over earlier laws also mean that—unless protected by a higher law—it must give way to any later inconsistent laws. That, in turn, would have meant that the rights protected in the Bill of Rights would have offered little protection against any new laws restricting those rights.

Once again, the clause in Article 39(1) of the Hong Kong Basic Law stating that the ICCPR as applied in Hong Kong "shall be implemented through the laws of the Hong Kong Special Administrative Region" came to the rescue of the Bill of Rights. That precise wording had been copied into the constitutional protection which the Bill of Rights enjoyed up until 1 July 1997 under Article VII(5) of the Letters Patent,[100] with the aim of mimicking the wording of the Hong Kong Basic Law.[101]

Byrnes (1999) explains that Britain's plan was that if the courts used this wording in the Letters Patent to protect the contents of the Bill of Rights prior to 1 July 1997, it could set a precedent for the courts to use the same wording in Article 39(1) of the Hong Kong Basic Law to continue to protect the contents of the Bill of Rights after that date.[102] Against expectations,[103] the plan worked with the courts concluding that the Bill of Rights continued to enjoy the same constitutional protection after 1 July 1997, with the only difference being that this was now provided by Article 39(1) of the Hong Kong Basic Law instead of by Article VII(5) of the Letters Patent.[104] In one early case, the Court of First Instance even referred to a "seamless transition" in the legal status of the Bill of Rights across 1997.[105]

That is unlikely to have been the intention of the drafters of the Hong Kong Basic Law, given that the Bill of Rights did not exist throughout most of the drafting of that document, and China's subsequent hostility towards the ordinance. Shiu (2001) complains

---

100. The first sentence of Article VII(5) of the Hong Kong Letters Patent 1917–1995 stated that: "*The provisions of the International Covenant on Civil and Political Rights,* adopted by the General Assembly of the United Nations on 16 December 1966, *as applied to Hong Kong, shall be implemented through the laws of Hong Kong*" (emphasis added, to highlight the words which are identical to those used in Article 39(1) of the Hong Kong Basic Law).
101. Byrnes (1999) notes that the wording of the amendment to the Letters Patent "was modelled closely on Article 39 of the Basic Law". See "And Some Have Bills of Rights Thrust Upon Them" (see note 75) at 335.
102. Ibid.
103. Ibid., where Byrnes express doubts "whether Article 39 of the Basic Law will bear this load".
104. See, for instance, *Swire Properties Ltd v Secretary for Justice* (2003) 6 HKCFAR 236, 258 where Justice Bokhary stated that the "Bill of Rights is entrenched by Article 39 of our constitution the Basic Law".
105. *Yau Kwong Man v Secretary for Security* [2002] 3 HKC 457, 492.

that the "Hong Kong courts misuse Article 39" by using it to protect the contents of the Bill of Rights.[106]

But, as we saw in the last chapter, the courts place their primary emphasis on the wording of any clear provisions in the Hong Kong Basic Law, rather than any statements of intent by the drafters, in deciding how those provisions should be interpreted.[107] Long before 1997, the courts had already concluded that, unless and until it was amended, the clear meaning of the wording of Article 39(1) of the Hong Kong Basic Law afforded constitutional protection to the Bill of Rights.[108]

Any such amendment seems improbable, especially given the procedural restrictions in Article 159 that make it extremely difficult to amend the Hong Kong Basic Law. Instead, when the Hong Kong SAR and Chinese Governments have considered it necessary to change the way in which a particular provision in the Hong Kong Basic Law is applied, this has usually been accomplished by asking the National People's Congress Standing Committee to issue a fresh interpretation of the relevant provision.[109] Such an interpretation then becomes binding on the Hong Kong courts, regardless of their own interpretation of the relevant provision in the Hong Kong Basic Law.[110]

Such a step could, if China so desired, be used to force the courts to adopt a different interpretation of Article 39 that no longer affords any special status to the Bill of Rights. This is strongly advocated by Shiu (2001), who claims that Article 39 "is crying out for an interpretation from the National People's Congress Standing Committee".[111] But an interpretation by the Standing Committee of the provision that lies at the heart of the human rights protections in the Hong Kong Basic Law would be bound to be extremely controversial,[112] and it is noticeable that for many years Shiu's call received virtually no support from any other quarter, including the Hong Kong SAR Government.[113]

---

106. Shiu Sin-por, "Abide by rule of law — not judges", *South China Morning Post*, 2 March 2001.
107. This was most clearly stated by the Court of Final Appeal in *Director of Immigration v Chong Fung Yuen* (2001) 4 HKCFAR 211, 213. For more on this aspect of the case, see further note 41 in Chapter 7 and the accompanying text.
108. In *R v Sin Yau Ming* [1992] 1 HKCLR 127, 154 Justice Kempster described the Bill of Rights as "entrenched" by the Hong Kong Basic Law unless "Article 39 of the Basic Law is amended after 30th June 1997".
109. Under Article 158(1) of the Hong Kong Basic Law. The exercise of this power is not subject to the same procedural restrictions that apply to amendments to the Hong Kong Basic Law. See further "7.2: Standing Committee" in Chapter 7.
110. As confirmed by the Court of Final Appeal in *Lau Kong Yung v Director of Immigration* (1999) 2 HKCFAR 300, 323. For more on this case, and criticism of the court's reasoning, see further notes 104–125 in Chapter 7 and the accompanying text.
111. Shiu, "Abide by rule of law — not judges" (see note 106).
112. See, for instance, the response to Shiu's call from Audrey Eu [in "Our judges, our law", *South China Morning Post*, 25 Feb 2001], stating: "If ever there is a sure way to destroy 'one country, two systems', this must be it."
113. See the subsequent assurances from Secretary for Justice Elsie Leung that Article 39 would always be interpreted according to common law principles (in "Letter to Hong Kong: The Chief Executive's Term of Office and the Rule of Law", *RTHK Radio 3*, 20 March 2005, at para. 13).

In the absence of such an interpretation by the Standing Committee, the courts continue to interpret the wording of Article 39(1) as giving constitutional protection to the contents of the Bill of Rights. That has led to the ordinance being invoked in several cases to invalidate parts of new laws that go too far in restricting these rights, even when these laws were enacted after 1 July 1997.[114]

As a result, the ordinance remains a very important part of the legal framework protecting human rights in Hong Kong. That means the long list of rights which originated in the ICCPR and are now incorporated into Hong Kong law through the Bill of Rights supplement those directly listed in the Hong Kong Basic Law. These include:

- Entitlement to rights without distinction of any kind, including on grounds of race, sex, language or religion, and equal enjoyment of civil and political rights by men and women (Article 1 of Bill of Rights/Articles 2(1) and 3 of ICCPR);
- Inherent right to life, with the death sentence only permitted for the most serious crimes (Article 2 of Bill of Rights/Article 6 of ICCPR);
- Freedom from torture and cruel, inhuman or degrading treatment or punishment (Article 3 of Bill of Rights/Article 7 of ICCPR);
- Freedom from slavery and servitude (Article 4 of Bill of Rights/Article 8 of ICCPR);
- The right to liberty and security of the person and freedom from arbitrary arrest. This includes the right to be informed of the reasons for an arrest, promptly brought before a judicial officer, tried within a reasonable time, and compensated for any unlawful arrest or detention (Article 5 of Bill of Rights/Article 9 of ICCPR);
- The right of all detainees to be treated with humanity and respect, including segregating juvenile detainees from adults[115] (Article 6 of Bill of Rights/Article 10 of ICCPR);
- The right not to be imprisoned for breach of a contract (Article 7 of Bill of Rights/Article 11 of ICCPR);
- Freedom of movement and to choose a residence, except where it is necessary to restrict this right for certain specified reasons (Article 8 of Bill of Rights/Article 12 of ICCPR);
- Restriction on the expulsion of those lawfully in Hong Kong, and the right to a review except in cases of national security[116] (Article 9 of Bill of Rights/Article 13 of ICCPR);

---

114. See, for example, *Leung Kwok Hung v HKSAR* (2005) 8 HKCFAR 229, 263–264 where the Court of Final Appeal cited the protection of freedom of assembly under the Bill of Rights and ICCPR in striking down one of the amendments made by the Public Order (Amendment) Ordinance (No. 119 of 1997). For more on this aspect of the case, see further note 390 in Chapter 6 and the accompanying text.
115. Except where there is a lack of suitable prison facilities, or this is considered mutually beneficial. See Section 10 of the Hong Kong Bill of Rights Ordinance (Cap. 383), implementing a reservation made by Britain when it ratified the ICCPR in 1976.
116. Or where that person does not have the right of abode in Hong Kong. See Section 12 of the Hong Kong Bill of Rights Ordinance (Cap. 383), implementing a reservation made by Britain when it ratified the ICCPR in 1976.

- Equality before the law and the right to a fair and public hearing, except where it is necessary to exclude the press and public for certain specified reasons (Article 10 of Bill of Rights/Article 14(1) of ICCPR);
- Guarantee of detailed rights for criminal defendants, including the right to be presumed innocent until proved guilty, promptly informed in detail of any charges, have adequate time to prepare a defence and communicate with a lawyer of the defendant's choosing, be present at the trial and have a lawyer assigned at public expense if the defendant cannot afford to pay for one, call witnesses and cross-examine those who testify against the accused, have the use of an interpreter if necessary, not to be compelled to testify against oneself or to confess guilt, not to be retried for an offence after being acquitted, and the right to have any conviction and sentence reviewed by a higher court (Article 11 of Bill of Rights/Article 14(2)–14(7) of ICCPR);
- The right not to be held guilty of any retrospective criminal offence, i.e., for any acts or omissions that were legal at the time they occurred but which later became criminal offences (Article 12 of Bill of Rights/Article 15(1) of ICCPR);
- The right to recognition as a person before the law (Article 13 of Bill of Rights/Article 16 of ICCPR);
- Protection of privacy, family, home, correspondence, honour and reputation (Article 14 of Bill of Rights/Article 17 of ICCPR);
- Freedom of thought, conscience and religion (Article 15 of Bill of Rights/Article 18 of ICCPR);
- Freedom of opinion and expression, except where it is necessary to restrict this right for certain specified reasons (Article 16 of Bill of Rights/Article 19 of ICCPR);
- The right of peaceful assembly, except where it is necessary to restrict this right for certain specified reasons (Article 17 of Bill of Rights/Article 21 of ICCPR);
- Freedom of association, except where it is necessary to restrict this right for certain specified reasons (Article 18 of Bill of Rights/Article 22 of ICCPR);
- The right to marry and found a family (Article 19 of Bill of Rights/Article 23 of ICCPR);
- The rights of children (Article 20 of Bill of Rights/Article 24 of ICCPR);
- The right to participate in public life without unreasonable restrictions, including voting and being elected in genuine periodic elections held by secret ballot using universal and equal suffrage,[117] and access to public service (Article 21 of Bill of Rights/Article 25 of ICCPR);

---

117. However, this does not require the establishment of an elected Executive or Legislative Council. See Section 13 of the Hong Kong Bill of Rights Ordinance (Cap. 383), implementing a reservation made by Britain when it ratified the ICCPR in 1976. The meaning of this reservation is disputed by the Hong Kong SAR Government and the UN Human Rights Committee. For more on the argument over the different possible meanings of this reservation, see further notes 264–265 in Chapter 5 and the accompanying text.

- Equality before the law and protection against discrimination on a wide range of grounds, including race, colour, sex, language and religion (Article 22 of Bill of Rights/Article 26 of ICCPR);
- The rights of ethnic, religious and linguistic minorities (Article 23 of Bill of Rights/Article 27 of ICCPR)

As can be seen from this long list, most of the rights listed in the Bill of Rights are very similar, or often identical, to those listed in various other articles of the Hong Kong Basic Law. These are what Young (2004) calls "parallel Basic Law rights",[118] and by far the most common type of rights listed in the two documents. For example, the presumption of innocence in Article 11(1) of the Bill of Rights repeats a similar statement contained in Article 87(2) of the Hong Kong Basic Law.

But the Bill of Rights and ICCPR generally provide far more detail about the precise content of these "parallel" rights than the relatively brief, and much more general, statements of the same rights in the Hong Kong Basic Law. Take, for instance, Article 11 of the Bill of Rights which contains a detailed list of the rights guaranteed to criminal defendants, many of which are not specifically mentioned in the Hong Kong Basic Law. These include such crucial rights as the right to have a lawyer assigned at public expense for those who cannot afford to pay. This, in effect, amounts to a right to legal aid in certain circumstances and led to the expansion of Hong Kong's legal aid system after the enactment of the Hong Kong Bill of Rights Ordinance (Cap. 383).[119] Note also that all the rights listed under the Bill of Rights and ICCPR can be enforced by anyone in Hong Kong, including visitors and illegal immigrants, unlike the rights listed in the Hong Kong Basic Law—some of which are restricted to Hong Kong residents. That has important implications for legal aid, with the Hong Kong Government recognizing that the Bill of Rights and ICCPR do not allow legal aid to be restricted to those resident in Hong Kong.[120] As a result, legal aid has been used to fund applicants not initially lawfully resident in Hong Kong in many court battles, including such landmark cases as *Ng Ka Ling v Director of Immigration*[121] and *Director of Immigration v Chong Fung Yuen*.[122]

In some cases, the Bill of Rights and ICCPR add further rights not mentioned in the Hong Kong Basic Law at all. These "exclusive Bill of Rights rights" include freedom from slavery, the right not to be imprisoned for breach of a contract and the right not to be held guilty of any retrospective criminal offence. Since the courts have held that Article 39(1) of the Hong Kong Basic Law protects the contents of the Bill of Rights, the effect is much the same as if they were directly mentioned in the Hong Kong Basic Law. In *Ng*

---

118. Simon N.M. Young, "Restricting Basic Law Rights in Hong Kong" (2004) 34 *HKLJ* 109, 119.
119. Legal aid in the magistrates' courts, which had previously only been available to defendants charged with six specified offences, was extended to cover more than 300 offences under the Duty Lawyer Scheme, following the enactment of the Bill of Rights Ordinance.
120. See Legal Aid Services Council, *Legal Aid in Hong Kong* (2006) at 105.
121. (1999) 2 HKCFAR 4.
122. (2001) 4 HKCFAR 211.

Ka Ling, for instance, the court struck down a provision in the Immigration Ordinance (Cap. 115) that imposed retrospective criminal punishment on some children entering Hong Kong from China without proper permission, partly on the grounds that it violated the prohibition against this in the ICCPR and Bill of Rights.[123]

Confusingly, there are also a few rights which are only mentioned in the Hong Kong Basic Law, and do not appear in the Bill of Rights or ICCPR. These "exclusive Basic Law rights" include the right to travel[124] and social welfare. The result is what Young (2004) aptly describes as "a complex legal matrix of overlapping constitutional rights both in and outside the Basic Law".[125]

But by far the most significant aspect of the more detailed description of rights in the Bill of Rights and ICCPR is that unlike most of the more general descriptions in the Hong Kong Basic Law, these more detailed description of those rights often offer more precise guidance on when it may be necessary to restrict those rights for certain specified reasons. As we will see in the next section of this chapter, it is those specific reasons, which are not listed in the Hong Kong Basic Law, that often form the most important factor in court cases determining whether or not a particular restriction on rights is constitutionally permissible in Hong Kong.

8.2 Restrictions on Rights

For all their importance, there are very few rights which are absolute and can never be restricted under any circumstances. Take, for instance, the right to life, which has been

---

123. Although these entry restrictions were only enacted into law under the Immigration (Amendment)(No. 3) Ordinance (No. 124 of 1997) on 10 July 1997, Section 1(2) of the ordinance stated that they came into effect nine days earlier—on 1 July 1997. In *Ng Ka Ling*, the Court of Final Appeal held (at 38–40) that this retrospective provision was invalid because it contravened Article 15(1) of the ICCPR. The court's decision on the issue of retrospectivity was separate from the main issue it decided in this case, in holding that the entry restrictions as a whole were invalid because they contravened the court's interpretation of Article 22(4) of the Hong Kong Basic Law (see further note 78 in Chapter 7). As a result, although a subsequent interpretation from the NPC Standing Committee effectively reversed the court's decision on the main issue in the case (see further note 89 in Chapter 7 and the accompanying text), this interpretation did not affect the court's separate decision on the retrospectivity issue. See *Lau Kong Yung v Director of Immigration* (1999) 2 HKCFAR 300, 327.
124. While Article 31 of the Hong Kong Basic Law specifically refers to "freedom to travel and to enter or leave the region", Article 8 of the Bill of Rights only refers to freedom of movement, including the right "to leave Hong Kong". See *Gurung Kesh Bahadur v Director of Immigration* (2002) 5 HKCFAR 480, 493–495 where the court held that the Immigration Department's power to prevent non-permanent Hong Kong residents returning to Hong Kong after travelling overseas violated their rights protected under Article 31 of the Hong Kong Basic Law.
125. Young, "Restricting Basic Law Rights in Hong Kong" (see note 118) at 110. See also the court's description of three different categories of rights, depending on whether they are listed in the Hong Kong Basic Law and/or the Bill of Rights in *Gurung Kesh Bahadur* at 490.

described by the UN Human Rights Committee as "the supreme right".[126] Yet even this supreme right is not absolute. Although Hong Kong has not executed anyone since 1966, and formally abolished the death penalty in 1993,[127] there is nothing in the Hong Kong Basic Law that would stop the death penalty from being reintroduced.[128] Article 28 of the Hong Kong Basic Law only forbids "arbitrary or unlawful deprivation of the life of any resident". As Hor (2011) notes, what is most striking about the wording of Article 28 is "the implicit recognition that one *can* be deprived of life, providing it is not 'unlawful' or 'arbitrary'".[129] The Bill of Rights and ICCPR make this more explicit, directly recognizing the death penalty as an exception to the right to life.[130]

The fact that exceptions exist even to this "supreme right" reflects the reality that no society can function without sometimes imposing restrictions on the rights which individual members of that society enjoy, if only to protect the rights of other members of that society. One obvious example is the law of defamation, which restricts freedom of expression but only in order to protect the rights of others, by penalizing certain false communications that harm the reputation of another person. Another is legislation allowing the government to impose restrictions on freedom of movement during times of medical emergency, in order to prevent the spread of infectious diseases that might otherwise claim large numbers of victims.[131]

Very few rights do not fall into the category of those which sometimes need to be restricted. One rare example is the right not to be tortured, a right which both the Bill of Rights and ICCPR do not permit to be restricted, even under the most extreme circumstances.[132] The same is true of freedom of thought and conscience,[133] together with a

---

126. Office of the UN High Commissioner for Human Rights, *General Comment No. 06: The Right to Life (Art. 6)* (30 April 1982) at para. 1.
127. Under the Crimes (Amendment) Ordinance (No. 24 of 1993). For more on the history of the death penalty in Hong Kong, see Athena Liu, "The Right to Life", in Wacks (ed.), *Human Rights in Hong Kong* (see note 6) at 270–274.
128. Ibid. at 275.
129. Michael Hor, "Right to Life" in Chan and Lim (eds.), *Law of the Hong Kong Constitution* (see note 3) at 513.
130. Article 2(2) of the Bill of Rights and Article 6(2) of the ICCPR. Note, however, that Articles 2(5) and 6(5) of these two documents ban the execution of pregnant women and persons who commit crimes while under the age of 18.
131. See Section 7(2)(f) of the Prevention and Control of Disease Ordinance (Cap. 599), allowing the Secretary for Food and Health to make regulations on the isolation or quarantine of any person in order to prevent the spread of disease. This power was exercised on 27 April 2009 to impose a seven-day quarantine on the Metropark Hotel in Wanchai, after the arrival of a guest with an infectious disease.
132. Article 3 of the Bill of Rights and Article 7 of the ICCPR. Note also the wording of Article 28 of the Hong Kong Basic Law which prohibits, without any qualification, "[t]orture of any resident". This is in contrast to most of the other rights in Article 28 which (as already observed in relation to the right to life) are qualified by the wording "arbitrary or unlawful". See also *Ubamaka Edward Wilson v Secretary for Security* [2013] 2 HKC 75, 108–111 where the Court of Final Appeal reviewed international jurisprudence on the issue and concluded this shows "the absolute character of the protection against torture".
133. Article 15 of the Bill of Rights and Article 18 of the ICCPR.

small number of other rights which both the Bill of Rights and ICCPR do not allow to be restricted, even in times of public emergency.[134]

Those rare examples aside, for as long as Hong Kong has had laws protecting human rights, it has been recognized that there will sometimes be situations when it is necessary to restrict most fundamental rights. That basic principle was recognized in *R v Sin Yau Ming*,[135] the first case involving the Bill of Rights to reach the Court of Appeal. Although the presumption of innocence, the right at issue in that case, is stated in absolute terms in the Bill of Rights, the court nonetheless held that the presumption of innocence could be restricted under certain circumstances.[136]

Later cases have extended the same principle to the rights protected under the Hong Kong Basic Law,[137] once again recognizing that some restrictions on almost every right are necessary in any society. Justice Yeung put this most starkly in one of Hong Kong's most important cases on freedom of assembly, when he observed that: "Rights and freedoms cannot be absolute or else they are no different from anarchy and can lead to mayhem and lawlessness."[138]

While not allowing any restrictions on rights might, in the most extreme scenario, lead to anarchy, allowing rights to be restricted too easily risks rendering them almost meaningless. Nor is it necessary to look very far to find an example of this, since the Constitution of the People's Republic of China 1982 includes many generously worded provisions that supposedly protect a wide variety of fundamental rights, often in language almost identical to the equivalent provisions in the Hong Kong Basic Law.[139] Take, for instance, freedom of speech, press, assembly, association, procession and

---

134. Section 5(2)(b)–5(2)(c) of the Bill of Rights and Article 4(1)–4(2) of the ICCPR. According to Young [in "Restricting Basic Law Rights in Hong Kong" (see note 118) at 120], the fact that these rights cannot be restricted even in times of public emergency suggests it is very likely the courts would view them as absolute rights.
135. [1992] 1 HKCLR 127. For more on this case see note 79.
136. Ibid. at 142. Article 11(1) of the Bill of Rights, states: "Everyone charged with a criminal offence shall have the right to be presumed innocent until proved guilty according to law." The Court of Appeal held that some restrictions could be implied into this provision, although not the restrictions that were at issue in this case.
137. See *HKSAR v Lam Kwong Wai* (2006) HKCFAR 574, 593 where the court held that restrictions on the presumption of innocence could be similarly implied into the Hong Kong Basic Law.
138. *HKSAR v Leung Kwok Hung* [2004] 3 HKLRD 729, 795 (CA). For criticism of some aspects of the Court of Appeal's decision in this case, see Janice Brabyn, "Leung Kwok Hung and Others Through the Hong Kong Courts" (2006) 36 *HKLJ* 83, 91–94. For more on the significance of the Court of Final Appeal's subsequent decision in this case, see further note 390 in Chapter 6 and the accompanying text.
139. Albert Chen notes [in "Civil Liberties in Hong Kong: Recent Controversies, Evolving Consciousness and Future Legal Protection" (1988) 2 *Journal of Chinese Law* 137, 149] that the language used in the "brief and simple" rights provisions in the Hong Kong Basic Law is "stylistically closer" to the rights provisions in the PRC Constitution 1982 than those in either the ICCPR or constitutional documents in many other countries.

demonstration—rights which are all supposedly protected in absolute terms under Article 35 of the PRC Constitution 1982.[140]

In reality, any protection afforded by these human rights provisions is rendered largely worthless by the constitution's accompanying list of often generally worded duties.[141] These include, for instance, the duty not to exercise these rights in any way which infringes the interests of the state or society,[142] and not to do anything "detrimental" to China's security, honour and interests.[143] Such duties are often written into Chinese laws in a way which so greatly restricts the rights listed in the constitution that these rights can hardly be said to exist in any meaningful sense in China.[144] In addition, the courts in China generally refuse to hear cases seeking to enforce rights supposedly protected under the constitution.[145]

The China experience shows the importance of having not only an independent judiciary prepared to enforce such rights, but also strict rules which can be used to decide whether or not to allow any particular restriction on rights, and so control how far such rights can be restricted. While the PRC Constitution 1982 lacks such rules, they are present in the Hong Kong Basic Law. In one of the most important rights-related provisions in the document, Article 39(2) imposes two crucial rules (or tests) that are used to judge whether or not any particular restriction on the rights and freedoms of Hong Kong residents is permissible under the Hong Kong Basic Law. These are firstly that any such restriction must be "prescribed by law", and secondly that the restriction is not inconsistent with the international human rights treaties, including the ICCPR, that apply to Hong Kong under Article 39(1) of the Hong Kong Basic Law.

The Article 39(2) requirement that any restrictions on rights must be "prescribed by law" gives rise to what has become known as the "legality test". This protects against arbitrary restrictions on human rights, as it requires that all restrictions on rights must

---

140. It is instructive to compare Article 35 of the PRC Constitution 1982 with Article 27 of the Hong Kong Basic Law, which lists these same rights and uses similar wording. Note, however, that Article 27 also protects the following rights not mentioned in the 1982 Constitution: freedom of publication, the right and freedom to form and join trade unions, and to strike.
141. Duties are listed in 8 out of the 24 articles in Chapter II of the PRC Constitution 1982, which is titled "Fundamental Rights and Duties of Citizens". Contrast this with the similarly titled Chapter III of the Hong Kong Basic Law, "Fundamental Rights and Duties of the Residents", where only one out of 19 articles mention duties. This is Article 42 which states that: "Hong Kong residents and other persons in Hong Kong shall have the obligation to abide by the laws in force in the Hong Kong Special Administrative Region."
142. Article 51.
143. Article 54.
144. See, for instance, Article 4 of the Law of the PRC on Assemblies, Processions and Demonstrations 1989. Among other restrictions, this bans freedom of assembly, procession and demonstration from being used in any way which challenges the leadership of the Communist Party, or "impairs state, public or collective interests". For more on the rights in the 1982 Constitution, and how they are restricted, see Albert Chen, "Human Rights in China: A Brief Historical Review" in Wacks (ed.), *Human Rights in Hong Kong* (see note 6) at 188–194.
145. See further note 123 in Chapter 6.

be prescribed (or authorized) by law. Since the executive branch of government lacks the power to make laws,[146] this means that the government cannot, by itself, impose any restrictions on rights. Instead, all such restrictions must be authorized by a law, either enacted by the legislature or developed at common law by the courts. As Chan and Lim (2011) note: "This, in turn, means that the restriction will have been debated in the (democratic) process of legislation, or will have gone through a rational process of law-making in the case of common law."[147]

The legality test not just requires any restriction to be authorized by law, but imposes important controls on what type of laws can pass this test. In *Shum Kwok Sher v HKSAR*,[148] drawing on a landmark European Court of Human Rights decision[149] on the meaning of the term "prescribed by law", the Court of Final Appeal held that any law restricting rights must firstly be "adequately accessible" and secondly "formulated with sufficient precision to enable the citizen to regulate his conduct".[150]

That reflects a basic principle of fairness. Given the importance of fundamental freedoms, it is surely correct that any law restricting such freedoms, even for the most justifiable of reasons, must be both accessible by those affected and worded sufficiently precisely so that those affected can understand what they can and cannot do without being in breach of this law. That is especially important when breaking the law in question may lead to criminal punishment, such as a jail sentence.

This protects against a scenario in which the executive persuades a government-friendly legislature to enact a law giving the government wide-ranging powers to restrict human rights, a scenario some critics might fear is not impossible in Hong Kong, given the current lack of popular elections for the entire legislature.[151] If that law is too wide ranging, it may be struck down by the courts under the legality test for failing to explain in sufficiently precise terms when the executive can, and cannot, restrict those rights. That is well demonstrated by *Leung Kwok Hung v HKSAR*,[152] one of Hong Kong's most famous cases on how far freedom of assembly can be restricted under the Hong Kong Basic Law. In that case, the Court of Final Appeal struck from the Public Order Ordinance (Cap. 245) a provision allowing the police to restrict or ban public protests on the grounds of "*ordre public*".[153] This is a term which even the court had struggled to

---

146. For an example of the Chief Executive's inability to make laws, see further notes 58–64 in Chapter 5 and the accompanying text.
147. Chan and Lim, "Interpreting Constitutional Rights and Permissible Restrictions" (see note 3) at 488.
148. (2002) 5 HKCFAR 381.
149. *Sunday Times v United Kingdom (No 1)* (1979–80) 2 EHRR 245. This was the culmination of a long and successful challenge by one of the Britain's largest newspaper to contempt of court laws on the grounds that these infringed freedom of expression.
150. Ibid. at 271, adopted by the Court of Final Appeal in *Shum Kwok Sher* at 402.
151. For more on the system of elections to the Legislative Council, see further "5.5: Elected Legislature" in Chapter 5.
152. (2005) 8 HKCFAR 229.
153. Ibid. at 261–264. See further note 390 in Chapter 6 and the accompanying text.

define in other cases, and which the court held was far too vague to be written into law without further explanation.[154]

That does not mean every vague law will fail the legality test. Much depends on the particular circumstances. The rule adopted in Hong Kong from the European Court of Human Rights is that any law must be formulated with sufficient precision that ordinary citizens can regulate their conduct "to a degree that is reasonable in the circumstances".[155] That does not require "absolute certainty", something expressly rejected by the court, noting that: "[M]any laws are inevitably couched in terms which, to a greater or lesser extent, are vague".[156]

Such vagueness is particularly likely when it comes to common law offences, which have been developed by the courts in previous cases. By their very nature, such offences may only be discoverable by reading through past court judgments dating back many decades.[157] It is difficult to see how this satisfies the "prescribed by law" requirement that any law restricting rights be both adequately accessible and sufficiently precise. Nonetheless, the courts are reluctant to conclude that laws which they developed in previous cases are too vague to satisfy the legality test, and may adopt a lower standard of what constitutes sufficient precision when it comes to common law offences.[158]

Common law offences aside, normally it should be relatively easy to draft legislation using wording which meets the "prescribed by law" requirement. As long as the law is adequately accessible, all that is required is wording which is sufficiently precise, a requirement which can easily be satisfied by many harsh and repressive laws, as long as they are worded clearly enough. Take, for instance, the hypothetical example of a law requiring a fixed number of executions of specified members of the public every month.

---

154. Ironically this term seems to have been added to the ordinance (by amendments in 1997 which are explained further in note 94 earlier in this chapter) in what has been described as a "good faith attempt" to comply with the ICCPR, Article 21 of which lists *ordre public* as one of the legitimate reasons for restricting freedom of assembly. See Brabyn, "Leung Kwok Hung and Others Through the Hong Kong Courts" (see note 138) at 93. As the Court of Final Appeal explained in the *Leung Kwok Hung* case (at 263–264), such wording is acceptable in the ICCPR which, as a constitutional instrument, is inevitably worded in "relatively abstract terms". However, that does not make the same wording acceptable in a law restricting rights, "where a degree of precision appropriate to the subject matter" is required.
155. *Sunday Times v UK (No 1)* at 271.
156. Ibid., noting that it may sometimes be necessary for an ordinary citizen to take "appropriate advice", presumably from a lawyer, in order to understand how a particular law restricts his or her rights.
157. A good example is the common law offence of misconduct in public office. This dates back to 1701 and had rarely been used for several centuries, until it was used to prosecute a Hong Kong civil servant in *Shum Kwok Sher v HKSAR* (2002) 5 HKCFAR 381.
158. Ibid. at 410–412 where the Court of Final Appeal concluded that the common law offence of misconduct in public office, although "cast in general terms", was not so imprecise as to fail the "prescribed by law" requirement in Article 39(2) of the Hong Kong Basic Law. See also Chan and Lim, "Interpreting Constitutional Rights and Permissible Restrictions" (see note 3) at 489.

Although utterly repulsive, such a law might well be judged sufficiently precise to satisfy the legality test.

That is because the "prescribed by law" requirement focuses on whether the wording of a law is sufficiently precise in explaining any restriction it imposes on human rights. It does not consider the arguably more crucial issue of whether there is any justification for such restrictions at all. So, while the legality test plays a useful role in preventing some arbitrary and vague restrictions on human rights, it is far from a sufficient safeguard against harsh and repressive laws on its own. Instead, it needs to be accompanied by some further tests that consider both the validity of the objectives (or reasons) for imposing any restriction on those rights, and the extent of the restriction imposed.

The need for such tests has been recognized by the courts ever since they began hearing cases on the Bill of Rights. This is an area in which international human rights judgments have had a considerable impact. So the Hong Kong courts look to developments elsewhere in the common law world, as well as the often influential judgments of the European Court of Human Rights, for guidance on the most appropriate tests to apply in deciding which restrictions on rights will, and will not, be allowed in Hong Kong.

That process of borrowing from rights-related case law overseas can be traced back to *R v Sin Yau Ming*,[159] the Court of Appeal's first case on the Bill of Rights. The Court of Appeal adopted the two tests then used to judge whether human rights restrictions are allowed in Canada, despite some significant differences between that country's framework for protecting human rights and Hong Kong's.[160] The first of these two tests is a "rationality test". It considers the objectives (now usually referred to as "legitimate purposes") for imposing any restriction on rights and, in particular, whether there is a rational (or logical) connection between those objectives and the restrictions themselves.[161] The second is a "proportionality test", which considers the extent of the restriction on rights, in particular whether or not any restriction is too wide and goes any further than is necessary to achieve its stated objective.[162]

In the years since *Sin Yau Ming*, the tests used by the Hong Kong courts to determine the permissible objectives for, and extent of, any restrictions on rights have evolved in

---

159. [1992] 1 HKCLR 127. For more on this case, see note 79 earlier in this chapter.
160. Unlike Hong Kong's Bill of Rights, the Canadian Charter of Rights and Freedoms, a bill of rights entrenched in the Constitution of Canada, contains an express provision (in Section 1 of the Charter) allowing for "reasonable limits" on the rights and freedoms listed in the Charter. In *Sin Yau Ming*, the Court of Appeal noted this difference (at 142 and 163) but said it did not stop similar provisions from being "implied" into the Hong Kong Bill of Rights.
161. See *Sin Yau Ming* at 163, where the court held that a restriction on the presumption of innocence could be implied into the Bill of Rights if it can be proved: "[T]hat the fact to be presumed *rationally* and realistically follows from that proved and also if the presumption is *no more than proportionate* to what is warranted by the nature of the evil against which society requires protection" (emphasis added). The term "rational connection" was subsequently used by the High Court in another case on the presumption of innocence. See *R v Lum Wai Ming* [1992] 2 HKCLR 221, 225.
162. *Sin Yau Ming* at 163.

line with developments elsewhere in the common law world. Just as proportionality has emerged as an increasingly important area of judicial review in many other jurisdictions,[163] in Hong Kong it has largely subsumed the former "rationality test", which is now rarely referred to by the courts as a separate test.[164] In 2005, the Court of Final Appeal noted that, while the exact wording might vary from one country to another, the Hong Kong courts apply "essentially the same" test in determining what restrictions on rights are permissible as in many other jurisdictions around the world.[165]

That is, however, subject to the Hong Kong Basic Law, Article 39(2) of which serves as the starting point for deciding how to apply any restrictions. As we saw earlier, this important provision explicitly mentions two tests against which most restrictions on rights must be judged. The first test requires that any restriction be "prescribed by law" (meaning that it is both adequately accessible and sufficiently precise), and the second test considers whether or not the restriction complies with the international human rights treaties that apply to Hong Kong under Article 39(1) of the Hong Kong Basic Law.

In most cases, this means the ICCPR. As noted earlier, this important international human rights treaty contains a long list of fundamental rights,[166] which are incorporated into Hong Kong law through the Hong Kong Bill of Rights Ordinance (Cap. 383).[167] From equality before the law to freedom of expression and the right of peaceful assembly, the ICCPR and Bill of Rights list the vast majority of freedoms which arise in court cases on restriction of rights.

In many cases, those same rights are also directly mentioned in various articles of the Hong Kong Basic Law, so giving rise to the term "parallel Basic Law rights".[168] However, as we saw earlier, these parallel provisions in the Hong Kong Basic Law are much less detailed than the corresponding provisions in the ICCPR and Bill of Rights.[169] In most cases, the human rights provisions in the Hong Kong Basic Law offer only general descriptions of the rights they purport to protect, in a manner reminiscent of the similarly general wording often used to describe those rights in the PRC Constitution 1982.[170] With only a few exceptions, those general descriptions mean the individual rights provisions in

---

163. For more on the growth of proportionality in recent years, see further notes 242–245 in Chapter 6 and the accompanying text.
164. See, for instance, *Leung Kwok Hung v HKSAR* (2005) 8 HKCFAR 229, 253, where the term "rational connection" was instead explicitly described as part of the proportionality test.
165. Ibid.
166. See further pages 282–284.
167. See further page 274.
168. See Young, "Restricting Basic Law Rights in Hong Kong" (see note 118) at 119.
169. See further page 284.
170. See note 140 earlier in this chapter for an example of the similarity between the general wording used to describe the same rights in both the Hong Kong Basic Law and the PRC Constitution 1982.

the Hong Kong Basic Law offer little or no guidance as to the circumstances under which those rights can, and cannot, be restricted.[171]

That does not mean those rights can never be restricted. The point is well illustrated by the case of *Secretary for Justice v Oriental Press Group Ltd*,[172] where a popular newspaper group sought to invoke the "clear and wide words" protecting freedom of expression in Article 27 of the Hong Kong Basic Law, which makes no mention of any circumstances under which that right can be restricted, to defend themselves against criminal charges over a series of abusive articles about various judges.[173] The court swiftly dismissed any idea that this clear and wide wording meant freedom of expression could never be restricted under the Hong Kong Basic Law. Instead, it noted that Article 39(2) allows for restrictions to be imposed on rights protected under other provisions of the Hong Kong Basic Law, even where the wide wording of those provisions makes no mention of any restrictions.[174]

What it does mean is that the courts need to look beyond the generalized wording of the human rights provisions in the Hong Kong Basic Law to find the objectives (or "legitimate purposes", as they are now usually called) that justify restricting any particular right listed in the Hong Kong Basic Law. That usually means turning to the more detailed descriptions of those same rights in the ICCPR, detailed descriptions which often, although not always, contain a list of legitimate purposes for restricting that right.

The effect of Article 39(2) is to import the legitimate purposes for restricting rights listed in the ICCPR into the parallel provisions listing the same rights in the Hong Kong Basic Law. The more detailed descriptions of those rights in the ICCPR are used to fill the gaps left by the more generalized provisions on the same rights in the Hong Kong Basic Law. That is not always a simple exercise, since the wording of some rights differs significantly between the two documents.[175] Young (2004) criticizes this approach arguing, "that the task of finding identical rights is more fiction than reality".[176] Despite such criticism, the approach of looking to the ICCPR to fill the gaps left by the generalized

---

171. One rare exception is Article 30 of the Hong Kong Basic Law. This notes that the freedom and privacy of communication of Hong Kong residents may be restricted, "in accordance with legal procedures to meet the needs of public security or of investigation into criminal offences". For more on the leading case relating to this article, see further notes 58–61 in Chapter 5 and the accompanying text.
172. [1998] 2 HKLRD 123. Appeal dismissed by Court of Appeal in *Wong Yeung Ng v Secretary for Justice* [1999] 2 HKLRD 293.
173. Ibid. at 164. The defendants argued that the common law offence of scandalizing the court, with which they had been charged, contravened Article 27, in which freedom of expression "is expressed in absolute terms".
174. Ibid. at 165.
175. See, for example, the difference in the wording of the presumption of innocence between Article 87(2) of the Hong Kong Basic Law and Article 14(2) of the ICCPR/Article 11(1) of the Bill of Rights. Cited by Young in "Restricting Basic Law Rights in Hong Kong" (see note 118) at 124.
176. Ibid.

provisions in the Hong Kong Basic Law has been applied by the courts in numerous cases and is now firmly established in law.[177]

The result is that the task of determining whether or not a particular restriction is permissible under the Hong Kong Basic Law often depends more on the wording of the corresponding provision in the ICCPR than it does on the wording of the right in the Hong Kong Basic Law itself. Since the ICCPR as applied to Hong Kong is implemented in Hong Kong law through the Bill of Rights, that points to another reason for the continuing significance of this ordinance.[178]

While the legitimate purposes for restricting rights listed in the ICCPR vary from one right to another, in some cases the same purpose is listed for several different rights. Most notably, the ICCPR[179] states that freedom of movement, choice of residence, opinion/expression, association and the right of peaceful assembly can all be restricted where this is necessary[180] to protect:

(1) National Security;
(2) Public order (*ordre public*);
(3) Public health or morals:
(4) Rights and freedoms of others.[181]

For peaceful assembly and freedom of association, the ICCPR adds[182] a fifth legitimate purpose, also allowing these rights to be restricted where this is necessary[183] to protect public safety.[184] The significance of this list of legitimate purposes is that they

---

177. See, for example, the use of this approach by the Court of Final Appeal in two of its most important rights-related decisions: *HKSAR v Ng Kung Siu* (1999) 2 HKCFAR 442, 454–455 and *Leung Kwok Hung v HKSAR* (2005) 8 HKCFAR 229, 247–248 and 252. In addition, in *HKSAR v Lam Kwong Wai* (2006) 9 HKCFAR 574, 597 the Court of Final Appeal held that there is no difference between the protection of the presumption of innocence under the Hong Kong Basic Law and the ICCPR/Bill of Rights (despite the different wording highlighted in note 175).
178. For more on the constitutional protection afforded to the Bill of Rights by the courts, see further note 104 earlier in this chapter and the accompanying text.
179. Articles 12(3), 19(3), 21 and 22(2) respectively.
180. Articles 21 and 22(2) use the term "necessary in a democratic society". In this context, the term "democratic society" refers to a pluralistic, tolerant and broadminded society, and not necessarily the system used to conduct elections in that society. See *Leung Kwok Hung* at 252.
181. Article 19(3) on freedom of opinion and expression expresses this legitimate purpose in slightly different wording, referring instead to: "[R]espect of the rights or reputations of others".
182. In Articles 21 and 22(2) respectively.
183. Again, the actual term used is "necessary in a democratic society".
184. In addition, Article 18(3) lists "public safety, order, health or morals or the fundamental rights and freedoms of others" as legitimate purposes for restricting freedom of religion, while Article 14(1) lists "morals, public order (*ordre public*) or national security" as legitimate purposes for restricting the right to a public hearing.

are the only purposes that the court will take into account in deciding whether or not to uphold a restriction on that particular right.[185] So any restriction risks being struck down by the courts unless the government can prove that it is necessary for one of the legitimate purposes listed in the ICCPR in relation to that particular right.

In most cases, it is fairly easy to find an applicable legitimate purpose. Chan and Lim (2011) note that, "given the breadth of these terms, it is normally not difficult to show that the objectives to be pursued fall within one of these legitimate objectives".[186] For example, any restrictions imposed on these freedoms by the legislation required under Article 23 of the Hong Kong Basic Law could be justified on the grounds that the ICCPR lists national security as a legitimate purpose for restricting such freedoms.[187] Equally, restrictions on freedom of movement to prevent the spread of a deadly disease would appear to fall within the legitimate purpose of protecting public health.

The task of finding an applicable legitimate purpose is made even easier by the unfortunately wide definition given to the second of these legitimate purposes—public order (*ordre public*). While the term "public order" is generally understood in common law as referring to the maintenance of law and order and prevention of crime,[188] the addition of the two obscure French words "*ordre public*" gives this legitimate purpose a much broader meaning.

Unlike the other, usually fairly self-explanatory,[189] legitimate purposes listed in the ICCPR, the meaning of *ordre public* is far from clear. In *HKSAR v Ng Kung Siu*, the Court of Final Appeal described it as an "imprecise and elusive" concept, with boundaries which "cannot be precisely defined" and may vary according to the "time, place and circumstances".[190] In that case, the court adopted such a wide definition of *ordre public* that it could include almost anything, so potentially allowing this legitimate purpose

---

185. *Leung Kwok Hung* at 253.
186. See Chan and Lim, "Interpreting Constitutional Rights and Permissible Restrictions" (see note 3) at 491.
187. Article 23 requires Hong Kong to enact legislation against treason, secession, sedition, subversion, theft of state secrets and certain offences involving foreign political organizations. During its failed attempt to enact this legislation in 2003 (see further note 94 in Chapter 4 and the accompanying text), the Hong Kong SAR Government eventually agreed to include what became known as the "Pannick clauses" (which was the name of the English Queen's Counsel who proposed the clauses) explicitly stating that the Article 23 legislation would be "interpreted, applied and enforced" in accordance with the provisions on human rights in Chapter III of the Hong Kong Basic Law. See Clauses 7, 7A and 14 of the National Security (Legislative Provisions) Bill.
188. See, for example, *HKSAR v Ng Kung Siu* (1999) 2 HKCFAR 442, 457.
189. If further guidance is needed on the meaning of these terms, it can be found in the Siracusa Principles, agreed by a group of international human rights experts at a conference in 1984. See UN Commission on Human Rights, *The Siracusa Principles on the Limitation and Derogation Provisions in the International Covenant on Civil and Political Rights* (28 Sept 1984). The Siracusa Principles have been cited by the Hong Kong courts on several occasions. See, for example, *Leung Kwok Hung* at 252.
190. *Ng Kung Siu* at 459–460.

to apply to a wide range of restrictions on freedom of movement, choice of residence, opinion/expression, association and the right of peaceful assembly.

Ng Kung Siu was a highly sensitive case decided at a highly sensitive time for the Court of Final Appeal. The decision, in December 1999, came at the end of a year in which the court had been embroiled in a constitutional crisis over its January 1999 judgment in the *Ng Ka Ling* case,[191] some aspects of which had intensely angered Chinese authorities.[192] Faced in *Ng Kung Siu* with another case that could have easily ignited fresh controversy with Beijing, Chen (2006) observes that the Court of Final Appeal "acted strategically in choosing the 'line of least resistance' from the political point of view".[193] Or, to adopt a famous Shakespeare phrase, the court decided that discretion was the better part of valour when it came to defending human rights in this case.

The case revolved around the extent to which the Chinese national flag is protected under Hong Kong law, with two pro-democracy protesters appealing against their conviction for desecrating both the Chinese national flag and Hong Kong's regional flag. These are offences under two Hong Kong laws,[194] one of which is a localized version of one of the few Chinese national laws that the National People's Congress Standing Committee has decided should apply in Hong Kong.[195] While flag desecration may be an unpopular act in Hong Kong which only a minority would ever contemplate, it is nonetheless a form of expression, in this case of the two protesters' opposition to the system of government in mainland China. That means, like any other restriction on freedom of expression, the ban on flag desecration is only allowable under the Hong Kong Basic Law if it can be shown to be necessary for one of the legitimate purposes for restricting this freedom that are listed in the ICCPR.

Unable to find any legitimate purpose in the ICCPR which justified this particular restriction on freedom of expression, the Court of Appeal overturned the conviction of the two protesters for flag desecration.[196] That provoked an angry response from some members of the National People's Congress,[197] anger which would most likely have

---

191. (1999) 2 HKCFAR 4.
192. China was particularly angered by the court's assertion of a power to invalidate actions of the NPC and its Standing Committee that breach the Hong Kong Basic Law. For more on this aspect of the case, and China's criticism of it, see further notes 186–194 and 202–205 in Chapter 6 and the accompanying text.
193. Chen, "Constitutional Adjudication in Post-1997 Hong Kong" (see note 8) at 663.
194. Section 7 of the National Flag and National Emblem Ordinance (No. 116 of 1997) and Section 7 of the Regional Flag and Regional Emblem Ordinance (No. 117 of 1997) make it a criminal offence to desecrate either of these flags "by publicly and willfully burning, mutilating, scrawling on, defiling or trampling on it".
195. This is the Law of the PRC on the National Flag. For more on the application of Chinese national laws in Hong Kong, see further "4.2: Legislative Power" in Chapter 4.
196. *HKSAR v Ng Kung Siu* [1999] 1 HKLRD 783, 790–791. The two defendants had been originally convicted in the Magistrates Court, and were allowed to appeal directly to the Court of Appeal.
197. See May Tam, "Court crisis after flag row", *The Standard*, 25 March 1999.

erupted into another constitutional crisis had these acquittals been upheld by the Court of Final Appeal.[198] In theory, all the Court of Appeal actually decided was that the provisions criminalizing flag desecration in two Hong Kong laws contravened the Hong Kong Basic Law. But since one of those two laws had been enacted in order to implement a Chinese national law, the Court of Appeal's decision carried with it the potentially explosive implication that Hong Kong courts had the power to defy a decision of the National People's Congress Standing Committee on applying a Chinese national law to Hong Kong.[199]

When *Ng Kung Siu* reached the Court of Final Appeal, it averted the threat of another constitutional crisis by reversing the Court of Appeal's decision and reinstating the conviction of the two protesters for flag desecration. The court reached this conclusion by focussing on the meaning of "public order (*ordre public*)" which, as we saw earlier, is listed in the ICCPR as a legitimate purpose for restricting freedom of expression. In *Ng Kung Siu*, the Court of Final Appeal held that the Court of Appeal was "not correct" in considering this legitimate purpose purely in terms of public order (or law and order), and had failed to consider the broader nature of the term *ordre public*.[200] In a politically flavoured judgment, which saw the Chief Justice quote from a speech by then Chinese President Jiang Zemin,[201] the Court of Final Appeal adopted an expansive definition of *ordre public* as including "what is necessary for the protection of the general welfare or for the interests of collectivity as a whole".[202] In other words, the court concluded that anything necessary for the interests of Hong Kong society as a whole falls into the category of *ordre public*, and can be used to justify imposing restrictions on several fundamental rights under the ICCPR.

---

198. See, for example, Chen's prediction [in "Constitutional Adjudication in Post-1997 Hong Kong" (see note 8) at 663] that such a decision by the Court of Final Appeal "would bring the Hong Kong courts into direct conflict with the NPCSC". See also Yap's analysis [in "Constitutional Review under the Basic Law: The Rise, Retreat and Resurgence of Judicial Power in Hong Kong" (2007) 37 *HKLJ* 449, 459] of how China would have been likely to respond to such a decision by the Court of Final Appeal.
199. The Court of Appeal appeared aware of the sensitivity of this issue, and its judgment both avoided any reference to the PRC Law on the National Flag and was careful to describe the national flag in respectful terms (at 790) as "poignantly symbolizes the pride and spirit of togetherness which unify a nation".
200. (1999) 2 HKCFAR 442, 457.
201. Ibid. at 447, citing a speech during the 1 July 1997 handover from Britain to Hong Kong which began by noting how both the national and regional flags "have now solemnly risen over this land". After deciding (at 459) that what falls within the legitimate purpose of *ordre public* may vary according to the "time, place and circumstances", the court then (at 461) cited this extract from President Jiang's speech as evidence that prohibiting desecration of the two flags fell within the legitimate purpose of *ordre public* at a time so soon after the 1997 handover.
202. Ibid. at 459, adopting a similar definition put forward by the French legal scholar Professor Alexandre Kiss in "Permissible Limitations on Rights", in Louis Henkin (ed.), *The International Bill of Rights: The Covenant on Civil and Political Rights* (Columbia University Press, 1981) at 301–302.

Wacks (2000) has harshly criticized the Court of Final Appeal judgment in this case, labelling its reasoning "unconvincing" and "a setback for the protection of rights".[203] However, the general reaction was more measured,[204] and it is not difficult to defend the actual decision, at least in relation to upholding the law criminalizing flag desecration. Many other countries have similar laws,[205] which essentially accord a special status to the national flag as the symbol of the nation and so allow freedom of expression to be restricted in this one specific instance. Even in the United States, with its strong constitutional guarantees of individual liberties, the courts have been sharply divided about whether these guarantees extend as far as protecting freedom to damage the national flag.[206]

The problem lies in the wide definition of *ordre public* adopted by the Court of Final Appeal, which sets a precedent that could be used to justify numerous other less acceptable restrictions on freedom of movement, choice of residence, opinion/expression, association and the right of peaceful assembly. Only one judge in the case seemed troubled by this. In a separate concurring judgment, Justice Bokhary sought to uphold the law restricting freedom to damage the two flags on much narrower grounds, arguing that these restrictions "lie just within the outer limits of constitutionality".[207] In other words, that the flag desecration laws lie at the very edge of the restrictions on rights permitted under the Hong Kong Basic Law, and so could not serve as a precedent for imposing broader restrictions on fundamental freedoms. Ghai (2012) describes this as a "near dissent" that "brought some comfort to civil-society activists".[208]

No such qualifications are evident in the majority judgment from the other four judges in *Ng Kung Siu*, which instead offers several examples of the wide range of circumstances in which the court's broad interpretation of *ordre public* could be used as a legitimate purpose for restricting fundamental freedoms. These include economic issues such as consumer protection, as well as what are described in very general terms as "aesthetic and moral considerations".[209]

It is difficult to avoid the conclusion that, in their apparent eagerness to avoid another confrontation with China so soon after the *Ng Ka Ling* case, the majority in *Ng Kung Siu* delivered a judgment in such unnecessarily broad terms that it undermines the

---

203. Raymond Wacks, "Our Flagging Rights" (2000) 30 *HKLJ* 1, 2.
204. For instance, Johannes Chan [in "Basic Law and Constitutional Review" (2007) 37 *HKLJ* 407, 422] describes the decision as "understandable at a time when the relationship between the Court and the NPCSC was rather uneasy, if not tense". See also Po Jen Yap's description of Wacks' criticism as "unnecessarily harsh on the Court of Final Appeal in this instance" [in "Freedom of Expression" in Chan and Lim (eds.), *Law of the Hong Kong Constitution* (see note 3) at 608].
205. Including Italy, Germany and Portugal, all of which are cited in Justice Bokhary's separate concurring judgment upholding Hong Kong's flag desecration laws. See *Ng Kung Siu* at 466.
206. In both *Texas v Johnson* (1989) 491 US 397, 402–420 and *United States v Eichman* (1990) 496 US 310, 313–319 the US Supreme Court decided by a narrow margin of 5 to 4 not to uphold laws restricting freedom to desecrate the national flag.
207. *Ng Kung Siu* at 468.
208. Yash Ghai, "Solid foundation", *South China Morning Post*, 17 April 2012.
209. *Ng Kung Siu* at 459–460. Again, these are taken from similar examples put forward by Prof. Kiss (see note 202 above).

protection of human rights under the Hong Kong Basic Law, an important aspect of Hong Kong's high degree of autonomy. A parallel can be drawn with another judgment two weeks earlier in *Lau Kong Yung v Director of Immigration*,[210] a case where the Court of Final Appeal has been similarly criticized for delivering a judgment in unnecessarily broad terms that damaged another important element of Hong Kong's high degree of autonomy—in that instance the extent of the National People's Congress Standing Committee's power to interpret the Hong Kong Basic Law.[211]

Whatever the motives behind the *Ng Kung Siu* judgment, the adoption of such a broad definition of *ordre public* renders the list of legitimate purposes in the ICCPR far less effective in providing any meaningful protection against restrictions on freedom of movement, choice of residence, opinion/expression, association and the right of peaceful assembly.

That places restrictions on these freedoms in a similar category to those on some other rights protected under the Hong Kong Basic Law, where the ICCPR offers far less guidance on the legitimate purposes for which they may be restricted. For instance, Article 25 of the ICCPR simply states that the right to vote and participate in public affairs should not be subject to "unreasonable restrictions", without any elaboration on what that means. In addition, some rights do not appear in the ICCPR at all. As we saw earlier, there are a few "exclusive Basic Law rights", such as the right to travel and social welfare. Since these do not appear in the ICCPR, that document offers no assistance on when it may be necessary to restrict them. Instead, in *Gurung Kesh Bahadur v Director of Immigration*,[212] the Court of Final Appeal concluded that this would have to be determined by the courts based upon "the nature and subject matter of the rights in issue".[213]

With the "prescribed by law" test focusing only on the accessibility and wording of any law restricting rights, and the legitimate purposes listed in the ICCPR sometimes formulated in such broad terms that they could potentially be used to justify a wide range of restrictions on rights, a vital role falls on the proportionality test in keeping such restrictions to a minimum. For instance, since national security is explicitly listed in the ICCPR as a legitimate purpose for restricting several fundamental freedoms, if legislation is ever enacted fully implementing Article 23 of the Hong Kong Basic Law, the issue of proportionality is likely to be one of the major battlegrounds in determining whether such legislation goes further in restricting fundamental freedoms than is permissible under the Hong Kong Basic Law.[214]

---

210. (1999) 2 HKCFAR 300.
211. For more on this case, and criticism of the court's reasoning, see further notes 104–125 in Chapter 7 and the accompanying text.
212. (2002) 5 HKCFAR 480.
213. Ibid. at 490. For more on this case, see further note 124 earlier in this chapter.
214. For an argument that parts of the Article 23 legislation unsuccessfully proposed by the Hong Kong SAR Government in 2003 would have failed the proportionality test, see Lison Harris, Lily Ma and C.B. Fung, "A Connecting Door: The Proscription of Local Organizations" in Fu Hualing, Carole J. Petersen and Simon N.M. Young (eds.), *National Security and Fundamental Freedoms: Hong Kong's Article 23 Under Scrutiny* (Hong Kong University Press, 2005) at 321–323.

As we saw earlier,[215] a proportionality test has been part of the approach of the Hong Kong courts to determining permissible restrictions on fundamental freedoms since the earliest cases on the Bill of Rights. Since then, its role has expanded, in line with the growing general importance of proportionality as an area of judicial review,[216] subsuming what was described as a separate "rationality test" in some early cases.[217] Unlike the "prescribed by law" requirement laid down in Article 39(2) of the Hong Kong Basic Law and the legitimate purposes listed in the ICCPR, the proportionality test is not explicitly mentioned in either document. However, such a test can be inferred from the many provisions in the ICCPR which stipulate that any such restriction must be "necessary" for one of those legitimate purposes,[218] with the proportionality test being used by the courts to determine what is necessary and what is not.[219]

In practice, the importance attached to the proportionality test means it now seems to be almost universally applied by the courts, regardless of whether or not this is actually required by the wording of the particular provisions in the Hong Kong Basic Law, ICCPR and Bill of Rights that are at issue in any particular case. Panditaratne (2011) notes that the varied approaches formerly applied by the courts to the various different categories of rights listed in these documents "appear to have converged in recent years into a general test of proportionality which courts are apt to apply in all rights-based cases".[220]

The significance of the proportionality test is that it imposes much stricter requirements on justifying any restriction than simply identifying a legitimate purpose for which it is permitted to restrict that right under the ICCPR. As now formulated by the courts,[221] it requires that the:

(1) Restriction must be rationally connected with one or more of the legitimate purposes; and the

---

215. See further notes 161–162 earlier in this chapter and the accompanying text.
216. For more on the growth of proportionality in recent years, see further notes 242–245 in Chapter 6 and the accompanying text.
217. See further note 164 earlier in this chapter.
218. Or, in some cases, "necessary in a democratic society". See further note 180 earlier in this chapter and the accompanying text.
219. Chan and Lim note [in "Interpreting Constitutional Rights and Permissible Restrictions" (see note 3) at 490] that "by a slight turn of phrase, the principle of necessity in international human rights law has been turned into a principle of proportionality under the Basic Law".
220. Panditaratne, "Basic Law, Hong Kong Bill of Rights and the ICCPR" (see note 71) at 446. One intriguing example of the court's growing trend towards applying the same proportionality test in all cases cited by Panditaratne (at 453) is the decision in *Official Receiver & Trustee in Bankruptcy of Chan Wing Hing v Chan Wing Hing* (2006) 9 HKCFAR 545. In that case, the Court of Final Appeal claimed (at 559) to be following the same proportionality test it had previously applied in *Gurung Kesh Bahadur v Director of Immigration* (2002) 5 HKCFAR 480, apparently ignoring the fact that, in reality, it had (at 492) expressly refused to apply a proportionality test in that earlier case. For more on this case, see further note 161 in Chapter 6.
221. *Leung Kwok Hung v HKSAR* (2005) 8 HKCFAR 229, 255.

(2) Means used to impair the right must be no more than is necessary to accomplish the legitimate purpose in question.

In other words, any restriction must have a strong connection with a legitimate purpose for restricting that right. Most crucially of all, it usually should be a narrow restriction on that right, since the wider the restriction the more likely it is to be judged to have gone further than is necessary to accomplish the legitimate purpose in question.[222]

That means even when a particular restriction on rights satisfies the "prescribed by law" test and a legitimate purpose can be identified for restricting that right, the restriction may still fail the much tougher requirements imposed by the proportionality test. That is precisely what happened in *Chan Kin Sum v Secretary for Justice*,[223] where the court was prepared to accept that a precisely worded ban on all prisoners voting in Hong Kong both satisfied the "prescribed by law" requirement and served a legitimate purpose, by imposing an additional punishment on prisoners and so helping to deter others from committing crimes.[224]

But primarily because the voting ban was imposed on all prisoners, regardless of the severity of their crimes or length of prison sentence, the court held that it went further than was necessary to accomplish this legitimate purpose, which could have been better achieved by a more limited ban on certain categories of prisoners.[225] That meant the blanket ban preventing all prisoners from voting failed the proportionality test,[226] and the government was forced to change the law.[227] That decision shows the valuable role that the proportionality test can play in preventing often widely worded legitimate purposes for restricting rights from being used to impose wide restrictions on those rights.

Similarly, in *Ng Kung Siu*, the Court of Final Appeal was only prepared to uphold the provisions criminalizing desecration of the national and Hong Kong flags because it found these constituted a very limited restriction on freedom of expression and so were "proportionate to the aims sought to be achieved".[228] It held that flag desecration is only

---

222. *Ng Kung Siu* at 456.
223. [2009] 2 HKLRD 166.
224. Ibid. at 187 and 197–201. Since Article 25 of the ICCPR only states in general terms that the right to vote shall not be subject to "unreasonable restrictions", the court accepted that it fell into a different category from other rights such as peaceful assembly where the only legitimate purposes for restricting those rights are expressly listed in the ICCPR. As a result, the court accepted the government's argument that deterring crime, enhancing civic responsibility and respect for the rule of law were, in principle, legitimate purposes for restricting the right to vote.
225. Ibid. at 201–209, describing such a wide ban as "arbitrary" and "unreasonable".
226. Ibid. at 221–222, where Justice Cheung stressed that a more limited ban that selectively prevents certain categories of prisoners from voting would not necessarily fail the proportionality test.
227. Although the court decision in *Chan Kin Sum* left open the possibility of maintaining a selective ban preventing certain categories of prisoners from voting, after a public consultation exercise the Hong Kong SAR Government decided to allow all prisoners the right to vote. This was implemented through the Voting by Imprisoned Persons Ordinance (No. 7 of 2009).
228. *Ng Kung Siu* at 461.

a "mode" (or method) of expressing an opinion, rather than an opinion in itself.[229] In most circumstances, the opinion being expressed through flag desecration is opposition to the country or government which those flags are taken to represent.[230] From newspaper articles to waving banners at public protests, there are many other methods through which that opposition can be expressed. So the court found that a restriction on the freedom to desecrate flags does not affect the "substance" of any views which protesters' may wish to express. It simply imposes the narrow restriction of requiring them to use another "mode" of expressing those same views.[231] As noted by Justice Bokhary, the judge most hesitant about upholding the flag desecration laws: "They place no restriction at all on what people may express. ... No idea would be suppressed by the restriction. Neither political outspokenness nor any other form of outspokenness would be inhibited."[232]

That application of the proportionality test goes a long way to ease concerns about the wide interpretation of *ordre public* adopted by the Court of Final Appeal in *Ng Kung Siu*. Although, as a result of that case, it is now relatively easy to use *ordre public* as a legitimate purpose to justify a wide range of restrictions on rights, this is still subject to the safeguard that it will often be much more difficult to show any such restriction goes no further than is absolutely necessary to achieve this legitimate purpose.

It also demonstrates how the various tests used by the courts to judge which restrictions on rights are permissible are best viewed as different aspects of a combined package. Some restrictions may fail the "prescribed by law" test, because they are not sufficiently precise. Others may, occasionally, fail because it is impossible to identify a legitimate purpose for that restriction.[233] Still more may fail at the final, and perhaps most difficult, hurdle of the proportionality test that acts as a particularly valuable protection against wide restrictions on fundamental rights. The combined effect of these tests, which must all be satisfied if any restriction is to be upheld by the courts, adds up to a generally rigorous approach to considering the legality of any attempt to restrict fundamental rights in Hong Kong. This goes a long way towards ensuring that the generous rights conferred by both the Hong Kong Basic Law and ICCPR/Bill of Rights continue to exist as an important feature of Hong Kong's way of life.

---

229. Ibid. at 456.
230. Ibid. Note, however, the intriguing suggestion by the court "that scrawling words of praise on the flags" might also breach those same provisions in Hong Kong's flag desecration laws. For the wording of these provisions, see further note 194 earlier in this chapter.
231. Ibid. See also Justice Bokhary's separate concurring judgment (at 463–465) for a clear explanation of the importance of the distinction between restrictions on the "mode" and "substance" of rights.
232. Ibid. at 468.
233. This is likely to be rare, given the breadth of many of the legitimate purposes listed in the ICCPR. See further note 186 earlier in this chapter and the accompanying text. One exception might be the power often used in the past by the Hong Kong Government (until it was abolished by the Film Censorship (Amendment) Ordinance (No. 63 of 1993)) to ban the broadcast of films in Hong Kong which might anger China. See Chan and Lim, "Interpreting Constitutional Rights and Permissible Restrictions" (see note 3) at 492.

Chapter 9
What Will Happen After 2047?[1]

As we saw at the beginning of this book, the Joint Declaration, the 1984 agreement on Hong Kong's future setting out China's "basic policies" on "one country, two systems", seeks to guarantee that these will "remain unchanged for 50 years".[2] Like the other promises in the Joint Declaration, that promise was then written into the Hong Kong Basic Law, Article 5 of which states that:

> The socialist system and policies shall not be practised in the Hong Kong Special Administrative Region, and the previous capitalist system and way of life shall remain unchanged for 50 years.

Although Article 5 does not mention any dates, since the Hong Kong Basic Law came into effect on 1 July 1997, the clear implication is that this 50-year period ends on 30 June 2047. But neither document addresses the issue of what will happen after that date, an issue which—although still far in the future—has already begun to attract some concern.

Some are pessimistic about Hong Kong's future. Kenneth Chan (2004) argues that, "'one country, two systems' should be seen as a transitory arrangement with an expiry date of 30 June 2047".[3] On this view, the special treatment that Hong Kong enjoys for those 50 years is a temporary measure to ease the territory's reintegration back into China, and once that process is complete there will be no need for the city to be treated differently from any other part of the country. That argument is put forward most emphatically by Morris (2005), who argues that the Hong Kong Basic Law "by its own terms is to have a lifespan of 50 years from 1997 to 2047".[4]

Others adopt a more nuanced view. Johannes Chan (2002) notes the ambiguity over what will happen to Hong Kong in the long term: "It is unclear whether the ultimate goal

---

1. This chapter is updated and rewritten from an article originally published by the author as "What Will Happen to Hong Kong After 2047?" (2011) 42 *California Western International Law Journal* 37–60.
2. Paragraph 3(12). See further "2.2: Sino-British Joint Declaration" in Chapter 2.
3. Kenneth Ka-lok Chan, "Taking Stock of 'One Country, Two Systems'" in Yiu-chung Wong (ed.), *"One Country, Two Systems" in Crisis* (Lexington Books, 2004) at 54.
4. Robert J. Morris, "The 'Replacement' Chief Executive's Two-Year Term: A Pure and Unambiguous Common Law Analysis" (2005) 35 *HKLJ* 17, 22 and 24, which also refers to "the 2047 end-date of the Basic Law itself".

is to retain two equally thriving but different systems, or whether it is to assimilate Hong Kong into the mainland politically, legally, culturally and ideologically."[5]

That raises the question of whether the two systems will necessarily remain so different over the long term. Already the differences between the capitalist system practised in Hong Kong and the socialist system as now practised in China have narrowed greatly in the decades since the Joint Declaration.[6] If that trend continues, it is entirely possible that such differences may have narrowed even further by the time 30 June 2047 arrives.

But even if, in the most optimistic scenario, by that date China has become a liberal democracy, practising the rule of law and respect for human rights, the issue of the future of Hong Kong's special privileges would remain. Take, for instance, the existence of a Court of Final Appeal with the power of final adjudication in Hong Kong. As we saw earlier in this book, such a power is very unusual in autonomous areas elsewhere in the world.[7]

Some, such as Kenneth Chan (2004), argue these special privileges will automatically end together with all aspects of one country, two systems after the 50-year period expires on 30 June 2047.[8] But, as we will see, that is not what the Hong Kong Basic Law says. As Tai (2007) points out, "it is legally possible for the constitutional game of Hong Kong to continue to operate under the Basic Law after 2047".[9]

9.1 Future of Property Rights

As we saw at the beginning of this book, concern over the future of land leases in Hong Kong beyond 30 June 1997 was often portrayed as a major driving force behind the Joint Declaration. Britain repeatedly cited its lack of any legal right to issue government land leases over most parts of Hong Kong that expired after that date as one of the main reasons for needing to reach an agreement with China on Hong Kong's future.[10] Annex III of the Joint Declaration resolved that problem by giving Britain the legal authority to

---

5. Johannes Chan, "Civil Liberties, Rule of Law and Human Rights: The Hong Kong Special Administrative Region in Its First Four Years" in Lau Siu-kai (ed.), *The First Tung Chee-hwa Administration: The First Five Years of the Hong Kong Special Administrative Region* (The Chinese University Press, 2002) at 116.
6. See, for instance, the changes to the PRC Constitution 1982. At the time of the 1984 agreement on Hong Kong's future this prohibited any form of private land-use rights. Since then, Article 10 of the constitution has been amended to permit private land-use rights, and Article 13 to strengthen private property rights. See further note 20 later in this chapter.
7. See further notes 191–193 in Chapter 4 and the accompanying text.
8. Chan, "Taking Stock of 'One Country, Two Systems'" (see note 3) at 54.
9. Benny Y.T. Tai, "Basic Law, Basic Politics: The Constitutional Game of Hong Kong" (2007) 37 *HKLJ* 503, 577
10. For more detail on this point, including discussion of how far this was really the main factor behind Britain's drive to reach an agreement with China on Hong Kong's future, see further notes 8–12 in Chapter 2 and the accompanying text.

issue and renew land leases beyond 30 June 1997—providing that their expiry date was no later than 30 June 2047.[11]

Given that historical background, it is scarcely surprising that similar concerns are now being raised about what will happen to land leases in Hong Kong after 30 June 2047. This is especially so because, ever since Britain's departure on 30 June 1997, the Hong Kong SAR Government has no longer considered it necessary to apply a 30 June 2047 expiry date to the issuance and renewal of land leases.[12] Instead, most land leases are now issued or renewed for a period of 50 years, which means that large numbers of leases extend beyond 30 June 2047.[13] In one well-known example, involving the land used to construct the Hong Kong Disneyland theme park, this includes a right to renew the lease for a second 50-year period, a right which (if exercised) would allow this lease to continue until 2100.[14]

Some have expressed doubts about the legality of this practice. Citing the 50-year limit in the Joint Declaration and the Hong Kong Basic Law on the guarantees against fundamental changes, Ng (2007) has questioned the legal basis for the Hong Kong SAR Government granting leases that extend beyond 2047.[15] Lee (1998) warns it "does not take long for developers and property owners to realize that the validity of government leases is not absolutely certain".[16]

Such concerns are perhaps understandable, given the historical background. But they overlook some very important differences between the land lease problems that arose during the final decades of British rule and the situation that exists in Hong Kong today. Prior to 1 July 1997, land leases were being issued under the authority of British rule which was, itself, subject to a 30 June 1997 time limit on the lease granted to Britain over most parts of Hong Kong. Now, however, there is no equivalent time limit since Hong Kong has reverted to Chinese sovereignty and all land and natural resources in the territory belong to the Chinese state in perpetuity.[17]

The power to manage, use and develop that land, including granting land leases, is currently delegated to the Hong Kong SAR Government by the Chinese state.[18] But even in the most extreme scenario of Hong Kong being abolished as a separate entity after 30 June 2047, and the disappearance of Hong Kong SAR Government that granted those

---

11. See Annex III(2)–III(3). Under Annex III(4), the issue of new land leases was subject to a 50-hectare annual limit. However this limit could be, and frequently was, increased with China's consent through a bilateral body known as the Sino-British Land Commission.
12. See Hong Kong SAR Government, "HKSARG land policy and first Land Disposal Programme announced", 15 July 1997.
13. See the Hong Kong SAR Government's justification of this practice in *Granting of Leases After 30 June 1997 With Term Extending Beyond 30 June 2047* (12 Dec 2006).
14. See Hong Kong SAR Government, "Land Lease Term for Disneyland Project", 4 Nov 1999.
15. Margaret Ng, "The land we stand on", *South China Morning Post*, 1 June 2007.
16. Alice Lee, "Leases Beyond 2047?" in Lee (ed.), *Law Lectures for Practitioners 1998* (Hong Kong Law Journal Ltd., 1998) 177, 184.
17. Hong Kong Basic Law, Article 7.
18. Ibid.

leases, the rights granted under those land leases would not necessarily disappear. Chen (2009) notes that responsibility for any unexpired portion of those land leases would simply pass to the body under whose delegated authority they were originally issued by the Hong Kong SAR Government, namely the Central People's Government.[19]

Some might justifiably object to seeing responsibility for land leases granted by Hong Kong authorities pass into the more uncertain hands of Chinese national authorities. However, this is no longer unthinkable in the way it was the last time that fears arose over the future of land leases, during British rule in the early 1980s. At that time, the Chinese constitution still prohibited any form of land leases.[20] Now, by contrast, private property rights are explicitly protected under the Chinese constitution,[21] and there is a long-established legal framework for granting land-use rights in other parts of China.[22]

Nor can it be argued that the Hong Kong SAR Government has exceeded its legal authority in issuing land leases that extend beyond 30 June 2047. Article 123 of the Hong Kong Basic Law, which grants the Hong Kong SAR Government broad authority to renew land leases "in accordance with laws and policies formulated by the Region on its own", makes no mention of a 30 June 2047 time limit. That omission is of particular significance because Article 121 of the Hong Kong Basic Law on the renewal of land leases in Hong Kong by British authorities *before* 1 July 1997 does refer to a 30 June 2047 time limit on those land leases that were renewed during the period when Hong Kong was still under British rule.

As the Hong Kong SAR Government has argued, in defence of its practice of issuing and renewing land leases beyond this date: "It also seems illogical to assume that the SAR government could only grant leases for an excessively short period as we approach 30 June 2047."[23] Wang Shuwen, a prominent mainland legal scholar who played an important role in the drafting of the Hong Kong Basic Law, has put it more bluntly. Pointing to the omission of any time limit in Article 123 of the Hong Kong Basic Law, he has dismissed as "groundless and unreasonable"[24] any concern that the Hong Kong SAR Government lacks the legal authority to issue land leases extending beyond 30 June 2047.

---

19. Professor Albert Chen, Chair Professor in Constitutional Law at the University of Hong Kong. Interviewed on "Backchat", *RTHK Radio 3*, 8 Dec 2009, a radio panel discussion on the legal implications of 2047 co-hosted by the author.
20. See Article 10 of the PRC Constitution 1982. Despite this constitutional prohibition, there were many experiments with land-use rights in China during the 1980s, and Article 10 was finally amended in 1988 to recognize this. It now states that: "The right to the use of land may be transferred in accordance with law."
21. Article 13, as amended in 2004.
22. This dates back to the PRC General Principles of the Civil Law, enacted by the NPC in 1986, and now includes the PRC Property Rights Law enacted in 2007.
23. *Granting of Leases After 30 June 1997* (see note 13) at para. 2.
24. Wang Shuwen, *Introduction to the Basic Law of the Hong Kong Special Administrative Region* (Law Press, 2nd English edition, 2009) at 614–615.

However, there have been some expressions of concern that Article 123 of the Hong Kong Basic Law does not grant an automatic right to renew land leases, instead leaving it at the discretion of the Hong Kong SAR Government whether or not to allow renewals in each case. Some scholars have suggested this could cause concern in the run up to 30 June 2047, perhaps making banks reluctant to grant mortgages which extend beyond that date.[25]

9.2 What Does 50 Years Mean?

Apart from these specific provisions on the renewal of land leases while Hong Kong was still under British rule, there is no explicit mention of the date 30 June 2047 in either the Joint Declaration or the Hong Kong Basic Law. That is not necessarily surprising, given that the primary focus of all parties at that time was on providing reassurance about continuity beyond 1997. With considerable doubts then being expressed about whether Hong Kong would survive as a separate entity beyond 30 June 1997, little attention seems to have been paid to what would happen half a century beyond that.[26]

In the absence of any further direct references to 30 June 2047 in either the Joint Declaration or the Hong Kong Basic Law, the significance of this date must instead be inferred from the provisions in both documents guaranteeing no fundamental change for a period of 50 years beyond 30 June 1997.

Article 5 of the Hong Kong Basic Law, which repeats identical wording used in Annex I(I) of the Joint Declaration, is cited by those who believe that one country, two systems will automatically come to an end on 30 June 2047 and that the socialist system (if it still exists in the rest of China at that date) will be applied to Hong Kong after that date. Morris (2007), for instance, argues that: "The destination is indeed 'to assimilate Hong Kong into the mainland politically, legally, culturally and ideologically,' using force if necessary, at whatever place may exist there in 2047."[27]

But it is open to question whether this is the correct interpretation of Article 5. Wang (2009), when discussing this provision, refers to a time period of "50 years and beyond".[28] Note, in particular, the comma separating Article 5 into two separate clauses in the English text of the Hong Kong Basic Law (the exact wording is shown at the start of this chapter). The second clause, promising that the "previous capitalist system and

---

25. See Olga Wong and Gary Cheung, "2047 is not all that far away", *South China Morning Post*, 29 June 2012, citing Professor Chau Kwong Wing as warning that the "current practice of discretionary renewal ... has given the public a false impression" and such lease renewals are "not guaranteed to continue after the 50-year term".
26. For one of the earliest discussions of this issue, C.K. Lau, "Why 2047 matters even now", *South China Morning Post*, 18 July 1997.
27. Robert J. Morris, "Forcing the Dance: Interpreting the Hong Kong Basic Law" in Hualing Fu, Lison Harris and Simon N.M. Young (eds.), *Interpreting Hong Kong's Basic Law: The Struggle for Coherence* (Palgrave Macmillan, 2007) at 100.
28. Wang, *Introduction to the Basic Law of the Hong Kong Special Administrative Region* (see note 24) at 102.

way of life shall remain unchanged", is expressly limited to a specific time period of 50 years. But the first clause, promising that "the socialist system and policies shall not be practised in the Hong Kong Special Administrative Region" is not expressly limited in this way, and may not necessarily be subject to a specific time restriction.

That is significant because the two promises in these two clauses separated by a comma in Article 5, although closely related, are not necessarily identical. The promise that the socialist system and policies will not be practised in Hong Kong is an essential precondition for the implementation of the promise that Hong Kong's previous capitalist system and way of life will be maintained. But the same is not true in reverse. After all, it would be perfectly possible to make many changes to Hong Kong's previous capitalist system and way of life that stopped short of introducing a socialist system, and which left Hong Kong, even after such changes, still following some form of one country, two systems.

In the Chinese text of the Hong Kong Basic Law, which prevails in any discrepancy between the two texts,[29] the structure of Article 5 is slightly different.[30] It could be argued that this blurs how far the wording on "no change for 50 years" can be interpreted as only referring to the minimum period during which Hong Kong's previous system and way of life must be maintained unchanged, and not the period during which China is barred from introducing a full socialist system in Hong Kong. But Article 5 needs to be interpreted in the context of the clear wording of the Preamble of the Hong Kong Basic Law. In both the Chinese and English texts this states, without any time limit, "that under the principle of 'one country, two systems', the socialist system and policies will not be practised in Hong Kong". Wang (2009) describes this provision in the Preamble as evidence of the "great importance" that China attaches to this principle.[31]

In fact, Chinese leaders have never suggested that they intend to impose a socialist system on Hong Kong after 30 June 2047. Quite the contrary. Deng Xiaoping, China's leader during the signing of the Joint Declaration and drafting of the Hong Kong Basic Law, repeatedly suggested that one country, two systems would remain in force beyond that date. In 1988, for instance, he told an international conference that:

> As a matter of fact, 50 years is only a vivid way of putting it. Even after 50 years our policy will not change either. That is, for the first 50 years it cannot be changed and for the second there will be no need to change it.[32]

Some Chinese officials have even suggested that China originally intended the guarantees about the maintenance of Hong Kong's previous capitalist system and way of life

---

29. Decision of the Standing Committee of the NPC on the English Text of the Basic Law of the Hong Kong SAR of the PRC (28 June 1990).
30. The Chinese text of Article 5 states as follows: 香港特別行政區不實行社會主義制度和政策，保持原有的資本主義制度和生活方式，五十年不變。
31. Wang, *Introduction to the Basic Law of the Hong Kong Special Administrative Region* (see note 24) at 102.
32. *Deng Xiaoping on the Question of Hong Kong* (Foreign Languages Press, 1993) at 61.

to apply indefinitely. According to these accounts, it was only because of suggestions from Hong Kong that guarantees linked to a specific time period would carry more credibility that these guarantees were subsequently framed in terms of a 50-year period.[33]

Viewed in this context, it seems unlikely that it was ever the purpose of Article 5 of the Hong Kong Basic Law to provide for an automatic end to one country, two systems and the imposition of a socialist system in Hong Kong after 30 June 2047. Instead, the reference to 50 years in Article 5 should be interpreted as only referring to the minimum period during which the promise not to make any fundamental changes to Hong Kong's capitalist system and way of life applies.

What that means is that while one country, two systems can continue to exist after 30 June 2047 under the Hong Kong Basic Law, fundamental changes to how that policy is applied in practice will become legally possible—changes, which are not, at least in theory, permissible before that date.

Even this conclusion is not free from challenge, since there is no expiry date mentioned in the provision in Article 159(4) prohibiting any amendments to the Hong Kong Basic Law that violate the fundamental tenets of one country, two systems.[34] On a literal interpretation, that prohibition of such amendments arguably continues to apply indefinitely.

But, as we saw earlier, a purposive approach needs to be taken in interpreting the Hong Kong Basic Law.[35] Since the original guarantee in the Joint Declaration only stated that these basic policies would remain unchanged for the first 50 years after 1 July 1997,[36] Ghai (1999) persuasively argues that on a purposive interpretation of the Hong Kong Basic Law the restriction on amendments imposed by Article 159(4) should be read as only applying for the same 50-year period.[37]

9.3 How Much Change?

The fact that fundamental changes to the Hong Kong Basic Law will become legally possible after 30 June 2047 inevitably gives rise to concern. After all, there are many possible ways of amending the Hong Kong Basic Law (such as by removing provisions protecting human rights or eroding the power of the judiciary) which, while still falling far short of imposing a socialist system, would so severely erode Hong Kong's separate system as to make it seem virtually meaningless.

But 30 June 2047 is also starting to be seen as an opportunity rather than a threat in some quarters. On that view, it offers Hong Kong the chance to make other changes to

---

33. Wong Man Fong, a senior Chinese official involved in formulating policy on Hong Kong. Cited in C.K. Lau, "Why 2047 matters even now" (see note 26).
34. For more on Article 159(4), and the procedure for amendments to the Hong Kong Basic Law, see further "7.5: Amendment" in Chapter 7.
35. For more on the purposive approach, see further "7.1: Hong Kong Courts" in Chapter 7.
36. Paragraph 3(12).
37. Yash Ghai, *Hong Kong's New Constitutional Order: The Resumption of Chinese Sovereignty and the Basic Law* (Hong Kong University Press, 2nd edition, 1999) at 143.

the Hong Kong Basic Law to rid itself of the shackles imposed by specific provisions which have become outdated with the passage of time, while continuing to preserve the bulk of the provisions in the Hong Kong Basic Law that protect the one country, two systems concept. That would require some kind of consultation process in Hong Kong prior to 2047, to try to reach a consensus on recommendations on which provisions in the Hong Kong Basic Law should be retained and which ones should be changed. Parallels could be drawn with the original process of writing the Hong Kong Basic Law during the 1980s, which involved the publication of two initial drafts and extensive public consultation in Hong Kong.[38]

The Hong Kong SAR Government has already floated the idea of such a discussion in relation to at least one provision in the Hong Kong Basic Law, calling for discussions on the future of the Small House Policy, which controversially offers every male indigenous inhabitant of the New Territories aged 18 or above a concessionary grant of land.[39] Since this policy is widely viewed as a right protected under Article 40 of the Hong Kong Basic Law,[40] the government has suggested that it could be possibly withdrawn from those indigenous inhabitants who will not turn 18 until after 30 June 2047.[41]

Another provision which some see as possibly in need of change is Article 111(1)'s guarantee of the continued existence of the Hong Kong dollar as a separate currency. At the time this was first written into the Joint Declaration in 1984, when the Chinese economy was much weaker and less open than it is today, a separate currency was seen as vital to Hong Kong's survival as an international financial centre. Chen (2003) identifies it as one of the most unique features of Hong Kong's high degree of autonomy.[42] Now, with China's Renminbi increasingly acquiring the status of a major international trading currency, Chen (2009) predicts the situation could change: "Maybe, by 2047, we will prefer not to have our own currency and to use the Renminbi."[43] Joseph Yam, former Chief Executive of the Hong Kong Monetary Authority, predicts it may be only a matter of time before the Renminbi starts to be widely used to buy goods and pay salaries in Hong Kong.[44]

---

38. See further "2.3: Drafting the Hong Kong Basic Law" in Chapter 2.
39. For more on the small house policy, and the problems it has caused, see further notes 38–43 in Chapter 8 and the accompanying text.
40. Article 40 protects the "lawful traditional rights and interests of the indigenous inhabitants of the New Territories", although it does not define what they are.
41. The idea of withdrawing this right for those born after 2029, which is 18 years before 2047, was first raised by then Secretary for Development Carrie Lam in a press interview in June 2012. See further Olga Wong and Joyce Ng, "End small-house policy, says Lam", *South China Morning Post*, 14 June 2012.
42. Albert H. Chen, "The Concept of 'One Country Two Systems' and Its Application to Hong Kong" in C. Stephen Hsu (ed.), *Understanding China's Legal System: Essays in Honor of Jerome A. Cohen* (New York University Press, 2003) at 364–365.
43. Interviewed on *Backchat* (see note 19).
44. Joseph Yam, *The Future of the Monetary System in Hong Kong* (Institute of Global Economics and Finance, Chinese University of Hong Kong, June 2012) at para. 22.

But the extent to which the existing provisions in the Hong Kong Basic Law impede such change is easily exaggerated. It is far from clear how far the Small House Policy is protected from change under Article 40 of the Hong Kong Basic Law.[45] In any case, since there was no mention in the Joint Declaration of the rights of indigenous inhabitants of the New Territories, there appears to be nothing to stop Article 40 from being amended, even before 30 June 2047.[46] Yam (2012) notes there is also nothing to stop China's Renminbi from circulating alongside the Hong Kong dollar, as is already increasingly the case.[47]

Nor has the Hong Kong Basic Law prevented the Hong Kong SAR Government from introducing major changes to Hong Kong's political structure, without any amendment of the Hong Kong Basic Law. Perhaps the most remarkable example of this came with the introduction in 2002 of a "ministerial" system,[48] under which the top posts in the Hong Kong SAR Government are filled by political appointees rather than civil servants, the system that existed at the time of the drafting of the Hong Kong Basic Law. The Hong Kong SAR Government justified this radical change on the somewhat remarkable grounds that there was nothing in the Hong Kong Basic Law that specifically prohibited it[49]—an argument which, if taken to its logical conclusion, would appear greatly to expand the boundaries of what can be done within the confines of the existing provisions of the Hong Kong Basic Law.

In a series of cases, the courts have held that the provisions in the Hong Kong Basic Law should not be interpreted in a way which unnecessarily inhibits change. In *Ng Ka Ling v Director of Immigration*,[50] the Court of Final Appeal laid down the general principle that the Hong Kong Basic Law is "a living instrument intended to meet changing needs and circumstances".[51] In *Secretary for Justice v Lau Kwok Fai*,[52] the court set a very high threshold which would have to be passed before any change to Hong Kong's current systems would be held to be in beach of the Hong Kong Basic Law. Referring to

---

45. For instance Johannes Chan argues persuasively [in "Rights of New Territories Indigenous Inhabitants" in Chan and Lim (eds.), *Law of the Hong Kong Constitution* (Sweet & Maxwell, 2011) at 894–900] that only a small part of what is today known as the Small House Policy falls within the rights protected under Article 40. See further notes 41–42 in Chapter 8 and the accompanying text.
46. Under Article 159(4) of the Hong Kong Basic Law, only those provisions which reflect the contents of China's promises in the 1984 Sino-British Joint Declaration are protected from change prior to 30 June 2047.
47. Yam, *The Future of the Monetary System in Hong Kong* (see note 44) at para. 21.
48. For more on the introduction of the ministerial system, officially known as the Principal Officials Accountability System, see further "5.4: Hong Kong SAR Government" in Chapter 5.
49. See further on this point, Christine Loh and Richard Cullen, "Politics Without Democracy: A Study of the New Principal Officials Accountability System in Hong Kong" (2003) 4 *San Diego International Law Journal* 127, 134.
50. (1999) 2 HKCFAR 4.
51. Ibid. at 28.
52. (2005) 8 HKCFAR 304.

Article 103, which preserves the civil service system that existed before 1 July 1997,[53] Sir Anthony Mason held that this provision "does not entail preservation of all the elements of which the system consists", and any change would only become a breach of the Hong Kong Basic Law if it was "such a material change that it resulted in the abandonment of the previous system".[54]

The court's reluctance to find that changes initiated by the Hong Kong SAR Government are in breach of the provisions in the Hong Kong Basic Law on maintaining Hong Kong's previous systems is illustrated by the Court of Final Appeal's subsequent decision in *Catholic Diocese of Hong Kong v Secretary for Justice*.[55] Despite strenuous opposition from the local Catholic Church to legislation they perceived as introducing a major—and unwelcome—change to the system of managing publicly funded schools,[56] the court held there was nothing in the Hong Kong Basic Law to stop Hong Kong's educational system from evolving in this way.[57]

Given the court's decisions in these cases, there is ample scope for arguing that it is possible to accommodate almost any change which might be considered desirable in Hong Kong within the confines of the existing wording of the Hong Kong Basic Law.

9.4 Parallels With 1997

The possibility of change after 30 June 2047 is sometimes seen as presenting an attractive opportunity to rid Hong Kong of outdated provisions. However, opening up the issue of selective amendments to the Hong Kong Basic Law carries risks. That is because it would present an opportunity for anyone in mainland China resentful of Hong Kong's special privileges to suggest changes which might be considered less desirable in Hong Kong. Lee (2009) warns, "it would be very foolish of Hong Kong people to say we want to change this and then to keep the rest because the reaction of Beijing would also be then we want to change this."[58] High on the list of provisions in the Hong Kong Basic Law which might then become vulnerable to change would be the power of final adjudication

---

53. Article 103 specifically refers to the continuation of the "previous system of recruitment, employment, assessment, discipline, training and management for the public service".
54. *Lau Kwok Fai* at 330.
55. [2012] 1 HKC 301.
56. This was Education (Amendment) Ordinance (No. 27 of 2004) requiring all such schools to set up incorporated management committees which the Catholic Diocese of Hong Kong feared would result in them losing full control over the publicly funded schools that they run.
57. *Catholic Diocese* at 321–322. The main argument in the case revolved around Article 136(1) of the Hong Kong Basic Law, which states that the Hong Kong SAR Government will formulate educational policies "[o]n the basis of the previous educational system". The Court of Final Appeal held that not only did this not prevent the introduction of new policies, but also that the policy at issue in this case was simply an evolution of a policy which had been already in place before 1 July 1997.
58. Martin Lee, Senior Counsel and former chairman of the Democratic Party. Interviewed on *Backchat* (see note 19).

granted to the Hong Kong courts, especially as this has resulted in many court rulings that China strongly disapproves of.[59]

Nonetheless, it is doubtful whether trying to ignore altogether the approach of 30 June 2047 is a realistic alternative. Whatever the precise meaning of the relevant provisions in the Hong Kong Basic Law, as a practical reality, concern about what will happen after that date is already starting to grow.[60] China appears to recognize that the date has some legal significance, judging by an official statement from the Central People's Government which sets a 30 June 2047 expiry date on Hong Kong's jurisdiction over a small area of land in Shenzhen.[61] However, a mainland legal expert has been quoted as stating that the Central Government does not want uncertainty about 2047 to undermine confidence in Hong Kong and, if the issue becomes a major cause for concern, would be prepared to offer some form of public reassurance that the "one country, two systems" formula would continue to apply in Hong Kong beyond that date.[62]

Easing such uncertainty need not involve making major changes to the Hong Kong Basic Law. Lee (1998) notes it might be sufficient simply to amend Article 5 of the Hong Kong Basic Law to explicitly state that Hong Kong's capitalist system and way of life will continue beyond 30 June 2047[63] — something arguably already implied by the lack of any reference to that date in the Preamble of the Hong Kong Basic Law. Chen (2009) suggests this could be accomplished by issuing a separate Decision of the National People's Congress on this point.[64] A common practice in China, this acts as a supplement to the original law and avoids the need to directly amend its text.[65]

Even if China does decide it wants to implement radical changes to the current system in Hong Kong, these need not necessarily happen in 2047. A historical parallel is instructive. Prior to 1 July 1997, there were many apocalyptic forecasts of the radical changes that were expected to occur in Hong Kong immediately after China's resumption of sovereignty.[66] In the event, these failed to materialize and 1 July 1997 saw a high degree

---

59. The most famous example was the Court of Final Appeal judgment in *Ng Ka Ling v Director of Immigration* (1999) 2 HKCFAR 4. For more on China's criticism of some aspects of this judgment, see further notes 202–205 in Chapter 6 and the accompanying text.
60. Former Chief Justice Andrew Li has predicted the issue will have to be resolved by "around 2030". See Simpson Cheung, "Hong Kong must iron out 'one country, two systems' as early as 2030, warns former chief justice", *South China Morning Post*, 9 Nov 2012.
61. This is around 40 hectares in Shenzhen Bay Port which has been placed under Hong Kong's jurisdiction to allow the operation of a Hong Kong customs station there. See further Official Reply of the State Council Concerning the Area of the "Hong Kong Port Area at the Shenzhen Bay Port" Over Which the Hong Kong Special Administrative Region is Authorized to Exercise Jurisdiction and the Land Use Period (30 Dec 2006).
62. Wong and Cheung, "2047 is not all that far away" (see note 25).
63. Lee, "Leases Beyond 2047?" (see note 16) at 185.
64. Interviewed on *Backchat* (see note 19).
65. See Albert Chen, *An Introduction to the Legal System of the People's Republic of China* (LexisNexis, 4th edition, 2011) at 143.
66. One of the most famous examples was the magazine cover story "The Death of Hong Kong", *Fortune*, 26 June 1995, subsequently retracted by the same magazine in "Oops! Hong Kong is hardly dead", *Fortune*, 28 June 2007.

of continuity, especially in Hong Kong's legal system. Instead, change has been a more gradual process, beginning long before 1997 and continuing after that date.

Much the same may well prove true in the run-up to 30 June 2047, especially as the guarantees in the Hong Kong Basic Law against fundamental change prior to that date are far less watertight than they might seem at first sight. As we saw earlier, it is now accepted that there are no legal constraints on the National People's Congress Standing Committee's unlimited power to interpret any part of the Hong Kong Basic Law at any time.[67] This power has already been used in 2004 to take away from Hong Kong the power to decide on any changes to how the Legislative Council is elected, a power which lay within Hong Kong's high degree of autonomy under the original text of the Hong Kong Basic Law.[68] What has been done once could easily be done again in future should China wish to do so. Indeed it would be far easier for the Standing Committee to introduce any radical changes—whether before or after 30 June 2047—through this power of interpretation, which is not subject to the same procedural restrictions as are supposed to apply to amending the Hong Kong Basic Law.[69]

Given the great changes that have already taken place in Hong Kong since the terms for "one country, two systems" were first agreed in the Joint Declaration between Britain and China in 1984, and the further changes which seem likely to continue to occur over the coming years, it would be wrong necessarily to see the date of 30 June 2047 as certain to mark a major turning point in Hong Kong's future. As we have seen, radical change is far from inevitable immediately after that date, nor necessarily the most likely scenario. Much will depend on decisions to be taken by future generations of Chinese leaders in coming decades, balancing the advantages and disadvantages to China of changing or maintaining Hong Kong's present system. Although far from certain, it is quite possible that the Hong Kong Basic Law may survive largely in its present form long beyond 30 June 2047.

---

67. See further note 105 in Chapter 7 and the accompanying text.
68. For more on this interpretation, and how it changed the original meaning of the text of Annex II(III) of the Hong Kong Basic Law, see further notes 206 and 208 in Chapter 5 and the accompanying text.
69. In addition, there are doubts about whether the restrictions on fundamental amendments to the HK Basic Law prior to 1 July 2047 are legally enforceable. See further note 266 in Chapter 7 and the accompanying text.

Appendix 1
Full Text of the Hong Kong Basic Law

The Basic Law of the Hong Kong Special Administrative Region
of the People's Republic of China

(Adopted at the Third Session of the Seventh National People's Congress on 4 April 1990)

Table of Contents

Preamble		316
Chapter I	General Principles	316
Chapter II	Relationship Between the Central Authorities and the Hong Kong Special Administrative Region	318
Chapter III	Fundamental Rights and Duties of the Residents	321
Chapter IV	Political Structure	323
Chapter V	Economy	335
Chapter VI	Education, Science, Culture, Sports, Religion, Labour and Social Services	340
Chapter VII	External Affairs	343
Chapter VIII	Interpretation and Amendment of the Basic Law	344
Chapter IX	Supplementary Provisions	345
Annex I	Method for the Selection of the Chief Executive of the Hong Kong Special Administrative Region	346
Annex II	Method for the Formation of the Legislative Council of the Hong Kong Special Administrative Region and Its Voting Procedures	347
Annex III	National Laws to be Applied in the Hong Kong Special Administrative Region	349

Preamble

Hong Kong has been part of the territory of China since ancient times; it was occupied by Britain after the Opium War in 1840. On 19 December 1984, the Chinese and British Governments signed the Joint Declaration on the Question of Hong Kong, affirming that the Government of the People's Republic of China will resume the exercise of sovereignty over Hong Kong with effect from 1 July 1997, thus fulfilling the long-cherished common aspiration of the Chinese people for the recovery of Hong Kong.

Upholding national unity and territorial integrity, maintaining the prosperity and stability of Hong Kong, and taking account of its history and realities, the People's Republic of China has decided that upon China's resumption of the exercise of sovereignty over Hong Kong, a Hong Kong Special Administrative Region will be established in accordance with the provisions of Article 31 of the Constitution of the People's Republic of China, and that under the principle of "one country, two systems", the socialist system and policies will not be practised in Hong Kong. The basic policies of the People's Republic of China regarding Hong Kong have been elaborated by the Chinese Government in the Sino-British Joint Declaration.

In accordance with the Constitution of the People's Republic of China, the National People's Congress hereby enacts the Basic Law of the Hong Kong Special Administrative Region of the People's Republic of China, prescribing the systems to be practised in the Hong Kong Special Administrative Region, in order to ensure the implementation of the basic policies of the People's Republic of China regarding Hong Kong.

Chapter I   General Principles

Article 1
The Hong Kong Special Administrative Region is an inalienable part of the People's Republic of China.

Article 2
The National People's Congress authorizes the Hong Kong Special Administrative Region to exercise a high degree of autonomy and enjoy executive, legislative and independent judicial power, including that of final adjudication, in accordance with the provisions of this Law.

Article 3
The executive authorities and legislature of the Hong Kong Special Administrative Region shall be composed of permanent residents of Hong Kong in accordance with the relevant provisions of this Law.

Article 4
The Hong Kong Special Administrative Region shall safeguard the rights and freedoms of the residents of the Hong Kong Special Administrative Region and of other persons in the Region in accordance with law.

Article 5

The socialist system and policies shall not be practised in the Hong Kong Special Administrative Region, and the previous capitalist system and way of life shall remain unchanged for 50 years.

Article 6

The Hong Kong Special Administrative Region shall protect the right of private ownership of property in accordance with law.

Article 7

The land and natural resources within the Hong Kong Special Administrative Region shall be State property. The Government of the Hong Kong Special Administrative Region shall be responsible for their management, use and development and for their lease or grant to individuals, legal persons or organizations for use or development. The revenues derived there from shall be exclusively at the disposal of the government of the Region.

Article 8

The laws previously in force in Hong Kong, that is, the common law, rules of equity, ordinances, subordinate legislation and customary law shall be maintained, except for any that contravene this Law, and subject to any amendment by the legislature of the Hong Kong Special Administrative Region.

Article 9

In addition to the Chinese language, English may also be used as an official language by the executive authorities, legislature and judiciary of the Hong Kong Special Administrative Region.

Article 10

Apart from displaying the national flag and national emblem of the People's Republic of China, the Hong Kong Special Administrative Region may also use a regional flag and regional emblem.

The regional flag of the Hong Kong Special Administrative Region is a red flag with a bauhinia highlighted by five star-tipped stamens.

The regional emblem of the Hong Kong Special Administrative Region is a bauhinia in the centre highlighted by five star-tipped stamens and encircled by the words "Hong Kong Special Administrative Region of the People's Republic of China" in Chinese and "HONG KONG" in English.

Article 11

In accordance with Article 31 of the Constitution of the People's Republic of China, the systems and policies practised in the Hong Kong Special Administrative Region, including the social and economic systems, the system for safeguarding the fundamental rights and freedoms of its residents, the executive, legislative and judicial systems, and the relevant policies, shall be based on the provisions of this Law.

No law enacted by the legislature of the Hong Kong Special Administrative Region shall contravene this Law.

Chapter II Relationship Between the Central Authorities and the Hong Kong Special Administrative Region

Article 12
The Hong Kong Special Administrative Region shall be a local administrative region of the People's Republic of China, which shall enjoy a high degree of autonomy and come directly under the Central People's Government.

Article 13
The Central People's Government shall be responsible for the foreign affairs relating to the Hong Kong Special Administrative Region.

The Ministry of Foreign Affairs of the People's Republic of China shall establish an office in Hong Kong to deal with foreign affairs.

The Central People's Government authorizes the Hong Kong Special Administrative Region to conduct relevant external affairs on its own in accordance with this Law.

Article 14
The Central People's Government shall be responsible for the defence of the Hong Kong Special Administrative Region.

The Government of the Hong Kong Special Administrative Region shall be responsible for the maintenance of public order in the Region.

Military forces stationed by the Central People's Government in the Hong Kong Special Administrative Region for defence shall not interfere in the local affairs of the Region. The Government of the Hong Kong Special Administrative Region may, when necessary, ask the Central People's Government for assistance from the garrison in the maintenance of public order and in disaster relief.

In addition to abiding by national laws, members of the garrison shall abide by the laws of the Hong Kong Special Administrative Region.

Expenditure for the garrison shall be borne by the Central People's Government.

Article 15
The Central People's Government shall appoint the Chief Executive and the principal officials of the executive authorities of the Hong Kong Special Administrative Region in accordance with the provisions of Chapter IV of this Law.

Article 16
The Hong Kong Special Administrative Region shall be vested with executive power. It shall, on its own, conduct the administrative affairs of the Region in accordance with the relevant provisions of this Law.

Article 17

The Hong Kong Special Administrative Region shall be vested with legislative power.

Laws enacted by the legislature of the Hong Kong Special Administrative Region must be reported to the National People's Congress Standing Committee for the record. The reporting for record shall not affect the entry into force of such laws.

If the National People's Congress Standing Committee, after consulting the Committee for the Basic Law of the Hong Kong Special Administrative Region under it, considers that any law enacted by the legislature of the Region is not in conformity with the provisions of this Law regarding affairs within the responsibility of the Central Authorities or regarding the relationship between the Central Authorities and the Region, the Standing Committee may return the law in question but shall not amend it. Any law returned by the National People's Congress Standing Committee shall immediately be invalidated. This invalidation shall not have retroactive effect, unless otherwise provided for in the laws of the Region.

Article 18

The laws in force in the Hong Kong Special Administrative Region shall be this Law, the laws previously in force in Hong Kong as provided for in Article 8 of this Law, and the laws enacted by the legislature of the Region.

National laws shall not be applied in the Hong Kong Special Administrative Region except for those listed in Annex III to this Law. The laws listed therein shall be applied locally by way of promulgation or legislation by the Region.

The National People's Congress Standing Committee may add to or delete from the list of laws in Annex III after consulting its Committee for the Basic Law of the Hong Kong Special Administrative Region and the government of the Region. Laws listed in Annex III to this Law shall be confined to those relating to defence and foreign affairs as well as other matters outside the limits of the autonomy of the Region as specified by this Law.

In the event that the National People's Congress Standing Committee decides to declare a state of war or, by reason of turmoil within the Hong Kong Special Administrative Region which endangers national unity or security and is beyond the control of the government of the Region, decides that the Region is in a state of emergency, the Central People's Government may issue an order applying the relevant national laws in the Region.

Article 19

The Hong Kong Special Administrative Region shall be vested with independent judicial power, including that of final adjudication.

The courts of the Hong Kong Special Administrative Region shall have jurisdiction over all cases in the Region, except that the restrictions on their jurisdiction imposed by the legal system and principles previously in force in Hong Kong shall be maintained.

The courts of the Hong Kong Special Administrative Region shall have no jurisdiction over acts of state such as defence and foreign affairs. The courts of the Region shall obtain a certificate from the Chief Executive on questions of fact concerning acts of state such as defence and foreign affairs whenever such questions arise in the adjudication of cases. This certificate shall be binding on the courts. Before issuing such a certificate, the Chief Executive shall obtain a certifying document from the Central People's Government.

Article 20
The Hong Kong Special Administrative Region may enjoy other powers granted to it by the National People's Congress, the National People's Congress Standing Committee or the Central People's Government.

Article 21
Chinese citizens who are residents of the Hong Kong Special Administrative Region shall be entitled to participate in the management of state affairs according to law.

In accordance with the assigned number of seats and the selection method specified by the National People's Congress, the Chinese citizens among the residents of the Hong Kong Special Administrative Region shall locally elect deputies of the Region to the National People's Congress to participate in the work of the highest organ of state power.

Article 22
No department of the Central People's Government and no province, autonomous region, or municipality directly under the Central Government may interfere in the affairs which the Hong Kong Special Administrative Region administers on its own in accordance with this Law.

If there is a need for departments of the Central Government, or for provinces, autonomous regions, or municipalities directly under the Central Government to set up offices in the Hong Kong Special Administrative Region, they must obtain the consent of the government of the Region and the approval of the Central People's Government.

All offices set up in the Hong Kong Special Administrative Region by departments of the Central Government, or by provinces, autonomous regions, or municipalities directly under the Central Government, and the personnel of these offices shall abide by the laws of the Region.

For entry into the Hong Kong Special Administrative Region, people from other parts of China must apply for approval. Among them, the number of persons who enter the Region for the purpose of settlement shall be determined by the competent authorities of the Central People's Government after consulting the government of the Region.

The Hong Kong Special Administrative Region may establish an office in Beijing.

Article 23
The Hong Kong Special Administrative Region shall enact laws on its own to prohibit any act of treason, secession, sedition, subversion against the Central People's Government, or theft of state secrets, to prohibit foreign political organizations or bodies from conducting political activities in the Region, and to prohibit political organizations or bodies of the Region from establishing ties with foreign political organizations or bodies.

Chapter III Fundamental Rights and Duties of the Residents

Article 24
Residents of the Hong Kong Special Administrative Region ("Hong Kong residents") shall include permanent residents and non-permanent residents.

The permanent residents of the Hong Kong Special Administrative Region shall be:

(1) Chinese citizens born in Hong Kong before or after the establishment of the Hong Kong Special Administrative Region;
(2) Chinese citizens who have ordinarily resided in Hong Kong for a continuous period of not less than seven years before or after the establishment of the Hong Kong Special Administrative Region;
(3) Persons of Chinese nationality born outside Hong Kong of those residents listed in categories (1) and (2);
(4) Persons not of Chinese nationality who have entered Hong Kong with valid travel documents, have ordinarily resided in Hong Kong for a continuous period of not less than seven years and have taken Hong Kong as their place of permanent residence before or after the establishment of the Hong Kong Special Administrative Region;
(5) Persons under 21 years of age born in Hong Kong of those residents listed in category (4) before or after the establishment of the Hong Kong Special Administrative Region; and
(6) Persons other than those residents listed in categories (1) to (5), who, before the establishment of the Hong Kong Special Administrative Region, had the right of abode in Hong Kong only.

The above-mentioned residents shall have the right of abode in the Hong Kong Special Administrative Region and shall be qualified to obtain, in accordance with the laws of the Region, permanent identity cards which state their right of abode.

The non-permanent residents of the Hong Kong Special Administrative Region shall be persons who are qualified to obtain Hong Kong identity cards in accordance with the laws of the Region but have no right of abode.

Article 25
All Hong Kong residents shall be equal before the law.

Article 26
Permanent residents of the Hong Kong Special Administrative Region shall have the right to vote and the right to stand for election in accordance with law.

Article 27
Hong Kong residents shall have freedom of speech, of the press and of publication; freedom of association, of assembly, of procession and of demonstration; and the right and freedom to form and join trade unions, and to strike.

Article 28

The freedom of the person of Hong Kong residents shall be inviolable.

No Hong Kong resident shall be subjected to arbitrary or unlawful arrest, detention or imprisonment. Arbitrary or unlawful search of the body of any resident or deprivation or restriction of the freedom of the person shall be prohibited. Torture of any resident or arbitrary or unlawful deprivation of the life of any resident shall be prohibited.

Article 29

The homes and other premises of Hong Kong residents shall be inviolable. Arbitrary or unlawful search of, or intrusion into, a resident's home or other premises shall be prohibited.

Article 30

The freedom and privacy of communication of Hong Kong residents shall be protected by law. No department or individual may, on any grounds, infringe upon the freedom and privacy of communication of residents except that the relevant authorities may inspect communication in accordance with legal procedures to meet the needs of public security or of investigation into criminal offences.

Article 31

Hong Kong residents shall have freedom of movement within the Hong Kong Special Administrative Region and freedom of emigration to other countries and regions. They shall have freedom to travel and to enter or leave the Region. Unless restrained by law, holders of valid travel documents shall be free to leave the Region without special authorization.

Article 32

Hong Kong residents shall have freedom of conscience.

Hong Kong residents shall have freedom of religious belief and freedom to preach and to conduct and participate in religious activities in public.

Article 33

Hong Kong residents shall have freedom of choice of occupation.

Article 34

Hong Kong residents shall have freedom to engage in academic research, literary and artistic creation, and other cultural activities.

Article 35

Hong Kong residents shall have the right to confidential legal advice, access to the courts, choice of lawyers for timely protection of their lawful rights and interests or for representation in the courts, and to judicial remedies.

Hong Kong residents shall have the right to institute legal proceedings in the courts against the acts of the executive authorities and their personnel.

Article 36
Hong Kong residents shall have the right to social welfare in accordance with law. The welfare benefits and retirement security of the labour force shall be protected by law.

Article 37
The freedom of marriage of Hong Kong residents and their right to raise a family freely shall be protected by law.

Article 38
Hong Kong residents shall enjoy the other rights and freedoms safeguarded by the laws of the Hong Kong Special Administrative Region.

Article 39
The provisions of the International Covenant on Civil and Political Rights, the International Covenant on Economic, Social and Cultural Rights, and international labour conventions as applied to Hong Kong shall remain in force and shall be implemented through the laws of the Hong Kong Special Administrative Region.

The rights and freedoms enjoyed by Hong Kong residents shall not be restricted unless as prescribed by law. Such restrictions shall not contravene the provisions of the preceding paragraph of this Article.

Article 40
The lawful traditional rights and interests of the indigenous inhabitants of the "New Territories" shall be protected by the Hong Kong Special Administrative Region.

Article 41
Persons in the Hong Kong Special Administrative Region other than Hong Kong residents shall, in accordance with law, enjoy the rights and freedoms of Hong Kong residents prescribed in this Chapter.

Article 42
Hong Kong residents and other persons in Hong Kong shall have the obligation to abide by the laws in force in the Hong Kong Special Administrative Region.

Chapter IV Political Structure

Section 1 *The Chief Executive*

Article 43
The Chief Executive of the Hong Kong Special Administrative Region shall be the head of the Hong Kong Special Administrative Region and shall represent the Region.

The Chief Executive of the Hong Kong Special Administrative Region shall be accountable to the Central People's Government and the Hong Kong Special Administrative Region in accordance with the provisions of this law.

Article 44

The Chief Executive of the Hong Kong Special Administrative Region shall be a Chinese citizen of not less than 40 years of age who is a permanent resident of the Region with no right of abode in any foreign country and has ordinarily resided in Hong Kong for a continuous period of not less than 20 years.

Article 45

The Chief Executive of the Hong Kong Special Administrative Region shall be selected by election or through consultations held locally and be appointed by the Central People's Government.

The method for selecting the Chief Executive shall be specified in the light of the actual situation in the Hong Kong Special Administrative Region and in accordance with the principle of gradual and orderly progress. The ultimate aim is the selection of the Chief Executive by universal suffrage upon nomination by a broadly representative nominating committee in accordance with democratic procedures.

The specific method for selecting the Chief Executive is prescribed in Annex I: "Method for the Selection of the Chief Executive of the Hong Kong Special Administrative Region".

Article 46

The term of office of the Chief Executive of the Hong Kong Special Administrative Region shall be five years. He or she may serve for not more than two consecutive terms.

Article 47

The Chief Executive of the Hong Kong Special Administrative Region must be a person of integrity, dedicated to his or her duties.

The Chief Executive, on assuming office, shall declare his or her assets to the Chief Justice of the Court of Final Appeal of the Hong Kong Special Administrative Region. This declaration shall be put on record.

Article 48

The Chief Executive of the Hong Kong Special Administrative Region shall exercise the following powers and functions:

(1) To lead the government of the Region;
(2) To be responsible for the implementation of this Law and other laws which, in accordance with this Law, apply in the Hong Kong Special Administrative Region;
(3) To sign bills passed by the Legislative Council and to promulgate laws;
   To sign budgets passed by the Legislative Council and report the budgets and final accounts to the Central People's Government for the record;
(4) To decide on government policies and to issue executive orders;
(5) To nominate and to report to the Central People's Government for appointment the following principal officials: Secretaries and Deputy Secretaries of Departments, Directors of Bureaux, Commissioner Against Corruption, Director of Audit,

Commissioner of Police, Director of Immigration and Commissioner of Customs and Excise; and to recommend to the Central People's Government the removal of the above-mentioned officials;
(6) To appoint or remove judges of the courts at all levels in accordance with legal procedures;
(7) To appoint or remove holders of public office in accordance with legal procedures;
(8) To implement the directives issued by the Central People's Government in respect of the relevant matters provided for in this Law;
(9) To conduct, on behalf of the Government of the Hong Kong Special Administrative Region, external affairs and other affairs as authorized by the Central Authorities;
(10) To approve the introduction of motions regarding revenues or expenditure to the Legislative Council;
(11) To decide, in the light of security and vital public interests, whether government-officials or other personnel in charge of government affairs should testify or give evidence before the Legislative Council or its committees;
(12) To pardon persons convicted of criminal offences or commute their penalties; and
(13) To handle petitions and complaints.

Article 49

If the Chief Executive of the Hong Kong Special Administrative Region considers that a bill passed by the Legislative Council is not compatible with the overall interests of the Region, he or she may return it to the Legislative Council within three months for reconsideration. If the Legislative Council passes the original bill again by not less than a two-thirds majority of all the members, the Chief Executive must sign and promulgate it within one month, or act in accordance with the provisions of Article 50 of this Law.

Article 50

If the Chief Executive of the Hong Kong Special Administrative Region refuses to sign a bill passed the second time by the Legislative Council, or the Legislative Council refuses to pass a budget or any other important bill introduced by the government, and if consensus still cannot be reached after consultations, the Chief Executive may dissolve the Legislative Council.

The Chief Executive must consult the Executive Council before dissolving the Legislative Council. The Chief Executive may dissolve the Legislative Council only once in each term of his or her office.

Article 51

If the Legislative Council of the Hong Kong Special Administrative Region refuses to pass the budget introduced by the government, the Chief Executive may apply to the Legislative Council for provisional appropriations. If appropriation of public funds cannot be approved because the Legislative Council has already been dissolved, the Chief Executive may, prior to the election of the new Legislative Council, approve provisional short-term appropriations according to the level of expenditure of the previous fiscal year.

Article 52

The Chief Executive of the Hong Kong Special Administrative Region must resign under any of the following circumstances:

(1) When he or she loses the ability to discharge his or her duties as a result of serious illness or other reasons;
(2) When, after the Legislative Council is dissolved because he or she twice refuses to sign a bill passed by it, the new Legislative Council again passes by a two-thirds majority of all the members the original bill in dispute, but he or she still refuses to sign it; and
(3) When, after the Legislative Council is dissolved because it refuses to pass a budget or any other important bill, the new Legislative Council still refuses to pass the original bill in dispute.

Article 53

If the Chief Executive of the Hong Kong Special Administrative Region is not able to discharge his or her duties for a short period, such duties shall temporarily be assumed by the Administrative Secretary, Financial Secretary or Secretary of Justice in this order of precedence.

In the event that the office of Chief Executive becomes vacant, a new Chief Executive shall be selected within six months in accordance with the provisions of Article 45 of this Law. During the period of vacancy, his or her duties shall be assumed according to the provisions of the preceding paragraph.

Article 54

The Executive Council of the Hong Kong Special Administrative Region shall be an organ for assisting the Chief Executive in policy-making.

Article 55

Members of the Executive Council of the Hong Kong Special Administrative Region shall be appointed by the Chief Executive from among the principal officials of the executive authorities, members of the Legislative Council and public figures. Their appointment or removal shall be decided by the Chief Executive. The term of office of members of the Executive Council shall not extend beyond the expiry of the term of office of the Chief Executive who appoints them.

Members of the Executive Council of the Hong Kong Special Administrative Region shall be Chinese citizens who are permanent residents of the Region with no right of abode in any foreign country.

The Chief Executive may, as he or she deems necessary, invite other persons concerned to sit in on meetings of the Council.

Article 56

The Executive Council of the Hong Kong Special Administrative Region shall be presided over by the Chief Executive.

Except for the appointment, removal and disciplining of officials and the adoption of measures in emergencies, the Chief Executive shall consult the Executive Council before making important policy decisions, introducing bills to the Legislative Council, making subordinate legislation, or dissolving the Legislative Council.

If the Chief Executive does not accept a majority opinion of the Executive Council, he or she shall put the specific reasons on record.

Article 57
A Commission Against Corruption shall be established in the Hong Kong Special Administrative Region. It shall function independently and be accountable to the Chief Executive.

Article 58
A Commission of Audit shall be established in the Hong Kong Special Administrative Region. It shall function independently and be accountable to the Chief Executive.

Section 2   The Executive Authorities

Article 59
The Government of the Hong Kong Special Administrative Region shall be the executive authorities of the Region.

Article 60
The head of the Government of the Hong Kong Special Administrative Region shall be the Chief Executive of the Region.

A Department of Administration, a Department of Finance, a Department of Justice, and various bureaux, divisions and commissions shall be established in the Government of the Hong Kong Special Administrative Region.

Article 61
The principal officials of the Hong Kong Special Administrative Region shall be Chinese citizens who are permanent residents of the Region with no right of abode in any foreign country and have ordinarily resided in Hong Kong for a continuous period of not less than 15 years.

Article 62
The Government of the Hong Kong Special Administrative Region shall exercise the following powers and functions:

(1) To formulate and implement policies;
(2) To conduct administrative affairs;
(3) To conduct external affairs as authorised by the Central People's Government under this Law;
(4) To draw up and introduce budgets and final accounts;
(5) To draft and introduce bills, motions and subordinate legislation; and
(6) To designate officials to sit in on the meetings of the Legislative Council and to speak on behalf of the government.

Article 63
The Department of Justice of the Hong Kong Special Administrative Region shall control criminal prosecutions, free from any interference.

Article 64
The Government of the Hong Kong Special Administrative Region must abide by the law and be accountable to the Legislative Council of the Region: it shall implement laws passed by the Council and already in force; it shall present regular policy addresses to the Council; it shall answer questions raised by members of the Council; and it shall obtain approval from the Council for taxation and public expenditure.

Article 65
The previous system of establishing advisory bodies by the executive authorities shall be maintained.

Section 3 The Legislature

Article 66
The Legislative Council of the Hong Kong Special Administrative Region shall be the legislature of the Region.

Article 67
The Legislative Council of the Hong Kong Special Administrative Region shall be composed of Chinese citizens who are permanent residents of the Region with no right of abode in any foreign country. However, permanent residents of the Region who are not of Chinese nationality or who have the right of abode in foreign countries may also be elected members of the Legislative Council of the Region, provided that the proportion of such members does not exceed 20 percent of the total membership of the Council.

Article 68
The Legislative Council of the Hong Kong Special Administrative Region shall be constituted by election.

The method for forming the Legislative Council shall be specified in the light of the actual situation in the Hong Kong Special Administrative Region and in accordance with the principle of gradual and orderly progress. The ultimate aim is the election of all the members of the Legislative Council by universal suffrage.

The specific method for forming the Legislative Council and its procedures for voting on bills and motions are prescribed in Annex II: "Method for the Formation of the Legislative Council of the Hong Kong Special Administrative Region and Its Voting Procedures".

Article 69
The term of office of the Legislative Council of the Hong Kong Special Administrative Region shall be four years, except the first term which shall be two years.

Article 70

If the Legislative Council of the Hong Kong Special Administrative Region is dissolved by the Chief Executive in accordance with the provisions of this Law, it must, within three months, be reconstituted by election in accordance with Article 68 of this Law.

Article 71

The President of the Legislative Council of the Hong Kong Special Administrative Region shall be elected by and from among the members of the Legislative Council.

The President of the Legislative Council of the Hong Kong Special Administrative Region shall be a Chinese citizen of not less than 40 years of age, who is a permanent resident of the Region with no right of abode in any foreign country and has ordinarily resided in Hong Kong for a continuous period of not less than 20 years.

Article 72

The President of the Legislative Council of the Hong Kong Special Administrative Region shall exercise the following powers and functions:

(1) To preside over meetings;
(2) To decide on the agenda, giving priority to government bills for inclusion in the agenda;
(3) To decide on the time of meetings;
(4) To call special sessions during the recess;
(5) To call emergency sessions on the request of the Chief Executive; and
(6) To exercise other powers and functions as prescribed in the rules of procedure of the Legislative Council.

Article 73

The Legislative Council of the Hong Kong Special Administrative Region shall exercise the following powers and functions;

(1) To enact, amend or repeal laws in accordance with the provisions of this Law and legal procedures;
(2) To examine and approve budgets introduced by the government;
(3) To approve taxation and public expenditure;
(4) To receive and debate the policy addresses of the Chief Executive;
(5) To raise questions on the work of the government;
(6) To debate any issue concerning public interests;
(7) To endorse the appointment and removal of the judges of the Court of Final Appeal and the Chief Judge of the High Court;
(8) To receive and handle complaints from Hong Kong residents;
(9) If a motion initiated jointly by one-fourth of all the members of the Legislative Council charges the Chief Executive with serious breach of law or dereliction of duty and if he or she refuses to resign, the Council may, after passing a motion for investigation, give a mandate to the Chief Justice of the Court of Final Appeal to form and chair an independent investigation committee. The committee shall

be responsible for carrying out the investigation and reporting its findings to the Council. If the committee considers the evidence sufficient to substantiate such charges, the Council may pass a motion of impeachment by a two-thirds majority of all its members and report it to the Central People's Government for decision; and

(10) To summon, as required when exercising the above-mentioned powers and functions, persons concerned to testify or give evidence.

Article 74

Members of the Legislative Council of the Hong Kong Special Administrative Region may introduce bills in accordance with the provisions of this Law and legal procedures. Bills which do not relate to public expenditure or political structure or the operation of the government may be introduced individually or jointly by members of the Council. The written consent of the Chief Executive shall be required before bills relating to government polices are introduced.

Article 75

The quorum for the meeting of the Legislative Council of the Hong Kong Special Administrative Region shall be not less than one half of all its members.

The rules of procedure of the Legislative Council shall be made by the Council on its own, provided that they do not contravene this Law.

Article 76

A bill passed by the Legislative council of the Hong Kong Special Administrative Region may take effect only after it is signed and promulgated by the Chief Executive.

Article 77

Members of the Legislative Council of the Hong Kong Special Administrative Region shall be immune from legal action in respect of their statements at meetings of the Council.

Article 78

Members of the Legislative Council of the Hong Kong Special Administrative Region shall not be subjected to arrest when attending or on their way to a meeting of the Council.

Article 79

The President of the Legislative Council of the Hong Kong Special Administrative Region shall declare that a member of the Council is no longer qualified for the office under any of the following circumstances:

(1) When he or she loses the ability to discharge his or her duties as a result of serious illness or other reasons;
(2) When he or she, with no valid reason, is absent from meetings for three consecutive months without the consent of the President of the Legislative Council;
(3) When he or she loses or renounces his or her status as a permanent resident of the Region;

(4) When he or she accepts a government appointment and becomes a public servant;
(5) When he or she is bankrupt or fails to comply with a court order to repay debts;
(6) When he or she is convicted and sentenced to imprisonment for one month or more for a criminal offence committed within or outside the Region and is relieved of his or her duties by a motion passed by two-thirds of the members of the Legislative Council present; and
(7) When he or she is censured for misbehaviour or breach of oath by a vote of two-thirds of the members of the Legislative Council present.

Section 4   The Judiciary

Article 80
The courts of the Hong Kong Special Administrative Region at all levels shall be the judiciary of the Region, exercising the judicial power of the Region.

Article 81
The Court of Final Appeal, the High Court, district courts, magistrates' courts and other special courts shall be established in the Hong Kong Special Administrative Region. The High Court shall comprise the Court of Appeal and the Court of First Instance.

The judicial system previously practised in Hong Kong shall be maintained except for those changes consequent upon the establishment of the Court of Final Appeal of the Hong Kong Special Administrative Region.

Article 82
The power of final adjudication of the Hong Kong Special Administrative Region shall be vested in the Court of Final Appeal of the Region, which may as required invite judges from other common law jurisdictions to sit on the Court of Final Appeal.

Article 83
The structure, powers and functions of the courts of the Hong Kong Special Administrative Region at all levels shall be prescribed by law.

Article 84
The courts of the Hong Kong Special Administrative Region shall adjudicate cases in accordance with the laws applicable in the Region as prescribed in Article 18 of this Law and may refer to precedents of other common law jurisdictions.

Article 85
The courts of the Hong Kong Special Administrative Region shall exercise judicial power independently, free from any interference. Members of the judiciary shall be immune from legal action in the performance of their judicial functions.

Article 86
The principle of trial by jury previously practised in Hong Kong shall be maintained.

Article 87

In criminal or civil proceedings in the Hong Kong Special Administrative Region, the principles previously applied in Hong Kong and the rights previously enjoyed by parties to proceedings shall be maintained.

Anyone who is lawfully arrested shall have the right to a fair trial by the judicial organs without delay and shall be presumed innocent until convicted by the judicial organs.

Article 88

Judges of the courts of the Hong Kong Special Administrative Region shall be appointed by the Chief Executive on the recommendation of an independent commission composed of local judges, persons from the legal profession and eminent persons from other sectors.

Article 89

A judge of court of the Hong Kong Special Administrative Region may only be removed for inability to discharge his or her duties, or for misbehaviour, by the Chief Executive on the recommendation of a tribunal appointed by the Chief Justice of the Court of Final Appeal and consisting of not fewer than three local judges.

The Chief Justice of the Court of Final Appeal of the Hong Kong Special Administrative Region may be investigated only for inability to discharge his or her duties, or for misbehaviour, by a tribunal appointed by the Chief Executive and consisting of not fewer than five local judges and may be removed by the Chief Executive on the recommendation of the tribunal and in accordance with the procedures prescribed in this Law.

Article 90

The Chief Justice of the Court of Final Appeal and the Chief Judge of the High Court of the Hong Kong Special Administrative Region shall be Chinese citizens who are permanent residents of the Region with no right of abode in any foreign country.

In the case of the appointment or removal of judges of the Court of Final Appeal and the Chief Judge of the High Court of the Hong Kong Special Administrative Region, the Chief Executive shall, in addition to following the procedures prescribed in Articles 88 and 89 of this Law, obtain the endorsement of the Legislative Council and report such appointment or removal to the National People's Congress Standing Committee for the record.

Article 91

The Hong Kong Special Administrative Region shall maintain the previous system of appointment and removal of members of the judiciary other than judges.

Article 92

Judges and other members of the judiciary of the Hong Kong Special Administrative Region shall be chosen on the basis of their judicial and professional qualities and may be recruited from other common law jurisdictions.

Article 93

Judges and other members of the judiciary serving in Hong Kong before the establishment of the Hong Kong Special Administrative Region may all remain in employment and retain their seniority with pay, allowances, benefits and conditions of service no less favourable than before.

The Government of the Hong Kong Special Administrative Region shall pay to judges and other members of the judiciary who retire or leave the service in compliance with regulations, including those who have retired or left the service before the establishment of the Hong Kong Special Administrative Region, or to their dependants, all pensions, gratuities, allowances and benefits due to them on terms no less favourable than before, irrespective of their nationality or place of residence.

Article 94

On the basis of the system previously operating in Hong Kong, the Government of the Hong Kong Special Administrative Region may make provisions for local lawyers and lawyers from outside Hong Kong to work and practise in the Region.

Article 95

The Hong Kong Special Administrative Region may, through consultations and in accordance with law, maintain juridical relations with the judicial organs of other parts of the country, and they may render assistance to each other.

Article 96

With the assistance or authorization of the Central People's Government, the Government of the Hong Kong Special Administrative Region may make appropriate arrangements with foreign states for reciprocal juridical assistance.

Section 5   District Organizations

Article 97

District organizations which are not organs of political power may be established in the Hong Kong Special Administrative Region, to be consulted by the government of the Region on district administration and other affairs, or to be responsible for providing services in such fields as culture, recreation and environmental sanitation.

Article 98

The powers and functions of the district organizations and the method for their formation shall be prescribed by law.

Section 6   Public Servants

Article 99

Public servants serving in all government departments of the Hong Kong Special Administrative Region must be permanent residents of the Region, except where otherwise provided for in Article 101 of this Law regarding public servants of foreign nationalities and except for those below a certain rank as prescribed by law.

Public servants must be dedicated to their duties and be responsible to the Government of the Hong Kong Special Administrative Region.

Article 100

Public servants serving in all Hong Kong government departments, including the police department, before the establishment of the Hong Kong Special Administrative Region, may all remain in employment and retain their seniority with pay, allowances, benefits and conditions of service no less favourable than before.

Article 101

The Government of the Hong Kong Special Administrative Region may employ British and other foreign nationals previously serving in the public service in Hong Kong, or those holding permanent identity cards of the Region, to serve as public servants in government departments at all levels, but only Chinese citizens among permanent residents of the Region with no right of abode in any foreign country may fill the following posts: the Secretaries and Deputy Secretaries of Departments, Directors of Bureaux, Commissioner Against Corruption, Director of Audit, Commissioner of Police, Director of Immigration and Commissioner of Customs and Excise.

The Government of the Hong Kong Special Administrative Region may also employ British and other foreign nationals as advisers to government departments and, when required, may recruit qualified candidates from outside the Region to fill professional and technical posts in government departments. These foreign nationals shall be employed only in their individual capacities and shall be responsible to the government of the Region.

Article 102

The Government of the Hong Kong Special Administrative Region shall pay to public servants who retire or who leave the service in compliance with regulations, including those who have retired or who have left the service in compliance with regulations before the establishment of the Hong Kong Special Administrative Region, or to their dependants, all pensions, gratuities, allowances and benefits due to them on terms no less favourable than before, irrespective of their nationality or place of residence.

Article 103

The appointment and promotion of public servants shall be on the basis of their qualifications, experience and ability. Hong Kong's previous system of recruitment, employment, assessment, discipline, training and management for the public service, including special bodies for their appointment, pay and conditions of service, shall be maintained, except for any provisions for privileged treatment of foreign nationals.

Article 104

When assuming office, the Chief Executive, principal officials, members of the Executive Council and of the Legislative Council, judges of the courts at all levels and other members of the judiciary in the Hong Kong Special Administrative Region must, in accordance with law, swear to uphold the Basic Law of the Hong Kong Special Administrative Region of the People's Republic of China and swear allegiance to the Hong Kong Special Administrative Region of the People's Republic of China

Chapter V Economy

Section 1 Public Finance, Monetary Affairs, Trade, Industry and Commerce

Article 105
The Hong Kong Special Administrative Region shall, in accordance with law, protect the right of individuals and legal persons to the acquisition, use, disposal and inheritance of property and their right to compensation for lawful deprivation of their property.

Such compensation shall correspond to the real value of the property concerned at the time and shall be freely convertible and paid without undue delay.

The ownership of enterprises and the investments from outside the Region shall be protected by law.

Article 106
The Hong Kong Special Administrative Region shall have independent finances.

The Hong Kong Special Administrative Region shall use its financial revenues exclusively for its own purposes, and they shall not be handed over to the Central People's Government.

The Central People's Government shall not levy taxes in the Hong Kong Special Administrative Region.

Article 107
The Hong Kong Special Administrative Region shall follow the principle of keeping the expenditure within the limits of revenues in drawing up its budget, and strive to achieve a fiscal balance, avoid deficits and keep the budget commensurate with the growth rate of its gross domestic product.

Article 108
The Hong Kong Special Administrative Region shall practise an independent taxation system.

The Hong Kong Special Administrative Region shall, taking the low tax policy previously pursued in Hong Kong as reference, enact laws on its own concerning types of taxes, tax rates, tax reductions, allowances and exemptions, and other matters of taxation.

Article 109
The Government of the Hong Kong Special Administrative Region shall provide an appropriate economic and legal environment for the maintenance of the status of Hong Kong as an international financial centre.

Article 110

The monetary and financial systems of the Hong Kong Special Administrative Region shall be prescribed by law.

The Government of the Hong Kong Special Administrative Region shall, on its own, formulate monetary and financial policies, safeguard the free operation of financial business and financial markets, and regulate and supervise them in accordance with law.

Article 111

The Hong Kong dollar, as the legal tender in the Hong Kong Special Administrative Region, shall continue to circulate.

The authority to issue Hong Kong currency shall be vested in the Government of the Hong Kong Special Administrative Region. The issue of Hong Kong currency must be backed by a 100% reserve fund. The system regarding the issue of Hong Kong currency and the reserve fund system shall be prescribed by law.

The Government of the Hong Kong Special Administrative Region may authorize designated banks to issue or continue to issue Hong Kong currency under statutory authority, after satisfying itself that any issue of currency will be soundly based and that the arrangements for such issue are consistent with the object of maintaining the stability of the currency.

Article 112

No foreign exchange control policies shall be applied in the Hong Kong Special Administrative Region. The Hong Kong dollar shall be freely convertible. Markets for foreign exchange, gold, securities, futures and the like shall continue.

The Government of the Hong Kong Special Administrative Region shall safeguard the free flow of capital within, into and out of the Region.

Article 113

The Exchange Fund of the Hong Kong Special Administrative Region shall be managed and controlled by the government of the Region, primarily for regulating the exchange value of the Hong Kong dollar.

Article 114

The Hong Kong Special Administrative Region shall maintain the status of a free port and shall not impose any tariff unless otherwise prescribed by law.

Article 115

The Hong Kong Special Administrative Region shall pursue the policy of free trade and safeguard the free movement of goods, intangible assets and capital.

Article 116

The Hong Kong Special Administrative Region shall be a separate customs territory.

The Hong Kong Special Administrative Region may, using the name "Hong Kong, China", participate in relevant international organizations and international trade agreements (including preferential trade arrangements), such as the General Agreement on Tariffs and Trade and arrangements regarding international trade in textiles.

Export quotas, tariff preferences and other similar arrangements, which are obtained or made by the Hong Kong Special Administrative Region or which were obtained or made and remain valid, shall be enjoyed exclusively by the Region.

Article 117
The Hong Kong Special Administrative Region may issue its own certificates of origin for products in accordance with prevailing rules of origin.

Article 118
The Government of the Hong Kong Special Administrative Region shall provide an economic and legal environment for encouraging investments, technological progress and the development of new industries.

Article 119
The Government of the Hong Kong Special Administrative Region shall formulate appropriate policies to promote and co-ordinate the development of various trades such as manufacturing, commerce, tourism, real estate, transport, public utilities, services, agriculture and fisheries, and pay regard to the protection of the environment.

Section 2   Land Leases

Article 120
All leases of land granted, decided upon or renewed before the establishment of the Hong Kong Special Administrative Region which extend beyond 30 June 1997, and all rights in relation to such leases, shall continue to be recognized and protected under the law of the Region.

Article 121
As regards all leases of land granted or renewed where the original leases contain no right of renewal, during the period from 27 May 1985 to 30 June 1997, which extend beyond 30 June 1997 and expire not later than 30 June 2047, the lessee is not required to pay an additional premium as from July 1, 1997, but an annual rent equivalent to 3 per cent of the rateable value of the property at that date, adjusted in step with any changes in the rateable value thereafter, shall be charged.

Article 122
In the case of old schedule lots, village lots, small houses and similar rural holdings, where the property was on 30 June 1984 held by, or, in the case of small houses granted after that date, where the property is granted to, a lessee descended through the male line from a person who was in 1898 a resident of an established village in Hong Kong, the previous rent shall remain unchanged so long as the property is held by that lessee or by one of his lawful successors in the male line.

Articles 123

Where leases of land without a right of renewal expire after the establishment of the Hong Kong Special Administrative Region, they shall be dealt with in accordance with laws and policies formulated by the Region on its own.

Section 3   Shipping

Article 124

The Hong Kong Special Administrative Region shall maintain Hong Kong's previous systems of shipping management and shipping regulation, including the system for regulating conditions of seamen.

The Government of the Hong Kong Special Administrative Region shall, on its own, define its specific functions and responsibilities in respect of shipping.

Article 125

The Hong Kong Special Administrative Region shall be authorized by the Central People's Government to continue to maintain a shipping register and issue related certificates under its legislation, using the name "Hong Kong, China".

Article 126

With the exception of foreign warships, access for which requires the special permission of the Central People's Government, ships shall enjoy access to the ports of the Hong Kong Special Administrative Region in accordance with the laws of the Region.

Article 127

Private shipping businesses and shipping-related businesses and private container terminals in the Hong Kong Special Administrative Region may continue to operate freely.

Section 4   Civil Aviation

Article 128

The Government of the Hong Kong Special Administrative Region shall provide conditions and take measures for the maintenance of the status of Hong Kong as a centre of international and regional aviation.

Article 129

The Hong Kong Special Administrative Region shall continue the previous system of civil aviation management in Hong Kong and keep its own aircraft register in accordance with provisions laid down by the Central People's Government concerning nationality marks and registration marks of aircraft.

Access of foreign state aircraft to the Hong Kong Special Administrative Region shall require the special permission of the Central People's Government.

Article 130

The Hong Kong Special Administrative Region shall be responsible on its own for matters of routine business and technical management of civil aviation, including the management of airports, the provision of air traffic services within the flight information region of the Hong Kong Special Administrative Region, and the discharge of other responsibilities allocated to it under the regional air navigation procedures of the International Civil Aviation Organization.

Article 131
The Central People's Government shall, in consultation with the Government of the Hong Kong Special Administrative Region, make arrangements providing air services between the Region and other parts of the People's Republic of China for airlines incorporated in the Hong Kong Special Administrative Region and having their principal place of business in Hong Kong and other airlines of the People's Republic of China.

Article 132
All air service agreements providing air services between other parts of the People's Republic of China and other states and regions with stops at the Hong Kong Special Administrative Region and air services between the Hong Kong Special Administrative Region and other states and regions with stops at other parts of the People's Republic of China shall be concluded by the Central People's Government.

In concluding the air service agreements referred to in the first paragraph of this Article, the Central People's Government shall take account of the special conditions and economic interests of the Hong Kong Special Administrative Region and consult the government of the Region.

Representatives of the Government of the Hong Kong Special Administrative Region may, as members of the delegations of the Government of the People's Republic of China, participate in air service consultations conducted by the Central People's Government with foreign governments concerning arrangements for such services referred to in the first paragraph of this Article.

Article 133
Acting under specific authorizations from the Central People's Government, the Government of the Hong Kong Special Administrative Region may:

(1) renew or amend air service agreements and arrangements previously in force;
(2) negotiate and conclude new air service agreements providing routes for airlines incorporated in the Hong Kong Special Administrative Region and having their principal place of business in Hong Kong and providing rights for over-flights and technical stops; and
(3) negotiate and conclude provisional arrangements with foreign states or regions with which no air service agreements have been concluded.

All scheduled air services to, from or through Hong Kong, which do not operate to, from or through the mainland of China shall be regulated by the air service agreements or provisional arrangements referred to in this Article.

Article 134
The Central People's Government shall give the Government of the Hong Kong Special Administrative Region the authority to:

(1) negotiate and conclude with other authorities all arrangements concerning the implementation of the air service agreements and provisional arrangements referred to in Article 133 of this Law;
(2) issue licences to airlines incorporated in the Hong Kong Special Administrative Region and having their principal place of business in Hong Kong;
(3) designate such airlines under the air service agreements and provisional arrangements referred to in Article 133 of this Law; and
(4) issue permits to foreign airlines for services other than those to, from or through the mainland of China.

Article 135
Airlines incorporated and having their principal place of business in Hong Kong and business related to civil aviation functioning there prior to the establishment of the Hong Kong Special Administrative Region may continue to operate.

Chapter VI   Education, Science, Culture, Sports, Religion, Labour and Social Services

Article 136
On the basis of the previous educational system, the Government of the Hong Kong Special Administrative Region shall, on its own, formulate policies on the development and improvement of education, including policies regarding the educational system and its administration, the language of instruction, the allocation of funds, the examination system, the system of academic awards and the recognition of educational qualifications.

Community organizations and individuals may, in accordance with law, run educational undertakings of various kinds in the Hong Kong Special Administrative Region.

Article 137
Educational institutions of all kinds may retain their autonomy and enjoy academic freedom. They may continue to recruit staff and use teaching materials from outside the Hong Kong Special Administrative Region. Schools run by religious organizations may continue to provide religious education, including courses in religion.

Students shall enjoy freedom of choice of educational institutions and freedom to pursue their education outside the Hong Kong Special Administrative Region.

Article 138
The Government of the Hong Kong Special Administrative Region shall, on its own, formulate policies to develop Western and traditional Chinese medicine and to improve medical and health services. Community organizations and individuals may provide various medical and health services in accordance with law.

Article 139

The Government of the Hong Kong Special Administrative Region shall, on its own, formulate policies on science and technology and protect by law achievements in scientific and technological research, patents, discoveries and inventions.

The Government of the Hong Kong Special Administrative Region shall, on its own, decide on the scientific and technological standards and specifications applicable in Hong Kong.

Article 140

The Government of the Hong Kong Special Administrative Region shall, on its own, formulate policies on culture and protect by law the achievements and the lawful rights and interests of authors in their literary and artistic creation.

Article 141

The Government of the Hong Kong Special Administrative Region shall not restrict the freedom of religious belief, interfere in the internal affairs of religious organizations or restrict religious activities which do not contravene the laws of the Region.

Religious organizations shall, in accordance with law, enjoy the rights to acquire, use, dispose of and inherit property and the right to receive financial assistance. Their previous property rights and interests shall be maintained and protected.

Religious organizations may, according to their previous practice, continue to run seminaries and other schools, hospitals and welfare institutions and to provide other social services.

Religious organizations and believers in the Hong Kong Special Administrative Region may maintain and develop their relations with religious organizations and believers elsewhere.

Article 142

The Government of the Hong Kong Special Administrative Region shall, on the basis of maintaining the previous systems concerning the professions, formulate provisions on its own for assessing the qualifications for practice in the various professions.

Persons with professional qualifications or qualifications for professional practice obtained prior to the establishment of the Hong Kong Special Administrative Region may retain their previous qualifications in accordance with the relevant regulations and codes of practice.

The Government of the Hong Kong Special Administrative Region shall continue to recognize the professions and the professional organizations recognized prior to the establishment of the Region, and these organizations may, on their own, assess and confer professional qualifications.

The Government of the Hong Kong Special Administrative Region may, as required by developments in society and in consultation with the parties concerned, recognize new professions and professional organizations.

Article 143

The Government of the Hong Kong Special Administrative Region shall, on its own, formulate policies on sports. Non-governmental sports organizations may continue to exist and develop in accordance with law.

Article 144

The Government of the Hong Kong Special Administrative Region shall maintain the policy previously practised in Hong Kong in respect of subventions for non-governmental organizations in fields such as education, medicine and health, culture, art, recreation, sports, social welfare and social work. Staff members previously serving in subvented organizations in Hong Kong may remain in their employment in accordance with the previous system.

Article 145

On the basis of the previous social welfare system, the Government of the Hong Kong Special Administrative Region shall, on its own, formulate policies on the development and improvement of this system in the light of the economic conditions and social needs.

Article 146

Voluntary organizations providing social services in the Hong Kong Special Administrative Region may, on their own, decide their forms of service, provided that the law is not contravened.

Article 147

The Hong Kong Special Administrative Region shall on its own formulate laws and policies relating to labour.

Article 148

The relationship between non-governmental organizations in fields such as education, science, technology, culture, art, sports, the professions, medicine and health, labour, social welfare and social work as well as religious organizations in the Hong Kong Special Administrative Region and their counterparts on the mainland shall be based on the principles of non-subordination, non-interference and mutual respect.

Article 149

Non-governmental organizations in fields such as education, science, technology, culture, art, sports, the professions, medicine and health, labour, social welfare and social work as well as religious organizations in the Hong Kong Special Administrative Region may maintain and develop relations with their counterparts in foreign countries and regions and with relevant international organizations. They may, as required, use the name "Hong Kong, China" in the relevant activities.

Chapter VII External Affairs

Article 150
Representatives of the Government of the Hong Kong Special Administrative Region may, as members of delegations of the Government of the People's Republic of China, participate in negotiations at the diplomatic level directly affecting the Region conducted by the Central People's Government.

Article 151
The Hong Kong Special Administrative Region may on its own, using the name "Hong Kong, China", maintain and develop relations and conclude and implement agreements with foreign states and regions and relevant international organizations in the appropriate fields, including the economic, trade, financial and monetary, shipping, communications, tourism, cultural and sports fields.

Article 152
Representatives of the Government of the Hong Kong Special Administrative Region may, as members of delegations of the People's Republic of China, participate in international organizations or conferences in appropriate fields limited to states and affecting the Region, or may attend in such other capacity as may be permitted by the Central People's Government and the international organization or conference concerned, and may express their views, using the name "Hong Kong, China".

The Hong Kong Special Administrative Region may, using the name "Hong Kong, China", participate in international organizations and conferences not limited to states.

The Central People's Government shall take the necessary steps to ensure that the Hong Kong Special Administrative Region shall continue to retain its status in an appropriate capacity in those international organizations of which the People's Republic of China is a member and in which Hong Kong participates in one capacity or another.

The Central People's Government shall, where necessary, facilitate the continued participation of the Hong Kong Special Administrative Region in an appropriate capacity in those international organizations in which Hong Kong is a participant in one capacity or another, but of which the People's Republic of China is not a member.

Article 153
The application to the Hong Kong Special Administrative Region of international agreements to which the People's Republic of China is or becomes a party shall be decided by the Central People's Government, in accordance with the circumstances and needs of the Region, and after seeking the views of the government of the Region.

International agreements to which the People's Republic of China is not a party but which are implemented in Hong Kong may continue to be implemented in the Hong Kong Special Administrative Region. The Central People's Government shall, as necessary, authorize or assist the government of the Region to make appropriate arrangements for the application to the Region of other relevant international agreements.

Article 154

The Central People's Government shall authorize the Government of the Hong Kong Special Administrative Region to issue, in accordance with law, passports of the Hong Kong Special Administrative Region of the People's Republic of China to all Chinese citizens who hold permanent identity cards of the Region, and travel documents of the Hong Kong Special Administrative Region of the People's Republic of China to all other persons lawfully residing in the Region. The above passports and documents shall be valid for all states and regions and shall record the holder's right to return to the Region.

The Government of the Hong Kong Special Administrative Region may apply immigration controls on entry into, stay in and departure from the Region by persons from foreign states and regions.

Article 155

The Central People's Government shall assist or authorize the Government of the Hong Kong Special Administrative Region to conclude visa abolition agreements with foreign states or regions.

Article 156

The Hong Kong Special Administrative Region may, as necessary, establish official or semi-official economic and trade missions in foreign countries and shall report the establishment of such missions to the Central People's Government for the record.

Article 157

The establishment of foreign consular and other official or semi-official missions in the Hong Kong Special Administrative Region shall require the approval of the Central People's Government.

Consular and other official missions established in Hong Kong by states which have formal diplomatic relations with the People's Republic of China may be maintained.

According to the circumstances of each case, consular and other official missions established in Hong Kong by states which have no formal diplomatic relations with the People's Republic of China may be permitted either to remain or be changed to semi-official missions.

States not recognized by the People's Republic of China may only establish non-governmental institutions in the Region.

Chapter VIII   Interpretation and Amendment of the Basic Law

Article 158

The power of interpretation of this Law shall be vested in the National People's Congress Standing Committee.

The National People's Congress Standing Committee shall authorize the courts of the Hong Kong Special Administrative Region to interpret on their own, in adjudicating cases, the provisions of this Law which are within the limits of the autonomy of the Region.

The courts of the Hong Kong Special Administrative Region may also interpret other provisions of this Law in adjudicating cases. However, if the courts of the Region, in adjudicating cases, need to interpret the provisions of this Law concerning affairs which are the responsibility of the Central People's Government, or concerning the relationship between the Central Authorities and the Region, and if such interpretation will affect the judgments on the cases, the courts of the Region shall, before making their final judgments which are not appealable, seek an interpretation of the relevant provisions from the National People's Congress Standing Committee through the Court of Final Appeal of the Region. When the Standing Committee makes an interpretation of the provisions concerned, the courts of the Region, in applying those provisions, shall follow the interpretation of the Standing Committee. However, judgments previously rendered shall not be affected.

The National People's Congress Standing Committee shall consult its Committee for the Basic Law of the Hong Kong Special Administrative Region before giving an interpretation of this Law.

Article 159

The power of amendment of this Law shall be vested in the National People's Congress.

The power to propose bills for amendments to this Law shall be vested in the National People's Congress Standing Committee, the State Council and the Hong Kong Special Administrative Region. Amendment bills from the Hong Kong Special Administrative Region shall be submitted to the National People's Congress by the delegation of the Region to the National People's Congress after obtaining the consent of two-thirds of the deputies of the Region to the National People's Congress, two-thirds of all the members of the Legislative Council of the Region, and the Chief Executive of the Region.

Before a bill for amendment to this Law is put on the agenda of the National People's Congress, the Committee for the Basic Law of the Hong Kong Special Administrative Region shall study it and submit its views.

No amendment to this Law shall contravene the established basic policies of the People's Republic of China regarding Hong Kong.

Chapter IX   Supplementary Provisions

Article 160

Upon the establishment of the Hong Kong Special Administrative Region, the laws previously in force in Hong Kong shall be adopted as laws of the Region except for those which the National People's Congress Standing Committee declares to be in contravention of this Law. If any laws are later discovered to be in contravention of this Law, they shall be amended or cease to have force in accordance with the procedure as prescribed by this Law.

Documents, certificates, contracts, and rights and obligations valid under the laws previously in force in Hong Kong shall continue to be valid and be recognized and protected by the Hong Kong Special Administrative Region, provided that they do not contravene this Law.

Annex I Method for the Selection of the Chief Executive of the Hong Kong Special Administrative Region

1. The Chief Executive shall be elected by a broadly representative Election Committee in accordance with this Law and appointed by the Central People's Government.
2. The Election Committee shall be composed of 800 members from the following sectors:

Industrial, commercial and financial sectors	200
The professions	200
Labour, social services, religious and other sectors	200
Members of the Legislative Council, representatives of district-based organizations, Hong Kong deputies to the National People's Congress, and representatives of Hong Kong members of the National Committee of the Chinese People's Political Consultative Conference	200

    The term of office of the Election Committee shall be five years.
3. The delimitation of the various sectors, the organizations in each sector eligible to return Election Committee members and the number of such members returned by each of these organizations shall be prescribed by an electoral law enacted by the Hong Kong Special Administrative Region in accordance with the principles of democracy and openness.

    Corporate bodies in various sectors shall, on their own, elect members to the Election Committee, in accordance with the number of seats allocated and the election method as prescribed by the electoral law.

    Members of the Election Committee shall vote in their individual capacities.
4. Candidates for the office of Chief Executive may be nominated jointly by not less than 100 members of the Election Committee. Each member may nominate only one candidate.
5. The Election Committee shall, on the basis of the list of nominees, elect the Chief Executive designate by secret ballot on a one-person-one-vote basis. The specific election method shall be prescribed by the electoral law.
6. The first Chief Executive shall be selected in accordance with the "Decision of the National People's Congress on the Method for the Formation of the First Government and the First Legislative Council of the Hong Kong Special Administrative Region".
7. If there is a need to amend the method for selecting the Chief Executives for the terms subsequent to the year 2007, such amendments must be made with the endorsement of a two-thirds majority of all the members of the Legislative Council and the consent of the Chief Executive, and they shall be reported to the National People's Congress Standing Committee for approval.

Amendment to Annex I

(Approved at the Sixteenth Session of the Standing Committee of the Eleventh National People's Congress on 28 August 2010)

1. The Election Committee to elect the fourth term Chief Executive in 2012 shall be composed of 1200 members from the following sectors:

Industrial, commercial and financial sectors	300
The professions	300
Labour, social services, religious and other sectors	300
Members of the Legislative Council, Hong Kong deputies to the National People's Congress, representatives of members of the District Councils, representatives of Hong Kong members of the National Committee of the Chinese People's Political Consultative Conference, and representatives of the Heung Yee Kuk	300

   The term of office of the Election Committee shall be five years.

2. Candidates for the office of Chief Executive may be nominated jointly by not less than 150 members of the Election Committee. Each member may nominate only one candidate.

Annex II Method for the Formation of the Legislative Council of the Hong Kong Special Administrative Region and Its Voting Procedures

I. Method for the formation of the Legislative Council

1. The Legislative Council of the Hong Kong Special Administrative Region shall be composed of 60 members in each term. In the first term, the Legislative Council shall be formed in accordance with the "Decision of the National People's Congress on the Method for the Formation of the First Government and the First Legislative Council of the Hong Kong Special Administrative Region". The composition of the Legislative Council in the second and third terms shall be as follows:

   Second term

Members returned by functional constituencies	30
Members returned by the Election Committee	6
Members returned by geographical constituencies through direct elections	24

   Third term

Members returned by functional constituencies	30
Members returned by geographical constituencies through direct elections	30

2. Except in the case of the first Legislative Council, the above-mentioned Election Committee refers to the one provided for in Annex I of this Law. The division of geographical constituencies and the voting method for direct elections therein; the delimitation of functional sectors and corporate bodies, their seat allocation and election methods; and the method for electing members of the Legislative Council by the Election Committee shall be specified by an electoral law introduced by the Government of the Hong Kong Special Administrative Region and passed by the Legislative Council.

II. *Procedures for voting on bills and motions in the Legislative Council*

Unless otherwise provided for in this Law, the Legislative Council shall adopt the following procedures for voting on bills and motions:

The passage of bills introduced by the government shall require at least a simple majority vote of the members of the Legislative Council present.

The passage of motions, bills or amendments to government bills introduced by individual members of the Legislative Council shall require a simple majority vote of each of the two groups of members present: members returned by functional constituencies and those returned by geographical constituencies through direct elections and by the Election Committee.

III. *Method for the formation of the Legislative Council and its voting procedures subsequent to the year 2007*

With regard to the method for forming the Legislative Council of the Hong Kong Special Administrative Region and its procedures for voting on bills and motions after 2007, if there is a need to amend the provisions of this Annex, such amendments must be made with the endorsement of a two-thirds majority of all the members of the Council and the consent of the Chief Executive, and they shall be reported to the National People's Congress Standing Committee for the record.

Amendment to Annex II

(Recorded at the Sixteenth Session of the Standing Committee of the Eleventh National People's Congress on 28 August 2010)

1. The fifth term Legislative Council in the year 2012 shall be composed of 70 members, and the composition shall be as follows:

Members returned by functional constituencies	35
Members returned by geographical constituencies through direct elections	35

Annex III National Laws to be Applied in the Hong Kong Special Administrative Region

The following national laws shall be applied locally with effect from 1 July 1997 by way of promulgation or legislation by the Hong Kong Special Administrative Region:

1. Resolution on the Capital, Calendar, National Anthem and National Flag of the People's Republic of China;
2. Resolution on the National Day of the People's Republic of China;
3. Declaration of the Government of the People's Republic of China on the Territorial Sea;
4. Nationality Law of the People's Republic of China;
5. Regulations of the People's Republic of China Concerning Diplomatic Privileges and Immunities;
6. Law of the People's Republic of China on the National Flag;
7. Regulations of the People's Republic of China concerning Consular Privileges and Immunities;
8. Law of the People's Republic of China on the National Emblem;
9. Law of the People's Republic of China on the Territorial Sea and the Contiguous Zone;
10. Law of the People's Republic of China on the Garrisoning of the Hong Kong Special Administrative Region;
11. Law of the People's Republic of China on the Exclusive Economic Zone and the Continental shelf;
12. Law of the People's Republic of China on Judicial Immunity from Compulsory Measures Concerning the Property of Foreign Central Banks.

Appendix 2
Full Text of Related Decisions and Interpretations

Selected Decisions and Interpretations of the National People's Congress and Its Standing Committee on the Basic Law of the Hong Kong Special Administrative Region of the People's Republic of China

Table of Contents

Decision of the NPC on the Basic Law of the Hong Kong SAR of the PRC (4 April 1990)	353
Decision of the NPC on the Establishment of the Hong Kong SAR (4 April 1990)	353
Decision of the NPC on the Method for the Formation of the First Government and the First Legislative Council of the Hong Kong SAR (4 April 1990)	354
Decision of the NPC Approving the Proposal by the Drafting Committee for the Basic Law of the Hong Kong SAR on the Establishment of the Committee for the Basic Law of the Hong Kong SAR Under the Standing Committee of the NPC (4 April 1990)	355
Decision of the Standing Committee of the NPC on the English Text of the Basic Law of the Hong Kong SAR of the PRC (28 June 1990)	356
Decision of the Standing Committee of the NPC on Treatment of the Laws Previously in Force in Hong Kong in Accordance With Article 160 of the Basic Law of the Hong Kong SAR of the PRC (23 February 1997)[1]	357
The Interpretation by the Standing Committee of the NPC of Articles 22(4) and 24(2)(3) of the Basic Law of the Hong Kong SAR of the PRC (26 June 1999)	362
The Interpretation by the Standing Committee of the NPC of Article 7 of Annex I and Article III of Annex II to the Basic Law of the Hong Kong SAR of the PRC (6 April 2004)	364

---

1. English translations of Decisions and Interpretations from 1997 onwards are prepared by the Department of Justice for reference purposes and reproduced © The Hong Kong SAR Government.

Decision of the Standing Committee of the NPC on Issues Relating to 366
the Methods for Selecting the Chief Executive of the Hong Kong SAR
in the Year 2007 and for Forming the Legislative Council of the Hong Kong
SAR in the Year 2008 (26 April 2004)

Interpretation of Paragraph 2, Article 53 of the Basic Law of the Hong Kong 368
SAR of the PRC by the Standing Committee of the NPC (27 April 2005)

Decision of the Standing Committee of the NPC on Issues Relating to the 370
Methods for Selecting the Chief Executive of the Hong Kong SAR and
for Forming the Legislative Council of the Hong Kong SAR in the Year
2012 and on Issues Relating to Universal Suffrage (29 December 2007)

Interpretation of Paragraph 1, Article 13 and Article 19 of the Basic Law of 372
the Hong Kong SAR of the PRC by the Standing Committee of the NPC
(26 August 2011)

Note:

For English translations of all Decisions of the NPC and its Standing Committee on the Hong Kong Basic Law, and other related documents, see Instruments A101–A211 on the Department of Justice Bilingual Laws Information Services, at http://www.legislation.gov.hk/eng/home.htm.

Decision of the National People's Congress on the Basic Law of the Hong Kong Special Administrative Region of the People's Republic of China

(Adopted at the Third Session of the Seventh National People's Congress on 4 April 1990)

The Third Session of the Seventh National People's Congress adopts the Basic Law of the Hong Kong Special Administrative Region of the People's Republic of China, including Annex I: Method for the Selection of the Chief Executive of the Hong Kong Special Administrative Region, Annex II: Method for the Formation of the Legislative Council of the Hong Kong Special Administrative Region and Its Voting Procedures, Annex III: National Laws to Be Applied in the Hong Kong Special Administrative Region, and the designs of the regional flag and regional emblem of the Hong Kong Special Administrative Region. Article 31 of the Constitution of the People's Republic of China provides: "The State may establish special administrative regions when necessary. The systems to be instituted in special administrative regions shall be prescribed by law enacted by the National People's Congress in the light of the specific conditions." The Basic Law of the Hong Kong Special Administrative Region is constitutional as it is enacted in accordance with the Constitution of the People's Republic of China and in the light of the specific conditions of Hong Kong. The systems, policies and laws to be instituted after the establishment of the Hong Kong Special Administrative Region shall be based on the Basic Law of the Hong Kong Special Administrative Region.

The Basic Law of the Hong Kong Special Administrative Region of the People's Republic of China shall be put into effect as of July 1, 1997.

Decision of the National People's Congress on the Establishment of the Hong Kong Special Administrative Region

(Adopted at the Third Session of the Seventh National People's Congress on 4 April 1990)

In accordance with the provisions of Article 31 and sub-paragraph 13 of Article 62 of the Constitution of the People's Republic of China, the Third Session of the Seventh National People's Congress decides:

1. The Hong Kong Special Administrative Region is to be established on July 1, 1997.
2. The area of the Hong Kong Special Administrative Region covers the Hong Kong Island, the Kowloon Peninsula, and the islands and adjacent waters under its jurisdiction. The map of the administrative division of the Hong Kong Special Administrative Region will be published by the State Council separately.

Decision of the National People's Congress on the Method for the Formation of the First Government and the First Legislative Council of the Hong Kong Special Administrative Region

(Adopted at the Third Session of the Seventh National People's Congress on 4 April 1990)

1. The first Government and the first Legislative Council of the Hong Kong Special Administrative Region shall be formed in accordance with the principles of State sovereignty and smooth transition.

2. Within the year 1996, the National People's Congress shall establish a Preparatory Committee for the Hong Kong Special Administrative Region, which shall be responsible for preparing the establishment of the Hong Kong Special Administrative Region and shall prescribe the specific method for the formation of the first Government and the first Legislative Council in accordance with this Decision. The Preparatory Committee shall be composed of mainland members and of Hong Kong members who shall constitute not less than 50 per cent of its membership. Its chairman and members shall be appointed by the Standing Committee of the National People's Congress.

3. The Preparatory Committee for the Hong Kong Special Administrative Region shall be responsible for preparing the establishment of the Selection Committee for the First Government of the Hong Kong Special Administrative Region (hereinafter referred to as the Selection Committee).

    The Selection Committee shall be composed entirely of permanent residents of Hong Kong and must be broadly representative. It shall include Hong Kong deputies to the National People's Congress, representatives of Hong Kong members of the National Committee of the Chinese People's Political Consultative Conference, persons with practical experience who have served in Hong Kong's executive, legislative and advisory organs prior to the establishment of the Hong Kong Special Administrative Region, and persons representative of various strata and sectors of society.

    The Selection Committee shall be composed of 400 members in the following proportions:

Industrial, commercial and financial sectors	25 per cent
The professions	25 per cent
Labour, grass-roots, religious and other sectors	25 per cent
Former political figures, Hong Kong deputies to the National People's Congress, and representatives of Hong Kong members of the National Committee of the Chinese People's Political Consultative Conference	25 per cent

4. The Selection Committee shall recommend the candidate for the first Chief Executive through local consultations or through nomination and election after consultations,

and report the recommended candidate to the Central People's Government for appointment. The term of office of the first Chief Executive shall be the same as the regular term.

5. The Chief Executive of the Hong Kong Special Administrative Region shall be responsible for preparing the formation of the first Government of the Region in accordance with the Basic Law of the Hong Kong Special Administrative Region.

6. The first Legislative Council of the Hong Kong Special Administrative Region shall be composed of 60 members, with 20 members returned by geographical constituencies through direct elections, 10 members returned by an election committee, and 30 members returned by functional constituencies. If the composition of the last Hong Kong Legislative Council before the establishment of the Hong Kong Special Administrative Region is in conformity with the relevant provisions of this Decision and the Basic Law of the Hong Kong Special Administrative Region, those of its members who uphold the Basic Law of the Hong Kong Special Administrative Region of the People's Republic of China and pledge allegiance to the Hong Kong Special Administrative Region of the People's Republic of China, and who meet the requirements set forth in the Basic Law of the Region may, upon confirmation by the Preparatory Committee, become members of the first Legislative Council of the Region. The term of office of members of the first Legislative Council of the Hong Kong Special Administrative Region shall be two years.

Decision of the National People's Congress Approving the Proposal by the Drafting Committee for the Basic Law of the Hong Kong Special Administrative Region on the Establishment of the Committee for the Basic Law of the Hong Kong Special Administrative Region Under the Standing Committee of the National People's Congress

(Adopted at the Third Session of the Seventh National People's Congress on 4 April 1990)

The Third Session of the Seventh National People's Congress decides:

1. to approve the proposal by the Drafting Committee for the Basic Law of the Hong Kong Special Administrative Region on the Establishment of the Committee for the Basic Law of the Hong Kong Special Administrative Region under the Standing Committee of the National People's Congress; and

2. to establish the Committee for the Basic Law of the Hong Kong Special Administrative Region under the Standing Committee of the National People's Congress when the Basic Law of the Hong Kong Special Administrative Region of the People's Republic of China is put into effect.

Appendix

Proposal by the Drafting Committee for the Basic Law of the Hong Kong Special Administrative Region on the Establishment of the Committee for the Basic Law of the Hong Kong Special Administrative Region Under the Standing Committee of the National People's Congress

1. Name: The Committee for the Basic Law of the Hong Kong Special Administrative Region under the Standing Committee of the National People's Congress.

2. Affiliation: To be a working committee under the Standing Committee of the National People's Congress.

3. Function: To study questions arising from the implementation of Articles 17, 18, 158 and 159 of the Basic Law of the Hong Kong Special Administrative Region and submit its views thereon to the Standing Committee of the National People's Congress.

4. Composition: Twelve members, six from the mainland and six from Hong Kong, including persons from the legal profession, appointed by the Standing Committee of the National People's Congress for a term of office of five years. Hong Kong members shall be Chinese citizens who are permanent residents of the Hong Kong Special Administrative Region with no right of abode in any foreign country and shall be nominated jointly by the Chief Executive, President of the Legislative Council and Chief Justice of the Court of Final Appeal of the Region for appointment by the Standing Committee of the National People's Congress.

Decision of the Standing Committee of the National People's Congress on the English Text of the Basic Law of the Hong Kong Special Administrative Region of the People's Republic of China

(Adopted on 28 June 1990)

The 14th Meeting of the Standing Committee of the Seventh National People's Congress decides: the English translation of the Basic Law of the Hong Kong Special Administrative Region of the People's Republic of China, examined and approved under the aegis of the Law Committee of the National People's Congress, shall be the official English text and shall be equally authentic as the Chinese text. In case of any discrepancy in the meaning of wording between the English text and the Chinese text, the Chinese text shall prevail.

Decision of the Standing Committee of the National People's Congress on Treatment of the Laws Previously in Force in Hong Kong in Accordance With Article 160 of the Basic Law of the Hong Kong Special Administrative Region of the People's Republic of China

(Adopted at the Twenty-Fourth Session of the Standing Committee of the
Eighth National People's Congress on 23 February 1997)

Article 160 of the Basic Law of the Hong Kong Special Administrative Region of the People's Republic of China (hereinafter referred to as "the Basic Law") stipulates—

"Upon the establishment of the Hong Kong Special Administrative Region, the laws previously in force in Hong Kong shall be adopted as laws of the Region except for those which the Standing Committee of the National People's Congress declares to be in contravention of this Law. If any laws are later discovered to be in contravention of this Law, they shall be amended or cease to have force in accordance with the procedure as prescribed by this Law."

Article 8 stipulates—

"The laws previously in force in Hong Kong, that is, the common law, rules of equity, ordinances, subordinate legislation and customary law shall be maintained, except for any that contravene this Law, and subject to any amendment by the legislature of the Hong Kong Special Administrative Region."

In accordance with the above provisions, the Standing Committee of the Eighth National People's Congress examined the proposals made by the preparatory Committee of the Hong Kong Special Administrative Region on treatment of issues relating to the laws previously in force in Hong Kong, and decides at its Twenty-Fourth Session as follows—

1. The laws previously in force in Hong Kong, which include the common law, rules of equity, ordinances, subordinate legislation and customary law, except for those which are in contravention of the Basic Law, are adopted as the laws of the Hong Kong Special Administrative Region.

2. Such of the ordinances and subordinate legislation previously in force in Hong Kong as set out in Annex 1 to this Decision are in contravention of the Basic Law and are not adopted as the laws of the Hong Kong Special Administrative Region.

3. Such provisions of the ordinances and subordinate legislation previously in force in Hong Kong as set out in Annex 2 to this Decision are in contravention of the Basic Law and those provisions are not adopted as the laws of the Hong Kong Special Administrative Region.

4. Such of the laws previously in force in Hong Kong which have been adopted as the laws of the Hong Kong Special Administrative Region shall, as from 1 July 1997, be applied subject to such modifications, adaptations, limitations or exceptions as are necessary so as to bring them into conformity with the status of Hong Kong

after resumption by the People's Republic of China of the exercise of sovereignty over Hong Kong as well as to be in conformity with the relevant provisions of the Basic Law. For example, the New Territories Land (Exemption) Ordinance should conform with the above principles in its application.

Apart from conforming with the above principles, the following shall be observed, that is to say, in the ordinances and subordinate legislation previously in force–

- (1) laws relating to foreign affairs in respect of the Hong Kong Special Administrative Region which are inconsistent with the national laws applied in the Hong Kong Special Administrative Region shall be subject to the national laws and shall be consistent with the international rights and obligations of the Central People's Government;
- (2) provisions conferring privileges on the United Kingdom or other Commonwealth countries or territories, other than provisions relating to reciprocal arrangements between Hong Kong and the United Kingdom or other Commonwealth countries or territories, are not retained;
- (3) provisions relating to the rights, exemptions and obligations of military forces stationed in Hong Kong by the United Kingdom are retained subject to the provisions of the Basic Law and the Law of the People's Republic of China on the Garrisoning of the Hong Kong Special Administrative Region of the People's Republic of China, and shall apply to the military forces stationed in the Hong Kong Special Administrative Region by the Central People's Government of the People's Republic of China;
- (4) provisions relating to the superior legal status of the English language as compared with the Chinese language shall be construed as providing that both the Chinese and English languages are to be official languages;
- (5) provisions applying any English law may continue to be applicable by reference thereto as a transitional arrangement pending their amendment by the Hong Kong Special Administrative Region, provided that they are not prejudicial to the sovereignty of the People's Republic of China and do not contravene the provisions of the Basic Law.

5. Subject to the provisions of paragraph 4, the names or expressions appearing in the laws previously in force in Hong Kong that are adopted as the laws of the Hong Kong Special Administrative Region shall, unless the context otherwise requires, be construed or applied in accordance with the principles of substitution provided for in Annex 3 to this Decision.

6. If any laws previously in force in Hong Kong which have been adopted as the laws of the Hong Kong Special Administrative Region are later discovered to be in contravention of the Basic Law, they shall be amended or shall cease to have force in accordance with the procedure as prescribed by the Basic Law.

Annex 1

The following ordinances and subordinate legislation previously in force in Hong Kong, which contravene the Basic Law, are not adopted as the laws of the Hong Kong Special Administrative Region–

1. Trustees (Hong Kong Government Securities) Ordinance (Cap 77, Laws of Hong Kong);
2. Application of English Law Ordinance (Cap 88, Laws of Hong Kong);
3. Foreign Marriage Ordinance (Cap 180, Laws of Hong Kong);
4. Chinese Extradition Ordinance (Cap 235, Laws of Hong Kong);
5. Colony Armorial Bearings (Protection) Ordinance (Cap 315, Laws of Hong Kong);
6. Secretary of State for Defence (Succession to Property) Ordinance (Cap 193, Laws of Hong Kong);
7. Royal Hong Kong Regiment Ordinance (Cap 199, Laws of Hong Kong);
8. Compulsory Service Ordinance (Cap 246, Laws of Hong Kong);
9. Army and Royal Air Force Legal Services Ordinance (Cap 286, Laws of Hong Kong);
10. British Nationality (Miscellaneous Provisions) Ordinance (Cap 186, Laws of Hong Kong);
11. British Nationality Act 1981 (Consequential Amendments) Ordinance (Cap 373, Laws of Hong Kong);
12. Electoral Provisions Ordinance (Cap 367, Laws of Hong Kong);
13. Legislative Council (Electoral Provisions) Ordinance (Cap 381, Laws of Hong Kong);
14. Boundary and Election Commission Ordinance (Cap 432, Laws of Hong Kong).

Annex 2

The following provisions in ordinances and subordinate legislation previously in force in Hong Kong, which are in contravention of the Basic Law, are not adopted as the laws of the Hong Kong Special Administrative Region–

1. the definition of "Hong Kong permanent resident" in section 2 of the Immigration Ordinance (Cap 115, Laws of Hong Kong) and the provisions relating to "Hong Kong permanent residents" in Schedule 1 to that Ordinance;
2. any provision giving effect to the British Nationality Act as applied in Hong Kong;
3. provisions relating to election in the Urban Council Ordinance (Cap 101, Laws of Hong Kong);
4. provisions relating to election in the Regional Council Ordinance (Cap 385, Laws of Hong Kong);
5. provisions relating to election in the District Boards Ordinance (Cap 366, Laws of Hong Kong);

6. the Urban Council, Regional Council and District Board Election Expenses Order (sub. leg. A) and the Resolution of the Legislative Council (sub. leg. C) made under the Corrupt and Illegal Practices Ordinance (Cap 288, Laws of Hong Kong);
7. provisions relating to the interpretation and application of the Ordinance in section 2(3), the effect on pre-existing legislation in section 3 and the interpretation of subsequent legislation in section 4 of the Hong Kong Bill of Rights Ordinance (Cap 383, Laws of Hong Kong);
8. provisions relating to the overriding status of the Personal Data (Privacy) Ordinance (Cap. 486, Laws of Hong Kong) in section 3(2) of that Ordinance;
9. major amendments to the Societies Ordinance (Cap 151, Laws of Hong Kong) since 17 July 1992;
10. major amendments to the Public Order Ordinance (Cap 245, Laws of Hong Kong) since 27 July 1995.

Annex 3

Names or expressions in the laws previously in force in Hong Kong that are adopted as the laws of the Hong Kong Special Administrative Region shall generally be construed or applied in accordance with the following principles of substitution–

1. In the case of any provision in which any reference is made to "Her Majesty", "the Crown", "the British Government" or "the Secretary of State" or to a similar name or expression, where the content of the provision relates to title to land in Hong Kong or involves affairs provided for in the Basic Law for which the Central People's Government is responsible or involves the relationship between the Central People's Government and the Hong Kong Special Administrative Region, the name or expression shall be construed as the Central People's Government or other competent authorities of the People's Republic of China. In other cases, the name or expression shall be construed as the Government of the Hong Kong Special Administrative Region.
2. In the case of any provision in which any reference is made to "Her Majesty in Council" or "the Privy Council", where the content of the provision relates to appellate jurisdiction, the name or expression shall be construed as the Court of Final Appeal of the Hong Kong Special Administrative Region. In other cases, the name or expression shall be dealt with in accordance with the provisions of paragraph 1 hereof.
3. In the case of a Government agency or a semi-official agency bearing a name with the word "Royal", the word "Royal" shall be removed from its name and the agency shall be construed as the corresponding agency of the Hong Kong Special Administrative Region.
4. Any reference to "the Colony" shall be construed as a reference to the Hong Kong Special Administrative Region and any description of the territories of Hong Kong

shall be construed and applied by reference to the map of the administrative division of the Hong Kong Special Administrative Region published by the State Council.

5. Any reference to such name or expression as "the Supreme Court" or "the High Court" shall be construed respectively as a reference to the High Court or the Court of First Instance of the High Court.

6. Any reference to such name or expression as "the Governor", "the Governor in Council", "the Chief Secretary", "the Attorney General", "the Chief Justice", "the Secretary for Home Affairs", "the Secretary for Constitutional Affairs", "the Commissioner of Customs and Excise" and "Justice" shall be construed respectively as a reference to the Chief Executive of the Hong Kong Special Administrative Region, the Chief Executive in Council, the Administrative Secretary, the Secretary for Justice, the Chief Justice of the Court of Final Appeal or Chief Judge of the High Court, the Secretary for Home Affairs, the Secretary for Constitutional Affairs, the Commissioner of Customs and Excise or Judge of the High Court.

7. Any reference in the Chinese text of any law previously in force in Hong Kong to such name or expression as the Legislative Council, the Judiciary or the Executive Authorities or the officers of those bodies shall be construed and applied in accordance with the relevant provisions of the Basic Law.

8. In the case of any provision in which any reference is made to "the People's Republic of China" or "China" or to a similar name or expression, such reference shall be construed as a reference to the People's Republic of China as including Taiwan, Hong Kong and Macau; and in the case of any provision in which any reference is made to such name or expression as the Mainland, Taiwan, Hong Kong or Macau, whether separately or concurrently, such reference shall be construed respectively as a reference to the Mainland, Taiwan, Hong Kong or Macau, as a part of the People's Republic of China.

9. In the case of any provision in which any reference is made to "foreign state" or "foreign country" or to a similar term or expression, such reference shall be construed as a reference to any state, country or territory other than the People's Republic of China, or as a reference to "any place other than the Hong Kong Special Administrative Region", as the context of the relevant law or provision requires; and in the case of any provision in which any reference is made to "alien" or to a similar term or expression, such reference shall be construed as a reference to a person other than a citizen of the People's Republic of China.

10. Any reference in any provision to "nothing in this Ordinance shall affect or be deemed to affect the rights of Her Majesty the Queen, Her heirs or successors" shall be construed as a reference to "nothing in this Ordinance shall affect or be deemed to affect the rights of the Central People's Government or the Government of the Hong Kong Special Administrative Region under the Basic law or other laws".

The Interpretation by the Standing Committee of the National People's Congress of Articles 22(4) and 24(2)(3) of the Basic Law of the Hong Kong Special Administrative Region of the People's Republic of China

(Adopted at the Tenth Session of the Standing Committee of the Ninth National People's Congress on 26 June 1999)

The Standing Committee of the Ninth National People's Congress examined at its Tenth Session the "Motion Regarding the Request for an Interpretation of Articles 22(4) and 24(2)(3) of the Basic Law of the Hong Kong Special Administrative Region of the People's Republic of China" submitted by the State Council. The motion of the State Council was submitted upon the report furnished by the Chief Executive of the Hong Kong Special Administrative Region under the relevant provisions of Articles 43 and 48(2) of the Basic Law of the Hong Kong Special Administrative Region of the People's Republic of China. The issue raised in the Motion concerns the interpretation of the relevant provisions of the Basic Law of the Hong Kong Special Administrative Region of the People's Republic of China by the Court of Final Appeal of the Hong Kong Special Administrative Region in its judgment dated 29 January 1999. Those relevant provisions concern affairs which are the responsibility of the Central People's Government and concern the relationship between the Central Authorities and the Hong Kong Special Administrative Region. Before making its judgment, the Court of Final Appeal had not sought an interpretation of the Standing Committee of the National People's Congress in compliance with the requirement of Article 158(3) of the Basic Law of the Hong Kong Special Administrative Region of the People's Republic of China. Moreover, the interpretation of the Court of Final Appeal is not consistent with the legislative intent. Therefore, having consulted the Committee for the Basic Law of the Hong Kong Special Administrative Region under the Standing Committee of the National People's Congress, the Standing Committee of the National People's Congress has decided to make, under the provisions of Article 67(4) of the Constitution of the People's Republic of China and Article 158(1) of the Basic Law of the Hong Kong Special Administrative Region of the People's Republic of China, an interpretation of the provisions of Articles 22(4) and 24(2)(3) of the Basic Law of the Hong Kong Special Administrative Region of the People's Republic of China as follows:

1. The provisions of Article 22(4) of the Basic Law of the Hong Kong Special Administrative Region of the People's Republic of China regarding "For entry into the Hong Kong Special Administrative Region, people from other parts of China must apply for approval" mean as follows: People from all provinces, autonomous regions, or municipalities directly under the Central Government, including those persons of Chinese nationality born outside Hong Kong of Hong Kong permanent residents, who wish to enter the Hong Kong Special Administrative Region for whatever reason, must apply to the relevant authorities of their residential districts for approval in accordance with the relevant national laws and administrative

regulations, and must hold valid documents issued by the relevant authorities before they can enter the Hong Kong Special Administrative Region. It is unlawful for people from all provinces, autonomous regions, or municipalities directly under the Central Government, including persons of Chinese nationality born outside Hong Kong of Hong Kong permanent residents, to enter the Hong Kong Special Administrative Region without complying with the appropriate approval procedure prescribed by the relevant national laws and administrative regulations.

2. It is stipulated in the first three categories of Article 24(2) of the Basic Law of the Hong Kong Special Administrative Region of the People's Republic of China that the "permanent residents of the Hong Kong Special Administrative Region shall be:
    (1) Chinese citizens born in Hong Kong before or after the establishment of the Hong Kong Special Administrative Region;
    (2) Chinese citizens who have ordinarily resided in Hong Kong for a continuous period of not less than seven years before or after the establishment of the Hong Kong Special Administrative Region;
    (3) Persons of Chinese nationality born outside Hong Kong of those residents listed in categories (1) and (2)".

The provisions of category (3) regarding the "persons of Chinese nationality born outside Hong Kong of those residents listed in categories (1) and (2)" mean both parents of such persons, whether born before or after the establishment of the Hong Kong Special Administrative Region, or either of such parents must have fulfilled the condition prescribed by category (1) or (2) of Article 24(2) of the Basic Law of the Hong Kong Special Administrative Region of the People's Republic of China at the time of their birth. The legislative intent as stated by this Interpretation, together with the legislative intent of all other categories of Article 24(2) of the Basic Law of the Hong Kong Special Administrative Region of the People's Republic of China, have been reflected in the "Opinions on the Implementation of Article 24(2) of the Basic Law of the Hong Kong Special Administrative Region of the People's Republic of China" adopted at the Fourth Plenary Meeting of the Preparatory Committee for the Hong Kong Special Administrative Region of the National People's Congress on 10 August 1996.

As from the promulgation of this Interpretation, the courts of the Hong Kong Special Administrative Region, when referring to the relevant provisions of the Basic Law of the Hong Kong Special Administrative Region of the People's Republic of China, shall adhere to this Interpretation. This Interpretation does not affect the right of abode in the Hong Kong Special Administrative Region which has been acquired under the judgment of the Court of Final Appeal on the relevant cases dated 29 January 1999 by the parties concerned in the relevant legal proceedings. Other than that, the question whether any other person fulfils the conditions prescribed by Article 24(2)(3) of the Basic Law of the Hong Kong Special Administrative Region of the People's Republic of China shall be determined by reference to this Interpretation.

The Interpretation by the Standing Committee of the National People's Congress of Article 7 of Annex I and Article III of Annex II to the Basic Law of the Hong Kong Special Administrative Region of the People's Republic of China

(Adopted at the Eighth Session of the Standing Committee of the Tenth National People's Congress on 6 April 2004)

The Standing Committee of the Tenth National People's Congress examined at its Eighth Session the motion regarding the request for examination of "The Draft Interpretation of Article 7 of Annex I and Article III of Annex II to the Basic Law of the Hong Kong Special Administrative Region of the People's Republic of China" submitted by the Council of Chairmen. Having consulted the Committee for the Basic Law of the Hong Kong Special Administrative Region under the Standing Committee of the National People's Congress, the Standing Committee of the National People's Congress has decided to make, under the provisions of Article 67(4) of the Constitution of the People's Republic of China and Article 158(1) of the Basic Law of the Hong Kong Special Administrative Region of the People's Republic of China, an interpretation of the provisions of Article 7 of Annex I "Method for the Selection of the Chief Executive of the Hong Kong Special Administrative Region" to the Basic Law of the Hong Kong Special Administrative Region of the People's Republic of China regarding "If there is a need to amend the method for selecting the Chief Executives for the terms subsequent to the year 2007, such amendments must be made with the endorsement of a two-thirds majority of all the members of the Legislative Council and the consent of the Chief Executive, and they shall be reported to the Standing Committee of the National People's Congress for approval" and the provisions of Article III of Annex II "Method for the Formation of the Legislative Council of the Hong Kong Special Administrative Region and Its Voting Procedures" regarding "With regard to the method for forming the Legislative Council of the Hong Kong Special Administrative Region and its procedures for voting on bills and motions after 2007, if there is a need to amend the provisions of this Annex, such amendments must be made with the endorsement of a two-thirds majority of all the members of the Council and the consent of the Chief Executive, and they shall be reported to the Standing Committee of the National People's Congress for the record" as follows:

1. The phrases "subsequent to the year 2007" and "after 2007" stipulated in the two above-mentioned Annexes include the year 2007.
2. The provisions in the two above-mentioned Annexes that "if there is a need" to amend the method for selecting the Chief Executives for the terms subsequent to the year 2007 or the method for forming the Legislative Council and its procedures for voting on bills and motions after 2007 mean they may be amended or remain unamended.

3. The provisions in the two above-mentioned Annexes that any amendment must be made with the endorsement of a two-thirds majority of all the members of the Legislative Council and the consent of the Chief Executive and shall be reported to the Standing Committee of the National People's Congress for approval or for the record mean the requisite legislative process through which the method for selecting the Chief Executive and the method for forming the Legislative Council and its procedures for voting on bills and motions are amended. Such an amendment may take effect only if it has gone through the said process, including the approval or recording ultimately given or made by the Standing Committee of the National People's Congress in accordance with law. The Chief Executive of the Hong Kong Special Administrative Region shall make a report to the Standing Committee of the National People's Congress as regards whether there is a need to make an amendment; and the Standing Committee of the National People's Congress shall, in accordance with the provisions of Articles 45 and 68 of the Basic Law of the Hong Kong Special Administrative Region of the People's Republic of China, make a determination in the light of the actual situation in the Hong Kong Special Administrative Region and in accordance with the principle of gradual and orderly progress. The bills on the amendments to the method for selecting the Chief Executive and the method for forming the Legislative Council and its procedures for voting on bills and motions and the proposed amendments to such bills shall be introduced by the Government of the Hong Kong Special Administrative Region into the Legislative Council.

4. If no amendment is made to the method for selecting the Chief Executive, the method for forming the Legislative Council and its procedures for voting on bills and motions as stipulated in the two above-mentioned Annexes, the provisions relating to the method for selecting the Chief Executive in Annex I will still be applicable to the method for selecting the Chief Executive, and the provisions relating to the method for forming the third term of the Legislative Council in Annex II and the provisions relating to its procedures for voting on bills and motions in Annex II will still be applicable to the method for forming the Legislative Council and its procedures for voting on bills and motions.

This Interpretation is hereby proclaimed.

Decision of the Standing Committee of the National People's Congress on Issues Relating to the Methods for Selecting the Chief Executive of the Hong Kong Special Administrative Region in the Year 2007 and for Forming the Legislative Council of the Hong Kong Special Administrative Region in the Year 2008

(Adopted at the Ninth Session of the Standing Committee of the Tenth National People's Congress on 26 April 2004)

The Standing Committee of the Tenth National People's Congress examined at its Ninth Session the "Report on whether there is a need to amend the methods for selecting the Chief Executive of the Hong Kong Special Administrative Region in 2007 and for forming the Legislative Council of the Hong Kong Special Administrative Region in 2008" submitted by Tung Chee-hwa, the Chief Executive of the Hong Kong Special Administrative Region, on 15 April 2004 and, before the Session, had consulted the Hong Kong deputies to the National People's Congress, the Hong Kong members of the National Committee of the Chinese People's Political Consultative Conference, different sectors of Hong Kong, the Hong Kong members of the Committee for the Basic Law of the Hong Kong Special Administrative Region under the Standing Committee of the National People's Congress, and the Constitutional Development Task Force of the Government of the Hong Kong Special Administrative Region, and had also sought the views of the Hong Kong and Macao Affairs Office of the State Council. The Standing Committee of the National People's Congress was, in the course of the examination, fully aware of the recent concerns of the Hong Kong society about the methods for selecting the Chief Executive and for forming the Legislative Council after the year 2007, including the views of some bodies and people that they wish to see the selection of the Chief Executive by universal suffrage in the year 2007 and the election of all the members of the Legislative Council by universal suffrage in the year 2008.

The Session is of the view that Articles 45 and 68 of the Basic Law of the Hong Kong Special Administrative Region of the People's Republic of China (hereinafter referred to as "Hong Kong Basic Law") already expressly provide that the methods for selecting the Chief Executive of the Hong Kong Special Administrative Region and for forming the Legislative Council of the Hong Kong Special Administrative Region shall be specified in the light of the actual situation in the Hong Kong Special Administrative Region and in accordance with the principle of gradual and orderly progress, and that the ultimate aims are the selection of the Chief Executive by universal suffrage upon nomination by a broadly representative nominating committee in accordance with democratic procedures and the election of all the members of the Legislative Council by universal suffrage. The methods for selecting the Chief Executive of the Hong Kong Special Administrative Region and for forming the Legislative Council of the Hong Kong Special Administrative Region shall conform to the above principles and provisions of the Hong Kong Basic

Law. Any change relating to the methods for selecting the Chief Executive of the Hong Kong Special Administrative Region and for forming the Legislative Council of the Hong Kong Special Administrative Region shall conform to principles such as being compatible with the social, economic, political development of Hong Kong, being conducive to the balanced participation of all sectors and groups of the society, being conducive to the effective operation of the executive-led system, being conducive to the maintenance of the long-term prosperity and stability of Hong Kong.

The Session is of the view that since the establishment of the Hong Kong Special Administrative Region, Hong Kong residents have enjoyed democratic rights that they have never had before. The first Chief Executive was elected by the Selection Committee, which was composed of 400 members. The second Chief Executive was elected by the Election Committee, which was composed of 800 members. Out of the 60 members of the Legislative Council, the number of members returned by geographical constituencies through direct elections increased from 20 in the Legislative Council in the first term to 24 in the Legislative Council in the second term and will reach 30 in the Legislative Council in the third term to be formed this September. Hong Kong does not have a long history of practising democratic elections. Until now, Hong Kong residents have exercised the democratic right to participate in the selection of the Chief Executive of the Special Administrative Region for less than 7 years. Since the reunification of Hong Kong with the motherland, the number of members of the Legislative Council returned by geographical constituencies through direct elections has already substantially increased. When the set-up is such that half of the members are returned by geographical constituencies through direct elections and half of the members are returned by functional constituencies, the impact on the operation of the Hong Kong society as a whole, especially the impact on the executive-led system, remains to be examined through practice. Further, at present, different sectors of the Hong Kong society still have considerable differences on how to determine the methods for selecting the Chief Executive and for forming the Legislative Council after the year 2007 and have not come to a broad consensus. In the circumstances, conditions do not exist for the selection of the Chief Executive by universal suffrage upon nomination by a broadly representative nominating committee in accordance with democratic procedures as provided for in Article 45 of the Hong Kong Basic Law and the election of all the members of the Legislative Council by universal suffrage as provided for in Article 68 of the Hong Kong Basic Law.

In the light of the above and pursuant to the relevant provisions of the Hong Kong Basic Law and "The Interpretation by the Standing Committee of the National People's Congress of Article 7 of Annex I and Article III of Annex II to the Basic Law of the Hong Kong Special Administrative Region of the People's Republic of China", the Standing Committee of the National People's Congress makes the following decision on the methods for selecting the Chief Executive of the Hong Kong Special Administrative Region in the year 2007 and for forming the Legislative Council of the Hong Kong Special Administrative Region in the year 2008:

1. The election of the third Chief Executive of the Hong Kong Special Administrative Region to be held in the year 2007 shall not be by means of universal suffrage. The election of the Legislative Council of the Hong Kong Special Administrative Region in the fourth term in the year 2008 shall not be by means of an election of all the members by universal suffrage. The ratio between members returned by functional constituencies and members returned by geographical constituencies through direct elections, who shall respectively occupy half of the seats, is to remain unchanged. The procedures for voting on bills and motions in the Legislative Council are to remain unchanged.

2. Subject to Article 1 of this Decision not being contravened, appropriate amendments that conform to the principle of gradual and orderly progress may be made to the specific method for selecting the third Chief Executive of the Hong Kong Special Administrative Region in the year 2007 and the specific method for forming the Legislative Council of the Hong Kong Special Administrative Region in the fourth term in the year 2008 according to the provisions of Articles 45 and 68 of the Hong Kong Basic Law and the provisions of Article 7 of Annex I and Article III of Annex II to the Hong Kong Basic Law.

The Session is of the view that developing democracy in the Hong Kong Special Administrative Region in the light of the actual situation and in a gradual and orderly manner according to the provisions of the Hong Kong Basic Law has all along been the resolute and firm stance of the Central Authorities. With the development and progress in all aspects of the Hong Kong society and through the joint endeavours of the Government of the Hong Kong Special Administrative Region and Hong Kong residents, the democratic system of the Hong Kong Special Administrative Region will certainly be able to progress forward incessantly, and ultimately attain the aims of selecting the Chief Executive by universal suffrage upon nomination by a broadly representative nominating committee in accordance with democratic procedures and electing all the members of the Legislative Council by universal suffrage provided for in the Hong Kong Basic Law.

Interpretation of Paragraph 2, Article 53 of the Basic Law of the Hong Kong Special Administrative Region of the People's Republic of China by the Standing Committee of the National People's Congress

(Adopted at the 15th Session of the Standing Committee of the Tenth National People's Congress on 27 April 2005)

The Standing Committee of the Tenth National People's Congress at its 15th session deliberated the State Council's Proposal on Requesting Interpretation of Paragraph 2,

Article 53 of the Basic Law of the Hong Kong Special Administrative Region of the People's Republic of China. In accordance with Item 4, Article 67 of the Constitution of the People's Republic of China and Paragraph 1, Article 158 of the Basic Law of the Hong Kong Special Administrative Region of the People's Republic of China, and after consulting the Committee for the Basic Law of the HKSAR under the NPC Standing Committee, the Standing Committee of the National People's Congress hereby makes the following interpretation on Paragraph 2, Article 53 of the Basic Law of the Hong Kong Special Administrative Region of the People's Republic of China.

Paragraph 2, Article 53 of the Basic Law stipulates, "In the event that the office of Chief Executive becomes vacant, a new Chief Executive shall be selected within six months in accordance with the provisions of Article 45 of this Law." The phrase "a new Chief Executive shall be selected ... in accordance with the provisions of Article 45 of this Law" implies that both the method of selecting and the term of office of the new Chief Executive shall be as prescribed and determined by the said Article.

Paragraph 3, Article 45 of the Basic Law stipulates, "The specific method for selecting the Chief Executive is prescribed in Annex I 'Method for the Selection of the Chief Executive of the Hong Kong Special Administrative Region'." Clause 1 of Annex I stipulates, "The Chief Executive shall be elected by a broadly representative Election Committee in accordance with this Law and appointed by the Central People's Government." Clause 2 of Annex I stipulates, "The term of office of the Election Committee shall be five years." Clause 7 of Annex I stipulates, "If there is a need to amend the method for selecting the Chief Executives for the terms subsequent to the year 2007, such amendments must be made with the endorsement of a two-thirds majority of all the members of the Legislative Council and the consent of the Chief Executive, and they shall be reported to the Standing Committee of the National People's Congress for approval." These provisions make it clear that prior to the year 2007, when the Chief Executive is selected by the Election Committee with a five-year term of office, in the event that the office of Chief Executive becomes vacant as he (she) fails to serve the full term of office of five years as prescribed by Article 46 of the Basic Law, the term of office of the new Chief Executive shall be the remainder of the previous Chief Executive; and that after 2007, the above-mentioned method for selecting the Chief Executives could be amended, and should the office of the Chief Executive then become vacant, the term of office of the new Chief Executive shall be determined in accordance with the amended method for the selection of the Chief Executive.

This Interpretation is hereby announced.

Decision of the Standing Committee of the National People's Congress on Issues Relating to the Methods for Selecting the Chief Executive of the Hong Kong Special Administrative Region and for Forming the Legislative Council of the Hong Kong Special Administrative Region in the Year 2012 and on Issues Relating to Universal Suffrage

(Adopted at the Thirty-First Session of the Standing Committee of the Tenth National People's Congress on 29 December 2007)

The Standing Committee of the Tenth National People's Congress considered at its Thirty-first Session the "Report on the Public Consultation on Constitutional Development and on whether there is a need to amend the methods for selecting the Chief Executive of the Hong Kong Special Administrative Region and for forming the Legislative Council of the Hong Kong Special Administrative Region in 2012" submitted by Tsang Yam-kuen, the Chief Executive of the Hong Kong Special Administrative Region, on 12 December 2007. The Session is of the view that appropriate amendments may be made to the specific method for selecting the fourth Chief Executive and the specific method for forming the fifth term Legislative Council of the Hong Kong Special Administrative Region in the year 2012; that the election of the fifth Chief Executive of the Hong Kong Special Administrative Region in the year 2017 may be implemented by the method of universal suffrage; that after the Chief Executive is selected by universal suffrage, the election of the Legislative Council of the Hong Kong Special Administrative Region may be implemented by the method of electing all the members by universal suffrage. Pursuant to the relevant provisions of the Basic Law of the Hong Kong Special Administrative Region of the People's Republic of China and "The Interpretation by the Standing Committee of the National People's Congress of Article 7 of Annex I and Article III of Annex II to the Basic Law of the Hong Kong Special Administrative Region of the People's Republic of China", the Standing Committee of the National People's Congress hereby makes the following decision:

1. The election of the fourth Chief Executive of the Hong Kong Special Administrative Region in the year 2012 shall not be implemented by the method of universal suffrage. The election of the fifth term Legislative Council of the Hong Kong Special Administrative Region in the year 2012 shall not be implemented by the method of electing all the members by universal suffrage. The half-and-half ratio between members returned by functional constituencies and members returned by geographical constituencies through direct elections shall remain unchanged. The procedures for voting on bills and motions in the Legislative Council shall remain unchanged. Subject to the aforementioned, appropriate amendments conforming to the principle of gradual and orderly progress may be made to the specific method for selecting the fourth Chief Executive of the Hong Kong Special Administrative Region in the year 2012 and the specific method for forming the fifth term Legislative Council of the Hong Kong Special Administrative Region in the year 2012 in accordance with the provisions of Articles 45 and 68, and those of Article 7 of Annex I and Article III of

Annex II to the Basic Law of the Hong Kong Special Administrative Region of the People's Republic of China.

2. At an appropriate time prior to the selection of the Chief Executive of the Hong Kong Special Administrative Region by universal suffrage, the Chief Executive shall make a report to the Standing Committee of the National People's Congress as regards the issue of amending the method for selecting the Chief Executive in accordance with the relevant provisions of the Hong Kong Basic Law and "The Interpretation by the Standing Committee of the National People's Congress of Article 7 of Annex I and Article III of Annex II to the Basic Law of the Hong Kong Special Administrative Region of the People's Republic of China"; a determination thereon shall be made by the Standing Committee of the National People's Congress. The bills on the amendments to the method for selecting the Chief Executive and the proposed amendments to such bills shall be introduced by the Government of the Hong Kong Special Administrative Region to the Legislative Council; such amendments must be made with the endorsement of a two-thirds majority of all the members of the Legislative Council and the consent of the Chief Executive and they shall be reported to the Standing Committee of the National People's Congress for approval.

3. At an appropriate time prior to the election of all the members of the Legislative Council of the Hong Kong Special Administrative Region by universal suffrage, the Chief Executive shall make a report to the Standing Committee of the National People's Congress as regards the issue of amending the method for forming the Legislative Council and the issue of whether any corresponding amendment should be made to the procedures for voting on bills and motions in the Legislative Council in accordance with the relevant provisions of the Hong Kong Basic Law and "The Interpretation by the Standing Committee of the National People's Congress of Article 7 of Annex I and Article III of Annex II to the Basic Law of the Hong Kong Special Administrative Region of the People's Republic of China"; a determination thereon shall be made by the Standing Committee of the National People's Congress. The bills on the amendments to the method for forming the Legislative Council and its procedures for voting on bills and motions and the proposed amendments to such bills shall be introduced by the Government of the Hong Kong Special Administrative Region to the Legislative Council; such amendments must be made with the endorsement of a two-thirds majority of all the members of the Legislative Council and the consent of the Chief Executive and they shall be reported to the Standing Committee of the National People's Congress for the record.

4. If no amendment is made to the method for selecting the Chief Executive, the method for forming the Legislative Council or its procedures for voting on bills and motions in accordance with the legal procedures, the method for selecting the Chief Executive used for the preceding term shall continue to apply, and the method for forming the Legislative Council and the procedures for voting on bills and motions used for the preceding term shall continue to apply.

The Session is of the view that in accordance with the provisions of Article 45 of the Hong Kong Basic Law, in selecting the Chief Executive of the Hong Kong Special Administrative Region by the method of universal suffrage, a broadly representative nominating committee shall be formed. The nominating committee may be formed with reference to the current provisions regarding the Election Committee in Annex I to the Hong Kong Basic Law. The nominating committee shall in accordance with democratic procedures nominate a certain number of candidates for the office of the Chief Executive, who is to be elected through universal suffrage by all registered electors of the Hong Kong Special Administrative Region, and to be appointed by the Central People's Government.

The Session is of the view that with the joint efforts of the Government of the Hong Kong Special Administrative Region and the people of Hong Kong, the democratic system of the Hong Kong Special Administrative Region will definitely make progress continuously, and that the aim of the selection of the Chief Executive and the election of all the members of the Legislative Council by universal suffrage will be realized in accordance with the Hong Kong Basic Law and this Decision.

Interpretation of Paragraph 1, Article 13 and Article 19 of the Basic Law of the Hong Kong Special Administrative Region of the People's Republic of China by the Standing Committee of the National People's Congress

(Adopted at the Twenty-Second Session of the Standing Committee of the Eleventh National People's Congress on 26 August 2011)

The Standing Committee of the Eleventh National People's Congress examined at its Twenty-second Session the motion regarding the request for examination of *The Draft Interpretation of Paragraph 1, Article 13 and Article 19 of the Basic Law of the Hong Kong Special Administrative Region of the People's Republic of China by the Standing Committee of the National People's Congress* submitted by the Council of Chairmen. The motion of the Council of Chairmen was submitted upon the report by the Court of Final Appeal of the Hong Kong Special Administrative Region requesting the Standing Committee of the National People's Congress to interpret the relevant provisions of *the Basic Law of the Hong Kong Special Administrative Region of the People's Republic of China*, in accordance with the provisions of Paragraph 3, Article 158 of *the Basic Law of the Hong Kong Special Administrative Region of the People's Republic of China*.

The Court of Final Appeal of the Hong Kong Special Administrative Region needs to ascertain, in adjudicating a case involving the Democratic Republic of the Congo, whether the Hong Kong Special Administrative Region should apply the rules or policies on state immunity as determined by the Central People's Government. For this purpose, in accordance with the provisions of Paragraph 3, Article 158 of *the Basic Law of the Hong Kong Special Administrative Region of the People's Republic of China*, the Court of Final Appeal of the Hong Kong Special Administrative Region, seeks an interpretation from the Standing Committee of the National People's Congress on the following questions: "(1) whether on the true interpretation of Paragraph 1, Article 13, the Central People's Government has the power to determine the rule or policy of the People's Republic of China on state immunity; (2) if so, whether, on the true interpretation of Paragraph 1, Article 13 and Article 19, the Hong Kong Special Administrative Region (HKSAR), including the courts of the HKSAR: ① is bound to apply or give effect to the rule or policy on state immunity determined by the Central People's Government under Paragraph 1, Article 13; or ② on the other hand, is at liberty to depart from the rule or policy on state immunity determined by the Central People's Government under Paragraph 1, Article 13 and to adopt a different rule; (3) whether the determination by the Central People's Government as to the rule or policy on state immunity falls within 'acts of state such as defence and foreign affairs' in the first sentence of Paragraph 3, Article 19 of the Basic Law; and (4) whether, upon the establishment of the HKSAR, the effect of Paragraph 1, Article 13, Article 19 and the status of Hong Kong as a Special Administrative Region of the People's Republic of China upon the common law on state immunity previously in force in Hong Kong (that is, before 1 July 1997), to the extent that such common law was inconsistent with the rule or policy on state immunity as determined by the Central People's Government pursuant to Paragraph 1, Article 13, was to require such common law to be applied subject to such modifications, adaptations, limitations or exceptions as were necessary to ensure that such common law is consistent with the rule or policy on state immunity as determined by the Central People's Government, in accordance with Articles 8 and 160 of *the Basic Law* and the *Decision of the Standing Committee of the National People's Congress* dated 23 February 1997 made pursuant to Article 160." The above request for interpretation by the Court of Final Appeal of the Hong Kong Special Administrative Region complies with the provisions of Paragraph 3, Article 158 of *the Basic Law of the Hong Kong Special Administrative Region of the People's Republic of China*.

In accordance with Subparagraph (4), Article 67 of the Constitution of the People's Republic of China and Article 158 of *the Basic Law of the Hong Kong Special Administrative Region of the People's Republic of China*, and after consulting the Committee for the Basic Law of the Hong Kong Special Administrative Region under the Standing Committee of the National People's Congress, the Standing Committee of the National People's Congress, in relation to the request for interpretation by the Court of Final Appeal of the Hong Kong Special Administrative Region, hereby makes the following interpretation of the provisions of Paragraph 1, Article 13 and Article 19 of *the Basic Law of the Hong Kong Special Administrative Region of the People's Republic of China* and related issues:

1. On question (1) on which an interpretation is sought by the Court of Final Appeal of the Hong Kong Special Administrative Region. According to Subparagraph (9), Article 89 of *the Constitution of the People's Republic of China*, the State Council as the Central People's Government exercises the function and power to conduct

the foreign affairs of the State; as the rules or policies on state immunity fall within diplomatic affairs in the realm of the foreign affairs of the state, the Central People's Government has the power to determine the rules or policies of the People's Republic of China on state immunity to be given effect to uniformly in the territory of the People's Republic of China. Based on the above, in accordance with the provisions of Paragraph 1, Article 13 of *the Basic Law of the Hong Kong Special Administrative Region of the People's Republic of China* that "[t]he Central People's Government shall be responsible for the foreign affairs relating to the Hong Kong Special Administrative Region", the conduct of the foreign affairs relating to the Hong Kong Special Administrative Region falls within the power of the Central People's Government. The Central People's Government has the power to determine the rules or policies on state immunity to be applied in the Hong Kong Special Administrative Region.

2. On question (2) on which an interpretation is sought by the Court of Final Appeal of the Hong Kong Special Administrative Region. According to the provisions of Paragraph 1, Article 13 of *the Basic Law of the Hong Kong Special Administrative Region of the People's Republic of China* and Article 1 of this Interpretation, the Central People's Government has the power to determine the rules or policies on state immunity to be applied in the Hong Kong Special Administrative Region. According to the provisions of Article 19 of *the Basic Law of the Hong Kong Special Administrative Region of the People's Republic of China* and Article 3 of this Interpretation, the courts of the Hong Kong Special Administrative Region have no jurisdiction over the act of the Central People's Government in determining the rules or policies on state immunity. Therefore, when questions of immunity from jurisdiction and immunity from execution of foreign states and their properties arise in the adjudication of cases, the courts of the Hong Kong Special Administrative Region must apply and give effect to the rules or policies on state immunity determined by the Central People's Government as being applicable to the Hong Kong Special Administrative Region. Based on the above, in accordance with the provisions of Paragraph 1, Article 13 and Article 19 of *the Basic Law of the Hong Kong Special Administrative Region of the People's Republic of China*, the Hong Kong Special Administrative Region, including the courts of the Hong Kong Special Administrative Region, is under a duty to apply or give effect to the rules or policies on state immunity that the Central People's Government has determined, and must not depart from the abovementioned rules or policies nor adopt a rule that is inconsistent with the abovementioned rules or policies.

3. On question (3) on which an interpretation is sought by the Court of Final Appeal of the Hong Kong Special Administrative Region. State immunity concerns whether the courts of a state have jurisdiction over foreign states and their properties and whether foreign states and their properties enjoy immunity in the courts of a state. It directly relates to the state's foreign relations and international rights and obligations.

Therefore, the determination as to the rules or policies on state immunity is an act of state involving foreign affairs. Based on the above, "acts of state such as defence and foreign affairs" as stipulated in Paragraph 3, Article 19 of *the Basic Law of the Hong Kong Special Administrative Region of the People's Republic of China* includes the act of determination by the Central People's Government as to the rules or policies on state immunity.

4. On question (4) on which an interpretation is sought by the Court of Final Appeal of the Hong Kong Special Administrative Region. According to the provisions of Articles 8 and 160 of *the Basic Law of the Hong Kong Special Administrative Region of the People's Republic of China*, the laws previously in force in Hong Kong shall be maintained only if there is no contravention of *the Basic Law of the Hong Kong Special Administrative Region of the People's Republic of China*. In accordance with the provisions of Paragraph 4 of the *Decision of the Standing Committee of the National People's Congress on Treatment of the Laws Previously in Force in Hong Kong in accordance with Article 160 of the Basic Law of the Hong Kong Special Administrative Region of the People's Republic of China*, such of the laws previously in force in Hong Kong which have been adopted as the laws of the Hong Kong Special Administrative Region shall, as from 1 July 1997, be applied subject to such modifications, adaptations, limitations or exceptions as are necessary so as to bring them into conformity with the status of Hong Kong after resumption by the People's Republic of China of the exercise of sovereignty over Hong Kong as well as to be in conformity with the relevant provisions of the Basic Law. The Hong Kong Special Administrative Region, as a local administrative region of the People's Republic of China that enjoys a high degree of autonomy and comes directly under the Central People's Government, must give effect to the rules or policies on state immunity as determined by the Central People's Government. The laws previously in force in Hong Kong relating to the rules on state immunity may continue to be applied after 1 July 1997 only if they comply with the above requirements. Based on the above, in accordance with the provisions of Paragraph 1, Article 13 and Article 19 of *the Basic Law of the Hong Kong Special Administrative Region of the People's Republic of China*, such of the laws previously in force in Hong Kong concerning the rules on state immunity which have been adopted as the laws of the Hong Kong Special Administrative Region according to the *Decision of the Standing Committee of the National People's Congress on Treatment of the Laws Previously in Force in Hong Kong in accordance with Article 160 of the Basic Law of the Hong Kong Special Administrative Region of the People's Republic of China*, when applied as from 1 July 1997, must be subject to such modifications, adaptations, limitations or exceptions as are necessary so as to be consistent with the rules or policies on state immunity that the Central People's Government has determined.

The Interpretation is hereby announced.

Bibliography

Books

Alston, Philip (ed.), *Promoting Human Rights Through Bills of Rights: Comparative Perspectives* (Oxford: Oxford University Press, 1999).

Asmerom, Haile K., and Reis, Elisa P. (eds.), *Democratization and Bureaucratic Neutrality* (London: Macmillan, 1996).

Barnett, Hilaire, *Constitutional and Administrative Law* (London: Routledge, 8th edition, 2011).

Bokhary, Justice Kemal, *Recollections* (Hong Kong: Sweet & Maxwell, 2013).

Chan, Johannes M.M., Fu. H.L., and Ghai, Yash (eds.), *Hong Kong's Constitutional Debate: Conflict Over Interpretation* (Hong Kong: Hong Kong University Press, 2000).

Chan, Johannes, and Harris, Lison (eds.), *Hong Kong's Constitutional Debates* (Hong Kong: Hong Kong Law Journal Ltd., 2005).

Chan, Ming K., and Clark, David J., *The Hong Kong Basic Law: Blueprint for "Stability and Prosperity" Under Chinese Sovereignty* (Hong Kong: Hong Kong University Press, 1991).

Chan, Ming K., and So, Alvin Y. (eds.), *Crisis and Transformation in China's Hong Kong* (Hong Kong: Hong Kong University Press; New York: M.E. Sharpe, 2002).

Chen, Albert, *An Introduction to the Legal System of the People's Republic of China* (Hong Kong: LexisNexis, 4th edition, 2011).

Chen, Jianfu, *Chinese Law: Towards an Understanding of Chinese Law, Its Nature and Development* (The Hague: Kluwer Law International, 1999).

_____, *Chinese Law: Context and Transformation* (Boston: Martinus Nijhoff Publishers, 2008).

Cheng, Joseph (ed.), *Political Development in the HKSAR* (Hong Kong: The Chinese University Press, 2001).

Cheng, Joseph Y.S., and Kwong, Paul C.K., *The Other Hong Kong Report 1992* (Hong Kong: The Chinese University Press, 1992).

Chiu, Hungdah (ed.), *The Draft Basic Law of Hong Kong: Analysis and Documents* (Maryland: School of Law, University of Maryland, 1988).

Corne, Peter Howard, *Foreign Investment in China: The Administrative Legal System* (Hong Kong: Hong Kong University Press, 1997).

Cottrell, Robert, *The End of Hong Kong: The Secret Diplomacy of Imperial Retreat* (London: John Murray, 1993).

Cradock, Percy, *Experiences of China* (London: John Murray, 1999).

Crawford, James, *Rights in One Country: Hong Kong and China* (Hong Kong: Faculty of Law, University of Hong Kong, 2005).

_____, *The Creation of States in International Law* (Oxford: Clarendon Press, 2nd edition, 2006).

De Smith, Stanley, and Brazier, Rodney, *Constitutional and Administrative Law* (London: Penguin, 8th edition, 1998).

Deng, Xiaoping, *Deng Xiaoping on the Question of Hong Kong* (Beijing: Foreign Languages Press, 1993).

Dicey, A.V., *An Introduction to the Study of the Law of the Constitution* (London: Macmillan, 10th edition, 1959).
Dimbleby, Jonathan, *The Last Governor: Chris Patten and the Handover of Hong Kong* (London: Little, Brown, 1997).
Edwards, George, and Chan, Johannes, *Hong Kong's Bill of Rights: Two Years Before 1997* (Hong Kong: Faculty of Law, University of Hong Kong, 1996).
Enright, M.J., Scott, E.E., and Dodwell, D., *The Hong Kong Advantage* (Hong Kong: Oxford University Press, 1997).
Fu, Hualing, Harris, Lison, and Young, Simon N.M., *Interpreting Hong Kong's Basic Law: The Struggle for Coherence* (New York: Palgrave, 2007).
Fu, Hualing, Petersen, Carole J., and Young, Simon N.M. (eds.), *National Security and Fundamental Freedoms: Hong Kong's Article 23 Under Scrutiny* (Hong Kong: Hong Kong University Press, 2005).
Gaylord, Mark S., Gittings, Danny, and Traver, Harold (eds.), *Introduction to Crime, Law and Justice in Hong Kong* (Hong Kong: Hong Kong University Press, 2009).
Ghai, Yash, *Hong Kong's New Constitutional Order: The Resumption of Chinese Sovereignty and the Basic Law* (Hong Kong: Hong Kong University Press, 2nd edition, 1999).
Ginsburg, Tom, and Chen, Albert (eds.), *Administrative Law and Governance in Asia* (London; New York: Routledge, 2008).
Gordon, Richard, and Mok, Johnny, *Judicial Review in Hong Kong* (Hong Kong: LexisNexis, 2009).
Hannikainen, Lauri, and Horn, Fran (eds.), *Autonomy and Demilitarisation in International Law: The Aland Islands in a Changing Europe* (The Hague: Kluwer Law International, 1997).
Hannum, Hurst, *Autonomy, Sovereignty and Self-Determination* (Philadelphia: University of Pennsylvania Press, revised edition, 1996).
_____ (ed.), *Documents on Autonomy and Minority Rights* (Dordrecht: Martinus Nijhoff Publishers, 1993).
Henkin, Louis (ed.), *The International Bill of Rights: The Covenant on Civil and Political Rights* (New York: Columbia University Press, 1981).
Herzer, Eva, *Options for Tibet's Future Political Status: Self-Governance Through an Autonomous Arrangement* (New Delhi: Tibetan Parliamentary & Policy Research Centre, 2002).
Hsu, C. Stephen (ed.), *Understanding China's Legal System: Essays in Honor of Jerome A. Cohen* (New York: New York University Press, 2003).
Lam, Wai-man, Lui, Percy Luen-tim and Wong, Wilson (eds.), *Contemporary Hong Kong Government and Politics* (Hong Kong: Hong Kong University Press, 2nd edition, 2012).
Lapidoth, Ruth, *Autonomy: Flexible Solutions to Ethnic Conflicts* (Washington, D.C.: United States Institute of Peace, 1997).
Lau, Siu-kai (ed.), *The First Tung Chee-hwa Administration: The First Five Years of the Hong Kong Special Administrative Region* (Hong Kong: The Chinese University Press, 2002).
Lee, Alice (ed.), *Law Lectures for Practitioners 1998* (Hong Kong: Hong Kong Law Journal Ltd., 1998).
Legal Aid Services Council, *Legal Aid in Hong Kong* (Hong Kong, 2006).
Leung, Priscilla, Mei-fun, *The Hong Kong Basic Law: Hybrid of Common Law and Chinese Law* (Hong Kong: LexisNexis, 2006).
Leung, Priscilla M.F., and Zhu, Guobin (eds.), *The Basic Law of the HKSAR: From Theory to Practice* (Hong Kong: Butterworths, 1998).
Liu, Nanping, *Opinions of the Supreme People's Court: Judicial Interpretation in China* (Hong Kong: Sweet & Maxwell Asia, 1997).
Lo, P.Y., *The Hong Kong Basic Law* (Hong Kong: LexisNexis, 2011).

Lo, Sonny, *The Dynamics of Beijing-Hong Kong Relations: A Model for Taiwan* (Hong Kong: Hong Kong University Press, 2008).
Loh, Christine, *Underground Front: The Chinese Communist Party in Hong Kong* (Hong Kong: Hong Kong University Press, 2010).
Loh, Christine, and Civic Exchange (eds.), *Functional Constituencies: A Unique Feature of the Hong Kong Legislative Council* (Hong Kong: Hong Kong University Press, 2006).
Ma, Ngok, *Political Development in Hong Kong: State, Political Society, and Civil Society* (Hong Kong: Hong Kong University Press, 2007).
McLaren, Robin, *Britain's Record in Hong Kong* (London: Royal Institute of International Affairs, 1997).
Miners, Norman, *The Government and Politics of Hong Kong* (Hong Kong: Oxford University Press, 5th edition, 1998).
Mushkat, Roda, *One Country, Two International Legal Personalities: The Case of Hong Kong* (Hong Kong: Hong Kong University Press, 1997).
One Country Two Systems Research Institute, *Seminar on Review and Prospect of the Basic Law: Collection of Articles 2007* (Hong Kong, 2010).
Otto, Jan Michel, Polak, Maurice V., Chen, Jianfu, and Li, Yuwen, *Law-Making in the People's Republic of China* (The Hague: Kluwer Law International, 2000).
Roberti, Mark, *The Fall of Hong Kong* (London: John Wiley, 1996).
Russell, P.H., and O'Brien, D.M., *Judicial Independence in the Age of Democracy: Critical Perspectives From Around the World* (Charlottesville: University Press of Virginia, 2001).
Suksi, Markku (ed.), *Autonomy: Applications and Implications* (The Hague: Kluwer Law International, 1998).
———, *Sub-State Governance Through Territorial Autonomy: A Comparative Study in Constitutional Law of Powers, Procedures and Institutions* (Heidelberg: Springer, 2011).
Tsang, Steve, *Democracy Shelved: Great Britain, China, and Attempts at Constitutional Reform in Hong Kong, 1945–1952* (Hong Kong: Oxford University Press, 1988).
——— (ed.), *Judicial Independence and the Rule of Law in Hong Kong* (Hong Kong: Hong Kong University Press, 2001).
Wacks, Raymond (ed.), *The Law in Hong Kong 1969–1989* (Hong Kong: Oxford University Press, 1989).
——— (ed.), *Human Rights in Hong Kong* (Hong Kong: Oxford University Press, 1992).
——— (ed.), *The New Legal Order in Hong Kong* (Hong Kong: Hong Kong University Press, 1999).
Wang, Guiguo, and Wei, Zhenying, *Legal Developments in China: Market Economy and Law* (Hong Kong: Sweet & Maxwell Asia, 1996).
Wang, Shuwen, *Introduction to the Basic Law of the Hong Kong Special Administrative Region* (Beijing: Law Press, 2nd English edition, 2009).
——— (ed.), *Judicial Independence and the Rule of Law in Hong Kong* (Hong Kong: Hong Kong University Press, 2001).
Wesley-Smith, Peter, *Constitutional and Administrative Law in Hong Kong* (Hong Kong: Longman Asia, 2nd edition, 1994).
———, *Unequal Treaty 1898–1997: China, Great Britain and Hong Kong's New Territories* (Hong Kong: Oxford University Press, Revised edition, 1998).
Wesley-Smith, Peter, and Chen, Albert (eds.), *The Basic Law and Hong Kong's Future* (Hong Kong: Butterworths, 1988).
Wong, Yiu-chung, *"One Country, Two Systems" in Crisis* (Lanham: Lexington Books, 2004).
Xiao, Weiyun, *One Country, Two Systems: An Account of the Drafting of the Hong Kong Basic Law* (Beijing: Peking University Press, English edition, 2001).

Young, Jessica, and Lee, Rebecca (eds.), *The Common Law Lecture Series 2005* (Hong Kong: Faculty of Law, University of Hong Kong, 2006).

Young, Simon N.M., and Cullen, Richard, *Electing Hong Kong's Chief Executive* (Hong Kong: Hong Kong University Press, 2010).

Journals[1]

Barnes, E.E., "The Independence of the Judiciary in Hong Kong" (1976) 6 *HKLJ* 7–26.

Brabyn, Janice, "Leung Kwok Hung and Others Through the Hong Kong Courts" (2006) 36 *HKLJ* 83–116.

Burns, John, "China's *Nomenklatura* System" (1987) 36(5) *Problems of Communism* 36–51.

Cao, Erbao, "Governing Forces Under the Condition of 'One Country, Two Systems'" (29 Jan 2008) 422 *Study Times*, English translation at http://www.civicparty.hk/cp/media/pdf/090506_cao_eng.pdf.

Chan, Johannes, "Hong Kong's Bill of Rights: Its Reception of and Contribution to International and Comparative Jurisprudence" (1998) 47 *International & Comparative Law Quarterly* 306–336.

———, "Judicial Independence: Controversies on the Constitutional Jurisdiction of the Court of Final Appeal of the Hong Kong Special Administrative Region" (2000) 33 *International Law* 1015–1023.

———, "Basic Law and Constitutional Review" (2007) 37 *HKLJ* 407–447.

———, "Mainland mothers giving birth in Hong Kong" (Sept 2012) *Hong Kong Lawyer* 24–34.

Chan, Ming K., "Different Roads to Home: The Retrocession of Hong Kong and Macau to Chinese Sovereignty" (2003) 12(36) *Journal of Contemporary China* 493–518.

Chang, Denis, "Has Hong Kong Anything Special or Unique to Contribute to the Contemporary World of Jurisprudence?" (2000) 30 *HKLJ* 347–350.

Chen, Albert H.Y., "A Disappointing Draft of Hong Kong's Bill of Rights" (1988) 17 *HKLJ* 133–136.

———, "Civil Liberties in Hong Kong: Recent Controversies, Evolving Consciousness and Future Legal Protection" (1988) 2 *Journal of Chinese Law* 137–151.

———, "The Provisional Legislative Council of the SAR" (1997) 27 *HKLJ* 1–11.

———, "The Interpretation of the Basic Law—Common Law and Mainland Chinese perspectives" (2000) 30 *HKLJ* 380–431.

———, "Another Case of Conflict Between the CFA and the NPC Standing Committee?" (2001) 31 *HKLJ* 179–187.

———, "The NPCSC's Interpretation in Spring 2005" (2005) 35 *HKLJ* 255–264.

———, "The Fate of the Constitutional Reform Proposal of October 2005" (2005) 35 *HKLJ* 537–543.

———, "Constitutional Adjudication in Post-1997 Hong Kong" (2006) 15 *Pacific Rim Law & Policy Journal* 627–682.

———, "A New Era in Hong Kong's Constitutional History" (2008) 38 *HKLJ* 1–14.

———, "Constitutional Developments in Autumn 2009" (2009) 39 *HKLJ* 751–766.

———, "An Unexpected Breakthrough in Hong Kong's Constitutional Development" (2010) 40 *HKLJ* 259–270.

———, "Focus on the Congo Case: Introduction" (2011) 41 *HKLJ* 369–376.

———, "The 'Foreign Domestic Helpers Case': The relevance of the NPCSC Interpretation of 1999 and the Preparatory Committee Opinion of 1996" (2011) 41 *HKLJ* 621–633.

---

1. All Internet-based sources were last accessed on 12 Oct 2012, and were current as of that date.

Cheng, Jie, "The Story of a New Policy" (July 2009) 15 *Hong Kong Journal*, at http://www.hkjournal.org/archive/2009_fall/1.htm.

Cheng, Joseph Y.S., "The Constitutional Relationship Between the Central Government and the Future Hong Kong Special Administrative Region Government" (1988) 20 *Case Western Reserve Journal of International Law* 65–97.

Cheung, Anthony B.L., and Wong, Max W.L., "Judicial Review and Policy Making in Hong Kong: Changing Interface Between the Legal and the Political" (2006) 28 *Asia Pacific Journal of Public Administration* 117–141.

Cheung, Chor Yung, "The Quest for Good Governance: Hong Kong's Principal Officials Accountability System" (2003) 1(2) *China, An International Journal* 249–272.

Cheung, Eric T.M., "Undermining Our Judicial Independence and Autonomy" (2011) 41 *HKLJ* 411–420.

Cheung, Eric T.M., Gu Weixia and Zhang Xianchu, "Crown Immunity Without the Crown" (Nov 2010) *Hong Kong Lawyer* 12–25.

Ching, Frank, "How Beijing Plays Its Hand: As Seen From Hong Kong" (July 2009) 15 *Hong Kong Journal*, at http://www.hkjournal.org/archive/2009_fall/2.htm.

———, "Looking Back: How London and Beijing Decided the Fate of Hong Kong" (April 2010) 18 *Hong Kong Journal*, at http://www.hkjournal.org/archive/2010_summer/2.htm.

Cottrell, Jill, and Ghai, Yash, "Concurring and Dissenting Judgments in the Court of Final Appeal" (August 2010) *Hong Kong Lawyer* 31–35.

Forsyth, Christopher, and Williams, Rebecca, "Closing Chapter in the Immigrant Children Saga: Substantive Legitimate Expectations and Administrative Justice in Hong Kong" (2002) 10(1) *Asia Pacific Law Review* 29–47.

Fu, H.L., "The Battle of Criminal Jurisdictions" (1998) 28 *HKLJ* 273–281.

Fu, Hualing, and Cullen, Richard, "But Hong Kong Should Seek a Better Way" (April 2006) 2 *Hong Kong Journal*, at http://www.hkjournal.org/archive/2006_spring/fu.html.

Gewirtz, Paul, "Approaches to Constitutional Interpretation: Comparative Constitutionalism and Chinese Characteristics" (2001) 31 *HKLJ* 200–223.

Ghai, Yash, "The Continuity of Laws and Legal Obligations and Rights in the SAR" (1997) 27 *HKLJ* 136–151.

———, "Commentary" [1999] 1 HKLRD 360–366.

———, "Resolution of Disputes Between the Central and Regional Governments: Models in Autonomous Regions" (2002) 5 *Journal of Chinese and Comparative Law* 1–20.

———, "The Intersection of Chinese Law and the Common Law in the Hong Kong Special Administrative Region: Question of Technique or Politics" (2007) 37 *HKLJ* 363–406.

Ghai, Yash, and Cottrell, Jill, "The Politics of Succession in Hong Kong" (2005) 35 *HKLJ* 1–6.

Gittings, Danny, "Changing Expectations: How the Rule of Law Fared in the First Decade of the Hong Kong SAR" (July 2007) 7 *Hong Kong Journal*, at http://www.hkjournal.org/archive/2007_fall/2.htm.

———, "Hong Kong Courts are Learning to Live With China" (July 2010) 19 *Hong Kong Journal*, at http://www.hkjournal.org/archive/2010_fall/2.htm.

———, "What Will Happen to Hong Kong After 2047?" (2011) 42 *California Western International Law Journal* 37–60.

Hannum, Hurst, and Lillich, Richard, "The Concept of Autonomy in International Law" (1980) 74 *American Journal of International Law* 858–889.

Harhoff, Frederick, "Institutions of Autonomy" (1986) 55 *Nordic Journal of International Law* 31–40.

Hsu, Berry F.C., "Judicial Independence Under the Basic Law" (2004) 34 *HKLJ* 279–302.

Jones, Oliver, "In Defence of Crown Liability" (Jan 2011) *Hong Kong Lawyer* 41–47.

Lee, Siu K., "Much Ado About Something" (July 1999) *Hong Kong Lawyer* 26–31.

Leung, Elsie (Secretary for Justice), "Viewing the Jurisdictional Issue From a Proper Perspective" (Jan 1999) *Hong Kong Lawyer* 56–58.
Ling, Bing, "Subject Matter Limitation on the NPCSC's Power to Interpret the Basic Law" (2007) 37 *HKLJ* 619–646.
Lo, P.Y., "The Impact of CFA Jurisprudence Beyond Hong Kong" (August 2010) *Hong Kong Lawyer* 36–41.
_____, "The Gateway Opens Wide" (2011) 41 *HKLJ* 385–391.
Loh, Christine, and Cullen, Richard, "Politics Without Democracy: A Study of the New Principal Officials Accountability System in Hong Kong" (2003) 4 *San Diego International Law Journal* 127–188.
Mason, Sir Anthony, "The Place of Comparative Law in the Developing Jurisprudence on the Rule of Law and Human Rights in Hong Kong" (2007) 37 *HKLJ* 299–317.
_____, "A Non-permanent Fixture on the CFA", Interview in (August 2010) *Hong Kong Lawyer* 20–23.
_____, "The Rule of Law in the Shadow of the Giant: The Hong Kong Experience" (2011) 33 *Sydney Law Review* 623–644.
Morris, Robert J., "The 'Replacement' Chief Executive's Two-Year Term: A Pure and Unambiguous Common Law Analysis" (2005) 35 *HKLJ* 17–26.
Ng, Margaret, "PRC Constitution Made Part of Laws of Hong Kong?" (Oct 1998) *Hong Kong Lawyer* 21–22.
Scott, Ian, "The Disarticulation of Hong Kong's Post-Handover Political System" (2000) 43 *The China Journal* 29–53.
Shen, Simon, "Hong Kong's External Space: Defining a Grey Area" (April 2011) 21 *Hong Kong Journal*, at http://www.hkjournal.org/archive/2011_summer/4.htm.
Swede, Richard, "One Territory—Three Systems? The Hong Kong Bill of Rights" (1995) 44 *International & Comparative Law Quarterly* 358–378.
Tai, Benny Y T, "Basic Law, Basic Politics: The Constitutional Game of Hong Kong" (2007) 37 *HKLJ* 503–578.
_____, "The Constitutional Game of Article 158(3) of the Basic Law" (2011) 41 *HKLJ* 377–383.
Tamanaha, Brian Z., "Post-1997 Hong Kong: A Comparative Study of the Meaning of 'High Degree of Autonomy'" (1989) 20 *California Western International Law Journal* 41–66.
Wacks, Raymond, "Our Flagging Rights" (2000) 30 *HKLJ* 1–5.
Wang, Zhenmin, "The Significance of China's Decision on Universal Suffrage" (April 2008) 10 *Hong Kong Journal*, at http://www.hkjournal.org/archive/2008_summer/1.htm.
Wesley-Smith, Peter, "Maintenance of the Bill of Rights" (1997) 27 *HKLJ* 15–16.
_____, "Judges and Judicial Power Under the Hong Kong Basic Law" (2004) 34 *HKLJ* 83–107.
Wong, Yan Lung (Secretary for Justice), "The Secretary for Justice as the Protector of the Public Interest—Continuity and Development" (2007) 37 *HKLJ* 319–349.
Wu, Jianfan, "Several Issues Concerning the Relationship Between the Central Government of the People's Republic of China and the Hong Kong Special Administrative Region" (1988) 2 *Journal of Chinese Law* 65–82.
Xiao, Weiyun, "A Brief Discussion of the Judgments of the Court of Final Appeal and the NPCSC Interpretation" (2002) 5 *Journal of Chinese and Comparative Law* 93–108.
Xu, Xiaobing, and Wilson, George D., "The Hong Kong Special Administrative Region as a Model of Regional External Autonomy" (2000) 32 *Case Western Reserve Journal of International Law* 1–38.
Yang, Xiaonan, "Legislative Interpretations by the Standing Committee of the National People's Congress in China" (2008) 38 *HKLJ* 255–285.
Yap, Po Jen, "Constitutional Review Under the Basic Law: The Rise, Retreat and Resurgence of Judicial Power in Hong Kong" (2007) 37 *HKLJ* 449–474.

Yen, Tony, "The PRC Constitution and Hong Kong Law" (Dec 1998) *Hong Kong Lawyer* 16–17.
Young, Simon N.M., "Restricting Basic Law Rights in Hong Kong" (2004) 34 *HKLJ* 109–132.
———, "Constitutional Rights in Hong Kong's Court of Final Appeal" (2011) 27 *Chinese (Taiwan) Yearbook of International Law and Affairs* 67–96.
Young, Simon N.M., and Da Roza, Antonio, "Judges and Judging in the Court of Final Appeal: A Statistical Picture" (August 2010) *Hong Kong Lawyer* 23–30.
Zervos, Kevin, "Constitutional Remedies Under the Basic Law" (2010) 40 *HKLJ* 687–718.
Zhang, Youyu, "The Reasons for and Basic Principles in Formulating the Hong Kong Special Administrative Region Basic Law, and Its Essential Contents and Mode of Expression" (1988) 2 *Journal of Chinese Law* 5–19.

Papers and Reports[2]

Bokhary, Justice Kemal, *Hong Kong's Legal System: The Court of Final Appeal* (New Zealand Centre for Public Law, Occasional Paper No. 13, Nov 2002), at http://www.victoria.ac.nz/law/centres/nzcpl/publications/occasional-papers/publications/Bokhary-Paper.pdf.
Chaney, Christopher, *The Hong Kong Executive Authorities' Monopoly on Legislative Power: Analysis of the Legislative Council's Second Term Voting Records* (Centre for Comparative and Public Law, University of Hong Kong, Occasional Paper No. 13, June 2004), at http://www.law.hku.hk/ccpl/pub/Documents/ChaneyOP.pdf.
Chau, Pak Kwan, *A Threat to One Country, Two Systems: National Law Making for Hong Kong* (School of Oriental and African Studies, M.A. thesis, April 1988), at http://e-chaupak.net/thesis/national.pdf.
Chief Executive's Office, *Civil Liberties and Social Order: Consultation Document* (April 1997).
Consultative Committee for the Basic Law of the Hong Kong SAR, *Final Report on the Relationship Between the Basic Law and the Constitution* (Feb 1987), at http://ebook.lib.hku.hk/bldho/articles/BL0834.pdf.
———, *Consultation Report, Volume 1: Report on the Consultation of the Draft Basic Law for Solicitation of Opinions* (Oct 1988), at http://ebook.lib.hku.hk/bldho/articles/BL0217.pdf.
Electoral Affairs Commission, *Report on the 2008 Legislative Council Election Held on 7 September 2008* (4 Dec 2008), at http://www.eac.gov.hk/en/legco/2008lce_report.htm.
Her Majesty's Government, *White Paper on a Draft Agreement Between the Government of Great Britain and Northern Ireland and the Government of the People's Republic of China on the Future of Hong Kong* (26 Sept 1984).
———, *Six-monthly Report on Hong Kong: January–June 2004* (July 2004), at http://british.e-consulate.org/common/15thSixMonthlyReport.pdf.
Hong Kong Bar Association, *Press Statement Regarding Judicial Independence* (9 July 2008), at http://www.hkba.org/whatsnew/press-release/20080709.pdf.
———, *Hong Kong: A Step Taken in Development of Political System* (July 2010), at http://www.hkba.org/whatsnew/misc/HKBA_Constitutional-related_articles_July_2010.pdf.
———, *The Bar's Position Paper on the "Procedure for Seeking an Interpretation of the Basic Law Under Article 158(1) of the Basic Law"* (25 May 2012), at http://www.hkba.org/whatsnew/submission-position-papers/2012/20120525.pdf.
Hong Kong Judiciary, *Statement on the Administration's Decision on the New System for the Determination of Judicial Remuneration* (20 May 2008), at http://www.info.gov.hk/gia/general/200805/20/P200805200152.htm.

---

2. All Internet-based sources were last accessed on 12 Oct 2012, and were current as of that date.

Hong Kong SAR Government, *Administration's Responses to Points Raised on 7 May by Members of the Bills Committee on the Legislative Council (Amendment) Bill 1999* (21 May 1999), at http://www.legco.gov.hk/yr98-99/english/bc/bc66/papers/b662151a.htm.

_____, *Legal and Administrative Matters Relating to the Appointment of Judges of the Court of Final Appeal* (3 June 2000), at http://www.legco.gov.hk/yr99-00/english/panels/ajls/papers/2176e01.pdf.

_____, *Paper Prepared by the Director of Administration on "Process of Appointment of Judges"* (22 April 2002), at http://www.legco.gov.hk/yr01-02/english/panels/ajls/papers/aj0422cb2-1617-2e.pdf.

_____, *Twelve-month Report on the Implementation of the Accountability System for Principal Officials* (July 2003), at http://www.cmab.gov.hk/upload/20040219153857/12mthreport-e.pdf.

_____, *Legislative Council Panel on Constitutional Affairs, Article 50 of the Basic Law* (July 2005), at http://www.legco.gov.hk/yr04-05/english/panels/ca/papers/ca0718cb2-2255-2e.pdf.

_____, *Consultation Paper on Further Development of the Political Appointment System* (July 2006), at http://www.cmab.gov.hk/images/pa_consultation_e.pdf.

_____, *Granting of Leases After 30 June 1997 With Term Extending Beyond 30 June 2047* (12 Dec 2006), at http://www.legco.gov.hk/yr06-07/english/panels/plw/papers/plw1114cb1-503-1-e.pdf.

_____, *Green Paper on Constitutional Development* (July 2007), at http://www.cmab.gov.hk/doc/issues/GPCD-e.pdf.

_____, *Report on Further Development of the Political Appointment System* (Oct 2007), at http://www.cmab.gov.hk/doc/issues/report_en.pdf.

_____, *Public Consultation Report on the Green Paper on Constitutional Development* (Dec 2007), at http://www.cmab.gov.hk/doc/issues/MainReport_en.pdf.

_____, *Legislative Council Brief: System for the Determination of Judicial Remuneration and Interim Arrangement for the 2008–09 Judicial Service Pay Adjustment Exercise* (20 May 2008), at http://www.legco.gov.hk/yr07-08/english/panels/ajls/papers/aj0526-csoad-mcr6322102-e.pdf.

_____, *Statutory and Non-statutory Appointments of Judges to Offices Outside the Judiciary* (13 Jan 2009), at http://www.legco.gov.hk/yr08-09/english/panels/ajls/papers/aj0113cb2-601-8-e.pdf.

_____, *Consultation Report on the District Council Appointment System* (June 2012), at http://www.cmab.gov.hk/doc/issues/electoral_matters/district_council_appointment_system_en.pdf.

Hopkinson, Lisa, and Lao, Man Lei Mandy, *Rethinking the Small House Policy* (Civic Exchange, 2003), at http://www.civic-exchange.org/wp/rethinking-the-small-house-policy.

Information Office of the State Council, *Regional Ethnic Autonomy in Tibet* (23 May 2004), at http://english.gov.cn/official/2005-07/28/content_18017.htm.

Legislative Affairs Commission of the NPC Standing Committee, *Statement on Term of Office of the Chief Executive Returned at a By-election Upon the Occurrence of a Vacancy* (12 March 2005), English translation at http://www.legco.gov.hk/yr04-05/english/bc/bc56/papers/bc560414cb2-1278-1e-scan.pdf.

Legislative Council, *Report of Select Committee to Inquire Into the Circumstances Leading to the Problems Surrounding the Commencement of the Operation of the New Hong Kong International Airport at Chek Lap Kok Since 6 July 1998 and Related Issues* (Jan 1999), at http://www.legco.gov.hk/yr98-99/english/sc/sc01/papers/report.htm.

_____, *Minutes of Special Meeting of the Legislative Council Panel on Administration of Justice and Legal Services* (3 June 2000), at http://www.legco.gov.hk/yr99-00/english/panels/ajls/minutes/aj030600.pdf.

—, *Minutes of Special Meeting of the Legislative Council Panel on Administration of Justice and Legal Services* (17 June 2000), at http://www.legco.gov.hk/yr99-00/english/panels/ajls/minutes/aj170600.pdf.

—, *Minutes of Special Meeting of the Legislative Council Panel on Constitutional Affairs* (28 Jan 2004), at http://www.legco.gov.hk/yr03-04/english/panels/ca/minutes/ca040128.pdf.

—, *Report of the Select Committee to Inquire Into the Handling of the Severe Acute Respiratory Syndrome Outbreak by the Government and the Hospital Authority* (July 2004), at http://www.legco.gov.hk/yr03-04/english/sc/sc_sars/reports/sars_rpt.htm.

Legislative Council Secretariat, *Procedure in Dealing With the Introduction of Members' Bills as Provided in Article 74 of the Basic Law and the Interpretation of Article 48(10) of the Basic Law* (22 July 1998), at http://www.legco.gov.hk/yr99-00/english/procedur/papers/rp_45e.htm.

Le Sueur, Andrew, *A Report on Six Seminars About the UK Supreme Court* (Queen Mary School of Law, Legal Studies Research Paper No. 1/2008, Dec 2008), at http://ssrn.com/abstract=1324749.

Liu, Eva, *The Process of Appointment of Judges in Some Foreign Countries: The United States* (Research and Library Services Division, Legislative Council Secretariat, 24 April 2001), at http://www.legco.gov.hk/yr00-01/english/library/0001in12.pdf.

—, and Cheung, Wai Lam, *The Process of Appointment of Judges in Hong Kong and Some Foreign Countries: Overall Comparison* (Research and Library Services Division, Legislative Council Secretariat, 12 May 2001), at http://www.legco.gov.hk/yr00-01/english/library/0001rp12.pdf.

Mason, Sir Anthony, *Consultancy Report: System for the Determination of Judicial Remuneration* (Hong Kong Judiciary, February 2003), at http://www.judiciary.gov.hk/en/publications/consultancy_report_e.pdf.

Office of the UN High Commissioner for Human Rights, *General Comment No. 06: The Right to Life (Art. 6)* (30 April 1982), at http://www.unhchr.ch/tbs/doc.nsf/0/84ab9690ccd81fc7c12563ed0046fae3.

Public Opinion Programme (University of Hong Kong), *Popularity of Chief Executive* (1996–2012), at http://hkupop.hku.hk/english/popexpress/ce2005/index.html.

Tsang, Donald (Acting Chief Executive), *Report to the State Council Concerning the Submission of a Request to the Standing Committee of the NPC Regarding the Interpretation of Article 53(2) of the Basic Law of the Hong Kong SAR of the PRC* (6 April 2005), English translation at http://www.info.gov.hk/gia/general/200504/06/04060198.htm.

Tsang, Donald (Chief Executive), *Report on the Public Consultation on Constitutional Development and on Whether There is a Need to Amend the Methods for Selecting the Chief Executive of the Hong Kong SAR and for Forming the Legislative Council of the Hong Kong SAR in 2012* (Dec 2007), English translation at http://www.cmab.gov.hk/doc/issues/Report_to_NPCSC_en.pdf.

Tsang, Jasper (Legislative Council President), *President's Ruling on Closing the Joint Debate at the Committee Stage of the Legislative Council (Amendment) Bill 2012* (22 May 2012), at http://www.legco.gov.hk/yr11-12/english/pre_rul/pre0522-ref-e.pdf.

UN Commission on Human Rights, *The Siracusa Principles on the Limitation and Derogation Provisions in the International Covenant on Civil and Political Rights* (28 Sept 1984), at http://www.unhcr.org/refworld/docid/4672bc122.html.

UN Committee on Economic, Social and Cultural Rights, *Concluding Observations on the Initial Report of the Hong Kong Special Administrative Region* (11 May 2001), at http://www.unhchr.ch/tbs/doc.nsf/0/1f67bd3f2a811fddc1256a4c002ed71a.

UN Human Rights Committee, *Concluding Observations of the Human Rights Committee on the Fourth Periodic Report Relating to Hong Kong of the United Kingdom and Northern Ireland* (9 Nov 1995), reproduced in (1995) 5 HKPLR 641–645.

386 Bibliography

US Consulate in Hong Kong, *Rule of Law in Hong Kong* (28 August 2007), published by Wikileaks at http://wikileaks.org/cable/2007/08/07HONGKONG2244.html.

———, *Upon This Rock: Hong Kong Rule of Law Remains Solid (Part 1)* (26 Feb 2010), published by Wikileaks at http://wikileaks.org/cable/2010/02/10HONGKONG334.html.

Wade, Sir William, *The Court of Final Appeal of Hong Kong* (24 Oct 1991).

Yam, Joseph, *The Future of the Monetary System in Hong Kong* (Institute of Global Economics and Finance, Chinese University of Hong Kong, Working Paper No. 9, June 2012), at http://www.igef.cuhk.edu.hk/igef_media/working-paper/IGEF/igef_working_paper_no_9_eng.pdf.

Speeches[3]

Allcock, Robert (Solicitor General), "Application of Article 158 of the Basic Law", Constitutional Law Conference on Implementation of the Basic Law: A Comparative Perspective, 29 April 2000, at http://www.info.gov.hk/gia/general/200004/29/0428219.htm.

———, "Challenges to Hong Kong's Legal System in View of Hong Kong's Return to Chinese Sovereignty", Conference at the City University of Hong Kong, 9 Nov 2004, at http://www.info.gov.hk/gia/general/200411/09/1109202.htm.

Bokhary, Justice Kemal, "Current State of Judicial Review in Hong Kong", Speech to Peking University School of Transnational Law, 15 Sept 2009.

Chan, Anson (Chief Secretary for Administration), "Speech at LegCo's Motion Debate", Legislative Council, 3 Feb 1999, at http://www.info.gov.hk/gia/general/199902/03/0203238.htm.

Cohen, Jerome A., "Hong Kong's Basic Law: An American Perspective", International Symposium to Commemorate the 10th Anniversary of the Promulgation of the Hong Kong SAR Basic Law, 1 April 2000, at http://www.info.gov.hk/basic_law/upload/977133808/Cohen.

Ip, Regina, "Statement by Secretary for Security", Press Conference, 16 July 2003, at http://www.info.gov.hk/gia/general/200307/16/0716223.htm.

Lai, Benedict, "Recent Trends and Developments of Judicial Review in Hong Kong", 20th Biennial Lawasia Conference, 5–8 June 2007, at http://www.doj.gov.hk/eng/public/pdf/lo2007/0608e.pdf.

Leung, Elsie (Secretary for Justice), "Speech Moving a Resolution Under the Hong Kong Court of Final Appeal Ordinance (Cap. 484) in the Provisional Legislative Council", 23 July 1997, at http://www.info.gov.hk/isd/speech/723-just.htm.

———, "Speech on Legal Aspects of the Accountability System at LegCo Motion Debate on the Accountability System", Legislative Council, 30 May 2002, at http://www.info.gov.hk/gia/general/200205/30/0530237.htm.

———, "Understanding One Country, Two Systems Through Hong Kong's Constitutional Development", Basic Law Seminar Presentation, 29 May 2004, at http://www.doj.gov.hk/eng/archive/pdf/sj20040529e.pdf.

———, "Statement on the Term of the New Chief Executive", Press Conference, 12 March 2005, at http://www.doj.gov.hk/eng/archive/pdf/sj20050312e.pdf.

———, "Letter to Hong Kong: The Chief Executive's Term of Office and the Rule of Law", *RTHK Radio 3*, 20 March 2005, at http://www.info.gov.hk/gia/general/200503/20/03190102.htm.

Li, Andrew (Chief Justice), "Speech at the Opening of the Legal Year", 17 Jan 2000, at http://www.info.gov.hk/gia/general/200001/17/0117134.htm.

———, "Speech at the Opening of the Legal Year", 17 Feb 2005, at http://www.info.gov.hk/gia/general/200502/17/02170118.htm.

---

3. All Internet-based sources were last accessed on 12 Oct 2012, and were current as of that date.

_____, "Speech at the Ceremonial Opening of the Legal Year", 9 Jan 2006, at http://www.info.gov.hk/gia/general/200601/09/P200601090137.htm.

_____, "The Chief Justice's Address at His Farewell Sitting", 16 July 2010, at http://gia.info.gov.hk/general/201007/16/P201007160173_0173_67253.pdf.

Li, Zaishun, "The Comprehensive Grasping of the 'One Country, Two Systems' Concept Is the Key to the Correct Implementation of the Hong Kong Basic Law", Constitutional Law Conference on Implementation of the Basic Law: A Comparative Perspective, 29 April 2000, at http://law.hku.hk/hkconlaw/Lizaishun.htm.

Patten, Christopher (Governor), "Our Next Five Years: The Agenda for Hong Kong", Policy Address, 7 Oct 1992.

Suen, Michael (Secretary for Constitutional Affairs), "Speech in Respect of the Government Motion on the Accountability System for Principal Officials at the Legislative Council Meeting", Legislative Council, 29 May 2002, at http://www.info.gov.hk/gia/general/200205/29/0529263.htm.

Wong, Yan Lung (Secretary for Justice), "One Country, Two Systems", Speech to Chatham House, 9 June 2006, at http://www.doj.gov.hk/eng/archive/pdf/2006/sj20060609e.pdf.

_____, "Speech at Press Conference on Constitutional Reform Package", Press Conference, 21 June 2010, at http://www.info.gov.hk/gia/general/201006/21/P201006210168.htm.

Index

Notes:

For ease of reference, wherever possible index entries refer to footnotes accompanying the relevant text (using the abbreviation "n" for footnote). For example, "10n2" refers to footnote 2 on page 10. Authors of sources listed in the bibliography are included in the index wherever they are cited in the main text.

In addition to the main abbreviations listed on page ix and used throughout this book, the following additional abbreviations are used in the index:

CE	Chief Executive
CFA	Court of Final Appeal
CPG	Central People's Government
HK	Hong Kong
HKBL	Hong Kong Basic Law
HKSAR	Hong Kong Special Administrative Region
JD	Joint Declaration
JORC	Judicial Officers Recommendation Commission
Legco	Legislative Council
NPCSC	National People's Congress Standing Committee

30 June 2047, after, 8, 303–314
   50 years guarantee, end of, 307–309
      no change, 308n32, 309n33
      pessimistic view, 303n3–4, 307n27
   1997, parallels with, 312–314
   CPG, and, 313n61–62
   property rights, future of (*see also* land leases in HK), 304–307

abode, right of, 7, 264–266
   children
      adopted, 226n45, 248n180
      born in HK (*see also Chong Fung Yuen* (2001) judgment), 200n357, 242, 248n178, 265n18
      born outside HK (*see also Ng Ka Ling* (1999) judgment), 158, 178, 200, 253n212, 265n20
      illegitimate, 232n77, 234n85, 235n90
      one-way permit restriction, 233n78, 235n90, 236n96
      time of birth restriction, 232n77, 235n90, 236n96
   domestic helpers, 209n429, 250n193, 265n21
   ethnic minorities, 266n26
   foreigners, 265n22, 266n23
   fundamental right, 237n102
   JD, provisions in, 18
   ordinary residence, 95n8, 265

Preparatory Committee, Opinions of, 230n62, 242n138, 248n177
prisoners, 265n21
refugees, 266n26
academic freedom, 123n173
acts of state, 214–217
　Chinese legal system, 215n461
　common law, 214n460
　Congo (2011) judgment, 195n313, 216–217, 256n228
　facts of state, 64n60, 214, 216, 256n228
　HKBL, drafting of, 24, 26, 215n463–464
adjudicate, power to (*see also* final adjudication, power of), 80–81, 157n33
administrative officers, 118n140
Administrative Secretary (*see also* Chief Secretary for Administration), 115n126
Advisory Committee on Post-service Employment of Civil Servants, 157n38
air service agreements, 62n43–44
Aland Delegation, 89n235–237
Aland Islands, 56
　HK, comparison with, 56n8, 89n236
　legislative power, 72n115–116, 74n130
Allcock, Robert (Solicitor General), 28n63, 34n110
amendment of HKBL, 258–262
　30 June 2047, after, 309
　1999, rejected in, 234, 260n259
　Annex I, 109n89, 112n111, 129
　Annex II, 128–129
　Annex III, 76
　difficulties, 120, 259n247, 260
　HKBL, special status of, 45–46, 258
　interpretation, preferable to, 261n263
　restrictions on, 258–262
　　not legally binding, 261n265, 262n266, 314n69
　　prevent substantial change, 46n72, 259, 261–262
anti-discrimination laws, 144n280
Aristotle (Greek philosopher), 93n2
armed forces (*see* defence; People's Liberation Army)
arrest, rights on, 266, 270, 282
Article 23 (*see* national security; secession; sedition; state secrets, theft of; subversion; treason)

assembly, freedom of (*see also Leung Kwok Hung* (2005) judgment; Public Order Ordinance), 203–204, 266, 270, 275n72, 283, 287
　restrictions on, 263, 287, 288n144, 294, 298–299, 301n224
associated states, 83n192
association, freedom of (*see also* Falun Gong; national security; Societies Ordinance; trade unions, right to form and join), 266, 270, 283, 287
　restrictions on, 294, 298–299
Attorney General, 116n133
Audit Commission, 116, 120n149
Australia
　CFA, judges on (*see also* Mason, Sir Anthony), 192
　HK, comparison with, 65n66, 66n73, 158n40, 187n252
autonomous areas (*see also* dispute resolution mechanism; National Autonomous Areas)
　common characteristics, 58n19, 91
　elections, 68
　executive power, 58–59
　judicial appointments, 82n184
　judicial power, 80n172, 84n201
　　final adjudication, power of, 83n191, 189n265, 304
　legislative power, 72, 74n129
autonomy
　definition of, 55n3–4
　ethnic basis for, 55–57
autonomy in HK (*see also* basic policies of the PRC regarding HK)
　CE's defence of, 67, 89–90
　China's self-restraint, dependent on, 67, 85n207
　constitutional guarantees less secure, 65n65, 67
　economic basis for, 57
　human rights at heart of, 237n101
　international legal personality, 63–64
　NPCSC 2004 interpretation damaged, 3, 6, 70n99, 91, 129–130
　semi-sovereignty, 60n32
　sub-sovereignty, 64n57
aviation (*see also* air service agreements), 41n36

Bank of China, 111n104
barristers (*see also* Hong Kong Bar Association), 161n64
basic law (*see also* Hong Kong Basic Law; Macao Basic Law)
  category of laws, 2, 20, 42, 180n196
  NPCSC, amendment by, 42n47, 258n244, 260
Basic Law Committee (*see* Committee for the Basic Law of the HKSAR)
Basic Law Consultative Committee (*see* Consultative Committee for the Basic Law of the HKSAR)
Basic Law Drafting Committee (*see* Drafting Committee for the Basic Law of the HKSAR)
Basic Law of the HKSAR (*see* Hong Kong Basic Law)
Basic Law of the Macao SAR (*see* Macao Basic Law)
basic policies of the PRC regarding HK, 16–17, 55n1, 259n251
  amendment of HKBL, restriction on, 46n72, 259, 261–262
  HKBL, duplicated in, 38n7, 259n250
Big Spender (*see* Cheung Tze Keung)
Bill of Rights (*see* Hong Kong Bill of Rights Ordinance)
bills (*see also* government bills; private members' bills)
  amendment, 106, 144–145
  important, 100n37
Bokhary, Justice Kemal, 193n300, 195n318, 209n424
  China, criticized by, 164n85
  judgments, 193n296, 206n404–406, 226n45
    Congo (2011), 64n61, 84n199, 163n84, 216n473, 217n478, 256n227
    Leung Kwok Hung (2005), 199n347, 205n394, 206n404
    Ng Kung Siu (1999), 199n345–348, 298n207–208, 302n232
  resignation, considered, 164n85, 197n330
  retirement, 163–164, 207n413
Boundary Street, 10
Brennan, Sir Gerard (overseas judge), 192n291
Britain (*see* United Kingdom)
British Overseas Territories, 60n34

budget
  judiciary, 167
  Legco, approval by, 103, 142
  Legco, rejection by, 100–101
by-elections, 75n138–141, 138n251, 145n287
Byrnes, Andrew (Professor), 280n101–103

Caird, Brian (District Judge), 165n96
Canada,
  HK, comparison with, 65n66, 66n73, 182n221
  residual powers, 65n69
  rights, restrictions on, 291n160
Cao, Erbao (PRC official), 70n102, 70n106
Catalonia, 67n82, 86n212
Catholic Church, 312n56
Central Authorities (*see also* Central Military Commission; CPG; NPC; NPCSC)
  after 2003, change of policy on HK, 3, 69–71
  HKBL, powers under, 40–41, 225n36
  self-restraint in use of, 68, 77–78, 91, 98, 242n140
  second governing team, 70n102
Central Military Commission, 40n20
Central People's Government (CPG), also known as State Council (*see also* Hong Kong and Macao Affairs Office of the State Council; Ministry of Foreign Affairs; subversion against the CPG)
  30 June 2047, and, 313n61–62
  acts of state, 26, 214–215
  amendments to HKBL, 258
  businesses immune from HK courts, 213n453
  Chief Executive of HKSAR
    appointment, 16, 40n23, 67, 95
    dismissal, 102
    report from, 178n182, 235n87, 254n215
  Chief Justice, approved appointment of, 82n187, 161n66
  diplomatic immunity, decides on, 210n434
  foreign affairs of HK, 16, 40n22, 60n31, 62n45
  grant further powers to HK, 66n72
  highest organ of state administration, 40n20
  HKSAR territorial boundaries, Order on, 79n163
  land leases in HK, 306n19

legislation in China, power to enact, 42n49, 79n162
legislation in HK
  loophole in HKBL, 79n163–164
  pressure HK to enact, 75
  state of war or emergency, 79–80
mainland Chinese settling in HK, number of, 41n26
NPCSC interpretation, request, 235, 236n97
offices in HK (*see also* Liaison Office of the CPG in the HKSAR), 41n38–39
Principal Officials
  appointment, 40n23, 71, 98, 116
  rejected nomination of, 71n110, 98, 122n165
Central Policy Unit, 175n156
Chan, Anson (Chief Secretary for Administration), 115n126, 118n141, 147n299
Chan, Dominic (HK legislator), 32n97
Chan, Johannes M.M. (Professor), 33n100, 69n90, 80n174, 158n41, 162n76, 164n88, 169n114, 171n130, 172n138, 183n222, 186n243, 186n245, 186n249, 191n285, 193n301, 197n333, 198n339, 199n348, 202n368, 202n370, 203n378, 206n407, 217n477, 237n103, 249n186, 249n190, 250n195, 252n202–204, 259n247, 269n41–42, 298n204, 304n5, 311n45
  Lim, C.L., and, 263n4, 268n32, 279n99, 289n147, 295n186, 300n219
Chan, Kenneth (Associate Professor), 304n3, 305n8
charging effect, 144n279, 145n284
Chau, Pak Kwan (scholar), 79n164
checks and balances (*see also* separation of powers), 93, 103, 142, 156
Chek Lap Kok, 118, 147n298
Chen, Albert H.Y. (Professor), 38n7, 60n33, 65n65–66, 68n88, 70n99, 76n145, 87n222, 88n233, 112n110, 113n113, 113n117, 139n255–256, 171n130, 172n136, 173n144, 182n218, 182n221, 195n313, 198n338, 200n355, 203n372, 205n394, 206n401, 225n36, 238n113, 241n131, 242n140, 246n166, 253n214, 261n263, 261n265, 264n8, 296n193, 297n198, 306n19, 310n42–43, 313n64
Cheng, Albert (talk-show host), 199
Cheng, Jie (Associate Professor), 69n95–96, 111n106
Chen, Zuoer (PRC official), 95n9
Cheung, Eric T. M. (Assistant Professor), 65n63, 208n418
  Gu, Weixia and Zhang, Xianchu, and, 213n454
Cheung, Tze Keung (also known as Big Spender) (criminal), 43–44
Chief Executive of the HKSAR (*see also* Chief Executive election), 95–102
  appointment powers, 4, 93, 96–98
    JORC members, 161n64
    judges (*see also* judicial appointments), 82n185, 98n24, 161–162
    reject judicial nominations, 162n70–73
    retirement age, beyond, 164n87, 165n93, 207n413
    tribunal to investigate Chief Justice, 164n89
    NPC deputies, 90n250
    Principal Officials, nomination of, 71, 98, 116, 121, 122n165
  constraints on, 4, 93, 103–106
  CPG, and
    accountable to, 67, 75, 89, 95
    appointed by, 16, 40n23, 67, 95, 108
    implement directives from, 67, 95
    legislation, pressure to enact, 75
    mediating role with, 89–90
    report to, 178n182, 235n87, 254n215
  democratic mandate, lack of 4, 68, 89, 108, 151
  Executive Council, 96–97
  executive orders, issue, 105n59, 177n176
  financial powers
    amendments, 145n284
    motions, 104, 143
    provisional funding, 103n50
  foreign presidents, comparison with, 93, 96n12–13, 100n35, 108, 116
  HKSAR, accountable to, 89, 95
  impeachment, 102

judicial powers
    acts of state, 214
    pardons, issue, 101
    sentencing, 101n41
legislative powers
    bills, introduction of, 75n133, 99, 104, 144
    bills, refusal to sign, 74n132, 100–101
    laws, cannot make, 42n48, 100, 105
    Legco, dissolve, 100–101, 106n71
    Legco summons, prevent, 147n293
    legislative process, control over, 100
    national laws, proclamation of, 76, 77n149–150
nationality requirement, 95, 266n24
policy making, 93, 98, 157n30
resignation, 100–102, 106n72, 107, 243n147
term of office, 243–244
unpopularity, 107
Chief Executive election (*see also* Election Committee), 107–114
    1996 election, 32, 108
    2005 election, 110
    2007 election, 110
    2012 election, 70, 110–111, 113
    HKBL, drafting of, 21, 23–24, 26, 28
    nomination procedures (*see also* nominating committee), 5, 24n47, 28n65, 109–114
    pro-democracy candidates, 110, 113–114
    universal suffrage, 4–5, 28n65, 90, 112–114, 124, 131
Chief Judge of the High Court (*see also* Ma, Geoffrey), 82, 98n26, 154n10
Chief Justice of the CFA (*see also* Li, Andrew; Ma, Geoffrey), 167, 190
    CFA appointments beyond retirement age, 164n87, 165n93, 207n413
    JORC, chairs, 161
    nationality requirement, 154n10, 190n277
    non-permanent judges, choice of, 191n279, 191n284
    tribunal to investigate judges, 164
Chief Secretary for Administration (*see also* Chan, Anson; Lam, Carrie; Lam, Stephen; Tang, Henry), 115, 120n149
    2012, nomination in, 71n111, 120n151, 121n159

CE, stepping stone to, 115n127
deputy, 115n128, 116n129
title, 115n126
children (*see also* abode, right of; *Ng Ka Ling* (1999) judgment)
    prisoners, 101n41, 157n37
    rights, 270, 282n115, 283
China (*see* People's Republic of China)
Chinese citizen
    naturalization in HK, 66n72, 183n226
    PRC Criminal Law, and, 44n57, 45n65
    requirement for
        Chief Executive, 95, 266n24
        judicial posts, 154n10, 190n277
        Legislative Councillors, 154n9, 266n25
        NPC deputies, 90
        principal officials, 33n102, 115, 122n162, 154n9
Chinese Communist Party
    decision to reclaim HK, 13
    Legco debate, 149n311
    NPCSC controlled by, 87, 221n12–13
    Supreme People's Court controlled by, 180n200
Chinese legal system (*see also* Supreme People's Court)
    acts of state, 215n461
    constitutional review, 86n218, 170n123–125, 174
    crimes in HK, jurisdiction over, 43–45
    interpretation of laws (*see also* interpretation of HKBL by NPCSC), 25, 83, 130, 158, 220–221, 232n72, 235n91–92, 241n135
    judicial independence, absence of, 160n61, 167
    judicial review, 169n121
    law-making bodies, proliferation of, 42–43
Chinese People's Political Consultative Conference, 90n250, 109n86
Chinese state
    definition, 32n99
    HK laws, exemption from, 32n98, 33n101
    Hua Tian Long (No 2) (2010) case, 213
    land in HK is property of, 305n17
Ching, Frank (journalist), 13n15, 14n16
Chong Fung Yuen (2001) judgment, 200–202
    1999 NPCSC interpretation, and, 160n60, 201n364, 248–249

abode, right of, 200n357–358, 227
HKBL, interpretation of, 201n363, 227
  purposive approach redefined, 226n40
judicial referral, rejection of, 254–255
legislative interpretation, 202n367,
    249n185, 261n262
  common law system, comparison with,
    178n185, 202n368, 249–250,
    252n203
  NPCSC, criticism from, 202n365, 242, 249
Chung, Sir S.Y. (Executive Councillor), 14n20
Civic Exchange, 122n165
Civic Party, 110n94, 122n164
civil aviation (*see also* air service agreements),
    41n36
civil service (*see also* administrative officers),
    117–118
  continuity, 312n53
  policy-making role, 117n134
  political neutrality, 117–118
  post-service employment, 157n38
  principal official posts, fill (*see also*
    Principal Officials of the HKSAR
    Government), 94, 117, 121
  public dissatisfaction with, 118–119
  resignations, 119n146, 123
Cohen, Jerome (Professor), 66n76, 198n337,
    238n114, 239n121
collective bargaining, right to, 271n55
Commissioner of Police (*see also* Hong Kong
    Police), 116, 120n149, 199n347,
    204n388–389
Commissioner on Interception of
    Communications and Surveillance,
    158n39
Committee for the Basic Law of the HKSAR
    (*see also* dispute resolution
    mechanism), 87–89
  1999 NPCSC interpretation, 89n241
  composition, 88n228
  consultation with, 73, 76, 259n248
  rubber-stamp, 89n242
common law offences, 39n15, 290n157–158,
    293n173
common law system
  continuity, 39
  HKBL prevails over, 247n172, 256n228
  judges from other jurisdictions (*see* overseas
    judges on CFA)

  precedents from other jurisdictions, 81
  rights, protection of, 263n3
  treaties not directly enforceable, 18,
    172n135, 273n61–62
communications, freedom and privacy of (*see
    also* covert surveillance), 267,
    293n171
communism (*see* Chinese Communist Party)
Congo (2011) judgment, 207–209, 255–257
  acts of state, 195n313, 216–217, 256n228
  Central Government, and, 208
  common law, and, 195n313, 247n172,
    255n226
  judicial independence, effect on, 84n199,
    208n420–422, 256n227
  NPCSC, interpretation by, 257n235
  NPCSC, referral to (*see also* judicial referral
    by CFA to NPCSC), 7, 84,
    208n415, 217n476, 255–257
  overseas judge, role of, 194
  provisional judgment, 256n232–233
conscience, freedom of, 267, 270, 283
  absolute right, 286n133
constitution (*see also* Constitution of the PRC
    1982; Hong Kong Letters Patent;
    United States Constitution)
  common characteristics, 47n81–83
  power sharing arrangements, 65n67
constitutional conventions, 122n166
  ministerial resignation, 123n167
constitutional court
  autonomous areas (*see also* dispute
    resolution mechanism), 86n212
  China, lacking in, 86–87
constitutional review, 170–184
  HKBL, drafting of, 174n152
  HK, power exercised by courts in, 173–175
  colonial era, 171–173
  declarations of unconstitutionality,
    175–178
  Ma Wai Kwan (1997) judgment,
    173n143
  Ng Ka Ling (1999) judgment, 173–174,
    196
  NPC and NPCSC, over actions of, 5,
    87n224, 159n52, 179–183
  objections to, 175n153–154
  judicial system, integral part of, 175n155

NPCSC, power of
    China, in, 86n218, 170n125, 174
    HK, in, 47n86, 73–74, 174n150
    UK, in, 171n126–128
    US, in, 170n122, 173
Constitution of the PRC 1982
    amendment of, 53n124, 53n130, 306n20–21
    Chinese courts, enforceability in, 53n129, 170n123, 288
    duties under, 288n141–144
    HK, application in, 3, 50
    HKBL, relationship with, 3, 50–54
    HK court cases, cited in, 50n110
    human rights, provisions on, 48
        HKBL, similarity with, 287n139, 288n140, 292
    NPC and NPCSC, supervised by, 53n127, 86n218
    one country, two systems, provision on, 51–54
    socialist system, provisions on, 50, 52, 304n6
    violations of, 53n130, 306n20
consultation, public, 23n45, 25, 104n55
Consultative Committee for the Basic Law of the HKSAR, 20–21, 25, 27, 53n125, 111n99
contextual approach, 224n30, 245–246
continuity
    change, degree of, 311–312
    civil service, 312n53
    common law system, 39
    economic system, 17, 57n15
    educational system, 312n57
    HKBL, purpose of, 225n37
    human rights, 16, 264
    judicial system, 5, 153–155, 210
conventions (*see* constitutional conventions)
Cooke of Thorndon, Lord (overseas judge), 192n292
Coroners' Court, 153n4
corporate voting (*see also* functional constituency elections), 135–136
    1995 elections, abolished in, 30n78, 135n235
    corporate bodies, 135n231, 136n239, 228n53
    legality of, 136n237–240, 142n267, 227–228

Council of Chairpersons of the NPCSC, 241n130
Court of Appeal, 153, 154n12
    CFA, appeals to, 195n317
    rights, conservative approach on, 206–207
Court of Final Appeal (*see also* judicial referral by CFA to NPCSC), 188–209
    appeals to, 195n315–316
    common law, development of, 186n247, 199n350
    composition of, 188–195
    constitutional crisis, 49, 87, 181–182, 296–297
    constitutional role (*see also* constitutional review), 195–209
    dissenting judgments, 194n306
        Bokhary, by (*see also* Bokhary, Justice Kemal), 64n61, 84n199, 163n84, 194n311, 199n347, 206n404–405, 216n473, 217n478, 226n45
    establishment of, 34, 78n156, 149n310, 155, 189–190, 215
    final adjudication, power of, 82, 188n264
    inherent jurisdiction, 181n210, 181n212
    judges on (*see also* Chief Justice of the CFA)
        appointment of, 82, 98n26
        non-permanent judges, 190–195 (*see also* overseas judges on CFA)
            Chief Justice, chosen by, 191n279, 191n284
            HK judges, 191n283, 191n287, 192n288
        permanent judges, 190n276, 191n278
    overseas court cases, cited in, 193n302–303
    pragmatic approach of, 202n371, 206n403
    retreat, period of, 6, 159, 197–199, 239, 298–299
    rights, role in protecting (see also *Ng Kung Siu* (1999) judgment), 6–8, 196, 198–199, 203–206
Court of First Instance, 153, 154n12
courts of HK (*see* Coroners' Court; Court of Appeal; Court of Final Appeal; Court of First Instance; District Court; High Court; interpretation of laws by HK courts; Judiciary; Labour Tribunal; Lands Tribunal;

396   Index

magistrates courts; restrictions on jurisdiction of HK courts; special courts)
covert surveillance
 executive order, 105n59, 177n176
 judicial oversight of, 105n62, 158n39
 judicial review of, 105, 177n175, 185n239
 legislation on, 105n62, 105n64, 177n177
Cradock, Sir Percy (UK diplomat), 13, 15
Crawford, James (Professor), 55n4, 130n210, 251n201
Criminal Law of the PRC
 crimes in HK, jurisdiction over, 43–45
 extra-territorial jurisdiction of, 44n57, 44n61, 45n65
 HKBL, not listed in, 43n56
Crown, 32n98, 213n455
Cullen, Richard (Professor), 188n262
 Yang, Xiaonan and Loh, Christine, and, 117n134, 122n163, 124n177,
Cultural Revolution, 9, 11, 35, 51n111
currency (*see* Hong Kong dollar; Renminbi; United States dollar)
Customs and Excise, 116, 120n149, 313n61
customs territory, separate, 60

Dalai Lama (Tibetan spiritual leader), 57n11
Davies, Sir John (Governor), 164n90
death penalty (*see also* life, right to), 282, 286n127–130
Decisions of NPCSC on HK
 30 June 2047, after, 313n64
 1995 elections, 31n85, 127n196
 functional constituencies, retention of, 130n211, 137, 139, 151
 HKBL drafters, expulsion of, 27n61
 laws previously in force in HK, 34, 47n86, 146n292, 278n92, 279n95
 universal suffrage after 2017, 68n86, 112n108, 131n214–215
declarations of unconstitutionality, 175–178
defamation, 199, 286
defence (*see also* People's Liberation Army), 16, 40n21, 214
defendants, rights of, 267, 283
Democratic Alliance for the Betterment of HK, 118n138
Democratic Party (formerly United Democrats of HK), 32n97, 110n93, 110n96, 122n164, 234n82

demonstration, freedom of (*see* assembly, freedom of)
Deng, Xiaoping (PRC leader), 2, 9, 11–14, 17n29, 94n5, 308n32
Denmark, 56, 88n234
Department of Administration, 115n128
Department of Finance, 115n128
Department of Justice, 114, 115n128
detention, rights in, 266, 270, 282
Dicey, A.V. (UK jurist), 122n166, 168n106, 171n126, 261n264
diplomatic immunity, 210, 216n468
Directors of Bureaux, 116, 120n149
discrimination (*see* anti-discrimination laws)
dispute resolution mechanism (*see also* constitutional court), 85–91
 autonomy, part of, 58, 86n211
 Chief Executive (*see also* Chief Executive of the HKSAR), 89–90
 HK, lacking in, 3, 91
 joint commission, 86n211, 88–89
 NPC deputies (*see also* National People's Congress deputies from HK), 90–91
District Boards (*see also* District Councils), 30n81, 126n192
District Councillors, 22n40, 30n82, 109, 127n195
District Councils (formerly known as District Councils), 97n16–18, 126n192
 functional constituencies, 132, 138–139
District Court, 105n62, 153, 164n88
Dowdle, Michael (Assistant Professor), 42n42, 46n78–79
Drafting Committee for the Basic Law of the HKSAR (*see also* drafting of HKBL), 20–21, 24n51, 27, 174n152, 215n464
 sub-groups, 21, 23–25, 28n70, 229n59, 231n68, 272n59
drafting of HKBL (*see also* Drafting Committee for the Basic Law of the HKSAR), 1, 18–29
 constitutional review, and, 174n152
 drafting deadline, 21, 27
 final draft, changes in, 27–28
 first draft, 23–25, 215n463
 HK drafters (*see also* Lee, Martin; Li, Ka Shing; Pao, Sir Y.K.; Szeto, Wah; Wu, Raymond), 20, 27–28

mainland drafters (*see also* Shao, Tianren; Xiao, Weiyun; Wang, Shuwen; Wu, Jianfan; Zhang, Youyu), 24–25, 29, 277n78
second draft, 25–27
UK involvement in, 28n66
Duty Lawyer Scheme, 284n119

Education Department, 97n19
election (*see also* Chief Executive election; Election Committee; functional constituency elections; Legislative Council elections; village elections; vote, right to)
stand for election, right to, 139n254, 140n262
Election Committee (*see also* Chief Executive election)
CE chosen by, 24, 26, 28, 108n80, 109–111, 132
composition, 109
functional constituency electorate, 109n87–88
legislators chosen by, 30, 127n195, 128n203, 134n226
nominating role (*see also* nominating committee), 109–111
NPC deputies chosen by (*see also* National People's Congress deputies from HK), 90n250
size, 24n48, 30, 68n85, 109n89–90, 110, 138n249–250
sub-sectors, 110n95
emergency (*see* state of war or emergency)
English, use in courts of, 81, 169n115
equality, right to, 266, 270, 282–284, 292
Equal Opportunities Commission, 97, 144n280
European Court of Human Rights, 289n149, 290n155, 291
European Court of Justice, 251n199, 256n232
European Union, 171n128, 251n199–200, 256
Executive Council, 33, 96–97
executive discretion, 101n41, 157n37
executive-led government
colonial era, 101–102
HKBL, under, 4, 93, 95n9, 142, 151
executive order, 105n59, 177n176
executive power, 3, 16, 58–71

expression, freedom of (*see also* Ng Kung Siu (1999) judgment), 270, 275n72, 283
Cheng v Tse (2000) judgment, 199–200
restrictions on (*see also* legitimate purpose), 289n149, 292–23, 294n180–181, 296–298, 301
contempt of court, 289n149
defamation, 199, 286
mode versus substance, 302
external affairs powers
autonomy, part of, 60–63
Congo (2011) judgment, 64n61
foreign affairs, distinction from, 62–63, 65n64
extradition, 62, 63n52, 213n451
extra-territorial jurisdiction
Criminal Law of the PRC, 44n57, 44n61, 45n65
extrinsic materials (*see also* purposive approach), 224, 228–230

facts of state (*see also* acts of state), 64n60, 214, 216, 256n228
fair trial, right to, 267
judicial referral by CFA to NPCSC, effect of, 252n204, 257
Falun Gong (*see also* association, freedom of)
attempt to ban in HK, 69n91, 75n135, 204n382
autonomy, test of, 69n90
members denied entry to HK, 61n38, 207n412
Yeung May Wan (2005) judgment, 203–204, 207
Faroe Islands, 60
federal system
China, experiment in, 66n76
division of powers under, 65n67
final adjudication, power of, 83n193
residual powers in, 65n68
filibuster, 145n287
final adjudication, power of
autonomous areas, 83n191, 189n265, 304
federal system, 83n193
HKSAR, 82–83, 188–189
JD, promised in, 16, 19n33, 24
Macao SAR, 83n191

Financial Secretary (*see also* Leung, Antony; Tsang, Donald; Tsang, John), 115, 120n149, 121n159
  deputy, 115n128, 116n129
Finland, 56, 74n130, 89
flags (*see* national flag, regional flag)
foreign affairs, 16, 40n22, 60n31, 255, 256n228
foreign judges (*see* overseas judges on CFA)
Forsyth, Christopher (Professor)
  Williams, Rebecca, and, 247n171
Free Building Licence (*see also* Small House Policy), 269n41
freedoms (*see* rights and freedoms)
Free Territory of Trieste, 61n40
Fu, Hualing (Professor), 45n65, 52n122
  Choy, D.W., and, 91n256
  Cullen, Richard, and, 90n251
functional constituencies (*see also* functional constituency elections), 131–142
  abolition, 5, 75, 131, 138n251
  ad-hoc allocation, 132n219
  China's support for, 140n260, 142n269
  definition, lack of, 29–30, 131, 137, 139n255
  Election Committee, link with, 109n87–88
  IIKBL, drafting of, 23 24
  HKSAR Government, supportive of, 134n227, 145n286
  Legco, powerful role in, 28, 134–135
  NPCSC requires retention, 130n211, 137, 139, 151
  origins, 133n221
functional constituency elections (*see also* corporate voting; individual voting; Legislative Council elections), 131–142
  1985 elections, 22, 127, 133
  1991 elections, 133
  1995 elections, 29–31, 127, 133, 136–137
  1998 elections, 137n247
  2012 elections, 139n253
  agency voting, 135n235
  foreign passport holders, 266n25
  super functional constituencies, 138–140

garrison (*see* People's Liberation Army)
Garrison Law, 40n20, 77n148
  HK courts, restriction on, 211–212
  state of war or emergency, 80n167

Geng, Biao (PRC official), 14n20
Gewirtz, Paul (Professor), 240n125
Ghai, Yash (Professor), 35n113, 56n8, 57n16–17, 60n32, 65n64, 74n127, 81n180, 85n209, 86n210, 86n213, 88n234, 89n238, 89n244, 183n223, 194n306, 199n346, 206n404, 220n6, 221n13, 224n32, 225n38, 226n41, 232n73, 244n148, 246n165, 252n207, 253n213, 259n252, 298n208, 309n37
  Cottrell, Jill, and, 156n25, 161n68, 162n73
goods and services tax, 104n55
governmental systems (*see* federal system; unitary system)
government bills (*see also* bills), 100
Governor of Hong Kong (*see also* Davies, Sir John; MacLehose, Sir Murray; Patten, Christopher; Wilson, Sir David)
  election, proposal for, 22n39
  powers, 101, 102n44, 144n279
  judges, appointment of, 161n67–68
  legislators, appointment of, 22, 102, 126, 133–134
Greenland, 56, 88n234

Hannum, Hurst (Professor), 57n13, 89n237
  Lillich, Richard, and, 55n3, 58n18–20, 59n25, 59n27, 67n83, 72n113–114, 74n129, 80n172, 82n184, 84n201, 86n211, 91n259
harbour reclamation, 187n253, 187n256
Heintze, Hans-Joachim (Professor), 55n2, 57n13
Her Majesty's Pleasure, 101n41, 157n37
Herzer, Eva (lawyer), 59n24, 60n34
Heung Yee Kuk, 132, 268n35
High Court (*see also* Chief Judge of the High Court; Court of Appeal; Court of First Instance), 153, 154n12
high degree of autonomy (*see* autonomy in HK)
Ho, Albert (HK legislator), 110n96–97
Hong Kong and Macao Affairs Office of the State Council, 95n9, 142n269
Hong Kong Bar Association, 140n259, 161n64, 181n209, 190n270, 234n82

Hong Kong Basic Law (*see also* amendment
of HKBL; drafting of HKBL;
interpretation of HKBL by
NPCSC; interpretation of laws by
HK courts), 37–54
   constitutional dimension of, 37, 46–50, 67
      constitution, described by HK courts as,
49n6, 179n193, 180
      higher source of law in HK, 47
   Constitution of the PRC 1982, relationship
with, 3, 50–54
      special law of, 49n104
   international dimension, 37–40
   JD, divergence from, 38n6, 80n168
   JD, duplicated in, 38n7
   living instrument, 223n22, 311n51
   national law of the PRC, 40–46, 180n196,
194n310
      conflicts with other basic laws, 43–45
      superior to other national laws, 45–46,
76, 258
   NPC, enacted by, 2, 29, 53n124
   provisions on
      Central Authorities, relationship with,
40–41
      duties, 288n141
      governmental structure, 47–48, 93–151
      judiciary, 5, 153–155
      rights, 7, 48, 237, 264–267, 280–281
         exclusive HKBL rights, 285n124, 299
         PRC Constitution, similarity with,
287n139, 288n140, 292n170
Hong Kong Bill of Rights Ordinance, 274–287
   1997, changes in, 34, 35n113, 278–279
   China's attitude towards, 34, 277–278
   constitutional revolution, 7, 172n136,
264n8
   enactment, 7, 29, 172, 274–276
   HKBL, constitutional protection under,
280–282
   HK laws, impact on, 277
   HK Letters Patent, entrenchment in, 264n7,
276–277, 280n100
   ICCPR incorporated into HK law (*see
also* International Covenant on
Civil and Political Rights), 63,
274–275, 292
   judicial hostility towards, 173n139, 276n80
   parallel HKBL rights, 284n118, 292n168
   private citizens, disputes between, 275n76

   rights, list of, 282–284
   UK, change of policy by, 29, 264n6
Hong Kong deputies to NPC (*see* National
People's Congress deputies from
HK)
Hong Kong Disneyland, 212n445, 305n14
Hong Kong dollar, 15, 60, 61n35, 68, 310n43,
311n47
Hong Kong General Chamber of Commerce,
132, 133n221
Hong Kong Housing Authority (*see* Housing
Authority)
Hong Kong Institute of Education, 123n173
Hong Kong International Airport, 118,
147n298
Hong Kong Letters Patent, 101n43, 171n129
   executive-led government, 101–102
   Governor made laws, 102n44
   rights, protection of, 171–172, 263n2,
264n7, 276–277, 280n100
Hong Kong Police (*see also* Commissioner of
Police), 62n45, 80, 116, 120n149,
158n39, 212n442
Hong Kong Royal Instructions, 101n43,
171n129
   private members' bills, 144n279
   rights, protection of, 263n2
Hong Kong Special Administrative Region
(HKSAR)
   PRC, inalienable part of, 55
   territorial boundaries, 79n163
Hong Kong Special Administrative Region
Government (*see also* Central
Policy Unit; civil service;
Customs and Excise; Department
of Administration; Department
of Finance; Department of
Justice; Education Department;
Immigration Department;
Independent Commission Against
Corruption; principal officials
of the HKSAR Government),
114–124
   accountability to (*see also* Principal
Officials Accountability System)
      legislature, 125n181, 145n289, 146–147
      public, 118–120, 123–124, 148
   bills, priority in Legco of, 100
   CE can rule like dictator, 97n15, 114
   economic and trade missions, 62n42

powers, 114
   judiciary's budget, 167
   land in HK, management of, 305n18
   policy formulation, 114, 117, 157n30
Hong Kong Special Administrative Region passport, 16, 60, 183n226
CPG, delegation of power by, 230n66
Hong Kong-Zhuhai-Macao bridge, 187–188
Hor, Michael (Professor), 286n129
Hospital Authority, 97, 148n304, 267n30
House of Commons, 96, 149n312
House of Lords, 155n16, 171n127, 181n208, 228n56, 229n57, 233n81
Housing Authority, 97, 119n146, 150
  judicial review cases, 99n32, 185n237, 187n254
Hsu, Berry F.C. (Professor), 155n21, 162n69
Huang, Hua (PRC official), 14n20
Hulme, John (Chief Justice), 164n90
human rights (*see* Hong Kong Bill of Rights Ordinance; restrictions on rights; rights and freedoms)
Hu, Yaobang (PRC leader), 27

identity card, 264n12, 266n27
illegal immigrants, 265, 267, 284
immigration, 60–61
Immigration Department, 66n72, 116, 120n149, 183n226
immunity (*see also* diplomatic immunity; judicial immunity; restrictions on jurisdiction of HK courts; state immunity), 210–214
impeachment, 102
implied repeal, doctrine of, 276n81
Independent Commission Against Corruption (ICAC), 105n62, 146
  Commissioner, 116, 120n149, 123n174
indigenous inhabitants of the New Territories (*see also* Heung Yee Kuk; Small House Policy; village elections), 268–269
individual voting (*see also* functional constituency elections), 30n78, 110n95, 136
innocence, presumption of, 263, 267, 283–284, 293n175
  court cases, 276n79, 287n136–137, 291n161, 294n177

Insider Dealing Tribunal, 157n38, 177n169
International Covenant on Civil and Political Rights (ICCPR), 270–302
  HKBL, continues under, 7, 63, 141, 271–272
  implemented through HK law, provision on (*see also* Hong Kong Bill of Rights Ordinance), 272n59, 278n90, 280n100
  HK courts, enforceability in, 272–273, 275, 277n88
  HK Letters Patent, entrenchment under, 172n132, 264n7, 277, 280n100
  Ng Ka Ling (1999) judgment, and, 234n85
  PRC signed, 273n65
  reporting requirement, 273–274
  reservations, 141, 142n267, 271–272, 282n115–116
  Siracusa Principles, 295n189
  universal and equal suffrage, 140–142
International Covenant on Economic, Social and Cultural Rights (ICESCR), 270–274
  aspirational, 270, 274n68
  HK courts, enforceability in, 272–274
  PRC ratified, 273n65
  reporting requirement, 273–274
  reservations, 271n50, 272
international labour conventions, 271n54
international organizations, HK's participation in, 61n39, 62n41
interpretation of HKBL by NPCSC (*see also* judicial referral by CFA to NPCSC; *Lau Kong Yung* (1999) judgment), 219–223, 230–240
  1999 interpretation (*see also Ng Ka Ling* (1999) judgment), 158n44, 160n60, 178n183, 201n364, 203n374, 226n44, 235–237, 239n122, 245, 248, 250n193, 254n216, 260, 285n123
  2004 interpretation, 69–70, 91, 112n111, 129–130, 142, 151, 241
  China's most significant intervention, 70n99, 241n131
  different system of interpretation, example of, 130n210, 241n135
  HKBL changed by, 175n158, 314

2005 interpretation, 236n94, 243–246, 261n261
  HKSAR Government changed position, 244n151
2011 interpretation (*see also* Congo (2011) judgment), 247n172, 257n235
amendment, alternative to, 260–261, 281
cautious approach, 6–7, 84n203, 240, 242
Chinese legal system, part of, 25, 83, 221–222
contextual approach, 245–246
courts limit effect of, 246–248
courts must follow, 85n204, 281n110
HKBL, drafting of, 25, 219n1, 221n11, 231n67–68, 237n107
JD, not mentioned in, 220n5
judicial independence, effect on, 84n199, 158–160, 240
legislative intent, 225, 236n95, 245
legislative interpretation, 202n367, 249n185, 261n262
  common law system, comparison with, 178n185, 202n368, 249–250, 252n203
previous judgments, effect on, 85n205, 159n47, 246n168, 247n169
procedural limitation, 231–232
safeguards, lack of, 261, 281n109
subject-matter limitation, 231, 236–237
unrestricted power, 6, 84, 87n220, 87n226, 159n50, 237n105, 248n181
interpretation of laws by HK courts (*see also* constitutional review; judicial referral; purposive approach), 223–230
common law approach, 201n363
declarations of unconstitutionality, 175–178
extrinsic materials, use of, 224, 228–230
HKBL, drafting of, 25, 219n1, 221n11
HKBL, excluded provisions in, 231n69, 251n196, 253–256
judicial power, part of, 158n41
Ng Ka Ling (1999) judgment, 223–225, 253
remedial interpretation, 176n163–165, 241n134
rights, generous approach towards, 196n323, 203n381, 223n21
severance, 176n167

interpreter, right to, 283
Ip, Regina (Secretary for Security), 118n139, 123n169–170, 194n310, 242n142
irrationality (*see also* judicial review), 168n109, 185n241

Jennings, Sir Ivor (UK jurist), 122n166
Jiang, Zemin (PRC President), 33, 108n84, 297n201
Ji, Pengfei (PRC official), 229n58
Joint Declaration on the Question of Hong Kong (*see also* basic policies of the PRC regarding HK), 2, 9–10, 13–18
  50-year guarantee, 18, 303n2
  after 1997, UK attempts to invoke, 40n18
  Annex I, elaboration in, 17–18, 259n252
  economic issues, emphasis on, 17
  HKBL, origins of, 2, 18, 37–38
  HK courts, use in, 2, 39, 224n29, 228n54–55
    not directly enforceable, 18n31–32, 273n61
  negotiations over, 14–15, 125
  treaty, status as, 18n30, 37n3
Joint Declaration on the Question of Macao, 134n224
Joint Liaison Group, 16, 23n44
judges (*see also* judicial appointments)
  covert surveillance overseen by, 105n62, 158n39
  executive posts, appointments to, 157–158
  HKBL, nationality requirements under, 154n10, 190n277
  remuneration, 166–167
  resignations, 165n94–96
  retirement age, 165n92
judicial appointments (*see also* Judicial Officers Recommendation Commission), 160–163
  autonomy, part of HK's, 82
  CE, made by, 82n185, 98n25, 161
  CE, rejection by, 162n70–73
  colonial era, 161n67–68
  CPG consulted, 82n187, 161n66
  Legco approval, 98n26–27, 161n65
  NPCSC notified, 82n186, 98n26, 129n204, 161, 164
  other countries, comparison with, 162–163
  politicisation of, 163

retirement age, beyond, 164n87, 165n93
    Bokhary denied extension, 163–164
Judicial Appointments Commission (UK), 163n81–82
Judicial Committee of the Privy Council, 5, 82, 155n16, 165n91, 193n303, 276n80
judicial immunity, 211n436
judicial independence (*see also* judicial appointments), 155–167
    Bokhary, concerns of (*see also* Bokhary, Justice Kemal), 84n199, 164n87, 208–209, 256n227
    China, lacking in, 160n61, 167
    colonial era, lacking in, 156n25–26, 164n90
    definition, 156n23, 166n97
    executive posts, appointments to, 157–158
    financial security (*see also* judicial remuneration), 5, 166
    HKBL, provisions in, 5, 81, 155n20
    HKSAR Government's failure to defend, 159–160
    institutional independence, 167
    judicial referral by CFA to NPCSC, 84n199, 208n420–422
    Ng Ka Ling (1999) judgment, 158–160, 182–183
    NPCSC interpretations (*see also* interpretation of HKBL by NPCSC), 158–159, 240
    Secretary for Justice's presence on JORC, 162n74
    security of tenure of judges, 5, 164–165
    Yeung May Wan (2005) judgment, 204n384
Judicial Officers Recommendation Commission (JORC) (formerly Judicial Service Commission), 82n185, 161–162
    composition, 161n64
    retirement age, beyond, 165n93
    Secretary for Justice, presence of, 161, 162n74
judicial power (*see also* judicial remedies), 80–85
    adjudicate, power to, 80–81, 157n33
    autonomy, part of, 3, 16, 58
    difficult to define, 80n174, 157n32
    interpretation, includes, 158n41
    NPC and NPCSC actions, jurisdiction over (*see also Ng Ka Ling* (1999) judgment), 179n194

pardon, CE's power to, 101
quasi-judicial, 115n122
sentencing, 101
judicial referral by CFA to NPCSC (*see also* interpretation of HKBL by NPCSC), 83–84, 250–257
    autonomy, effect on, 196n322, 225n35, 252n206
    CFA control over process, 7, 231n70, 256–257
    CFA, only applies to, 251
    Chong Fung Yuen (2001) judgment, 201n362, 254–255
    classification condition, 252–253, 255
    Congo (2011) judgment, 7n4, 208n415, 255–257
    European Court of Justice, comparison with, 251–252, 256
    excluded provisions, 231n69, 239n122–123, 251n196, 253–256
    fair trial, effect on right to, 252n204, 257
    institutional reluctance, 252n205, 254–255
    judicial independence, effect on, 84n199, 208n420–422
    necessity condition, 202n366, 209n429, 252n208, 255–256
    Ng Ka Ling (1999) judgment, 196n322, 224–225, 252–254
    predominant provision test, 208n416, 232n71, 253–254
    substantive effect test, 201n362, 255n222
    Vallejos (2013) judgment, 202n366, 209n429, 243n143, 250n193
judicial remedies (*see also* declarations of unconstitutionality; prospective overruling; remedial interpretation; severance; suspension of court declaration), 175–177
judicial remuneration, 166–167
judicial review (*see also* constitutional review), 168–188
    cases, 184–185
        covert surveillance, 105, 177n175, 185n239
        harbour reclamation, 187n253, 187n256
        HK-Zhuhai-Macao bridge, 187n258
        public housing, 99n32, 185n237, 187n254
    categories (*see also* irrationality; legitimate expectation; proportionality), 168, 185

Index   403

China, in, 169n121
criticism of, 186–188
growth in, 156, 169, 172n137, 184, 264, 276
HKBL, provision in, 93, 267
judicial independence, importance of, 156
political process, alternative to, 186–187
standing to bring cases, 185n238
Judicial Service Commission (replaced by Judicial Officers Recommendation Commission), 161n63
judicial system
China, separate from, 81
constitutional review integral part of, 175n155
Judiciary (*see also* Coroners' Court; Court of Appeal; Court of Final Appeal; Court of First Instance; District Court; High Court; interpretation of laws by HK courts; judges; Judicial Officers Recommendation Commission; Labour Tribunal; Lands Tribunal; magistrates courts; special courts), 153–217
administrator, 167
budget, 167
executive and legislature, support, 167n104
HKBL, lack of detail in, 5, 153
jurisdiction (*see also* restrictions on jurisdiction of HK courts), 44n58, 154, 210n431
other members of, 154, 160n62
June Fourth crackdown (*see* Tiananmen Square protests)
Justices of the Peace, 133n221

Kiss, Alexandre (Professor), 297n202
Kuomintang, 11, 61, 214n460

Labour Tribunal, 153n4
Lam, Carrie
Chief Secretary for Administration, 71n111, 120n151, 121n159, 160n58
Secretary for Development, 310n41
Lam, Stephen (Chief Secretary for Administration), 71n111, 120n151
land leases in HK, 304–307
30 June 1997, expiring before, 12–13
30 June 2047, extended after, 305–306
mortgages for, 307n25

30 June 2047, extended until, 16, 305n11
part of autonomy, 41n32
Lands Tribunal, 153n4
land-use rights in China, 53n130, 304n6, 306n20–22
Lapidoth, Ruth (Professor), 58n22
Lau Kong Yung (1999) judgment, 197–198, 237–240
common law system, strange for, 194n309, 238n111
constitution cited in, 50n110
unqualified NPCSC power of interpretation, 87n220, 159n50, 197n335, 237n105
law and order, 16, 59n24
state of war or emergency, 38n6, 80n168
Law, Fanny (civil servant), 123n173–174
Law Society of HK, 52, 161n64, 190
leases (*see* land leases in HK; land-use rights in China)
Lee, Alice (Associate Professor), 305n16, 313n63
Lee, Martin
HKBL drafter, 19n33, 20, 23, 25, 27, 220n5
HK legislator, 22, 68n88, 133, 216n467, 312n58
Lee Wing Tat (HK legislator), 110n93
legal aid, 184n231, 247n170, 284n119–120
legality test (*see also* restrictions on rights), 288–291
common law offences, 290n157–158
legal procedures, 72, 105n61, 293n171
legal profession (*see also* barristers; solicitors), 22, 88, 133, 163n81, 190, 191n278, 191n283, 215, 263n5
Legislative Affairs Commission of the NPCSC
Chong Fung Yuen (2001) judgment, and, 202n365, 242, 249
Ng Ka Ling (1999) judgment, and, 181n204, 182n219
Legislative Council (*see also* Legislative Council elections; Legislative Councillors; President of Legco; Provisional Legislative Council of the HKSAR)
1997, dissolved in, 31, 127, 137
appointments to, 22, 102, 126
abolition of, 133–134, 136n242
CE's power to dissolve, 100–101
consultation with, lack of, 99, 187n255

origins, 102
party politics, introduction of, 118n138
powers, 124, 142–151
  executive scrutiny
    inquiries, conduct (*see also* Select Committees of Legco), 119, 123n171, 146–148
    issues, debate, 98n21, 148–149
    no confidence motions, 98n21, 119n146, 148–151
    policy address, debate, 98
    witnesses, summon, 119, 146–147
  filibuster, 145n287
  financial powers, 103–104, 142–143
    judicial remuneration, 167n102
    line-item veto, 104, 142
    other countries, comparison with, 104n53–54
    HKBL, exceed powers explicitly granted under, 142n271, 150–151
  judicial appointments, 98n26–27, 161n65
  legislative powers, 42, 72–73, 143–145
    amendments, 145
    budget or important bill, reject, 100
    national laws, enact, 76, 77n152
voting system (*see also* split voting system), 100n36
Legislative Council elections (*see also* functional constituency elections)
  1985 elections, 22, 127, 133, 141
  1991 elections, 23, 102n45, 118, 127
  1995 elections, 29–31, 34, 127n195, 133, 136–137, 278
  1998 elections, 127n195, 128, 137n247
  2000 elections, 127n195, 128, 134n226
  2004 elections, 128
  2012 elections, 139n253
  2020 elections, 131, 139
  direct elections, introduction of, 22–23, 118, 127
  electoral college (*see also* Election Committee, 22n40, 23, 127n195
  HKBL, drafting of, 21, 23–24, 26n57, 28, 125–126
  HKBL, provisions in, 126
  JD, promised in, 15n25, 19, 124–125, 133n222
  Omelco consensus, 28n69, 126n187

one person, two votes, 139–140
universal suffrage, 4–5, 131, 139–141, 151, 271
Legislative Councillors (*see also* President of Legco)
  appointed members, 22, 102, 126
  Chinese nationality requirement, 154n9, 266n25
  prosecution, immunity from, 211n437
  rejectionist attitude, 94
legislative intent (*see also* interpretation of HKBL by NPCSC), 225–226, 236n95, 245
legislative interpretation (*see also* interpretation of HKBL by NPCSC), 202n367, 249n185, 261n262
  common law system, comparison with, 178n185, 202n368, 249–250, 252n203
legislative power (*see also* Legislative Council), 72–80
  autonomy, part of, 3, 16, 58, 72n112–113
  HKBL, wide power under, 72
  limits, 72n114, 74n129
  national security legislation, power to enact, 73
legitimate expectation (*see also* judicial review), 186, 203n375, 247
legitimate purpose (*see also* national security; *ordre public*; public health; public order; public safety; restrictions on rights), 291, 293–302
Leong, Alan (HK legislator), 110n94
Letters Patent (*see* Hong Kong Letters Patent)
Leung, Antony (Financial Secretary), 123, 150n313
Leung, Chun Ying
  Chief Executive
    election, 70, 110–111
    impeachment, attempt at, 102n48
    Liaison Office, visit to (*see also* Liaison Office of the CPG in the HKSAR), 71n107, 96n10
    popularity, 107n78
    principal officials, nomination of, 71, 120n150, 121n159
  Consultative Committee for the Basic Law of the HKSAR, 111n99

Leung, Elsie (Secretary for Justice), 44n61, 116n133, 150n314, 160n58, 209n425, 220n3, 244
Leung Kwok Hung (2005) judgment, 204–205, 207n411, 282n114
  Court of Appeal judgment, 287n138
  declaration of unconstitutionality, 176n166, 205n390, 289n153
  dissenting judgment, 199n347, 205n394, 206n404
  majority judgment, 205n392
  proportionality, use of, 185n242, 205n391
Leung, Laurence (Director of Immigration), 146n290
Leung, Priscilla (Associate Professor), 45n66
Liaison Office of the CPG in the HKSAR, 70n101
  Chief Executive election, 70n105, 111n103
  HK affairs, intervention in, 70, 111
  HK laws, exemption from, 32n99, 41n39
  Leung Chun Ying, visit by, 71n107, 96n10
Li, Andrew (Chief Justice), 167n103, 169n116, 183n224, 193n296, 313n60
  appointment, 33n104
  Court of Appeal, criticized, 207n411
  defence of courts, 159n54
  mainstream view within CFA, 206n402
  overseas judges, choice of, 191n285
  retirement, 207, 240n127
Liao, Chengzhi (PRC official), 13n14
liberty, right to, 270, 282
life, right to, 266, 270, 282, 285–286
  death penalty, 282, 286n127–130
  supreme right, 286n126
Li, Huijuan (PRC judge), 160n61, 170n124
Li, Ka Shing (HKBL drafter), 20
Lim, C.L. (Professor)
  Chan, Johannes M.M., and, 89n239
  Mushkat, Roda, and, 63n53, 64n58
Lin, Feng (Associate Professor)
  Lo, P.Y., and, 246n164
Ling, Bing (Professor), 46n73, 197n336, 230n65, 238n108, 238n115, 239n122, 262n266
Link REIT, 99, 187n254–255
Li, Pang Kwong (Associate Professor), 143n275
Li, Yahong (Associate Professor), 67n79
Li, Yuhui (criminal), 44

Li, Zaishun (PRC official), 49n101
local people's congresses, 43n52, 86n215, 160n61
Loh, Christine (Under Secretary for the Environment), 71n110, 122n165
Lo, P.Y. (HK barrister), 84n200, 193n303, 248n173, 252n205, 257n238
Lui, Percy Luen Tim (Assistant Professor), 104n57
Luk Yu teahouse murder, 44n63
Luo, Haocai (PRC judge), 215n461

Macao Basic Law, 42, 83n191, 134n224, 244n157
  amendment, 46n71, 258n241, 258n244
  interpretation, 244n157
Macao SAR, 51n112
  Chief Executive, 134n224, 244n157
MacLehose, Sir Murray (later Lord) (Governor), 12–13
Ma, Geoffrey, 207–209
  Chief Judge of the High Court, 207
  Chief Justice, 82n187, 161n66, 209n428–430
magistrates, 160n62, 164n88, 211n436
magistrates' courts, 153, 167, 284n119
mainland China (*see* People's Republic of China)
mainland mothers (*see also* abode, right of), 200, 227, 242
Major, John (UK Prime Minister), 29
Ma, Ngok (Associate Professor), 95n7, 96n12, 97n15, 104n53, 104n56, 106n66, 114, 116
Manila, 64
marriage, freedom of, 267, 270, 283
martial law, 27, 79–80
Mason, Sir Anthony (overseas judge), 221n10, 230n63, 235n92
  Australia, comparison with, 158n40, 187n252
  Court of Final Appeal, role on, 192–195, 206n403, 209n430
    Congo (2011) judgment, 194, 208n421–422
    Lau Kong Yung (1999) judgment, 194n309–310, 238n111, 239n117
  judicial remuneration report, 166n98
Mathews, Jeremy (Attorney General), 116n133

Ma Wai Kwan (1997) judgment
  common law system, continuity of, 39
  constitutional review, power of, 173
  HKBL, nature of, 37n1–2, 40n19, 225n37
  Ng Ka Ling (1999) judgment, overruled in, 179n191
military courts of the PRC, 212n441
military service, 78n157–158
Miller, Tony (civil servant), 119n146
ministerial system (*see also* Principal Officials Accountability System), 94, 119–124, 148, 150, 311
Ministry of Foreign Affairs (*see also* Central People's Government; foreign affairs)
  Congo (2011) judgment, letters in, 208n417, 217n474, 256n228, 257n239
  diplomatic immunity, 210
  HK, office in, 62n44
mischief rule, 223–224
misconduct in public office, 290n157–158
Montesquieu, Baron de (French philosopher), 93n2
Morris, Robert (scholar), 243n145, 303n4, 307n27
movement, freedom of, 267, 270, 275n76, 282, 285n124
  restrictions on, 271n49, 286n131, 294–296, 298–299
Mugabe, Grace (Zimbabwean President's wife), 210n433
municipal councils (*see* district organizations)
murder, 44n63, 101n41, 157n37, 205n396, 213n451

National Autonomous Areas, 56–57, 76n146
national flag (*see also Ng Kung Siu* (1999) judgment)
  desecration, criminal penalties for, 77n154, 296n194
  legislation in HK, 77n152, 198n342
  legislation overseas, 298n205
  US Supreme Court cases, 298n206
nationality (*see* Chinese citizen)
national laws, application in HK of, 40n24, 41n28, 75–80
  HKBL, compliance with, 47n85, 77n151
  implementation by legislation or proclamation, 76–77
  NPCSC, self-restraint of, 77–78
  other categories of legislation, 78–79, 90n249
  state of war or emergency, 79–80
  wider definition, 78n156
National People's Congress (NPC) (*see also* National People's Congress deputies from HK)
  basic laws, enacts, 20, 42n41
  Committee for the Basic Law, created (*see also* Committee for the Basic Law of the HKSAR), 88n227
  constitutional jurisdiction, 53n127, 86n218
  constitution, amends, 258n246
  court president, appoints and removes, 86n216, 180n195
  highest organ of state power, 20, 41n40, 180n197
  no legal limit on powers, 261–262
  HK, can grant further powers to, 66n72
  HKBL, amends (*see also* amendment of HKBL), 258, 262
  HKBL, Decision on constitutional validity of, 53n126
  HKBL, enacted, 2, 29, 53n124
  Special Administrative Regions, power to establish, 42n41, 51n113
  Supreme People's Court, and, 86n214, 180n195
National People's Congress deputies from HK
  bridging institution, 91n252, 91n255
  election, 90n249–250
  HKBL, propose amendments to, 258
  speaking restrictions, 68n87, 68n89, 91
  unrepresentative, 90n251
National People's Congress Standing Committee (*see also* Decisions of NPCSC on HK; judicial referral by CFA to NPCSC; Legislative Affairs Commission of the NPCSC)
  basic laws, amends, 42n47, 258n244, 260
  Committee for the Basic Law, and (*see also* Committee for the Basic Law of the HKSAR), 73, 76, 88
  Communist Party control, 87, 221n12–13
  conflicts between laws, resolves, 45n68
  constitutional jurisdiction, 53n127, 86n218, 170n125
  Council of Chairpersons, 241n130
  HKBL, cannot amend, 258, 260

Index   407

HKBL, propose amendments to (*see also* amendment of HKBL), 258
HK, can grant further powers to, 66n72
HK laws, power to invalidate, 41n25, 47, 73–74, 278
  ambiguity about extent of power, 34n106, 47n84, 73n124, 174n150
  amendment prohibited, 74n126
  interprets laws (*see also* interpretation of HKBL by NPCSC), 25, 83, 221
  rarely exercised power, 222n16
  judges in China, appoints and removes, 86n216, 180n195
  judges in HK, notified of appointment of, 82n186, 98n26, 129n204, 161, 164
  laws, power to enact, 42n47
  laws reported to, 72n117, 73n123
  national laws in HK, power over, 40n24, 75–76, 296n195
  not impartial arbiter, 87n222
  NPC, handles work of, 15n26, 86n219
  Preparatory Committee, established, 31n87, 230n62
  state of war or emergency in HK, declare, 79
national security (*see also* secession; sedition; state secrets, theft of; subversion against the CPG; treason)
  HKBL, drafting of, 26–28
  legislation proposed in 2003, 73n119, 106
    autonomy, part of HK's, 73n120–121
    Falun Gong, use against, 69n91, 75, 204n382
    proportionality and, 299n214
    protests against, 1, 3, 27, 69, 73, 106, 111
    resignation of Regina Ip, 123n169–170
    withdrawal, 75, 106n70, 143
    restricting rights, legitimate purpose for, 294–295, 299
naturalization in HK, 66n72, 183n226
necessity (*see also* proportionality; restrictions on rights), 300n219
New Territories (*see also* Heung Yee Kuk; indigenous inhabitants of the New Territories; Small House Policy)
  99-year lease to UK, 2, 10
  land leases (*see also* land leases in HK), 12–13, 18n32

Regional Council, 128
village elections, 177, 205–206, 269n40
New Zealand, 192
Ng Ka Ling (1999) judgment, 173–174, 178–183, 195–196, 232–236, 251–254
  aftermath, 197–199
  children
    illegitimate, 232n77, 235n90
    numbers involved, 178n181, 200, 232n75
    one-way permit restriction, 233n78, 235n90
    time of birth restriction, 232n77, 235n90
  constitutional crisis, 49, 87, 181–182, 244, 296–297
  constitutional review, power of (*see also* constitutional review), 5, 173–174, 196
    NPC and NPCSC, jurisdiction over, 5, 87n224, 159n52, 179–180, 196
    criticism of, 180–181, 196, 225n36, 253n214, 296n192
  judicial independence, effect on, 158–160, 182–183
  judicial referral, rejection of (*see also* predominant provision test), 196n322, 224–225, 252–254
  legitimate expectation after judgment, 186n247, 203n375, 247
  NPCSC interpretation (*see also* interpretation of HKBL by NPCSC), 6, 158n44, 178n183, 196, 235–237, 254n216, 260
  Provisional Legislature, legality of, 32n96
  purposive approach, 223–225, 253
  resignation considered by judges, 164n85, 197n330
  retrospective criminal punishment, 285n123
  supplementary judgment, 87n225, 160n56, 181–183, 196
Ng Kung Siu (1999) judgment (*see also* national flag; *ordre public*), 77n155, 198–199, 239, 296–299, 301–302
  Bokhary's near dissent, 199n346, 298n208, 302n232
  civil liberties, retreat on, 8, 159n51, 198
  Court of Appeal judgment, 296n196, 297n199

408   Index

judicial referral, rejection of, 254n220
  mode of expression, 302
  other countries, comparison with, 298n205
Ng, Margaret (HK legislator), 305n15
Nicholls of Birkenhead, Lord (overseas judge), 193n299, 193n303, 200n353
no confidence motions, 98n21, 119n146, 148–151
nominating committee (*see also* Chief Executive election; Election Committee)
  Election Committee, nominating role of, 109–111
  HKBL, drafting of, 24n47
  universal suffrage, election by, 28n65, 112–114
    primary election, 113n115
non-permanent residents, 266

occupation, freedom of, 267
O'Dea, Justice Patrick, 165n95
Official Receiver, 176n161
Omelco consensus, 28n69, 126n187
one-child policy, 52
one country, two systems, 2, 9, 11, 13–15, 17, 20, 25, 29, 35–36, 43, 153, 222, 228, 259, 261–262
  30 June 2047, future after, 303–304, 307–309, 313–314
  constitution, provision in, 51–54
  JD, and (*see also* basic policies of the PRC regarding HK), 13–18
ordinary residence, 95n8, 115n124, 265
ordre public (*see also Ng Kung Siu* (1999) judgment; restrictions on rights), 198n344, 205n390, 289n153, 290n154, 294–299
  imprecise concept, 205n390, 295n190
  wide definition, 295, 297–299
overseas judges on CFA, 189–195
  CJ, chosen by, 191n279, 191n284
  criticism of, 193n299, 200n353
  influence (*see also* Mason, Sir Anthony), 192
  JD, promised in, 15n23, 18, 189
  number, controversy over, 189–190
  politically sensitive cases, 194–195

Panditaratne, Dinusha (Adjunct Assistant Professor), 300n220

Pannick, Lord (English Queen's Counsel), 208n419, 295n187
Pao, Sir Y.K. (HKBL drafter), 20
parliamentary sovereignty, 171n126–127, 261n264
parliamentary system, 96, 117n134, 149
passport (*see* Hong Kong Special Administrative Region passport)
Patten, Christopher (Governor), 29, 33, 102n45
  political reforms, 29–31, 97n16, 135–137, 190n272
penny stocks fiasco, 124n175
People's Liberation Army, 11, 19, 78n157–158
  HK courts, jurisdiction of, 211–213
  HK, decision to station in, 14n20
  state of war or emergency in HK, powers in, 80n167
People's Republic of China (PRC)
  federalism, experiment with, 66n76
  government officials, term of office of, 243n146
  unitary system, 64n57, 66n70, 67n79
permanent resident (*see also* abode, right of), 264–266
  government posts, requirement for, 95, 115, 154n11, 266n24
  voting rights, requirement for, 125n185, 265
person, freedom of, 266, 282
Petersen, Carole J. (Professor), 75n134
Philippines, 64
Piggott, Sir Francis (Chief Justice), 164n90
police (*see* Hong Kong Police)
Political Assistants (*see also* Principal Officials Accountability System), 121
political parties (*see* Chinese Communist Party; Civic Party; Democratic Alliance for the Betterment of HK; Democratic Party; United Democrats of HK)
political system in HK (*see also* executive-led government; separation of powers), 93–95
  hybrid system, 117n134
  other countries, comparison with, 96, 100n35
Portugal (*see also* Joint Declaration on the Question of Macao), 298n205
PRC Constitution 1982 (*see* Constitution of the PRC 1982)

Index   409

PRC Criminal Law (*see* Criminal Law of the PRC)
PRC legal system (*see* Chinese legal system)
predominant provision test (*see also* judicial referral by CFA to NPCSC), 208n416, 232n71, 253–254
pregnancy, 263n1, 286n130
Preparatory Committee
  1996 Opinions on right of abode, 230n62, 242n138, 248n177, 250n193
  provisional legislature, and, 31–32
prescribed by law (*see also* legality test), 288–292, 299–302
presidential system, 96, 98, 101–102, 117n134
President of the Legislative Council, 88, 145n284, 145n288, 148n307, 174n149
press, freedom of (*see also* expression, freedom of), 48n91, 266, 287
presumption of innocence (*see* innocence, presumption of)
Principal Officials Accountability System (*see also* ministerial system), 99, 119–124
  democratic accountability, lack of, 124n177
  other countries, comparison with, 121n161, 122, 124
  Political Assistants, 121
  Under Secretaries, 121, 122n165
Principal Officials of the HKSAR Government (*see also* Chief Secretary for Administration; Commissioner of Police; Directors of Bureaux; Financial Secretary; Secretary for the Civil Service; Secretary for Health, Welfare and Food; Secretary for Justice; Secretary for Security), 115–116
  CE, nominated by, 71, 98, 116, 121, 122n165
  continuity, 33, 116
  CPG, appointed by, 16, 40n23, 71, 98, 116
  nationality requirements, 33n102, 115, 122n162, 154n9
  resignations, 123
prisoners, 101n41, 157n37, 265n21, 282n115
  vote, right to, 186n244, 301
privacy, right to, 266–267, 270, 283

private members' bills, 144, 271n55, 275n76
  CE's approval needed to introduce, 75n133, 99, 104, 144
  not brought into force, 105n62
Private Treaty Grant (*see also* Small House Policy), 269n42
privatization, 99n32, 187n254–255
Privy Council (*see* Judicial Committee of the Privy Council)
procedural impropriety (*see also* judicial review), 168n109
procession, freedom of (*see* assembly, freedom of)
property ownership, right to, 266n28, 267n31
  30 June 2047, after, 304–307
proportionality, 168n110, 185–186, 292
  restricting rights, test for, 291–292, 299–302
  necessity, relationship with, 300n219
  tougher test, 301
  universally applied, 300n220
prospective overruling, 177n172
Provisional Legislative Council of the HKSAR (Provisional Legislature)
  establishment, 31–32, 127, 137
  laws enacted by (*see also* Public Order Ordinance; Societies Ordinance), 31n89, 32n98, 35, 155n15, 233n78, 275n76, 279n94, 282n114, 290n154
  legality, 32, 127n197
  rule of law, legacy for, 32–33
publication, freedom of (*see* expression, freedom of)
public health
  legitimate purpose for restricting rights, 294–295
  quarantine, 286n131, 295
public housing (*see also* Housing Authority)
  judicial review cases, 99n32, 185n237, 187n254
  short-piling scandal, 118–119, 147n300
public order, 204n389, 294–295, 297
Public Order Ordinance (*see also* assembly, freedom of; *Leung Kwok Hung* (2005) judgment)
  colonial era, 263n5, 277n86
  NPCSC deleted amendments, 35, 278
  Provisional Legislature enacted restrictions, 35, 279n94, 282n114, 290n154

410   Index

public safety, 204n289, 294n184
purposive approach, 223–228
    Chong Fung Yuen (2001) judgment,
        redefined in, 226
    extrinsic materials, use of, 224, 228–230
    JD, 2, 39, 224n29, 228n54–55
    post-enactment materials, 230n62
    Ng Ka Ling (1999) judgment, 223–225, 253
    problems with, 225n38

Qiao, Xiaoyang (PRC official), 113n114,
        140n257, 140n260
Qing dynasty, 10, 14
quarantine, 286n131, 295
quasi-judicial power, 115n122

reclamation, 187n253, 187n256
referendum, 75, 138n251
Regional Council, 22n40, 128
regional flag, 159n51, 296n194, 297n201
religion, freedom of, 52n119–120, 267, 270,
        283, 294n184
remedial interpretation, 176n163–165,
        241n134
Renminbi, 60, 61n35, 310, 311n47
residual powers, 65n68–69
restrictions on jurisdiction of HK courts (*see
        also* acts of state; state immunity),
        210–217
    diplomatic immunity, 210, 216n468
    NPC and NPCSC, jurisdiction over,
        179–183
    PLA Garrison in HK, 211–213
restrictions on rights (*see also* legitimate
        purpose) 7–8, 285–302
    defamation, 199, 286
    emergencies (*see also* state of war or
        emergency), 80, 287n134
    legality test, 288–291
    proportionality test (*see also*
        proportionality), 291–292,
        299–302
    quarantine, 286n131, 295
    rational connection, 291n161, 292n164, 300
    Siracusa Principles, 295n189
retrospective criminal punishment
    prohibition of, 283–284, 285n123
rights and freedoms (*see also* Hong Kong Bill
        of Rights Ordinance; restrictions
        on rights), 263–302

absolute rights, 286n132–133, 287n134
autonomy, at heart of, 237n101
common law, protection under, 247n170,
        263n3
generous interpretation, 196n323, 203n381,
        223n21
HKBL, protection under, 7, 48, 237,
        264–267, 280–281
JD, preserved under, 16
non-residents, 267, 284
three categories, 285n125
Roberts, Sir Denys (Chief Justice), 165n96
Rules of Procedure of Legco, 145

sales tax, 104n55, 143
Sanitary Board, 126n191
SAR passport (*see* Hong Kong Special
        Administrative Region passport)
scandalizing the court, 293n173
Scotland, 56n6, 60, 83n191
Scott, Ian (Professor), 94n6, 118n137
secession (*see also* national security), 26n60,
        295n187
Secretary for Justice (*see also* Leung, Elsie;
        Wong, Yan Lung; Yuen, Rimsky),
        114–115, 120n149
    JORC member, 161, 162n74
    quasi-judicial power, 115n122
    title, 116n133
Secretary for the Civil Service, 121n157
security of tenure of judges, 5, 164–165
sedition (*see also* national security), 26n60,
        106n68, 295n187
Select Committees of Legco, 123n171,
        146–148, 151
Selection Committee, 31–32, 108
separation of powers, 93–94, 103–107,
        157–158
    checks and balances, 93, 103, 142, 156
    China, and, 42, 94n5
    court cases, 94n4, 101n41, 147n297,
        157n35–37
    HKBL, system in, 4, 94n3
    treaties, ratification of, 273n61
severance, 176n167
Severe Acute Respiratory Syndrome (SARS),
        123n171, 147n294, 148n304
sex discrimination, 144n280, 271n50, 284
Shao, Tianren (HKBL drafter), 129n206,
        278n91, 279n96

Shen, Simon (Associate Professor), 64n57
Shenzhen, 31n88, 44n63, 107n75
  customs post under HK jurisdiction, 313n61
shipping, 41n35, 62, 72, 111n104
Shiu, Sin Por (head of Central Policy Unit), 96n11, 100n35, 125n183, 142n271, 150n318, 175n154, 175n156, 274n66, 281n106, 281n111
short-piling scandal, 118–119, 147n300
Sino-British Joint Declaration (*see* Joint Declaration on the Question of Hong Kong)
Sino-British Joint Liaison Group, 16, 23n44
Sino-British Land Commission, 305n11
Sino-Portuguese Joint Declaration (*see* Joint Declaration on the Question of Macao)
Siracusa Principles, 295n189
slavery, freedom from, 270, 282, 284
small-circle selection process (*see also* Chief Executive election), 107–114
Small House Policy, 269, 311n45
  30 June 2047, abolition after, 269, 310n41
socialist system
  30 June 2047, after, 308–309
  HK, not practised in, 52, 303
  PRC Constitution 1982, provisions in, 3, 50, 52
social welfare, right to, 267, 270
  exclusive HKBL right, 285, 299
Societies Ordinance (*see also* association, freedom of)
  colonial era, 277n86
  NPCSC deleted amendments, 35, 278
  Provisional Legislature enacted restrictions, 35, 279n95
solicitors (*see also* Law Society of HK), 161n64
Spain, 67n82, 86n212
Special Administrative Regions
  NPC, establishment by, 42n41, 51n113
special courts, 153n4
speech, freedom of (*see also* expression, freedom of), 48n91, 203n381, 208n419, 266, 287
split voting system, 28, 100n36, 134
  amendments, impact on, 145, 151n320
  debates, impact on, 149n309
  functional constituencies, power of, 28, 134–135

Standing Committee of the National People's Congress (*see* National People's Congress Standing Committee)
Standing Committee on Judicial Salaries and Conditions of Service, 166
state (*see* Chinese state)
State Council (*see* Central People's Government)
state immunity (*see also* Congo (2011) judgment), 64, 195n313, 208, 216–217, 255n226, 256n228
state of war or emergency, 38n6, 41n27, 79–80, 287n134
state secrets, theft of (*see also* national security), 26n60, 295n187
stock market, 68, 124n175
strike, right to, 266, 270, 288n140
subsidiary legislation, 34n112, 99, 103n52, 121n155
substantive effect test (*see also* judicial referral by CFA to NPCSC), 201n362, 255n222
subversion against the CPG (*see also* national security), 26–27, 295n187
Suen, Michael (Secretary for Constitutional Affairs), 119n147
Suksi, Markku (Professor), 73n121, 74n125, 77n150, 85n208
Supreme Court (HK), 154n12
Supreme Court of the UK, 155n16
Supreme People's Court (PRC), 82n189, 154n12
  Chinese Communist Party, subordinate to, 180n200
  constitutional jurisdiction, lack of, 86n217
  interprets laws, 220n8
  NPC, subordinate to, 86n214, 180n195
  PLA Garrison in HK, jurisdiction over, 212n449
suspension of court declaration, 105n163, 177n171
Szeto, Wah (HKBL drafter), 20, 22–23, 27, 133

Tai, Benny Y.T. (Associate Professor), 81n177, 85n206–207, 100n38, 160n57, 167n105, 196n321, 198n340, 199n352, 209n428, 304n9
Taiwan, 2, 11, 13–14, 17, 61
Tamanaha, Brian (Professor), 67n81

Tang, Henry (Chief Secretary for Administration), 110–111, 115n127
Tang, Justice Robert, 163n83
taxation
　autonomy, part of, 16, 41n34, 59n28, 60
　Legco, approval by, 103–104, 142
　sales, 104n55, 143
Telford Gardens poisoner (*see* Li Yuhui)
Thatcher, Margaret (UK Prime Minister), 14–15, 149n312
thought, freedom of, 270, 283
　absolute right, 286n133
through train across 1997, 31, 33–36
Tiananmen Square protests
　HKBL, impact on, 1–2, 19–20, 27–28, 35, 126
　UK policy, impact on, 29, 264n6
Tibet, 56–57, 61n37
torture, freedom from, 80, 266–267, 282
　absolute right, 286n132
trade unions, right to form and join, 263n1, 266, 270–271, 288n140
transformation theory, 273n61
travel, right to, 39n17, 48n93–94, 228n55, 267
　exclusive HKBL right, 285n124, 299
treason (*see also* national security), 26n60, 295n187
Tsang, Donald
　Chief Executive, 64, 70, 97n19, 121n158, 131n213, 213n452, 244n148
　　election, 110–112
　　popularity, 107
　Chief Secretary for Administration, 115n127, 150n319
　colonial era, 33n103, 112n107
　Financial Secretary, 71n109
Tsang, John (Financial Secretary), 121n159
Tsang, Steve (Professor), 44n62
Tsui, Alex (ICAC officer), 146n290
Tung, Chee Hwa
　Chief Executive, 97, 106, 111n104, 143, 147n294
　　CE election, 32, 108
　　Jiang Zemin, handshake with, 33, 108n84
　　popularity, 107, 110n91
　　principal officials, nomination of, 116n133
　　protests against, 69, 106–107
　　resignation, 70n100, 107, 110, 243n147
　Executive Councillor, 33
　turmoil (*see also* state of war or emergency), 79

ultra vires (*see also* judicial review), 168n108
Under Secretaries (*see also* Principal Officials Accountability System), 121, 122n165
unequal treaties, 11
unitary system, 64n57, 66n70–71, 67n79
United Democrats of HK (became Democratic Party), 118n138
United Kingdom
　CFA cited in UK court cases, 193n302
　CFA, English judges on, 192n290
　constitutional review, 171n126–128
　governmental system, 66, 96
　HK, comparison with, 104n54, 121n161, 122–123, 149, 181n208
　HK, control over, 10–13, 29–33
　　armed forces, 211n438, 212n447, 213n451
　　democracy (*see also* Patten, Christopher), 21–23, 29–31, 126–127
　JD, negotiations over, 13–15
　passports for HK people, 112n107
　judicial appointments, 163n80–82
　parliamentary sovereignty, 171n126–127, 261n264–265
United Nations,
　committees, 141n265, 273n64, 274n69, 283n117, 286n126
　General Assembly, 270, 280n100
　JD registered with, 18n30
United States,
　Constitution, 1, 48
　constitutional review, 170n122, 173
　dollar, 15, 60n34
　HK, comparison with, 65n66, 66n73, 93, 96, 100n35, 102, 108, 163n78
　　political system, similarities of, 96n11
　HK, separate treatment of, 63n50–52
　judicial appointments, 163n78–79
　Supreme Court, 48n94, 83, 170n122, 173, 298n206

Universal Declaration of Human Rights, 270
universal suffrage (*see also* Chief Executive election; Legislative Council elections), 4–5, 19, 90, 95, 97, 112–114, 139–141, 151, 186n249, 188n262, 271
   Decisions of NPCSC, 68n86, 112n108, 130n211, 131n214–215
   equal suffrage, 140–141, 283n117
   HKBL, drafting of, 23–24, 125–126
   quasi, 139n256
   ultimate aim, 28n65, 112
Urban Council, 22n40, 126n191, 128

village elections, 177, 205–206, 269n40
visa abolition agreements, 62
vote, right to (*see also* corporate voting; election; individual voting; universal suffrage), 136n237, 140n262, 283
   permanent residency requirement, 125n185, 265
   prisoners, 186n244, 301
   reservation under ICCPR, 141–142, 271, 283n117
   unreasonable restrictions, without, 140n262, 283, 299, 301n224

Wacks, Raymond (Professor), 298n204
Wade, Sir William (Professor), 52n121, 53n123, 190n271
Wang, Shuwen (HKBL drafter), 260n255, 306n24, 308n31
Wang, Zhenmin (Professor), 112n109
war (*see* state of war or emergency)
Wednesbury unreasonableness (*see* irrationality), 185n241
Weng, Byron S.J. (Professor), 79n165, 80n171
Wesley-Smith, Peter (Professor), 103n49, 153n1, 214n458
Wilson, Sir David (later Lord) (Governor), 29, 102n45
Woolf of Barnes, Lord (overseas judge), 192n290, 276n80
Wong, Ada (Principal Official nominee), 71n110
Wong, Rosanna (Housing Authority Chair), 119n146, 150

Wong, Yan Lung (Secretary for Justice), 71n109, 115n122, 240n126
Woo, Peter (CE election candidate), 108n83
World Trade Organization, 62
Wu, Anna (Equal Opportunities Commission Chair), 97n19, 144
Wu, Jianfan (HKBL drafter), 66n70, 78n156
Wu, Raymond (HKBL drafter), 28n70

Xiao, Weiyun (HKBL drafter), 54n132, 66n74, 79n166, 150n317, 175n153
Xi, Jinping (PRC leader), 167
Xinhua News Agency
   CFA, criticism of, 180n202
   HK branch (*see also* Liaison Office of the CPG in the HKSAR), 22n43, 32n99, 70n101, 125n184
Xu, Jiatun (PRC official), 22n43, 125n184
Xu, Xiaobing (Associate Professor)
   Wilson, George, and, 61n40

Yam, Joseph (HK Monetary Authority CE), 61n35, 310n44, 311n47
Yang, Sir Ti Liang (Chief Justice), 108n83, 173n139
Yang, Xiaonan (lecturer), 235n91, 241n135
Yap, Po Jen (Associate Professor), 203n377, 203n379, 204n386, 205n393, 247n171, 249n189, 298n204
Yeoh, Eng Kiong (Secretary for Health, Welfare and Food), 123n171, 148
Young, Simon N.M. (Professor), 175n160, 176n162, 192n288, 193n297, 194n305, 206n402, 206n406, 229n59, 284n118, 285n125, 287n134, 293n176
   Cullen, Richard, and, 108n82, 114n118,
   Da Roza, Antonio, and, 191n287, 192n294
   Law, Anthony, and, 132n219, 135n232, 135n235,
Yuen, Rimsky (Secretary for Justice), 115n123

Zhang, Xiaoming (PRC official), 74n131, 142n269
Zhang, Youyu (HKBL drafter), 46n76, 49
Zhao, Lianhai (PRC dissident), 91n255
Zhou, Enlai (PRC leader), 11n4
Zhu, Guobin (Associate Professor), 66n75